PRAISE FOR
Lutheranism vs. Calvinism

The 1586 Colloquy of Montbéliard should not have been forgotten. Here we see what the real issues were between classic Lutheranism and classic Calvinism. The differences were real and important, but this Colloquy also shows where the two sides agreed. In order to avoid mischaracterizing classic, confessional Lutheranism and Calvinism, the Colloquy of Montbéliard should be required reading.

— Rev. Dr. Benjamin T. G. Mayes
Assistant Professor of Historical Theology,
Concordia Theological Seminary, Fort Wayne, IN
Co-General Editor, Luther's Works: American Edition,
Concordia Publishing House

Due to this splendid translation and commentary by Dr. Clinton Armstrong, confessional Lutherans will be able to appreciate the contribution of Jakob Andreae's defense of the Lutheran Symbols. Appearing six years after the Book of Concord, the record of this debate reveals the reliance of Lutheran theologians such as Andreae and Martin Chemnitz on the patristic Fathers who appeared first in the Catalogue of Witnesses (Testimonies) to the original Concordia and here again in Andreae's debate with Theodore Beza. The Chalcedonian Christology of Martin Luther and his contemporaries emerges here in renewed clarity in the tradition of Augustine, John Chrysostom, Gregory Nazianzus, Gregory of Nyssa, and John of Damascus, to name but a few.

— Rev. Fr. Anthony Roeber
Emeritus Professor of History & Religious Studies, Penn State University
Professor of Church History, St. Vladimir's Orthodox Theological Seminary,
Yonkers, NY

Jakob Andreae's *Acts of the Colloquy of Montbéliard,* his own report of the great theological dialogue with Theodore Beza, is a point-by-point accounting of one of the most important debates between Lutherans and the Reformed in the sixteenth century. Addressing distinctions and differences in doctrines such as Christology, the Lord's Supper, Baptism, and predestination, this debate tackled what ultimately were practical-theological questions, which still have bearing in pastoral practice, in teaching, and in broader theological conversations in current contexts. This English translation makes this debate accessible in the most detailed terms and is a valuable resource for historical understanding and theological engagement today.

—Rev. Dr. Gerhard H. Bode
Associate Professor of Historical Theology,
Concordia Seminary, St. Louis, MO

In 1586, spokesmen for the Reformed and Lutheran pastors within the French-speaking county of Montbéliard, ruled by the Lutheran duke of Württemberg, met in public debate over their confession of the faith. Theodore Beza and Jakob Andreae set down formative summaries of the positions of the two confessions. C. J. Armstrong's translation of the Lutheran record of this historic confrontation opens a significant window upon the roots and development of the two confessional positions. Twenty-first century readers will better understand their own tradition's teaching on the Sacraments, predestination, and public worship from this volume.

—Rev. Dr. Robert Kolb
Emeritus Professor of Systematic Theology,
Concordia Seminary, St. Louis, MO

For Lutherans and Reformed to remain true to their distinctive Reformation core beliefs, each must know how they came to believe what they do. Disparaging a widely held belief of a "one size fits all Protestantism" is the publication in English translation of the transcript of the 1586 debate between Jakob Andreae, an author of the Lutheran Formula of Concord, and Theodore Beza, John Calvin's successor in Geneva. The 1586 debate between theological giants of the two great Reformation traditions opens the door to learn how they handled their differences on the Lord's Supper, the person of Christ, Baptism, and predestination without compromising respect for each other. Even after more than 400 years, the debate makes for fascinating reading.

—Rev. Dr. David P. Scaer
The David P. Scaer Chair of Biblical and Systematic Theology
Chairman, Department of Systematic Theology,
Concordia Theological Seminary, Fort Wayne, IN
Editor, Concordia Theological Quarterly

This record of the 1586 Colloquy of Montbéliard between confessional Lutheran and Reformed pastors and theologians reflects the work of their contemporaneous churches, ministers, and theologians who were working out their own confession of the Word of God and simultaneously engaging those with whom they earnestly (and sometimes heatedly) disagreed. Rather than downplaying and obscuring genuine theological and practical differences, these discussions explored the differences honestly and even brutally. We are indebted to Dr. Armstrong and to the publisher for making available for the first time an important source document in the study of the history of confessional Protestant theology.

—Rev. Dr. R. Scott Clark
Professor of Church History and Historical Theology,
Westminster Seminary California, Escondido, CA

This translation of the Colloquy of Montbéliard opens a fascinating window into the second generation of the Reformation. Theodore Beza and Jakob Andreae discuss at length the divisive points between Lutherans and Reformed: the Lord's Supper, Baptism, images, and predestination. Even after more than 400 years, the patience and diligence with which Beza and Andreae conduct their discussion impresses and rewards the reader. Dr. Armstrong is to be thanked for making accessible this piece of history which has relevance for today.

—Rev. Dr. Roland Ziegler
Robert D. Preus Associate Professor of Systematic Theology and
Confessional Lutheran Studies, Concordia Theological Seminary, Fort Wayne, IN

Hitherto I have encountered the famous Colloquy of Montbéliard as a beckoning but foreboding footnote in the history of Lutheran-Reformed relations: a must for the historian of theology, but who has the linguistic proficiency these days, not to mention the time, to plough through a lengthy Latin manuscript? Dr. Armstrong has rendered signal service by putting this gripping debate into our hands, helping us to see that Lutheran-Reformed differences go all the way down, all the way across, and all the way up. His patient and skilled toil will help us put Jakob Andreae more accurately on the late sixteenth-century Lutheran map and will also make it plain that classic Reformed theology was governed more by philosophical a priori judgments than by exegetical findings.

—Rev. Dr. John R. Stephenson
Registrar and Professor of Historical Theology,
Concordia Lutheran Theological Seminary,
St. Catharines, Ontario

LUTHERANISM VS. CALVINISM

THE CLASSIC DEBATE AT THE COLLOQUY OF MONTBÉLIARD 1586

TRANSLATED BY CLINTON J. ARMSTRONG
FOREWORD BY JEFFREY MALLINSON

Cover images:
Theodore Beza © University Library of Tuebingen, Image Database
Jakob Andreae, Archive.org/Public Domain

Manufactured in the United States of America

Library of Congress Cataloging-in-Publication Data

Names: Andreae, Jakob, 1528-1590, author. | Beze, Theodore de, 1519-1605,
    author. | Armstrong, Clinton J., translator.
Title: Lutheranism vs. Calvinism : the classic debate at the Colloquy of
    Montbeliard / translated by Clinton J. Armstrong.
Other titles: Acta Colloquii Montis Belligartensis. English.
Description: St. Louis : Concordia Publishing House, 2017. | Includes
    bibliographical references and index.
Identifiers: LCCN 2017034612 (print) | LCCN 2017045267 (ebook) | ISBN
    9780758650788 | ISBN 9780758650771 (alk. paper)
Subjects: LCSH: Lutheran Church--Relations--Reformed Church--History--16th
    century. | Reformed Church--Relations--Lutheran Church--History--16th
    century. | Religious disputations--France--Montbeliard--History--16th
    century. | Lutheran Church--Doctrines--History--16th century. | Reformed
    Church--Doctrines--History--16th century. | Montbeliard (France)--Church
    history--16th century.
Classification: LCC BX8063.7.R4 (ebook) | LCC BX8063.7.R4 A5313 2017 (print)
    | DDC 230/.41--dc23
LC record available at https://lccn.loc.gov/2017034612

---

2   3   4   5   6   7   8   9   10   26 25 24 23 22 21 20 19 18 17

Table of Contents

Foreword

For those who believe in the Council of Constantinople's (381) commitment to the "one holy, catholic, and apostolic Church," almost all the sixteenth-century colloquies mark the beginning of a heartbreaking time of division within Western Christianity. This fragmentation of the Church continues to this day, despite various attempts at ecumenical bridge building. Some readers will be familiar with the Colloquy of Marburg (1529), which revealed an irreconcilable difference between Martin Luther and Ulrich Zwingli concerning the nature of the Lord's Supper. That was indeed an important turning point in Church history. Nonetheless, the records of the Colloquy of Montbeliard (1586) offer far more insight into the division between Reformed and Lutheran theologians during the sixteenth century. At that gathering, the principal participants were able to display mature, developed, and relatively consistent expressions of their theological traditions. This makes a document valuable not only for understanding the past but also for understanding the issues that divide Protestants.

Observers today might be inclined too easily to dismiss the concerns of those assembled at Montbéliard. They might, for instance, wish to simply dispense with the nitpicking of the old theologians and reunite the various evangelical sects. Alternatively, some might brush off the controversies of the past as overly abstract, intellectual, and scholastic.[1] The precise and technical language of colloquy, even with translation, may further cause some to think the whole matter revolved around trivial controversies. As understandable as such thinking may be, there are several reasons why these old disputes remain important to examine closely.

---

1   For important insights into the role of the Protestant Scholastics, which tend to emphasize the theological consistency among the reformers, and their later academic consolidators, see Robert Preus, *The Theology of Post-Reformation Lutheranism*, 2 Vols. (St. Louis, MO: Concordia, 1970–72); Richard A. Muller, *Post-Reformation Reformed Dogmatics*, 4 Vols. (Grand Rapids, MI: Baker 1987–1993); Carl R. Trueman and R. Scott Clark eds., *Protestant Scholasticism: Essays in Reassessment* (Eugene, OR: Wipf and Stock, 2007); Eef Dekker and Willem J. van Asselt, *Reformation and Scholasticism: An Ecumenical Enterprise* (Grand Rapids, MI: Baker, 2001); and my book, *Faith, Reason, and Revelation in Theodore Beza (1519–1605)* (Oxford University Press, 2003).

First of all, proto-scholastics had concrete, life and death reasons for being precise and polemical with their theological writing and dialogue. Princes and city councils operating under the policy of *cuius regio, eius religio* or "whoever's realm, his religion [is the official religion]" cultivated the best and brightest theological minds to explain and defend distinct confessions. Failure in the public square meant not only embarrassment but also the concrete loss of rights to worship and teach within a region. This means that, even in cases where the disposition of individuals such as Beza and Andreae might have been courteous and irenic, the political and ecclesiastical context all but required these men to become polemic if they were to accomplish the task assigned by both the princes and churches.

Second, the colloquy reflects the fundamental differences between the formal principles (that is, the authoritative sources of theology and the relative positions of those sources) of the Reformed and Lutherans. Specifically, the role of instrumental reason as a tool for interpreting biblical passages was elevated within Reformed circles. Likewise, logical consistency of various doctrines was valued more highly by the Reformed than the Lutherans. The following exchange between Beza and Andreae illustrates this difference well:

Dr. Jakob:
Paul writes, 1 Corinthians 10[:16], The bread which we break is a communication of the body of Christ. He does not say, it is a communication of the remission of sins, but rather it is a communication of the body of Christ.

Dr. Beza:
Prove it with a Syllogism.

Dr. Jakob:
Sayings of holy Scripture do not need to be proven with a Syllogism; they are rather believed on account of divine authority.

Dr. Beza:
Make a Syllogism.

Dr. Jakob:
This is a novelty and unheard of in any school, that testimonies of Scripture are proved with a Syllogism.

Dr. Beza:
Make a Syllogism.

Dr. Jakob:
The genuine meaning of the saying of Scripture should not be proved with a Syllogism, but should rather be demonstrated from Scripture. And what kind of communication is it where there is no reception?[2]

Similarly, Andreae says repeatedly that he wants biblical backing for the axiom *finitum non capax infiniti* (the finite is not able to contain the infinite), which the Reformed frequently employed: "I still hear no testimony of Scripture, but rather just a philosophical principle, that the finite is not capable of containing the infinite. This has its own place in Philosophy and the natural sciences. But it cannot hold a place in this mystery."[3]

Third, there is an important connection between Eucharistic theology and Christology. Neither party at the colloquy thought that the Lord's Supper was merely a memorial ritual. Rather, they believed it had something to say about the very nature of God's presence in the world, before and after the Ascension. In the following pages, one finds that for the Lutherans, the bread in Communion emphatically remains bread. It is redeemed. Sanctified. It has the privilege of being part of God's intervention in His creation. It is no mere superstition or affectation that caused the Lutherans to insist that in the Lord's Supper one finds the real Jesus. Jesus is right there: not in some faint imaginary way, but *right there*. No metaphysical explanations are needed.

Moreover, to deny this presence is at least as misguided as to deny the dignity of the bread's presence. In God's plan, the Lutherans believed, Spirit and matter unite. To insist on the divide between spirit and matter,

---

2   Original pages 118–119.

3   Original page 280.

as the Reformed did, was tantamount to rejecting the very core of the Eucharistic mystery itself, and ultimately the mystery of the Incarnation. Thus, for Andreae, a two-natured Christ is able to do two-natured things where and when He pleases. Beza, on the contrary, maintained that Jesus' body remains at the right hand of God in heaven, and thus cannot logically be in more than one place at the same time when Christians around the world celebrate Holy Communion. The Christological implications here were obvious to both parties. For this reason, the reader will find Lutherans calling the Reformed "Nestorians," after the condemned teaching of Nestorius, who emphasized the strict division between the two natures of Christ. The Reformed, in turn, called the Lutherans "Eutychians," believing that they inordinately confused the two natures.

Fourth, though the issues debated at Montbeliard might appear abstract and academic, they had deeply *pastoral* implications. Both Beza and Andreae recognized this. Beza, for instance, was concerned not to give the sense that a believer could fall out of God's favor, and so rejected Andreae's endorsement of the idea of mortal sin. On the other side, Andreae was startled that Beza could say, with respect to Baptism, that infants were only "probably" elect:

> *Beza: "I answer: Infants sprinkled by water Baptism are PROBABLY, probably I say, considered sons of God. But we think that it is absurd to assert that they are renewed at that moment when they are baptized, such that they become new people with the old man destroyed. The reason for this is that children do not have faith, especially actual faith. But they are baptized in the faith of their parents."[4]*

Such teaching, for Andreae, threatened to take away a believer's confidence in the redeeming work of God *extra nos* (outside ourselves), and dangerously turned a person inward, leading to a desperate attempt to find inward assurance that one was indeed elect. Andreae believed that pastors could point a troubled conscience to the words of his or her Baptism whenever they doubted God's love and mercy.

---

4 Original page 485.

Getting Along

Fifth and finally, the exchanges within this unsuccessful colloquy may provide a humane model for inter-confessional dialogue today. Beza and Andreae maintained simultaneously both (1) a commitment to courtesy and respect for their opponents and (2) an unwillingness to discard important doctrines for the sake of unity. They were thus principled, rather than stubborn in their effort at reconciliation. For instance, both explicitly stated they would be glad for the uncharitable and false writings found in their respective camps to be destroyed, if such a move could restore peace. In other words, they were not so much committed to their egos or writings, but rather committed what they understood about the very nature of Christ.

Toward the end of the colloquy, their discussion branched into a few other tricky topics, including predestination, the use of images and iconoclastic measures, the sort of music appropriate to churches, and the perseverance of the saints. But the nature of Christ—and what Christ means for poor, miserable sinners—remained the central topic for both Andreae and Beza. For that reason, we can return to this account with respect for all those assembled, including the laity and nobility, grateful for those who took their faith seriously enough to explore it in detail. We may be free to skim sections here and there in this book, just as the 1586 audience might have snoozed here and there during longwinded monologues, but we ought not dismiss the sincerity and earnestness with which they sought to understand their Christian faith.

Jeff Mallinson, D. Phil.
Professor of Theology and Philosophy
Concordia University Irvine

Introduction and acknowledgments

Near the border that France shares with Germany and Switzerland, between Strasbourg and Geneva, just west of Basel, lies the county of Montbéliard, home to a Peugeot factory and a population of which the majority claim to be Roman Catholic. This religious identity is rather a recent development, though, due to changes that took place over the last century. From the time of the Reformation the population had been majority Lutheran, ruled by the house of Württemberg until the French Revolution. Despite the modern world's changes, however, the county enjoys a heritage that today still boasts Lutheran churches. The reasons for this include, in no small part, the political landscape and religious disagreements that shaped this borderland at the end of the sixteenth century.

This book is a translation of a document prepared by the German Lutheran theologian Jakob Andreae in 1587. The bulk of it is a transcript of a conference that had taken place the year prior, between him and the French successor of John Calvin at Geneva, Theodore Beza. The Colloquy of Montbéliard is, like other instances of dialogue among reformers that pepper the history of the sixteenth century, fraught with tensions both political and theological. This one, coming forty years after Martin Luther's death, reprises in some ways the more famous Colloquy of Marburg that had involved that reformer and Ulrich Zwingli, more than half a century before Andreae would meet Beza at Montbéliard. The topic of the Lord's Supper and examination of its attendant presuppositions regarding the person of Christ constituted the bulk of both colloquies. "*Is* means *is*" proved to be a sticking point on the Lutheran side at both. And just as Luther had refused to shake hands with Zwingli at Marburg, so also Andreae refused his hand to Beza at the end of Montbéliard. But the Colloquy of Montbéliard is significantly different in that it illustrates not the early Evangelical struggle between Luther's German Reformation and the radical Swiss, but rather, the tensions involving what were now Lutherans and Calvinists, reformers in churches that had grown up in an age of religious war and suspicion, churches that reached their adolescence in an age of concession as much as of confession.

Space does not permit a thorough historical introduction, and it is probable that those interested in reading Andreae's Acts of the Colloquy are already sufficiently grounded in the history of the later sixteenth century to know what has led to the drama about to unfold between these pages. For a fuller treatment, the reader is directed to Jill Raitt's 1993 Oxford monograph, *The Colloquy of Montbéliard: Religion and Politics in the Sixteenth Century*. Her study broadly surveys the religious and political background of the 1586 Colloquy and outlines the debates covered in the week of the Colloquy via the primary sources that recorded it. The first and most comprehensive of these is the first edition of Andreae's transcript: *Acta Colloquii Montis Belligartensis: Quod Habitum est, Anno Christ 1586* (Tübingen: George Gruppenbach, 1587). An English translation has been published here for the first time. Count Frederick's Preface to the Acts claims that their publication in 1587 was inspired by false gossip on the Reformed side that the Lutherans at Montbéliard had had their hat handed to them; the last straw was a certain "notorious Epistle," promulgated by the Reformed, that had included a document maintaining the Huguenot exiles seeking sanctuary in Montbéliard had been given official permission to receive the Eucharist under their own confession. Beza's response to Andreae's publication followed. Andreae then published a refutation of Beza's response. Far from being conciliatory, these responses and counter-responses illustrate how entrenched the reformers were in their own positions, and how theologically far apart their churches were. When looking at the modern world and new world churches that have grown from their adolescent, confessional forebearers, it appears we still are.

One might well wonder what advantage is gained by the existence of an English translation of Andreae's *Acts of the Colloquy of Montbéliard*. After all, chances are that those who are entrenched sufficiently in the study of the history and theology of the sixteenth century even to know about the 1586 Colloquy probably have sufficient skill in the Latin language and the history of Reformation debate to read the text, publicly accessible these days via digital copy, in the original language. No attempt has been made here to modernize or beautify the language; it has some rough edges and often sacrifices fluid English for Latinate construction and vocabulary. But it is hoped that having the text available in English will help an Anglophone readership to explore the text more, to dig deeper into Reformed-Lutheran dialogue of the sixteenth century, and perhaps further that dialogue more in the twenty-first.

Accessibility is key, and though rendered into what is perhaps an easier language for a reader, the topics themselves do not become less vexing even into our twenty-first century. I have been shocked just this year to have been made aware of shots fired via social media in the continuing exchanges of both amateur and professional theologians, showing our celebration of 500 years of Reformation comes with plenty of baggage: a Calvinist charges a Lutheran of stercoranism (the idea being that Lutheran communication involves the reception of Jesus' real body, therefore naturally, as with all food, its digestion, the end of which is solid waste in defecation); a Lutheran calls a Calvinist a Muslim (the idea being that Reformed denial of communication of majesty to Christ results in a Jesus who was endowed with created gifts (rather than uncreated), and who is therefore no more than a special prophet, not the Son of God). Accessibility to one's native tongue is not a quick cure for the corruption of the human nature, curved inward to such a degree that it delights in such backstabbing. If nothing else, the modern reader of this translation will be able to see this in action 500 years ago; what the reader does with it at that point I do not know, but hazard a prayer that it may tend toward the more productive and edifying rather than the vitriolic and histrionic as in the case of Beza and Andreae.

For as devoid of style as this stark translation may seem, there is something of the character of the interlocutors that yet peeks out in their dialogue. Neither seems altogether likeable in a modern sense of *politesse*. Sure, as product of their cultural circumstances, they use the correct forms of address with nobles and guests, but when it comes down to it, these men are at table with a bone to pick, and a worldview that is absolutely positive that there is one, and only one, capital-T truth, and *their* read of Scripture, orthodox history, and their place in it has led them to believe that their confession of that truth is the only confession there is, all others be damned (quite literally). This is the spirit of Luther's "Here I stand," certainly, but the standing up for oneself on display in these reformers can aim blows below the belt quite often. Which, I'll confess, is some of the fun of working with this text. There are some pretty good zingers here, most on the side of Andreae pointing up the inadequacy of Beza's logical system and conclusions in light of his (Andreae's) contrary hermeneutical presuppositions. This should remind the reader that this is a very *Lutheran* document. For a more comprehensive sense of the conversation (avoiding the adjective "fair and balanced," as probably no writing in the sixteenth century can fairly be so described), the reader will need to engage the responses from 1587 and 1588 that followed this initial publication.

The text you see before you attempts to reflect, in some small way, the printing conventions of the 1587 text. Diamond brackets (<>) enclose page numbers original to the text. Gruppenbach's publication set type so as to distinguish one speaker from the other, and so the translation attempts to do so as well. Marginalia in the 1587 text are here normally at the head of the paragraph they refer to, unless they are lettered annotations that follow (like our practice with footnotes) after the paragraph they treat. We are used to seeing certain words capitalized, e.g., "New Testament," "Holy Spirit." The 1587 text writes these as "new Testament" and "holy Spirit," capitalizing the first word only in abbreviated form. The text you see before attempts as much as possible to keep the capitals capitalized, as the original printer often indicated emphasis by doing so. When whole words or phrases needed emphasis, the printer put words in all caps; the convention of this translation has been to italicize these words and phrases instead. In place of quotation marks, the sixteenth-century text used parentheses; these have been changed to quotation marks as appropriate. Greek in the printed text of 1587 has been retained intact where translation was provided by the Colloquy's interlocutors. Where translation was not provided in the Acts, it is offered here with the Greek in brackets. The table of contents reflects the basic practice of the colloquy — reading of theses from both sides, responses to objected dogmas, and so on. I attempted to make the table of contents fairly consistent so that readers might find their place more quickly.

Finally, a word of thanks to those whose assistance allowed this manuscript to come to completion. The generosity of Christ College at Concordia University, Irvine, in awarding me the Harry and Caroline Trembath Chair in Confessional Theology in 2015–2016, allowed me to begin this work, following the encouragement of Rev. Dr. Benjamin Mayes, who models the mission of making more and more accessible the Reformation and post-Reformation world for a modern readership. Dr. Jeffrey Mallinson's expertise in Reformation theology, philosophy, and in particular Theodore Beza, was a *sine qua non* for this project; his editorial eye and his ability to follow Beza's logic helped to untangle not a few quandaries of rendering the language into a more understandable idiom. Several students of CUI had their first taste of late-medieval Latin under my tutelage, whose contributions in the section on the person of Christ led to a deeper understanding of the *communicatio idiomatum*, as well as keen translational insights: Kayla Biar, Aubrie Bogle, Kimberly Olivar, Bradley Smith, James Virant, and Phoebe Weaver. My family, of course, puts up with the brunt of the dark side of writing and research, as their father and husband is away while writing, even when present. Their support in reading, commenting, and even indexing are sacrifices I cherish, but that pales in comparison to their love, patience, and encouragement.

Acts of the Colloquy
of Montebéliard,

Which was held in the year of Christ 1586,
with the help of God Almighty,

THE HONORABLE PRINCE AND LORD,
THE LORD FREDERICK,
Count of Württemburg and
Montebéliard, etc., presiding,

Between the very renowned men,
DR. JAKOB ANDREAE,
Provost and Chancellor of the University of Tübingen,
and
DR. THEODORE BEZA,
Professor and Pastor in Geneva,

Published now in the year of our Lord 1587
BY THE AUTHORITY OF THE AFOREMENTIONED PRINCE FREDERICK, ETC.

THESE ACTS HAVE BEEN SEALED,
honestly and in good faith, and will amply refute the
very ridiculous rumors scattered abroad regarding this
Colloquy, especially a certain letter, replete with
falsehoods and slanders, and printed in type.

Frederick

By God's grace the Count of Württemburg and Montebéliard, etc.

To the Christian reader, eager for heavenly truth, Greetings.

Christian Emperors once discharged a duty pleasing to God and worthy of his person, and in our generation many pious Electors, Princes and Orders of Government, although very anxiously, have weighed in on it with tireless zeal (sparing neither efforts nor costs), in order that Religious controversies, having arisen in Christ's Church, might be laid to rest as soon as possible, or else might promptly be eliminated in a lawful manner. In their own pious attempt, they maintained their determined goal, that if they should wander off track, they would be led back into the way, and avoid the destruction of their souls, that both the sweetest consensus of heavenly truth and harmony in Christ's Church, to the praise of God Almighty, might be restored, and might be heeded everywhere in the Churches.

With exactly this intention, and toward the same end, in the month of March, of the Year that most recently passed, We summoned to our castle at Montebéliard the Honorable Theologians Dr. Jakob Andreae, Provost and Chancellor of the Academy of Tübingen, and Dr. Theodore Beza, Professor and Pastor of Geneva, in order that there in our presence they might confer peaceably concerning articles that are controversial between themselves and might converse together. We organized all this for no other reason at all than that we might agree for certain amongst ourselves on something about the truth of our

Confession. Indeed for some time we, with the Emperor's Electors and the rest of the Princes and Nobles, have subscribed to the pure Evangelical doctrine, and have given public testimony to heavenly truth, <preface 3> from which, aided by divine grace, we will never depart. But we wish it to be furthermore confirmed and established, and to stand prominently for our posterity. But French exiles, who made a break from the Papist religion, had asked us humbly and resolutely to organize a Colloquy between those very famous Theologians, and besides this had conceived a great hope that a holy concord would be established concerning the controversial articles in which the French Churches disagree with ours. Through this salutary cure, it was hoped, the French Churches and certain other foreign ones would more suitably blend with ours.

As in time past, out of compassion we granted the French exiles lodging in our city of Montbéliard, mindful of the Prophetic word, "Lead needy wanderers into your home" (Isaiah 58[:7]) and the Apostolic one, "Do not forget hospitality" (Hebrews 13[:2]). We had no wish to refuse a Colloquy (since they were requesting it so humbly and resolutely) lest we seem to neglect anything that could be effective for <preface 4> the peace of Christ's Church or our own eternal salvation.

But when the Theologians of whom we made mention above had convened in our castle, together with those whose names are registered in the Acts elsewhere, we admitted to the Colloquy not only our own Aides and courtiers, but also the French exiles, as many as desired to be present and were not ignorant of the Latin language. Nor did we wish to be absent from the Colloquy even for a moment; we considered moreover that amid such an important affair we should not consider other Political business, so that we might the more readily be at our leisure to address this one matter. Now this was the process of the Colloquy that was established and observed: the Theologians of our party would first hand over to the opposing party their Theses on each of the controversial Articles, and then receive in turn a written response from them. After the different writings were publicly read out loud in the presence of all of those in attendance,

<preface 5> Dr. Jakob Andreae and Dr. Theodore Beza conversed peacefully about each article (of which they treated the Theses and response). The Articles discussed were these: 1. Concerning the Lord's Supper. 2. Concerning the Person of Christ. 3. Concerning Images, temples, and similar matters. 4. Concerning Baptism. 5. Concerning Predestination. For it was well-known to us that between us and the French Doctors there was no consensus regarding these Articles.

Although it is often customary in Colloquies of this sort for public and sworn Notaries to be appointed to record every single one of the things said by either party, nevertheless at the beginning of this Colloquy it was determined and agreed upon by both parties that Notaries would not be used, so as not to protract the time of spoken presentations to allow transcription, and lest the slower speech be harder to understand by both the collocutors and the audience, since the attempt to accommodate dictation would involve breaking the conversation into many small bits. For it was our desire in this Colloquy that both parties, by joining together in friendly discussion, <preface 6> would lay out and explain their opinion to the other as simply as possible. Thus neither party could complain (as has happened often up to this point) that they were never sufficiently heard or rightly understood, since the opposing party would comprehend fully our intention in each and every one of the chief points of controversy, and in turn would declare their own opinion fully and abundantly.

In the meantime, though, each presenter was free to annotate whatever he wished. And since we did not doubt even from the beginning of this Colloquy but that many who were absent would very much want to procure these Acts, certain members of our court made it their business to ensure that each and every thing that was said by either party was recorded very faithfully and as swiftly, skillfully, and diligently as possible. They were also collected into papers lest anything in the Acts that was necessary to be known be left out, if they were ever made public. But the result was that both parties were compelled to confess that the Acts of that colloquy had been collected in good faith.

It was not a source of trouble for us, moreover, to annotate by hand, **\<preface 7\>** *what was being said, and obstinately asserted, by the opposing party, contrary to the pious, simple, and sincere doctrine understood in our Christian Catechesis. Such things included that we have no presence of Christ's body and blood in the Lord's Supper except that which Abraham had in the old Testament during his era (p. 67),[1] when in fact the Son of God had not yet become incarnate, and his flesh and blood was not yet in existence; that the infinite properties of his divinity are in no way able to be communicated to Christ's human nature (p. 290), and so omnipotence, omniscience, omnipresence, and adoration all fail to come together in Christ's assumed humanity, even though they are personally united with the Son of God, but those things communicated to the human nature in Christ are only finite and created (p. 247); that countless children are baptized who nevertheless are not regenerated (p. 473), and for this reason it cannot be said for certain that a baptized infant is born again,* **\<preface 8\>** *even though we ought to hold out good hope for it (p. 484); that Christ did not die for the sins of the whole world, but only for the elect, and that the rest perish by God's hidden and eternal decree (p. 547); that David retained the holy Spirit and faith even in the midst of his adultery (p. 463), etc. These and similar things we particularly noted by pen. But afterward, when all our notes and signatures were collected together, we bid them be arranged as carefully and faithfully as possible into one corpus, that the context of the disputation also might be established. There are no gaps in the record of each oration, and nothing which pertained to the substance of the entire Colloquy was left wanting. Moreover, since we knew it could be pleasing and useful to a young scholar were the reproofs to be annotated, at the margin of those writings which the opposing party in this Colloquy presented, which briefly list the errors and the causes of the errors, we gladly gave our assent to this, even though the same errors are refuted abundantly in our responses.* **\<preface 9\>**

---

1   These page numbers refer to the printed 1587 document, referred to throughout in diamond brackets (e.g. **\<67\>**).

*Our consideration in this matter was in fact based on the need
to maintain the approach of the Alumni of that renowned Academy, of which our very praiseworthy Ancestors and Kin were
founders. We once served as Dean at this illustrious University,
where we gladly support singular students (for the service of
our Churches and Schools). The usefulness of this document for
these students and others who study Theology, which they will
receive from the edition of the Colloquy organized by us, had to
be considered of greater value than the viciousness of slanderers,
who hold this opinion (from the wisdom of Theognis): Slander
boldly: something will always stick.[2] We have judged that the
slanders of these wicked people are of little value in comparison
with the benefit we can offer so many people. We publicly swear,
in fact, that in the collection of these Acts, nothing at all has
been inserted or left out which pertained to the CHIEF CON-
TROVERSIES. Indeed, nothing in this entire business has been
presented either out of favor or animosity toward the one party
or the other.*

    \<preface 10\> *And yet, however, at the start we did not summon
the two aforementioned very renowned Theologians to a colloquy with the plan to publish the Acts of that colloquy. For this
reason indeed we thought that public and sworn Notaries (as
we said above) should not be employed, inasmuch as we thought
these Acts could lie hidden (for the sake of peace and the greater
tranquility) as if within private walls. Nevertheless necessity
compelled us to change our plan, lest our silence defraud the
glory of the divine name and the salvation of the Church. For
as soon as the Colloquy concluded, various empty and stormy
rumors scattered far and wide (brought up to us partly in speech,
partly in letters), namely that our pious confession (which nevertheless rests on the immovable word of God) had been refuted,
defeated, and rejected by the opposing party, and that the confes-*

---

2   This pithy aphorism is actually not to be found among the nearly 2800 lines of extant *Theognidea*;
a closer comparandum may be found in Plutarch, relating in his essay "How to Tell a Flatterer from a
Friend" the story of Medius, a sycophant of Alexander: "Now he urged them not to be afraid to assail
and sting with their calumnies, pointing out that, even if the man who is stung succeeds in healing the
wound, the scar of the calumny will still remain" (*Moralia* 1.4.65B–5E (Frank Cole Babbitt, trans., *Plutarch:
Moralia I*, Cambridge, MA: Harvard University Press, 1927).

sion's defenders had brought home confusion and disgrace. And
though we were able to consider these hollow boasts worthless,
since we knew (taught by experience) **\<preface 11\>** that spreading
even gross falsehoods was very agreeable to the opposing party,
and not in the least unusual for them, nevertheless once a certain
Letter about the Colloquy of Montbéliard, published in print,[3]
was brought to light, stuffed full of figments and falsehoods, and
even published under a false author and imprint (which is still
universally against the laws and statutes of the Roman Empire),
it became necessary to assert the truth and dignity of our person,
by means of this edition of the Acts of the Colloquy, against the
insults of that light-shunning reprobate who spared no lie against
us in his own report. So might the falsehood of that person be
refuted in this way. And of course the opposing party, even
had they not been able to prevent the aforementioned Epistle
from being spread among themselves widely, and being retailed
publicly in the marketplaces, should rightly have taken care to
suppress that notorious writing, if pious concord and the tranquility of the Churches were dear to their heart. But the opposing
party, by turning a blind eye to so shameless a fiction, **\<preface 12\>**
now spread abroad far and wide, has by this very oversight sufficiently betrayed their own consensus with that hollow joker
and slanderer, according to the old saying: The one who is silent
seems to agree.

That groundless Epistle, and other things written also by the
opposing party from that point, have therefore both provided us
the occasion and imposed the necessity of bringing the Acts of
the Colloquy to the light, sealed truly and in good faith, and to
determine that they be recognized by Christ's Church, so that
the holy cause of our party might be burdened the less henceforth
by slanders, and so that our person might be vindicated from the
insult of those slanders. And since the truth of our confession is
splendidly demonstrated anew in those Acts, by this a true and
God-pleasing peace is offered to our adversaries. This peace can

---

3 The "notorious Epistle" (as Count Frederick will call it later in this Preface) is discussed in Raitt,
160–4.

be easily established if it is willing to embrace the heavenly truth with us in unanimous consent, the heavenly truth proposed and expressed in God's word. This is our heart-felt desire, and we pray to God that it may come to pass. In fact we do not rejoice in the least in strife (especially in the business of religion), <preface 13> and so it has neither been our intention to introduce new disagreements, nor to offer reason for greater discord of spirits by the publication of the Colloquy.

The author of that notorious Epistle even bears false witness against us, as if we assumed to ourselves the role of JUDGE, and PARTIAL one at that, in the Colloquy so frequently mentioned already. In this matter he does us a considerable injustice.

In fact, with the blessing of God we learned long ago, through repeated reading of holy writ and testimonials of the Historians, that the one and only Christ was judge over the things expressed in the Prophetic and Apostolic writings, all controversies of religion, and even ones that rose up before (who alone the heavenly Father bid be listened to as our sole Teacher, Matthew 28[:20], Matthew 17[:5]). And we know well that Constantine the great (in name and in deed) seriously charged the Bishops gathered for the Council of Nicea to put aside hostile strife amongst themselves in order that they might take up the solution of present questions, <preface 14> from God's book, the ordinances of the ancient Prophets, the Evangelists, and the Apostolic books. We were delighted when we heard that happening with our own ears, as our party maintained their affirmation of the first and unaltered holy Augsburg Confession, proceeding with care by a defense of the same truth. This made us exceedingly glad, confirmed in faith and our conscience. But on the other hand we were grieved when we observed that the opposing party made thoughtless sport of those most well-known and unshakable testimonies of sacred letters, in which they ought rightly to have been educated and called back to the right way, or when they twisted them by some human interpretation, and granted no place at their table for heavenly truth. To be sure, this most malicious obstinacy violently troubled our spirit.

The author of the aforementioned Epistle seriously and unjustly injured us in the following, shamelessly daring to concoct the story that after the Colloquium had been held, we gave permission to the French exiles that they could commune, together with our citizens, under the free declaration **<preface 15>** *that they wished to retain their French Confession, and take the holy Supper of the Lord. This is what before the Colloquy (as that joker maliciously makes up) we were unwilling to permit them. From this he opines that it must be deduced that we have become more acquiescent to the Confession of the opposing party. Therefore he tries to draw us into this suspicion before Christ's Church, as if we began to incline toward the teaching of the opposing party, and to make some concession to it. In this entire claim the author of that Epistle is entirely without ground. For we are endowed with enough understanding of sacred things to know that the holy Supper of the Lord possesses, besides other ends, this use as well, that it makes known the religion and Confession which each man professes. For those who commune with any Church in the taking of this Sacrament profess publicly by this action that they embrace the teaching of the same Church and reject the contrary teaching, and separate themselves from others, just as when someone* **<preface 16>** *communes with Popes under one kind (as they say), shows that he approves of Papal religion, but those who with Lutherans take the Lord's Supper (as they call it) under both kinds bear witness that they profess the pure teaching of the Gospel and reject the contrary.[4] And so we have always judged that there should in no way at all be any deception in taking the Lord's Supper, or any kind of pretending, a thing from which our spirit recoils. Because of this, as many times as the French exiles desired to commune with us (they made this petition rather often, though they had not been invited by anyone), we always sent them back to our Confession, follow-*

---

4   By "both kinds," the Preface refers to the practice in churches of the Reformation to distribute the Sacrament of the Altar entirely, both the bread and the chalice, for all to receive both elements. In the late 16th century Roman Catholic practice denied the chalice to the laity, distributing the Sacramental element under one *species* or "kind" only, namely the bread. The practice continued as an extension of medieval practice intended to curb the possibility of irreverence, and also in response to the churches of the Reformation which considered the withholding of the chalice as a Papist abuse.

ing the Colloquy just as before the Colloquy, admonishing them that they should only commune if they embraced our Confession sincerely. However we were never willing to permit them to take the Lord's Supper with our people under their unrestrained declaration (of retaining their French Confession), even though they petitioned resolutely and humbly. This will be treated more abundantly in the Appendix (which is to be appended to the Acts of the Colloquy). **<preface 17>** *For we readily understood that such permission would detract significantly from our pious Confession, and be a source of injury to sincere religion. We would come under suspicion, as if we were either defending yet another Confession, or at least secretly sponsoring it.*

And indeed in this matter we have imitated Christian Emperors, who did not yield to the Arians' demand, when they sought to be received back into communion with the Orthodox, before such time as they could confirm the doctrine of the Orthodox: though even then they found it impossible to guard against them even with saintly vigilance, since many professed one thing by mouth and pen rather than holding it close to their heart. In such a way therefore did we send away the French exiles who sought communion with our people, to read and approve our Confession. Our purpose was that we might in the meantime advise them seriously but gently, lest they do anything with an uncertain conscience, since they would otherwise **<preface 18>** *in doubt not take care of their conscience, and receive the body and blood of the Lord unworthily and to their judgment, since this salutary Sacrament instituted for life and salvation could result in death and condemnation for them. And so at Christmas (before the Colloquy was held) they abstained from the Lord's Supper. But after Easter, which followed the Colloquy, they communed together with our citizens, and they did the same thing the following Pentecost. Then we gathered together, and amassed a considerable part of the audience of the Colloquy, so that they might understand that our opinion about the Lord's Supper rested on the firm and immovable words of Christ, and a pious person's conscience could safely acquiesce to these.*

But then while we were traveling abroad, certain of the French exiles made a declaration in the presence of some of the Ministers of the Church at Montbéliard, namely that they intended to commune under the opinion of their French Confession, but afterwards <preface 19> with the departure of the Ministers (who spoke against their declaration) the French even brought up an Instrument[5] in addition to their declaration through a Notary public. Not only did we not approve it, but we also consider it worthless, and are unwilling to think it of any value; we publicly spoke against it. For the Instrument clearly contends against true piety and our decrees, so often given regarding this matter, and it was produced without the knowledge of the Ministers of our Churches. Our Ministers of the Gospel did their duty and were unwilling to admit the French to the communion of the Lord's Supper, being instructed by our decrees, unless they should first assent to our Confession and following a friendly explanation of their French Confession, acquiesce to our holy opinion.

We undertook an embassy into France on behalf of those exiles (elected from great Men), not with the purpose of approving their errors which they continue to have in the business of religion, <preface 20> but rather to try to bring relief to those who, besides being expelled from their ancestral homes, wander in exile, and shun the tyranny of the Roman Pontiff in the Church and the manifold Papal Idol-madness: for these we attempted to obtain a repatriation, and security and tranquility, but we never intended to encourage or propagate their errors. Rather, moved by pity, we wished to discharge our obligation of piety by interceding with the almighty King of France on behalf of the poor exiles. Certainly it was in the same spirit that our relative Duke Christoph of Württemberg of blessed and happy memory once gave generous alms to the French exiles dwelling at Frankfurt-

---

5   The "Instrument," which is mentioned in the "notorious Epistle," claims permission for the French exiles to receive the Sacrament from the church at Montbéliard from their own priests, under their own confession, authorized by Frederick himself; this is the reason he so vehemently attacks it as a falsehood. See Raitt, 161–68; she includes a transcription of the French text of the "Instrument" in her Appendix, 203–5.

am-Main, with this declaration attached: that he gave alms not to their religion, but to their need.

But we pray the eternal God, Father of our Lord Jesus Christ, to <preface 21> cause the Colloquy of Montbéliard to produce such fruit through the holy Spirit, that those who are yet remediable, and who prefer not their own little glory to their soul's salvation, may approach us in approval and Confession of heavenly truth, and in such a way a pious and hoped for peace and concord may be established between the French Churches and ours. Amen. Written at Montbéliard in our castle, February 2, in the Year from the birth of our Savior Jesus Christ, 1587.

<1>

Concerning the Occasion of the Colloquy of Montbéliard.

THE CONVERSATION OF THE BARON OF CLERVANT WITH DR. JAKOB ANDREAE CONCERNING THE ORGANIZATION OF A COLLOQUY.

In the Year of Our Lord 1586, on the 13th day of January, the Ambassador of the judicious Lord, King Henry, Duke of Navarre, the Baron of Clervant, had come to Stüttgart, and had learned also that Jakob Andreae was there. He sent a messenger to him and invited him to a friendly Colloquy. He told him to bring with him others he would want to have there. Since this quite satisfied Dr. Jakob's good pleasure, he brought with him a few things concerning French matters, and used his brother as interpreter, Baron Malroy, because Dr. Jakob did not understand the French language, and the Baron of Clervant could not speak Latin without difficulty.

WHY DR. JAKOB DOES NOT TAKE JUDGMENT TO HIMSELF CONCERNING POLITICAL BUSINESS. THE ORACULAR BREASTPLATE OF THE HIGH PRIEST.

After this, Dr. Jakob swore that he did not assume for himself the power of judgment concerning the French affairs which related to Politics (especially rebellions in the realm of France), since they were better referred to those skilled in law and their judgments. The Lord Baron insisted that in the old Testament, the Priests had also been consulted by the Israelites. Dr. Jakob replied that the model of the high Priest gave him an even better reason not to answer, as he was lacking one thing, namely the breastplate, in which were inscribed the names of the 12 tribes of the Israelites on twelve gems. When the high Priest, ordained by God was dressed in it, he would answer the people when they asked. But then

Dr. Jakob said to himself, Who decided that I should be Judge between <2> you and your brother? (Luke 2 [12:14]) Smiling at this answer, the Baron of Clervant let it go. He began a discussion about Theological topics, especially about the conflict which has endured now these many years between the German Churches which profess the Augsburg Confession and the French Churches which he himself called reformed, that is, which had thrown off the yoke and Papal Tyranny. This is what he wanted to converse about with Dr. Jakob.

THE OPINION OF THE BARON OF CLERVANT REGARDING OUR DIFFERENCE OF OPINION.

It seemed to him that the Disagreement between the Theologians of either party was centered around merely one part of Christian doctrine, namely the Lord's Supper, but that in the rest of the articles of faith and confession, he was himself indeed of the opinion that there was a holy consensus in every respect.

THE BARON OF CLERVANT'S PLAN REGARDING ESTABLISHING CONCORD.

Nevertheless (asking the pardon of Dr. Jakob), it seemed therefore to him that the most convenient and expeditious way forward towards establishing holy peace and strong concord would be if precisely nothing further were disputed about Christ's words by either party. Since Christ said, Take, eat, this is my body, etc. Take and drink, this is my blood of the new Testament (Matthew 26[:26–28], Mark 14[:22–24], Luke 22[:19–20], 1 Corinthians 11[:24–25]), then these words of Christ should be embraced in simple faith, and the mode of presence ought to be entrusted to his omnipotence and divine wisdom, who is true, omnipotent, and wisest of all. And for this reason he is able to fulfill whatever he promises, so that he supremely exceeds the folly of human capacity and intelligence (as do the other countless works of God).

DR. JAKOB'S ANSWER. AN EXPEDITIOUS WAY TOWARDS CONCORD IN THE CONTROVERSY ABOUT THE LORD'S SUPPER. LUTHER'S DOCTRINE CONCERNING THE LORD'S SUPPER.

Dr. Jakob answered, This reasoning is indeed very expeditious and a way towards establishing holy concord — not only is this so, but it is also the same one as had been proposed by our people already from the moment <3> when that unfortunate controversy arose. Had the Zwinglians entered on this path, this conflict either would never have arisen or it could have been very easily laid to rest again, since Luther, and those who agree with him, urged this simplicity of faith in all his writings and orations, namely that we understand the words of Christ's Testament simply, just as the words themselves read, and that we trust simply that in the administration of the consecrated bread and wine there are distributed to us truly the body and blood of Christ, and they are received by all those eating in the Supper by mouth (for he thus teaches us to eat in the Supper). The mode of the presence, however, of Christ's body and blood must be entrusted *to God* and his omnipotence (since it is not natural or Physical, but heavenly and divine, and a Capernaitic[6] eating is not happening either).

How Luther's doctrine about the Lord's Supper is condemned by Zwinglians and Calvinists.

But Zwinglians and Calvinists have condemned this doctrine of the Sacramental eating of Christ's body in the holy Supper, which up to this day they denounce as if it were Capernaitic carnage and cyclopic,[7] carnivorous cannibalism [κρεοφαγίαν, καὶ ἀνθρωποφαγίαν] of Christ. And they have obstinately maintained that Christ's words should not be understood as they read, but that this simple faith which we teach consistently is a horrible Idolatry, which all Christians ought to flee.

Strife between Calvinist doctors and doctors of the Augsburg Confession in many articles of Christian religion.

Besides this, there is controversy between the Calvinists and our theologians in many other articles, not merely in this one article, and they are not of minor importance. Namely, in regard to the person of Christ, in

---

6 "Capernaitic" is a word used throughout this document to refer to the belief that Jesus' body in the Lord's Supper is to be regarded as substantial, meaty flesh, and compares the eating in the Sacrament of the Altar to cannibalism. The word derives from the misunderstanding of the people of Capernaum addressed by Jesus in John 6: "The Jews then disputed among themselves, saying, 'How can this man give us his flesh to eat?'" (v. 52); "When many of his disciples heard it, they said, 'This is a hard saying; who can listen to it?'" (v. 60)

7 "Cyclopic," another adjective referring to the belief in a cannibalistic reception of the Lord's body, ultimately derives from Homer's depiction of the anthropophagous, one-eyed Polyphemus of *Odyssey* 9. The term is apt in a conversation with Beza, he had written a pamphlet condemning what he called Lutheran consubstantiation under the title Κρεωφαγία, *sive Cyclops*, published in Geneva in 1561.

which all the articles of the Apostolic creed are involved, concerning the incarnation of the son of God, his nativity, <4> passion, death, resurrection, ascension, and his being seated at the right hand of God. Also, concerning his omnipotence, his infinite and inestimable knowledge and wisdom, the presence of the same in the management of all creatures, the devout adoration and invocation of him in all tribulations, Baptism, Predestination of the elect to eternal life, and other things. Their explanations give birth to these errors one after another in great number. Unless a holy consensus is established regarding all these matters too, the intention to work at effecting concord in merely the one article (regarding the Lord's Supper) will be in vain.

To this the Baron of Clervant answered: these things had not been heard by him before, and were by and large unknown also among the French. Thus far in fact he and most other French people were of the mind that the Lord's Supper was the only difference of opinion between their and our Churches.

THE BARON'S PLAN REGARDING A COLLOQUY ESTABLISHED BETWEEN DR. JAKOB AND DR. BEZA. WHAT PROFIT SHOULD BE EXPECTED FROM THE COLLOQUY.

Concerning these things, after the brief conversation had taken place between the Baron of Clervant and Dr. Jakob, the Baron asked Dr. Jakob whether or not it would be possible to set up a friendly conversation between himself and Dr. Beza. The most convenient place for the business would be either Strasbourg or Montbéliard, where they could meet and peacefully discuss this issue. Dr. Jakob answered that as far as he was concerned, he would always be ready and willing. And he hoped especially that if consensus and concord could not be reached, that this would not be something to be despised, but that a certain fruit could be expected from it: namely, that with mutual accusations done away with, the perpetual and consistent opinion of each party and its proper foundations <5> could be demonstrated to everyone, just as if painted in a small picture.

HOW THE CHURCHES OF THE AUGSBURG CONFESSION ARE ACCUSED BY BEZA.

For he noted that the parties of both sides complain that the disputants falsely attribute many things to the other which are not to be found in their writings. For example, Dr. Beza, with his colleagues, makes a public, written accusation not only in France, but also throughout the entire Christian world, that the Churches of Germany, of the Augsburg Confession, teach a Cyclopic and Capernaitic eating of Christ's body in the Lord's Supper, in which Christ's body is ground with the teeth, passes through the throat into the belly, is digested in the stomach, and with its honor preserved, ejected through excrement.

WHY THE FRENCH VARY FROM THE REFORMED CHURCHES IN GERMANY.

The French have become convinced that our Churches teach this, as many as listen to Dr. Beza and trust him. They publicly attest that they shy away from our Lord's Supper, especially because of just this one charge.

CAPERNAITIC EATING OF CHRIST'S FLESH ALWAYS CONDEMNED BY LUTHER.

But since none of these things ever were imagined by Luther or us, nor can be produced in a single letter of any of our writings that Dr. Beza or any other like-minded critics could point to — rather to the contrary, they have condemned at every time in very clear words exactly this Capernaitic eatingx — we all need to agree that a step towards concord has been made by the sincere denial of Capernaitic eating on both sides. This fact should not be disregarded. Likewise, Dr. Beza could show with his brothers that he is not rightly understood, if our party were not comprehending their opinion and that of their people, but that what they would least wish to maintain is attributed to them against their will.

But in other matters if neither party were able to relax or yield from their own position or opinion <6> once those false accusations have been removed and the true status of the controversy has been assessed, the foundations of each doctrine, briefly represented, would be brought forward for argument. From these could all pious people, even those of middling intelligence, easily judge which party affirms its doctrine by the express word of God or, on the other hand, by human interpretation. So also in the remaining controverted Articles could it come to pass that, with a peaceful conversation taking place, those they call Zwinglians and Calvinists might be compelled to agree with us, whom they call Lutherans; either that, or they would understand that they were asserting things so absurd and impious from which their pious minds would wholeheartedly recoil, and would so disprove themselves by means of their own absurdity and impiety, that there would be no further need of a wordier refutation.

When these things had been treated in this manner between the Baron of Clervant and Dr. Jakob, the rest of the conversation continued on regarding the meeting and colloquy organized between Dr. Jakob and Dr. Beza.

CONVERSATION OF THE BARON OF CLERVANT WITH DR. OSIANDER REGARDING THE COLLOQUY TO BE ORGANIZED BETWEEN DR. BEZA AND DR. JAKOB.

For this reason, once the Baron of Clervant had conversed with Dr. Lucas Osiander in the Court of the Prince of Württemberg, he earnestly asked the same man to advance as much as possible this meeting of the Theologians Dr. Beza and Dr. Jakob. He said furthermore that he would take care that Dr. Beza should appear also, and declare himself eager for peace and truth.

REQUEST OF THE FRENCH BEFORE THE HONORABLE PRINCE FREDERICK OF WÜRTTEMBERG, ETC., REGARDING THE COLLOQUY TO BE ORGANIZED.

A few weeks later, while it was unknown to Dr. Jakob what the Baron of Clervant was doing in the meantime, the Honorable Prince Frederick, Count of Württemberg and Montbéliard, was solicited several times by French people exiled on account of Religion to Montbéliard, exhorting him, if it were in any way possible, to organize the Colloquy between Dr. Beza and Dr. Jakob. Prince Frederick was unwilling to agree to their request, <7> though, unless it should be agreeable to Beza himself, and if Dr. Beza should request this in writing.

THE HONORABLE PRINCE, COUNT FREDERICK, ASKS DUKE LUDWIG THAT DR. JAKOB BE SENT TO THE COLLOQUY. DR. JAKOB SUMMONED TO THE COLLOQUY BY TWO LETTERS OF THE HONORABLE PRINCE, COUNT FREDERICK.

Once this was done, Count Frederick wrote his relative, the Honorable Prince Ludwig, Duke of Württemberg, and asked that Dr. Jakob be sent to Montbéliard for the purpose of the peaceful conference sought with Dr. Beza. 13 March had been set for it. He gently requested the same thing also with two letters written to Doctor Jakob himself, lest he wish to decline the Colloquy with Dr. Beza that was being sought after so eagerly by the French.

<hr>

COMPANIONS OF DR. JAKOB ANDREAE'S JOURNEY.

<hr>

Since therefore Prince Ludwig was in willing agreement and desired to gratify his relative Count Frederick, he joined to Dr. Jakob the Theologian Dr. Lucas Osiander and two Political Counselors, men outstanding in the nobility of their birth and education, Johann Wolfgang von Anweil and Frederick Schütz, Doctor of both kinds of law.

<hr>

DR. JAKOB WITH THE AMBASSADORS RECEIVED MOST COURTEOUSLY BY THE FRENCH.

<hr>

After the Württemberg Theologians and Politicians had arrived at Montbéliard on 14 March, they were received and greeted most courteously in the Castle by the French exiles, by Baron Beluoës, Baron Vesines, and many noble, learned men.

<hr>

THESES DRAWN UP BY THE WÜRTTEMBERG THEOLOGIANS CONCERNING THE CONTROVERTED ARTICLES.

<hr>

POINT 1.

Dr. Beza was still absent with his people, but the Württemberg Theologians in the meantime drew up very brief and clear Theses regarding each of the controverted Articles, chief among them these five: the Lord's Supper, the person of Christ, Predestination, Baptism, and the reformation of Pontifical church buildings, etc. And so that the conference would be the more expedient, the Theses were presented at the beginning in each single article, by which it is briefly shown what there is no controversy about between both parties, <8> or ever had been. In this way many unnecessary disputations could be cut off.

POINT 2.

Then, the true and proper status of the controversy was presented, concerning which there is especially in each single article something being disputed and fought over on either side.

POINT 3.

Third, the foundations of the assertion and confession of the Churches of the Augsburg Confession as comprehended in the book of Concord are proposed, drawn from the word *of the Lord.* By these do his Doctors and Pastors defend their teaching.

POINT 4.

Fourth, the teaching of the opponents and their dogmas are recited, and those are rejected which are in conflict with the express word of God.

THE COMPANIONS OF DR. BEZA'S JOURNEY.

After these things had come to completion, Dr. Beza arrived at Montbéliard on 20 March with those he had brought with him, Theologians Abraham Musculus of Bern and Antoine de La Faye of Geneva, ministers of the Church, as well as Peter Hiebnerus the public Professor of the Greek language in the Gymnasium of Bern, Dr, Claude Albery, Professor of Philosophy at the University of Lausanne, and politicians Samuel Mayer, Senator of the Republic of Bern, Antoine Maris, Senator of Geneva. The Honorable Prince Frederick summoned them to the castle, and they wanted immediately to greet the Württemberg Theologians. When this was made known to those from Württemberg, they also desired to make known the same courtesy to them.

FIRST MEETING OF THE THEOLOGIANS IN THE CASTLE OF MONTBÉLIARD.

When this first meeting happened, therefore, once Dr. Beza had willingly sworn that he had brought a teachable spirit to this peaceful conference, eager as he was for truth and concord, the Württemberg Theologians likewise declared their own [9] will in turn to them, promising categorically that they would prove their spirit of truth, not merely in word but also in deed at the scheduled conference, and that they had never been found wanting in zeal for pious and holy concord, nor would they ever.

THE FRENCH EXILES ASK ALSO TO BE ADMITTED TO THE COLLOQUY.

On the following day, which was 21 March, the Honorable Prince, Count Frederick, was asked by the French (who were staying at this time at Montbéliard as exiles on account of religion) to be allowed also to be present at the Colloquy. His Highness indulged them, granting the concession to those who knew Latin, lest they be excluded from it.

1

Conference on
the Lord's Supper

Commenced 21 March.

ASSEMBLY OF COLLOCUTORS IN THE COLLOQUIUM.

Therefore at the seventh hour, when the Honorable Prince, Count Frederick had come to the place appointed for the Colloquy, together with his Counselors and Noble courtiers, the Theologians of either party also arrived, and at the same time French exiles in great number were present. There were two tables in the room, separated not very far away from each other, and the Honorable Prince Frederick occupied the first with the Theologians and civic Ambassadors of Württemberg named above (to whom he joined his Courtier Marcus Gaspar Lutz as Spokesman). At the other Dr. Beza placed himself along with the Theologians of Geneva and Bern, Professors of Philosophy and Greek language, and those politicians accompanying him from both Republics.

\<10\>

Everything was therefore ready for the commencement of the Colloquy. In the following oration, Prince Frederick, through his Chancellor, solemnly gave thanks to the Theologians for their fortunate arrival and gently exhorted them toward a readiness for peace and truth.

Speech of the Chancellor of Montbéliard, Dr. Hector Vogelmann.

THANKSGIVING OF THE HONORABLE PRINCE, COUNT FREDERICK.

For some time the Honorable Prince, Lord Frederick, Count of Württemberg and Montbéliard, etc., my most Merciful Prince, had been urged, more than once in former years, by certain distinguished men of the glorious French nobility, to grant them a place in this town and by the court of his Highness for organizing a conference regarding certain controverted Articles in the business of Religion. This place could provide a most convenient opportunity for such a gathering, especially because we can enjoy the use of the French language and the Realm. The recent Lord exiles also ‹11› have repeatedly followed up their request. And so my most Merciful Prince, by virtue of his own innate integrity, in order that he might relieve in some measure their burdensome exile and their conscience (with the changing fortunes of which he sympathizes in a pious and Christian way), was unwilling to come short of their desire and prayers. And so after he had reported the business, as difficult as it was salutary, to the relative of his Highness, the Honorable Duke Ludwig of Württemberg, etc., he conducted the entire affair such that his Highness gave his approval in view of his own pious love for the Christian Religion, and he dispatched here his own very Reverend Theologians, eager for peace and concord, with certain noble Politicians, something which appears also to have been done by you. My most Merciful Prince wholeheartedly rejoices at the arrival of all of these people, and begs God Almighty with his prayers above all that by the grace of his presiding holy Spirit, everything said may be to the glory of his ‹12› name, and opinions be unanimously expressed by you to the salutary concord of the Republic. And as the matter has in this way commenced with a good beginning, may it also continue on to a desired outcome. My very Kindhearted Prince bids you, Reverend Dr. Beza, by virtue of your singular courtesy, to lay open your mind and that of your Colleagues. And the Theologians of the Honorable Duke

Ludwig, etc., will do the same. And please be convinced that his Highness will endeavor with his whole strength to satisfy, with public vows, the desire of everyone, above all and as much as possible, without violation of truth.

After the Chancellor had delivered this speech, Dr. Beza conferred the honor upon Dr. Jakob that he should respond first to these things. But since Dr. Beza had been specially addressed by the Chancellor's Speech, Dr. Jakob entreated and urged Dr. Beza to answer the bidding of the Honorable Prince Frederick, and lay open his mind concerning the process of the Colloquy.

\<13\>

Dr. Beza:

BEZA'S PREFACE. BEZA WOULD DESIRE THE CONFERENCE TO BE ORGANIZED WITH WRITINGS.

Dr. Beza therefore first gave thanks to the Honorable Prince, Count Frederick, for his pious prayer and very kindhearted will, by whose piety this conference was organized at the request of the French. But as to the process of the Colloquy, he was of the opinion that everything should be executed in writing. For it would be possible in the instituted conference for someone to let fall an inconsiderate word, but in writing one could take care, in a place where all things could be accurately considered, and each thing written more judiciously.

DR. BEZA'S CONSENSUS ABOUT THE PROCESS OF THE COLLOQUY.

But he agreed that that way was satisfactory which was made known to him a short time earlier by the Prince, Count Frederick, immediately upon his arrival, on the opinion of the Württemberg Theologians, namely that very brief Theses would be presented first about the controverted articles, in which the points at issue in the single articles would be sent beforehand between the disputing Theologians. Then the status of the controversy would be presented distinctly, clearly, and briefly, in order that the audience might understand why it was being discussed.

Third, the Foundations of the opinion of either party would be presented from God's word alone, by which one or the other party might confirm their teaching in the controverted articles.

Finally, the dogmas would be repeated which seem, either by this or the other party, to be in conflict with holy Scripture.

Furthermore, a passing over from one Article to another would not happen in the scheduled conference, but the Theologians would converse about only one at a time, until such time as either a pious consensus may be established in it, or else it be plainly demonstrated that concession could be made on either side in these matters.

Dr. Jakob:

SUMMARY OF DR. JAKOB ANDREAE'S RESPONSE TO THE SPEECH OF BEZA CONCERNING THE PROCESS OF THE COLLOQUY.

Dr. Jakob, when a space for speaking had been given to him also, first gave thanks to the eternal God, the father of our Lord Jesus Christ, <14> for this scheduled conference, and asked him to be willing to be present by his grace, to direct the hearts of either party by his own holy Spirit, and to aim the thoughts and speech of each man towards the glory of his name and the salvation of the Church.

He gave thanks also to the Honorable Prince, Count Frederick, that this Colloquy had been undertaken because of His piety and most compassionate will for the propagation of the truth of heavenly doctrine and for achieving a harmony that is holy and pleasing to God. And he said that God would repay him abundantly for sparing no expense in promoting it.

THE WORD OF GOD THE NORM AND RULE OF JUDGMENT.

But as far as the process of the Colloquy is concerned, he attested that the proposed procedure met his approval, and that the Württemberg Theologians thought too that they could not envision a better way to conduct and expedite everything thus in brief. But he also declared that the only and sole norm and rule of evaluating all controversies was the word of God, which would suffice in the Church for bringing all fights to an end, and is the best interpreter of itself, to which all things are subject.

DR. JAKOB PUSHES FORWARD THE COLLOQUY.

That the business would take place only in writing seemed to him not at all well advised. If in fact this approach to the discussion had been entered into, it would indeed have been possible for both parties to spare expenses and to be relieved of as many vexations as possible, which would have to be endured by going on a journey and returning, especially given the nastiness of the weather.

But then again, he said, the audience would not have reached the desired goal. Although they had read the writings of each party for a long time, nevertheless they had not always been able to explain themselves in them. Therefore it was his wish and desire that the business be conducted in the form of a friendly conference, in which each party might explain its beliefs lucidly and clearly by means of live speech (which possesses a kind of latent energy), responding to the questions of the other party. He hoped that this would be no source of trouble or burden for Dr. Beza, adding that there was no need to fear that there would be any treachery or deceit in this matter, for business would be done honestly and sincerely, since the whole point was the search for truth. Furthermore, he would remain free of bias for both parties, if anything happened to be said carelessly, either retracting what was said or more clearly explaining his position.

<15>

WHY THE COLLOQUY SHOULD START WITH THE LORD'S SUPPER.

Because the start of the controversy, which has endured for many years between the French Churches and the German ones of the Augsburg Confession, originally began with the Article concerning the Lord's Supper (from which thereafter other controversies have also arisen), it seemed good to them to decide that the commencement of the peaceful meeting should also begin with this same article.

In this regard, in order that the meeting might be more expedited, Dr. Jakob put on display a few Theses included in Dr. Beza's writing, and asked that he not only carefully consider them with his own Colleagues, but also examine and discuss what was in them one by one. He asked that after they had themselves expressed it in a brief essay, they would willingly give to the Württemberg Theologians the explanation of their position on the Lord's Supper. When both parties had read through them, they then would proceed to a friendly meeting in the presence of the Honorable Prince and the rest of the audience.

1A. THESES OF THE THEOLOGIANS OF WÜRTTEMBERG CONCERNING THE LORD'S SUPPER.

THE DISTINCTION BETWEEN EATING THE FLESH OF CHRIST IN JOHN 6 AND SACRAMENTAL EATING.

1.

It is beyond dispute, that all faithful people eat spiritually the flesh of the son of man, and drink his blood; according to that saying of Christ: Unless you eat the flesh of the son of man, and drink his blood, you will not have life in you (John 6[:53]). This spiritual eating happens through faith, even without the use of the Lord's Supper; and it is always salutary. Christ in fact states thus: He who eats my flesh, and drinks my blood, has eternal life, John 6[:54]. But sometimes the eating in the Lord's Supper is dangerous, and leads to judgment. And so it stands that the one is different than the other: though reception of the Sacrament of the Lord's Supper is beneficial, a spiritual eating is necessary.

<16>

THE CAPERNAITIC EATING OF CHRIST'S FLESH CONDEMNED.

2.

We have never been of the same mind, nor ever will be, as the Capernaitans who thought that the flesh of Christ is rent in pieces by the teeth, and is to be eaten after the fashion of cow's flesh or as other food is eaten. Wherefore it is not necessary to dispute concerning Capernaitic rending or eating.

PAPISTIC TRANSUBSTANTIATION CONDEMNED.

3.

Nor do we accept transubstantiation of the Pontiffs, who teach that the bread in the holy Lord's Supper is changed into the substance of the body of Christ, and the wine transformed into the blood of Christ: but we confess that in the holy Supper we eat true bread and drink true wine, without the intervention of transubstantiation.

THE PRESENCE OF THE BODY AND BLOOD OF CHRIST IS NOT LOCAL.

4.

Nor do we assert a Physical and local presence or limitation of the body and blood of Christ in the holy Supper.

THE STATUS OF THE CONTROVERSY.

5.

It has come into controversy however: Whether the true body and true blood of our Lord Jesus Christ are really and substantially present in the holy Supper; and distributed with the bread and wine, and taken by mouth by all those who use the Sacrament, whether worthy or unworthy, good or evil, faithful or unfaithful; in so far as the faithful receive in the Lord's Supper comfort and life; the unfaithful however take it to their judgment. Concerning this question we embrace and defend the affirmative thesis.

CONCERNING THE TERMS *IN, UNDER, WITH* THE BREAD, ETC. CONCERNING THE
WORDS SUBSTANTIALLY, BODILY, REALLY, ORALLY, ESSENTIALLY, ETC.

6.

By the words In, With, and Under the bread, we understand nothing other than this: that those who eat the bread and drink the wine
in the Lord's Supper, really take the very body and blood of Christ at
the same time. Thus indeed the words substantially, bodily, really,
essentially, and orally, in our estimation, mean nothing other than
the true presence and eating of the body and blood of Christ in the
holy Supper.

7.

The foundations of these beliefs are as follows: In the first place
<17> the words of Christ, God and man, who in the institution of the
holy Lord's Supper (offering bread to his disciples) said: Eat, this
is my body, which is given for you. And producing a cup of wine,
he said: This is my blood, which is poured out for you (Matthew
26[:26–28]; Mark 14[:22–24]; Luke 22[:19–20]). And Paul, speaking concerning this Sacrament, attests: The cup of blessing, which
we bless, is it not a *fellowship* in the blood of Christ? And the bread
which we break, is it not a participation in the body of Christ? (1
Corinthians 10[:16]) In this first foundation of the words of Christ's
Testament are also included those that follow.

8.

In the second place, Christ, who is God, does not know how to lie
(Titus 1[:2]), and no deceit is found in his mouth (1 Peter 2[:22]).

9.

In the third place, Christ is God and man, in one inseparable
person. For this reason nothing is impossible for him. Things that
are impossible among men are possible with God, as Christ says
(Luke 18[:27]). And the Angel Gabriel said, No promise will be impossible with God (Luke 1[:37]). And concerning the man Christ, John

said, Jesus knew that his father gave to him all things into his hands (John 13[:3]). And Scripture testifies that Christ the son of man was seated at the right hand of God (Ephesians 1[:20], what is the infinite power of God (Hebrews 1[:3]), and that all authority has been given to him in heaven and on earth (Matthew 28[:18]). And so Christ is able to provide all the things that he promises. Therefore, since he has promised in the words of his Testament that *he wants* to give us his body for eating and his blood for drinking, and that *he is able* to provide all the things he has promised, it is most certainly true that we eat the body of Christ with the bread in the holy Supper, and we drink his blood with the wine.

CONCERNING THE MODE OF THE PRESENCE, AND OF THE EATING, OF CHRIST'S BODY, THERE IS NO DEBATE.

10.

However, *how* the worthy and unworthy take the body and blood of the *Lord* in the holy Supper with the bread and the wine is not expressly stated in Sacred scripture. For this reason we can say only this concerning the *mode*, that it is supernatural, and incomprehensible to human reason. <18> Up to this point there can be no dispute concerning it. For God can invent more reasons and modes (by way of his immense wisdom and Omnipotence) than merely the Physical and natural mode (which alone human reason understands), by which he may achieve his end, that Christ's body and blood can be anywhere and delivered to those feeding on it. And so in this divine Mystery, we consider our reason captive, and rest in simple faith on the words of Christ, "This is my body, This is my blood," with a healthy and untroubled conscience.

1B. WE JUDGE THE FOLLOWING DOGMAS TO BE IN CONFLICT WITH HOLY SCRIPTURE.

1.

That the words of Jesus Christ's Testament should not be understood simply, or according to the plain, literal meaning [κατὰ δ' ῥητόν], as they read. That they are in fact obscure, and for this reason their true sense must be sought from other places in Scripture.

2.

That in the holy Supper only bread and wine are received orally, but the true body of Christ is taken only in a spiritual way, truly *by faith*. For by faith there is an ascension into heaven with the result that we become participants there with body and blood of Christ, since Christ's body after his ascension into heaven is never anywhere before the last day except in heaven.

3.

That God is incapable, even by his universal Omnipotence, of making it possible for Christ's body to be present in more places than one only, at one and the same time.

4.

And likewise that Christ's body is present for us in the Sacrament of the Eucharist in a manner no different on earth today than it was once for Abraham.

<19>

5.

That in the holy Supper is dispensed merely the virtue, working, and merit of the absent body and blood of Christ.

6.

That they may be numbered among those who eat unworthily, and (in their reception of the Lord's Supper) take judgment upon themselves, who suffer because of some weakness of faith or other infirmities, although they nevertheless possess true faith.

THEODORE BEZA IN VOLUME 2 OF *THEOLOGICARUM TRACTATIONUM*, PAGE 450.

7.

What some people affirm (not without horrible blasphemy), namely that sacramental eating entails the idea that Christ's body passes through into the belly and is there digested or not digested, and thereafter is finally either defecated or not. We also disavow similar things that are shocking to hear and unworthy of Christian people, whether they are spoken or written down.

Dr. Beza:
Since it seemed good to the Württemberg Theologians to proceed thus, he was saying that he also did not disapprove the proposed manner of discussion, and had no wish to oppose it.

Therefore once the audience was dismissed, that same day Dr. Beza read and considered with his brothers the Theses about the Lord's Supper that were delivered, and on the following day before lunchtime delivered to the Württemberg Theologians his own written opinion on both the Lord's Supper as well as the Theses. Concerning these, a friendly and peaceful conversation commenced at the first hour of the Afternoon of the same day.

<20>

1c. The writing of Dr. Beza, in which is contained the Confession of himself and his colleagues concerning the Lord's Supper.

Summary of our doctrine concerning the Lord's Supper.

Declaration of Dr. Beza and his brothers concerning the established Colloquy.

Reverend gentlemen, with whom we now must engage, we testify to this above all: that we who have come to this conference, at the will of the Honorable Prince Frederick, Count of Württemberg and Montbéliard, and by the consensus of the Church at Bern and Geneva, are acting as private persons, with absolutely no prejudgment of any Church or any pastor. (a)

We set before you the things that follow in order that, once you have possession of a brief summary of our whole teaching concerning the Lord's Supper, comparing it with your writing, it may be possible the more easily to observe from both sides where we agree or disagree.

Refutatory annotation of Dr. Jakob Andreae: (a) Although we also do not prejudge our churches in any way, nevertheless we testify that we are not in the least uncertain or doubtful of our doctrine, as it rests on the clear and express Word of God.

---

1. Concerning signs.

What Beza's Sacraments signify.

In this argument we are calling the things that occur to the external senses signs, or symbols, or sacraments, (b) when this word is accepted with a narrower connotation. They have been determined from the Lord's institution and mandate since spiritual and holy things must be signified for us by common and natural use. <21> Of this kind are bread and wine in the Lord's Supper, together with the rites prescribed by Christ in their correct administration.

REFUTATORY ANNOTATION OF DR. JAKOB ANDREAE: (B) THE EQUIVOCATION OF THE TERM "SACRAMENT" IS A HIDING-PLACE OF ERROR, WHICH IN OUR CHURCHES ALWAYS EMBRACES TWO THINGS, AN EARTHLY AND A HEAVENLY THING, SACRAMENTALLY AND REALLY JOINED TOGETHER.

But we say that this sacramental signification (c) is not in the least an empty external representation of things signified, by which the mind may be directed to conceive something held before the senses, as is the common way with images and pictures, but rather that it pertains to God, and so has always had conjoined with it what is furnished: the true thing itself that belongs to the signified things, offered to our souls.

REFUTATORY ANNOTATION OF DR. JAKOB ANDREAE: (C) CHRIST HAS NOT ARRANGED THE EXTERNAL ORGANS FOR SIGNIFICATION, BUT FOR DELIVERY OF SPIRITUAL THINGS.

Foundation of this Thesis.

In this matter we judge that we have consensus (d) in every way, with one exception, that we teach that the things signified are presented only to the Mind, which you think are delivered also to the mouth to be taken. Because of this it should be stated in another question, in one which we deal with the delivery of signs and things signified.

REFUTATORY ANNOTATION OF DR. JAKOB ANDREAE: (D) THERE IS NO CONSENSUS HERE, BUT RATHER OPEN DISSENT. FOR THE EXTERNAL ELEMENTS IN THE SACRAMENTS HAVE BEEN APPOINTED FOR THE DELIVERY, NOT SIGNIFICATION, OF SPIRITUAL THINGS.

2. Concerning things signified sacramentally.

We teach that by means of the bread, the body of Christ has been given for us; by means of the wine, the blood has been poured out for

us; that in the breaking of the bread and the pouring of the wine, the
dire torments have been endured by Christ for us both in body and
in soul; that by the exterior giving of the same symbols, an interior
and spiritual offering is made to our minds by Christ; and finally by
external acquisition of the same symbols, a spiritual reception of the
same Christ through faith is sacramentally, but nevertheless (as we
have said) by the ordination of Christ himself, signified. (e)

REFUTATORY ANNOTATION OF DR. JAKOB ANDREAE: (E) BREAD AND WINE ARE
PUT TO USE BY DIVINE ARRANGEMENT NOT FOR THE SAKE OF SIGNIFICATION,
BUT FOR THE SAKE OF COMMUNICATION.

<22>

Foundation of the second Thesis.

Since the Lord has shown not only what signs must be used in
these Mysteries, but also has instructed the thing to be done which
he has done, we teach that what must be observed is not only the
bread and wine but also the rites of their administration. (f) Indeed,
they do not lack their own signification, and they are not in the least
meaningless.

REFUTATORY ANNOTATION OF DR. JAKOB ANDREAE: (F) RITES SHOULD BE
OBSERVED IN SACRAMENTS WHICH CHRIST TAUGHT OUGHT TO BE PRESERVED.

---

3. Concerning the juxtaposition of signs and things signified, or sacramental union.

Since Sacraments are signs by a narrower (as has been said) meaning, we posit sacramental union in reciprocal relation and habitude[8]
of signs and things signified. By this it comes to pass that those
things meeting the senses, by Christ's ordaining, by common and
natural use, are put to use for holy things that need both to be signified for us and really divinely offered to us.

---

8   "Habitude" translates Latin habitudo. As a Scholastic term for relative connection or ordered condition, it is a synonym of "relation" here. It is not rendered here into more modern English vocabulary in
order to reflect Beza's category and reliance on Scholastic reasoning.

Foundation of this Thesis.

Point 1.

The first foundation of this Thesis is the truth of Christ's body, truly circumscribed and local, (h) both before and after its glorification. This truth cannot stand if it should be said that Christ's body is present in the bread in another way than by means of that relative habitude. And so as many times as that truth of Christ's body is affirmed by testimonies (and these are almost innumerable), thus real consubstantiation is refuted by many biblical proofs.

Refutatory annotation of Dr. Jakob Andreae: (h) The truth of Christ's circumscribed and local body is not in conflict with the presence of the same body of Christ in the real Sacrament, since it is not physical and local, but sacramental.

<23>

Point 2.

Second, in as many passages as the true and Physical departure of Christ's body from earth to heaven is affirmed, and the return of the same from heaven finally on the last day to come, in just so many passages is that very dogma refuted, conflicting diametrically with the former passages.

Refutatory annotation of Dr. Jakob Andreae: (i) So also the physical departure of Christ's body from earth is not in conflict with sacramental presence.

Point 3.

Third, Paul expressly says in 2 Corinthians 5[:6], Now we are absent, away from the Lord; (k) Paul desires to be released in order that he may be with Christ, and orders us to seek things above, and purposely adds, where Christ is seated at the right hand of God, which would be superfluous if he were still dwelling on earth with us.

And again (in order that we may pass over other innumerable testimonies), Christ bears witness with the express words that he goes to prepare a place, where he intends to receive his own (John 14[:2]; John 3[:31]).

From this two things are realized: One, that he himself has gone away into a certain place, since he has left this world. (l) The other, that those who are in the world are not with Christ, that is, not in the place where Christ's flesh now is, but going out of the world are received into that place where Christ is now, that is, in Paradise, just as he himself explains as he addresses the thief, Luke 23[:43].

REFUTATORY ANNOTATIONS OF DR. JAKOB ANDREAE: (K) THE BODILY OR EARTHLY TRAVEL BY CHRIST IS NOT IN CONFLICT WITH SACRAMENTAL PRESENCE, AND JUXTAPOSITION WITH CHRIST'S BODY, WHICH IS NOT AN EARTHLY ONE, BUT HEAVENLY AND SUPERNATURAL. (L) BEZA THINKS, WITH HIS PEOPLE, THAT WE CANNOT EXIST OTHERWISE WITH CHRIST, NOR CHRIST OTHERWISE WITH US, EXCEPT IF IT HAPPENS LOCALLY AND BY MEANS OF PHYSICAL PRESENCE, WHICH IS THE FOUNDATION OF THIS WHOLE ERROR CONCERNING THE LORD'S SUPPER.

POINT 4.

Fourth, we affirm that this was the ancient Church's perpetual consensus about the true absence of the essence of Christ's flesh from us, from the time he ascended into heaven, and the perpetual organic circumscription and locality of the essence of Christ's flesh, not located on the earth but rather now in heaven. These cannot be connected by another sacramental union, a union which is composed in a way that is σχετική, that is, relative, any more than contradictions can stand together.

REFUTATORY ANNOTATIONS OF DR. JAKOB ANDREAE: (M) IT HAS BEEN DEMONSTRATED THAT THIS IS NOT THE CONSENSUS OF THE ANCIENT AND PURER CHURCH IN THE SOLID REFUTATION OF THE ORTHODOX CONSENSUS. (N) THE JOINING OF CHRIST'S BODY WITH SIGNS ON THE EARTH IS NOT VIRTUAL [σχετική] AND RELATIVE, BUT REAL, HEAVENLY, DIVINE, AND SUPERNATURAL.

<24>

4. Concerning the reception of signs and things signified in the administered rite of the Lord's Supper.

Since Sacraments (understood in the wider sense) consist of two things, one, namely, the earthly, and the other heavenly, (o) we teach that the earthly thing, that is, bread and wine, are received by earthly organs, the hand and mouth. In the same manner, Sacramental rites are performed by bodily organs. The heavenly thing, on the other hand, that is, whatever is signified sacramentally by those things, is grasped by the Mind alone through faith, just as it is submitted to the Mind alone.

REFUTATORY ANNOTATION OF DR. JAKOB ANDREAE: (o) EQUIVOCATION REGARDING THE TERM "SACRAMENT" IS A HIDING-PLACE OF ERROR. IT MEANS TWO THINGS TO THE DOCTORS OF THE PURER CHURCH, AN EARTHLY AND A HEAVENLY, JUST AS IT ALSO IS REGARDING THE TERM EUCHARIST [εὐχαριστία] ACCORDING TO IRENAEUS AND OTHER ECCLESIASTICAL WRITERS.

Foundation of this Thesis.

Even though Christ's body, which is offered to be taken in the Supper, is a true organic body, nevertheless by analogy this indicates that as it is like nourishment and nourishment's purpose, so the mode of receiving it is like that of receiving nourishment. (p) And those things that belong to the sacramentally signified things, that is, Christ's very flesh and blood, are spiritual nourishment and its purpose, that is, they regard a spiritual connection with Christ and eternal life to be derived from him. (q) It is necessary therefore that the mode of receiving these same things should be spiritual, and that it should be carried out by the soul's proper instrument, that is, by faith, just as in the simple word, so also in the Sacraments. (r) Then the earthly taking of earthly signs is a pledge of something else, the spiritual thing. And the language of eating and drinking is used for this reason, just as it is when taking the signs, but it is used FIGURATIVELY (s) about the things signified, by Sacramental METONYMY, in which what corresponds with the signs is attributed to the thing signified.

REFUTATORY ANNOTATIONS OF DR. JAKOB ANDREAE: (P) CHRIST, IN THE WORDS OF THE TESTAMENT, BIDS HIS BODY BE EATEN BY MOUTH; NO MENTION MADE OF MIND OR FAITH. (Q) CHRYSOSTOM BEARS WITNESS THAT CHRIST DISPENSES SPIRITUAL THINGS THROUGH BODILY ONES, WHEN OFFERING THE BREAD HE SAYS, TAKE, EAT, THIS IS MY BODY. SO ALSO DOES HE BID RECEPTION THROUGH A BODILY ORGAN, THAT IS, BY MOUTH. THEREFORE THIS IS THE BEST ANALOGY THAT BEST AGREES: JUST AS CHRIST'S BODY IS GIVEN *WITH* BREAD, SO ALSO IS IT RECEIVED *BY MOUTH*. (R) CHRIST'S WORDS DEMONSTRATE THAT THE MODE OF RECEPTION IS BODILY: TAKE, EAT, WHICH HAPPENS BY MOUTH. HE DOES NOT SAY, BELIEVE. (S) EATING OF CHRIST'S BODY IN THE LORD'S SUPPER IS IN NO WAY FIGURATIVE, BUT TRUE AND REAL, WHAT IS IN THE MYSTERY, TO THE DEGREE THAT METONYMY DOES NOT HAVE A PLACE HERE.

<25>

Therefore taking both of these by mouth neither can nor should happen, [(t)] since either one of the things would be in this manner the pledge of a third something, totally different in kind, or the other of them would be the sign of itself and pledge, either at the same time sign and thing signified, or the pledge and the thing itself, of which it is the pledge. In either case this is very absurd. For this reason also in this very argument, the thing is called heavenly by Irenaeus, and distinguished from the earthly.

REFUTATORY ANNOTATION OF DR. JAKOB ANDREAE: (T) TAKING BOTH BY MOUTH CAN HAPPEN, ALTHOUGH THE MANNER OF THESE IS DIFFERENT. JUST AS MARY GAVE BIRTH TO GOD AND MAN IN ONE BIRTH, ALTHOUGH IN ONE WAY GOD, IN ANOTHER MAN. THEREFORE THEIR CONCLUSIONS ARE ABSURD AND DO NOT FOLLOW. SINCE THE MYSTICAL EATING OF CHRIST'S BODY IS IN THE PHYSICAL EATING OF THE CONSECRATED BREAD IN THE SACRAMENT.

In the second place, if the substance of the very body of Christ were being received by mouth, it would also remain at all events in the pious and faithful who would become therefore the substantial members of Christ. What would follow from this would be quite absurd, namely that the Church would not be the mystical body of CHRIST, but a certain body of the substance of Christ's very body, and really and essentially fused together with the bodies of all the pious. (u)

REFUTATORY ANNOTATION OF DR. JAKOB ANDREAE: (U) IF THE EATING OF CHRIST'S FLESH IN THE LORD'S SUPPER WERE PHYSICAL, THOSE ABSURDITIES WOULD FOLLOW. BUT SINCE IT IS HEAVENLY, AND SUPERNATURAL, AS INDEED THE MODE IS PLAINLY SPIRITUAL, THEN THIS IS NOT THE CONSEQUENCE. AND JUST AS THE CHURCH IS A MYSTICAL BODY WITH CHRIST, SO ALSO THIS RECEPTION HAPPENS IN MYSTERY.

In the third place, since the flesh of Christ is a bond by which all the pious coalesce into one mystical body, there should of necessity not be separate substances or persons of the pious, but just as with Christ as the head, so also among themselves they should cohere with their actual essences and persons. (x) But although it is spiritual, the connection of the faithful members between themselves is nevertheless also very true and close, indeed to the degree that they are called one heart and one soul. It follows that they are joined spiritually also by that connection and through faith with their head. (y) Since on account of these things they are one body, namely the Mystic one, (z) so also they are called one spirit and Christ dwells in them through the spirit. (z)

REFUTATORY ANNOTATIONS OF DR. JAKOB ANDREAE: (X) CHRIST'S MEMBERS, BY VIRTUE OF THEIR SUBSTANCES, FOR THEIR PART, REMAIN SEPARATE PERSONS, WHICH NEVERTHELESS ARE JOINED TOGETHER MYSTICALLY WITH CHRIST, THAT IS, REALLY, NOT VIRTUALLY [σχετικῶς], OR RELATIVELY, BUT TRULY IN THIS MYSTERY, IN A SUPERNATURAL WAY. (Y) BUT THE JOINING TOGETHER IS NOT VIRTUAL [σχετική] OR RELATIVE, BUT REAL, NOT SIGNIFIED BUT DELIVERED (1 CORINTHIANS 6[:15]). (Z) THE DISTINCTION BETWEEN [διάστημα] LOCATIONS DOES NOT REMOVE THIS JOINING TOGETHER, SINCE THERE IS NEITHER PLACE NOR TIME BEFORE THE FACE OF GOD OR IN THE PRESENCE OF GOD.

In the fourth place, the joining together of Christ, God and Man, with his bride the Church, is merely spiritual and accomplished by the organ of faith, (a) as is evident from those who are like the children of this marriage, who are called the fruits of righteousness. [26] It is like the creation of offspring: it should go the way of conception first, then begetting, then also the way of marriage itself.

REFUTATORY ANNOTATIONS OF DR. JAKOB ANDREAE: (A) THIS SPIRITUAL JOINING TOGETHER, HOWEVER, HAPPENS THROUGH BODILY AND EXTERNAL ORGANS, IN WHICH SPIRITUAL THINGS ARE JOINED TOGETHER WITH EXTERNAL THINGS.

5. Concerning the effects of the Lord's Supper.

It is certainly true that the Lord's Supper was not instituted on account of bread and wine but for the salvation of men. Therefore its true character is realized worthily, that is, when those approaching it with penitence and faith come to salvation, through the confirmation of their spiritual association with Christ, by which it happens of course as in the same way as in the natural animated body members naturally cohere with the head, then receive sense and motion: so also those spiritually joined with Christ reach more and more all spiritual gifts, the characteristics of the regenerate, and finally even eternal life itself, flowing from Christ the head into the members that cohere in him. On account of this they are called his members individually, and collectively called the mystical body; because of this also the gift of grace is increased through the holy Spirit, since members separated from each other do not completely form one body, nor can it be one body of one and the same head. Another thing is formed unworthily however, that is, judgment for those approaching with ignorance of this Mystery, or when the totally unbelieving and impenitent approach it. The judgment flows not from the supper itself, but from the unworthy accidental [κατὰ συμβεβηκός] use of it. (b)

REFUTATORY ANNOTATIONS OF DR. JAKOB ANDREAE: (A) EVEN THOUGH THE LORD'S SUPPER WAS NOT INSTITUTED ON ACCOUNT OF BREAD AND WINE, NEVERTHELESS IT PLEASED CHRIST TO JOIN HIS BODY AND BLOOD SACRAMENTALLY WITH BREAD AND WINE, AND TO DISTRIBUTE IT TO THOSE DINING IN THE LORD'S SUPPER, JUST AS HIS EXPRESS WORDS SAY, TAKE, EAT, THIS IS MY BODY, ETC. (B) CHRIST WORKS JUDGMENT ON THE UNWORTHY IN HIS SUPPER AS EFFICACIOUSLY AS HE DOES LIFE AND CONSOLATION IN THE WORTHY DINNER GUESTS. SINCE HE IS NOT ONLY AN ODOR OF LIFE FOR LIFE BUT ALSO AN ODOR OF DEATH FOR DEATH (2 CORINTHIANS 2[:15–16]).

---

6. Concerning the causes of the salutary effects of the Supper.

We distinguish cooperating causes in this Mystery in this way: concerning the holy Spirit's infinite and ineffable power (c)[27] we bear an association accepted wholly, our association with CHRIST, *which Paul calls on this account a great Mystery (Ephesians 5[:32]). But we believe all those heavenly gifts of which we have spoken, and at length even that eternal life of body and soul, flow into us from CHRIST alone, God and Man, crucified for us, and finally lifted up over all things in that flesh, by the ordaining of God the Omnipotent father.*

REFUTATORY ANNOTATION OF DR. JAKOB ANDREAE: (C) ALTHOUGH CHRIST ACTS THROUGH THE HOLY SPIRIT, NEVERTHELESS IN THE LORD'S SUPPER THE SAYING IS NOT, <27> TAKE, EAT, THIS IS THE HOLY SPIRIT. THEREFORE CHRIST'S FLESH OUGHT NEVER TO BE ROBBED OF THIS EFFICACY BY ATTRIBUTING IT TO THE HOLY SPIRIT ALONE, BY WHOSE PARTICIPATION THE FLESH VIVIFIES.

But we agree that the instrumental causes with respect to God himself are partly the Pastor doing what he does in God's name and by his mandate, partly the words of institution, and partly the symbols and sacramental rites. But in respect to our faith, it is planted in us as a gift of God. (d) We teach however that God uses these instruments in such a way that he nevertheless introduces with them no intrinsic efficient power, (e) but merely the fact that he himself alone works inwardly, testifying to us through these things, namely that spiritual union of Christ with us, and whatsoever we encounter thereafter.

REFUTATORY ANNOTATIONS OF DR. JAKOB ANDREAE: (D) SACRAMENTAL RECEPTION OF CHRIST'S BODY AND BLOOD IS NOT ONLY BY FAITH BUT ALSO BY THE MOUTH OF THE BODY, SINCE HE SAYS, TAKE, EAT; HE DOES NOT SAY, TAKE, AND BELIEVE. (E) ONCE THIS INTRINSIC SACRAMENTAL POWER IS REMOVED, THE SUBSTANCE IS DISSOLVED FROM THE SACRAMENT. FOR IT DOES NOT TESTIFY ONLY, BUT IT WORKS, AND CHRIST EXERCISES HIS POWER IN THE USE OF THIS SACRAMENT.

We judge that there is no deficiency of approval among you in regard to these two latter Theses. (f)

REFUTATORY ANNOTATION OF DR. JAKOB ANDREAE: (F) THE DEFICIENCY IS QUITE GREAT, SINCE THEY ROB THE SACRAMENTS OF THEIR SPIRITUAL POWER.

At Montbéliard, 22 March 1586.
Signed:
Theodore Beza, Minister of the Church at Geneva.

Abraham Musculus, Minister of the Church at Bern.

Antoine de La Faye, Minister of the Church at Geneva.

Pierre Hübner, Professor of Greek, in the Gymnasium at Bern.

Claude Albery, Bachelor and Professor of Philosophy in the Academy at Lausanne.

<28>

1D. RESPONSES TO THE THESES OF THE WÜRTTEMBERG THEOLOGIANS.

ON THESIS 1.

We acknowledge NO OTHER reception of Christ himself, (g) whether in a simple word, as in John 6, or in the Sacraments, as in the institution of the Lord's Supper, except a spiritual one, that is, one that takes place by virtue of the holy Spirit and the organ of faith. (h) We nevertheless acknowledge that there is a difference, at least in external form, between the reception of the simple word and a sacramental one, but not really in what is signified and offered, (i) nor the reception of that. For in a simple word God works with us through the ears only, but in the Sacraments he also delivers other things, breaking into the rest of our senses. From this it comes to pass that unless the unworthiness of those approaching obstructs the efficacy of the Sacraments, Sacramental communication is more powerful and distinct than merely spiritual communication through the simple word.

REFUTATORY ANNOTATIONS OF DR. JAKOB ANDREAE: (G) THIS IS IN OPEN CONFLICT WITH THE WORDS OF CHRIST'S TESTAMENT, WHO SPEAKS ABOUT RECEPTION BY MOUTH WHEN HE SAYS, TAKE, *EAT*, THIS IS MY BODY. BESIDES, THE EATING OF CHRIST'S BODY, WHICH HAPPENS BY MOUTH, WAS INSTITUTED FOR THE CONFIRMING OF EATING DONE THROUGH FAITH. (H) IT IS CALLED SPIRITUAL BECAUSE THE MODE IS SPIRITUAL; THE ONE INDEED WHO CAN COME TO JUDGMENT WITHOUT FAITH WHEN EATING UNWORTHILY DOES NOT DISCERN THE BODY OF THE LORD, 1 CORINTHIANS 11[:29]. (I) THEY DIFFER NOT ONLY IN OUTWARD FORM BUT ALSO IN REALITY, SINCE THE MODE OF EATING IS UNIQUE IN THE SACRAMENT.

ON THESIS 2.

Though the eating of Christ's body is essential, (k) as is drinking his blood, we should consider that it differs in mode from that of common eating and drinking, (l) the one happening invisibly, the other visibly. Nevertheless we do not see (m) how the mode of eating is one and the same, so far as the thing itself is concerned, nor as the circumstance of visibility or invisibility is concerned, if it should be considered that the very substance of the Lord's body and blood is being eaten and drunk orally.

REFUTATORY ANNOTATIONS OF DR. JAKOB ANDREAE: (K) WE SAY THAT THE EATING IS SACRAMENTAL. (L) THEY DIFFER NOT ONLY IN THE MODE, BUT ALSO IN THE FACT THAT THE NATURE OF THE LORD'S BODY IS ENTIRELY A SPIRITUAL ONE IN THIS MYSTERY. THIS IS IN CLEAR CONFLICT WITH THE CRASS FORMULATIONS OF THE CAPERNAITISTS. (M) WHAT YOU SEE IS NOT THE QUESTION, NOR WHAT YOU CAN SEE, BUT WHETHER THESE THINGS ARE IN CONFLICT WITH CHRIST'S WORD AND WILL.

<29>

ON THESIS 3.

We agree.

ON THESIS 4.

In so far as the substance of Christ's very body and blood has been glorified, we do not see that it is really possible to determine that it is present with bread and wine, (n) other than by means of physical and local circumscription. (o) Since glorification, as Augustine rightly says in perpetual agreement with the entire Church, gave immortality to Christ's body, it did not take away its nature.

REFUTATORY ANNOTATIONS OF DR. JAKOB ANDREAE: (N) WHAT YOU SEE IS NOT THE QUESTION, NOR WHAT YOU CAN SEE, BUT RATHER WHAT CHRIST SAYS AND COMMANDS: TAKE, EAT, THIS IS MY BODY. (O) NOTHING CONTRADICTS OUR TEACHING THEREFORE, SINCE WE DO NOT AT ALL ASSERT THAT CHRIST'S BODY IS PRESENT BY MEANS OF PHYSICAL LOCATION IN THE LORD'S SUPPER.

ON THESIS 5.

We uphold the negative, but nevertheless do not deny that the true body and the true blood of the Lord Jesus Christ are offered (p) to whoever truly approaches in the proper act of the Supper. But this happens in the mind, not the body; these things must be received by faith, not by mouth. (q) This is why it happens that those who approach unworthily, lacking the organ of faith, though they also are offered the whole Sacrament, [(r)] nevertheless they receive only the signs, and in such a way that they become guilty of the body and blood OF THE LORD; they do not take it, but rather despise it. (s)

REFUTATORY ANNOTATIONS OF DR. JAKOB ANDREAE: (P) THIS IS SNEAKINESS IN WORDS, AND AN EQUIVOCATION OF THE TERM "OFFER," WHICH RIGHTLY PRESUPPOSES THE PRESENCE OF A THING IN PLAIN WORDS. (Q) CHRIST, ON THE CONTRARY, MADE NO MENTION OF FAITH, BUT SAID: TAKE, EAT, THIS IS MY BODY. (R) THE WHOLE SACRAMENT IS NOT OFFERED TO THE ONE WHO RECEIVES JUST A PART OF IT, AND THAT THE LEAST PART, NAMELY, ONLY THE EXTERNAL SIGNS. (S) THEY RECEIVE JUDGMENT BY EATING, NOT BY NEGLECTING OR DESPISING (1 CORINTHIANS 11[:27–30]).

ON THESIS 6.

We indeed know that the ancients employed those formulas. But it was not considered that the substance of the things signified IN, UNDER, or WITH (t) was present in the same place as the signs themselves, (u) but rather that what was offered to the true faith of those approaching was understood to be the very body and blood of the Lord, as truly as was promised in the words of institution, and the external symbols are evidence to the senses of those who approach. <30> Nevertheless, since we see these formulas being treated in another way now, (x) namely for the Real consubstantiation, (y) for this reason we avoid those terms as dangerous and less suitable. These terms though, SUBSTANTIALLY, BODILY, ESSENTIALLY, if they should refer to the things themselves which are offered, we acknowledge they are used in the right sense, but not if they are used for a sacramental union or a mode of presence. (z) We confess that "really" is rightly said, and "in reality," and "not feignedly," (a) but we nevertheless think those terms should be used deliberately. (b) We reject *"orally,"* however, as both false in sense and barbaric in form, (c) just as we also entirely reject the Papistic term *"sensually."*

REFUTATORY ANNOTATIONS OF DR. JAKOB ANDREAE: (T) THEREFORE OUR ADVERSARIES HOLD THOSE AGAINST US UNFAIRLY, AS IF WE THOUGHT THEM UP, ALTHOUGH ORTHODOX ANTIQUITY EMPLOYED THEM. (U) TWO THINGS CAN BE PRESENT IN THE SAME PLACE, OF WHICH ONE OR THE OTHER IS NEVERTHELESS NOT PRESENT PHYSICALLY OR LOCALLY, JUST AS GOD HIMSELF AND THE SAINTS ARE PRESENT IN THE SAME PLACE, HE NOT LOCALLY, THEY LOCALLY. BUT FOR YOU BEING PRESENT IN THE SAME PLACE AND BEING LOCALLY PRESENT ARE EQUIVALENT. THIS IS FALSE. <30> (X) THEY ARE TREATED BY US IN NO WAY OTHER THAN FOR TRUE AND REAL PRESENCE, WHICH THEY HANDED DOWN TO US UNDER THESE PHRASES. (Y) THERE IS NO CONSUBSTANTIATION, BUT SACRAMENTAL AND SUPERNATURAL PRESENCE. (Z) WE REFER NOT TO A MODE OF PRESENCE BUT TO THE THINGS THEMSELVES, WHICH ARE TRULY PRESENT. (A) WE ASSERT THE SAME THING. (B) WHY? UNLESS THEY ARE CONTRARY TO YOUR ERROR. (C) ORALLY, THOUGH BARBARIC IN YOUR OPINION, IS NEVERTHELESS TRUE IN SENSE, PIOUS, AND IN AGREEMENT WITH THE WORD OF CHRIST, EAT, WHICH HE BIDS BE DONE BY MOUTH. (D) PAPISTS, HOWEVER RUDE THEY MAY BE, HAVE NOT ASSERTED "SENSUALLY."

ON THESIS 7.

Far be it from us that we would not agree with the words of institution of the Lord's Supper. (e) We assert only that they should of necessity be understood in relation to the Analogy and norm of the whole Christian faith, comprehended faithfully in the Apostolic Creed, just like all the rest of the passages of Scripture without any exception. But if this should be the case, we think that the consubstantiation of the signs and the body and blood of Christ, opposite from the virtual [σχετική] which we put forward, not only is not proved but also is manifestly and of necessity overturned. (f) Certainly it cannot be said that the cup of blessing is a communion of the blood of Christ, and the bread that we break is a communion of the body of Christ, without a literary device. (g)

REFUTATORY ANNOTATIONS OF DR. JAKOB ANDREAE: (E) SINCE YOU DO NOT RECEIVE THE WORDS OF CHRIST WITHOUT INTERPRETATION, IT IS CLEAR THAT YOU DO NOT AGREE WITH THEM. (F) WE SAID ABOVE THAT WE DO NOT PUT FORWARD CONSUBSTANTIATION. WE REJECT RELATIVE AS IT ACCOMPLISHES NOTHING. (G) WE OPENLY CONDEMN LITERARY DEVICE IN PAUL'S WORDS AS AN EVACUATION OF THE SACRAMENT.

ON THESIS 8.

We believe and preach that what is said is true, but we affirm that it is applied badly to the point at issue. (h)

REFUTATORY ANNOTATION OF DR. JAKOB ANDREAE: (H) IT IS NO SURPRISE THAT YOU FEEL THIS WAY, SINCE SWISS PASTORS REFUSE TO DISPUTE THE LORD'S SUPPER WITH US SO LONG AS WE PUT FORWARD OMNIPOTENCE AS A FOUNDATION OF OUR FAITH IN THIS MYSTERY TOGETHER WITH THE WORDS OF THE LORD'S SUPPER.

<31>

ON THESIS 9.

We ourselves also profess that nothing is impossible for Christ, God and Man, but in such a way that the interpretation of this saying and that which is bound up with this, be examined according to the rule of faith. Therefore, first we affirm that the Omnipotence is unique. It is not duplex, such that there is one Omnipotence that is uncreated and proper to Deity that can be transferred to no created thing, and another, created Omnipotence, which is the quality that is infused into the humanity of Christ. And we say that it is not less false or absurd than to establish more Omnipotences than there are Omnipotent Ones, that is, Gods. Therefore Christ's Humanity is not in itself Omnipotent, but Christ the man is Omnipotent in the Word [Λόγος], just as the Humanity is not Deity, but that man is God the Word [Λόγος]. Second, we say that God is Omnipotent, as far as his power is considered in itself, in such a way that the things he has decreed not to do, or the things contrary to those things which he has decreed, cannot ACTUALLY be done. The reason for this is not that he is not Omnipotent, but that being able to change his will and to be changed in turn would not be a mark of power but of weakness, an attribute of one who could lie. We number among these things the unchangeable circumscription and locality of Christ's body, since God decided that what he once assumed he would never destroy, which would happen if, before or after glorification, the substance of Christ's body were to be able to exist in many places, much less all places, at once. Third, though he has received authority over all created things, we deny that it follows that his Essence is everywhere.

For it is one thing to explain what is possible about something, and another to explain what it is in itself, since in creatures without any exception at all, what it is potential is other than what it is. However, now that we have said these things, we do affirm, nevertheless, that the true body (which is now in heaven and nowhere else), in the rightly administered Lord's Supper, should be taken by us who are now on earth and not elsewhere, very truly and efficaciously through faith, for the salvation of soul <32> and body. We affirm that it is offered by the ineffable virtue of the holy Spirit. (r) And for this reason we think that the inexplicable power of Christ—God and Man—is put forward by us much more distinctly, (s) than by those who think that it is not possible for us to be united with CHRIST himself, except that he himself be present on earth with his own essence, clinging inseparably to the bread and wine. (t)

REFUTATORY ANNOTATIONS OF DR. JAKOB ANDREAE: (I) THEY DO NOT CONCEDE THAT GOD IS ABSOLUTELY AND SIMPLY OMNIPOTENT. (K) ONE WORD CANNOT BE IDENTIFIED IN OUR WRITINGS THAT THEY HAVE EVER TAUGHT A CREATED OMNIPOTENCE. THERE IS IN FACT ONE OMNIPOTENCE, AND IT IS ETERNAL AND INFINITE, BUT IN CHRIST ITS MANNER IS DUPLEX. (L) CHRIST'S HUMANITY *IN ITSELF*, THAT IS, *PER SE*, IS NOT OMNIPOTENT BY THE PROPERTY OF ITS OWN NATURE, BUT RATHER BY THE PERSONAL PARTICIPATION OF THE DIVINE NATURE. (M) MAN IN THE WORD [λόγος] IS OMNIPOTENT: AN AMBIGUOUS STATEMENT, CONCERNING WHICH THERE WILL BE MORE IN ITS OWN PLACE. (N) IT IS DENIED THAT GOD IS ABSOLUTELY OMNIPOTENT. (O) THEY DENY THAT GOD CAN BY HIS OWN OMNIPOTENCE BRING IT ABOUT THAT CHRIST'S BODY, WITH ITS PROPERTY INTACT, MAY BE IN MANY LOCATIONS AT ONE AND THE SAME TIME. THIS IS AN OPEN DENIAL OF GOD'S OMNIPOTENCE. (P) HUMAN FANTASY CONCERNING CHRIST'S AUTHORITY OVER ALL HEAVENLY AND EARTHLY CREATURES, WITHOUT HIS TRUE AND REAL PRESENCE. (Q) IN GOD THE *CAN* BE (*POSSE ESSE*) AND THE *TO* BE (*ESSE*) ARE THE SAME. CHRIST'S FLESH HAS BECOME A PARTAKER IN THIS VIRTUE. <32> (R) SINCE THIS VIRTUE IS INFINITE, THEY DENY THAT HUMAN NATURE HAS BECOME A PARTAKER IN HIM. THEREFORE THEY ATTRIBUTE TO THE HOLY SPIRIT WHAT CHRIST ATTRIBUTES TO HIS OWN FLESH. (S) THEY ARE ABSOLUTELY ROBBING CHRIST'S FLESH OF PARTICIPATION IN THIS VIRTUE; HOW THEN IS THIS POWER ATTRIBUTED TO IT? (T) BEZA ASSERTS THIS ABOUT THE PHYSICAL AND LOCAL PRESENCE, WHICH NOBODY TEACHES. FOR THIS REASON HE FIGHTS AGAINST A FIGMENT OF HIS OWN IMAGINATION.

ON THESIS 10.

The mode, by which the thing signified is joined together with signs by divine ordaining, the name of the signs itself explains, (u) and shows it is Relative to God's covenant, which has a place also even in human and ordinary contracts. (x) But the mode of receiving the thing signified, or in what manner it can happen, such that the body remaining in heaven may be communicated to us who are on the earth by the intervention of an instrumental cause, faith, (y) so efficaciously that we are to drink in eternal life therefrom, and already now receive so many spiritual benefits—this mode, we confess with the Apostle, is truly a great mystery, and accordingly should be believed and adored and not over-examined. But if in fact it is true that the essence of Christ's body and blood is actually present on earth with bread and wine, and nevertheless received, though invisibly, by all who approach, in one and the same oral taking, then we do not see it, since that mode cannot be called inscrutable, which is merely natural and common, sometimes by signs, sometimes by things signified. (z)

REFUTATORY ANNOTATIONS OF DR. JAKOB ANDREAE: (U) THIS RELATIVE MODE IS A HUMAN FANTASY, THOUGHT UP IN ORDER TO COVER AN ERROR. THERE IS NO RELATION HERE, BUT RATHER A TRUE AND REAL DELIVERY OF SPIRITUAL THINGS THROUGH BODILY ONES HAS BEEN INSTITUTED. (X) THERE IS A VAST DIFFERENCE BETWEEN CIVIL CONTRACTS AND EVANGELICAL SACRAMENTS. (Y) THEY ATTRIBUTE MORE POWER TO FAITH THAN TO CHRIST, SUCH THAT IT ASCENDS TO CHRIST IN HEAVEN, THOUGH HE CANNOT BE PRESENT ON EARTH BY PARTAKING OF HIS OWN DIVINE POWER. (Z) ON THE CONTRARY, IT IS CLEAR THAT IT DOES NOT HAPPEN BY A PHYSICAL OR NATURAL MODE.

<33>

1E. IN RESPONSE TO THE DOGMAS WHICH THE COLLOCUTORS JUDGE TO BE IN CONFLICT WITH HOLY SCRIPTURE.

ON DOGMA 1.

We think on the contrary that the words of the Lord's institution, as also the interpretation of the passages of Scripture, without any exception, ought to be brought back to the rule of faith comprehended in the Apostles' creed, as was said above, and explained from a comparison of Scriptures. (a) We think also that it is impossible for them to be accepted according to the plain, literal meaning [κατὰ δ' ῥητόν], if the analogy of faith is to be preserved. (b) Another reason that could be cited is that the institution of the Lord's Supper should be considered unclear, in that a metaphor exists in it.

REFUTATORY ANNOTATIONS OF DR. JAKOB ANDREAE: (A) OBSCURE PASSAGES ARE IN NEED OF SUCH ILLUSTRATION. BUT THE WORDS OF THE LORD'S SUPPER ARE PLAIN AND CLEAR. (B) THIS IS SIMPLY FALSE, AS THE FOLLOWING COMPARISON TEACHES.

ON DOGMA 2.

We appear to have proved sufficiently what is here rejected. (c)

REFUTATORY ANNOTATION OF DR. JAKOB ANDREAE: (C) IT HAS BEEN SHOWN FROM THE WORDS OF CHRIST THAT ABSOLUTELY NOTHING HAS BEEN PROVED.

ON DOGMA 3.

God would not cease to be Omnipotent, even if he were not able to bring it about that Christ's body was essentially present in many places at the same time, or was now somewhere other than in heaven. (d) We have said this at Thesis 9.

REFUTATORY ANNOTATION OF DR. JAKOB ANDREAE: (D) PATENT DENIAL OF GOD'S OMNIPOTENCE: SINCE WITH GOD NOT *ANY WORD* IS IMPOSSIBLE, THAT IS, ANY THING (LUKE 1[:37]).

ON DOGMA 4.

We confess that Christ is God and Man, as he who is Mediator could not be otherwise, though in action he was not man before the actual incarnation. (e) Nevertheless we teach that he was present to Abraham's faith <**34**> *(which is called the substance [ὑπόστασις] of things that are not), (f) not by some false conjecture, but truly and efficaciously, as also to the rest of the holy patriarchs. (g) For Abraham saw the day of the Lord, and there was no other identical Christ coming who pertains to the faith of the patriarchs than the Christ who came to us. (h) This is why Augustine asserts rightly that the Sacraments of the ancients were like ours in substance but different in their signs. (i)*

REFUTATORY ANNOTATIONS OF DR. JAKOB ANDREAE: (E) THERE IS ONE PRESENCE OF THE MAN CHRIST AT THE TIME OF ABRAHAM AND ANOTHER PRESENCE OF THE SAME IN THE NEW TESTAMENT AFTER THE INCARNATION HAPPENED. <**34**> (F) PAUL DOES NOT SAY THAT FAITH IS THE SUBSTANCE [ὑπόστασις] OF THINGS THAT ARE NOT (HEBREWS 11[:1]), BUT OF THINGS THAT ARE TO BE HOPED FOR, AND NOT SEEN. (G) THE PATRIARCHS WERE PARTICIPANTS IN CHRIST'S BENEFITS, BUT THEY DID NOT HAVE CHRIST PRESENT ACCORDING TO HIS HUMANITY, WHICH THEY BELIEVED WAS GOING TO COME. (H) HE WAS OF COURSE THE SAME CHRIST, BUT NOT PRESENT TO THEM AFTER THE SAME MANNER. (AUGUSTINE, *TRACT.* 20 ON JOHN) (I) IN RESPECT OF THE PURPOSE AND OF THE POWER, BUT NOT EQUALLY IN RESPECT OF CHRIST'S PRESENCE ACCORDING TO HIS HUMANITY.

ON DOGMA 5.

This is so far from being the case that we separate Christ's power and benefits in THE LORD'S SUPPER from the communication of Christ himself; in fact we assert the contrary also in the simple word and in Baptism, that these things are inseparably joined to each other, and presented to be taken by the Mind through faith. (k)

REFUTATORY ANNOTATION OF DR. JAKOB ANDREAE: (K) CHRIST DOES NOT OFFER AND PRESENT HIS OWN FLESH AND BLOOD TO BE TAKEN IN THE SACRAMENT *TO THE MIND* ALONE, BUT TO THE MOUTH OF THE BODY, WHETHER SOMEONE BELIEVES OR DOES NOT BELIEVE.

On Dogma 6.

It has never entered our mind that we in any way were proposing perfect faith, since this perfection cannot exist with the remnants of flesh. This is so far from being the case that we do not distinguish true faith from perfect, nor struggling under that weakness of faith do we keep our distance from the Supper. Rather to the contrary we say that it has been instituted for this very reason, that we may be strengthened and nourished in faith. (l)

REFUTATORY ANNOTATION OF DR. JAKOB ANDREAE: (L) WHY THEREFORE DO YOU MAKE TWO TYPES OF UNWORTHY PEOPLE, AND WHY ASSERT THAT THOSE TRULY BELIEVING TAKE IT ALSO TO THEIR JUDGMENT?

On Dogma 7.

We readily believe that this came to the mind of neither the defenders of Transubstantiation nor the defenders of consubstantiation, such that they might affirm these monstrosities. But we confess that we are not able to see which <35> of these, however absurd, false, and blasphemous they may sound, do not of necessity follow that oral eating, unless they should prefer to establish that the substance of Christ's flesh and blood vanish once they pass through the teeth and palate. (m) We wish this to be said nevertheless in the good peace of all.

REFUTATORY ANNOTATION OF DR. JAKOB ANDREAE: (M) IT IS HORRENDOUS TO HEAR, SHOULD CHRIST'S BODY BE RECEIVED WITH THE BREAD BY MOUTH, THAT THE SAME IS ALSO ELIMINATED THROUGH EXCREMENT.

At Montbéliard, 22 March, 1586.
Signed:
Theodore Beza, Minister of the Church at Geneva.
Abraham Musculus, Minister of the Church at Bern.
Antoine de La Faye, Minister of the Church at Geneva.
Pierre Hübner, Professor of Greek, in the Gymnasium at Bern.
Claude Albery, Bachelor and Professor of Philosophy in the Academy at Lausanne.

<36>

1F.I. 2 P.M., 22 MARCH.

After the Theologians of Württemberg had read the two tracts now mentioned, and had scrutinized them, they admitted the president and Honorable Prince, Count Frederick, with his select Courtiers, and also the ministers of the Church at Montbéliard, and as many French exiles as possible. Dr. Jakob began the colloquy with a pious prayer.

THE PRAYER OF DR. JACOB. THE TESTIMONY OF HIS DESIRE AND THAT OF HIS COLLEAGUES. THE SCOPE OF THE DISPUTATION IS ESTABLISHED.

In the name of the Lord and our Savior Jesus Christ, Amen. We pray with our whole heart that he be willing to direct this scheduled colloquy by his holy Spirit and to the glory of his name, and aim at a righteous and salutary peace for our Churches. Amen. O Reverend and very learned Dr. Beza, your two tracts on the Lord's Supper were shown to us a little before lunch, from which we have read, for our part, and reread, and carefully scrutinized in the fear of the Lord. We will respond to them briefly and clearly, as much as possible hereafter. And let the Gentlemen here gathered persuade themselves for certain, that as far as we are concerned, nothing other than the glory of God, the truth of the divine word, pious peace and concord for our Churches, as much as this has been established as a peaceful conference, is the one single target proposed here. Wherefore do we call upon Jesus Christ by name, our one and only savior, the one who searches our hearts, the one who bears witness above our rational thoughts. But if from time to time we seem to anyone to be rather too terse or too vague, we wish to be so advised; with the holy Spirit guiding us, we will actually make known the gentleness of spirit we bring along with us and promised by us, and we will passionately strive to maintain it. Not only do we pledge this on our part, but also graciously pray the same of Your Lordships.

<37>

THE TWO CHIEF POINTS OF CONTROVERSY CONCERNING THE LORD'S SUPPER.

Therefore, on your two tracts on the Lord's Supper which you published, here is what obtains: even though they contain as many things as possible, nevertheless we judge that all their contents can be understood best under two headings. The first of these concerns the true and real presence of the body and blood of our Lord Jesus Christ in the holy Supper of the Lord. And the other concerns the true and sacramental reception of these same elements, their eating and drinking, as we say accordingly. After we have taken up these initial questions, it then will be a simple matter to answer all the things that seem to be challenged in this article. At that time it will be evident to all what the true state of controversy in this article is. We will take care, however, as much as possible, not to seem to have disregarded anything in silence, so that what we had to answer is made note of in both of your writings.

THE CONFESSION OF THE WÜRTTEMBERGERS CONCERNING THE PRESENCE OF CHRIST'S BODY AND BLOOD IN THE LORD'S SUPPER.

First of all, though, we want to testify before the eternal God and father of our Lord Jesus Christ, before our Honorable Prince and Lord, Lord Frederick, Count of Württemberg and Montbéliard, our most kindhearted Lord, whose Highness, after God Almighty, acts as president of this conference, and before all those who listen to these proceedings, that we and our Churches teach about the Lord's Supper consistently and by unanimous consensus, that we must not move even a hair's breadth away from the words of the Testament of Jesus Christ, namely, when giving bread to his disciples, he said, "Take, eat, *this is my body, which is given for you,* and offering the cup, said, Take, drink from this all of you, *this is my blood of the new testament, which is poured out for you, and for many, for the remission of sins.*" We teach that these words must be understood in simple faith, and that they must not be referred to the scrutiny of human reason. Indeed, human reason is not able to comprehend this mystery, but our understanding must be led captive into obedience to Christ, and the simple meaning should be maintained, in the way that the words themselves sound, [38] and in whatever way it does or even can happen, that way must be entrusted to Christ.

WHY THE LITERAL AND SIMPLE MEANING OF THE WORDS OF THE LORD'S SUPPER IS NOT TO BE ABANDONED.

Since Christ is in fact the truth itself, which is not able to lie, and not only is omnipotent, but is omnipotence itself as well, so that he has the ability to fulfill what he promises in spoken words; since this is the case, we teach that the righteous and faithful have no reason to abandon the literal and simple meaning of (and trust in) these words, or to seek some other sense, than that which the words themselves demonstrate to us clearly.

Since therefore he has said, *this is my body*, and again, *this is my blood of the new testament*, etc., in the first place we teach our hearers that having faith in these clear and very simple words, they ought not doubt in the least, that the body and blood of Christ is truly and really present in this holy meal, and indeed is distributed with the bread and wine; that they are received moreover truly and really by all who make use of the Lord's Supper, whether they be worthy or unworthy. Those who are worthy indeed and truly faithful make use of it unto life, while the unworthy and impenitent, on the other hand, to their judgment, either temporal judgment only, if they should be repentant, or eternal judgment, if they should continue in their disbelief and impenitence.

THE CONFESSION OF THE WÜRTTEMBERG THEOLOGIANS CONCERNING THE SACRAMENTAL EATING OF CHRIST'S BODY AND BLOOD IN THE LORD'S SUPPER. WHAT "EATING" MEANS IN THE WORDS OF CHRIST'S TESTAMENT.

Next, when Christ also says, *eat*, we teach our hearers likewise that the word "*eat*" does not mean the same thing as believe, in the manner of John's sixth chapter, in which the words of Christ are taken Metaphorically for believing, when Christ says, unless *you eat* the flesh of the son of man. And again, the one who *eats my flesh* remains in me and I in him, etc. But eating in the words of Christ's Testament means *to receive by mouth*, which Christ shows.

Since therefore Christ did not say, take and eat, this is bread; take, drink, this is wine, but said instead, *this is my body, this is my blood*, we believe and teach that with that bread and wine [39] (according to the very clear words of institution of this Sacrament) is given also his body and blood. And indeed his disciples obeyed his mandate and received it *by mouth*.

THE UNDERSTANDING OF THE SACRAMENT OF THE SUPPER HAS ALWAYS BEEN THE SAME IN ALL TIMES AND PLACES.

And since there is not another understanding of this Sacrament in our Church besides that which was in the first Supper celebrated by Christ and his Apostles, we affirm the same thing also concerning the Lord's Supper, celebrated at all times in the whole world.

CAPERNAITIC AND CYCLOPIC EATING OF THE FLESH OF CHRIST IS CONDEMNED.

But we have first of all publicly attested in our Theses that in no way is there taught by us a Capernaitic eating and Cyclopic carnage of Christ's flesh in the Lord's Supper, nor have these ever been the traditional teaching of our Churches. We have always condemned such teaching in fact, and here and now we also publicly condemn it.

CONCERNING SPIRITUAL EATING THERE HAS NEVER BEEN A CONTROVERSY.

There has never been a controversy either concerning the way in which the eating happens, which is through faith, called spiritual eating by our adversaries. This is nothing other than to believe that the body of Christ has been given for us and his blood poured out for our sins.

This is our honest and public confession and assertion concerning the Lord's Supper, the true and real presence of Christ's body and blood, and sacramental eating. The presence of the body and blood of our Lord *Jesus Christ* and sacramental eating were not in the old Testament.

THE DIFFERENCE BETWEEN THE PRESENCE AND EATING OF CHRIST'S BODY AND BLOOD IN THE SACRAMENTS OF THE OLD AND NEW TESTAMENT.

Though in fact the Patriarchs of the old Testament also had true flesh and real blood in their own Sacraments; nevertheless they were not the real flesh and blood *of Christ*, but merely a figure, type and

shadow of the flesh and blood of Christ, which were only prefiguring, signifying, and foreshadowing the flesh of Christ and his blood.
The evidence of Scripture testifies in what way this is true: Hebrews
10[:1], The Law was a shadow of good things to come, not the image
itself of those things. Furthermore, they are the shadow of things to
come, but the body is Christ's, Colossians 2[:17].

<40>

THE BLOOD OF THE SACRAMENTS OF THE OLD TESTAMENT A SHADOW AND TYPE OF CHRIST.

Thus we read in Exodus 24[:8] that Moses sprinkled the people
with the blood of offered calves after reciting the book of the covenant, saying, This is the blood of the covenant, which the Lord has
fastened upon all these words. This was true blood, substantial and
natural blood of calves, but symbolic, signifying, and figurative only
in respect of the Christ to come, and of the son of God yet to be incarnate, upon whom they believed as one promised who would come to
them. We believe in what has been delivered.

THE BLOOD OF THE SACRAMENT OF THE NEW TESTAMENT IS NOT REPRESENTATIVE, BUT TRUE, AND THE REAL BLOOD OF CHRIST.

In his own Testament, however, Christ says, *this is my blood*, and
adds, *of the new Testament*, in order to mark a distinction between
the Old and New Testaments. Christ did not in fact say, This wine
signifies my blood, or is a sign or figure of my blood, signifying,
representing, or foreshadowing my blood, but said *is, is, is my* blood *of
the new Testament.*

DISTINCTION OF THE SACRAMENTS OF THE OLD AND NEW TESTAMENT.

If in fact he had wished merely to signify or represent his blood,
Moses also could have said, This is the blood of Jesus Christ, of that
true lamb, who takes away the sins of the world, inasmuch as it
represents and signifies him. But Christ wanted to show a distinction
among the Sacraments of the Old and New Testaments, in order that
we may know that in the Sacraments of the old Testament, Christ's
real blood was merely foreshadowed and prefigured through the real

blood of calves, but in the Sacrament of the Eucharist the body and blood of Christ is really present, distributed and received.

FIGURES AND SHADOWS ARE TAKEN AWAY IN THE NEW TESTAMENT.

In fact in the New Testament, all figures and shadows are taken away, and his body takes their place, as the Apostle testifies (Colossians 2[:17]), that he is Christ, the Son of God incarnate, delivered and present according to the flesh, just as it is written, The Law was given through Moses, but truth through Jesus Christ. Hebrews 10[:1]: The Law was a shadow of good things to come.

As great as the difference is, then, between a shadow and the body, between a figure and the thing represented, so great is the difference between the Sacraments of the Old and New Testaments, since in the Sacraments <41> of the old Testament there existed merely a shadow of Christ according to the flesh. Nevertheless, through these the Lord was not to a lesser degree bestowing the benefits of a Mediator to his people, who would acquire them for us by his death, than through the Sacraments of the New Testament, which contain his body, that is, Christ according to his humanity or flesh now manifest, and who is truly and really present in his true flesh in the usage of the Sacraments of the New Testament; he bestows these same benefits to his faithful.

BEZA'S CONFESSION CONCERNING THE PRESENCE OF CHRIST IN ALL THE SACRAMENTS. BEZA IN THE CALM RESPONSE TO BRENZ'S ARGUMENTS, PAGE 27.

Therefore this stands as the first chief point of controversy in this article, namely what concerns the true and real presence of the body and blood of Christ in the Lord's Supper. Since the opposing party publicly writes, "The Body of Christ was present to Abraham in the same way as it is present to us in the Sacrament of the Eucharist," we leave it to the judgment of all hearers in what way this opinion is in accord with the words of Christ's Testament.

For truly it is clear to all that the body of Christ was not yet manifest at the time of Abraham, nor had it been born. In what way therefore could it be present to Abraham (seeing as it did not yet exist) in the same way as it is present to us now, after it has become really manifest, since it was not then? And a little while ago it was said that the law was merely a shadow, not a body or truth.

The Patriarchs indeed had a shadow, an image, and a figure signifying and foreshadowing Christ, as well as also same benefits of Christ procured through his death, namely the grace of God, the remission of sins, on account of Christ who would be sacrificed, and the certain hope of eternal life to follow.

Likewise, in spite of the way in which their Sacraments are in common with ours, namely, what is concerned with the chief efficient cause and end of their Sacraments, they were nevertheless quite a bit different in substance and form, as will be explained shortly. Therefore there is a vast difference between these benefits, and the body of Christ, which has won for us these benefits.

<42>

The words of Christ's Testament clearly and carefully commend and deliver this body to us, when he says, Take, Eat, This is *my body*, which is given for you. I say the body of Christ, not a shadow, figure, or sign of Christ's body; these things are very different from each other.

For the blood of calves was not poured out for the sins of the world, but the blood of Christ, the figure and shadow of which was the blood of bulls. In fact Christ's blood has been poured out for our sins, and Christ testifies that he delivers this blood to us in this Sacrament, in words that are clear and not in the least vague.

THE CONFESSION OF THE WÜRTTEMBERG THEOLOGIANS CONCERNING THE MODE OF THE PRESENCE OF CHRIST'S BODY IN THE LORD'S SUPPER

Now as regards the mode of the sacramental presence of Christ's body and blood, we have always taught, written, and publicly testi-fied that it is not a Physical one, natural, fleshly, or localized one, in the way that Christ dwelt with people on earth.

CARNAL MUSINGS CONCERNING CHRIST'S BODY IN THE BREAD.

In fact they are nothing other than carnal musings concerning this mystery, when simple men imagine for themselves that some little body, with its limbs drawn in, lurks hidden in the offered host. On the contrary we say that the mode of this presence is supernatural, heavenly, one that neither the sense nor the reason of man may comprehend, nor something that can be comprehended in this life, but one that must be left to the infinite wisdom of God, who knows the way, and can even effect by his own infinite power what he promises in his own Testament, as he is omnipotent, and he is true, and he cannot lie and deceive.

THE PIOUS AND HOLY CONFESSION OF CHRYSOSTOM CONCERNING THE LORD'S SUPPER.

Ranking highly among words that ought to be commended to righteous and faithful people are Chrysostom's, which survive in a sermon to the people of Antioch in regard to the Lord's Supper (Homily 60 to the people of Antioch):[9]

WHY GOD DISPENSES SPIRITUAL GIFTS THROUGH CORPOREAL ONES IN THE SACRAMENTS.

Let us submit to God in all things, *and let us not contradict him*, even if he seems to disagree with our *concepts* and *that which is affirmed* by our eyes. On the contrary, let his *speech* be *worthier* than both your concepts and vision. Let us act in such a way in his *mysteries* also, having regard for those things that are placed not *only before our eyes*, but also <43> *concentrating on his words*. For his speech is infallible; our sense is however *easily seduced*. His speech never fails, but our sense *is mistaken* most of the time. Therefore since the word says, *This is my body, so also let us submit, and let us trust*, and let us gaze at it carefully with the eyes of understanding. For Christ handed over to us nothing just for the senses, but what things are indeed perceptible to the senses, are nevertheless all perceptible to the understanding. So also in Baptism, the gift is bestowed through a thing most assuredly sensible, namely water, but what is accomplished is perceived by the understanding, namely regeneration

---

9   Actually Homily 82, on Matthew 26:26–28.

and renewal. If you existed without a body, he would have given you undisguised, incorporeal gifts. But since the soul has been mingled with a body, he delivers *to you* things perceptible to the understanding, *in* things that are perceptible to the senses. How many say nowadays, I should wish to gaze on his form, his figure, his clothing, his sandals? *Behold, you see him, you touch him, you eat him.* Yet you want to see his clothes. But he grants you not only to see but also *to eat and to touch and to take him within you.*

And a little later he says:

> And no small punishment is in store for those partaking in an unworthy fashion. Think about your outrage against his betrayer and those who crucified Christ. And then reflect maturely, lest *you also be guilty of the body and blood of Christ.* Those men murdered his most hallowed body, *but you take within your polluted soul so many benefits.* It was not enough, you see, that he became man, that he was beaten and slain, but his very self he also *commingles with us, and not only by faith, but really and truly makes us his own body.*

Thus far Chrysostom's words.

If we all equally followed these very venerable words, every controversy in this article would have been utterly done away with already. Indeed, for our part, we do follow them, and we advise our hearers carefully and conscientiously to do the same. In doing so, they reflect on the reason for their salvation most correctly and fearlessly.

<44>

Theodore Beza:

Dr. Beza began in a similar fashion with prayers that God would attend the conference with his Holy Spirit, direct the same to the glory of his name, and aim at the salvation and concord of the Church. Beza also prayed that God, in the same way he promised to attend his Church, and send it the spirit of truth,

... also bestow it on me.[10] I see that this is necessary for me on account of the momentous scale of the matter and because of my own infirmity.

THE WITNESS OF THEODORE BEZA, OF HIS OWN WILL.

But we can bear witness by our souls that we bring a spirit desirous of learning the truth, and if we would wish to be taught the better things, then we should be teachable. Nevertheless, I see that we disagree, even though the Holy Spirit does not disagree with himself. But this is nothing strange; nay rather, if it were otherwise, it would be something strange. Indeed we see that not all people judge rightly, and therefore it remains that I pray again that the Lord open our eyes, and that it be understood which party is in error.

A BRIEF REVIEW OF THE CHIEF POINTS OF DR. JAKOB'S CONFESSION.

Now in order that I may begin the matter, O Reverend Doctor, Sir, you have embraced many arguments at the same time. Everything has proceeded from a simple interpretation of Christ's words of institution, from which you have drawn out the proof of your Doctrine in this controversy, which you have established in the real presence of the body and blood of Christ, in the reception of which the worthy and the unworthy coincide. And of course we also do not in the least deny the presence of Christ's body in the holy Supper, and the true eating of it.

From that point you came down to a comparison of the Old and New Testament, and the Sacraments of the same. It seems to me that I have followed your train of thought, <45> namely, that our ancestors enjoyed only a shadow with benefits, but did not have Jesus Christ Himself. From this it would follow that even in their Sacraments they had only a shadow, not Christ himself present.

---

10   The speech of Beza becomes direct at this point, and the colloquy proceeds essentially as back-and-forth between Theodore Beza and Jakob Andreae. The dramatic organization of the 1587 printed text, including the identification of each speaker as well as a different typesetting style to match the speaker, are reflected in the distinct type of this translation.

BEZA ASKS THAT IT BE DONE IN THE WAY OF SYLLOGISM.

I would very gladly ask, though, that we do this in the way of Syllogism, and whenever we have digested a lot of arguments, that we explain each bit in order, one by one. For it would thus improve things to lay everything out in the open; they could be understood more easily. And because you have got wisdom, you are not ignorant that although it may be one thing to be intellectual [λογικὸς], and another to be a Theologian, nevertheless even reason [λόγος] has its place in Theology, in the way that axioms and proofs are sought from sacred Theology.

REITERATION OF DR. JAKOB'S ARGUMENT.

Your opinion seems to be: Christ's words in the holy Supper are to be understood just as they sound. This is your opinion, and the proof of it: THE LORD said, This is my body. Therefore it must be understood simply, just as the words sound. However this does not seem to follow.

DR. BEZA'S ANSWER TO DR. JAKOB'S ARGUMENT.

There are in fact many such, and similar, ways of speaking in holy Scripture. If we were to understand them simply, many obvious and clear absurdities would follow. For example, Christ says at John 14[:28], My Father is greater than me. The Fathers understood and interpreted these words differently than the Arians, who accepted the sentence simply, just as the words sound. And they attempted to prove from it that Christ was not true God, but merely man, a creature subject to God.

Thus you know how Scripture talks about God: The Mouth of the Lord has spoken; and again: The eye of the Lord sees. When heretics interpret such anthropomorphisms [ἀνθρωπομορφήται] literally, they have maintained falsely against the substance of his divinity that God exists bodily. I deny therefore, when you argue in this manner: The Lord Said, This is my body; therefore it must be understood simply.

<46>

Dr. Jakob:

AN APOLOGY FOR HIS WORDINESS IN STATING HIS CONFESSION CONCERNING THE LORD'S SUPPER. WHY THE PROPER AND GENUINE MEANING OF THE WORDS OF CHRIST'S TESTAMENT SHOULD BE RETAINED.

I beg the forgiveness of the audience if I was a bit verbose at the introduction of the Colloquy. This occurred in fact in order best to establish for everyone the real point of argument and our confession in this controversy, and, as they will be disputed in succession, that they might the more easily be able to understand it. Seeing that Dr. Beza is asking that my arguments be refashioned in the form of an argument, I will do what he asks. I am arguing in this way, then: In all Testaments, the proper and genuine meaning of the words must be carefully heeded and maintained. How much the more, therefore, must this happen in this Testament of Christ, and the proper and genuine meaning of Christ's words heeded and maintained, seeing that concentrated in his Testament are, by far, even more excellent benefits that have been bequeathed to the Church.

The premise is proved. In fact there would otherwise be no certainty in Testaments, and of the last will and testament of the Testator (and also in the same way of bequests: what, and how much to whoever, is granted), if there were such incomprehensibility of a Testament's words, with the result that from the words of the Testator his wishes could not be understood or demonstrated, nor what and how much to each inheritor in the testament had been bequeathed.

For this reason, testators devote serious attention and care that they speak distinctly and clearly, lest they leave behind lawsuits and quarrels among their inheritors, or sow the seeds of them. So much the more ought we to judge Christ to have done in establishing his own Testament, with the result that even the simplest faithful Christians, the number of whom is always very great in the Church, may be able to understand what has been delivered and sealed for themselves by Christ in this Testament. No one understands Christ's Testament better than the simplest Christians, who submit to his very simple words in simple faith, and since they are bidden by Christ to trust and do this, they do it in simple faith and obedience.

Dr. Beza:

WHETHER THE LORD'S SUPPER IS RIGHTLY CALLED A TESTAMENT: POINT 1.

Indeed I am astonished, Honorable Doctor, sir, that the Lord's Supper is being called <47> *by you a Testament, which frankly seems to me strange. The Lord's Supper is in fact itself not a Testament, but only part of the Testament of Christ, namely its seal.*

POINT 2.

And again I say that your argument does not follow. What is not said properly is vague. For often figures and literary devices are cited and used to illustrate the things through themselves.

POINTS 3 AND 4.

Meanwhile, there is no possible way to deny that in the words of institution, a figure of speech is being used, and it is being said figuratively, when Luke says, This cup is the New Testament in my blood. For a cup cannot be a Testament. Nor can Luke's words be harmonized with those of Matthew and Mark without a figure of speech: This is my blood of the New Testament, although I always read "THIS" ["HOC"] for "THIS" ["HIC"].[11] And again, one place says blood of the Testament, and another says the Testament itself. And again, how many literary devices and figures does the Testament of Jacob the Patriarch have in it? There is no way to deny this.

Dr. Jakob:

POINT 1.

O Reverend Beza, sir, in turn it seems to me utterly strange and unheard of that anyone would deny that the Lord's Supper is Christ's

---

11   The distinction in gender for these demonstratives is lost in English; Beza claims to read the neuter *hoc* (which would properly refer to the cup or the testament, *poculum* or *testamentum*) instead of the masculine *hic* (which would properly refer to the blood of Christ, *sanguis*).

Testament, contrary to the clear words from the Evangelist Luke you related: This cup is the New Testament in my blood (Luke 22[:20]).

THE EUCHARIST HAS ALL THE CONVENTIONS OF A TRUE TESTAMENT. 1. A TESTATOR. 2. THE WORDS OF THE TESTATOR. 3. HEIRS. 4. BEQUESTS. 5. 12 WITNESSES. 6. A SEAL.

Then again, it is clear to all that it possesses all the essential elements needed for a legitimate and customary Testament. For in the first place, the Testator, Our Lord Jesus Christ, is expressly named as the one who established this Testament. In the second place are the Testator's official words, by which he makes known his will. In the third place, heirs are chosen, namely, all those who trust in Christ, on behalf of whom Christ's blood was poured out, and his body handed over unto death. In the fourth place, bequests are described, namely, the remission of sins and eternal life: This is my blood, which is poured out for you and for many for the remission of sins. In the fifth place, the twelve Apostles are Witnesses. In the sixth, seals are added too, partly visible, partly invisible: not only bread and wine, <48> but also the body and blood of Christ, just as the clear words sound, by which the promise of the bequests is sealed. For he communicates to us with bread and wine this very body and this very blood, which have been given on our behalf. And Christ strengthens our faith by these things, and the strengthening of faith is the purpose of the Sacrament of the Lord's Supper. From these points it stands that the holy Supper of the Lord very justly, and not without the authority of the Holy Spirit, is called a Testament, by which the promise of grace and of the remission of sins is sealed and confirmed in those who believe.

MEANING AND INTENTION OF CHRIST'S TESTAMENT. COMFORT OFFERED IN THE LORD'S SUPPER.

This is the intention and meaning of Christ's words: to the extent you have heard how mercifully and gently I have invited all sinners and promised them, as much as they work repentance and truly trust in me, they will have, on account of my obedience to the law being fulfilled, and my death which I am about to undergo, full remission of all their sins and eternal life. Let no one be in doubt concerning the truth and certainty of this promise. Behold, I give you a most certain pledge with this consecrated bread, this very body, which I have handed over to death for the sins of the whole world, and the same blood—and not another—which I have poured out for the sins of the world. Amid very serious trials this is by far the greatest and surest consolation which they possess, stored up, in the usage of this Sacrament. But they regard instead the word of Christ and they embrace it with firm faith.

POINT 2. NO FIGURE OF SPEECH IN THE WORDS OF CHRIST'S TESTAMENT.

Then again, I do not deny, but rather concede, that occasionally things are not obscured but rather brought to light through figures of speech and literary devices. But Christ had no desire to explain or to illustrate in his own Testament. Rather, he wished to establish and set forth in clear, obvious, and very few words, what it was that he was giving and delivering with bread and wine, to his disciples and the whole Church of the New Testament. And there was not there the least need of a literary device or a figure of speech to illustrate it.

A FIGURE OF SPEECH DOES NOT ILLUSTRATE THE WORDS OF CHRIST'S TESTAMENT.

Furthermore, the literary device that you affix to Christ's words does not illustrate, but rather destroys the thing that is proposed in Christ's words [49] and delivered to the Church. By means of this, the body and blood of Christ are done away with in the Lord's Supper, and mere signs, symbols, figures, and shadows offered in place of Christ's body and blood, to such a degree that the Church of God is left with only the leftover shells, the remainder once the nut has been removed.

POINT 3. WHETHER TO RESORT TO A LITERARY DEVICE IN PAUL'S WORDS CONCERNING THE CUP. THE HARMONY OF PAUL'S WORDS WITH THE WORDS OF MATTHEW AND MARK CONCERNING THE CUP OF THE LORD'S SUPPER. THE HEBREW PHRASE USED IN SCRIPTURE. IN WHAT WAY THE CUP OF THE LORD'S SUPPER IS THE NEW TESTAMENT. WHAT THE NEW TESTAMENT IS.

But Rev. Dr. Beza appends the following: in Luke it is necessary to revert to a figure of speech, if we would trust the words by which he describes the institution of the Lord's Supper: This cup is the New Testament in my blood, which cannot be harmonized otherwise with the words of Matthew and Mark, which read thus: This is my blood of the New Testament. I answer: Instead of understanding Luke (with Paul, in his description of the words of the Lord's Supper), as presenting a really big disparity in his words concerning the cup, and therefore finds it unavoidable to revert to a figure of speech for the sake of their harmony; much to the contrary, I will demonstrate very clearly that they use the very same words, equally about the cup and the bread. The difference, however, is only in the diversity of their phrases. For Matthew and Mark spoke after the customary usage of the Greeks: This [Hic] or this [hoc] is my blood of the New Testament. Luke and Paul, however, used a Hebrew phrase: This cup is the New Testament in my blood. This phrase is used by the Hebrews and occurs often in Scripture. Genesis 32[:10], the Patriarch Jacob says, On my staff I crossed the Jordan, that is, with my staff. Judges 15[:16], In the jawbone of an ass, in the jaw of the foal of an ass, did I destroy them, and have struck down a thousand men, that is, with a jawbone. Psalm 63 [66:13], I will enter into your house in whole burnt offerings, that is, with whole burnt offerings. Joshua 24[:12], Not in a sword and in your bow have I cast out the two Kings of the Amorites, that is, with a sword. In such a way Luke says with Paul, not simply and conclusively, this cup is the New Testament, but adds to it with a Hebrew phrase: *in my blood*, that is, with my blood. For without the blood of Christ it cannot be the New Testament. But since the blood of Christ is joined with this cup according to the words of promise, it does not signify the New Testament, but *it really is*. For the presence of Christ's blood, and its efficacy, makes effective the New Testament, <50> the blood which was merely foreshadowed in the old Testament.

THE EVANGELISTS DESCRIBED THE LORD'S SUPPER USING THE SAME WORDS AS PAUL, BUT A DIFFERENT PHRASE.

All hearers therefore see in what way the words of the three Evangelists and Paul are the same in the earlier part of the Sacrament: This is my body. Thus indeed concerning the cup the same words exist in the four descriptions, but the phrasing is various merely on account of Idiosyncracies of languages. For if you were to enumerate the words, This, blood, new Testament, *is*, the same words will be found in all of them. Their context is now one and now another, because of each language. So for this reason we by no means need a figure of speech to harmonize the words of the Evangelists and Paul, but only an explanation of the diversity of their phrases, since this very thing shows that Christ's words have been retained accurately by all of them.

POINT 4. CONCERNING THE WORDS OF THE TESTAMENT OF THE PATRIARCH JACOB.

But as far as the words of the Testament of the Patriarch Jacob are concerned, this manner of speaking is quite different. He in fact addressed his sons in his own last words regarding the fortune of each of them more than he established a Testament. There is the place for literary devices and figures. However Christ in his own Testament is not making an address after this fashion. Rather, he ordained bread and wine for the dispensing of his own body and blood. He likewise prescribed how they are to be administered for the strengthening of faith and our eternal salvation; here there is no use of literary devices and figures.

Dr. Beza:

POINT 1.

Since you have made use of this general foundation, namely, that in Testaments there is no place for figures or literary devices, to that end I produced the example of the Patriarch Jacob.

POINT 2.

And I add, you have affirmed that the Lord's Supper is the New Testament. I said that it was not properly a Testament, but a pledge.

POINT 3.

And again, if Christ had not instituted the Lord's Supper, would the New Testament really not have been instituted in the meantime?

<51>

POINTS 4 AND 5.

Also, if you understand by New Testament nothing except for the Lord's Supper, what then shall we say about Baptism? Surely this Sacrament will not also be able to be called, for the same reason, a Testament? For here the Testator is Christ, who instituted Baptism. Here are Christ's bequests, the remission of sins. And I say also that Baptism also has the blood of Christ. And you are not unaware that the Papists have derived the madness of Transubstantiation from the simple understanding of the words of institution.

POINT 6.

Therefore in the same way that the signature attached to a document is not the document itself, but is merely its validation, by which it is rendered authentic, so also the Lord's Supper is not a Testament, but merely a signature, and signification of a Testament.

POINT 7.

I could not be more astonished, besides, that the same man is Testator and Testament. You are in fact confusing the Testator and the Testament.

POINT 8. POINT 9. CONCERNING SACRAMENTAL PHRASES.

And in a similar way also, it does not seem like what you have said can stand, that there can be no place in Christ's Testament for figures of speech, since Christ here did not wish to illustrate. The argument does not hold water. For it really seems there was need of illustration, since the disciples were seeing Christ holding bread, and that it was pure bread and wine that he offered with his hands. They were also seeing that this bread was not essentially Christ's body. So for this reason they were in need of such an explanation and illustration, for which Christ used a Literary device, which fights against the madness of the Papists concerning Transubstantiation. This literary device was not overlooked by the disciples in the least. For even if they were otherwise rather ignorant, nevertheless they *were experienced with his ways of speaking, with the result that they understood them rightly. They had gotten used to them not only in Mysteries and Sacraments, but otherwise also in common speech. Thus it is said, <52> Circumcision is a covenant, a Lamb is a Passover or the passing over of the Lord, that is, this signifies, whether it is a sign of a covenant, or it signifies the passing over of the Lord.*

Points 10, 11, and 12.

So it is also, when a judge installs someone into the occupation of exercising justice, he offers him a sword and says, This power has been given to you. And again, in contracts when letters are presented, Behold, with these letters I hand you a meadow, a field, a house, etc. even if they are other things. And these figurative manners of speech are always employed in Scripture. For example, Luke 13[:32], Christ said about Herod, tell that fox, which is said by literary device, by which he declared the more significantly the wickedness of Herod than if he had spoken without a literary device, and had said wicked and cunning person. So also he said to Peter, Get behind me Satan. There, more is said with the word Satan, and it is stated more clearly when he names him Satan or Devil, than if he had said that he was an adversary. Similarly, it is certain that Christ also wanted to speak by literary device when he said, This is my body. Let us not partake only of bread, but of such bread as is a sign and figure of Christ's body, such as represents and offers Christ's body most efficaciously to the mind of pious people.

Point 13.

And when Paul says with Luke, This cup is the new Testament IN MY BLOOD, I prefer to render it through my blood, rather than with my blood.

Dr. Jakob:

Reverend Doctor Beza has said many things. If I do not respond to all of them in order, it is the fault of my memory, and I ask that it be pardoned me and that I be reminded. For I myself acknowledge that my memory is weak.

POINTS 1, 2, AND 3.

What was said therefore from the beginning by me about the Testament, that the Lord's Supper is thus named by Luke and Paul, has been proved sufficiently above. <53> And we have demon-strated clearly after what fashion a Testament is brought about, in which every customary feature that pertains to the substance of a Testament is observed. I thus concede also that a new Testament would have existed, even if the Lord's Supper had not been instituted. But that the Lord's Supper is not a Testament or able to be called one, I deny. The reasons have been mentioned by me earlier. And this Testament would have lacked another seal, which Christ hangs on the Lord's Supper.

POINT 4. WHY BAPTISM IS NOT CALLED A TESTAMENT. WHENCE A DISTINCTION OF SACRAMENTS SHOULD BE SOUGHT.

It has been brought up that Baptism can be equally called a Testament after this manner. I answer: we should talk about the Sacraments individually from the word of God. Therefore since Scripture does not say this about Baptism, we also remain silent. As far as a distinction beteween the Sacraments is concerned, this is taken from the word of God and the external signs. For even though Christ is one and the same in number in all the Sacraments, the nature of the Sacraments is not for this reason the same in every respect. Thus Baptism in the word of God is not called a Testament, but a washing of regeneration and renewal in the holy Spirit.

And concerning Baptism Christ has not said, This is my blood, but rather, he joined together water and the Spirit for regeneration, when he said, Unless someone has been born again of water and spirit, etc. (John 3[:5]). Concerning the Testament of the Patriarch Jacob we said a little earlier that it was more a Prophetic address concerning the fortune and success of his sons and their posterity rather than a Testament. It follows that the Patriarch wanted to illustrate with literary devices. In the Lord's Supper however there is by far another matter. And it remains forever a true rule: in Testaments, people customarily use not literary devices or figures, but very simple and clear words, in order that the Testator's will may be established.

POINT 5. TRANSUBSTANTIATION DOES NOT FOLLOW FROM A SIMPLE UNDERSTANDING OF THE WORDS OF THE LORD'S SUPPER.

But regarding the fact that Popes introduced the fiction and madness of Transubstantiation into the Church out of a simple understanding of the words of Christ's Testament, it is manifest in what way this does not follow. For just as from a literal and simple sense of John's words (John 3 [1:32–33]) something could be put together erroneously as when it is said: Upon whom you will see the spirit descending, in the <54> form of a dove (Luke 3[:22]), therefore a dove is transubstantiated into the holy Spirit; thus also does it not follow that Christ, showing them bread, said This is my body, and therefore the bread is transubstantiated into the body of the Lord.

For just as the substance of the dove and of the holy Spirit remained distinct in this revelation of the holy Spirit, and no confusion of their substances happened, or change of one substance into the other, so also in the Lord's Supper, no transmutation of the substances of bread and body, of wine and Christ's blood, has happened according to substance. But what is expressed merely by these words is the presence of Christ's body, and the sacramental union, which has happened between the bread and Christ's body, by virtue of the words of institution.

NO LITERARY DEVICE IN THE WORDS OF CHRIST'S TESTAMENT.

Therefore, in the same way as there is no literary device in these words when it is said, This dove is the holy Spirit, in fact truly it was the holy Spirit, which descended in the form of a dove, and not merely a sign of the holy Spirit; so also is there no literary device in the words of Christ's Testament, This is my body. Nor does Transubstantiation follow from the literal sense.

So also, the fact that the disciples see Christ holding bread, in its essence, in his hand, to distribute to the Apostles, does not manifest a literary device. For not only did they gaze upon the bread with their own eyes, but they were directed to the words of Christ in true faith, this is my body, which they trusted simply without any literary device.

POINT 7.

And I do not see in what way a confusion of Testator and Testament follows from our way of thinking, seeing as the same man is Testator and Testament. For Christ's body (by which name the Testator can be understood) is not totally and fully a Testament, just as Christ's Testament is also something other than Christ's body. But in Christ's Testament his body and blood comprise a seal of promise, as it were.

DISTINCTION BETWEEN A TESTAMENT AND THE SEAL OF A TESTAMENT.

So also a Testament is and remains one thing, which is the promise of grace, on account of the body and blood of Christ given for us, and poured out for the remission of sins. And Christ's body and blood, with the bread and wine of the Lord's Supper, are another thing <55> by which this promise is sealed. But just as in another case it is necessary for a whole and complete Testament not to be just plain paper but also to have a seal affixed, so also in Christ's Testament, the promise is not only described on paper but a seal is affixed, so that all truly penitent sinners may be most certain about the grace of God.

POINT 8. NO LITERARY DEVICE IN THE WORDS OF THE SACRAMENTS OF THE OLD TESTAMENT.

I am very much astonished however that you say, In the Lord's Supper there was need of illustration, for which Christ made use of this kind of speech, which was understood rightly by his disciples, since there is no example of these extant in the old Testament.

POINT 9.

For what you brought forward concerning sacramental say-ings of the old Testament, not unknown to Christ's disciples, were: Circumcision is a covenant, that is, a sign of a covenant; and again,

The lamb is the Passover, or the passing over of the Lord, that is, it was signifying the passing over of the Lord. But I simply and categorically deny that these sayings are figurative literary devices.

IN WHAT WAY "CIRCUMCISION IS A COVENANT" SHOULD BE UNDERSTOOD.

For when we say, Circumcision is a covenant, the term "*is*" must be taken hyparctically, that is, just as it reads, namely, not as "*signifies*" but as it *truly is*. For circumcision did not represent a covenant, but *was* a true covenant between God and the posterity of Abraham, to whom it was given.

WHAT CIRCUMCISION EMBRACES.

But circumcision does not signify only cutting off or amputation of the foreskin, as if it consisted entirely in that cutting off of skin, but it requires also the word of God, just like the substantial part of a covenant, without which the external circumcision is not a covenant, but an idle ceremony.

CIRCUMCISION OF THE TURKS IS AN IDLE CEREMONY.

Likewise we can see it among Turks and Jews, who in our time employ this external ceremony, and have their boys circumcised, They do not, however, have the true circumcision, since it lacks God's word, his mandate, and the promise given to Abraham, which alone had to endure up to the advent of Christ, and was abrogated by Baptism, which succeeded in the place of circumcision.

It is clear, therefore, since what is needed for circumcision is not only an outward ceremony but also the word of God, [56] that circumcision is no way merely a sign of a covenant, but really and truly is the covenant itself.

When Scripture speaks merely, though, about an outward ceremony, then we say rightly that it was a sign and seal of a covenant, as a part of it. This is how Paul speaks in Romans 4 about Abraham. And he received the sign of circumcision, a mark of the righteousness of faith.

THE PASCHAL LAMB IS NOT THE PASSOVER OF THE LORD. THE LAMB DID NOT SIGNIFY THE PASSING OVER OF THE LORD.

Thus we read nowhere in scripture, The lamb is the Passover of the Lord. Nor can Dr. Beza demonstrate this phrase or way of speaking in the cited passage of Moses in Exodus 12, such that he could argue from it for the purpose of confirming his assertion of the literary device in the words of the Lord's Supper. Therefore just as the lamb is not said to be the Passover of the Lord, nor did it signify this Passover, so also is a false conclusion made from this that the bread of the supper is not the Lord's body, but exists only to signify the Lord's body.

THE PASCHAL LAMB A FIGURE AND TYPE OF CHRIST.

For the Paschal lamb signifies merely the true lamb of God who is Jesus Christ; in no way did it signify the Passover of God. This is a clear stratagem of composition that Beza has joined together from the words of Moses described in Exodus chapter 12, which he has removed from context. Indeed Moses reports the reason why they should put some of the lamb's blood on the posts and lintel of the homes, and eat its flesh quickly: Thus however you will eat, says Moses, You will gird your loins and you will have shoes on your feet, holding staves in your hands, and you will eat *quickly*. For it is the Passover, or passing over of the Lord. The following words of Moses will show more clearly in the light of day that these final words cannot refer to the lamb. For he continues, And I will pass over throughout the land of Egypt on that night, and I will strike every firstborn in the land of Egypt, from man to cattle.

Here is spoken nothing about a sign, figure, figurative speech or signification of the Lord's Passover, but rather about a real Passover, because the Lord was in fact about to pass over. The lamb did not stand for this Passover, or signify it, but its blood foreshadowed the blood of Christ, by whose merit they were saved, who is today, yesterday, and forever. <57> The following words of Moses indicate this more clearly, when he says, And when your sons say, what is that sacred rite? You will say, it is the sacrifice of the Lord's Passover, when the

Lord passed over the houses of Israel, etc. Nothing is said there about a signification of the Lord's Passover, but the distinct things are rehearsed, namely the sacrifice of the lamb, and the time when the Lord passed over, and spared Israel in the killing of the firstborn of Egypt.

Since therefore circumcision is a true and real covenant, and does not signify a covenant, and the Paschal lamb is not called the Lord's Passover, nor does it signify the Lord's Passover as if a thing absent, a duplicitous transgression has taken place in the assertion of these examples. First, they attach a false meaning to Moses' words. Then, they adapt that twisted meaning to the words of the Lord's Supper, and thus attempt to show by this uncertain, or rather manifestly false sense, an uncertain, or rather false sense in the words of Christ's Testament, when the phrases about circumcision and the Paschal lamb are in no way figurative, as has been demonstrated.

Because of this it is falsely stated, These figurative expressions were known to the disciples, if indeed they were not figurative, as has been shown.

POINT 10. REFUTATION OF THE ARGUMENT PRODUCED FROM THE ANALOGY OF THE SWORD.

The analogy of the judge delivering the sword to his minister is also erroneously adapted to this point. For some phrases are Sacramental, but others are employed in political matters. God, in the Sacraments, has willed not to signify spiritual things compre-hended by the word, but to distribute and deliver them to his own, and he also really and truly delivers them.

POINT 11. REFUTATION OF THE ARGUMENT FROM CIVIL CONTRACTS.

Thus also the letters of contracts in civil actions are erroneously adapted to Christ's words, as if the nature of each would seem to be the same. For the customary manner of speaking when delivering letters of a contract is not that someone would say, take it, This is a house, a field, a meadow, even if they are other things. But Christ delivering bread says, Take, Eat, This is my body. [58] This phrase and expression is by far something other than those customary in contracts.

POINT 12.

In the example offered about Herod, I confess that there is a literary device present, which is called a Metaphor. But this is not a Sacramental expression.

POINT 13.

But about Peter, I deny that a literary device is present in the word Satan, since in the Hebrew language Satan is a general term, which means adversary.

NO LITERARY DEVICE IN THE WORDS OF CHRIST.

Answer has been made above to the citation of Paul, that he does not say simply, The cup is the new Testament. If in fact these words had been placed absolutely in Paul or Luke, then I might admit a literary device in these words, but since he adds, *in my blood*, any literary device is left out of this Hebrew phrase. The words of Luke and Paul read the same way in fact, This cup is the new Testament in my blood, as Matthew's and Mark's words, This [*Hic*] or this [*hoc*] (for I regard there is no difference) is my blood of the new Testament.

It still remains therefore firm and unshaken: The words of Christ's Testament, This is my body, must be understood according to the plain, literal meaning [κατὰ δ' ῥητόν], that is, literally, just as the words read, apart from every literary device.

Dr. Beza:
The reason I asserted the Patriarch Jacob's Testament, was so that I might prove that it is possible that a literary device can take place in Testaments. But you answer that there is another nature in Christ's words.

WHETHER JOHN SAW THE HOLY SPIRIT.

Moreover you bring this up concerning the holy Spirit, whom you say was seen by John. I do not concede that it can be said without a literary device, that John saw the holy Spirit, since he saw a dove, and not the very substance of the holy Spirit. It is necessary therefore, since it was a dove, and not the holy Spirit, but a sign of the holy Spirit, that these things be said by way of a literary device.

<59>

POINT 2.

But when it is said in regard to the Son of God, He was seen, it is said according to the hypostatic union, because God and man are in Christ one person. But in regard to the holy Spirit and the dove it is not possible that this can take place, because the dove and the Holy Spirit were not united hypostatically; rather the dove was only a sign of the holy Spirit.

POINT 3.

With your permission, you seem to me also to err in this, and not to act rightly, because you think that an explanation of the words of the Lord's Supper should not be cited from other Testaments and references in Scripture.

POINTS 4 AND 5.

And although I confess that the nature of Baptism and of the Lord's Supper is not simply the same, nevertheless it is not able to be denied that the Sacraments have something in common. And this, not only in the new, but also in the old Testament, if the Sacraments of the new Testament should be compared to those, just as has been said about circumcision, that it is a covenant, that is, the sign of a covenant. Thus also can it be said that the bread in the Lord's Supper is Christ's body, that is a sign of Christ's body.

POINT 6.

You spoke about Peter, whom Christ named Satan, and there you understand by the term Satan, not the devil but an adversary. I confess, I think I have not read such an explanation, nor has it been explained this way by anyone.

POINT 7.

And you are not unaware that Bernard explained the words of the Lord's Supper by way of analogy, that is, with the example of the ring which is given by a husband to his wife when he sets out to go abroad, to preserve the memory of her husband, until such time as he has returned. Thus also did Christ give his bride the Church the bread of the supper for preserving the memory of her spouse, until such time as he returns for judgment. It is not possible that what is said there is said without a literary device, that the ring is the husband, but rather that it is a sign and a memorial of the husband, intended perpetually to remind the wife of his return.

<60>

Dr. Jakob:

POINT 1. JOHN SAW THE HOLY SPIRIT HIMSELF.

In the example of the holy Spirit and the dove, in which the Holy Spirit revealed himself, we have said sufficiently above that there is no literary device in it. For John is said to have seen not a sign of the holy Spirit, but the holy Spirit himself, just as the words of the text plainly read, *And he saw the Holy Spirit descending like* a dove, and coming upon him (Matthew 3[:16]). It does not say, And John saw a dove descending, which signified the holy Spirit. Again, The Holy Spirit descended in corporeal form, with a dove on him as it were (Luke [3:22]). I ask at this place, in which term is there a figure of speech or literary device, if you examine each and every one of them?

THE ANALOGY OF THE VEILED MAN.

But even if John did not see the holy Spirit in the property of his substance and Divine essence, since with respect to the spirit he is not at all corporeal, but invisible, nevertheless he saw the holy Spirit himself in the form in which he revealed himself, namely in the appearance of a dove. The appearance of a dove is not a literary device or Grammatical figure of speech. In the same way if someone were to see a veiled man, his whole body clothed in a habit, it could truly be said that he saw a man like this, but merely in the form which met his own eyes. In a similar fashion also, no literary device can obtain here, as if one saw merely a sign and not the man present himself. Nowhere is it written, moreover, that John saw a dove, which signified the holy Spirit, but it is plainly said, John saw the holy Spirit descending. What is attributed to the holy Spirit there, on account of the form and appearance in which he appeared, and on account of his real presence, not a figurative or signified one, was what is proper not to the holy Spirit, but to a dove. This is according to the plain, literal meaning [κατὰ δ' ῥητόν], without a figure of speech or literary device.

THE FORM OF SPEAKING CUSTOMARY, NOT FIGURATIVE. DEMONSTRATION OF THE PRONOUN *HOC*.

Then again, everybody knows that, when two things are joined together and shown at the same time, only the more noble and excellent is named, and a substitution occurs from the nobler. In this way a host, serving different types of wine in different cups or glasses, says, <61> This is red wine, this is white wine, this is from the Rhineland, this is from Alsace. Here in all of these expressions there are two things demonstrated by means of the Pronoun "*this*" ["*hoc*"] namely the glass that contains wine, and the wine contained in the glass. Nevertheless the wine only, and not the glass, is being named, as the more noble and excellent thing.

FROM THE RULE REGARDING THE COMMON FORM OF SPEAKING IN ALL LANGUAGES. WHAT THE PRONOUN *"THIS"* ["*HOC*"] SHOWS IN THE WORDS OF CHRIST.

This way of speaking is not in the least literary or figurative, but simple and customary in all languages. The words mean what they sound like, as they are intended. Since the thing itself that is given is really wine of the type that is named. For what is said or meant is not, This glass signifies red wine or white wine, or This glass is a figure and sign of wine, signifying wine. But in the same way that we say, this is red wine, so also does the Pronoun "*hoc*" indicate two things, bread and Christ's body, but only the nobler is named, and the bread serves the distribution and reception of it. Similarly there is also no literary device in the rest of the words, but a literal meaning, according to the rules of grammar, for every single one of them. *Is* really means and expresses *is*. Body means and expresses true body. *My* means and expresses Christ's and not another's. When therefore the meaning proper to every single term in Christ's words is retained, how can there be a literary device in them? From this it is understood not only that the way of speaking is not Metaphorical, but also that the Metaphorical explanation is so absurd that the thing itself cannot bear it, as has been explained.

POINT 2. WHETHER THE APOSTLES SAW THE SON OF GOD TRULY OR METAPHORICALLY.

The same reasoning obtains, of course, regarding the Son of God, about whom John writes, That which was from the beginning, which we have heard, which we saw with our eyes, which we have beheld, which our hands touched, concerning the Word of life (1 John 1[:4]). For even if a visible human nature was united with the Son of God in another way than a dove with the holy Spirit, indeed, hypostatically united, nevertheless it is plainly the same reasoning in so far as the external perception and real presence of both of these is concerned. For just as the Son of God and the holy Spirit are invisible with respect to the property of the Divine nature, so they were not seen except by way of an external, visible <62> nature assumed by them. But they were seen not by way of literary device, figuratively, or emblematically, but truly and really; present, not absent.

POINT 3. ANALOGY OF THE SACRAMENTS OF THE OLD AND NEW TESTAMENT.

As to what touches the Analogy between the Sacraments of the Old and New Testament, I confess that they have certain points in common, namely that they all consist of word and element, that they are seals of grace, of free remission in Christ, and promised on account of Christ. It does not in the least follow from this, however, that their nature is altogether the same.

For the distinction between the Sacraments of the old and new Testament is as great as the difference between a shadow and the body that casts it, as was shown above.

POINT 4. REGARDING THE COMPARISON OF BAPTISM TO THE LORD'S SUPPER.

And concerning the comparison of Baptism to the Lord's Supper it was also mentioned why Baptism was not called a Testament by the Evangelists, but only the Lord's Supper. The reason for this is that we must speak about and understand each of the Sacraments according to the convention of God's word. Christ is indeed present in each Sacrament. But in Baptism we are born again, not refreshed with food or drink. And in the Lord's Supper we are refreshed with food and spiritual drink, not born again.

POINT 5. WHEN AND HOW THE TERM "SIGN" OBTAINS IN THE SACRAMENTS.

I concede that the sign of a covenant and the covenant itself are different, since by the sign of a covenant is understood only the seal attached to it. I persistently deny however that circumcision consists only in an external ceremony without the word. For just as in external Testaments, parchment without a signature has no authority, and neither does a signature without the parchment, so also Christ, on account of the infirmity and weakness of our faith, joins together the parchment, that is, the promise of the Gospel, with the signature, and the signature with the parchment, that is, his promise and his seal. And in this way he entrusts and leaves behind a completed Testament as it were to his Church.

POINT 6. IN WHAT WAY PETER WAS CALLED SATAN.

For my understanding and explanation that not the devil, but an adversary, is in Christ's words spoken to Peter, Get behind me Satan, I appeal to the judgment of those skilled in the Hebrew language, to whom the meaning of this Chaldean term is known. This was the language in which Christ spoke <63> among the Jews, the vernacular, as it were, spoken by the Jewish people of the era after the return from Babylon. The general term Satan is attributed to the devil in this case since the devil is the supreme adversary of God, but this notwithstanding, Christ can employ it with a general meaning against Peter, who did not speak this deviating utterance as the Devil out of hatred, but out of love for Christ, on account of which he is rebuked by Christ and called Satan.

Point 7. Bernard in the sermon on the Lord's Supper. Analogy of the ring.

The analogy of the ring brought up from Bernard cannot be extended further than the words of the Author permit. This is how Bernard's words read:

> Let us take an everyday example. A ring is given absolutely for the sake of a ring, and its meaning is null. It is given for the sake of endowing a certain inheritance, and is a sign, such that the one who receives it can say, The ring is nothing, but the inheritance is, which I was seeking. It is the same as when a Canon is invested with a book, an Abbot with a staff, a Bishop with a Staff and a Ring at the same time. Just as in matters of this sort, so also, I say, are the *divisions of the graces* given by the different Sacraments.

From which it is clear that Bernard intended by the analogy of the ring to preach in no way about the substance of the Sacrament of the Supper, but only about its use and purpose. The analogy squares best with this understanding.

Abuse or perverse interpretation of the analogy of the ring. Bernard's faith and confession regarding the Lord's Supper.

But it never came to Bernard's mind that his point get twisted to the substance of the Sacrament, as if bread were merely a sign of Christ's body in the holy Supper. Rather, this is in conflict with his express words, which are extant in the following sermon concerning the Lord's Supper. He says:

> Although the Sacrament is one, there are *three distinct things* laid out there: namely the visible appearance, *the truth of the body*, and the virtue of spiritual grace. And again: You ought indeed to attend to three things in the Sacrament of the altar, the appearance of the bread, the truth of the flesh, and the virtue of spiritual grace.

Thus far Bernard's words. Therefore the analogy of the ring in no way confirms a literary device in the words of Christ's Testament, which neither Bernard's words, nor Christ's, admit.
<64>

PLAIN, LITERAL MEANING [Τὸ ῥητόν][12] OF CHRIST'S WORDS FIRM. SIMPLE FAITH OF CHRIST'S DISCIPLES REGARDING THE LORD'S SUPPER.

From all these things it is clear that we are pressed by no necessity at all to shrink back from the simple and literal sense of the words of Christ's Testament, but rather they must be understood according to the plain, literal meaning [κατὰ δ' ῥητόν], and accepted by simple faith, in the same way that Christ's disciples doubtless accepted them very simply by that faith, remembering the Apostle Peter's word: Where shall we go? You have the words of eternal life (John 6[:67]). The disciples trusted this, and did not curiously inquire into Christ's words, nor indulge in human reason or senses, which saw nothing but bread and wine with external eyes, but heeding Christ's words which they knew were words of life, they simply trust that Christ gives his body to be eaten. They entrust the *mode* of presence to Christ, but take obedience upon themselves, and do what Christ bids them. For unless they had trusted this simply, they would doubtless have asked Christ how these words of his, This is my body, should be understood. This was otherwise done by them often, as often as they did not understand something or doubted something.

THE LORD'S SUPPER IS A MYSTERY SURPASSING HUMAN INTELLECT.

---

12   Alternative translation—Precise, literal meaning—need to decide this

Elsewhere Calvin bids us do the same thing. He says, It is a Mystery, which surpasses every capacity of human aptitude, and which attempts more in itself than it understands. If we kept away from every counterfeit and Sophistic reasoning in this regard, we would not say one thing with the mouth and think something else with the heart. But this entire controversy would be happily settled and done away with straightway.

THE WORDS OF CHRIST'S TESTAMENT, AND THEIR SIMPLE, LITERAL SENSE, NOT TO BE SHRUNK BACK FROM.

But indeed for our part, from that point from which this controversy commenced, Luther and we together with him have borne witness that we do not examine the mode of the presence of Christ's body and blood in the Holy Supper, nor define it, but entrust it rather to the omnipotence and truth of Christ who knows the *mode*, which we do not understand. We have subjected ourselves to it simply by faith. And again, also before these Illustrious men, we wish it to be repeated before the Prince and all the present audience that we neither should, nor can, shrink away from the very simple words of Christ's Testament and their simple sense and understanding, unless we should be willing [65] to turn out to be corruptors and perverters of Christ's Testament, which ought not in the least to happen.

PUNISHMENT DECREED FOR VIOLATORS OF TESTAMENTS.

For if civil laws decree very severe punishments for violators of human Testaments, with the result that they are alluded to with disgrace, and forfeit the share of inheritance appointed to them and bequeathed in the Testament, what should be expected from Christ by violators of the Testament of the Son of God?

SECURITY AND CONFIDENCE OF THE SIMPLICITY OF FAITH. NO ONE SHOULD SHRINK BACK FROM THE SIMPLICITY OF FAITH.

For this reason, let us remain in the simple meaning of and faith in the words of Christ's Testament, even if our sense and reason should not grasp it. For the one who walks simply, says Solomon, walks securely and confidently, but the one who corrupts his ways will be found out (Proverbs 10[:9]). Nor should we fear that by chance we will be accused or condemned by Christ on the last day on account of this simplicity of faith. For indeed it attributes praise to him for his omnipotence and truth, however much what is believed seems absurd to human reason. And let us forever be mindful of Paul's very serious warning which appears at Corinthians: I joined you to one husband, so that I might deliver a chaste virgin to Christ, but I fear lest it somehow happen that just as the serpent deceived Eve by its cunning, so your minds may be corrupted from simplicity unto Christ (2 Corinthians 11[:3]).

SIMPLICITY OF FAITH MORE PLEASING TO GOD THAN THE WISDOM OF THE WORLD.

Simplicity is pleasing to God and necessary in the Church, since indeed there is a very great number of those who are not teachers, nor are learned, who are ignorant of literary devices and figures of speech, who are approved of more by God and please him more than wise men who are learned and erudite according to the flesh. Concerning these Christ says, I give thanks to you, Father, because you have hidden these things from the wise and clever, and have revealed them to the little ones (Matthew 11[:25]). Among these let us number ourselves also, and let us trust simply. In such a way we will be disciples very pleasing to God, and will walk most securely and safely.

<66>

Dr. Beza:

POINTS 1, 2, AND 3.

Reverend Doctor, Sir, you seem to me not to stay within the proposed question. For we do not deny that Christ's body and blood are truly present, and truly given and received in the Supper, and are signified by bread and wine in the Lord's Supper. And neither do we deny that the bread is Christ's body and that the wine is Christ's blood. But the dispute is, in what sense these are said. We say that the sacramental mode is generally known, common to all Sacraments in the old and new Testament, namely that by which Christ's body and blood is signified and represented. By this mode of presence they are said to be present to the mind, which, lifted up into heaven by its own thoughts, thoroughly enjoys Christ there.

POINT 4. SACRAMENTAL MEANING.

We say that this sacramental meaning is in no way an empty, external representation of things signified, by which the mind is only advised to take hold of that which is laid before the senses, in the manner we commonly employ with images and pictures. Rather, that which belongs to God always has joined with it a true representation of the very things signified, offered to our souls.

POINT 5.

But we say that the mode of reception is a Mystery. What reason does not understand, but faith alone grasps, must be trusted, namely that we are bone of his bones, and flesh of his flesh, that we are joined together as members to Christ as head, and are united with him.

POINTS 6 AND 7.

Calvin thinks in this way too, when he writes, It is a Mystery that exceeds the capacity of human aptitude and intellect. For he is not speaking about a joining together of signs and things signified, but about reception, which happens through faith in the use of the Lord's Supper. And this is itself remarkable: the body of Christ, absent and remaining in heaven, nevertheless present through faith in the holy Supper [67] offered and exhibited to those who believe. For Christ's body is present to the mind, not to the body or the bread, through faith.

POINT 8.

For this reason Christ said about Abraham, Abraham desired to see my day and saw it and rejoiced. In this way all the Patriarchs possessed Christ as present through faith, not less than us. They believed in the one to come; we believe in the one who has come.

POINT 9.

Now to Augustine's saying: Receive in the bread that which hung on the cross. Drink from the cup that which flowed from Christ's side. This must refer to the reception of offered things, not to the presence of Christ's body, in that place where the bread is. And this seems a greater mystery, that although the thing be absent, nevertheless it is said to be given.

POINT 10.

In this way was the holy Spirit seen in the dove, since it was signifying the holy Spirit. But he was not seen who is invisible. In this way the bread is the Sacrament of Christ's body, which signifies Christ's absent body, unless it is not in heaven and is rather existing on the earth.

POINT 11.

Besides this, the truth of Christ's body does not grant that Christ's body is present in that place where the bread of the Supper is distributed. It is only in heaven and not on the earth, up to the last day of Judgment.

POINT 12.

Nor can it be denied that Synechdoche is a literary device. Your people admit this in the words of the Lord's Supper.

POINTS 13 AND 14.

Regarding Baptism, it is also certain that it is a seal of Christ's Testament, by which remission of sins is sealed not less than in the LORD'S Supper. Therefore it can be said to be Christ's Testament just as much according to your understanding, though Christ did not say in the Lord's Supper that his body was a new Testament.

<68>

Dr. Jakob:

The New Testament.

I would like to respond to the last point first, that the Lord's supper is called a Testament by us. The reason why has been stated sufficiently above, and the Hebrew phrase in Luke's and Paul's words was explained. They openly call the cup of the Lord's Supper a Testament, though not simply, but in Christ's blood. Nor in fact is the cup this new Testament entirely, nor the bread, nor the body or blood of Christ, but the whole new Testament is that which the words of institution of the Lord's Supper embrace. This is it, truly and properly, and without any literary device, and it can be refuted by no argument. Since, therefore, we are following the words and phrase of the holy Spirit, this reproof is leveled against us unjustly.

Why Christ and the Apostles called the Lord's Supper the New Testament.

And we are not unaware that Christ did not say, My body is the new Testament. But since Luke and Paul say this plainly about the cup, who will accuse the holy Spirit of forgery in the Apostles? Following Christ as the originator, they doubtless looked back to the covenant of the old Testament (concerning which Exodus 24 was written and spoken about sufficiently above), so that the distinction between either Testament, the old and new, might rightly be emphasized in the Sacraments to all the faithful, in particular by these two terms "*New testament*."

Point 1. The controversy is not about the mode, but about the true and real presence of Christ's body and blood in the Lord's Supper.

Dr. Beza says that the contest is not about the true and real presence of Christ's body and blood in the Lord's Supper, but only about the mode of presence. Would that this were true. In this way in fact the entire controversy would be done away with, and the concord so long desired and awaited by the Church in this article would be restored.

TRUE STATUS OF THE CONTROVERSY IN THE CONTROVERSY ABOUT THE LORD'S SUPPER.

For not one time, but frequently and now from the point of commencement of this controversy, our people have always and openly borne witness that they are unwilling to contend with anyone regarding the mode of presence. This is hidden from us, unknown to human reason, and known to God alone. Only let our adversaries confess the true presence candidly and sincerely. But this very thing says that the dispute and controversy is not about the mode of presence, but is about the presence itself, <69> whether Christ's body is truly and really present on earth in the Supper, *not how it is present.*

DR. BEZA OPENLY DENIES THE TRUE PRESENCE OF CHRIST'S BODY AND BLOOD.

To this question Dr. Beza has now for a long time openly responded that Christ's body is present to us in the Lord's Supper in no other way than as it was present to Abraham. Here I call upon the judgment of the entire audience, whether or not this is openly denying the presence of Christ's body and blood in the Lord's Supper and asserting Christ's body is certainly not present? For at the time of Abraham Christ's body was not yet conceived or born. But is that not how it is possible for anyone really to be present? Once again here I appeal to the judgment of the audience. For I doubt not at all that all people with a basic education can understand this.

ASSERTION OF THE TRUE PRESENCE OF CHRIST'S BODY AND BLOOD IN THE LORD'S SUPPER.

For this reason we confess openly and frankly that we do not in the least approve this understanding or opinion, nor can we ever agree with our adversaries. For we openly teach the contrary, namely that Christ's body, which had not yet been born at the time of Abraham, is present not only when born, but also as positioned at the right hand of God's might, and truly and really in the Eucharist with respect to itself, according to the plain words of Christ, This is my body. This utterance did not happen for Abraham nor for any other of the Patriarchs or Prophets. To all these Christ was absent according to the flesh, and was not present.

DISTINCTION BETWEEN CHRIST'S BODY AND THE BODY OF PETER AND OTHER SAINTS. COMPARISON OF THE ANIMATED BODY TO THE DEIFIED BODY. DEIFIED PREROGATIVE OF CHRIST'S BODY.

For this reason all men see that we are disputing not about the mode of presence, but only whether he is present. Regarding the truth of Christ's body, they adduce in argument that it is not possible for it to be present in many places at the same time. We respond, there is a vast difference between the body of the Son of God and the body of Peter. For even if the substance and essence of Christ's body is similar to Peter's body, with the exception of sin, and even if our bodies, too, will be like Christ's glorious body, nevertheless, this fact notwithstanding, holy Scripture attributes properties and prerogatives to Christ's body, in respect of our bodies, of such a kind by which he surpasses all creatures, even Angelic ones. To be sure, this Analogy is also the comparative relation of an inanimate body to an animated one; the same, <70> and better by far, is that of the animated body to the Deified body, as the fathers have said. For example, this table at which we are sitting is a body, possessed of its own length, breadth, and depth. My eye is also a body, having its own dimensions, long, wide, and deep. My eye, however, though small, sees and in a moment embraces the dome of heaven, not because it is a body, but because it is animated, that is, when it is united to life. The table does not see, nor is it able to perform this function, because it lacks life. An eye does not on account of this cease to be a body, because it can perform some function beyond all other inanimate bodies, even bigger ones. If an animated body can perform this function, why should a Deified body not do so? That is, the one assumed by the Son of God under the personal union? For Christ does not simply say, Take, this is a body, but adds, *my*, that is, the body of the Son of God, which has taken to itself every life-creating power from the Son of God with the result that it can create life, something granted to the body of no sanctified person.

This body did not yet exist in the old Testament. It goes without saying that it was assumed by the Son of God under the personal union. For this reason it was not presence in its own essence. But now it exists; not only so, but it has become the body of the Son of God, and is stationed at the right hand of God's strength and omnipotence (which is neither a place nor in a place), and thereafter he possesses a divine, heavenly, and supernatural manner, with the result that he is present—a manner that is denied to the bodies of Peter, Paul, and all the Saints.

HOW ABRAHAM SAW CHRIST'S DAY.

But that which is brought up about Abraham from Christ's utterance, Abraham saw my day and rejoiced, adds nothing to the present matter. For Abraham neither saw Christ present nor possessed him, and Christ does not say this, but that he saw *his Day which would come*, and Christ *who would come*. For this reason it is said that he saw it.

ANOTHER VISION OF CHRIST IN THE APOSTLES THAN IN ABRAHAM.

This is why Christ said to his disciples, Blessed the eyes which see the things which you see, *and did not see* (Luke 10[:]). And we read it written about Simeon, that an answer was given to him, that he would not see death <71> before *he should see* the Lord's Christ. Holding him in his arms, he proclaimed, Now, Lord, you send your servant, because *my eyes have seen* your salvation. Therefore there is another presence of Christ in the new Testament than in the old, at the time of the Patriarchs and Abraham. For now this man promised his presence: Wherever two or three are gathered together in my name, I am in their midst (Matthew 18[:20]). The Fathers believed in him as the one who would come, but not as one present.

FAITH DOES NOT MAKE CHRIST PRESENT. ANALOGY OF THE FORT. BEZA IN THE PREFACE OF A BOOK ABOUT CYRIL'S WORDS. PRESENCE OF CHRIST'S BODY DOES NOT DEPEND ON OUR FAITH, BUT COMMUNICATED OMNIPOTENCE OF CHRIST HIMSELF.

Beza is deceived however (if I may beg his pardon) when he defines the presence of Christ according to the flesh by faith alone, that is, merely with respect to our faith. In this way faith, which is one at all times, makes it present. And he explains it by the analogy of a fort, which located at a distance, would constitute a present image, if one were to open one's eyes. But if he should close them, it would be absent. In the same way faith makes Christ's body present in the Lord's Supper, but if someone should lack it, Christ's body is not present for him as well, but is absent. This we openly deny. For presence of Christ's body in the Lord's Supper depends not on faith or our thinking about Christ. Faith does not produce the presence, nor does unbelief impede it. Rather it is defined by Christ's person, and his words of institution. For since it is the body of the omnipotent Son of God, for this reason it is able to be present, and really is present, whether someone should believe or not. And since he says, this is my body, for this reason it should not be doubted in the least that it is certainly present.

FAITH RENDERS THE PRESENCE OF CHRIST'S BODY SALUTARY.

Indeed, faith is required for Christ's salutary presence, lest his body be received unto judgment. But it does not in the least bring about the presence itself. For Christ is present not only to the pious, but reigns also in the midst of his enemies, not absent, as the fort remains perpetually absent whether someone opens his eyes or closes them, unless he were to approach it with his own body. Rather, he is present to his enemies, and reigns in all places and times. Indeed he is by far more present than are his enemies present to themselves.

PRESENCE OF CHRIST'S FLESH NOT LOCAL, BUT HEAVENLY AND SUPERNATURAL.

But this presence is not a local one, but divine, heavenly, and supernatural. Christ's flesh possesses it from the Son of God, with <72> whom he is one person. Therefore we do not approach him, but he approaches us, either unto life or unto judgment.

ANALOGY OF THE MAGISTRATE.

In fact, in the same way a Magistrate is, in respect to himself, present equally to the good and the wicked—the latter for the purpose of punishment, the former, favor. And one and the same man is Magistrate, who performs contradictory functions. Paul declares the very same thing about Christ's presence in the Lord's Supper. For

Christ is not only savior, but also judge, according to John 5[:22–23]: The Father judges no one, but has given all judgment to the son, because he is the son of man.

FROM WHAT VIRTUE THE SACRAMENTAL PRESENCE OF CHRIST'S BODY IN THE LORD'S SUPPER DEPENDS.

Therefore we define sacramental presence of Christ's body in no way at all by faith, but by the communication of divine virtue, to which Christ's flesh has been promoted, stationed at the right hand of God. We define it furthermore by the word of institution, the truth of which men's unbelief cannot render null and void.

HOW BEZA DEFINES THE PRESENCE OF CHRIST'S BODY IN THE LORD'S SUPPER.

Since my opponent denies this, it is clear that he believes in no true and real presence of Christ's body at all on earth, where the Lord's Supper is celebrated. For he defines this presence not by reason of the person involved in accordance with the word, but by reason of his belief only. This is in conflict with not only the express word of God, but also with the holy consensus of the whole of antiquity, as has been demonstrated elsewhere.

CONSENSUS CONCERNING PARTICIPATION OF CHRIST'S BENEFITS.

There has never been among us a dispute or controversy as regards what pertains to Christ's benefits and his merit. The Patriarchs and all the faithful in the Old Testament were made participants in them no less in their own Sacraments (which were shadows of things to come) than we have become through true faith in the usage of our own Sacraments. Because Christ is the same yesterday, today, and forever (Hebrews 13[:8]), and the lamb slain already from the creation of the world (Revelation 13[:8]); however, much to the contrary remains this argument for his presence, that now our salvation is nearer than when they first believed, as the Apostle bears witness (Romans 11 [13:11]).

But your Reverence will forgive me that I have been too wordy as regards the first part of your speech. I wanted in fact to explain these things a little more fully so that it might be understood what our opinion is, and what the true and proper status of our debate is. NowI will respond to the remaining parts briefly.

<73>

POINT 2. METONYMY IS IN CONFLICT WITH TRUE PRESENCE.

You say you do not deny that the bread is the body of Christ. Although you hold that it is a Metonymy, you think the opposite, which we will show in its proper place.

POINT 3. RELATIVE AND SIGNIFIED PRESENCE IS NOT PRESENCE OF A THING.

But it has now been abundantly explained and proven that the mode of sacramental presence is not the same in the old and new Testament.

POINT 4.

For even if you say that it is not an empty signification or representation, the kind commonly used of images or pictures, nevertheless this affords nothing for the true presence. For Christ's body and blood were supplied in this way even in the Sacraments of the old Testament, and Christ's benefits applied by them, and to this degree Christ himself was bestowed. But besides this it is not said that he was present to them in the substance of his flesh, as he now is present to us.

POINT 5. MYSTERY OF RECEPTION DOES NOT DO AWAY WITH MYSTERY OF PRESENCE.

There remains also the Mystery of reception, which happens through faith, by which we are joined together with Christ, and are made flesh of his flesh and bone of his bones. However through this presence of Christ's body, the Mystery is not done away with, by which Christ truly and really delivers his own body, really present with the bread, for the encouragement of eating done through faith.

POINT 6. SACRAMENTAL EATING OF CHRIST'S BODY A MYSTERY. *TO EAT* CHRIST'S BODY AND TO BELIEVE IN CHRIST DIFFER IN FORM AND IN ACTUALITY. IN RESPONSE TO THESIS 1.

It is clear that Calvin also understood his words about this latter Mystery from his commentary on John. He warns that they are entirely mistaken who think that the eating of Christ's body in John 6 and in the Lord's Supper are one and the same. And also, those who would think that *eating* Christ's body in the Lord's Supper, is what believing is in John 6. For this reason nothing is more certain than that he spoke about the conjunction of signs with things signified. On account of this it is false that you say in your Theses that the reception of Christ, whether by the simple word as in John 6, or in the Sacraments, as in the institution of the Lord's Supper, *is the same*.

Nothing wondrous in this regard, but rather customary.

But it is not astonishing that the body existing and remaining in heaven is on earth, through earthly things, Relatively signified and represented, and communicated by their usage. This is known to all.

<74>

Point 8. Abraham saw the Christ to come, not Christ present.

So Christ does not say, I was present to Abraham. But he says, Abraham desired to see my day, namely, the one to come, not present to him. And he saw Christ himself as one who would come, not as one present. This has been spoken about enough a little earlier.

Point 9. What it means to drink blood from the chalice.

As far as the passage of Augustine is concerned, since he bids one drink what flowed from Christ's side from the chalice, the words patently demonstrate that he is not talking about spiritual reception. For he bids to drink what flowed from Christ's side, not to believe what flowed from Christ's side, but the drink it from the cup. That reception happens by mouth, about which alone his sermon is concerned, not merely faith.

Point 10. The Holy Spirit was truly and really seen by corporeal eyes.

It was explained and demonstrated a little earlier that the holy Spirit was seen truly and not figuratively or symbolically. Though he was seen not in his proper form, but in an assumed one, rather, in the appearance of a dove.

POINT 11. THE TRUTH OF THE BODY DOES NOT DO AWAY WITH HIS PRESENCE IN THE LORD'S SUPPER.

But regarding the truth of Christ's body, that it is said how its true and real presence does not do away with the supernatural and heavenly presence, I have demonstrated by the analogy of the animated and Deified body.

POINT 12. IN WHAT MANNER LUTHER AND BRENZ WOULD HAVE CONCEDED A SYNECDOCHE. SYNECDOCHE IS NOT PROPERLY A LITERARY DEVICE. NO LITERARY DEVICE IN THE WORDS OF THE LORD'S SUPPER.

As far as Synecdoche is concerned, it is true enough that when Luther's opponents were so much seduced by figures of speech, Luther and Brenz responded in this way, why in place of Metonymy they did not rather snatch hold of Synecdoche, which was also counted among figures of speech, and would not remove the presence of Christ's body and blood from the supper. For although it is a figure of speech, nevertheless it is improperly referred to among literary devices. For in this case, a Noun is not used in substitution for a noun. Nor does Christ say, Bread is my body. Rather, he says, This is my body. In this place he demonstrates two things by means of the pronoun "*this*" ["*hoc*"]: the one for the sense, the other for the understanding. *What* he wanted to give to his disciples, he expressed by words when he said *this is my body.* He showed at the same time, however, by what organ or instrument he gives or gave it by the term "*this*" ["*hoc*"]. But he did not name the antecedent, lest the disciples seem to be bidden merely to eat bread.

POINTS 13 AND 14. DESCRIPTION OF THE LORD'S SUPPER IS A COMPLETE AND PERFECT TESTAMENT.

Why Baptism is not called a Testament has been said sufficiently above. And we also confess that Christ in the supper [75] did not say, My body is a Testament. But this does not in any way keep the complete description of the words of institution of the Lord's Supper from being a true, perfect, and complete Testament, whose parts are also the Lord's body and blood, just as was explained and proven above. Only so much thus far. I will be briefer after this.

Dr. Beza:

POINT 1.

Reverend Doctor, Sir, this business is not about presence, but about a literary device, whether a literary device should be admitted in the words of the Lord's Supper.

POINT 2. WHAT SORT OF PRESENCE OF CHRIST'S BODY DR. BEZA ESTABLISHES IN THE LORD'S SUPPER.

For we say about the presence that Christ's body and blood are truly present in the Supper. But present not to the body, but rather TO THE MIND. *Faith itself does not effect this presence, but the power and word of God.*

POINT 3.

From this we say that this presence, which happens through faith, is by far more certain than that one by which you say that it is present to the body. Since indeed we would receive things far more certainly with the mind than with the eyes. And from time to time we see that a man present to someone is absent.

POINTS 4 AND 5.

For what faith sees, it sees truly by virtue of the holy Spirit. That which it thinks it sees with the eyes often deceives. On account of this, we do not do away with every presence of Christ's body in the holy Supper, but merely that one by which Christ's body is said to be present to our bodies. On the contrary however, we establish the presence by which it is said to be present to the mind, through faith. But faith turns its attention to the words of God. On account of this it is not an imaginary presence, by which the mind and faith embraces Christ's body absent and remaining in heaven.

POINT 6.

Besides, this bodily presence about which you are talking is in conflict with the analogy and articles of faith about Christ. For the articles of the creed teach that the Son of God assumed from the virgin Mary a true and <76> *natural, circumscribed body, in which he suffered, was crucified, dead, buried, rose again, ascended into heaven, whence he will come again in this body for judgment.*

POINT 7.

And Christ himself celebrated the first Supper before he was situated at the right hand of God. For after his death, resurrection, and ascension into heaven, he was finally situated at the right hand of God in heaven. How therefore is this presence of Christ's body able to be proved from his session at the right hand of God? For indeed, when the cause ceases, the effect must cease too.

POINT 8. PERVERSE EXPLANATION OF THE DEIFICATION OF CHRIST'S BODY.

What has been brought up from John of Damascus about the Deification of Christ's body should not be understood regarding such Deification in the way that you say, by which Christ's body lost its own properties and became Deity. Nor does John of Damascus speak about such a Deification. For it belongs to Christ's body TO BE ENTIRELY finite and circumscribed. If therefore it be determined that Christ's body were present at one and the same time in more places than one, it would no longer be a true body, but would have lost its own quantity, and circumscription, which is proper to a body. What Christ assumed once, said John of Damascus, he never any longer set aside.

POINT 9. PERVERSE EXPLANATION OF GIFTS BROUGHT TOGETHER INTO CHRIST'S HUMANITY.

And when the Fathers speak about divine gifts brought together into Christ's flesh, they speak about a personal union by which the Son of God united to himself an assumed body, not however that he transformed into Deity or brought into it his divine properties. They are characteristic gifts of glorification, by which Christ not only is distinguished above all blessed Angels, but also surpasses all the angels in power, glory, and majesty. His humanity however did not become Deity itself.

POINT 10.

I confess also that Christ's body was not present ACTUALLY to Abraham, nor existed ACTUALLY at the time of Abraham. I deny however that it follows from that point that it was not simply present to him. <77> For faith is ὑπόστασις τῶν μὴ ὄντων, that is, the substance of things WHICH ARE NOT, just as the Epistle to the Hebrews testifies (Hebrews 11[:1]). Since faith looks to the word of the Lord, in which the thing promised is present in its own way.

POINT 11.

Thus we believe many things which we know have been done; we believe the age was begun. For though creation has passed by, nevertheless we believe that it existed, and in this way is present to faith. Thus we believe also many future things, which do not actually exist at this time.

POINT 12.

And of course I would be unwilling to say, Christ's body did not exist at the time of Abraham. For it was, but not actually.

POINT 13.

From this it follows that the real existence is not always required for true presence. For faith also travels out of the world.

POINT 14.

You said also, The benefits of Christ were conferred to the Fathers also in the old Testament, namely, the remission of sins, the imputation of righteousness, and eternal life. Surely you do not therefore desire, and believe, that those benefits commenced FROM SOMETHING NONEXISTENT? For those benefits regard Christ as present for their own EXISTENCE, not less for the Fathers than for us. They were also just as much participants in Christ's body and *blood as are we in the Lord's Supper, and all the Sacraments of the new Testament.*

POINT 15.

Nor can I concede to you the comparison of blood in the old and new Testament brought up from Moses. You say that that Mosaic blood was only a figure and a shadow of the absent blood of Christ, when Moses says, This is the blood of the covenant which THE LORD has fastened over all these words. Christ's true blood itself is in the Lord's Supper however, and not as merely as a figure or sign, since Christ says, This is my blood of the new Testament. For one and the same blood is in either Testament, and in the Sacraments of either Testament, <78> namely, the true blood of our Lord Jesus Christ, present to faith and the mind, although they believed in the One To Come, just as we believe in him who has come and poured out this blood for our sins.

For just as the true and natural blood of calves represented and signified Christ's true blood to the Israelites, and offered to their faith and mind that which was going to be poured out, thus does the consecrated wine in the Lord's Supper represent, signify to our faith and mind, and offer to it the true blood of Christ, which has now been poured out for our sins.

POINT 16.

From all this it stands that we do not in the least deny the true presence of Christ's body and blood in the Lord's Supper, but that we attack only that presence by which it is offered to our bodies and not our minds.

Dr. Jakob:

POINT 1. WHY A LITERARY DEVICE HAS BEEN INTRODUCED IN THE WORDS OF THE LORD'S SUPPER.

Reverend Dr. Beza, I do indeed know that there is a controversy concerning the literary device, whether it ought to be admitted in

Christ's words. But you cannot deny that this argument about a literary device has been introduced by you above all for this reason, that you openly deny that Christ's body is present in the bread. For this reason you have maintained up till now that it is necessary to understand Christ's words by way of literary device, We openly deny and contradict this—more on this a little later.

POINT 2.

But you are trying to convince us that you also believe and teach the true and real presence of Christ's body and blood in the Lord's Supper so that the controversy seems to be more about the mode of presence than about the presence itself. We will also respond briefly to that point.

POINT 3. HOW BEZA MAKES SPORT OF THE PRESENCE OF CHRIST'S BODY IN THE LORD'S SUPPER. DR. BEZA SPEAKS WITH US, BUT DOES NOT UNDERSTAND IN THE SAME WAY AS US.

You say that the body of Christ is represented, signified, and delivered by the bread of the *Lord's* Supper *to the mind*. You say also that faith does not effect this presence, but rather the virtue of the holy Spirit and the word. I confess, the words are splendid which are not immediately clearly comprehended and understood by everybody, according to your opinion. For any simple Christian, upon hearing these words, <79> judges that there is no conflict between us about the presence itself, but merely about the mode of presence.

HOW THIS FALLACY IS DISCOVERED.

But if we were to weigh the explanation and analyze the negative corollary, namely that *the agent does not* have present *a body*, then those brought up reasonably can immediately make note of the fact that no true and real presence is taught, established, or believed by you, and you openly contradict yourselves.

THAT CHRIST'S BODY IS NOT PRESENT AND OFFERED ONLY TO THE MIND, BUT ALSO TO THE MOUTH OF THE BODY.

For even if it is true that Christ's body is delivered by way of the bread to our mind and heart, it nevertheless does not follow consequently that he is not present to the bread, and not offered to our mouth. Rather, Christ's words openly testify that the contrary is true. For when Christ bid them eat this bread when he said, Take, eat, this is my body, it is clear that Christ's body is not only represented and signified, but just as you say, by the virtue of the holy Spirit according to Christ's word, it is also offered and delivered. Therefore how is Christ's body not present with the bread and not offered and delivered to the mouth, seeing as we receive the bread in no way except by mouth?

FROM BEZA'S ARGUMENT CHRIST'S PRESENT BODY IS NOT OFFERED TO THE MIND EITHER.

When you say therefore that Christ's body is not present to the bread and our mouth in the Lord's Supper, because it is eaten by way of this food unto immortality, then it necessarily follows that it is not even present or offered to the mind. For the mind is in the body, and it is not fed alone in the supper, but the whole person, consisting of soul and body, is restored spiritually by this food and drink.

And in the same way that the mind regards Christ's words, by which the one simply having faith cannot be deceived, the eyes regard the offered bread, which he bids be received by mouth in addition to something else—he adds, This is my body, and he makes no mention of faith or the mind, but speaks of eating, which happens by way of the body's exterior mouth.

If therefore the body is truly offered with the bread by way of Christ's word, Take, eat, This is my body, who, I ask, can deny that it is offered and truly delivered to the mouth of the body? Nevertheless it is offered and delivered the way Chrysostom says, spiritual things distributed through bodily things in the Sacraments, not Capernaitically or carnally,

<80>

But if it is not offered to the mouth of the body, and is not present to it, but merely to faith, and by faith to the mind, then Christ's body is absent, it is argued, until such time as deliberation of faith, and not God's power, makes it present, since Christ's body is present not by the virtue of the holy Spirit, but necessarily as faith elevates itself up to the place of heaven, where alone Christ's body is present, and not on earth. This is your opinion, and by naming it, we are not at all quibbling or playing the sophist. For we desire that the opinion of either party be understood rightly by everybody. It is for this reason above all that this peaceful conference was organized, without any bitterness of spirit.

POINT 4. BEZA AND HIS COLLEAGUES DENY EVERY PRESENCE OF CHRIST'S BODY IN THE LORD'S SUPPER.

From this it is clear that you deny every presence of Christ's body in the Lord's Supper, even if you do not at all wish to seem so. But this is what you actually do when you say openly, Christ's body, in the usage of the Supper on earth, is present *in no way* to bread and our mouth, and you confine it solely in heaven up to the final day of judgment, with the result that it is present to you in no way on earth.

POINT 5. IMAGINARY PRESENCES OF CHRIST'S BODY IN THE SUPPER, ACCORDING TO DR. BEZA'S DOCTRINE.

The presence you fashion is an imaginary one, and it is clear from it that when we think in our mind about absent things, that we place before us by the action things that are not present. But this is merely musing on our part, and the thing itself remains absent, just as I will demonstrate with the same examples that were brought up by you.

POINT 6. REAL PRESENCE OF CHRIST'S BODY AND BLOOD IN THE LORD'S SUPPER IS NOT IN CONFLICT WITH THE ANALOGY OF FAITH.

But you say that the presence of Christ's body which we have established in the Lord's Supper as true and real is in conflict with the analogy of faith and the articles of the Apostolic creed concerning Christ, in which it is taught that Christ's body was conceived and born of the virgin Mary, suffered, was crucified, died, was buried, that it rose again, ascended into heaven, etc. It is not however settled that he is present in rather many places at one and the same time he is able to retain his circumscription. We respond that, if a physical, natural, or local presence of Christ's body were being established by us in the Lord's supper, I admit that what you conclude here would follow.

<81>

However it is known from our theses that we do not establish the physical, natural, and local presence, nor ever have taught it. Our writings openly teach this.

THE GROSS OPINION OF BEZA AND HIS ALLIES CONCERNING THE PRESENCE OF CHRIST'S BODY AND BLOOD. BEZA ATTACKS HIS OWN FICTION. FOUNDATION AND CAUSE OF BEZA'S ERROR REGARDING THE LORD'S SUPPER.

However, when you say openly in your response to our fourth Thesis, that you cannot really see that the substance of the very body of Christ is established as present with the bread and wine *other than by means of physical and local circumscription*, then it is clear to all those who hear this, that in this entire disputation and in all your pamphlets, you are attacking not the doctrine of our Churches, but your own fiction, and that you attribute falsely to us an opinion that we have never asserted, but have openly condemned.

IN THE LORD'S SUPPER THERE IS NOT A PHYSICAL AND LOCAL PRESENCE OF CHRIST'S BODY.

Nor in fact was there ever a controversy between us whether the substance of Christ's body and blood was present to the bread and wine of the supper by means of physical and local circumscription, but we always openly denied this presence, just as will be taught more fully a little later.

TRUE STATUS OF THE CONTROVERSY REGARDING THE PRESENCE OF CHRIST'S BODY IN THE LORD'S SUPPER.

The question however is and always was proposed by us, whether there can be no other presence of Christ's body in the Supper than the visible, local, physical, and circumscribed one. We have always denied and still consistently deny this. For God possesses infinite ways by which he can produce present realities, and not only the local, physical, visible, and gross circumscribed way which our sense perceives.

THE SACRAMENTAL PRESENCE OF CHRIST'S BODY DOES NOT DEPRIVE CHRIST'S BODY OF LOCALITY AND CIRCUMSCRIPTION.

Therefore we say that Sacramental presence of Christ's body in the Lord's Supper does not do away with the truth, locality, and circumscription of Christ's body. For the way that in the first Supper Christ's body remained local, finite, and circumscribed, when he was distributing his body to his disciples in a heavenly way, so now also remains in glory finite and circumscribed by its own property of substance, and is present nevertheless according to the words of Christ's Testament in the Supper, <82> and is present, dispensed, and received by mouth, with bread, not only to the mind, but also to the mouth of the body, in a heavenly mode, which God alone knows. We attribute it to his power and truth, and adore this Mystery.

POINT 7. CONCERNING THE RIGHT HAND OF GOD.

Now, from the Analogy of faith and articles of the creed, you allege that Christ celebrated his own Lord's Supper with his disciples before he had been seated at the right hand of God, and that thus far from the point of this session, his presence is not able to be confirmed. I respond that the Article about his session at the right hand of God should be understood and explained rightly and in harmony with holy Scripture.

WHAT THE RIGHT HAND OF GOD IS. THE MAN CHRIST COMPLETELY EXALTED IN HIS MOTHER'S WOMB.

For Holy Scripture teaches that the Right Hand of God is nothing other than God's omnipotence, so completely that it is God himself. And although a rather wordy explanation of it pertains to the passage regarding the person of Christ, nevertheless I will respond in just a few to the Argument which has been constructed from this Article by the opponents now already from the time of the commencement of this controversy, and has been objected to by us: "Christ is stationed in heaven at the right hand of God. Therefore he is not able to be present in his own body in the Supper." For since the Right Hand of God is God himself, but Christ's body, since it was personally united with God in the womb of his mother, it is clear that Christ's body after the ascension into heaven was not able to be more highly exalted than he was when he was exalted in the womb of his mother, that is, when he was made one personally with God. No sane person can deny this, unless perhaps someone would want to assert that something can exist that is higher that God himself.

In what way God is highest. Who is highest after God.

Since God is the highest, therefore, not in place (since indeed God is not a place, nor is he in a place) but in Majesty, it follows from this that the one who is next to God, after God, is highest with respect to all creatures, and that it is not possible for another to be higher, unless he were to be transformed into Deity, which cannot happen.

Man by way of assumed humanity, the phrase of the Orthodox Fathers.

Christian religion and faith teaches, however, that *the assumed Man* (this is fact is how universal orthodox antiquity speaks, lest anyone object on the basis of our ignorance of concrete and abstract) became one person with the Son of God. For this reason he is also highest, [83] and just as the Epistle to the Hebrews says (Hebrews 7[:26]), became higher than the heavens themselves, even before he was conceived in this mother's womb at his conception.

Why it is said that Christ the man at last after death is sitting at the right hand of God.

However in the Apostles' Creed the session at the right hand of God is attributed to Christ not only after his conception and nativity, but also after his passion, death, resurrection, and ascension into heaven, by which he has been exalted over every principality, power and dominion. With respect to the form of a slave, it is attributed to Christ that he at last laid it aside after death.

EXPLANATION OF THE POINT FROM PHILIPPIANS 2 REGARDING THE FORM OF GOD AND THE FORM OF A SLAVE.

St. Paul explains this at Philippians chapter 2[:6–7], where he says, Christ, although he was in the form of God, did not judge it robbery to be himself equal to God, but completely emptied himself, taking on the form of a slave. There the Apostle does not say that Christ laid aside the form of God in the form of a slave, but he remained in the form of God, and assumed the form of a slave, by which he administered the form of God, which remained in him perpetually from the point of conception. In him the fullness of Deity dwelt bodily (Colossians 2[:9]). Nevertheless he did not show it, though from time to time he publicized it by working miracles, and offered a certain taste of it, so to speak, to people who were his friends and enemies.

CHRIST REMAINS LORD EVEN WHILE WEARING THE FORM OF A SLAVE.

Therefore just as Christ wore the form of a slave until he should accomplish the work of the Redemption of the human race, so also did he meanwhile always remain Lord, just as he said to his disciples: You call me Master and Lord, and you do so rightly, because I am (John 13[:13]). He was true Lord not only as God, but also as Man, since the one person, God and Man, is one Christ, not two.

DISTRIBUTION OF CHRIST'S BODY AND BLOOD IN THE FIRST SUPPER NECESSITATES COMMUNICATION OF INFINITE VIRTUE.

Therefore both in the state of humiliation and emptiness, and in the form of a slave, he always retained the form of God (which itself is the right hand of God and his omnipotence, to the degree that he is himself God), and *he was in it* according to his humanity, and never laid it aside, but with respect to his humanity he abdicated himself for a time from its full use. He particularly made use of the Majesty <84> in the first Supper when he distributed his body to his disciples.

This distribution of Christ's body and blood was work proper not to the form of a slave but to the form of the Lord, and his Majesty, communicated to the man Christ.

He made the same thing public likewise a little later in the garden to his enemies, before he was arrested. He also made it manifest when he was twelve years old among the learned of Jerusalem, and it became clear through miracles afterwards. It is written nevertheless that he grew in wisdom and became obedient to his parents (Luke 2[:52]).

SIMPLE, TRUE, AND GERMAN OPINION OF THE SESSION AT THE RIGHT HAND OF GOD.

After he completed the work of the redemption of the human race, however, and straightway laid aside the form of a slave, the article of the Apostolic creed states: *he sits* at the right hand of God the Father Almighty, that is, he governs all things not only as God, but also as man, in power equal with the father, just as it is written, Let all Israel know most certainly therefore that God made him both Lord and Christ, this Jesus, whom you crucified (Acts 2[:36]). Dr. Beza cannot deny that in the article of the creed, "to sit" in Scriptural diction refers not at all to a physical location, but means rather to rule with God in equal power.

ANALOGY OF A TRAVELING PRINCE.

But in order that the audience may understand this better, we will explain by analogy. A certain Prince (in a not unwonted manner) got ready to set out for a holy pilgrimage. He dressed in slave's attire for the sake of his safety, to avoid danger, lest he be recognized by everybody on his journey, and while on his journey he observed servile compliance, took care of his own board and horses, and washed the hose of those who were by far his inferiors, his very own slaves, even as he was himself their Lord, and remained so. He continued to do this until he finished his travel. Upon returning home, he laid aside the Slave's attire, and did not then finally become a Prince, because he was born a Prince, but merely undertook the administration of his reign, which he had abdicated for a certain time.

<85>

HOW CHRIST IS SAID TO BE STATIONED AT THE RIGHT HAND OF GOD AFTER HIS DEATH AND RESURRECTION.

In such a way was Christ, conceived according to the flesh by the holy Spirit and born of the virgin Mary, true Lord, not only according to God, but also according to man. He could have publicized his divine Majesty at the nativity itself, with the result that he would have rushed upon the eyes of the whole world with supreme amazement, but he did not want to. Rather, for the sake of our salvation, according to man he abdicated the use of that which according to God was unchangeably permanent, but never laid it aside or was able to lay it aside. After death, however, once he had laid aside the form of a slave, he undertook the administration of all creatures according to man, and now it is said that he sits, that is, that he reigns, something he did not do yet, according to his humanity, from the time of his conception and nativity, all the way up to his resurrection from the dead and his ascension into heaven.

AMBIGUOUS UNDERSTANDING IN THE WORDS "TO SIT AT THE RIGHT HAND OF GOD."

Therefore there is an ambiguity in the words "To sit at the right hand of God," because having this divine Majesty, and not openly using it, means one thing, but both having it and exercising it publicly means something else. The one is attributed to Christ in his state of humility, the other, only after his resurrection and ascension into heaven, where he at length is stationed, seated at the right hand of God, that is, wherever he is said to reign. And he is no longer slave, or in servile form, but will reveal himself in divine Majesty to the whole world.

CHRIST'S DIVINE MAJESTY ONE IN THE STATE OF HUMILIATION AND EXALTATION.

This subsequent Majesty, therefore, which consists in it full use, takes nothing away from the communication of majesty which Christ had in the first Supper, clothed in the form of a slave.

Therefore in the celebration of the Lord's Supper we have neither more nor less than the disciples had in the first Supper. But let a fuller explanation on the point about Christ's person be postponed, where everything will be treated more completely.

POINT 8. HOW CHRIST'S BODY IS SAID TO BE DEIFIED. VIVIFICATION PROPER TO DEITY, COMMUNICATED TO CHRIST'S FLESH. CYRIL.

To the point brought up from John of Damascus concerning the Deification of the man Christ, we respond, that not only John of Damascus but also Gregory Nazianzus and other Church Writers assert that Christ's body was Deified. ἐθεόθη, he says, it was Deified. Neither John of Damascus, nor we, have written or ever said that Christ's body was Deified in the sense <86> that it was changed into Deity or that Deity was effected. For this reason also he did not lose his own *degree of extent*, and his own circumscription. Rather, in the same way that an animated has different properties than an inanimate body on account of its union with life, so also John of Damascus attributes properties to Christ's body on account of the personal union with the Son of God which can be attributed to the body of no holy man, nor even to the Angels. Of the number of these properties, one is vivification, which is proper to God in a way such that nothing could be more proper to him. Christ's flesh took in its *entire* power, and embarked upon its dignity and operation with the result that it can itself also make alive, and truly does make alive. Just as the Orthodox Fathers teach and bear witness with one voice and with unanimous consensus, especially Cyril.

POINT 9. NOT JUST HABITUAL GIFTS WERE CONFERRED UPON CHRIST'S HUMANITY.

The Fathers openly bear witness that not only were habitual gifts conferred upon Christ's humanity by way of the personal union, but also properties of Divinity itself were communicated to him truly and really. So that we do not confuse articles, but rather treat them each in their own place, we will put a fuller treatment of Christ's person on display in another place, where we refer to Christ's person. Nevertheless, from this point it by no means follows that Christ's body was changed into Deity, or became Deity, just as it clearly appears.

POINT 10. FAITH IS NOT OF THE THINGS WHICH ARE NOT. HERE A MINISTER OF THE CHURCH AT GENEVA SHOWED BEZA A GREEK CODEX AND URGED HIM NOT TO FIGHT THE POINT IN VAIN, BECAUSE THE WORDS WHICH WERE ALLEGED BY HIM WERE NOT CONTAINED IN THE EPISTLE.

What Dr. Beza confesses, that Christ's body did not actually exist at the time of Abraham, we accept this as far as the confession goes. But he attempts to demonstrate from the Epistle to the Hebrews that it was absent not so much to the mind and faith of Abraham, because faith is ὑπόστασις τῶν μὴ ὄντων, that is, the substance of those things which are not (Hebrews 11[:1]). I respond: these words are not found in the Epistle to the Hebrews. The words of the Epistle read this way: ἔστιν δὲ πίστις ἐλπιζομένων ὑπόστασις, πραγμάτων ἔλεγχος οὐ βλεπομένων, that is, faith is the substance of things hoped for, and the evidence of those things which are not seen. A thing hoped for and not seen is one thing; a thing plainly not existing is something else entirely.

<87>

But even if faith trusts things that are either yet to be or which have already happened, nevertheless those things are not meanwhile present. For it is sufficient for faith when things that have been, are, or will be promised, even if they are not present at that time, are trusted, that is, looked at through faith.

PRESENCE BY WHICH THINGS ARE PRESENT TO THE MIND.

The presence, however, by which things are said to be present to the mind of a believer, things promised in the future or that have passed away, this is not the real and true presence of the things themselves, but rather is a very certain confidence of mind and will, that whenever these things should come to pass or have been, even if they have already passed, at least they are *not yet*.

POINT 12. CHRIST'S TRUE PRESENCE ON EARTH ACCORDING TO THE FLESH.

I am also not afraid to say, Christ's body was not present at the time of Abraham, since it was not in action. Indeed, I do not deny that he was in the loins of his Fathers before his appointed time was fulfilled. But we are speaking about the presence of Christ's body, which by communication of the Divine Majesty is efficacious in the Church, and by which Christ as a man also sees and hears the groans of his saints and consoles them. By this presence he is said now to be present to his Church in Word and Sacraments. This presence was certainly not at the time of Abraham.

POINT 13. REAL PRESENCE REQUIRES REAL EXISTENCE OF A THING.

From this it follows that real existence is always required for that presence by which actions are attributed to existing things. And even though faith steps outside of the world, nevertheless it is not the thing itself that is present, but faith is thinking merely about the things thought about through faith.

WHENCE CHRIST'S BENEFITS WERE CONFERRED TO THE PATRIARCHS.

But Dr. Beza asks, since I concede also that the Fathers became participants in Christ's benefits, and obtained the remission of their sins, surely I would not be willing or believe that those benefits commenced *from something that did not exist*, which considered Christ instead of *something existing*, present not less for the Fathers than for us?

THE MAN CHRIST ATTRIBUTED TO HIMSELF WHAT WAS PROPER TO GOD ALONE.

I respond, that these benefits commenced not at all from *something that did not exist*, but considered Christ as his own *thing existing* for certain. Not present though, but future, as one to come, who would suffer on behalf of the redemption of the human race. He was foreshadowed [88] in the sacrifices of the Old Testament. And on that account in the old Testament, all the circumstances had to be observed very accurately. No one was heard in their prayers, unless with respect to propitiation, which was signifying the true propitiation, Christ. To this propitiation the face had to be turned, where the Jews were on earth, and sacrifices had to be performed in a certain place and order, in order that they might correspond to the Archetype. The Israelites were bound to that type which was representing, prefiguring, and signifying Christ's flesh, in what way it would become incarnate, and would redeem the human race. In this shadow and through this shadow the Son of God (who is not out of *things not existing*) was conferring benefits to the fathers, not on account of the shadow, but on account of him who was represented and signified by this shadow. For remission of sins is the proper work of God. And on that account the Jews became angry at Christ when he said, Take heart, son, your sins are forgiven you, and in their heart they say within themselves, This man is blaspheming (Matthew 9[:3]). This was because a man, as it were, Christ, attributed to himself what was proper to God alone. God conferred this consequence to the Fathers through Mosaic shadows. For this reason not only the very work of Redemption, namely the obedience and death of Christ, but also his very human nature was truly absent to the fathers and not present.

ABSOLUTE PRESENCE OF THE MAN CHRIST NOT REQUIRED FOR PARTICIPATION OF CHRIST'S MERIT.

There was no need of the presence either of his very person, with respect to his human Nature, nor of its work, for participation of this work and merit, but it was sufficient that they trusted that *thing existing* of these benefits would be, and would fulfill this obedience.

In this way indeed nothing takes away from us this work of Redemption which was accomplished more than a thousand and five hundred years before, when we were not present. For faith is sufficient for participation in Christ's benefits, by which we firmly believe that this was done on our behalf.

HOW CHRIST IS NOW PRESENT TO OUR MIND AND FAITH.

Now however is there definitely another presence of Christ, even with respect to the mind and faith, than was at the time of Abraham. For Christ did not fulfill this work on earth such that he might be absent from us and our mind according to his humanity, <89> just as he was not present to Abraham. But because his human nature was personally united with God and stationed upon a Throne proper to Deity, which is limited to no place; on that account Christ really existing is also really and truly present to the elect, actually, according to his own humanity, without respect to faith or unbelief. And for this reason also he delivers his own body and blood really present in a heavenly way, according to the word and promise of his own Testament, which promise at the time of Abraham, or of the Patriarchs, he did not make, nor was it made, in the Mosaic Sacraments of the Old Testament.

Deity the chief cause of Christ's benefits. The distinction between the Sacraments of the Old and New Testaments confirmed.

Besides this, the results or benefits of Christ commence effectively, as it were, chiefly from his Divinity. For this reason the results, that is, the benefits of Christ, applied to the fathers through faith, are elicited in no way from things that do not exist, but the Word [λόγος] that would be incarnate, foreshadowed in sacrifices and Sacraments, conferred those benefits to them with respect to his future incarnation. On this account the distinction between the Sacraments of the old and new Testament will stand forever, and cannot be overturned for any reason, namely that the Sacraments of the old Testament are merely a shadow of Christ according to his humanity, but our Sacraments in the new Testament have his very body, which is really present, dispensed, and presently received in a heavenly way by mouth with the bread.

For even if Christ's blood, to which the blood of the Sacraments of the old Testament related, and the blood of the new Testament are one, since Christ is one, nevertheless it was only prefigured in that place, but here the figure is done away with and here it is really and truly present and dispensed through the bodily, or external, Elements of bread and wine.

And it was said above that the words of Christ's Testament offer his body not merely to the mind, but also to the mouth, since he said, Take, eat, this is my body.

<90>

No literary device in Sacraments of the Old and New Testament.

From this it follows that precisely no literary device must be admitted in the words of the Sacraments of the old or new Testament, since the blood of sacrifices was real blood, just as Moses says, This is *the blood of the covenant* (Exodus 24[:8]) and not that it signifies the blood of the covenant, though notwithstanding that it represents Christ's blood. For just as it is covenant, so also is it blood. And the blood of the new Testament also, is Christ's true blood, which does not signify or represent other than that it is Christ's blood.

ABSURDITY OF A LITERARY DEVICE IN THE WORDS OF CHRIST'S TESTAMENT.

For just as it would be absurd if Moses' words concerning the blood of calves were interpreted according to a literary device, This is the blood of the covenant, that is, it signifies the blood of this covenant, so also would it be absurd if the words of Christ's Testament were interpreted by the same literary device, This is my blood of the new Testament, which is poured out for you, as if there were some other blood of the new Testament which was poured out by Christ.

BLOOD OF THE OLD TESTAMENT SYMBOLIC. BLOOD OF THE NEW TESTAMENT NOT SYMBOLIC.

Therefore the blood of Mosaic calves and of his covenant was true, natural, and essential, but also symbolic, emblematic, and representative of Christ's true blood. The blood of the new Testament is likewise true, natural, and essential, however it is not figurative, emblematic, or representative. For what would it represent or signify? Rather it is the real blood of Jesus Christ, which was poured out for the sins of the whole World.

WHY CHRIST DISPENSES SPIRITUAL GIFTS THROUGH BODILY ONES.

That Christ employs wine in a cup for his dispensation was shown above from Chrysostom, namely that we are not only spiritual, but also corporeal. If in fact the whole person were spiritual, God would confer spiritual gifts, of which sort are Christ's body and blood offered in the Mystery, without bodily organs.

And if Christ wished, it would be as easy for him to feed and refresh us by means of his body and blood without bread and wine, as he does with bread and wine.

IN SACRAMENTS SPIRITUAL THINGS JOINED WITH BODILY ONES.

But since man is partly body and partly spirit, for this reason Christ joins together bodily things with spiritual ones.

<91>

EMPHASIS OF THE TERMS *"MY AND MINE"* [*"MEUS ET MEUM"*] IN THE WORDS OF CHRIST'S TESTAMENT.

It should be noted especially that the term *"my* and *mine"* is emphatic, and contradicts shadows and literary devices, and can admit no literary device. Otherwise we would slip back into the old Testament and transform the body into shadow.

Nor in fact is food for stomachs sought here, but food that is life-giving to eternal life, which is Christ's body, guaranteeing life to those eating in faith. For if otherwise we were eating a thousand men's bodies, we would not in any case be spiritually vivified. But the one who eats the flesh of the Son of God, he is vivified. With respect to life-giving food, a shadow and figure or sign cannot stand for this, which is Christ's flesh.

For this reason the Sacraments of the Old and New Testament must not be confused in the least, unless we should wish to become Jews and reject Christ's body. May this be absent from us.

THE ROCK IN THE PAULINE PHRASE DOES NOT SIGNIFY CHRIST. CHRIST IS THE TRUE AND REAL ROCK.

Paul speaks in this way when it is read, the rock that was following them is Christ (I forgot this above, so as to prevent me answering). In this place a rock does not signify a stone nor is understood to prefigure Christ. For a stony rock did not follow the Israelites, but remained perpetually in its own place and was prior to the Israelite people. The rock about which Paul speaks, though, was Christ himself, who followed long after the Israelites were living in the desert and redeemed the human race, Who indeed according to Divinity never deserted the people but perpetually attended them.

METAPHOR, NOT METONYMY, IN PAUL'S WORDS.

Therefore even if I admit a literary device in the term rock, I do not nevertheless concede that it is Metonymy, since here in no way is a noun situated in place of a noun. But it is a Metaphor, by which an inanimate object is situated in place of a live one. For at Matthew 16, Christ gives the name Rock by way of Metaphor, to signify the certainty and confirmation upon which the Church is built, against which the gates of hell will not prevail. For a Rock is very firm, which can sustain the Church against the storms of all the winds and the insults of the Devil and of the world lest it be overturned; rather, it remains immovable forever.

But it is enough to have pointed out to be seen that in the old Testament were merely shadows, which represented and foreshadowed Christ according to the flesh; in the New Testament however all those <92> figures are taken away, and in their place has followed the body, which we have according to the clear and perspicuous words of Christ, *this is my body*, etc., present in the holy Supper. We freely confess that we are ignorant of the mode of presence, however, which we commend to God's wisdom and omnipotence, who is truth itself, and is not able to lie.

Dr. Beza:

POINT 1.

I hear many things being said, but few being proved.

POINT 2. SUMMARY OF DOCTRINE CONCERNING THE LORD'S SUPPER, THESIS 1.

I too acknowledge that old figures and Sacraments were offered, but new ones instituted. But if they are Sacraments, they are therefore signs. Therefore they will signify. What? Christ. This is however not a mere signification, or representation, in such a way as dead men are represented in statues or other images, but in the Sacraments of the new Testament something is truly shown to the mind through faith, which is signified in signs. Namely, Christ's body and blood are shown to the mind, and are signified through bread and wine.

POINT 3.

I am very much amazed, however, that you have said that the session at the right hand of God commenced by way of the personal union, perhaps, that is, at the incarnation of the Son of God, since you are not ignorant that the incarnation and session at the right hand are distinct articles of faith and of the Apostles' creed.

POINT 4.

Then again, you seem always to take up the name "human" instead of "humanity," and in this way seem not to distinguish concrete words from abstract ones, but to confuse them, something we read was not done by the Fathers.

POINT 5.

Meanwhile in Paul's words to the Philippians, chapter 2, which is said concerning the person, you refer to his humanity, even though you know that the term "Christ" signifies a person, not only another Nature.

POINT 6.

Again, St. Paul is speaking not about the nature of his humanity, but about the [93] Divine nature, which you understand by the word "FORM OF GOD," just like form of a slave signifies not condition, status, or servile clothing, but the human Nature itself, which Christ assumed.

POINT 7. ANALOGY OF THE KING OF SPAIN.

I acknowledge, too, from that sentence of Paul, the supreme glory which attains to the man Christ, to whom every knee will bow, and that he exercises dominion over all things which can be named in this world and the world to come. But that glory does not derive its contours and truth from the body of Christ. In the same way every knee in India bows to the King of Spain on account of his dominion, and they recognize his rightful ownership, and subject themselves to it, they nevertheless abide in the sure location of his Realm.

POINT 8. WHETHER GOD CONFERRED GRACE THROUGH SHADOWS AND TYPES OF THE OLD TESTAMENT.

Clearly it is strange to me, though, that God should bestow the benefits of the remission of sins and his grace to the Patriarchs through shadows. The blood of bulls and calves did not purify consciences (Hebrews 9[:9]). And shadows did not have some hidden power to bestow life and other such things. It is for this reason that Christ was present as God and man to the Patriarchs and to their mind through faith, through whom and from whom they received all things in their rites.

POINT 9.

Thus the understanding of the Sacraments of either Testament is the same, in which Christ is offered to the mind through external things, and he is received by faith, and once received he communicates his gifts to the members of his own body. In these matters the Son of God does not deceive us.

POINT 10.

And it is for this reason that bread is Sacrament, that wine is Sacrament, that is, a sign, through which Christ who remains in heaven is offered to the mind, not less efficaciously than if by his own body he were present in the Supper, present to our body and to our mouth.

POINT 11. BEZA SEEKS CONCORD.

Since therefore we consent in many points of this article, namely concerning communion under both kinds, against the Papists on Transubstantiation and the sacrifice of the Mass, concerning spiritual[94] eating which happens through faith; furthermore, that Sacraments are signs, by which are signified the promises of grace *regarding the remission of sins; and likewise concerning the true and salutary presence of Christ's body; and since we are really only at odds concerning the mode of the presence; what, finally, is the reason that we are dissenting to such a great degree over such a trifling matter, and are fighting so bitterly and with such enmity? Nay, rather, let us engage in brotherly love and proclaim it mutually. For if by chance we prate on, it is not happening because of dishonesty or malice, but because of ignorance. May the Lord be willing to open the eyes of whichever party is in error, and to illuminate him with his Holy Spirit.*

Dr. Jakob:

POINT 1.

I leave it to the judgment of all hearers whether or not I have proved those things I have presented in favor of the statement of our teaching, from the words of Christ's Testament, and the clear testimonies of holy Scripture.

POINT 2. FALLACIES FROM A FALSE DEFINITION OF SACRAMENT.

However I do not concede in the least that your Lordship says that Sacraments are signs, and because of this deduces a proof against a real presence of Christ's body in the Lord's Supper. This is a fallacy by false definition of Sacrament, which is not a sign only, but also embraces the thing signified. Thus the Eucharist consists of two things, and earthly and a heavenly. Nor was this Sacrament instituted for the sake of signifying, but rather for the sake of presenting the body of the Lord. And not to the mind alone, either, but it is presented also to the mouth according to the clear word "*eat*," which in no way here means to believe, but to receive by mouth.

POINT 3. WHEN THE COMMUNICATION OF MAJESTY BEGAN IN HIS HUMAN NATURE.

Nor indeed am I unacquainted with the fact that the incarnation of the Son of God, and the man Christ's being seated at the right hand of God, are distinct articles of the Creed. However it does not follow therefore, that he did not receive his share in the Majesty (the complete usage of which is assigned to Christ according to the flesh only following the resurrection), nor that it had its start from the incarnation. These things are able to exist together at the same time very well without all the confusion of the articles of the creed, just as has been shown in Paul's words.

POINT 4. HUMAN AND HUMANITY USED CLEARLY.

No one who ordinarily reflects on their writings can deny, however, that the Church's Scribes have indiscriminately employed the words "human and humanity" in regard to Christ. [95] Among them St. Augustine easily deserves first place. For this reason, I have intentionally used "human" instead of "humanity," since this word avoids the danger of the Nestorian heresy. (See the solid refutation of the Orthodox Consensus.)

THE NAME "CHRIST" USED VARIOUSLY.

Nor is it unknown to Dr. Beza, even if the term "Christ" is the name of a person; to him nevertheless can be attributed different names for one reason or the other, now for this, now the other reason or with respect to one or the other nature, which cannot coexist and be true without real communication.

THE RULE OF THE ORTHODOX FATHERS IN REGARD TO THE EMPTYING AND EXALTATION OF CHRIST.

Since therefore it stands with the consensus of all the Orthodox Fathers that the divine Nature is able neither to be exalted nor humiliated (that which is proper to the human nature), the rule of the Orthodox Fathers in known also to Dr. Beza himself, namely that whatsoever is spoken of in holy Scripture concerning the humiliation and exaltation of Christ, such sayings are wholly to be understood concerning his humanity, or concerning Christ according to his humanity. But anyone who interprets such things as concerning his Divinity, Leo I says that Arius captures such a one to his own confederacy.[13]

POINT 6. TRUE AND PROPER INTENTIONS OF PAUL'S WORDS (PHILIPPIANS 2). CONCERNING THE FORM OF GOD AND THE FORM OF A SLAVE. ACCORDING TO WHICH NATURE CHRIST WAS EMPTIED. CHRIST THE MOST PERFECT EXAMPLE OF HUMILITY. CHRIST NO LONGER A SLAVE. WHAT IT IS TO BE IN THE FORM OF GOD.

However, Paul speaks not about the assumption of the human nature, but about the servile condition of the assumed man himself. The very words of the text teach and confirm very clearly what they say in this way (Philippians 2[:5–7]): Let that be in you which was also in Christ. He who although in the form of God, did not consider robbery to the end that he be the equal of God, but completely emptied himself, and took the form of a slave. Paul proposes however that the man Christ was a model of supreme humility, who although (he says) was in the form of God that is, the true God, and established in supreme Majesty, and for this reason was equal to God, who by the declaration of his Majesty could have utterly overwhelmed the entire world, just as will happen on the last day; nevertheless he assumed a servile form, in which nothing of the Divine Majesty was manifest. For which reason he completely emptied himself, or as the Apostle's voice says it, "evacuated," ἐκένωσε. This cannot be attributed to his absolute divinity without injury to the sense, because divinity cannot evacuate itself, since it is unchangeable. But according to <96> the nature he completely emptied and evacuated himself, in which nature the whole fullness of Deity was dwelling bodily, whose usage he had renounced, and was wearing the form of a slave, all the way up to his death; nevertheless he is ever and always Lord. He discharged a slave's duties to his disciples and all who find their refuge in him, for which reason Christ himself by his example also invites all people to learn humility: Learn from me, he says, since I am *humble of heart*. I ask: in the proper explanation of holy Scripture, and even of Paul himself, what is there that could be stated more clearly and more consistently with reason? Therefore even though after his resurrection and ascension into heaven he put away the

---

13   Epistle 59.3.

form of a slave, and is no longer a slave, nor can he be said to be according to the Scripture, but never put away his human nature; nevertheless, all people see that the words of Paul have to be understood as speaking about the servile condition. Although I should nevertheless not deny that the things understood by the Patriarchs concerning the divine nature have been made use of, also, against heretics for the purpose of asserting the Divinity of Christ, according to the Analogy of faith piously and rightly. In fact neither interpretation renders the other void, but by reason of his Divinity, the one confirms and results in the other and vice versa, since Christ is true God, and the man assumed is united with God. Which one may be more fitting, however, is easily recognized, should we consider the words precisely. In fact he says plainly that Christ is *in the form of God*. These words teach plainly that Paul is speaking about Christ according to his humanity. For it is one thing to be the very form of God, and another to be in the form of God. Each of these is attributed to Christ truly. For Christ himself is the form of God, in so far as he is God. However he is in the form of God, in so far as he is a man (which phrase refers to the communication of the form of God in the human Nature), since he is personally united with God. Therefore although he had been able, in so far as he is a man, to show forth his own glory (communicated to him by his Divinity and essentially proper to his Deity), since he was in the form of God (a condition which none of the angels could claim), and since he had been able to make that form openly known to all people, nevertheless he was unwilling to do so, but clothed his glory in a servile appearance and condition. Paul desires the same thing: that all pious men imitate him, and not become arrogant on account of the gifts of God, but each one serve the other after the example of Christ.

<97>

POINT 7. CHRIST'S RULE NOT A WORLDLY ONE.

Let the glory of his unlimited power take nothing away from the truth and compass of Christ's body; we have plainly shown this above. But just as the man Christ may have dominion over all things, like the king of the Spanish Indies, it is laying it on pretty thick of course, this thinking about the reign and dominion of Christ, which exchanges the spiritual and heavenly reign of Christ for a worldly reign. In fact he does not rule through substitutes like the king of Spain. On the contrary, he himself, being present, directs and administrates all things in all times and places, in a heavenly way, inscrutable and impenetrable to human reason.

POINT 8.

Nor is it less novel and strange that you dare to deny that God through the shadows of the old Testament Sacraments conferred grace to the Patriarchs. Even if he did not atone for their sins by the blood of bulls and calves, but purified them from all sins by the blood of Jesus Christ; nevertheless those who despised these Sacraments attained no grace. These Sacraments were in use, as Paul says (Galatians 4 [3:24–25]), as guardians until Christ came, leading to faith in him. Through these he conferred his grace upon them, and on account of Christ he received them into grace. They were prefiguring and foreshadowing him who was as yet absent according to his humanity.

POINT 9. DISTINCTION OF THE OLD AND NEW TESTAMENT.

Therefore there is in no way the same understanding of Sacraments of the old and new Testament, if indeed the body of Christ's body given in the Eucharist is given not only to the mind but also to the mouth, which in the rites of the old Testament was merely foreshadowed.

POINT 10. INTEGRITY OF THE SACRAMENT.

And bread and wine are not the Sacrament, but merely part of the Sacrament, the more ignoble part at that, to which a heavenly things joins of necessity, the body and blood of Christ. Otherwise it will not be the Eucharist, as has been said above.

Point 11.

As for the rest, it is true that in many things we agree, as you have mentioned now in part; concerning these things there is no dissent between us and there has not been controversy.

Concerning why there has always been controversy in this article.

However, in this matter there is still no consensus, and between your Churches and our there has been a controversy about it for so many years, namely <98> concerning the true and real presence of the body and blood of Christ in the supper. We would consent easily regarding the proper and true sense of the words of the supper if there were agreement about this issue. We still understand the words simply, literally, according to the plain, literal meaning [κατὰ δ' ῥητόν], just as the words sound, and without figure of speech, wherefore we do not doubt at all concerning this true and real presence, since Christ (who is true and omnipotent) has promised it in plain words, and his wisdom is infinite, who knows the way by which it must be undertaken.

Whether Beza and his people believe in the real presence of Christ's body in the Supper.

Here, although you would not dare deny openly a presence of every kind, nevertheless you wish to seem as if you assert the same presence as us, even though you would say openly that the body of Christ is present *in no other way* than as it was present for Abraham. We commit it to the judgment of all hearers, whether we do you wrong when we say that you believe in no presence, since indeed at the time of Abraham the body of Christ was not yet conceived and born, much less present to him or the other Patriarchs.

A different understanding of Christ's person in the Old and New Testament.

For this reason we keep on saying that so long as you persist in that opinion, no consensus can be established between us on this article. For just as there is one understanding of Christ's person in the old Testament, when the son had not yet become incarnate, and another in the new Testament, after he became incarnate; so also there is one and another understanding of his presence: they had merely the shadow of Christ according to his humanity is in their Sacraments, whereas we possess the body and the thing itself that had been foreshadowed, prefigured, and symbolized. We have no doubt at all that these things are understood rightly by all hearers.

A STEP MADE TOWARDS CONCORD. YOU SHOULD NOT BEAR FALSE WITNESS.

Since therefore on either hand we openly condemn Capernaitic eating and Cyclopic carnage of Christ's flesh in the Lord's Supper, (nevertheless under this name Doctors of our churches, not only throughout France, but also in other regions, where your writings have penetrated, wretchedly deformed, and most of you from our Churches, by this cause alone have been alienated, as if they teach this Cyclopic carnage, which we have never dreamt; and concerning the spiritual eating, which <99> is through faith, not only in use, but also outside of the usage of the Lord's Supper, no controversy has existed between us), the step is not to be despised by this open dec-laration of our will, we judge that it has been done for the purpose of holy concord.

CONCERNING WHY ESPECIALLY THERE IS STILL CONTROVERSY. CONCERNING SACRAMENTAL EATING, A QUESTION.

And there remains only a third mode of presence and eating of the body of Christ, namely the eating which is called sacramental, and happens in the mouth; concerning which it is asked, Whether it is only of external signs, bread and wine; or whether with the bread and wine, is there eating also of the body and blood of Christ. Concerning which we will devote more of our attention, Lord willing.

Dr. Beza:

I do not see how Christ's flesh is able to be omnipresent. If we are in one accord concerning its results, what need is there to argue about other things quite unrelated? The Fathers have many errors, and we do not reject them on account of these. We concede a sacramental mode of eating Christ's body. I would like it, though, if it could happen, that I could procure a peace with my death.

Dr. Jakob:

And I deeply feel the same way. From my heart do I desire and long for a true and in fact God-pleasing concord. I can consider easily indeed how pleasing each of us may be to the Pope, into whose hands (if we were to fall, with God's consent) he would attempt to purify the earth with our supplications. But for our part, we are not able to abandon the truth, nor to withdraw from the plain words of Christ's Testament on account of the fact that we do not see or understand how the body of Christ is able to be present, truly and really, in all places, and to be received by mouth, when the Lord's Supper is celebrated.

<100>

THE CONTROVERSY CONCERNING THE LORD'S SUPPER IS VERY SERIOUS.

Neither is it still, for our part, unnecessary, or of no great moment, in what way it seems to be for you, when in place of the body of Christ, it is forcefully insisted to be only the bread of the Church, and that which goes under the name of the body of Christ, is that which is only represented, and not, however, delivered with the bread. For this same reason, I have so forcefully summoned the words of Christ's Testament, which are clear, against their alien sense.

THE FATHERS TEACHABLE IN THEIR OWN ERRORS.

And to be sure, it is a fact that the Fathers possess errors of their own. Nevertheless, if they had been so accurately and carefully admonished about them, without doubt, they would have corrected them.

BEZA SPEAKS WITH US, BUT DOES NOT THINK WITH US.

You assert the sacramental mode of presence and eating to us indeed in words; but when the time has come for explanation, you understand nothing other than eating of bread, which happens in the absence of the body of Christ, a point which we are not able to concede. But more on these things tomorrow, Lord willing.

1F.II. 23 MARCH 1586, 7:00 A.M.

Dr. Jakob:

In the name of our Lord and Savior Jesus Christ, Amen. We wish to continue the comparison we have instituted and to make a beginning at that place where we left off yesterday evening; and may fortune favor our endeavor!

IN WHICH PARTS THERE IS CONSENSUS.
POINT 1.PHYSICAL OR LOCAL PRESENCE IN THE LORD'S SUPPER REJECTED.
POINT 2. CAPERNAITIC EATING ALWAYS CONDEMNED BY GERMAN THEOLOGIANS OF THE AUGSBURG CONFESSION.

In the first place among us there is agreement, that from either part concerning the presence and reception of the body and blood of Christ we feel, that it is not Physical, local, (in the way that he dwelt with people on earth) Capernaitic, or <101> Cyclopic carnage, by which the flesh of Christ, according to the likeness of calf-flesh should be ground by the teeth, passed through the throat into the belly, digested in the belly, and if there are any other things, the absurdities that are gathered together from these points. By which name nevertheless innocently, and without cause our Churches throughout France and in other regions have been maligned, as if they teach that in the Supper of Christ's blood there is a Capernaitic carnage of this sort, although in our writings this teaching cannot be shown, nor that we have ever taught such absurdities.

POINT 3. NO CONTROVERSY IN REGARD TO SPIRITUAL EATING.

Not only so, but it also applies to spiritual eating, which happens through faith, not only in use, but also outside of the use of the Lord's Supper; concerning these things also has there never been any controversy among us and our forerunners or yours. If indeed this eating is nothing other than to trust in Jesus Christ, on account of his body given over unto death, and his blood poured out, that we through faith have the forgiveness of sins and eternal life. To trust this, I say, is to eat the body and to drink the blood of Christ: concerning which we put forward John chapter 6.

POINT 4. DISTINCTION OF SACRAMENTS OF THE OLD AND NEW TESTAMENT.

Then we spoke also from our side, concerning the distinction of the presence of the body and blood of Christ in the Sacraments of the old and new Testament: That in the old Testament were only shadows and Figures; however in the New were the things themselves and his body.

POINT 5. FAITH DOES NOT ACCOMPLISH THE SACRAMENTAL PRESENCE OF CHRIST'S BODY.

That our faith does not effect this sacramental presence, but so far as this matter is concerned, he renders it salvific to those who receive the body and blood of Christ in their mouth; since Christ is present in himself and by means of his own virtue, whether we believe or do not believe; to the righteous and faithful unto their salvation, to the unrighteous and unbelieving unto their judgment.

POINT 6. WHY TYPES ARE DONE AWAY WITH IN THE SACRAMENTS OF THE NEW TESTAMENT. SACRAMENTS OF THE OLD TESTAMENT CLEARER BY REPRESENTATION THAN SACRAMENTS OF THE NEW TESTAMENT.

It was also mentioned briefly, concerning the reason why there cannot be in the Sacraments of the new Testament shadows, types, and symbols of the body and blood of Christ. If in fact the Sacraments and their substance consisted only in symbolism and representation of the body, the blood, and the death of Christ: the Sacraments of the old Testament had by far been more clear than the <102> Sacraments of the new Testament. For the flesh of Calves, Bulls, Sheep more clearly and symbolically represented the flesh of

Christ than the bread of the Lord's Supper. Thus with respect to the rite, moreover, by the slaughter of sheep and the pouring out of their blood, they represented the death of Christ more than the rite of the Sacrament of the Lord's Supper, which consists in the breaking of the bread, in eating and drinking.

THE TYPE OF THE PASCHAL LAMB CLEAR.

Since in fact the paterfamilias sacrificed the Paschal lamb, with his children and the whole family looking on, he was able to teach them in this way: in what manner you see the lamb killed by me, and his blood poured out, in such a way the promised Messiah, when he has come, will be killed and his blood poured out for the forgiveness of all sinners who will believe in him. This symbolism, I say, of the passion and death of Christ, was clearer by far in the old Testament than that which happens in the Lord's Supper, in the use of conse-crated bread and wine. This comparison to bread and wine is not even close to the likeness of the body and blood Christ, so far as they pertain to the external senses.

For that reason therefore, the substance of the Sacrament of the Lord's Supper does not consist in a shadowy semblance, symbolism, or representation of either the body or blood of Christ, nor even of his death; but it is the body and blood of Christ a *true presentation*, when Christ says: Take, eat, This is my body.

Upon this opinion the Reverend Dr. Beza himself has written (1. Tom. *Tract. Theologicarum* page 289): his words are these: that in the old Testament is represented by a mere symbol, what now is given *truly* and *substantially with* symbols becoming visible and subjected to sense; which words were indeed written piously and rightly by Beza. And if he were steadfast in this opinion, consensus in this part would indeed have been declared and established.

THE STATUS OF THE CONTROVERSY CONCERNING THE THIRD MODE OF PRESENCE AND EATING OF CHRIST'S BODY AND BLOOD.

Controversy remains, however, concerning the true presence of the body and blood of Christ in the Lord's Supper. Namely whether a third mode of presence, besides the two made mention of (namely the local or Capernaic mode, and that which occurs through faith), can be demonstrated in the scriptures, by which neither the flesh of Christ [103] is ground by the teeth and swallowed down, nor is represented in the mind alone and received by faith, but together with external symbols is delivered to the mouth and received by the mouth.

This third mode of eating or reception, is the chief point of controversy concerning the Lord's Supper. Whether it is proved or refuted, it will effect an end to this controversy.

SUMMARY OF HIS DOCTRINE CONCERNING THE LORD'S SUPPER, THESIS 3.

For Dr. Beza maintains, as the Theses he offered attest, that in Sacraments of the old and new Testament, there is not another mode of presence of the body and blood of Christ, than that which is offered and represented *to the mind* through these external symbols; which in the Sacraments of the old Testament attended the Fathers more presently, than if they had resided locally. He believes and teaches precisely the same thing and not another presence of the body and blood of Christ also in the Eucharist.

LOCAL PRESENCE OF CHRIST'S BODY REJECTED.

But as far as local presence is concerned, which alone Dr. Beza objects to against us continuously in his own writings, our writings bear witness that they have never taught it, but always and constantly have condemned it. They indeed cannot demonstrate it in our writings anywhere, and the same goes for Capernaitic eating. For this reason, when our adversaries dispute against it, they attack not our doctrine, but their own fabrication of these very things. Since concerning this matter also there has not ever been controversy, it is also clear that consensus exist among us.

LOCAL PRESENCE IN NO WAY BRINGS TO PASS THE SACRAMENTAL PRESENCE OF CHRIST'S BODY. LOCAL ABSENCE IN NO WAY HINDERS THE SACRAMENTAL PRESENCE OF CHRIST'S BODY. THE MODE OF SACRAMENTAL PRESENCE.

For just as in the first Supper Christ was locally by means of his body rather near to one of his disciples and more remote to another; which local presence neither accomplished nor hindered the dispensing of his body made in the Mystery; whether, however, the presence was sacramental or whether the dispensing was not at all local; thus now also after the body of Christ was received into heaven, a local absence would impede not at all the sacramental presence (if he were through all things in this way in the heavens, just as he dwelt with people on earth, nor yet had the body of Christ become glorious), which depends on the communication of the divine Majesty. Because of this, since the flesh of Christ is personally united with the son of God, just as it has drawn to itself every power of making alive, [104] so also it has a mode of presence, by which it may effect and work this vivification. We say that this mode is the divine mode, the heavenly, the supernatural, and that it is untraceable by human reason. For this reason simple faith must cling to the words the Testament of Christ, who said: This is my body. Therefore let us believe that it is.

Dr. Beza:

I. EXPLANATION OF BEZA'S OPINION CONCERNING THE PRESENCE OF CHRIST'S BODY IN THE SUPPER.

O Reverend Doctor, Sir, I have desired Eagerly that we be in agreement, not only in those matters concerning which your Reverence has discussed, but also in the rest. May the Lord give us the grace of his Spirit, in order that at the very last this may happen. But as much as I have been able to understand from your speech, your Reverence, either the opinion has not yet been explained sufficiently by us, or else has not been understood by you. Do you think that we are in agreement concerning the presence of Christ's body? Surely it is true, as has been established from both sides, that in the holy Supper the true body of Christ and his blood is present. But there is not agreement that it is present IN, WITH, or UNDER the bread. And likewise you understand that what we are saying is present to the mind, is the same as what is present to the mouth IN, WITH, or UNDER the bread, in the place where the bread is, and where we are in our bodies.

II.

We however are saying that the body of Christ is present to the mind; it is right to say that he is contained in one place of heaven, and is absent from the earth. If only the mind should gaze upon it through faith in the word, then also through faith will he be transported into heaven.

N.B. BEZA'S CONFESSION. BEZA ATTACKS ONLY THE LOCAL PRESENCE OF CHRIST'S BODY ON EARTH.

Besides this mode of presence, I confess that we are able to attribute to Christ's body NO OTHER MODE of presence than a LOCAL one. If in fact Christ should be in a place with his body, the way in which we are in our bodies, then it follows BY NECESSITY that his presence be a local one.

<105>

Here Dr. Jakob interrupted and advised that discussion take place regarding each point in order, one by one. Then Beza proceeded.

I have not yet begun to argue, but only wished to demonstrate, that there has not yet been established between us a consensus regarding the presence of the body and blood of Christ in the Supper.

III. DISAGREEMENT REGARDING THE PRESENCE OF CHRIST'S BODY AND THE EATING OF THE UNFAITHFUL.

We know that Christ is Judge and savior: the savior of them who embrace him in word and Sacraments; the Judge, though, to those who despise him. The question, however, remains: whether judgment and condemnation arises from the body of Christ itself, assumed or neglected? On account of which I say that there is not yet agreement concerning the presence, nor regarding the eating of the unworthy, which proceeds hereafter.

IV. COMPARISON OF THE SACRAMENTS OF THE OLD AND NEW TESTAMENT.

You have explained that chief point, concerning the comparison of the old Sacraments and ours, and you have added the reason that in the former is contained a shadow, but in the latter body and truth. And your Reverence did not remember his argument which you have now brought up: if the Sacraments were not established to be presented to us, for whom the body of Christ is not signified or represented, but truly delivered with external symbols, this absurdity would be entailed: that the Sacraments of the old Testament were far more clear in signifying and representing Christ and his death than the Sacraments of the new Testament.

NOTA BENE: BEZA'S CONFESSION. SACRAMENTS OF THE OLD TESTAMENT WERE CLEARER IN RITE AND SIGNIFICATION THAN SACRAMENTS OF THE NEW TESTAMENT.

I answer: Of course I say that the signs and significations were more perspicuous in the old Testament, and the types clearer. But I deny that on this account the condition of the old ones was better than ours. For even though the signs were clearer, nevertheless the promises made by them were more obscure.

For just as the man who needs two sticks to triumph over the man who relies on one is not stronger than the man with one stick, and the man who triumphs with a slender stick is braver than the one who does so with a big stick, so it is with the promises about Christ. <106> They were far more obscure for them than for us. Hence it happened that it was fitting for the Sacraments of the old Testament to be more clear and perspicuous in their rite and signification.

And since the promises are like the soul of the Sacraments, and Sacraments should not be thought about only in regard to their signification, by which the things promises are represented to the eyes, the Sacraments of the new Testament are more spiritual than those of the old Testament, which were more dim.

Therefore to the extent that they are more spiritual, they are more suitable for us than for the ancients. For we are not in need of those dim imaginings, but of spiritual things which call us away from the earthly to spiritual and heavenly things.

Augustine's passage (Epistle 118) applies to this, when he writes that Christ has gathered together a society of a new people by means of Sacraments which are very few in number, very easily observed, very evident in their signification, and which are more perfectly suited to us. Besides, Christ is today, yesterday, and forever (Hebrews 13[:8]). For this reason there is equal participation in the Sacraments of both people.

V.

On account of this the Sacraments of the old and new Testament do not differ in the thing, but in their dispensation. And Christ was the mediator in both Testaments, according to both natures. Therefore the ancients possessed the whole Christ also, God and man, or they were without a Mediator. Even though he could not be at that time according to the human nature, he was nevertheless by faith.

As far as my words are concerned that have been brought up from a certain writing of mine, even though I have no doubt that you brought them up in good faith, nevertheless what my intention was can be understood sufficiently from my other writings. For I want not to say that the Sacraments of the old Testament were bare symbols, [107] but rather that they also possessed Christ present, unless we should wish to say that he excluded the fathers from eternal salvation.

Dr. Jakob:

I.

Reverend Dr. Beza, as far as the first part of your speech is concerned, in which Your Reverence rehearsed the chief points about which we conferred yesterday, in which there was consensus between us and where there is still controversy, and added that there has not yet been decided a consensus between us regarding the presence of

Christ's body, I share the same opinion, as can be understood from the preceding friendly and peaceful conference.

DISTORTION OF THE DOCTRINE OF THE WÜRTTEMBERG THEOLOGIANS CONCERNING THE PRESENCE OF CHRIST'S BODY IN THE LORD'S SUPPER.

But I do not concede that the status of the controversy, which Your Reverence has proposed, is that we say that in the place where the bread is, there also the body of Christ is present, that we think the body of Christ is locally present and contained *in*, *with*, and *under* the bread.

For we expressly removed the local presence in the Lord's Supper from our argument, as not only the conference, but also our Theses about the Lord's Supper offered to you, openly demonstrate.

LOCAL PRESENCE OF CHRIST'S BODY IN THE LORD'S SUPPER CONDEMNED.

Therefore let the whole audience know that there neither is, nor ever was, any controversy between us regarding the local presence of Christ's body *in*, *with*, or *under* the bread, for as long as this unfortunate controversy has preoccupied our churches. We reject and condemn this local presence openly in all our writings (just as also Capernaitic carnage of Christ's flesh).

TRUE STATUS OF THE CONTROVERSY. CONCERNING THE SACRAMENTAL MODE OF PRESENCE OF CHRIST'S BODY.

But we are arguing over the *third mode* of presence, which is called Sacramental. Is nothing other than bread and wine delivered to the mouth of the body, and does the mouth receive nothing more than bread and wine? This is the status and scope of the dispute.

<108>

---

1. CANDID CONFESSION OF THE WÜRTTEMBERG THEOLOGIANS.

We for our part here have rejected first the figurative or signifying mode proper to the Sacraments of the old Testament, in which the body and blood of Christ were foreshadowed, signified, represented, but had not yet at that time come into existence, but were believe to be forthcoming.

2.

Next, we have also rejected the local, physical, natural and circumscribed or bodily mode, by which we have in no way asserted that Christ's body is present.

---

3. TRUE STATUS OF THE CONTROVERSY.

But we are talking about the third mode, which is neither signifying nor physical or local, but supernatural, divine, and heavenly: whether this mode is expressed in holy Scripture, by which it is demonstrated that the body of Christ is present and offered not only *to the mind*, but also *to the mouth*, and received by mouth. This is the status of the controversy; let the whole audience turn their attention to this.

TRUE PRESENCE OF CHRIST'S BODY IN THE LORD'S SUPPER.

Therefore as far as this presence is concerned, we for our part affirm frankly and openly, that we establish, believe, and teach this kind of presence of Christ's body in the Lord's Supper, for which Christ does not exactly stand in need of our faith. I would wish the whole audience to observe this attentively, and to weigh it carefully.

For Christ is present in himself, that is, by the power communicated by the Divinity uniquely to him, whether someone should believe it or not believe it. Faith does not bring about this presence, nor help it along, since Christ is sufficiently powerful in himself to be present without the help of our faith; nor can unbelief, impiety, or unworthiness of wicked men impede it.

WHENCE THE PRESENCE OF CHRIST'S BODY IN THE HOLY SUPPER.

Christ's body does not have this presence or this mode of presence in so far as it is a body. For in this way it is and remains finite and circumscribed by the property of its nature, even in its glory. But it possesses this from the Divinity of the Word [ὁ λόγος], the Son of God, with whom he has been personally united and exists as one person, something that cannot be said of any of the angels or the blessed saints.

<109>

Christ's body did not possess this mode of presence at the time of Abraham, even though Christ's body was represented to his mind through Sacraments. For since it did not exist at that time, it could not be present to him. For this reason it is one thing to say the Son of God is present, and it is another to say the incarnate Son of God is present, who was not yet incarnate at the time of Abraham. But now he is not only incarnate, and exists according to the flesh, but also is ruler of heaven and earth according to the flesh, neither of which he was at the time of Abraham according to the flesh.

DISTINCTION BETWEEN PRESENCE AND EFFECT OF CHRIST'S BODY.

But as far as the effect of this presence is concerned, presence is one thing, and the effect of the presence is another. In this respect the different effects which are attributed to Christ in the use and reception of this Sacrament also demand different causes, namely faith, unto vivification and comfort; but unbelief or impenitence, unto judgment and damnation. For Christ's flesh is the food of life in no way, save that he wishes to vivify believers, when he says, My flesh is true food (John 6[:55]). And again, The righteous will live by faith, as the Prophet says (Habakkuk 2[:4]). So Christ does not judge anyone without unbelief, as it is written: The one who does not believe will be condemned (Mark 16[:16]). And again, He who does not believe has already been judged (John 3[:18]).

WHO MADE CHRIST THE JUDGE.

But unbelief does not make Christ the judge and the one who con-demns, but rather the father established him as the judge; he gave him all judgment, since he is the son of man (John 5[:27]). But he judges or condemns no one, except the unbelieving and unfaithful.

WHENCE CHRIST POSSESSES THE POWER OF JUDGING.

So also in judgment elsewhere, which is exercised against the transgressors, when punishment is exacted from criminals, two causes run together: the first the crime of the offender or criminal, the second the justice and power of the magistrate. Here the Magistrate does not receive the power to judge and exercise justice from the criminal, but from God. So in the judgment which Christ exercises in the use of the Lord's Supper against the unfaithful, hypocrites, and Epicureans, two causes run together also: the one is the person's unbelief, on account of which <110> the person is judged; the other is Christ's power which Christ received not from the criminal, but from God the father, who established him as judge of all flesh.

CHRIST THE JUDGE IN SO FAR AS THE SON OF MAN.

But the Father did not give him this power since he is the Son of God who had this power from eternity, but rather in so far as he is the son of man, as the words of Christ plainly read in John 5[:27] *since he is the son of man.*

TWO CAUSES RUN TOGETHER IN JUDGMENT.

When this judgment is exercised against criminals, it cannot be defined only as one cause. For if he should not sin, the Magistrate indeed remains in himself a just judge, possessing the power to judge. But when there is no one who sins, even his judgment ceases. Thus when someone steals or perpetrates a murder, and the Magistrate does not punish, there is still no judgment. But if the criminal and judge run together, and the judge exercises his justice against the criminal, then we say that justice happens, that is the execution of justice.

EVERY MAGISTRATE LAUDABLE, JUST, AND MERCIFUL. SAME PRAISE OF JUSTICE AND MERCY IN CHRIST.

When therefore in the use of the Lord's Supper the impious eat judgment, the cause on account of which they are judged is in the impious themselves, namely, unbelief. But the power and execution of this punishment is in Christ, in the exercise of judgment, and from *Christ.* If it were never approaching, the impious would never be judged. For no one would condemn himself. But Christ is the one who saves and condemns, who brings life and death. And the same goes for a Magistrate, should he not punish evildoers. He would indeed be called benign and merciful in the company of evildoers. Meanwhile he would be accused of injustice, since he would not punish the wicked. But then the commendation of the good Magistrate has been completed when he is a benefactor to the good and protects them against the violence and injuries of the wicked. And it is as praise-worthy in him when he punishes the wicked justly as when he is benefactor to the good. So also is the same praise of justice in Christ, which is praise of goodness and mercy, since the virtues are equal in God, and for this reason it is not less praiseworthy and glorious in Christ when he judges and condemns the impious hypocrite, <111> who pretends piety, which otherwise saves a pious and faithful man by grace and mercy.

HOW JUDGMENT PROCEEDS FROM THE BODY OF CHRIST. HOW JUDGMENT PROCEEDS FROM THE IMPIOUS.

So judgment proceeds from Christ's body, and out of it, in so far as Christ the man exercises his judgment in the impious. Justice in fact stands in the way of him also working life in the impious, just as mercy is the cause that confers life on those who believe. But judg-ment proceeds from the impious in so far as they provide the reason of him exercising this judgment, to which the impious have been disposed by their own unbelief and impiety, just as believers have been disposed to life by faith. For this reason the impious eat and drink judgment on themselves by mouth, not simply by scorning and rejecting Christ, as Dr. Beza thinks and says, but also by receiving Christ in the use of this Sacrament.

IN WHAT WAY THE IMPIOUS EAT JUDGMENT *BY RECEIVING* CHRIST.

Now as to Christ's presence in this exercising of his judgment, the unbelief of the impious can in no way impede his presence, just as faith does not produce it. For this reason the impious and the unwor-thy partakers can indeed in their impious heart scorn and reject Christ as savior, but since they receive one and the same Sacrament with the pious, Christ is not only a Savior, but also a judge. Whether or not they are willing, they are even compelled against their will to admit the same Christ as judge, who being present works judgment just as effectively in them as he does salvation in those who believe.

In the same way the evildoer, when he is taken away to punish-ment, would happily keep the Judge, the executor of justice, away, so as not to be punished, but he cannot keep him away on account of the armed power which the judge possesses by his authority; so also the impious would happily reject and keep Christ the Judge away, but he himself is far more powerful than them, and does not allow him-self to be kept away by the impious in the exercise of his judgment.

3.

But Dr. Beza here declares openly that besides a representative or signifying mode of presence of Christ's body <112> and of his blood in the Lord's Supper, he can attribute to Christ's body *no other mode* of presence than a *local* one. Once again I bear witness before the Honorable Prince and all the audience, we have never believed in the local presence of Christ's body, never have preached it, never have written it. So too, there will nowhere be found in our writings even one syllable or letter about it, as if we assert this.

THOU SHALT NOT SPEAK FALSE TESTIMONY.

Since therefore Dr. Beza, with all the associates and brothers who share his opinion, attacks this one presence in all the writing which he has published against us, and the writings are sold through many regions, we leave it to their conscience how they will render to God their reason for attributing to us a mode of presence of this kind, and in this way have been eager to make us appear suspect and odious among the French Churches and others, even though they know that we think otherwise.

But as far as the last part of what was mentioned is concerned, regarding the comparison of the Sacraments of the old and new Testament, I do not want to repeat with many words what has been said by both of us. I leave it in fact to the judgment of the Audience,

who have just about heard everything, and can easily understand that what pertains to representation and signification, if the
Sacraments had to be defined by this only, was by far more descrip-
tive of the Sacraments of the old rather than the new Testament, a
fact that Mr. Beza also confesses.

AUGUSTINE.

Therefore when Augustine says that the Sacraments of the new
Testament are most excellent in signification, it is certain that he had
regard not at all for a bare signification or representation but rather
for the delivery of the things promised, the body and blood of Christ,
which he asserted.

---

5. DR. BEZA SPEAKS WITH US BUT DOES NOT THINK WITH US.

Regarding the recitation of Your Reverence's words, which you
wrote regarding the distinction between the Sacraments of the
old and new Testament, there is no doubt about what you wrote in
Volume 1 of your *Tractationes Theologicae*, page 289. So too, I could
likewise recite plenty of other passages in which you speak with
us <113> in such a way that the inexperienced reader could think
none other than that Your Reverence thinks with us entirely. So for
instance you say, Volume 1, page 282. I respond in a few words, the
thing of the Sacrament, that is, the very body and blood of Christ,
is absent from the Supper *leaving no more than* the symbols themselves. And again, page 262. Be assured finally that we do *not* have
a conflict regarding its *substance*, that is, regarding what it holds in
common [κοινωνία] with the very *body*, but rather regarding the brut-
ish and cyclopic eating, without which you vainly dream that holding
substance in common [κοινωνία] cannot stand. And in the same place:
We object to the Cyclopic eating, which you hold in common with the
Papists. These, my dear Beza, are your words.

---

6. CONSOLATION IN THE TRUE USE OF THE LORD'S SUPPER.

But as far as the analogy of the sticks is concerned, which you
brought up, I am not unaware that the same condition belongs to
all men and all times (by reason of our infirmity), especially when

people have been confused in agony and near death, such that they need many sticks. But the greatest consolation for us in the Lord's Supper is restored not by way of signification or representation, but rather by way of delivery, as we showed a little earlier. Since the troubled conscience is without doubt roused to the strengthening of its faith, the body of Christ is not represented, but rather is truly delivered, according to the words of institution, to be eaten by mouth, and his blood to be drunk by mouth, which was given into death for our sins. Behold, says the pastor, distributing the Lord's Supper to the sick, that you may know that you have not been cast aside by God on account of your sins, he has not only promised you his grace in words and confirmed it with an oath, but in this his Testament he delivers also this very body as a pledge for you, which was given into death for you, and this very blood, which was poured out for you unto the remission of sins. Therefore you should say to Satan, Get away from me Satan, you have no part in me, I am all Christ's, and Christ is mine, who is my righteousness, holiness, and life. This is by far the most efficacious consolation.

For the purpose of signifying the privilege of the people in the new Testament, Paul compares the Jewish people to little children (Galatians 4[:3]), who were preserved under the elementary princi-ples of the World, that is, under the shadow of the law, <114> as though under tutors and caretakers up to the fulfillment of time, until Christ should come. For just as a child is in no way different than a slave, as long as he is under a guardian, but when he is freed from the care of the guardian, then he himself manages his own goods, so also the people of God in the old Testament indeed had the good promises under a shadow, but in the new Testament, they have been fully delivered to them, and are delivered and communicated in the Sacraments.

CONSOLATION IN THE SACRAMENTS OF THE NEW TESTAMENT CLEARER THAN IN THE SACRAMENTS OF THE OLD TESTAMENT.

So not only is the consolation greatest in the patent promises, but also is clearer by far in the Sacraments of the new Testament than it was in the old Testament.

THE PURPOSE OF THE ESTABLISHED COLLOQUY.

This is why we must take pains in this matter, especially in this conference, that it may be clear to the audience of the Colloquy whether Christ's body truly and really is present in the Lord's Supper, and what either party's position is regarding the question, whether we agree or disagree.

DR. BEZA'S INTENTION.

For your part, you do not wish ever to appear to have denied the true presence of Christ's body and blood in the Lord's Supper, but rather fight against just a base and cyclopic eating of Christ's flesh, as your words were recited a little earlier.

DR. BEZA'S OPINION CONCERNING THE PRESENCE OF CHRIST'S BODY IN THE LORD'S SUPPER.

To this question we answer clearly and distinctly that no true and real presence of Christ's body and blood in the Lord's Supper is established on your side. You openly say: Christ's body is present in the Lord's Supper *in no other way* that it was present for Abraham. Moreover, the substance of Christ's body could not be present except for Physically, and in a local, circumscribed way. (We agree too that Christ's body is not present in the Lord's Supper in this way.) Pray tell, then, how can you establish a true presence? If in fact there is not another way possible, then he is present in no way. Since at the time of Abraham the body of Christ did not exist, how then could it have been present? Abraham indeed saw Christ's body from far off, in the Spirit, through faith, but he did not have him present. Now though, [115] after the fullness of time came (says Paul), God sent his son born of a woman, etc. (Galatians 4[:4]). He promised he would be present to his Church. But he is present not locally or in a circumscribed way, but rather in a divine and heavenly way, which he himself knows. For his promise cannot lie: I am with you always, even up to the consummation of the age (Matthew 28[:20]). And, where two or three are gathered in my name, I am in their midst (Matthew 18[:20]).

Dr. Beza:

1.

Reverend Doctor, I request that we do this in a Syllogism. That way we will understand your arguments from both sides more correctly and we will be able to answer more easily.

2. FOUNDATION AND CAUSE OF SACRAMENTAL ERROR. DR. BEZA KNOWS ONLY TWO MODES OF PRESENCE.

Your Reverence suggests three modes of presence, the local, figurative, and heavenly. I suggest only two, by which CHRIST is either represented and offered to the mind or is situated locally in the place where the bread is.

If in fact you name Christ personally, and understand him in his humanity, and say that he is present in the Supper, then I understand the spiritual presence, by which he is present to the mind through faith. But I establish another presence, by which Christ's body is now in heaven.

3.

This presence is local and circumscribed, pertaining to the essence of CHRIST'S humanity, which remains eternally the property of Christ's body, and which he does not lay aside.

4.

The third mode which you assert rests, I think, on the disputation regarding the PERSON OF CHRIST. I do not find that mode of presence in holy writ or the writings of the Fathers. <116> It appears to destroy the truth of the human Nature in Christ.

5.

As far as Christ the judge is concerned, we have no doubt but that he has been appointed judge. Indeed we know and confess with great and unanimous consent that the cause of damnation depends on unbelief. And we know that judgment has been given to Christ according to his humanity.

WHAT BEZA UNDERSTANDS BY JUDGMENT.

But when we say that Christ was given judgment according to his humanity, we do not restrict this to condemnation, but rather understand that it is dominion over heaven and earth, visible and invisible government. And when it is said that the father judges no one, we plainly do not exclude him from government, for he governs all things in the son and through the son.

QUESTION ABOUT THE EATING OF THE IMPIOUS.

But it is asked whether the impious share in the body of Christ just as the pious and faithful do, and whether the impious is as truly a participant in it as the pious.

IN WHAT WAY THE BODY OF CHRIST JUDGES AND CONDEMNS ACCORDING TO BEZA.

Here we say that Christ's body condemns when it is despised but not when it is received. And we assert that it is not received except by faith, and rejected by unbelief. For this reason, reception, or the mode of reception, is proper to the faithful. Christ's body is indeed offered to the impious, but it is not received by them.

And it is offered to all people with a condition which is not manifest in the impious, namely under the condition of faith. For no one can become a participant in Christ's body except he become his member.

But for those for whom Christ results in death, it happens that he is rejected, not that he is received.

I say that the difference between the old and new Testament does not depend on the thing, but rather on the dispensation. For the lamb was slain from the beginning of the world (Revelation 13[:8]). Therefore he was just as present to those in their own Sacraments as *he to us in our Sacraments. But again, I ask that we do this in the form of a syllogism.*

<117>

Dr. Jakob:

1.

Reverend Dr. Beza, it is fine to do this in the form of a syllogism. We will in fact explain ourselves more quickly in this way, and the conference itself will be less disagreeable to the audience.

2. DIFFERENCE BETWEEN CHRIST'S PRESENCE IN THE OLD AND IN THE NEW TESTAMENT.

But enough has been said about the difference between Christ's presence by reason of his humanity in the old and new Testament. Namely, in the old Testament Christ was only foreshadowed according to his humanity, signified, prefigured and represented. Through this shadow and these figures God distributed blessings to his people, and applied them when Christ's death was accomplished, namely the remission of sins, righteousness, and eternal life. But in the new Testament the very body, present in a heavenly way, is distributed in the Lord's Supper either unto life or unto judgment. Therefore I do not wish to add more concerning these things, concerning which enough has also been said in our Theses.

SPIRITUAL EATING THE SAME IN THE OLD AND NEW TESTAMENT. WHAT JUDGMENT MEANS IN PAUL.

Enough has also been said about spiritual eating, which happens through faith, about which there is no question. We are equal to the ancient Fathers themselves in this, who themselves also ate the body of Christ through faith. But regarding the presence of their substance *there is as big a difference* in the Sacraments of both Testaments *as the difference between what is and what is not.* What Dr. Beza says is plainly novel and unheard of, when he says that Christ's voice as a *"judge"* must be understood as a statement not about damnation but rather about government. So Paul also speaks about punishment, which God inflicted on the Corinthians on account of their abuse of the Lord's Supper. Paul himself explains this in his own words. If we judged ourselves, he says, we would not be judged, that is, not be getting punished by the Lord (1 Corinthians 11[:31]).

TWOFOLD JUDGMENT.

But this is judgment, either temporal punishment if they repent later; but if not, and they remain in impenitence, then it is damnation.

Christ plainly confirms the same thing also in John 5 when he says about judgment that the impious will endure it by reason of sustaining punishment, which Christ will inflict on them. For immediately after <118> the words, "every judgment he has given to the son," he adds, "Do not wonder at this, since the hour is coming in which all who are in their graves will hear the voice of the Son of God. And those who have done good works will go forth into the resurrection of life, but those who have done evil into the resurrection of Judgment," which others have rendered, condemnation.

THE IMPIOUS EAT JUDGMENT NOT BECAUSE OF REJECTING BUT RATHER BECAUSE OF RECEIVING CHRIST.

But the impious eat judgment not because of rejecting Christ but because of receiving him. This is clear from Paul's words, when he says, The bread which we break, is it not a communication of Christ's body, that is, whoever eats this bread, Christ's body is communicated with the bread. But not only do the pious eat this bread, but the impious as well. Therefore they eat judgment by eating, indeed by receiving *Christ's* body in the organ that *God* ordained, and not by rejecting it. But let us reduce this into the form of a syllogism.

SYLLOGISM. THE IMPIOUS EAT JUDGMENT *BY EATING* THE BODY OF CHRIST.

Whoever eats the bread of the Lord's Supper eats Christ's body.

The impious eat the bread of the Lord's Supper. Therefore the impious also eat Christ's body. And so they eat judgment not by rejecting it, but by receiving Christ's body.

Dr. Beza:
Please prove the major proposition.

Dr. Jakob:
Paul writes, 1 Corinthians 10[:16], The bread which we break is a communication of the body of Christ. He does not say, it is a communication of the remission of sins, but rather it is a communication of the body of Christ.

<119>

Dr. Beza:
Prove it with a syllogism.

Dr. Jakob:
Sayings of holy Scripture do not need to be proven with a Syllogism; they are rather believed on account of divine authority.

Dr. Beza:
Make a Syllogism.

Dr. Jakob:
This is a novelty and unheard of in any school, that testimonies of Scripture are proved with a Syllogism.

Dr. Beza:
Make a Syllogism.

Dr. Jakob:

THERE IS NO COMMUNICATION WITHOUT RECEPTION.

The genuine meaning of the saying of Scripture should not be proved with a Syllogism, but should rather be demonstrated from Scripture. And what kind of communication is it where there is no reception?

Dr. Beza:

Christ's body is communicated by God's will, that is, offered to all, but the impious do not accept it because they are not clothed with Christ, Galatians 3[:27].

Dr. Jakob:

It is not a communication but rather an offering when <120> something is offered and not received. But when it is offered and received, then it is communicated, according to the nature and law of relations. So communication is situated between the one communicating and the one receiving, otherwise there can be no communication nor can it be called communication.

COMMUNICATION OF CHRIST'S BODY, NOT OF BLESSINGS.

But Paul's words are plain. He does not say, The bread which we break is a communication of Christ's blessings. If he had said it this way, everyone would understand that the impious were excluded from the communication, since they do not become sharers in Christ's blessings. On the contrary, Paul says it is a communication of Christ's body. What could be said more plainly to prove that everyone who eats the bread of the Lord eats the body of Christ? He says that this is a communication of Christ's body, by whatever mode finally it happens in the end. And this is the genuine opinion and understanding of Paul, by the consensus of all learned men, without exception, namely that the body of Christ is communicated with this bread to all who eat this bread.

Dr. Beza:

Christ's body is indeed offered to all who eat the bread, but it is not received by all who eat the bread.

Dr. Jakob:

HOW THE IMPIOUS DO NOT RECEIVE CHRIST'S BODY.

If you are talking about reception which happens through faith, there is no controversy that the unfaithful do not receive Christ's body since they lack faith. But Paul is not here talking about eating of faith, but rather about oral eating, when he says, He who eats this bread, etc.

THE IMPIOUS EAT CHRIST'S BODY IN THE HOLY SUPPER BY MOUTH. EMPHATIC TERMS IN PAUL'S WORDS CAREFULLY TO BE OBSERVED.

But I will prove with another express testimony of Paul, who is the best interpreter of his own words, that this oral eating is directed towards not only the bread, but also Christ's body. <121> His words read this way: "Whoever eats *this* bread and drinks the cup *of the Lord* unworthily will be guilty of the body and blood of the Lord. But let a man test himself, and so eat of *that* bread and drink of the cup. For the one who eats and drinks unworthily eats and drinks judgment on himself, *Because he does not discern the body of the Lord.*" What, pray, could be said more plainly to explain the intention and meaning of Paul's words, which were considered a little while ago: "The bread which we break, is it not a communication of the body of Christ?" Here the Emphatic terms in Paul's words must be carefully observed, when he says *This* bread; of *that* bread; the cup *of the Lord.* The one who eats *this* bread, namely that which Christ gave to his disciples and said, This is my body. And again, concerning which he had himself spoken earlier: The bread which we break, is it not a communication of the body of Christ?

So also Paul does not say in this passage that those who eat unworthily eat judgment *since they do not discern this bread* from common bread, but rather that they do not discern *the body of the Lord*, and for this reason also that they become guilty *of the body and blood of Christ*. From this it appears more clear than the sun at noon that the body of Christ is not only offered but also received by the unworthy, but to their judgment, that is, to either temporal punishment, as befell the Corinthians, whom Christ punished with a particular sickness, or if they should remain impenitent, to eternal punishment.

THIRD MODE OF EATING THE BODY OF CHRIST IN THE LORD'S SUPPER. CORRUPT MEMBERS ALSO IN THE BODY OF THE CHURCH.

Since therefore it can in no way be denied that the unworthy and impious are able to eat Christ's body to their judgment, a fact unmistakably demonstrated by Paul's words, then it has also by this very fact been proved and demonstrated that a third eating exists, amid the eating that is through faith alone and the Capernaitic eating and carnage of Christ's flesh, namely a Sacramental eating, by which not only the bread which is broken, but also the body of Christ of which it is a communication, is received by mouth, and not only wine from the cup, but also the blood of Christ of which the blessed cup is a communication, <122> is drunk by all who share in this bread and cup, whether good or evil, just as Paul's words have disclosed: "Since the bread is one, we many are one body," (says Paul) "for we all share in one bread and one cup" (1 Corinthians 10[:17]). But he teaches in the same place that there were very many corrupt members in in this body among the Corinthians.

Dr. Beza:

Comparison of the Sacrament with the Preaching of the Word.

This is oration, not disputation. You asked a little bit ago what sort of communication there is of a thing where there exists no reception of it. I answer that the same thing happens in the word as in the Sacraments. It has been written: The gospel is the power of God for salvation of all who believe (Romans 1[:16]). It therefore does not follow that whoever hear the gospel also receive it.

Dr. Jakob:

Yes indeed, it is the same Gospel in the ears and heart of the impious, who perish and are damned, as it is in the ears and heart of the pious, who are saved. They receive it also by means of their ears who are damned and among whom it bears no fruit. I am happy you brought up this example, because it can illustrate the present controversy.

Argumentation regarding the preached word.

Your reverence is arguing from effect to cause, after this fashion: When the impious hear the Gospel, which is the power of God for salvation, they do not receive salvation. Therefore what they have received is not the power of God, indeed is not the word of God, but rather merely a certain noise without power. This argumentation is faulty.

THE GOSPEL ONE IN THE EARS OF THE PIOUS AND THE IMPIOUS. TWOFOLD POWER OF THE GOSPEL.

The reason I say this is that the Gospel and the word of God which the impious who will be judged hear is one and the same Gospel as that which the pious hear, those who will be saved. Just as Christ says: The speech which I have spoken will judge him on the last day (John 12[:48]). And it has a twofold effect, on the one hand for judging those who despise and do not accept it with true faith, on the other hand for saving those who accept it with true faith. Just as the Apostle also writes: We are before God the good fragrance of Christ, <123> among those who are being saved, *and among those who are perishing.* To the latter indeed we are *the odor of death and unto death,* but to the former the odor of life unto life (2 Corinthians 2[:16]). He testifies with these words: The word of the Gospel, which is the power of God for salvation of all who believe, is also the odor *of death* unto death in those who hear it but do not trust it. There are in fact at all times and places corrupt members of the Church militant, so long as it discharges its duty on earth.

Dr. Beza:
When the Impious hear the Gospel, the power of salvation is not present for them; rather only a noise strikes their ears, so that though listening they may not hear.

Dr. Jakob:
It is one and the same power of saving and damning, even though its manner is different. Christ does not say: The noise, but rather, the word which I have spoken will judge him on the last day, just as one and the same power will save the one who believes, but on the other

hand their effects are very different, according to the difference of the hearers.

And that this is not in the least absurd can be demonstrated in other created things, namely that the effects of a single cause can be different and contrary. It is one and the same ray from the sun that hardens liquid mud and melts hard wax; the ability of the sun ray is one and the same, and it works those two contrary effects. But the cause of the difference is not in the sun's ray, since it is one and the same ray, one and the same ability and power of the ray; there are not two rays or different rays, but rather the case of the different and contrary effects is in the difference of the subjected material, in which the sun's ray works according to its own nature.

Dr. Beza:

WHETHER THE BODY OF CHRIST POSSESSES A TWOFOLD ABILITY.

The sun hardens accidentally. But show me the twofold ability in Christ's body. For we say that Christ's body is only salvific and his flesh vivific.

<124>

Dr. Jakob:

TWOFOLD ABILITY IN CHRIST, OF SAVING AND DAMNING.

I trust that the fact that there is a twofold ability in Christ, of judging and of saving, has been established sufficiently and more than sufficiently above. From this he also is and is called at the same time both Judge and Savior. On account of his power to save he is named Jesus, that is, Savior, since he will save his people from their sins (Matthew 1[:21]). He is also called judge, since the Father has given him every judgment, not only in the manner of administration, but also in the manner of inflicting temporal and eternal punishment

(John 5[:25–29]). For this reason also he will not only say on that day, *come*, but he will also say, *go* into eternal fire (Matthew 25[:41]).

Christ is not idle in the impious.

Thus Christ on earth, when the impious approach the Lord's Supper mixed together with the pious, does not indeed work salvation in them, but just as he does not cease to be the savior in and of himself, so also he is not in the least idle in them, but rather he judges them, just as was said a little bit before, that they eat judgment, and become guilty of the body and blood of Christ.

Dr. Beza:

Whether the cause of damnation is in Christ.

I do not hear a proof. And I ask: is the cause of damnation in Christ? I hear an interpretation, not a Text.

Dr. Jakob:

Whether I bring up an interpretation or plain testimonies of Scripture, and these not in the least violently distorted, but perspicuous and quite plain, I leave to the judgment of the audience. For I do not think that it can be demonstrated more plainly in the words of the holy Spirit than what has been shown and proved by me in this passage from Paul's words.

Judgment of damnation is not the one cause defined.

But so that I may answer the proposed question clearly and perspicuously, it was said above: the cause of damnation on account of which a person is damned is in man and from man, not in God nor either from God. But it would damn no one except that the justice of God, of Christ the just Judge, and its execution assent to it. <125> Therefore damnation itself cannot be defined as the one and only cause, which revolves around two, namely, God condemning, and the person who is condemned by God.

Dr. Beza:
Again I ask whether the cause of damnation emanates from Christ in the same way as the cause of salvation does?

Dr. Jakob:

WHETHER THE CAUSE OF DAMNATION EMANATES FROM CHRIST IN THE SAME MANNER AS THE CAUSE OF SALVATION.

I answer: no, not at all. For even though the nature of the powers in God is the same, if God were being considered in the way of his nature, just as the power of vivification proceeds from him, thus also the power of judgment proceeds from the same one (for the same God is just and merciful, who saves and damns), but this notwithstanding, when it comes to the consideration of the judging and saving of man, the cause of these effects is by far a rather different matter. For the cause of divine judgment, which he exercises in men to be judged and condemned, and on account of which he damns people, does not flow forth from God like salvation does in those to be saved.

For God is not the cause of unbelief, on account of which people are condemned, nor does unbelief flow forth from God, but rather from the Devil, and from the perverted will of man.

When however people are saved, the cause of this salvation is not only the mercy of God, but also of faith as an instrumental cause, which is itself also a gift of God, and flows forth from God and his holy Spirit. For this reason there is no cause of salvation originating in man, but the cause of damnation is in man and originates in man.

Dr. Beza:
You move across from Christ to God, though Christ is our salvation and life, from whom they emanate. Here has been placed our one sole cause of salvation. <126> But the one sole efficient cause of damnation is our unbelief. For this reason we say that unbelief damns us, not Christ, or the Lord's Supper when it is received.

God and Christ ought to be considered in different ways. Since our salvation and life has been placed in Christ's merit alone, these things emanate thence into us, and they vivify us and save us.

Dr. Jakob:

OUR SALVATION EMANATES FROM CHRIST ALONE.

It is true that I put God in place of the word "Christ," but the meaning is exactly the same. Though in fact I said that our salvation emanates from God's mercy, I embraced and included Christ with the word mercy, since outside of Christ, who is true God, God is merciful and gracious to no one. Everything I said about God, then, is said about Christ, that our entire salvation emanates from his mercy and merit.

IN WHAT WAY UNBELIEF IS THE EFFICIENT CAUSE OF DAMNATION.

But even though unbelief is also called the efficient cause of damnation, since instrumental causes are also numbered among efficient ones, nevertheless Christ's justice is not excluded from the cause of damnation on this account. For Christ is the one who judges and condemns.

So also is faith the instrumental cause, and for this reason effects salvation and life in those believing to be saved. But that we should say this, that faith also is the efficient cause of our salvation, does not at all stand in the way of us ascribing the entire cause of our salvation to the merit of Christ alone. For Christ not only did away with all of our sins by his obedience, passion and death, but also through the holy Spirit works faith in the elect, by which they take hold of Christ together with his merit and are saved. Thus at the same time Christ is the chief efficient cause and faith the instrumental. The work is Christ's alone, not ours, such that all praise for salvation and life is attributed to him alone. As it is written, Your destruction is from you, O Israel, but your salvation is in me (Hosea 13[:4]).

<127>

TWO CAUSES RUN TOGETHER IN THE SALVATION AND DAMNATION OF MEN.

From this it is clear that it there exists not only one cause in men being saved or damned, but two always run together as has been said. Christ is the one who saves, as the efficient cause; faith is what saves as the instrumental cause with respect to man. So Christ is the one who judges and condemns, by reason of his justice, and unbelief also condemns, as the efficient instrumental cause, on account of which a person is condemned. For instrumental causes are also numbered among the efficient ones.

GOD CONDEMNS NO ONE BY MEANS OF HIS ABSOLUTE JUSTICE.

So faith is the instrumental cause of salvation, since God saves no one by means of his absolute mercy, but rather all are saved, as many as are saved, only through faith. So also Christ's absolute justice condemns no one, otherwise the entire world would have been condemned. Rather, the world is condemned on account of unbelief, which is the efficient cause with respect to man (John 3[:18]; Mark 16[:16]).

So also when the Gospel is preached (which is the power of God for salvation) not one but many causes run together. The chief is God's power, as the efficient cause of our salvation; the instrumental with respect to Christ is preaching, or the ministry the uttered word; with respect to men, it is the hearing of the preached word, through which God works faith according to what Paul says: Faith comes through hearing, hearing through the word of God (Romans 10[:17]).

So in the Lord's Supper are Christ's body and blood as food and drink for eternal life, with reference to the efficient cause of each, namely, salvation and judgment. The instrumental with respect to Christ is the word and the elements of the consecrated bread and wine; with respect to worthy or unworthy persons it is the person's mouth by which people are bidden by Christ to eat and drink the offered bread and cup. In this action Christ works either life or judgment relative to the condition of each man communing with this bread and cup.

<128>

Dr. Beza:

Can your Reverence say that unbelief is the instrumental cause of damnation? Just as faith is the instrumental cause of salvation, so also unbelief of judgment and damnation?

Dr. Jakob:

FAITH AND UNBELIEF THE INSTRUMENTAL CAUSES OF SALVATION AND DAMNATION.

Yes indeed, since the nature of the inverses is the same. For just as without faith no one is saved, so also unless unbelief were in those to be damned, no one would be damned.

Dr. Beza:

WHAT AN EFFICIENT CAUSE IS ACCORDING TO BEZA.

An efficient cause is really one that has an effect by itself [καθ' αὐτό], in itself and through itself, and possesses the power in itself that the effect naturally follows it. But faith is not this sort of cause. Therefore it is not an efficient cause.

At this point Antoine de La Faye showed Dr. Beza from Aristotle about instrumental causes, lest he contend longer about them with Dr. Jakob, that they also are numbered among efficient causes.

Dr. Jakob:

DISTINCTION BETWEEN EFFICIENT CAUSES.

The nature of efficient causes is not the same. For some are chief and efficient in themselves, by themselves [καθ' αὐτό], and some are instrumental. So God is an efficient cause by himself [καθ' αὐτό] and absolutely, and needed no instrument for the creation of all creatures. Now in the creation of man he employs instruments, Male and Female. But faith is not of the causes by themselves [καθ' αὐτό] effecting salvation, but only, as we said, an instrumental one, which cannot deliver salvation without Christ as the efficient cause.

<129>

WHAT CAUSES RUN TOGETHER IN THE CONVERSION OF MAN.

Thus it is written: and they will all be taught by God (John 6[:45]; Isaiah 48[54:13]). But this does not at all keep ministers of the word from also being counted among the efficient causes, not by themselves [καθ᾽ αὑτό] but instrumental, through whom the first and chief cause God converts men, who could convert them also without their ministry and voice.

GOD'S POWER NOT TO BE SEPARATED FROM THE SPOKEN WORD.

God's power ought not to be separated from the preached word of the Gospel, on account of which the spoken word, whether written or preached, is called by Paul the power of God. Whoever hears this hears not an empty sound but hears God's power.

But when faith and unbelief are compared together, whence they arise, without which no one is saved or damned, it is clear that their nature, while not the same, is not very different at all. For faith is God's gift and work, but unbelief in man is the Devil's work. And just as through faith, which is God's work in us, we are saved, so also through unbelief, which is the Devil's work, are we damned. But we are not saved on account of faith in the same way we are damned on account of unbelief. For unbelief merits damnation, but Faith is God's gift in us in such a way that it does not itself merit eternal life like a work, since it is incomplete, and no one believes as strongly (as he is thought to believe), but rather faith takes hold of Christ's merit, which is attributed to the obedience of Christ alone.

Dr. Beza:
I say that Christ, being not received but rejected, damns the impious. For this reason I say that unbelief alone is the efficient cause of damnation of the impious, not Christ.

Dr. Jakob:

I ask, then, Reverend Dr. Beza, whether the impious damn themselves?

<130>

Dr. Beza:
The impious give God a reason to damn them. Christ pronounces the sentence.

Dr. Jakob:

IN WHAT WAY CHRIST CONDEMNS.

I ask again, whether Christ only pronounces the sentence?

Dr. Beza:
Christ not only pronounces the sentence, but also brings it against the impious.

Dr. Jakob:

THE TWO CAUSES RUNNING TOGETHER IN JUDGMENT.

What I said therefore remains: judgment, which the impious eat, must be defined by not only one cause but two, namely, the unbelief of man and the justice of Christ, which run together in this judgment and condemnation.

CHRIST THE EXECUTOR OF JUSTICE. CHRIST THE EFFICIENT CAUSE OF JUDGMENT.

And the Corinthians found out that Christ not only pronounced and brought the sentence, but also executed justice by his judging work, that is, by punishing. This is certainly something other than just pronouncing and bringing a sentence. For this reason, since judgment is the execution of justice, which was handed over to Christ by the Father, Christ is and remains the efficient cause of it.

NO ONE IS SAVED OR DAMNED BY THE ABSOLUTE MERCY OR JUSTICE OF GOD. HOW THE CAUSE OF JUDGMENT AND SALVATION EXISTS IN MEN.

But since Christ saves no one by his absolute mercy nor damns them by his absolute justice, I say undauntedly that he is the cause of salvation in pious men as he is the cause of judgment in impious men. But with this distinction or this difference in place: that faith does not originate from men, or their strength, but from God, as God's gift, which operates by virtue of the holy Spirit through the preached word, but unbelief is from the Devil.

<131>

This is the efficient cause of damnation, as you yourself affirm in your Theses and in this conference, and do not in the least deny, and not this alone, as was said a little while ago. For unless Christ's justice and the execution of it were happening, neither the Devil nor impious people would be condemned, and they would never damn themselves if it were placed in their power.

Dr. Beza:
Christ decreed and pronounced sentence against the damned, not on account of receiving his body and blood but rather on account of scorning his body and blood.

Dr. Jakob:

CHRIST IS THE EXECUTOR OF GOD'S JUSTICE IN THE IMPIOUS.

Christ did not only decree and pronounce the sentence of judgment and damnation against the impious, but also executed his decree and pronounced sentence, without which execution, the decreed and pronounced sentence would be a flash in a pan.[14] Nor in fact will Devils cast themselves down or the damned, but God's

---

14 *Fulgur ex pelvi*: a proverb from Greek ἀστραπὴ ἐκ πυέλον. The sense is flash without real danger—"paper tiger" probably gets closer to this in English idiom today than "flash in the pan." Erasmus explains it in his *Adagia* 2.7.90: "A flash in the pan. Of the empty threats of those who have no power to harm. The flash which is produced, by some sort of imitation of lightning, by the oscillation of polished vessels or from water, has no power to damage and frightens only children. In our own day too there are mirrors which imitate a flash of lightning when oscillated in the sun; but that is not the true lighting, which, as Pliny says, 'strikes mountains and seas.' The proverb is listed by Diogenianus. It is also alluded to by Augustine, or the author whoever he was of the *De quinque heresibus*: 'Let us not be recalled by a crowd of enemies or the appearance of armed men, nor frightened by the glitter of weapons as though made of glass.' Though I think we should read *vitra*, 'Weapons that glitter like glass.'" (*Collected Works of Erasmus: Adages II vii 1 to III iii 100*, trans. and annot. By R.A.B. Mynors, Toronto: U of Toronto P, 1974–.)

justice will cast down both the Devils themselves and men. His command extends by reason of his justice all the way to hell, and not only his mercy to the heavens.

Dr. Beza:
Faith is not salvation, but rather the thing that takes hold of salvation, which is Christ. Thus Christ determines and pronounces sentence, but discovers the cause of judgment outside himself in the impious man, namely unbelief. For this reason he is not the cause of judgment or damnation, but the man is himself the sole and only efficient cause of this judgment.

Dr. Jakob:
It has now been said several times that faith is not the cause <132> of salvation in the same way that unbelief is of judgment. Rather, from Dr. Beza's argument, the contrary plainly follows, that he himself intends to prove.

INVERSE OF DR. BEZA'S ARGUMENT.

For just as faith is not itself salvation, but rather Christ is salvation, of whom faith takes hold, so unbelief is not itself judgment, but rather that which rejects Christ as savior, and rather takes hold of and motivates the judge, who is Christ, who judges the impious on account of unbelief. Therefore just as faith would never save without Christ, so unbelief would never damn without Christ. Since the father (as Christ himself says) judges no one (John 5[:22]), that is, outside of Christ, and without Christ God the father judges no one, but rather he has given judgment to the son *since he is the son of man.*

And that your Reverence may understand me correctly, since the disagreement about efficient and instrumental causes pertains to Philosophy, which few of our audience understand, let us speak about the thing itself and lay aside the dispute over the terms of the art, that is, over causes efficient by themselves [καθ' αὐτό] and efficient instrumentally.

HOW GOD SAVES AND DAMNS PEOPLE. CONDITION OF MAN FOR LIFE AND SALVATION.

For I say openly: God is the cause of neither the sin of unbelief nor damnation. For just as God does not desire sins (Ezekiel 18[:32]), so also does he not desire death. But he saves man not by his absolute will but rather he saves man disposed[15] for salvation. So also does he condemn no one by his absolute will but rather the one disposed for damnation. The condition[16] for salvation requires faith in man, which renders man fit for receiving salvation, which is wholly laid up in Christ. For without faith, says the Apostle, it is impossible to please God (Hebrews 11[:6]). And again, The righteous will live by faith (Hebrews 2 [10:38; Habakkuk 2:4]).

CONDITION OF MAN FOR DAMNATION.

The impious man also is so disposed for damnation through unbelief. For no one is damned except he be an unbeliever.

DISTINCTION BETWEEN THE CONDITION FOR LIFE AND DEATH WITH RESPECT TO GOD.

But the distinction appears in this, that Christ is not only salvation but is himself also the one who disposes man for receiving salvation, and works faith in him through the hearing of the Gospel. But in the impious he does not work unbelief, which is a work <133> of the Devil, which he discovers in the impious. Since they are and remain those who scorn God's word, and do not wish to learn from the father who speaks through the son, through the Apostles, through genuine ministers, for this reason he judges them as they remain and persevere in their unbelief, that is, not only does he decide and pronounce sentence, but also effectively executes it in them.

---

15 *dispositus*
16 *dispositio*

Dr. Beza:

The condition of faith and unbelief nevertheless differ in their nature. For faith indeed disposes a man, but not that on account of it man is saved but rather such that he is able to receive Christ who is salvation. But unbelief disposes man to damnation in such a way that it compels God to condemn him without respect to anything else. This happens not because he receives Christ but because he despises and scorns him.

ANALOGY OF A MAN SPEAKING AN UNKNOWN TONGUE.

In a similar way I hear someone speaking to me, but since he speaks German, I do not understand. This is just as if I were not hearing him and he were not speaking to me. Nay rather, the devils hear Christ and they understand him, but nevertheless do not receive his word, since they do not believe. But faith requires something more than merely hearing the preached word. For we are only talking about the faith of the elect which alone saves, which we not only receives the sound but receives the very thing expressed by the sound, and applies to itself the universal promises promised about grace in Christ.

Concerning this hearing Paul speaks in Romans chapter 10 where he says that faith is from the word of God. This is understood only about the hearing of the faithful, who not only receive the external sound but also understand, receive, and apply to themselves the thing expressed by the sound.

<134>

Dr. Jakob:

Unbelief damns no one simply and by itself, just as faith saves no one by itself and simply. Rather, just as faith saves only with respect to Christ, whose merit is applied to man through faith, so also unbelief damns with respect to Christ, whose merit he does not receive nor apply to himself. But he cannot push the judge away, which he receives by mouth in the Lord's Supper no less than the pious and faithful man.

DISTORTION OF PAUL'S WORDS, ROMANS 10.

This explanation of Paul's words is astonishing, though, in which your Reverence says that Paul is speaking only about the hearing of the faithful, since Paul teaches in this passage not how the faithful hear but rather how they become faithful from being unfaithful, namely through hearing the word of God. He is in fact speaking about the external hearing of the word, which is common to the faithful and unfaithful, just as he also speaks about external preaching, that is the voiced word, which is common to the pious and impious, faithful and unfaithful. How (he says) will they believe about what they have not heard? But how will they hear without someone preaching (Romans 10[:14])? All these words speak about external preaching and external hearing, which Dr. Beza refers to internal, and separates from the external, as if the elect hear a word other than that which the damned hear.

INVERSION OF THE ARGUMENT FROM THE ANALOGY OF THE PREACHED WORD TO THE LORD'S SUPPER.

But this passage is rightly suited to the explanation of Paul's words which we produced from 1 Corinthians 10: The bread which we break is a communication of the body of Christ. For in the same way that the power of God is offered through the externally preached word, equally for salvation for the believer and for judgment for the unbeliever, so through the bread of the Lord's Supper is offered Christ's body for all partaking in the Lord's Supper, either for salvation or for judgment. And just as the ears of unfaithful hearers do not receive only the sound of the preached word, but rather the thing brought up by the preached word, namely, plainly the same word which the ears of the pious receive, not separated from the power, so also the impious partaking in the Supper receive Christ's body *by their own mouth*, which the pious receive *by their own mouth*.

<135>

For just as the external word, that is the preaching and reading of God's word, is the organ through which God is made known in the minds of men, so the bread and wine of the Lord's Supper is the organ through which Christ communicates his own body and blood, either for the strengthening of our faith or for judgment.

But the holy Spirit plainly shows the reason that this does not convert the hearts of all people and that this power of the word does not work salvation in all people.

Rᴇᴀsᴏɴs ᴡʜʏ ɴᴏᴛ ᴀʟʟ ᴀʀᴇ ᴄᴏɴᴠᴇʀᴛᴇᴅ ᴛᴏ ꜰᴀɪᴛʜ ɪɴ Cʜʀɪsᴛ.

For certain people really are unwilling to hear, as it is written: How often I wished to gather your children as a Hen her chicks, *but you were unwilling* (Matthew 23[:37]). Acts 7[:57], They covered their ears lest they hear God's word from Stephan's mouth. Since these ones despise the organ of the holy Spirit, through which the holy Spirit works faith, for this reason they are never converted, but rather condemned. And such people are they who walk outside God's Church in the blindness of their mind.

Then there are impious people in the very gathering of the Church, and are even members of the Church by an external profession of faith, who indeed hear the word of the Gospel preached, but carelessly, because they do not happen to be eager to learn from the father (John 6[:46]). Therefore it is just as if they were not hearing, and for this reason it does not disclose to them its virtue for conversion, but for judgment. Just as Christ says, The words which I have spoken to them will judge them on the last day (John 12[:48]).

Dr. Beza:
Paul begins in this passage from faith; it is therefore not about external preaching alone. For God's word is able to be heard such that only the sound of it is heard, without the thing expressed by the sound, just as if someone speaks to a person in an unknown language. In the same way the impious indeed hear the preached word but do not receive the thing itself.

In the same way also the Sacraments have an external thing, bread and wine, and the impious apply these to themselves, but the body and blood of Christ which are signified by these things they do not receive, since they lack faith.

<136>

Dr. Jakob:

ROMANS 10, PAUL SPEAKS ABOUT THE EXTERNAL HEARING OF THE WORD.

Reverend Dr. Beza, Paul does not begin from faith, but rather from the preached word, and proceeds from the effect to the cause, which precedes faith. For the preaching of the word as cause precedes faith as effect, and not faith preaching. And the entire context of this passage indicates that Paul is speaking about the external hearing of the word. They are in fact correlated, preaching and hearing. How will they hear, he says, if they will not preach? And for this reason Paul recalls the Romans to the hearing of the external word. You should not say in your heart (he says), who will ascend into heaven? The word is near, in *your mouth and in your heart*. Do you hear the word is *in your mouth*? And also the same and not another word *in your heart*? For this reason Paul does not begin from faith, but rather from the external preaching of the word of the Gospel, and he says that they cannot believe unless the word be preached to them *prior*.

DISTINCTION OF JUDGMENT.

But even if they are damned who have not heard and not believed, nevertheless they who have heard but not believed are damned the more powerfully and their damnation is greater than those who have not heard, according to the word of Christ: If I had not come and spoken to them, they would not have sin (John 15[:22]). Thus in the Lord's Supper, even though those who despise the Sacrament are also judged, that they do not use it, nevertheless they are damned the more powerfully and their judgment is greater who receive the Sacrament, that is, not merely a sign but rather also the thing signi-fied, unworthily. Paul says about these that they eat judgment, since they do not discern the body of the Lord. All these things are so plain and clear that it is a wonder that a Christian person can be in doubt about them, much less argue against them.

Dr. Beza:

CONFIRMATION OF DR. BEZA, THAT CHRIST'S BODY IS NOT RECEIVED BY MOUTH.

The testimonies of Scripture that clearly confirm that Christ's body is not received nor able to be received by mouth are countless. Since it is now in heaven and not on <137> earth, just as we pray, Our father who art in heaven, to whom Christ ascended in his own body (Mark 16[:19]). And again, I go to prepare a place for you (John 14[:3]); I am leaving the world behind (John 16[:28]); We are on journey from the Lord (2 Corinthians 5[:7]); I desire to die and to be with Christ (Philippians 1[:23]); Seek things above, where Christ is at the right hand of the Father (Colossians 3[:1]); He will come in the clouds (Acts 1[:11]); and there are very many others like these. They all confirm together that Christ's body is in heaven, not on earth, and for this reason is not in the place where the bread is, nor received by the external mouth, but just by faith. Through the bread his body is presented just TO THE MIND, not to the body.

Moreover Paul's words, Who will ascend into heaven, etc., are words of doubt; Paul condemns this doubt. For he does not want us to rise up into heaven without a mediator. And we do not simply deny, that something cannot be understood from external hearing, but it is nevertheless certain that Paul is speaking about an interior hearing.

Dr. Jakob:

TWOFOLD CONSIDERATION OF CHRIST'S BODY.

As far as the testimonies of Scripture brought up by Dr. Beza are concerned, by which he attempts to show that Christ is in heaven in his Father's presence such that he is at the same time not present on earth with us, I answer that the alleged Testimonies are poorly suited to this Sacrament. For Christ is indeed in heaven, in his own body, in his Father's presence, a fact impossible to be denied, but Dr. Beza adds *and not on earth*, which we speak against. Indeed, we have no fewer plain testimonies about his presence on earth: I am with you always; Where two or three, etc. He ascended above all the heavens, such that he might fill up all things. For this reason even though Christ is one, and not two, one in heaven and the other on earth, nevertheless the consideration of his body, or his humanity, is twofold. On the one hand, in so far as the body is true and essential, it is similar to our bodies, with the exception of sin, and it retains the essential properties of a true body, and never lays them aside.

IN WHAT WAY CHRIST'S BODY IN HEAVEN AND NOT ON EARTH.

It is in this way that Christ's body is considered to be only <138> in heaven now, that is, in the state of another age, with God the father, and not on earth.

IN WHAT WAY CHRIST'S BODY CAN BE AT THE SAME TIME IN HEAVEN AND ON EARTH. CHRIST'S BODY SITUATED ON ITS PROPER THRONE OF DEITY.

But just as when we pray, Our father who are in heaven, the Father is not in heaven in such a way that he is not present on earth, nor is said to be. He is in fact also with us on earth, who fills heaven and earth (Jeremiah 23[:24]). So also Christ is not in heaven in the property of his own body, or as Augustine says, on account of the mode of a true body, such that he is not also able to be on earth with us in another mode with his own body, since his body has been translated to and situated upon his proper throne of divinity (which is not a place, nor in a place). Heaven, says the Lord (Isaiah 66[:1]), is my seat and earth the footstool of my feet. Upon this throne have none of the saints or angels been situated, but to the son of man Christ alone has it been appointed: Sit at my right hand (Psalm 110[:1]; Hebrews 1[:13]). How then would he not have a mode on that throne by which he could also be present to us on earth?

IN WHAT WAY PASSAGES OF SCRIPTURE TO BE UNDERSTOOD REGARDING THE ABSENCE OF CHRIST ON EARTH.

For this reason all the testimonies of holy Scripture that talk about Christ's absence on earth at the same time speak about Christ and ought to be understood *not simply* as if he is in no way present, but *what* exactly we consider and understand the essence of this true body, or property in the body, to be, without disregarding the nature of a body as such.

But nothing is taken away from Christ's majesty by these things, by which majesty he is situated on his proper throne of divine majesty, and is *wholly* present also on earth in word and Sacrament, *wholly* present to his Church, God and man, in his Divinity and humanity, concerning which, more in its own place.

Concerning Paul's words, Do not say in your heart, they do especially belong to a doubting person who blindly searches for the path of salvation. Nevertheless it is certain that by these words Paul calls people *to an external hearing of the external word*, as to the organ and instrument of the holy Spirit, through which people may come to a knowledge of Christ.

And that he understands an external hearing *only*, and not an internal hearing, [139] the words themselves expressly teach. For since the inner hearing is faith itself, of the effect of faith, it is clear that Paul speaks not about the internal hearing, since he teaches that the faith is given through *the hearing of the word*, which people lack before they hear, and the Lord works this faith through the preached word in hearers.

My argument stands unmoved then: in the same way that a person's ears are an organ and instrument through which they receive the eternal word of God in the external hearing of the preached word, which is actually the power of God for the salvation of everyone who believes, on account of which the external word also is and is called the power of God, so also in the Lord's Supper a person's external mouth is an organ and instrument with respect to the person, through which Christ's body is, with the bread or through the bread (for you avoid the term *in*, on account of the fear of opinion about local inclusion of Christ's body in the bread) presented, delivered, and also received orally, not only *to the mind*, but also *to the mouth*.

CHRIST'S BODY IS OFFERED AND DELIVERED THROUGH THE BREAD OF THE LORD'S SUPPER TO THE MOUTH AND THE MIND TOGETHER AT THE SAME TIME.

For just as *the mind* regards the word of promise through faith, This is my body, which is given for you, by which word Christ's body is offered and delivered *to the mind*, so the mouth of the body and the eyes regard the bread which is the communication of Christ's body, that is, the organ and instrument with respect to God, ordained by Christ for sacramental reception of his own body.

THE IMPIOUS ALSO RECEIVE WHOLE SACRAMENTS.

For this reason it is manifestly false to say that the Sacrament which is for the pious is, for the impious, only bread and wine. For our unbelief does not make faith in God void, and the substance of Sacraments does not depend on our worthiness or faith, but only on the word instituting the Sacrament. A person's unbelief cannot change this, if the institution and use instituted by Christ should be preserved.

PARABLE OF THE SEED (MATTHEW 13).

Christ's parable is known, of the man sowing good seed, which nevertheless only bears fruit in the fourth part. There is not another seed which falls on the road, upon the rock, and among the thorns, but the very seed which brings forth fruit in good soil. The strength of the seed is one and the same in all terrains, but it does not bear fruit in all of them.

<140>

THE PREACHED WORD PENETRATES TO THE HEARTS OF THE IMPIOUS.

It is the same way also with word preached in the ears and hearts of the pious and the impious, retaining the same power in itself everywhere, but not bringing forth fruit in all.

For the heard word penetrates not only ears but also the hearts of the impious, and renders them without excuse before God. Roused by the power of this word, they sometimes think about the emendation of their life, but at length return to their vomit, since Satan snatches the word from their heart, and then compels them to wickedness and vices (John 12[:31]; 15[:6–7]; Luke 8[:12]; Matthew 13[:19]).

From this it is understood that Paul's words agree with Christ's, and that they are both talking only about the external hearing of the word, which is common to the pious and the impious. But there is one and the same word in the ears of the pious and the impious.

Dr. Beza:

I myself have distinguished between the internal hearing and the external hearing of the word. For we need not only to be taught through the external word, but also internally, just as it is written in John 6[:45], And they will all be taught by God. Otherwise the exterior teaching will be of no profit at all. And Christ speaks in the parable of the seed about general faith. For faith has its kernels. Just as a fetus in a woman's uterus is formed first from the conceived seed, so also faith at the beginning of the hearing of the word is an incomplete fetus, which has its own increases and does not come into its own perfection entirely, since the word does not proceed among all. Just as the Devils also have faith, as James says [2:19], and tremble; so also their faith is not true faith, among whom are the seed that falls on the path, upon the rock, and among the thorns.

Dr. Jakob:

GOD'S LIVING WORD IN THE HEART OF THE IMPIOUS.

Reverend Dr. Beza, You were asked about the word, you answer about faith. I say in fact, and have proved clearly, that the word of God is true, living, and vivific, and remains with its own nature not only in <141> the ears, but also in the heart of the person *who does not believe*, even though it does not vivify the impious. For this was asked: whether the word which the impious hears and does not believe, and which penetrates into his heart, is merely *sound*, or in fact the true, living word of God itself, which bears fruit in the hearts of the pious, but bears no fruit in the impious. This is what you had to respond to, but you are arguing about faith and its increase, about general faith, the faith of devils, all of which has been placed outside of controversy.

Dr. Beza:
No one denies that.

Dr. Jakob:
Then why does your Reverence contend that it is not the word of God but a stark sound in the ears of the impious? And he goes on about the twofold word, the internal and external, when there is one word of God in the hearts of the pious and the impious.

HOW ALL PEOPLE BECOME TAUGHT BY GOD, AND ARE TAUGHT.

Then even though it is true that everyone ought to be taught by God, and not only externally, but even on the inside as well, nevertheless this also is true, that God does not teach on the inside except he do so through the external word, unless we should wish people to leave the word behind for hidden revelations, which is enthusiasm. For this reason I ask your Reverence whether the same word is in the ears and heart of the impious when it is preached as there is in the ears and heart of the pious? I want this a Categorical answer to this.

Dr. Beza:
The question is whether it is received by the impious.

Dr. Jakob:
It needs to be established first whether the word is the same, before we argue about reception. Once there has been an answer to this question, then the second question will also be answered, whether or not it is received by the impious. For there are two distinct <142> questions, the one about the word which is heard by the impious, whether it is the same and entirely true word of God as the word the pious hear. But the other is whether and how the pious and the impious receive it.

To each question we openly respond that one and the same true word of God exists in both, the pious and the impious, and that it is not only equally received in the ears by both but also penetrates into the heart. And thence from the argument which Dr. Beza brought up, I argue the inverse for the Sacrament of the Eucharist in this way:

One and the same body of Christ is presented and delivered by the bread of the Sacrament to the mouth of the pious and the impious in the use of the Supper, and both also receive it by mouth, just as has been clearly proved by the words of Christ's Testament, and Paul's two testimonies.

For just as the word is received into the heart through the ears, and pinches the heart of the impious and rouses them to some love of truth and their own salvation, but since they indulge in pleasures or are secure, it yields them not salvation but Judgment, so also they receive by mouth the whole Sacrament, not merely bread but the body of Christ also offered with the bread, and it yields them judgment and not salvation and life.

Dr. Beza:

Whether the heard word descends into the heart.

The word of God or rather the sound of the word does not go any farther in the impious than into the ears. It does not descend to their heart. If they were otherwise to receive it in their heart, they would also believe.

At this point Dr. Lucas Osiander, sitting by Dr. Jakob, recited Christ's words from the Gospel of Matthew (13[:19]) and Luke (8[:12]): The one who hears the proclamation of the kingdom and does not understand it, the evil one comes and snatches what *has been sown in his heart*. And again Luke: The ones along the path are they who hear, and then the Devil comes and takes away the word *from their heart*, lest they believe and be saved.

<143>

Dr. Jakob:

Here your Reverence sees and hears, my dear Beza, that the word of the kingdom, namely that by which people are led to the kingdom of God, has been sown not only in ears but also in *the heart*, and that the Devil takes it away from *the heart* of the impious, lest they believe and be saved. Therefore the heart can receive the word and nevertheless not believe.

Dr. Beza:

I concede that whole Sacraments are offered not only to the pious but also to the impious, but the whole are not received by the impious, but merely the external signs, and they are judged and condemned. Just as a sick man listening to Medicine being prepared for him, which is offered to him as much as possible, if nevertheless he either does not take it or immediately rejects it, the Medicine is of no profit to him at all, but he dies in his sickness. So also Christ's body is offered in fact with the bread to the impious, but so long as they do not receive it in true faith, but despise and reject it, they take judgment for themselves and die spiritually.

Dr. Jakob:

We swore at the beginning that there is between us no conflict or controversy about the eating and reception that is through faith, to which you are constantly running back. We agreed on this from both sides already from the point the dispute arose. Therefore since the impious do not possess true faith, who is there who would not see that they do not receive Christ's body through faith? In the same way we, from our side, also always reject and condemn Capernaitic eating or carnage of Christ's body.

THE EATING OF FAITH PRECEDES SACRAMENTAL EATING OF CHRIST'S BODY.

But the question and controversy is over the third mode of eating Christ's body, namely, the Sacramental mode, which happens by mouth in the use of the Lord's Supper, which we have proved plainly from Christ's words of institution and Paul's words, and have put on display. Here nothing is said either about true faith or temporary, but merely about the bread which is the body *of Christ,* <144> as the words of Christ sound, or as the Apostle says, a communication of Christ's body. And Christ bids us eat, which does not mean to believe, but to receive by mouth. Here also Dr. Beza was supposed to answer and show that a third such mode of sacramental eating has not been expressed in Christ's words or Paul's. This he never has done, and he cannot. And so as often as it is urged about this third eating of Christ's body, which is sacramental, since he does not dare affirm that the bread alone is being eaten, he always escapes to the eating which is by faith, although there is no question about this. For all are commanded to be faithful and believing, and to eat Christ's body through faith, before approaching the Sacrament and receiving it. For indeed eating Christ's body through faith is nothing other than believing that Christ gave his body over to death and poured out his blood for our sins. Whoever does not believe this truly, we command to abstain from the Lord's Supper. Otherwise he would communicate to his judgment, if he should receive the Lord's body without faith with the bread, which is a communication of the body of Christ. This communication is a mystery, which is not seen or understood, but believed and discerned spiritually, either for consolation and life, or for judgment. Concerning this communication, Beza does not answer at all categorically in this conference.

ANALOGY OF THE OFFERED MEDICINE.

Next, I accept the analogy of the Medicine offered to the sick man. But I have never heard of a medicine that keeps someone from death which is not taken. But Paul plainly says that people of this kind *eat* judgment for themselves. He does not say they take it or scorn or reject, but that *they do not discern* the body of the Lord, which according to the express words of Christ and Paul, they take in the Sacrament.

INVERSION OF BEZA'S ARGUMENT TAKEN FROM THE ANALOGY OF BODY'S MEDICINE.

This analogy can therefore be applied in another way and very suitably to the proposed business. Namely, in the same way that medicine is delivered sometimes to a sick man by a Doctor, <145> which the sick man does not scorn but takes, but on account of the weakness of his stomach and constitution he cannot make use of its power, and what kills the person is the medicine that was delivered and taken for the recovery of health. But it kills him, not because it brings death through itself, but on account of the bad condition of the body which is in the person. Nor is the doctor accused on this charge afterward, that he killed a person of this kind, for doctors are allowed to go unpunished when they kill, not people, but sick people. So Christ's body, delivered to and taken with the bread by a person of bad condition, on account of unbelief and impiety, kills the person spiritually, not by its own fault, since the flesh is vivific and the body is vivific, but rather by the fault of the one taking it, since he impious and profane. For this reason it yields him judgment, what brings others life and consolation.

After this fashion it can happen that two people take one and the same medicine, prepared from one and the same mass by a drug-maker, under the exact same Prescription written by a Doctor. And when each of them takes it, one escapes with his health, but the other dies immediately after taking the Medicine. So in the Lord's Supper does one take, do a thousand take it, this one as much as that, good men take it and evil men, nevertheless the outcome is *unequal*, and though eaten he is not diminished, as the holy ancient saying goes. [17]

CONCERNING CHRIST'S ASCENSION TO THE FATHER. WHETHER CHRIST'S ASCENSION TO THE FATHER IS LOCAL.

But since your Reverence objects to me so often with Christ's local ascension, and pushes against this third mode of eating which the Fathers call sacramental with his local dwelling in heaven, I ask therefore whether the ascension to God the father was local.

Dr. Beza:
I do not doubt it.

Dr. Jakob:
How great a journey was it then, and how many miles had to be completed by him, <146> until he arrived to his father to whom he ascended?

17 These lines come from the *Lauda Sion Salvatorem* from the Corpus Christi sequence (written by Thomas Aquinas around 1264).

Dr. Beza:
I have not measured it. The Lord knows.

Dr. Jakob:
I will point out for all the audience to see that what is to be understood cannot be a local ascension. For we read it written in John
chapter 14 that Christ said to Philip, Do you not believe that I am in
the father and the father is in me? Philip, the one who sees me sees
my father also (John 14[:7]). These clear words of Christ admit no
interpretation and openly testify that the father was not only with
Christ, *but was in Christ*, while he was still dwelling on earth. What
need was there, therefore, of a local ascension for him to go to his
father, according to your opinion? At this point I want you to answer
me Categorically.

Dr. Beza:
Christ intended to say that he was one with the father by reason
of his divinity. For he acts from the nature of divinity in which are
distinguished persons, not two essences. Therefore Christ speaks
about the Word [λόγος] incarnate, or the incarnate person, which
Philip was seeing. Therefore it must be understood that he only
fulfilled what he had said to Philip AT HIS DEPARTURE. And the
faith of the Centurion suffices for us.

Dr. Jakob:
I am asking about presence, whether the father was present with
Christ on earth, while he was saying these words. Answer now. For
the essence cannot be separated from the person. If the essence of
Divinity is present, therefore the person also is present, a fact that
can never be mistaken. And you are always saying, The father is in
the highest heavens <147> which are understood by the name the right
hand of God.

Dr. Beza:
The Father was not present to Christ on earth in the way that
Christ is in glory.

Dr. Jakob:

Here there is no mention of glory or humility, but his words rather speak simply about the presence of the Father in Christ. The father, says Christ, *is in me*, and I am in the father. The question is only about this presence, not about glory.

Dr. Beza:

The Father and the Son are one God. But Christ in this passage is not talking simply about himself as the Word [λόγος], that is, in the way of Divinity. But since he uses the vocabulary of seeing, for this reason he bids Philip see and regard him as a man, who is nevertheless true God, whom we no longer see now.

Dr. Jakob:

How Philip saw the Son of God.

The question is not really about seeing the Son of God in the way that Philip saw him. For it is outside of controversy that the son of God is not seen by external eyes like the body is seen. And for this reason it is certain that Philip did not see Christ the Son of God in the property of his divine essence, but in so far as he was made visible man.

And for this reason this answer as the prior ones about the sense of Christ's words, accomplishes nothing for the proposed question. For it is asked regarding presence, whether the father was present truly on earth, substantially, and essentially in Christ, when Christ was saying these words. From here it will be clearly established whether Christ's words should be understood regarding a local ascension, of which Christ had need *until* he should go to his father.

<148>

The visible ascension of Christ to heaven, historical.

For as far as the truth of Christ's visible ascension into heaven is concerned, the history of Acts chapter 1 is known to all, that Christ was raised from earth in his own body and lifted to the visible heavens. No sane person can deny that this local ascension took place.

But here is the question: did Christ need the local ascension to go to the Father, and was he not with the father before the local ascension into heaven, and could he not go to the father without it? This, I say, is the question, to which there should have been a Categorical answer, as has now been requested many times.

Dr. Beza:
We do not say that he needed such an ascension to go to the Father, but rather that he went to his heavenly glory which belongs to a place distant from earth IN LOCATION AND NATURE.

Dr. Jakob:

CHRIST ENTERED INTO HIS GLORY THROUGH THE RESURRECTION.

This commentary and interpretation of Christ's words likewise cannot hold a place. For Christ entered into his glory through his resurrection, as Scripture openly confirms, not to mention that he dwelt among his disciples for forty days on earth before the visible ascension. For this reason, as far as entering into his glory, there was not as much need for his visible ascension as for the presence by which he was with the Father.

HUMAN FANCIES ABOUT THE LOCATION AND GLORY OF THE HEAVENS.

But you are saying these things about *location and nature* of heaven and glory, to which Christ is believed by you to have ascended with the saints above the visible heavens. This is human and purely carnal imagination and fantasy, by which the heavenly and spiritual kingdom, which is defined by glory and blessedness, is transformed into the likeness of an earthly kingdom.

<149>

Dr. Beza:
Of course I concede that Christ entered into the beginning of his glory after his resurrection, and that from the resurrection to his

ascension he showed it through his dispensation[18] with his disciples. But he was not yet situated fully into his glory at the right hand of the father. For there is a middle status in the midst of glory, in which the Angels regard the face of God the father, and Christ was in this state of glory into which he entered until he ascended visibly into heaven. Men were not able on earth to bear the sight of angels in this middle state.

Dr. Jakob:

Therefore you cannot deny that Christ also entered into glory before he ascended visibly to heaven. From this it is clear, as you concede, that Christ had no need of a visible ascension either for his presence before the Father or for the acquisition of his glory.

THREEFOLD STATUS OF CHRIST. 1., 2., 3. CONCERNING THE STATUS OF THE ECONOMY OR DISPENSATION OF CHRIST. CHRIST SEEN ON EARTH AFTER THE VISIBLE ASCENSION INTO HEAVEN.

But you also are not unaware that a threefold status of Christ is taught among Church Writers: 1. The state of Humility. 2. Of Glory. 3. Of Dispensation. The state of humility lasted up to his resurrection. The state of glory followed after the resurrection, in which Christ is said to have entered into his glory. The third state, called the state of οἰκονομία or dispensation, lasted from resurrection to the visible ascension. For since the faith of the disciples had to be strengthened concerning his true resurrection, though they could not bear the glory of the resurrection on account of the weakness of their nature, he dwelt with them for a period of forty days. He assumed one and another appearance of body with his glory hidden, and made himself known to them now in the persona of a gardener as with Mary Magdalene, now as a traveler, like with the two disciples going to Emmaus. So also is it written that Christ stood by St. Paul *on earth* after the visible ascension into heaven, not only on the day of his conversion (Acts 9[:1–19]), but also <150> afterward when he was imprisoned in chains. And he encouraged Paul not to fear

---

18   *Dispensatio*: that is, the state of administratorship, economy, office, stewardship (= *oeconomia*, that is, *economy*, as below in the marginal note)

appearing before Caesar and presenting his testimony about him (Acts 28[:17–30]).

CHRIST HAD HIS GLORY WITH HIM, COVERED. IN THE MYSTERY OF THE LORD'S SUPPER ALL CARNAL NOTIONS ABOUT LOCAL GLORY TO BE REJECTED.

But as far as his glory is concerned, Christ had it with him, from his nativity, even in the state of humiliation. Just as it is written in John 2: This is the first of the signs which Jesus did in Cana of Galilee, and he manifested *his glory*. He desired to hide this glory until the work of redemption was completed. But he always had it with him, since the fullness of Divinity dwelt in him bodily (Colossians 2[:9]), a certain taste of which he presented to his disciples from time to time. Just as we read happened on Mt. Tabor, when Peter was so taken with his appearance that he forgot about his wife and his whole Household, and made no other request than one that thought he was in heaven (Matthew 17[:1–13]). But if our adversaries could reject the carnal notions about local glory which they imagine, they would be able to extract themselves from these labyrinths. So also he always had his father present with him, as he says: I am not alone, because my Father is with me (John 16[:32]). So he had no need for the visible ascension for the sake of this glory or presence.

Dr. Beza:
The revelation about which Acts 23 is written, in which Christ is said to have appeared to Paul, was a nocturnal vision. For Christ was never present on earth any longer in his own body after his ascension into heaven, but rather manifested himself through the vision from the third heaven.

Dr. Jakob:

DR. OSIANDER RECITED THESE WORDS FROM THE CODEX.

Were the text to be examined, it will be made clear to everyone that it would not admit this interpretation of yours. For the words read as follows: But the following night *the Lord stood near him*, ἐπιστὰς αὐτῷ ὁ κύριος, and said, Be of good spirit, Paul. For as you have testified ^{<151>} about me in Jerusalem, so you must testify also in Rome. Here the term ἐπιστάς, standing near, is expressly used, which cannot be understood as a vision. So long as your interpreters refuse the term, contrary to the express letter, they bring up interpretations so varied that they confute and silence each other. It is necessary that this happen when they are unwilling to yield to evident truth.

Dr. Beza:

It is written about Stephan that he saw the heavens open and Jesus standing at the right hand of God. This revelation like the others also happened from the third heaven, such that there he did not need to descend to earth.

Dr. Jakob:

I do not in the least deny that this appearance was a vision, but that it happened from the third heaven is a human notion which confutes itself. The reason is this: our eyes are scarce able to see the most splendid heavenly bodies in the firmament which are said to surpass the earth in their magnitude. How then could it be possible for the line of sight to penetrate there and see a body of human magnitude similar to ours? For this reason if it was a vision, it could happen on earth, such that there is no need of a third heaven. But if it happened from the third heaven, with the body of Christ standing there in that very place, then it was not a vision, nor could it be. And your interpreters furthermore do not agree among themselves, but confute one another.

THE GLORY OF CHRIST AFTER THE RESURRECTION IS NOT LOCAL.

In summary, Christ's glory, into which he entered following his resurrection, is not at all local. For this reason he used his dispensation in order to bring about revelations, so that he might not appear in the glory which he could have made known if he had wished, but rather in the way that the weakness of human nature requires and is able to endure. For it was truly Christ and not a specter that spoke with Paul on the road. I am Jesus, he said, whom you persecute (Acts

9[:5]), and stood by him at night when he was being held captive in Jerusalem.

<152>

WHY THE APPARITION THAT APPEARED TO STEPHAN WAS A VISION.

But seeing Christ standing at the right hand of God, this is not something that belongs to the eyes of the body, but of the mind, since the right hand of God is invisible. For this reason it needs to have been a vision concerning which Luke in Acts 7 writes, that Stephan *saw* the heavens opened and Christ *standing* at the right hand *of God.*

But in order that we may return whence we have digressed, Christ's glory, into which he is said to have entered, is not at all local, but rather is the majesty which he indeed had from the personal union, but in his state of humiliation covered under the assumed form of a slave, into the full possession and use of which he has arrived, having laid aside the form of a slave.

Dr. Beza:

DR. BEZA'S OPINION REGARDING CHRIST'S GLORY.

Christ always possessed glory, should you understand the Word [λόγος] and his divinity, but not if his humanity should be understood. For his humanity was indeed gifted with GREAT glory, above all the angels and saints, but not the glory which is proper to divinity. He exercised this glory from time to time when it pleased him to. And so he lacked the other glory by which he demands that he be glorified, namely the glory which he possessed in the presence of God, before this world existed, of which he had been deprived in certain measure.

Dr. Jakob:

CHRIST ALWAYS POSSESSED IN HIMSELF HIS OWN GLORY NOT ONLY AS GOD BUT ALSO AS MAN.

If Christ's words are to be interpreted in regard to glory that is proper to Divinity, how can you say he was deprived of it? Unless we wish somehow to say that the Divinity is changeable? But he possessed glory not only by reason of the Divinity but also according to his humanity, since the whole fullness of Deity dwelt in him bodily according to his humanity. This very glory of Divinity has not been excluded or separated from this fullness of Deity. Unless perhaps we were to say, he is God, that is, the whole fullness of Divinity without its own glory, or needing a glory from the outside for his glorification, a glory not naturally characteristic of him. <153> This is plainly absurd to think about God, who is sufficient for the most perfect glory in himself.

Since therefore this argument about the glory of Deity applies properly to the passage about Christ's person, where the glorification of Christ will have to be treated, and it is the lunch hour, and we should not detain the Honorable Prince any longer with trouble, we will postpone it till then.

IN WHICH POINTS THERE IS STILL DISAGREEMENT.

But it stands that out of all these points about which we have conversed so far, there is clearly no agreement between us about these two chief points. The one concerns the sacramental presence of the body and blood of Christ, by which the body of Christ is delivered with the bread to all who are offered it, and the other concerns sacramental reception, by which the body of Christ is present not only to the mind but to the mouth, and is said to be received by the mouth of the body. For on both counts we reject and condemn Capernaitic carnage and Cyclopic eating of Christ's body, as has now been repeated time and again. But regarding the eating which is through faith, there has never been any controversy.

Dr. Beza:
We say that Christ's body is represented, presented, and offered through the bread of the Lord's Supper to the mind, but not to the mouth of the body. And we affirm that its reception is only spiritual,

and therefore that it is received by mouth neither by the worthy or the unworthy but by faith alone.

But if we need to meet again at the second hour, we will not be able to get ready in writing our response to the Theses on Christ's person that have been brought forward. My brothers who have arrived with me need to return to their Churches.

Dr. Jakob:

Rᴇᴘᴇᴛɪᴛɪᴏɴ ᴀɴᴅ ᴇᴍᴘʜᴀsɪs ᴏғ ᴛʜᴇ sᴛᴀᴛᴜs ᴏғ ᴛʜᴇ ᴄᴏɴᴛʀᴏᴠᴇʀsʏ. Iɴ ᴡʜᴀᴛ ᴡᴀʏ ᴛʜᴇ ʙᴏᴅʏ ᴏғ Cʜʀɪsᴛ ɪs ᴏғғᴇʀᴇᴅ ᴀᴛ ᴛʜᴇ sᴀᴍᴇ ᴛɪᴍᴇ ᴛᴏ ᴛʜᴇ ᴍɪɴᴅ ᴀɴᴅ ᴛʜᴇ ᴍᴏᴜᴛʜ ᴏғ ᴛʜᴇ ʙᴏᴅʏ ɪɴ ᴛʜᴇ Sᴀᴄʀᴀᴍᴇɴᴛ.

We have so often already attested that there has never been between us any controversy concerning the presence by which the body of Christ is represented and offered to the mind, and regarding the reception <154> of the same, which happens through faith, just as also regarding Capernaitic and Cyclopic carnage of Christ's body. But there is one regarding the third mode only, which is Sacramental, by which we say not only that Christ's body is present with the bread, and not just to the mind, but also that it is offered to the mouth. Indeed, it is offered to the mind through the word, which only understands the word. But through the bread it is truly and really delivered to the mouth.

So also the mind takes hold of the body in the word, but the mouth takes hold of the body with the bread truly and really, not Capernaitically, but rather in mystery, in a heavenly mode imperceptible to human reason, according to Christ's word: Take, *eat*, This is my body, etc.

Mᴏᴅᴇ ᴏғ ᴘʀᴇsᴇɴᴄᴇ ᴛʀᴜsᴛᴡᴏʀᴛʜʏ [πιστός].

But we commend the mode in which this is able to happen to God's power and wisdom. He is in fact true and omnipotent; he cannot deceive.

THE HONORABLE PRINCE FREDERICK PUSHES FORWARD A CONTINUATION OF THE COLLOQUY.

As far as a continuation of the colloquy is concerned, it seems most satisfactory to the Honorable Prince that the article about the Lord's Supper be concluded before the Gentlemen supplement our Theses with their response in their own writing. This can happen in a short amount of time, unless by chance they should be willing to produce new arguments in favor of the assertion of their opinion. It is our view that sufficient answer has been made to what was brought up both in the Theses and your responses as well as the conference introduced by you. And you have plenty of time also to furnish more writing; in this there is no need to rush at all.

Dr. Beza:
I think then, for all you have said, that this one thing remains, that the first article, which is about the Lord's Supper, is being concluded by lunch.

Dr. Jakob:

---

1. SCOPE OF THE ESTABLISHED COLLOQUY.
2. COMMON AND PERNICIOUS ERROR IN MANY REGARDING THE SACRAMENTARIAN CONTROVERSY.

Yes indeed. For it ought to be clear to the audience in what matters we agree and in what we disagree, and on what foundations we rest and what you cannot yield to us, nor we to you. <155> They will be able to think accurately about each of the principles in turn, and decide which party they can embrace with better conscience and firmer faith. For almost all are convinced that you concede verbally with us the presence and eating, not only of bread, but also of the body of Christ, or that there is a very small disagreement, or none at all, concerning these things. The controversy can be easily reconciled and settled in this way.

1f.iii. 23 March, 1586, 2 p.m.

Dr. Jakob:

RECAPITULATION [Ἀνακεφαλαίωσις] OF THE PRINCIPAL POINTS OF THE DIALOGUE CONCERNING THE LORD'S SUPPER.

O Reverend and most erudite Dr. Beza, after we run through the largest part of the chief points in our peaceful conference, which have been put forward in the your Theses and responses and ours regarding the Lord's Supper, and they have been sufficiently treated in our opinion such that the whole audience may easily understand which party rests on the clear and not in the least distorted testimonies of holy Scripture, or on the other hand merely on human interpretation, seeming incapable of producing any more scriptures, it perhaps remains for us to draw this article to a close.

POINT 1. OPINION OF THE WÜRTTEMBERG THEOLOGIANS CONCERNING THE PRESENCE AND EATING OF THE BODY OF CHRIST.

First of all therefore we have borne witness several times that the Physical or local presence of the body and blood of Christ in the Lord's Supper has never been taught in our Churches and schools.

POINT 2.

Likewise also we have never taught Capernaitic and Cyclopic eating of the body of Christ, nor have we written this, nor can this be shown in any of the writings of our party, Luther, Brenz, my writings, or the writings of others.

<156>

POINT 3. FALSE TARGET OF THE ADVERSARIES. PROTEST OF THE WÜRTTEMBERG THEOLOGIANS AGAINST ALL THE WRITINGS OF BEZA AND HIS BROTHERS CONCERNING THE LORD'S SUPPER.

But seeing as these two errors are in all your writings not only attributed to ours, and falsely ascribed to them, but also comprises the sole goal of all your polemical writings, just as that of both your theses and responses, such that you refute the Physical and local presence of the body and blood of Christ with the bread, and Capernaitic and Cyclopic carnage of the flesh of Christ in the same Supper, we have testified to the Honorable Count Frederick and all the audience, Barons, Nobles, Doctors, and Renowned Men, that the dogmas regarding the Lord's Supper that are condemned by them do not in any way pertain to us. Rather throughout France and in other regions we have been treated unjustly and unfairly in the presence of the best men, as if we maintain so crass and impious an opinion regarding the Lord's Supper that all pious men rightly do, and should, shrink back from it in horror.

POINT 4. REGARDING EATING OF FAITH THERE HAS NEVER BEEN A CONTROVERSY.

Besides this, moreover, as our Theses maintain, we have testified every time about the eating of Christ's body which happens by faith, that there has never been a controversy between us. We have rather so consistently asserted this as we have taught and unremittingly reminded our audience, that unless they eat Christ's body by faith before they approach this holy Feast, they will receive the Lord's Supper not unto life, but rather unto judgment.

WHAT THE EATING OF CHRIST'S FLESH BY FAITH IS.

The reason I say this is that this eating is nothing other than believing that Christ's body has been handed over for us unto death and his blood has been poured out for the remission of sins.

SACRAMENTAL PRESENCE AND EATING OF CHRIST'S FLESH.

A third presence and eating of Christ's flesh remains, however, which is called sacramental. What is asserted by it is that it is Christ's body according to the words of Christ's Testament: This is my body, the very body, I say, without respect to faith or disbelief of man, truly and really is present with the bread of the supper, in a supernatural and heavenly way, and is presented not only to the mind, but also to the mouth of the body by virtue of Christ's word "*eat*," and is received by the mouth of the body by those who believe, for the confirmation of faith and life begun through faith, but by the impious to their judgment.

<157>

CHIEF POINT OF DISPUTE AND CONTROVERSY ABOUT THE LORD'S SUPPER. FOUNDATIONS OF THE ASSERTION OF SACRAMENTAL PRESENCE OF CHRIST'S BODY IN THE HOLY SUPPER.

The chief point of Dispute turns on the question concerning this third sacramental presence and eating. We have settled this by the very plain words of Christ's Testament, "Take, eat, this is my body, etc. Drink, this is my blood," and by the testimonies of St. Paul, "the bread which we break is a communion of Christ's body. And again, they who eat unworthily eat judgment, *because they do not discern* the Lord's body. And again, they are guilty of the body and blood of Christ." We have settled it in such a way that all might understand that we are departing not even a hair's breadth from the simple and genuine meaning of the words of Christ and Paul.

This teaching about the presence and eating of Christ's body is neither our interpretation, nor our conception, but rather the genuine and very plain sense of Christ's words and Paul's. Dr. Beza and his brothers had to refute this in the conference we had, and if they could not consent with us or wish to, they had to prove that this third eating could not exist, and that another presence of Christ's body could not exist than one that was local and Physical or Relative, that is, by signification. And again, that another eating of Christ's body could not exist than a Capernaitic and Cyclopic carnage of Christ's flesh, except for that which happens by faith, which is nothing other than believing in Christ.

If they demonstrate this from the word of the Lord, and not merely with human interpretation, we will confess that they have won the victory, and we are prepared to believe them and publicly revoke our doctrine. But if they cannot prove it, which they have of course not yet done, the whole audience sees that we cannot depart from the very simple words of Christ, and that no reason has been shown why we ought to depart from these and their very simple sense on account of a human interpretation which can be proved or demonstrated by no testimony of Scripture.

Dr. Beza:

Reverend Doctor, we thought the scope of this afternoon's confer-ence <158> was not to advance towards a new dispute. We have in fact argued enough both yesterday and today. Rather, the scope was for us to examine whether we could infer, from those points we had our conference about yesterday and today, where we agree or dis-agree. But if a new dispute must be pursued, let us pursue it. But it would seem to me very useful to examine where we agree or disagree, and in what matters one might be able to carry the other, such that some fruit may result from this conference. This gathering, as well as others who are absent, await this and seek it out very eagerly.

DR. BEZA'S PLAN ABOUT THE WAY TO ACHIEVE CONCORD.

For this reason, with the leave and kindness of the Honorable Prince, I will explain what has come to my mind. For in the article about the Lord's Supper, about which we have conversed so far, the way would have been most efficient if we were separately putting things down in writing, and this also happened on your part, with the result that then from a common collation of each writing (after we had conferred regarding the sense) a common document could come about which might be read in the assembly of our audience. It could be gathered from this whether any peace and concord could be established between us. For we have common enemies, and the fact of the matter teaches that they aroused by this strife and conceive a boldness not only because of this very controversy, but also from the way we have gone about this business, so bitterly fighting thus far, on either side. This way of doing business shows that passions have gotten espe-cially aggravated on both sides. I, for my own part, of course confess that I have written many things which I wish had not been written by me; some from your party will confess the same thing.

Let us proceed in the way I have proposed, if it please the Hon-orable Prince: we for our part are prepared to furnish something written of this kind.

Dr. Jakob:

SCOPE OF THE ESTABLISHED COLLOQUY. DESIRE OF PIOUS PEOPLE IN MANY REALMS FOR DETERMINING HOLYCONCORD. DESIRE OF PIOUS PEOPLE SATISFIED IN THIS CONFERENCE.

Reverend Beza, sir, what you have proposed about putting things down in writing is a way that pleases me and my brother [159] Dr. Lucas Osiander, and we are of exactly the same opinion, that once we make a collation of Scriptures we may deduce where we agree and disagree. For this was also the scope of the established Colloquy, especially if concord could not be determined in every way or be able to be (which nevertheless is especially to be hoped), that not only the present audience but also those absent, French and Germans, and pious people in other realms undecided in this controversy, might know for certain what issues exist between us, and on what we have consensus or disagreement. This is because pamphlets have been published from both sides, and have been found of complaints, in which both sides complain that they have suffered injury from the other side and that as many things as possible have been attributed falsely to them, which they never thought, believed, taught, or wrote. Whatever either party therefore has imputed unjustly to the other will be able to be shown in this peaceful conference. We think that this has happened in our conversation from the start of this article. Whoever knows what has been discussed together between us during these days will easily understand from these things what the consistent and perpetual opinion is that belongs to either party, and what are its foundations.

Therefore until the Gentlemen compose a document of faith and their Confession in the second controverted article concerning the Person of Christ, and include their opinion about the Theses we offered in writing, let us compose a writing of this sort. This will buy us time, too, if on both sides we are eager to get these things ready at the same time.

RECAP NECESSARY.

But a new Dispute was not established by me when I recited certain things from the conference in place of a Colophon.[19] They are especially in service to what has been established, as I briefly demonstrated in which parts we either agree or disagree, once the conference was done. First, that we have never taught or put down in writing a local and Physical presence of Christ's body with the bread. Then too, that we have just as plainly, always and consistently, condemned as impious Cyclopic and Capernaitic carnage of Christ's body in the Lord's supper.

A BIG STEP HAS BEEN MADE TOWARDS HOLY CONCORD.

But does it not seem because of this candid Confession of ours that a big step has been made towards holy Concord? Since in all your writings <160> about this article, you took up these two chief points above all to attack. If they were to be removed from your writings, *not even one argument* will be left that you have thus far produced against us and our doctrine. I pray and implore the esteemed Audience that they consider this carefully.

IN WHAT THE REMAINING DISAGREEMENT CONSISTS.

As far as the chief points of disagreement are concerned, we have shown that it is *only and entirely* in regard to the third mode of presence and eating of the body and blood of Christ in the Sacrament of the Lord's Supper, namely, whether the body of Christ is truly and really present, though not Physically and locally, and not relatively and in a signified way. And again, whether it be present not only to the mind, but also to our body in earth, and received by the mouth of those who eat it in the Supper with the bread.

Hence it is asked whether you flatly deny that mode, or you affirm that it is impossible, whether God himself cannot actually accomplish it by means of his own Omnipotence. This, I say, is the one thing being asked.

---

19 I.e., a summary, as in a publisher's finishing touch on the verso of a book's first leaf.

For thus far you have attacked this mode of presence in your writings, though always under the name of physical and local presence, despite not knowing another mode, not only as absurd, but also as plainly impossible. And so you deny straightway deny also the eating of the body which happens by mouth, either by the worthy or the unworthy. Your Theses and all your writings, and in addition the conference we just had, demonstrate that I am not accusing you falsely or attributing to you anything false; nor I think will this be denied by you.

PRIMARY CAUSE OF CALVIN'S ERROR CONCERNING THE LORD'S SUPPER. IN RESPONSE TO THE THIRD DOGMA.

In fact the Thesis advanced in your responses to our fourth Thesis has these words expressly:

> *We do not see* that it is possible for the substance of Christ's very body and blood, although glorified, to be considered actually present with the bread and wine *in a way other than physical and local circumscription.* Since glorification has given Christ's body immortality, but has not taken away its nature.

And again:

> <161>*God* does not cease to be omnipotent, even though *he cannot bring it about* that Christ's body be essentially present at one and the same time in many places, or that *it be now* anywhere else than in heaven.[20]

Dr. Beza:
That is a twofold question, it seems to me. The one contains the conjoining of Christ's body and blood with the signs. The other is our conjoining with Christ's body and blood.

---

20   This sentence in the printed edition has a printer's mark in the margin connected to a "N.B." (*nota bene*).

On the first question, whether God joins the essence of Christ's body and blood together with bread such that Christ's body and his blood are present invisibly IN, UNDER, AND WITH the bread, but not locally, in a circumscribed way, and visibly on earth: we do not see how this can be said truly and asserted or that they can subsist together. It conflicts with the truth of Christ's body, which does not admit a presence of this kind.

CONCERNING VIRTUAL [σχετική] AND RELATIVE PRESENCE.

But we say that the sacramental joining together of Christ's body and blood with the bread and wine of the Lord's Supper is σχετική, that is, a relative joining together of the signs of bread and wine on earth, relative to Christ's body and blood in heaven.

Now as far as the joining together of Christ's body and blood with the people who eat it in the supper is concerned, we confess that the body and blood of Christ is also communicated to us, and received by us through Faith, by which we become flesh of his flesh and bone of his bone. We say with Paul that this joining together of us with Christ's body and blood is a great mystery.

Dr. Jakob:

It is clear from this response that you hold exactly no presence of Christ's body and blood in the Lord's Supper, <162> but establish rather that Christ's body and blood are only signified in it by the bread and wine of the Lord's Supper, and on earth there is *really no mode* of presence, since Christ's body cannot be present in any other way than physically and in a circumscribed way, a mode of presence all of us deny.

But lest simple Christians pay attention to the fact that you hold precisely *no* presence, you employ ambiguous and obscure words which naïve and uneducated people do not understand, and even the erudite have a hard time following.

SOMETHING BEING PRESENT TO THE MIND IS SAID IN A TWOFOLD WAY.

For when you say that Christ's body is present and offered to the mind, this is ambiguous and can be understood in a twofold way.

1. A REAL AND EFFICACIOUS PRESENCE OF THINGS IN THE MIND OF MAN.

The one way is saying that something is truly and really present, as when Christ says, I and my father will come to him and make our dwelling place with him. So also the Holy Spirit is said to be present to the mind, who renews it for a true knowledge of God. This mode of the holy Spirit's presence is not representative or signifying, but the holy Spirit is *really* present, *in the place* where *the mind* of the man is.

2. PRESENCE OF THINGS ABSENT IN THE MIND.

But the other way is talking about things present to the mind about which the mind thinks, but such things are all the while absent. Like when a person thinks in the word concerning Christ's body, that (in your opinion) it is never present on earth all the way up to the last day, but is only in heaven. This is not a true and real presence, but only a thinking about a thing that is absent, by the merit of which a person may profit through faith in the Lord's Supper, just as it was present to Abraham and the Patriarchs in the old Testament.

REGARDING VIRTUAL [σχετική] AND RELATIVE PRESENCE OF CHRIST'S BODY IN THE LORD'S SUPPER.

Now, in order that it may be shown to everyone how the matter stands, I ask, Reverend Beza, sir, that you be willing to explain to the audience seated here and standing too in great number, what it means, or what you understand by relative [σχετική] presence of Christ's body and blood in the Lord's Supper. For I do not think that there is *one* among all of these gathered who understands it. But I do think this Mystery should be talked about and discussed such that even all the simplest hearers may understand. For the Lord instituted this supper not just for the learned and the erudite, but also for the uneducated and not in the least erudite, <163> the very great number of whom is in the Church of all places and times.

Dr. Beza:

EXPLANATION OF σχητικὴ παρουσία, THAT IS, OF THE RELATIVE PRESENCE OF CHRIST'S BODY IN THE LORD'S SUPPER. USE OF THE BREAD AND WINE IN THE LORD'S SUPPER ACCORDING TO BEZA.

I will explain. The Sacraments are signs, which are not consid-ered according to their own substance and material, but according to the use ordained by God in the Sacraments. Thus bread and wine are substances, considered in the way of material. But then the same things are considered in the way of the use for which they have been determined by the Lord in the Sacraments. Now the use of the bread and wine in the Lord's Supper is that they may be external, bodily signs that meet the senses, that they may represent spiritual things to the soul and the mind, namely, the body and blood of the Lord. This happens through the promise from Christ in the words of the supper, when he says about the bread, Take, eat, this is my body, etc. And about the cup, Take, drink, This is my blood of the New Testament. Christ promises by these words that he wants to make us partakers in his body and blood for the remission of sins and eternal life. Not that he begins to do this only now for the first time, when the faith-ful put the Sacrament to use; rather that this communication MAY BE INCREASED in them through the use of the Sacrament.

HOW SIGNS AND THINGS SIGNIFIED ARE JOINED IN THE SACRAMENT. LOCAL CONJUNCTION.

Now it is asked how the signs and the things signified are joined in this Sacrament, whether in such a way that where the essence of the signs exists, there also is present the essence of the things signified, the body and blood of Christ. Here we respond that the sacramental conjunction does not require that things signified be in the same place where the signs are, but it is sufficient that the signs possess a certain σχέσις, that is, a Relation and habitude to those things which they signify, represent, and offer and present to the mind. We call this conjunction or union a σχέσις or relation and habitude of signs to the things signified.

<164>

They are by this understanding in the Category of Relation. For a sign by reason of its use is in the Category of relation, and not in the Category of substance. Thus also the Sacraments of the old Testament possessed a σχέσις, that is, a relation and habitude to the body and blood of Christ, in plainly the same way and nature as the Sacraments of the new Testament possess. Christ's body is in fact not present to us in a way other than it was present to them in the use of the Sacraments, since Christ's body cannot be really present with respect to itself IN ANY WAY OTHER than LOCALLY AND IN A CIRCUMSCRIBED WAY. For the nature of the body has not been destroyed, and so it cannot exists illocally in the place where the bread of the Lord's Supper is. A third mode of presence, though, about which you are speaking, is a matter for a future conference.

Dr. Jakob:

POINT 1. SACRAMENTS ARE NOT JUST SIGNS.

Reverend Dr. Beza, if I have perceived your intention correctly, you are saying that the Sacraments are just signs. This we simply and categorically deny. Signs are in fact not Sacraments, but only part of the Sacraments. For two things are required for the substance of the Eucharist, a sign and a thing signified, or, as Irenaeus says, an earthly and a heavenly thing. The earthly, bread and wine; the heavenly, the body and blood of Christ.

POINT 2.

Next, to the point about relation [σχέσις] of signs, as it has been explained by you (but which I think very few people understood), this is the meaning of your words, that on earth there exist two things in the use of Sacraments: the one is the substance of signs, for which reason it is located in the Category of substance, and the other is σχέσις, a relation or habitude of the signs to the things signified. Except these two things nothing is present on the earth, according to your relative [σχετική] explanation, since Christ's body is and remains in heaven and (according to your opinion) is *in no way* <165> on earth. For you say that Christ's body cannot be present in any other way except locally and in a circumscribed way. When therefore the Sacrament of the Lord's Supper is celebrated, according to your opinion, what is given and presented to those who intend to commune is bread with σχέσις, or habitude and relation to the body of Christ, absent from earth, existing in heaven.

DR. BEZA'S WORD TRICKS, IN REGARD TO THE PRESENCE OF CHRIST'S BODY IN THE HOLY LORD'S SUPPER.

But, begging your pardon, please, what need is there of those word tricks? Those who are ignorant of Dialectic have absolutely no knowledge of these things, and meanwhile are occupied in this opinion and error since they hear in relative [σχετική] presence the term presence, so that they judge falsely from this that you also believe and teach the true presence of the body and blood of Christ, which you have not yet in the least demonstrated that you do.

RELATIVE [Σκετική] PRESENCE PRESUPPOSES NO REAL PRESENCE.

For the relative [σκετική] presence or habitude is nothing other than a representation and signification merely of the absent body of Christ. How much more satisfying it would prove to be, therefore, if you were simply to state what you are thinking in your heart, saying it without words that cover it up, so that everyone can understand what your opinion is? You could in this way, in fact, the more easily set yourselves and others free. Your constant and unchanging opinion would be known to all. Simple men cannot understand what you are concealing under the words you use that cover up your meaning.

EXPLANATION OF BEZA'S OPINION ABOUT THE PRESENCE OF CHRIST'S BODY IN THE LORD'S SUPPER. CHRIST DOES NOT ORDER US TO BE CARRIED UP INTO HEAVEN IN OUR MIND AND THROUGH FAITH.

For who does not know, when you say the bread of the Supper represents the body of the Lord, existing in heaven and absent from earth, that this manifestly asserts the absence of Christ's body in the Lord's Supper? This can be understood more easily by everyone than the many and splendid words you propose about the relative [σχετική] presence, which is not even understood by many learned folks. And where, please, are Christ's words? Or in what Testament of Christ is it to be found that he said in the institution of the holy Supper, Take, eat, this is bread joined together with a relation [σχέσις] or habitude of my body? Where did he say, Take and drink, this is a sign, that is, wine, joined together with a relation [σχέσις] or habitude of my blood? Nowhere is this said. And Paul does not <166> say, The bread is a communication of relation [σχέσις]. Nothing is said here about a habitude that signifies, but rather about real communication, either to life or to judgment: The bread is a communication of Christ's body; the cup is a communication of Christ's blood. What pious person, though, reflecting on his eternal salvation will allow himself to be seduced away from the express words of Christ's Testament, "This is my body; This is my blood," to the relation [σχέσις] and habitude of a body, by opinions so worthless? Of course no pious person of understanding will do this, who wishes to be certain of his faith, and to pacify his conscience in the use of this Sacrament. Nor does Christ order us to rise up in meditations of faith and be carried up into the place of heaven where Christ's body is, in order to enjoy it there. Rather in the words of his own Testament, he bids us pay attention to the bread and wine with the eyes of our body as external elements set before them, and to pay attention with the eyes of faith to *the words of his testament*, This is my body which is given for you, and This is my blood which is poured out for you for the remission of sin. He bids us pay attention to the word, I say, the word, Christ's word. Not into heaven. Let us trust him simply, as Chrysostom says, and not doubt both that Christ both is, and gives, what his words say.

RELATION [Σχέσις] CANNOT HAVE A PLACE IN THE WORDS OF CHRIST'S TESTAMENT.

From this it can be understood by everyone that the relation [σχέσις] cannot have a place in the words of the Testament. It is plainly in conflict with them.

CAUSE OF ERROR IN THE DOCTRINE OF THE LORD'S SUPPER.

Now, the cause of this error is that you judge, and have been persuaded, that no true and real presence of Christ's body and blood can be present on earth other than the local and circumscribed one. If this error could be removed from your minds, not only would an easy path to concord already have been achieved, but concord itself.

Sacramental presence does not destroy the truth of Christ's body.

For the truth of Christ's body is not destroyed if it is believed to be present in this Mystery in another mode than that by which it is now in heaven according to the property of a body. Give God glory, please, and do not detract from his omnipotence and truth. He knows the way, by virtue of his infinite wisdom, which we <167> do not know. And he is able to be present by means of his own omnipotent power, and he is also present, because of his infallible truth, according to the words of the Testament.

Dr. Beza:

Concerning ambiguity [ὁμωνυμία] of the term Sacrament. Whether Sacraments in the number of signs. Why Sacraments are called visible words. Dr. Beza, in his response.

There is ambiguity [ὁμωνυμία] in the term Sacrament. For a Sacrament is from time to time taken just as a Sacramental, substantial, and corporeal sign, which is used for signifying and representing spiritual things. So circumcision is called the sign of the covenant, and bread and wine are called the Sacraments of the body and blood of Christ, on account of the relation [σχέσις] and habitude which they possess in relation to the body and blood OF CHRIST. But from time to time as sign and thing signified at the same time, as when we say that the Sacrament of the Lord's Supper embraces not only bread and wine but also the body and blood of Christ. But this does not stand in the way of Sacraments being in the number of signs. This is why they are also called visible words by Augustine, as if visible signs are added to God's words, and confirm their power. Since the reception of Christ himself in the Sacrament is the same as that which is in the simple word. These indeed differ in external form, but not actually in what is signified and offered. In the word they meet us through the ears only, but in the Sacrament they meet the rest of the senses through signs of this kind. In this way the words give voice to the signs. Nevertheless we say that that Christ's body is also actually present, BUT NOT ON EARTH. For that which is signified is also offered at the same time, but not to the body, but rather to the mind through faith.

Now, if anyone should object, Does the benefit of Christ's body therefore reach only the mind? I respond: Even though Faith is the unique organ by which Christ is received, nevertheless the benefit <168> reaches the body too, since bodies are rendered immortal by the communication of this food.

Dr. Jakob:

FALLACY OF DIVISION. SACRAMENT CONSISTS OF TWO THINGS.

Reverend Dr. Beza, the fallacy of division is not unknown to you, by which are disjoined things which should be conjoined, and from that point we argue falsely. So in the present business of the Lord's Supper, we are not disputing about just one part, but about the entire Sacrament, which Irenaeus declares consists of two things, namely an earthly and a heavenly.[21] Irenaeus does not say that a Sacrament consists of *one thing*, namely bread and wine joined together with a σχέσις, that is, a habitude and relation to the absent body of Christ. For bread and wine is not the Sacrament; the body and blood of Christ also is not the Sacrament; but these two things together in the Mystery joined together by the words of the Testament are the Sacrament which is called the Eucharist. And this is the unanimous opinion of all the Orthodox Fathers, who all define the Sacrament not with one part only, but two at the same time.

AUGUSTINE MISUSED THE TERM SACRAMENT. AUGUSTINE IN THE SENTENCES OF ST. PROSPER 2 DE CONF. CAP. THIS IS.

But I am not unaware that Augustine misused the term Sacrament and often spoke of bread and wine as signs for one part

---

21   *Adv. Haer.* 4.18.5.

of it. The same man openly bears witness nevertheless that the Sacrament of the Eucharist consists of two things, just as his words plainly read. He says, His flesh is what we receive in the form of bread, *hidden* in the Sacrament, and his blood, which we drink *under* the appearance and taste of wine. And again, The Church's sacrifice (he uses the word sacrifice for Sacrament) *consists of two things*, the visible appearance of the elements, and the invisible flesh and blood of our Lord Jesus Christ. For this reason Your reverence cannot get away with the term ambiguity [homonymia], which has no foundation in Scripture.

But we flatly deny what you say, that Christ's body, with respect to itself, cannot be present on earth in any other way than locally and circumscribed. Anyone who is somewhat educated understands that this language undermines God's omnipotence. <169> Nor can it be taught or proved by any testimony of Scripture, either.

And it has already been stated by us, several times now, that we have never asserted a local or circumscribed presence in the Lord's Supper. You fight against this one thing as if we teach it, but this is pointless.

SUMMARY AND ARGUMENT OF THE BOOK OF ORTHODOX CONSENSUS. VERY BRIEF CONFUTATION OF ORTHODOX CONSENSUS.

What, may I ask, does the Orthodox Consensus, as they call it, accomplish as it teaches against Luther, Brenz, and us, in the first place saying that in the Lord's Supper the body of Christ is not present locally and in a circumscribed way? And then that the body of Christ in the Supper is not eaten Capernaitically? But why was so large a tome needed to prove this from the property of the body, the analogy of faith, and other arguments, when there is no one who asserts this? This is a confutation of their own making. Therefore negation of a local and physical presence of Christ's body in the Lord's Supper, and of Capernaitic eating of Christ's body, is the most concise and solid refutation of the entire book which is called the Orthodox Consensus, since there is no one who would assert that presence and eating of Christ's body, which we all condemn in like manner.

It goes on to teach that the bread of the Lord's Supper *is or is said to be* the body of Christ *in no other way* than only this: that it has obtained the name of Christ's body on account of signification, by which it signifies Christ's absent body. This we not only consistently deny, but also have solidly refuted by means of very strong arguments. For Christ did not say, Take and eat, this is bread, which has merely the name of my body, which it represents, but he said, This is my body, *is, is* my body (says Christ).

SWISS AGAINST LUTHER'S BRIEF CONFESSION CONCERNING THE LORD'S SUPPER.

Some of your people have also written that the body of Christ now living in heaven has so discharged his office on earth that he has no business any longer with us on earth. This is likewise in conflict with the words of Christ's Testament. For just as the sacrifice on the cross was for the sins of the whole *world*, thus in the Lord's Supper now there is food and drink, not for bellies, but rather <170> for eternal life, as spiritual nourishment, by which our faith is strengthened, and our body is truly fed for immortality.

BEZA AND HIS PEOPLE SPEAK WITH US, BUT DO NOT THINK WITH US.

But you often speak publicly so splendidly about the true and real presence of Christ's body and blood in the Lord's Supper that your simple hearers—and even the erudite—cannot judge or report otherwise than that you think with us, provided Cyclopic Flesheating is taken off the table. *I do not at all doubt* that the majority of pious people commune in this faith in your Churches and receive the Sacrament from you.

But I hope that the whole audience in the conference we have established has been able easily to understand that the fact of the matter is completely the opposite.

For when we arrived at the explanation, when you say, the body of Christ is truly and really present, you add σχετικῶς, that is, relatively, by a kind of sacramental, representative, and signifying habitude. And again, that the bread has the name body of Christ. And again, that it is meant metonymically [μετωνυμικῶς]. When you say this, you show that we have consensus only in words, and not in the things themselves.

We have *never* believed in that Cyclopic flesh-eating [κρεοφαγία] and Capernaitic carnage of Christ's flesh, have *never* taught it, have *never* written it, but rather condemn it and have always condemned it. In like manner also, I have displayed that you neither believe nor set forth *any* true and real presence of Christ's body and blood in the Lord's Supper, which is clear from the virtual [σχετική], relative habitude which you teach in the Lord's Supper.

METONYMY DOES NOT HAVE A PLACE IN THE LORD'S SUPPER.

Besides this, it is clear to all that Metonymy, which you attach to Christ's words in his Testament, cannot in the least coexist with words so plain. Nor in fact is there here a transmutation of words whereby one word is substituted for another. Neither Christ nor Paul says that the bread just has the name of Christ's body, nor that the body itself is joined to the bread in the Mystery.

<171>

And so all these things are rejected as they do not in the least match up with the words of Christ's Testament and this Mystery, in which this relation [σχέσις], habitude, and representation or signification does not have a place.

EFFICIENT PATH TOWARDS HOLY CONCORD.

For this reason, far and away the surest and safest path and way is if we should very simply have faith in Christ's words and trust that, by the power of those words which Christ once spoke, the body and blood of Christ in the Lord's Supper are not signified or represented, as happened in the types and figures of the Sacraments of the Old Testament, but rather that body and blood of Christ are truly present with the bread and wine of the supper, distributed with the bread, and received by mouth, in a heavenly and divine way, which is known to God alone. For in this way can a conscience be assuaged which rests on the undoubted word of God.

CRASS REASONING REGARDING EATING CHRIST'S FLESH. REFUTATION OF THE SAME. EATING OF CHRIST'S FLESH IN THE LORD'S SUPPER IS NOT CAPERNAITIC CARNAGE.

What more is said in the summary of the Confession of their doctrine concerning the Lord's Supper is stated in Foundation 4 of the Assertion: if the substance of Christ's body were being received by mouth and remaining also, at least in the pious and faithful, and if the faithful were becoming substantial members of Christ, then they would not be the mystical body of Christ the Church. This would have some appearance of truth, if a physical and local presence were established by us with Capernaitic carnage and Cyclopic eating of Christ's body in the Lord's Supper. Since however we do not at all do this, but rather have always condemned these as extravagant fictions, there is correspondingly no reason for this conclusion here. For the presence, and the sacramental reception of the body and blood of Christ with the bread and wine of the Supper, and what happens by mouth, is a Mystery, which neither reason nor sense grasps, but faith alone understands.

Dr. Beza:

RELATIVE PRESENCE. METONYMIC PREDICATION.

We say that Sacraments are signs because of the perpetual nature and property of Sacraments. But meanwhile we do not deny that the whole is contained by those signs, namely the sign and the thing signified, that is, the thing itself of the Sacrament, but virtually [σχετικῶς] and relatively. <172> Just as no one can conceive of his father mentally, unless he should at the same time think himself a son. But the predication is Metonymic, by which a name of something signified is attributed to a sign.

BREAD IS NOT ESSENTIALLY CHRIST'S BODY. NOTHING IS LESS TRUE.

Thus the Fathers say that Christ's body falls to earth, is worn away by teeth, and teeth are fixed into his body. These things do not actually happen to Christ's body, but they are attributed to it by relation [σχέσις] and the figure by which what happens to the sign

is attributed to the thing signified. Metonymy is the figure of speech
by which the nature of the Sacraments is explained. So also bread
is called the body of Christ. And we also say that the bread IS the
body of Christ, since God's son is not a liar. But it is not essentially
Christ's body. Thus we say that it is present in the mind, but not
in the bread, since it is present not on account of the bread but on
account of the person. And the Sacrament is not bread, but rather the
act. In sum, we agree that the body of Christ is present in the Lord's
Supper, but we do not agree about the mode of presence.

Dr. Jakob:

SACRAMENTS ARE NOT JUST SIGNIFYING SIGNS.

No one has ever denied that Sacraments are signs. But we have
never conceded, nor ever will concede, that they are just signs signifying and representative of things signified, through which the profit
of the things signified may be applied to those who receive them.

THE PRESENCE OF CHRIST'S BODY IN THE SACRAMENTS IS NOT VIRTUAL [σχετική].

Nor do we concede that this presence is Relative or virtual
[σχετική]. We have refuted now several times over the instance of
when someone thinks about a Son when the Father is present, and so
in the same way things signified are present with the signs that are
present. For even though the Father has a relation to the Son, considered in the mind of man, nevertheless the Son is not present on
account of this, when the Father is present.

IN WHAT WAY PARTS OF THE SACRAMENT IN PREDICATION OF RELATION. IN SACRAMENTS SPIRITUAL THINGS NOT TO BE PULLED APART FROM BODILY.

Nor are the parts of the substance of the Sacrament related
simply, but rather only by the nature in which they are constituted
among themselves. But in so far as they determine the substance
of the Sacraments, they are in no way <173> related, but have
an indissoluble nature, and are present, each one, in their own
nature, by which they serve the action of the Lord's Supper, not

independently and separately, but together on behalf of the nature of the Sacramental union, by which neither acts without the other in the use of the Supper. Nor in fact are bodily things to be pulled apart from spiritual in the use of the Sacrament of the supper; rather they must always be kept together, and ought to remain conjoined, just as the words of institution have joined them together.

REGARDING PHRASES OF THE ORTHODOX FATHERS, TEETH FIXED IN THE BODY OF CHRIST. JOHN SEES THE HOLY SPIRIT IS NOT METONYMIC LANGUAGE.

As far as the expressions employed by the Fathers about this Mystery are concerned, that teeth are fixed in Christ's body and other language, these are not Metonymic but rather are attributed to Christ's body on account of the true and real presence of Christ's body and the sacramental union effected with the bread of the supper. Just as was said above about the dove and the Holy Spirit who is said to have descended not Metonymically, as if the noun Holy Spirit is substituted for the dove, but rather the Holy Spirit was truly present in the appearance of a dove, and revealed himself according to this mode. So not a dove, which represented the holy Spirit, but rather the Holy Spirit himself, is said to have descended.

THE APOSTLES SAW THE WORD OF LIFE WITH EXTERNAL EYES.

Likewise also Metonymy should in no way be admitted in John's words: "That which we have seen, which we have looked at with our eyes, which our hands have handled concerning the word of life" (1 John 1[:1]). For even though the word of life cannot be seen and handled with hands in the property of its own essence, since it is spirit, nevertheless because of this the Apostles are correctly said to have handled not just a man, but truly to have handled God.

BREAD IS NOT ESSENTIALLY, BUT SACRAMENTALLY THE BODY OF CHRIST.

It does not follow from this, however, that the bread of the supper is essentially Christ's body, but it is sacramentally Christ's body, on account of the sacramental union with Christ's body. And it has been said, and we have explained several times now, that for this reason

Christ's body in the Eucharist is present not only to the mind but also to our body and mouth.

CHRIST'S BODY PRESENT NOT ON ACCOUNT OF THE BREAD BUT ON ACCOUNT OF THE MAN.

And we are not unaware that Christ is present not because of the bread but rather on account of the man. But it does not follow that on this account Christ's body is not present to the bread sacramentally, since <174> Christ said as he took the bread, Take, eat, This is my body. The Lord wished in this Mystery to dispense, and to be received, not bread without his body, nor his body without bread, but these spiritual things through the bodily, just as Chrysostom says.

SACRAMENT IS NOT THE ACT. IN WHAT THE SUBSTANCE OF THE SACRAMENTS CONSISTS.

So also we are not unaware that the bread is not the Sacrament, but part of the Sacrament. But on the other hand the Sacrament is not just the act. Rather the act is required for the Sacrament, without which it is not a Sacrament. For outside the use instituted by Christ it is not a Sacrament. Nevertheless the substance of the Sacrament, which is said to be offered and received, consists in these two absolute things, joined with God's word, namely an earthly thing and a heavenly thing (as Irenaeus bears witness and the words of the Testament teach), bread and wine, Christ's body and blood.

NO CONSENSUS REGARDING PRESENCE OF CHRIST'S BODY AND BLOOD IN THE SUPPER.

Since therefore Dr. Beza constantly and forcefully repeats that the body of Christ is only in heaven, and cannot be really present on earth in any other way than by means of a local and physical presence, which we consistently deny from both sides, we are seriously shocked how he dares so often to assert that there is consensus between us regarding the presence of Christ's body in the Supper.

For relation, which is not predicated for things that act, produces no presence, but rather only a respect in which a thing is able to be far absent. But we have proved plainly and very clearly a third mode of presence, which is neither physical nor relative, but true neverthe-less and real. It subsists in the Mystery which reason is not able to grasp, but faith apprehends in the word. It is necessary that Beza either approve this mode of presence with us, if there is to be any consensus determined between us, or refute it. He has done neither of these so far. And so disagreement still remains between us.

Dr. Beza:

WHETHER TEETH ARE FIXED IN CHRIST'S BODY.

We say that it cannot happen, even though there is a sacramen-tal union between the body and the bread, that teeth can be fixed in Christ's body in the proper sense. Rather, this happens only to a sign. Because of this it is said to be a Metonymy, <175> or to happen by way of Metonymy. For the fixing of teeth belongs to the sign of the body, not to the signified body itself.

Dr. Jakob:

WHAT STANDS IN THE WAY OF BEZA RECOGNIZING THE TRUTH. IN WHAT WAY TEETH BEING FIXED IN CHRIST'S BODY IS SAID IN THE USE OF THE SUPPER.

Reverend Dr. Beza, this one thing especially stands in the way of your being able to consent to our opinion. You constantly imagine that we are asserting a local and physical presence of Christ's body, a fact we have denied so often now. Hence your mental image, that you think we teach that teeth are fixed in Christ's body the same way as happens in the eating of veal, something we have never thought. Rather, Chrysostom attributes these things to Christ's body, because of the assertion of its presence. Since its presence is spiritual, teeth are in no way able to be fixed in it. But just as the word of life is said to have been truly seen by the Apostle, so also is it said piously and correctly about Christ's body, by Chrysostom and other doctors, even though nothing happens in the property of the substance of these things.

This is why I say that neither virtual relation [σχέσις] nor Metonymy have a place in this Mystery. For nothing is figurative here, but rather everything is heavenly, divine, and real in the Mystery, and nevertheless truly present, which except for the visible things are declared and expressed by the words of Christ's Testament.

Dr. Beza:
We do not deny that Christ is present in his own body and blood in the Supper, but we add TO THE MIND not TO THE BREAD, just as we have said now several times.

Dr. Jakob:
Therefore I ask, my dear Beza, where, oh where, is the Lord's Supper celebrated? In heaven or on earth?

Dr. Beza:
It is celebrated in the body on earth, and in the mind in heaven. For since Christ's body is in heaven, and not on earth, up to the last day, for this reason our mind needs to ascend into heaven where Christ's body is <176> in order that there we may fully enjoy that which has been granted to us by the Father with all of his blessings.

Dr. Jakob:

THE LORD'S SUPPER IS CELEBRATED ON EARTH IN BODY AND MIND.

Christ did not bid us who eat the bread to look to heaven in the words of his own Testament, or to be carried there in our mind. No word of Christ exists concerning such a Lord's Supper; rather he bids us raise our eyes to the bread laid before them and *our mind* to the words brought before it: Take, eat, This is my body, which is given for you. In this way he bids us celebrate this supper on earth both in body and mind until the day of his return for judgment, and also for remembrance of his death.

ON THE RESPONSES TO THE THESIS.

But that you say in your responses that you cannot *see* how the body and blood of Christ can with the bread and wine actually be

considered in a presence that is other than Physical or local circumscription, we confess that we also cannot *see* this, but believe it on
account of Christ's words and those of his Apostle (Hebrews 2[11:1]);
they attest to this presence, though we do not see it, since it is neither physical nor local, but there is nevertheless on this account a
conjoining which God can accomplish easily by means of his own
infinite power and wisdom. My appeal and counsel is this one thing,
that your Reverence consider this carefully. You are not unaware
that all the things that were seeming to be in service to the assertion of your opinion were brought together into a book whose Title
is Orthodox Consensus. In it the Author, or rather Authors (for the
preface attests that it was brought together by the work and incred-
ible exertion of many people), seemed to have transposed the status
of the entire controversy on purpose, and seriously to have wished to
wrap it in obscurity.

FALSE TESTIMONY OF THE AUTHORS OF ORTHODOX CONSENSUS AGAINST THE
THEOLOGIANS OF THE AUGSBURG CONFESSION CONCERNING THE LORD'S
SUPPER.

For the scope of the entire Book, as I brought up also a little while
ago, was located in these two chief points: one, to prove that the
presence of Christ's body in the supper was not physical, natural, or
local; the other, to prove that neither Capernaitic eating of Christ's
body nor Cyclopic carnage happens in the Lord's Supper. [177] All of
us, Luther, Brenz, and the rest of us, are accused of having asserted
and of still asserting these things with the universal Church in the
same book.

But since we have certainly never taught or thought these things,
and still do not, I ask, please, what do you think this Author will
answer our Lord Jesus Christ the righteous judge on the last day,
with all those who share his opinion, in regard to the false witness
published in public writings throughout so many realms? Indeed
there is no way the same things will cease to happen, now that it has
been brought up so repeatedly in public writings.

Dr. Beza:

The Author of the book, a very learned man, now lives with the Son of God. If he were present, perhaps he could answer and defend himself. But there is nothing more to say about this.

Dr. Jakob:

FRIVOLOUS PROOF OF THINGS THAT ARE FALSELY ATTRIBUTED TO LUTHER, BRENZ, DR. JAKOB, AND OTHERS.

But you do the same thing in your Response to the dogmas we did not approve of, where these monstrosities are attributed to us, and the horrors that follow from them. Instead of a proof you add that *you cannot see* how oral eating does not result in absurdities, falsehoods, and blasphemies as big as you please, namely that the body of Christ is ground with the teeth, swallowed down the throat, passed through into the stomach, digested, and finally defecated. These things are horrible to hear.

But it is insufficient to say that *you cannot see otherwise.* For that seeing is made possible by *not seeing.*

It has not yet in fact been proved that we have ever taught a Cyclopic eating of Christ's flesh, from which these blasphemies are inferred, but to the contrary, we always condemn this openly and have still consistently condemned it.

THE STATUS OF THE CONTROVERSY IS SET FORTH.

But the status of the dispute, and the chief point of the entire business, as I have said often now, turns on the question about <178> the third mode of presence of Christ's body, by which it is present not physically or locally, nor relatively, but nevertheless Christ's body truly and really is present, not Capernaitically, not symbolically, but nevertheless actually distributed with the bread and received by the mouth of the body in the way that God wishes spiritual things to be distributed and received through bodily ones.

You need to respond to this. This mode, which we have demon-strated clearly from the words of Christ and Paul, must be refuted.

But there is no response here, or in the Orthodox Consensus, nor in the writings of all the people who have written against us all the way to this very day. Rather, all their talk is either about Cyclopic carnage or about the eating of Christ's body which happens through faith, about both of which there has never been any controversy.

Dr. Jakob's exhortation to Dr. Beza.

Please consider these things carefully in your mind with your brothers, my dear Beza. For both of us, as you see, are grey and close to death, and will have to appear before the tribunal of our Lord and Savior Jesus Christ and render and account of the doctrine we have set forth for our hearers. Let us take care then, lest it seem as though we have settled on establishing a concord that is less than pious, holy, and God-pleasing.

In what way more consensus can be determined.

All consensus will be made at the point when on both sides we subject ourselves to Christ and his word with a humble spirit and, as the Apostle says, obediently lead our thought captive to Jesus Christ, and honoring the words of Christ's Testament in simple faith, rejecting Cyclopic carnage and Capernaitic eating of Christ's flesh, as well as its metonymic [μετωνυμική], virtual [σχετική], and relative presence, and attributing to him the praise of truth, wisdom, and power who does not deceive, and promises that he can accomplish it, though we may not understand it.

Many of the French approach the Lord's Supper in this simplicity of faith.

In the same way I do not doubt that very many, both of those French people who are standing here, and also in other places in your Churches, approach the Lord's table with the same faith and intention, and receive the body and blood of Christ with the bread and wine. They are not thinking about <179> σχέσις, about the relation and habitude about which you spoke here, but take this Sacrament gazing with their eyes at the elements set forth, and with their mind at Christ's words, in the most God-pleasing simplicity of faith. Their simplicity is approved more by God than arguing over made-up σχέσις, relation, and habitude in this meeting. If we were to do this *peace and concord would already* have been determined between us in this Article. Please, what danger is there in the assertion of this Sacramental presence, if Capernaitic eating should be condemned, and at the same time spiritual eating, which happens through faith before the reception of the Sacrament, be taught piously?

Dr. Beza:

Reverend Doctor, we also Desire peace and concord, and seek it out very eagerly, but a peace of the sort that does not trouble our consciences. But our consciences would be troubled if we were giving you our assent while you are in opposition. Perhaps what renders your consciences peaceful is the very thing that would trouble ours.

IT DOES NOT EXIST AT ALL.

But the disagreement is not about presence but rather about the mode of presence. As we approach the Lord's Supper we look back to the promise which Christ promises, that he does not want to nourish our bodies, but to offer the Sacraments to us in order that our soul may be nourished. For this reason we are not arguing about what we receive, but rather in what sense Christ's body is said to be eaten in the Lord's Supper. We are speaking not about substance but use. The substance on earth is bread. The substance in heaven is Christ's body. He is also on earth, since his words admonish us so that he may speak to us. And this mode of presence by which the substance of Christ's body is in heaven, and nevertheless is shared with us on earth, is more miraculous than if his substance should be said to be present. Namely when through faith we are by the power of the holy Spirit so conjoined to CHRIST'S body that we are flesh of his flesh and bone of his bones, [180] to the point that it is certain we become one body with Christ (who is our head). And it is clear that the truth of the body naturally stands in the way and does not admit that he is at the same time in heaven and on earth truly and really present.

Dr. Jakob:

POINT 1. POINT 2. HOW CHRIST'S BODY IS NOT FOOD FOR BELLIES. POINT 3. POINT 4. MIRACULOUS MODE OF SACRAMENTAL PRESENCE. EATING AN AMBIGUOUS [ὁμώνυμον] TERM.

We are returning to those things concerning which we have disputed over two days. Dr. Beza correctly discourses regarding spiritual eating, which happens through faith. But there was no controversy over this. And it is true indeed that Christ's body is not food for bellies by which either natural hunger may be repelled or the body naturally nourished. But this fact does not yet refute the notion that Christ, partly through his own bodily things, bread and wine, and partly by our reception, which happens in the mouth, wishes to confer and deliver to us these spiritual gifts, and for us to receive them.[22] This I say has not yet been refuted by this response. And we said above with approval that Christ's body was in heaven, and not on earth, by its own substance according to the property of a body and according to the mode of a true body. But we consistently deny that on this account it is mysteriously present *in no way really on earth* to the Sacraments. And this mode of presence is truly miraculous, that Christ's body, because of the mode of the true body existing and remaining in heaven, in another mode removed from all local motion, is present in all places, distributed, and received, where the Lord's Supper is celebrated. This mode of presence is neither physical or local, nor is it virtual [σχετικός] and relative, but mystical, as Antiquity said: the Mystery is believed but not understood. For the word eating is understood one way in John 6 and another way in the words of the supper; this needs no proof. In John 6 it means believe, but in the words of the Lord's Supper it means *to eat by mouth* and to receive by mouth. But what if someone were to conclude that this was about faith, how absurd would that be? For it would follow from this that it would have to be called into doubt whether the bread of the supper should be eaten by mouth, if eating in the words of Christ's Testament meant the same thing <181>

---

22   This sentence in the printed edition is specially referred to with "N.B." (*nota bene*).

as believing. And thus it would be received by mouth without Christ's mandate. This is plainly absurd.

Since therefore in regard to spiritual eating, which happens through faith, there has never been any controversy, and since Dr. Beza hears that Cyclopic carnage of Christ's flesh has been openly condemned by us, though he cannot refute a third mode of presence by which Christ presents his own body and blood with the bread and wine, and bids us eat it by mouth and so not only offers and presents spiritual things through bodily, but also wishes them to be received, since this be the case, what is the reason that he opposes himself to the truth any longer? Please, oh please yield to manifest truth!

For no one can deny that the sacramental distribution and reception of Christ's body, which happens with the bread and the mouth, has been instituted by Christ for the confirmation of the spiritual eating done through faith.

My dear Dr. Beza, I pray once again with all my strength that you weigh all these things carefully with your brothers, and so at length obtain the pious and salutary peace of God's Church. For your Reverence sees that I have brought forward not human fantasies nor human interpretations, but the express and indubitable word of the Lord. Let us subject our intellect to it in simple faith, and every controversy will be removed. For we for our part cannot retreat from the express words of Christ and their simple and genuine meaning when no necessity urges us to do so. For that presence does not fight against either the analogy of faith nor the truth of Christ's body, or any sentence of holy Scripture, but only seems absurd to our senses and human reason. The express, simple, plain, and clear word of God must be opposed to these, which is expressly set forth for us in the words of Christ's Testament. In these does our conscience most safely find repose, and ought rightly to, without any disagreement and in simplicity of faith, since they cannot deceive us, though the senses and reason can.

<182>

Dr. Beza:

Your Reverence is able to think sufficiently such that peace is so dear to us that nothing is more desirable to us than this. But we cannot purchase it with terror for consciences. You object with simplicity of faith; we think that we are seeking this and leading our thought captive in obedience to Christ. For flesh and blood do not teach that we possess the body of Christ remaining in heaven, present to the mind. Therefore we lead our mind captive to the word of the Lord, which joins us with the absent body of Christ. This perception is wonderful, when the body of Christ remaining in heaven is shown to us and perceived in the Sacraments, although we remain on earth.

Dr. Jakob:

We have never suggested that you purchase peace for the Church with terror of your consciences. But you could easily achieve it if you would not retreat from the simplicity of the words of Christ's Testament, leading captive the senses and human reason that is blind in spiritual matters.

DR. BEZA'S DOCTRINE IN THE LORD'S SUPPER DOES NOT BELONG TO FAITH BUT RATHER TO FLESH AND BLOOD.

For your Reverence says that flesh and blood does not teach that the body of Christ remains in heaven, is offered to our mind in the Sacraments, and that we remaining on earth are joined with them. I answer: if the presence of Christ's body and blood in the Lord's Supper is not other than virtual [σχετική] and relative as you have explained, then it is certain that this is taught and understood by flesh and blood. Unless you should wish to deny that Dialectic, of which part is treatment regarding relation, is taught and understood by reason. Certainly flesh and blood teaches and understands examples about contracts, from your interpretation of Christ's words above. For this reason your doctrine concerning the Lord's Supper, and interpretation of the words of Christ's Testament, is nothing other than flesh and <183> blood, that is, human conception about the Mystery, which flesh and blood does not understand.

DR. BEZA FIGHTS FROM FALSE PRESUPPOSITIONS.

We have said this often. When your Reverence says that our opinion is that the substance of Christ's flesh is joined together with the substance of the bread of the Lord's Supper, it is certain that you understand and attack nothing other than a physical and local presence and joining together. In this, for your part, you are in error.

IN WHAT WAY DISTRIBUTION OF CHRIST'S BODY, INVISIBLY PRESENT IN THE LORD'S SUPPER, SHOULD BE UNDERSTOOD.

For we also reject and condemn this presence and joining together. It is not a distinction between the local presence and what is in the Sacrament, as if the one belongs to the mode of eating Christ's flesh in the Lord's Supper and the other to the common way of eating by mouth, to the point that we arrange our categories to say that the one happens visibly, but the other invisibly. Nor in fact are these things done by Christ only invisibly, but rather spiritually, in such a way that nothing carnal can be considered here, which a common mode of eating brings with it. Since the mode of presence is plainly spiritual, though it is not merely the power of the holy Spirit, but rather the presence of the body of Christ himself, and the eating of it.

DR. BEZA'S CARNAL FANCY REGARDING THE DOCTRINE OF THE CHURCHES OF THE AUGSBURG CONFESSION ON THE ARTICLE CONCERNING THE LORD'S SUPPER. CONSUBSTANTIATION AND TRANSUBSTANTIATION CONDEMNED.

For this reason this pure carnal fancy of yours about our doctrine is not our doctrine. We certainly do not teach what you condemn in the writings you have published against us. Nor do we teach consubstantiation (which is how we are labeled) of Christ's body with the bread, but rather, just as we reject and condemn transubstantiation, so also do we flat out reject any such physical consubstantiation whether visible or invisible, and teach and assert only a sacramental conjunction.

JOINING TOGETHER OF BREAD WITH CHRIST'S BODY A MYSTERY.

For we say that the joining together of Christ's body with the bread is a Mystery, which flesh and blood does not grasp, that is, the human mind does not understand, but rather only faith comprehends in the words of the Testament, which it simply believes, and we commit the mode by which this happens and by which Christ can accomplish it to his infinite wisdom, power, and truth. We say only what is not, <184> namely that what does not happen is a physical and local presence, nor either a relation [σχέσις] or figure, which is involved between two absent things. And again, what does not happen is a Capernaitic eating and carnage of Christ's body, nor either an eating merely of faith, which is nothing other than belief in Christ. Rather it is a kind of eating by which faith may be confirmed in us, and which happens orally, as bread (which is the communication of Christ's body) is offered to the mouth and received by mouth. We ought not pull this apart or separate it from the bread in the use of the Lord's Supper.

IT IS A MYSTERY THAT GOD DISTRIBUTES SPIRITUAL THINGS THROUGH BODILY THINGS.

But how it happens that God distributes spiritual things through bodily ones, and we receive them via bodily organs, we do not know, but rather trust the word that bids us eat by mouth, making no mention of faith here. But if they could trust from your party, the entire controversy would be removed. We can see the same thing also from the comparison of participation in the table of Demons and the table of the Lord, which Paul employs when he censures the Corinthians who have been converted to faith in Christ but at the same time have become participants in the table of Demons. Those who eat what is sacrificed, says the Apostle, are participants in the altar, and just as however many used to eat of the Idol sacrifices that were sacrificed to Demons were the partners of Demons, so also however many ate of the bread of *the Lord's* Supper were participants in Christ's body.

Dr. Beza:

**WHETHER SOMEONE CAN BE AT THE SAME TIME A PARTICIPANT IN *THE LORD'S*
TABLE AND THE TABLE OF DEMONS.**

---

*Paul says, You cannot, you cannot, I say, drink the Lord's cup
and the cup of Demons; you cannot be participants in the Lord's
table and the table of Demons (1 Corinthians 10[:21]). Therefore they
were not participants in THE LORD'S table, that is, the body of
Christ, if they were participants in the table of Demons.*

Dr. Jakob:

There were Christians during Paul's time who were of the opinion that idols were nothing, and consequently that what <185> was
sacrificed to them was no different than common meat or food. So
they thought they could attend communal feasts, to which they were
invited by Idolaters, without offense to God. Just like certain people
are met in our own time who are taught that the sacrifice of the Mass
is nothing and so attend the feasts instituted for this occasion, something St. Paul censures the Corinthians for.

Dr. Beza:
Paul says, You cannot, you cannot.

Dr. Jakob:

INTERPRETATION OF PAUL'S WORDS BY PAUL'S WORDS.

Please, in what way can they not? For unless it were being done by
the Corinthians, Paul would not have convicted them on this count.
Therefore just as they accepted and ate by the external mouth what
was being sacrificed to Idols, so also they were eating by the external
mouth the bread of which Paul says that it is a communication of
Christ's body. And the phrase used by which it is said, You cannot at
the same time profess the Christian religion and commend yourself
as a Christian, while also applying yourself to greed, lusts, drunkenness, and other disgraces. But the best interpreter of Paul's words
is Paul himself, when he adds: all things are permissible to me, but
not all things are profitable; all things are permitted to me, but not

all things build up. Paul plainly teaches in these words that it is even possible for the Corinthian at the same time to approach the table of the Lord and the table of Demons, but this would be useful neither to themselves nor others. For God bids us flee idols, and cautions us away from stumbling blocks. The Corinthians were sinning against both mandates of God, attending the public feasts sacred to the gentiles, that polluted themselves with idols, gave offense to the weak in faith, and confirmed the Idolaters in their impiety. But meanwhile Paul does not deny that they are at the same time participants in the table of the Lord, but in any event also threatens judgment and punishment. For he does not want them to be partners with Demons.

<186>

Dr. Beza:

CHRIST'S BODY (THE CHURCH) JOINED TOGETHER OF MEMBERS OF THIS KIND.

Christ's true body is one, which consists only of living members, that is, those who truly believe. Partners with Demons do not belong to it. For no one can be at the same time a member of Christ and a member of the Devil.

Dr. Jakob:

MANY CORRUPT MEMBERS IN CHRIST'S BODY.

On the contrary, just as in one human body exist many bad humors which irritate the body, so in the Church, which is Christ's body, there exist many corrupt members also, that is, Christians by outward profession, but hypocrites, partners with Demons, who nevertheless also communicate in the rites of Christians, and the table of the Lord, yes, and meanwhile so shine before others that they seem to be very good.

But the Honorable Prince, Count Frederick, our very merciful Lord, thinks we have conversed enough about this article of the Lord's Supper. For nothing more that is new is being brought forward from your party. From this, I think that the whole audience could easily understand what both sides have said, which party has confirmed its doctrine by human interpretation or on the other hand by solid testimonies of holy Scripture. We commend it to their judgment.

But the other party's Theologians will be able to conclude also from this conference in what matters we agree and disagree. And they should know that we are very eager that peace and God-pleasing concord to be established. If they desire anything more in our doctrine, we will be prepared at any hour to explain and give an account. May *the Lord* bestow his holy Spirit, that solid concord may be established which can stand in the presence of God and his Church with the result that we are one in *Christ Jesus*.

Dr. Beza:

BEZA DECLARES EAGERNESS FOR PEACE AND CONCORD.

This is what we want, that it may become evident where we agree or disagree, even if we cannot agree entirely. I swear to God that I speak from my heart. And unless it be <187> annoying, I will recite a few things which I had jotted down at the end of what I wrote 27 years ago against [Joachim] Westphal [of Eisleben], who presented me the opportunity in the year [15]59.[23] There at the end of the Apology these are my words:

> *But come now, I swear to you all who intend to look at this Apology, I am least of all. But now let us finally consider seriously, not who aroused those flames, but rather in what manner they can be completely extin-guished. More than enough of quarreling, more than enough of reproaches, more than enough of accusations and defenses. We ought actually to repent that for so many years the progress of the Gospel has been retarded by such conflicts so lamentable. Therefore thus far we have fought with hatred (because this is what our sins have deserved). Why, pray, do we not fight rather with*

---

23   [15]59 for 69. *De Coena Domini*, 164–67.

charity? Certainly we have common enemies, we confess the same God, father, Son, and holy Spirit. We agree about his office as Mediator, about faith, good works, the word of the Lord, the Church, and Magisterial office. Whatever the point of disagreement is in the sacramental question, I ask you for heaven's sake whether it is of such a kind that we ought to be divided over it and make ourselves ridiculous before our enemies? We do not compare the proclamation of the simple word to that which is like clothing to the Sacraments. Regarding the true communication of the true body and blood in the Lord's Supper, the matter is decided between us, to the point that we confess that Christ is present such that he truly feeds us with his own flesh and blood for eternal life. There is controversy only over the mode of communication, since we are content with a spiritual one, which is by faith. We sufficiently understand that this controversy brings along two others with it, but I ask you for heaven's sake, what kind are they? We know that Christ ascended into heaven, that he has entered the realm of heaven in our name, that by his virtue, power, and charity alone we are ruled and saved. We declare that whatever good can proceed from us is entirely accepted by his spirit. Some confuse his session at the right hand with his ascension, but on this matter, on what does our salvation depend, that this is a dividing wall? However many times they eat of the holy bread unworthily, that is, without faith, <188> and drink unworthily from the holy cup, we know they are guilty of the Lord's body and blood. Therefore we also agree in this very thing. The controversy also remains here, whether they take symbols alone unworthily, with the body rejected through unbelief, or on the other hand whether they take the very body. I ask you for heaven's sake, will the spirits of the pious be very long troubled on account of this controversy about the impious? If the Lord has revealed something to anyone, let it be brought forth, but in a way that befits Christians. Let a Colloquy of learned and pious men be established; let the authority of Christian princes be set in its midst to mitigate any acrimony, and repress those unbridled gestures (since indeed the impudence of some requires this); let neither party bring forward some prejudice, but rather a spirit prepared to yield to those things which frank and simple truth will demonstrate. Nor as I write these things has it come into my mind that I am a small man among men of such great doctrine and authority, as though I am playing the part of arbiter or judge. For who am I that I should assume this? Nevertheless since the opportunity presented itself I wanted to swear to the Church of God what my mind is, and what my daily sighing is. I have put this present desire of mine to the test not only with several honorable princes, but also with the most learned Theologians of Germany, whom I had the pleasure of seeing just a short time ago. I urge and implore again in the name of the Lord that they think rather about patching up this wretched division of the Church than about any other business. I believe that no duty applies more to Christian Princes than this. And this is what I trust will be of consequence to our people: that however many free and Christian Colloquies are offered, in which some hope, even the least hope, of a future concord shines out, they will not only refrain from avoiding them, but also embrace them most eagerly.

Thus far the words of Beza.

This is still my opinion, may THE LORD grant peace.

<189>

Dr. Jakob:

DR. JAKOB WITH HIS PEOPLE EAGER FOR TRUE AND PIOUS PEACE AND CONCORD.
SCOPE AND PROFIT OF THE INSTITUTED COLLOQUY, FOR THE SAKE OF WHICH
DR. JAKOB DESIRED CONVERSATION WITH DR. BEZA.

Reverend Dr. Beza, I believe that you all have really discovered, in the conference we have begun, that we treat this controversy with no bitterness of spirit, but rather pursue it truthfully, peacefully, and in a spirit of concord. I think it has happened by means of a singular divine providence that we have been able to meet before we die in the presence of the Honorable Prince, Count Frederick our merciful Lord, and in that of very many nobles and very learned men, and converse peacefully about this and other controversies. I have longed for it a good deal for a long time, not because we have doubts about the truth and certainty of our doctrine, which I know has its foundation on the words of Christ's Testament, but rather since we from both sides have lamented in our public writings that many things are attributed to us by you and your brothers which we do not in the least teach, and the way things stand, your polemical books also are replete with similar complaints. My desire has been that it be shown to everyone, by a peacefully established conference, what has been imputed, fairly or unfairly, truly or falsely, to the one party by the other.

OPINION OF MOST PEOPLE ABOUT THE CONTROVERSY IN THE BUSINESS
CONCERNING THE LORD'S SUPPER.

And since most people on either side have thus far abided in their opinion, judging that we do not disagree with one another very much, if only the one side were willing to understand the other correctly and the other willing to interpret the words and the opinion of the one honestly, I hope that the present Audience has received this profit now from the peaceful and friendly conference, that they understand not only which of the two parties is enduring and consistent in its opinion and doctrine, but also which one is founded on the word of the Lord, or is contrary to it. From this they will easily be able to decide which one they might wish or be able to follow safe and secure, without the risk of eternal salvation.

BRIEF RECAPITULATION [ἀνακεφαλαίωσις] OF THE ENTIRE CONTROVERSY.

1. For regarding the eating of Christ's flesh which happens by faith, there has never been any controversy. 2. We have never taught Capernaitic eating and Cyclopic carnage of Christ's flesh. <190> 3. We have always rejected a Physical and local presence of Christ's body, whether visible or invisible. 4. We have demonstrated representation, signification, and shadows of Christ's body to belong to the old Testament. 5. But we believe the true and real presence and eating of the same body of Christ to be sacramental, by which, through bodily things, bread and wine, God presents and delivers spiritual things, namely Christ's body and blood, not only to our mind, but also to our body, 6. He bids us receive it by bodily instrument, that is, by mouth, when he says, Take, eat (which does not mean to believe, but to receive by mouth), This is my body; 7. Nothing carnal should be imagined as pertaining to the mode of presence or eating here, which is attributed to God's wisdom, power, and omnipotent truth. He alone knows the mode.

IN WHAT WAY HOLY CONCORD CAN BE ESTABLISHED. ADDRESS [Ἀποστροφή] AND EXHORTATION TO DR. BEZA.

All pious minds will judge that these things are true and in agreement with the words of Christ. Should you also believe, teach, and confess them, pious consensus has already been reached. This can happen easily, if only you reject carnal notions about this mystery. I beg over and over again that you do this and bring cheer to so many pious and faithful people, so that with one spirit we may, very soon, together appear and stand before the tribunal of Christ, our God and savior, joyous and of good cheer.

Dr. Beza:

DR. BEZA'S DECLARATION OF WILLINGNESS.

I can truly affirm that we have brought to this conference a peaceful and teachable spirit, eager for concord. Thus I trust that the Lord will bless this conference. God has his own time; if full consensus should not follow on this day, at least it will on another.

Although it has fallen out in a way other than what I had hoped for, and I see that there is still some disagreement between us, <191> I do not think nevertheless that it is such that the foundations of religion would be destroyed.

Dr. Jakob:
You have in fact come to realize that we also have equally brought a spirit eager for concord. And we trust also that this conference will not go off without fruit; the Lord will produce it in his own time. But let your Reverence with his brothers undertake the work of response to our other writing prepared on the person of Christ. We ask that you study it briefly.

Dr. Beza:
The seriousness of the argument demands time, and you have arrived prepared and equipped with books which we lack. But we will study briefly, as much as we can.

Dr. Jakob:
We can solemnly promise you that we did not write anything at all at home, but partly on the journey and partly here. And the chief reason for it was that we might save time, and we have not brought books with us.

Dr. Beza:
We pray God be willing to be present with us by his holy Spirit.

Dr. Jakob:
Amen.

After the first Article concerning the Lord's Supper was brought to a close, the Württemberg Theologians prepared their own text (as had been agreed between the speakers) <192> in which they showed in which parts there was consensus and in which was still disagreement. And they also demonstrated by what way holy concord could be established in this article without offense of consciences and with truth intact and uninjured. When this was delivered to the other party, they expressed their position in their own text, and when their own document was restored to each, nothing further was attempted for the purpose of achieving concord concerning this article. A great many things were explained both in the writings from either side communicated before the conference, and also in the context of the conference after it began, such that everyone could easily see in what things there was consensus or disagreement. What way exists for the purpose of establishing holy concord has been demonstrated clearly enough.

2

Concerning the Person of Christ

25 March
2 p.m.

Before the conference regarding the second controverted Article began, in the presence of the Honorable Prince, Count Frederick, and the rest of the Audience of the Colloquy, court councilors and French exiles, the Theses concerning the person of Christ which had been written by the Württemberg Theologians were first recited publicly by Dr. Lucas Osiander. Dr. Abraham Musculus followed him afterward and also recited the responses written up in the name of Dr. <193> Beza and his brothers. Dr. Beza and Dr. Jakob afterward discussed these in the presence of the whole audience in as peaceful a manner as they had the Article about the Lord's Supper.

2A. THESES OF THE WÜRTTEMBERG THEOLOGIANS CONCERNING THE PERSON OF CHRIST.

THESIS 1.

That the eternal Son of God assumed in time a human nature consisting of a body and soul, of the substance, flesh, and blood of the virgin Mary, is outside of controversy. In this way he was made similar to us his brothers in every way (with the exception of sin). He assumed the human nature into the unity of his person, such that in Christ there are not two persons, but one unique person, and one Christ only, and this person cannot be divided for all eternity.

THESIS 2.

But even though two natures have been joined together very closely, nevertheless no confusion of the natures <194> has occurred of the sort that happens when from two wholes a third results, as when water and honey produces mead. Nor is one nature changed into another. And as divinity is not turned into humanity, so neither is humanity changed into divinity, either before or after the ascension of Christ into heaven. For two natures are needed for the whole person of the mediator Christ.

THESIS 3.

It is established also that both natures in Christ possess and retain their own properties. Namely, the properties of the divine nature are to be omnipotent, eternal, infinite, etc. The properties of the human nature are to be bodily, creature, finite, circumscribed, that which can suffer, die, etc. Nor do the properties of one nature ever for all eternity become the properties of the other nature, for confusion of the natures would ensue from this, indeed even the obliteration of them.

THESIS 4.

Besides the properties of the natures in Christ there are also in Christ the man, created gifts, by which he is superior to all men and Angels. But these do not come into consideration when there is a dispute regarding the properties of the natures in Christ.

THESIS 5.

In the person of Christ there is a certain communication of properties by which what is proper to one nature is attributed to the whole person, and the property that one nature possesses is declared about the other. Whence has arisen the doctrine concerning the communication of Attributes in the Church.

THESIS 6.

When it is taught that the Son of God communicated his properties to the assumed human nature, namely, omnipotence, omnipresence, this should not be understood that it is as if the Son of God poured out his own properties into the assumed human nature (like something poured from one glass into another) such that the human nature possesses through itself and from itself (even in the abstract, that is, considered outside the personal union) a particular omnipotence which is now not only proper to it but also its own property. Christ would in this way in fact be made up of two Divinities, and it would follow that there would not be in God a trinity but rather a quaternity. And so it should be thought about in this way: that if it were possible to divide the personal union, and nevertheless for Christ's human nature to remain, then neither omnipotence nor omnipresence could be correctly attributed to the human nature.

THESIS 7.

And it should not be established that the human nature in Christ became <195> an infinite and uncircumscribed essence or that it is extended to all places in heaven and earth, or that it is everywhere in the kind of way that the Divinity is everywhere, or that it has been placed on the same level as the divine natures. For none of these follow from the true and real communication of properties.

THESIS 8.

When we say real communication of properties, we do not understand a physical one, by which one nature crosses over into the other, but rather we oppose the term "*real*" to the term *verbal* communication, which accomplishes for the natures only common *names* of the properties.

THESIS 9.

It is asked therefore whether some *real* communication happens between the divine and human nature in Christ on account of the personal union, that is, true and really subsisting in Christ's person, such that one nature communicates its own properties to the other. And it is asked moreover how far that real communication extends.

THESIS 10.

We believe that a real communication of properties follows from the personal union, of the sort by which the Son of God communicates to the assumed human nature his own omnipotence, omniscience, omnipresence, and power or virtue of vivifying, etc., by which the divine nature in Christ does not become weaker, though his human nature is exalted, not abolished. Ancient thought employed the analogy of soul and body to explain this mystery, as well as that of glowing hot iron. For the body really lives, but lives by virtue of the soul. And glowing hot iron really burns, but does so by virtue of fire. Nevertheless the body is not changed into soul, nor is abolished on account of the communication, nor is iron converted into fire, nor does it cease to be iron.

THESIS 11.

And so (on account of the personal union and communication of properties) **<196>** we believe that Christ also is omnipotent according to his humanity, or that the human nature in Christ is omnipotent (which is the same thing). For holy Scripture attributes all power (which is nothing other than omnipotence) to Christ in so far as he is a man. You have subjected all things (says the Psalter) under his feet (Psalm 8[:6]). And Paul, explaining this passage of David, proves from it that *all things* were subjected to Christ except for him who subjected all things under him (1 Corinthians 15[:27]). John the Evangelist says, Jesus knew that the father had given *all things* into his hands (John 13[:3]). And Christ himself (even before his passion) says, all things have been handed to me by my father (Matthew 11[:27]). And after the resurrection he says, All power has been given to me in heaven and on earth (Matthew 28[:18]). Here must be noted also Christ's miracles as undoubted testimonies of his omnipotence, that he cleansed the lepers with his touch, restored sight to the blind, that he called Lazarus back to life with his voice. Indeed, Christ performed these miracles not by alien power (as did the Prophets and Apostles) but rather by means of his own power.

THESIS 12.

We believe that according to the human nature (now in the state of glory and majesty), Christ perfectly knows all things that have been, are, and will be. For John the Baptist testifies that the spirit was given to Christ not in the same measure as to other men, but rather in such a way that we receive from his fullness (John 3[:34]). And Christ in the state of humiliation saw the *thoughts* of the Pharisees. And Paul, speaking of Christ, says, In whom are hidden *all the treasures* of wisdom and knowledge (Colossians 2[:3]). And it is necessary for Christ to know *all things*, since he is the future Judge of the living and the dead (John 5[:21]). That he did not know the day of judgment before his passion must be ascribed not simply to his humanity, but rather to the form of a slave which he has set aside.

THESIS 13.

Holy writ clearly testifies that Christ is present to all creatures, but especially <197> the Church and his elect, indeed everywhere in his humanity. Where (says Christ) there are two or three gathered in my name, there am I in the midst of them (Matthew 18[:20]). And elsewhere, Behold (he says), I am with you for all days, up to the consummation of the age (Matthew 28[:20]). There is no need in these utterances to tear the human nature away from the divine, since not even death could divide Christ's person. Paul writes concerning the ascension of the man Christ into heaven: He ascended above all the heavens *in order that he might fulfill all things* (Ephesians 4[:10]). And in the same letter he testifies concerning the man Christ that he fulfills all in all (Ephesians 1[:23]). To fulfill all things means, according to the Scripture's diction, to be present to all things in a heavenly mode. I fill heaven and earth, says the Lord (Jeremiah 23[:24]).

THESIS 14.

But the mode of this presence is not expressed in holy writ, and so we believe *the fact that* Christ is truly present to all creatures, not indeed locally and physically, but rather supernaturally, but *how* this happens, we freely confess, in true and pious humility, that we do not know.

THESIS 15.

To be sure, we believe with pious antiquity (which also confirmed the resurrection of the dead on the assumption of Christ's vivific flesh) that Christ's flesh also is truly vivific. For Christ says, I am the bread of life. Your fathers ate Manna in the desert and died. This is the bread coming down from heaven such that if anyone should eat of it he will not die. I am the living bread which came down from heaven, if anyone should eat of this bread, he will live forever. And the bread which I will give is my flesh for the life of the world, etc.

THESIS 16.

Christ possessed this Majesty of omnipotence, omniscience, and omnipresence, and the power of vivifying, <198> in so far as he was man (on account of the personal union), even when he was in the womb of his mother, but he did not put it into effect or use. But following his birth into this world, so often as there was need, he demonstrated it and used it in miracles and the distribution of his body and blood, so far as the nature of his calling and office was demanding. For Christ was then in the form of a slave, and humbled himself, that he might be able to suffer and die (Philippians 2[:8]).

THESIS 17.

But the state of humiliation and the form of a slave which lasted for a short time in Christ detract in no way from his Majesty, into which he fully entered when he ascended to heaven and sat at the right hand of God the father Almighty. This right hand of God is the Majesty of Christ, presently reigning in heaven and on earth according to both natures. And so now Christ governs all things in heaven and on earth In, With, and through his assumed human nature. For this is sitting at God's right hand. And so Christ worked together with the Apostles sent out into the world and confirmed the message of the Gospel with accompanying signs which were happening by the virtue and power, and in the name, of Jesus Christ (Mark 16[:17]).

THESIS 18.

It is also correct and true to say that on account of the indissoluble personal union, the man Jesus Christ is true God, and God eternal became man. John says none other than this when he says, *the Word became flesh* (John 1[:]). For the Word (by witness of the same Apostle in the same chapter) was *God*, but flesh means *man* according to the diction of Scripture. And so this proposition, the Word became flesh, means nothing other than that God became man. For this reason Paul writes this way about Christ: Christ is from them (the Jews) according to the flesh, *who* is *God* above all things, blessed into the ages (Romans 9[:5]).

THESIS 19.

For this reason it is correct and true to say, God suffered for [199] us, God died for the sins of the human race, even though we freely confess that the divine nature did not suffer in itself, nor die, but rather that Christ suffered in the flesh, as Peter says (1 Peter 4[:1]). But meanwhile, even though the divine nature cannot die, the abuses extended not to the son of man alone but also to the Son of God, since there are not two persons in Christ, but only one. For unless God's blood had been poured out for us, we would not have been redeemed from eternal death, nor cleansed from our sins. This is why Paul says, as he entrusts the care of the Church at Ephesus to the Ministers of the word, the holy Spirit placed you as overseers, to direct God's Church, which he acquired *with his own blood* (Acts 20[:28]). And John says, The blood of Jesus Christ his *son* cleanses us from every sin (1 John 1[:7]).

THESIS 20.

Now this Jesus Christ, our mediator and redeemer, is to be adored entirely with reverent worship according to both natures, since we do not have two Christs, of whom one is to be worshiped, and the other not worshiped. It is written concerning the whole Christ: let all his Angels adore *him* (Hebrews 1[:6]). And the blind directed their worship and invocation to him, not only to the Son of God, but also the son of David, that is, to the human nature in Christ, saying, Lord *Son of David*, have mercy on us, and they were not rebuked by Christ for this, but rather were cared for (Matthew 20[:30]; Mark 10[:47–48]; Luke 18[:39]). And Stephan Martyr, who certainly possessed a solid knowledge of Christ the mediator, entrusting the care of his soul to Christ in agony said, *Jesus*, receive my spirit, entrusting his soul to God and man *Jesus* Christ.

THESIS 21.

This sound and pious doctrine concerning the inseparable personal union of two natures in Christ, the real communication of Attributes, the exaltation of the human nature to the right hand, that is to the Majesty and power of God, still does not **<200>** remove the presence of Christ's body and blood from the holy Supper, but rather confirms the same. Since the human nature in Christ was *indissolubly* united with the Son of God, and made a sharer in his divine properties, and was situated at the right hand of God, he is not only always present in the holy Supper of the Lord, but also in the entire Church. Moreover in the holy Supper the flesh and blood of Christ are distributed, etc.

2B. WE JUDGE THAT THE FOLLOWING DOGMAS CONFLICT WITH HOLY SCRIPTURE.

POINT 1.

That in the Person of Christ there is no other communication of properties with respect to the natures than that which effects common names, for which reason the Humanity in *Christ* would receive nothing from the Divinity, nor would those things that happen to the humanity pertain in any way to the eternal Son of God. And affirming, when we say God is man and man is God, that this is only an expression and a certain manner of speaking. That God in fact has nothing *really* in common with humanity and humanity has nothing *really* in common with Divinity, that is, truly and actually. And that in the proposition, Man is God, the term "Man" does not mean a true man, but rather the Son of God, who supports the human nature. And so they interpret the proposition "God suffered" as follows: God, that is humanity united to Divinity, suffered, and man is omnipotent, that is, Divinity united to humanity, is omnipotent. This is the dogma of Nestorius, who said, Boast not, Jews, you did not crucify God but a man. This dogma in fact creates two Christs, one of which would possess Majesty, while the other would have nothing in common with it. <201> One would have suffered for the human race, but it would have nothing altogether in common with the other in regard to suffering.

POINT 2.

That every power in heaven and on earth which has been given to Christ in time has been given to the person of the savior according to *both* natures. And that every power in heaven and on earth was again *restored* to Christ according to his *divine* nature in the resurrection and ascension to heaven, just as if while he was in the state of humiliation he had laid down and set aside the power even according to his divinity. This dogma smacks of Arianism since it sets up a kind of divinity in Christ which suffers increase and decrease, though nothing can be added to, nor subtracted from, true divinity.

POINT 3.

That the whole person of Christ, according to *both* natures, with respect to the office, remains *under divinity*. This also stinks of Arianism, for a kind of divinity is attributed to Christ which is *under divinity*, with respect to which it is itself at length accomplished.

POINT 4.

That Christ is really not capable, according to his humanity, of omnipotence and other properties of the divine nature, and he (according to the human nature) has no communication with the omnipotence of God, but rather possesses a power in the middle between the divine one and that of Angels and people.

POINT 5.

That it is asserted that certain limits have been placed on Christ according to his human spirit, namely how much is fitting for him to know, and that he does not know more than is appropriate for him and required necessarily for the execution of his office, of judge no doubt. And that Christ possesses not even today a perfect knowledge of God of all his works. And that it is impossible for Christ <202> to know by means of his human spirit whatever has been from eternity, what already now is happening everywhere, and what will be in all eternity.

POINT 6.

That it is impossible for Christ, on account of the property of human nature, to be *in many places* at one and the same time, much less that he is able to be in all places with his own body. And that Christ according to his humanity has no business with us any longer following his passion and death to redeem us.

POINT 7.

That it is taught that no other power and virtue of vivifying should be attributed to Christ's flesh except in so far as Christ has redeemed us by his passion in the flesh.

POINT 8.

That he who directs his worship or invocation to the flesh of Christ itself (even that remaining in the union of the person) is cursed by the mouth of God himself. That Christ in fact is our *fellow servant* (as if he is not the Lord of glory), and so the one who would adore Christ's flesh, even glorified and remaining in the union of person, etc., is Idolater and blasphemer against God.

> *Signed:*
> Dr. *Jakob Andreae*
> Dr. *Lucas Osiander*

<203>

2C. RESPONSE TO THE THESES CONCERNING THE PERSON OF CHRIST, DELIVERED BY THE COLLOCUTORS, MARCH 23.

TO THESES 1 AND 2.

We approve both.

TO THESIS 3.

We agree and especially approve the formula by which it is said that properties never depart from their subjects. (a)

DR. JAKOB ANDREAE'S MARGINAL NOTES: (A) WE DID NOT USE THIS SENTENCE, THOUGH IT IS NOT CONDEMNED IF RIGHTLY UNDERSTOOD. BUT YOU ARE ABUSING IT TO BRING UP VERBAL COMMUNICATION.

TO THESIS 4.

We agree and approve here the distinction between the grace of union, (b) by which the man is God, and the grace which they call habitual, by which the man is adorned with habits, both of so many kinds and such sizes as no other created thing can be adorned.

DR. JAKOB ANDREAE'S MARGINAL NOTES: (B) THE DISAGREEMENT IS OVER WHAT THE GRACE OF UNION IS AND WHAT IT EMBRACES.

TO THESIS 5.

Concerning Christ's person sometimes language is used that is appropriate to either nature or to the whole Christ, as when Christ is named, and Jesus, and Mediator, and the rest of the names like this. But other times on account of the unity of person, (c) only one nature is specifically designated from the other, and it is ambiguous. For sometimes there are predicates that are suitable for the one nature by which it is denoted, (d) as when God is called blessed, eternal, omnipotent, etc., just as though you would say, the man <204> *suffered, died, was crucified for us, etc. And statements of this sort are entirely appropriate. (e) But from time to time a statement predicated to the whole Christ, because he is a single, indissoluble person, is truly and properly suitable; nonetheless the particular natures are not changed into each other, not even with respect to the union, by which he is named, as when it is said that God redeemed the Church with his own blood, and the Lord of glory was crucified, and again, the son of man on earth speaking with Nicodemus was in heaven: this type of speaking is called by the older theologians exchange [ἀντίδοσις], and by our more recent ones communication of* attributes. But this predication cannot be used except with concrete nouns (h); since the whole person of Christ is never denoted in the abstract, but by either of his own two natures. And from ignorance of this distinction between concrete and abstract ways of speaking heresy has arisen, first that of Nestorius, who denied that God (that is the Word [ὁ λόγος]) was both the son of Mary and had been crucified; (i) and then that of Eutyches, who asserted that the Divinity of Christ suffered. (k) The universal rule stands therefore, that one cannot be attributed to the other, neither one nature about the other, nor the properties of the one nature. (l)

DR. JAKOB ANDREAE'S MARGINAL NOTES: (C) YOU UNDERSTAND AND ARE DESCRIBING THIS UNITY BY COMBINATION ALONE, WITHOUT A REAL COMMUNICATION OF PROPERTIES; THIS WILL BE SHOWN TO BE FALSE. (D) IT IS NOT ONLY DENOTED, BUT REALLY COMMUNICATED TO THE OTHER NATURE. <204> (E) THE STATEMENTS ARE NOT PARTICULAR BUT UNUSUAL, SINCE THE THING, THAT IS, THE MYSTERY OF THE UNION OF THE NATURES, IS UNUSUAL. (F) IN ITSELF IS AMBIGUOUS, SOMETIMES DENOTING THE PROPERTY OF A NATURE, OTHERWISE MEANING THE REAL COMMUNICATION THAT HAS HAPPENED. (G) THIS IS NOT JUST A GRAMMATICAL DESIGNATION, BUT RATHER A REAL COMMUNICATION. (H) THE ERROR OF THE ADVERSARIES LIES HIDDEN IN CONCRETE TERMS, WHICH ABSTRACT TERMS DISCLOSE. (I) THE HERESY OF NESTORIUS NEVER AT ALL AROSE FROM IGNORANCE OF THESE WAYS OF SPEAKING. NESTORIUS CONFESSED ONE SINGLE PERSON, BUT DENIED THE COMMUNICATION OF ATTRIBUTES. THIS IS WHERE HIS HERESY ORIGINATED. (K) THIS DOES NOT NECESSARILY MAKE HIM A HERETIC, SINCE SAID THE SAME THING; HIS ERROR IS RATHER THAT HE ASSERTED ONLY ONE NATURE IN CHRIST AFTER HIS ASSUMPTION INTO HEAVEN. (L) THE PRINCIPLE THAT PROPERTIES OF ONE NATURE CANNOT BE ATTRIBUTED TO THE OTHER IS QUITE FALSE. FOR THIS WAS THE NESTORIAN HERESY.

TO THESES 6 AND 7.

We explained in our previous response that we teach from the definition of the hypostatic union that neither the Divinity nor the Divine properties can rightly be attributed to the Humanity in any way (m), not even as it pertains to the union.

DR. JAKOB ANDREAE'S MARGINAL NOTES: (M) THIS HERESY IS FAR WORSE THAN THE NESTORIAN. FOR NESTORIUS MERELY CALLED INTO QUESTION THE COMMUNICATION OF THE PROPERTIES OF HUMANITY. BUT THESE PEOPLE ALSO DENY THE COMMUNICATION OF THE PROPERTIES OF DIVINITY.

TO THESES 8 AND 9.

Equivocation [Ὁμονυμία] (n) exists in the one term "communication," which is taken to refer on the one hand to the hypostatic union, and on the other hand to its effects. (o) And so we admit a real communication, that is, <205> a union of the natures, in which the individual natures remain in themselves, even in the union, distinct with respect to their properties, apart from any other communication. And so we say that there is not even a verbal communication of the sort mentioned here, by which the Humanity is said to be everywhere and omnipotent in its own special way, (p) but rather we judge that this is just as false (q) as to say that the humanity departed from the Deity. Although, as we said above, whatever God's properties are, are rightly and truly attributed to the man united with the Word [λόγος], that is, to the whole person concretely, from the other nature, namely that called humanity, whether Christ is considered entirely [ὅλως] and not according to parts [κατὰ μέρη], or considered distinctly in the natures. (r)

DR. JAKOB ANDREAE'S MARGINAL NOTES: (N) THERE IS NO EQUIVOCATION HERE, BUT INNATE SIGNIFICATION OF THE MEANING OF COMMUNICATION, WHICH IS ATTRIBUTED ON ACCOUNT OF THE UNION BOTH OF THE NATURES AND THEIR PROPERTIES. <205> (O) THIS IS THE SAMOSATIAN HERESY, TO ASSERT A UNION OF THE NATURES WITHOUT COMMUNICATION. (P) THIS ASSERTION IS BLASPHEMY: THAT HE IS NOT EVEN VERBALLY OMNIPOTENT, CONTRARY TO CHRIST'S WORD: ALL AUTHORITY HAS BEEN GIVEN TO ME (MATTHEW 28[:18]). (Q) IT DOES NOT FOLLOW THAT OMNIPOTENT DEITY IS TALKED ABOUT IN ONE WAY, NAMELY, IN AND OF ITSELF, AND HUMANITY IN CHRIST IN ANOTHER WAY, WITH RESPECT TO PARTICIPATION IN OMNIPOTENCE. (R) A TRICK OF WORDS, BY WHICH THE EYES OF THE INEXPERIENCED ARE HOODWINKED. ALL THINGS ARE VERBAL, NOT REAL, AND THIS IS TO DECEIVE WITH EMPTY WORDS.

TO THESIS 10.

Regarding the humanity's omnipotence, omnipresence, and omniscience, we have responded many times that they are attributed not to the united humanity, but rather to the man in another way [κατ' ἄλλο], (s) and we will say it again below point by point. As far as the analogies of glowing hot iron and the body joined to the soul are concerned, (t) the hypostatic union cannot be defined by these, but rather merely illustrated, provided communication is not able to arise therefrom, as you hold. For there are very many differences among these, and accordingly they should be treated in no other way than in the sense these analogies were applied by the Orthodox fathers. For example, as far as the analogy of the glowing-hot iron is concerned, they were teaching against the Eutychians and the Monothelites that it is just not true that the properties and operations of the natures communicate with each other in spite of their union, (u) or step beyond their own limits, as you hold. And the analogy of the union of soul and body for making up a person, as is known, <206> differs just as greatly from the union of the two natures in Christ. (x) It was applied by the Orthodox brothers in no other way than for the need to show the unity of the person, in two perfect natures, and was not treated further than this. Finally, this rule prevails: in this hypostatic union, the natures themselves remain distinct, and each does distinctly what is proper to itself; (y) accordingly the Word [ὁ λόγος] is distinctly that which is Word [λόγος], and it does distinctly that which belongs to the Word [ὁ λόγος]. (z) Just so, flesh remains also distinctly that which is flesh, and accomplishes that which distinctly belongs to flesh. Hence, to make a long story short: just as we can say there are two distinct essences [οὐσίαι], not separate, but nevertheless distinct in number, so there are also two wills and operative functions [ἐνέργιαι], and two operations [ἐνεργήματα] but one end purpose [ἀποτέλεσμα], just as the person is one only. (a) Nor should Athanasius' saying be understood in another way: it pleased the Word [ὁ λόγος] to reveal its own divine power through the flesh, in and with itself. (b)

DR. JAKOB ANDREAE'S MARGINAL NOTES: (S) IT IS PLAYING WITH WORDS AND A PERVERSION OF MARKED PHRASES, WHICH SHOWS NOT ONLY WHICH NATURE IT IS PROPER TO, BUT ALSO INDICATES THE REASON WHY WHAT IS PROPER TO ONE NATURE IS ATTRIBUTED TO THE OTHER, NAMELY ON ACCOUNT OF THE UNION WITH THE OTHER NATURE, WITH WHICH IT IS PERSONALLY, TRULY, AND REALLY COMMUNICATED TO IT. (T) BY THESE ANALOGIES THE FATHERS DECLARE THE MYSTERY OF UNION AND REAL COMMUNICATION OF PROPERTIES, WHICH CAN HAPPEN WITHOUT CONFUSION OF THE NATURES. (U) MUCH TO THE CONTRARY, IT IS TRUE, FOR THEY THEREFORE DEMONSTRATE REAL COMMUNICATION. SO INDEED AGAINST THE EUTYCHIANS, BECAUSE NO CONFUSION OF THE NATURES OR ABOLITION OF ONE OR THE OTHER FOLLOWS

FROM IT. (X) NO ANALOGY RUNS ON FOUR FEET; RATHER IT SQUARES UP WITH WHAT THE FATHERS WERE ADAPTING IT FOR. <206> (Y) THIS IS A FALSE RULE. FOR THE ACTIONS IN THE PERSON OF CHRIST ARE NEVER ATTRIBUTED DISTINCTLY, THAT IS, SEPARATELY OR DISJOINTEDLY WITH RESPECT TO NATURES, BUT RATHER TO THE ENTIRE PERSON. (Z) WORD [λόγος] DOES NOTHING WITHOUT THE FLESH, JUST AS THE SOUL WORKS NOTHING DISTINCTLY WITHOUT THE FLESH, NOR THE FLESH WITHOUT THE SOUL, EVEN THOUGH THEIR NATURES ARE AND REMAIN DISTINCT, BUT RATHER CHRIST WORKS IN HIS WHOLE PERSON. (A) THE CRASSEST NESTORIANISM. THERE ARE TWO DISTINCT WILLS IN CHRIST, AND TWO DISTINCT ESSENCES [οὐσίαι] AND OPERATIVE FUNCTIONS [ἐνέργιαι], BUT THEIR ACTIONS ARE IN COMMON, DIRECTED TOWARD ONE END. (B) THIS SENTENCE OF ATHANASIUS DOES NOT DEFEND THE ERROR ABOUT THE DISTINCT ACTIONS OF THE NATURES, BUT RATHER REFUTES AND OVERTURNS IT.

TO THESIS 11.

We agree that this entire power, as from all the testimonies which you cite here, is totally different than that which is considered essential and absolutely in God. It is in fact nothing other than the supreme power, according to God, for administrating all created things, (c) to which also the thing itself is referred, and it must accordingly be considered among the gifts conferred to Christ's flesh, that is, to habitual grace, (d) which you nevertheless excluded in thesis 4 from your communication. And as far as the miracles performed by Christ are concerned, we follow the universal consensus of the ancient Orthodox Church, prompted by the analogy of faith, by which the Nestorians, Eutychians, and Monothelites were struck down. It is sufficient to have described these things from the fathers. From Tertullian against Praxeas, we see a twofold status not confused, but conjoined in <207> one person, God and the man Jesus, and in this way the property of each substance is preserved, as also the spirit, that is, the Divinity worked its own things in him, that is, powers, works, signs, and the flesh discharged its own passions, hungering when tempted by the Devil, and thirsting when with the Samaritan woman. (e)

DR. JAKOB ANDREAE'S MARGINAL NOTES: (C) THESE THINGS ARE SAID NOT ONLY WITHOUT ANY WITNESS OF HOLY SCRIPTURE, BUT CONTRARY TO IT. THEY ARE THEREFORE FALSE. (D) THAT POWER CONFERRED TO THE MAN CHRIST SHOULD NEVER BE NUMBERED AMONG THE CREATED GIFTS IS THE PLAIN

CONSENSUS OF HOLY SCRIPTURE AND THE FATHERS. **<207>** (E) THE ORTHODOX FATHERS DESIRED TO SHOW WITH THESE SAYINGS THE ACTIONS THAT WERE PROPER TO WHICH NATURE, BUT THEY NEVER DREAMED THAT THEY WERE EXECUTED DISTINCTLY AND WITHOUT COMMUNICATION. THUS THEY TEACH THAT THE SAYINGS OF TERTULLIAN, CYRIL, AND THE BEST INTERPRETERS OF THEIR WORDS SHOULD BE ACCEPTED.

From Cyril, On the Trinity, Book 5. Those things that are done by Christ in a divine way should not be attributed to the human creation [κτίσις] but rather to the ineffable nature that transcends all thought. From Gregory of Nyssa against Eunomius: The human nature does not vivify Lazarus, nor does the impassible power weep over the one lying in the tomb; rather tears are proper to the man, but those things which belong to true life are proper to life. (f)

DR. JAKOB ANDREAE'S MARGINAL NOTES: (F) GREGORY OF NYSSA IS NOT AN INTERPRETER OF HIS OWN WORDS AS MUCH AS HE IS OF THOSE OF TERTULLIAN AND CYRIL, SPEAKING ABOUT THE PROPERTIES OF THE NATURES, NOT THEIR COMMUNICATION. THEY ARE NOT IN CONFLICT. JOHN OF DAMASCUS ALSO OPENLY CONFIRMS THIS. FOR EVEN IF IT IS NOT PROPER TO THE HUMAN NATURE TO RAISE LAZARUS, NEVERTHELESS IT WAS NOT DIVINE POWER WITHOUT THE HUMAN NATURE THAT RAISED LAZARUS, JUST AS IT WAS NOT PURE MAN, BUT GOD WHO WEPT, THOUGH WEEPING IS NOT PROPER TO GOD.

From John of Damascus, On the Orthodox Faith, Book 3, chapter 15. The human nature did not raise Lazarus from the dead, nor either does the divine power weep. For tears are the certain property of humanity, but life is proper to the life of him who is life subsisting in himself.

TO THESIS 12.

Whatever knowledge Christ had in his state of humiliation, and now has in glory, in so far as he is a man (g) was and is a created gift, and ingrafted subjectively in Christ's soul, and accordingly applies not at all to the communication you suggest. But far be it from us that we would teach that Christ laid aside the form of a slave, that is, his humanity, or ever will, (h) in as much as he has transferred it from humility to distinction, even over all the angels themselves, seated above all the heavens.

DR. JAKOB ANDREAE'S MARGINAL NOTES: (G) THESE THINGS ARE SAID CONTRARY TO THE PLAIN TESTIMONIES OF SCRIPTURE: IN HIM ARE HIDDEN ALL THE TREASURES OF WISDOM AND KNOWLEDGE (COLOSSIANS 2[:3]). (H) THE FORM OF A SLAVE IS NOT THE HUMANITY, BUT THE SERVILE CONDITION OF THE MAN CHRIST. HE IS THE LORD, JOHN 13[:13]: YOU CALL ME LORD, AND DO SO RIGHTLY, FOR I AM.

TO THESES 13 AND 14.

We draw a different conclusion too about omnipresence, which is derived from the two superior things, namely power and knowledge, with which <208> *we acknowledge that the flesh assumed by the Word [λόγος] was most abundantly and ineffably endowed and furnished. But that omnipresence which necessarily presupposes the infinite essence, (i) which is proper to the one Divinity of course, as well as what they call a fourth mode,[24] (k) we can in no way acknowledge in Christ's humanity, though it is united hypostatically and now glorified, but nevertheless retains its own circumscription. Finally, we completely distinguish the matters surpassing nature [ὑπερφυσικά] which we know, and with which Christ's humanity was supremely furnished, from those that are contrary to nature [ἀντιφυσικά], by which the humanity would be abolished. (l) The testimonies you offer here partly concern the unique Divinity of the Word [λόγος] (m) (we can say not separate from the humanity, but nevertheless distinct), and partly pertain to the power he as head brings to bear in his own members*

---

24   Beza uses this language on the two natures in his book *Quaestionum et responsionum Christianarum*, in the section on "idioms." Kirk Summers' modern English translation of the work (*A Little Book of Christian Questions and Responses*, Allison Park: Pickwick Publications, 1986) offers the following answer to the question "what are idioms?" (Q45): "That which the dialectics call proper to the fourth mode: of which manner is (for example) infinity in the divine nature, and quantity in all things created, especially bodily things." Beza is likely going back to John Scotus Eriugena, who asserted five modes of being and non-being. The first mode refers to empirically sensible and understandable things. God in his own essence is not in this first mode. The second mode negates a higher or lower being. For instance, to say a person is a peasant is to deny that they are a king. The third mode distinguishes actually existing things from things that may be or are potential. The fourth mode (mentioned here) involves a Platonic way of thinking and refers to the reality of ideal things, comprehended only by the intellect. This may help to make sense of Beza's concept that the spiritual or intellectual presence of Christ in the supper is in this way of thinking *more real* than the first mode. The fifth mode relates to the difference between believers and nonbelievers. Believers have authentic existence, whereas unbelievers do not, according to this system of thought.

DR. JAKOB ANDREAE'S MARGINAL NOTES: (I) ABSOLUTE OMNIPRESENCE PRESUPPOSE INFINITE ESSENCE. BUT IT IS SUFFICIENT FOR THE PARTICIPATING NATURE THAT THE NATURE BECOMES A PARTICIPANT, BY PARTICIPATION IN WHICH IT POSSESSES THAT WHICH IS IN ITS ESSENCE AN INFINITE NATURE. (K) IT IS NOT SUFFICIENT TO SAY THAT THIS CAN HAPPEN IN NO WAY, BUT RATHER IT NEEDS TO BE PROVED. FOR HOLY SCRIPTURE PLAINLY TESTIFIES TO THE CONTRARY, EPHESIANS 1:4. (L) OMNIPOTENCE, OMNISCIENCE, AND OMNIPRESENCE ARE NOT MATTERS CONTRARY TO NATURE [ἀντιφυσικά] BUT RATHER SURPASSING NATURE [ὑπερφυσικά], ABOVE THE HUMAN NATURE, NOT CONTRARY TO IT, SO THEY ALSO DO NOT OVERTURN IT. (M) CHRIST'S WORDS ARE PLAIN. HE IS HIS OWN INTERPRETER, AND ATTRIBUTES THE POWER *TO THE FLESH* WHICH WAS COMMUNICATED TO IT BY THE WORD [λόγος], AND WHICH IS DERIVED FROM CHRIST AS THE HEAD.

TO THESIS 15.

As far as vivification is concerned, we do not deny that Christ's flesh is vivific, but not in the sense we are concerned with here. (n) For it is vivific, but not by means of that power which is proper to Divinity and utterly incommunicable [ἀκοινώνητος], but rather first, since Christ abolished death for us in this flesh, once all the things which were demanded for winning eternal life for us were fulfilled, and Second, since we do not obtain that eternal life from Christ, God and man, except by the intervention of this flesh communicated to us spiritually, through faith. The testimonies of the Scriptures offered by you should be adapted in this way.

DR. JAKOB ANDREAE'S MARGINAL NOTES: (N) THE ENTIRE CHORUS OF THE ORTHODOX FATHERS CONFIRMS THAT CHRIST'S FLESH IS VIVIFIC *BY THE POWER PROPER TO THE DIVINITY.* THEREFORE WHAT IS ASSERTED IN THIS RESPONSE IS AN OBVIOUS FALSEHOOD.

TO THESIS 16.

That the gifts lavished subjectively on Christ's flesh (of which kind are those you recount here) were conferred neither immediately nor perfectly, as they have now been conferred to CHRIST'S soul and body, (o) is clear from the fact that <209> his body grew in stature, as also his soul in wisdom and grace, as Luke 2[:52] truly says, (p) and he did not know the last day, Matthew 24[:36]. And the Apostle says that he was truly susceptible to all the infirmities of

our flesh, with the exception of sin, during the time of his humiliation. In this sense he is called subject to suffering [παθητός] (Acts
26[:23]), but not merely according to appearance [κατὰ δόκησιν], as
Marcion blasphemously said. Now this flesh could not possibly be
at one and the same time subject to suffering [παθητή] (q) and also
the sort of thing that we judge it to have been like at the time of his
dereliction. Whence it follows that, by his ascension to heaven and
his session and the right hand of the Father, Christ's flesh has not
attained merely the declaration and use of this glory and power, but
rather the consummation of its glory and power. (r)

DR. JAKOB ANDREAE'S MARGINAL NOTES: (O) IT WAS SHOWN ABOVE THAT THE
GIFTS LAVISHED ON CHRIST'S FLESH SUBJECTIVELY ARE NOT OMNIPOTENCE,
OMNIPRESENCE, OMNISCIENCE, AND THE POWER OF VIVIFYING. SINCE THESE
ARE NOT ACCIDENTS EITHER IN *GOD* OR IN THE ASSUMED HUMAN NATURE, BUT
RATHER ESSENCES IN GOD, PERSONALLY GRANTED IN THE ASSUMED MAN.
<209> (P) ALL THESE TESTIMONIES SHOULD BE REFERRED TO THE STATE OF
HUMILIATION AND EMPTINESS. (Q) ON THE CONTRARY, PAUL, WHO SAYS THAT
CHRIST WAS IN THE FORM OF GOD AND AT THE SAME TIME TOOK ON THE FORM
OF A SLAVE, PHILIPPIANS 2([:6-7]). (R) THIS CONSUMMATION WAS THE
REVELATION OF COMMUNICATION OF MAJESTY, WHICH WAS FORMERLY HIDDEN
UNDER THE FORM OF A SLAVE.

To Thesis 17.

We agree with this thesis with the exception of two points. First,
that you accept that the form of a slave, and the state of humiliation
as you call it, (s) are one and the same thing, and think that each
was laid aside by Christ. But by form of a slave we understand the
humanity itself, (t) according to which it always was, is, and will
be inferior to the Word [λόγος] itself, (u) and of the same substance
[ὁμοούσιος] with us, even though he laid aside all infirmities after
the ministry of our redemption was accomplished. But circumscription must not in the least be counted among those infirmities, (x)
inasmuch as it formally constitutes humanity itself. Otherwise
when he comes visibly on the last day, and accordingly, by means
of circumscribed bodily substance, it would then have to be said
that he would appear not as the most glorious, but humble, with
this infirmity taken up again. Second, we confess that Christ indeed

rules now, and possesses all authority, both in heaven and on earth, according to both natures. But not presently, (y) as far as **<210>** *the flesh is concerned. The Apostle says that we are absent from Christ now on earth, not at home, and desire to leave the body to be joined to him. (z) On this account we say that he has indeed not yet come, nor is present in his flesh, but will certainly appear again, visibly from the invisible, or rather will come for all to see. (a)*

DR. JAKOB ANDREAE'S MARGINAL NOTES: (S) LOOK AT PAUL'S WORDS, AND THE MATTER WILL BE CLEAR. (T) YOU SAY IT BUT DO NOT PROVE IT, WHICH DOES NOT SUFFICE. (U) EVEN IF THE HUMANITY WAS ALWAYS INFERIOR IN NATURE TO THE WORD [λόγος], NEVERTHELESS HE IS NO LONGER A SLAVE. (X) COMMUNICATION OF MAJESTY DOES NOT CONFLICT WITH CIRCUMSCRIPTION, NOR ABOLISH IT, OR OVERTURN NATURE, BUT RATHER EXALTS TO THE HIGHEST DEGREE OF GLORY ON THE THRONE PROPER TO GOD. (Y) VERY PRESENT, SINCE HE RULES NOT THROUGH SUBSTITUTES, BUT RATHER BY HIS VERY SELF, AS WAS SAID ABOVE. **<210>** (Z) THE PILGRIMAGE IS PHYSICAL AND LOCAL, WHICH DOES NOT TAKE AWAY FROM THE SPIRITUAL PRESENCE, BY WHICH CHRIST IS VERY PRESENT TO US. (A) VISIBLY, WHO NOW IS PRESENT INVISIBLY HERE ON EARTH IN A HEAVENLY WAY.

TO THESES 18 AND 19.

We agree, but are missing this from you besides, that just as you rightly and piously attribute by the communication of Attributes to God incarnate, on account of the hypostatic union and with respect to the whole person, what things are proper to the assumed humanity, you should attribute also to the man what things are proper to the assuming Divinity of the Word [ὁ λόγος]. (b) And lest we seem to request of you something novel, we say that we are asking what Dr. Luther once wrote should be done in so many words in the last words of David: just as two natures are united into one person, (c) so also the names of each nature are united into the name of the one person, which is called the communication of attributes or properties. As a man is called and is born of the virgin Mary, and was crucified by the Jews, the same name ought also to be attributed to the son of God, and it should be said that God was born from the virgin Mary, and was crucified by the Jews, since God and Man is one person, and there are not two sons, the one of God, the other of Mary, but he is one and the same Son of God and Son of man. But even though the assuming nature excels in all ways and especially in this, that subsisting in and of itself it furnishes subsistence for the human nature, nevertheless it is united not in a different way, but in the way of one and the same union, Word with the flesh, and flesh with the Word. *(d)* And that vast difference, by which it happens that the assuming Divinity receives nothing from the human nature that it assumes, but rather the humanity is thereafter enriched, pertains not to the hypostatic union itself, but rather to its effect, which we have said is called habitual grace. *(e)*

DR. JAKOB ANDREAE'S MARGINAL NOTES: (B) THE WAY OF COMMUNICATION IS DIFFERENT ON ACCOUNT OF THE DIFFERENCE BETWEEN THE NATURES, AND THE IMMUTABILITY OF THE DIVINE NATURE. (C) WE EMBRACE BOTH THE WORDS AND THE MEANING OF LUTHER. BUT WE DO NOT UNDERSTAND IT AS MERELY A VERBAL, BUT RATHER AS A REAL UNION. YET YOU ACCEPT ONLY A VERBAL ONE, WHICH IS FALSE. (D) THIS IS MOST UNTRUE. SINCE THE TWO NATURES ARE UNITED IN SUCH A WAY THAT THE ONE GIVES AND THE OTHER RECEIVES. BUT HERE THE DIVINE NATURE CAN ACCEPT NOTHING FROM THE HUMAN NATURE EITHER OF PERFECTION OR IMPERFECTION, ON ACCOUNT OF ITS OWN SUPREME PERFECTION AND IMMUTABILITY. FOR THIS REASON THE WAY OF UNION IS QUITE DIFFERENT. (E) BY THE GRACE OF UNION THE HUMAN NATURE POSSESSES THOSE THINGS THAT ARE PROPER TO DIVINITY.

<211>

TO THESIS 20.

We do not in the least divide the person of our one sole mediator in worship solely directed according to either nature, *(f)* but rather correctly distinguish the natures. The Word [Λόγος] is in fact the true and absolute object of our worship, inasmuch as it is owed to God alone. *(g)* But we do not exclude the assumed flesh from our worship, lest we divide the person with Nestorius, with the result that we worship the flesh at the same time (not in itself), *(h)* but rather respectively, (that is, in so far as it is the flesh of the son of God, constituting a unique person with and in the Word [Λόγος]). *(i)* For simply the humanity considered in itself *(k)* and not in another respect, says Cyril,[25] numbers itself among those who worship, and Christ also worships, as a man, after he has become man. But he is

---

25   Cyril, *Commentary on John* (as referred to in Andreae's marginal note).

always worshiped with Father and Spirit, since he is true God by nature. And the same thing regarding the right faith to Theodosius: Surely we will not worship Immanuel as a man (namely in himself, absolutely, even considered in the union)? May this not be! This would in fact be nonsense and deception and error. For in this we would be no different at all from those who worship the creature more than the creator and maker. To put it all finally in a few words, following the eighth Anathema of the Council of Chalcedon, we worship Immanuel with one worship, but accordingly as the son of God essentially became flesh by the hypostatic union.

DR. JAKOB ANDREAE'S MARGINAL NOTES: <211> (F) YOU ARE UNWILLING TO SEEM TO DO SO IN WORDS, BUT YOU ACTUALLY DO THIS, SO LONG AS YOU TAKE AWAY FROM CHRIST ACCORDING TO HIS HUMANITY WHAT THINGS ARE NECESSARILY REQUIRED FOR RELIGIOUS WORSHIP, NAMELY THE COMMUNICATION OF OMNIPOTENCE. (G) YOU ARE ASSERTING THAT IT IS NOT POSSIBLE FOR WHAT IS OWED TO GOD ALONE TO BE ATTRIBUTED ON THAT ACCOUNT TO THE FLESH WITHOUT BLASPHEMY. (H) YOU ARE CLEARLY LEAVING OUT THAT YOU UNDERSTAND THE SUBSTANCE OF THE HUMAN NATURE *IN ITSELF*, WHICH SHOULD NOT BE CALLED UPON, BUT RATHER THE WORD [λόγος], TO WHICH IT HAS BEEN UNITED. (I) JUST LIKE THE HAT, THAT IS, THE KING'S CROWN, WHEN THE KING IS REVERED, WHICH NO ONE ADDRESSES. BOOK ON JOHN 2, CHAPTER 92, IN THESE WORDS. WE WORSHIP WHAT WE KNOW.[26] (K) IN ITSELF. CYRIL UNDERSTANDS IN THIS PASSAGE AND THIS SENTENCE THE PROPERTY OF THE SUBSTANCE OF THE HUMANITY, IF IT IS CONSIDERED IN ITSELF, AND AT THE SAME TIME EMBRACES THE STATE OF HUMILIATION. (M) THEY APPROVE THE ANATHEMA VERBALLY, BUT ACTUALLY DISAPPROVE IT.

TO THESIS 21.

We confess the sound and pious doctrine about the inseparable hypostatic union. We acknowledge a real communication of attributes with respect to the unity of person. (n) We acknowledge also, against Nestorius, that the man has been elevated by the hypostatic union to Divinity itself, and it goes without saying to his majesty and power, <212> with the result that through the communication he has become God and Word [Θεὸς καὶ λόγος], (o) and then by his ineffable gifts, extolled above the angels themselves. But we deny, against Eutyches, that humanity itself has become Divinity by the

---

26 *Commentary on John*, Book 2, cp. 5.

hypostatic union, or been made a sharer in divine properties by any communication arising therefrom. *(p)* But we think that his situation at the right hand of God should not in the least be credited to the incarnation, but rather partly to declare that the time of the humiliation of the Word *[ὁ λόγος]* was at an end, and partly to declare the consummation of his glory and the habitual grace of Christ's flesh. *(q)* Finally, the presence of Christ's flesh in the Lord's Supper we do not credit to the hypostatic union, but rather to the words of sacramental institution, the way we said in our writing above, namely, a spiritual presence. *(r)* In this way is he present to the entire Church according to the flesh, partly by his own power, partly since it is the one person of Jesus Christ, and we learn from holy writ that he will be present to the consummation of the age. Since in other respects by the substance of his real body just as when he was on earth he was absent from heaven, thus now situated in heaven he is absent from earth. *(s)* Nevertheless he makes his flesh known, to his own for eternal life, very truly and very efficaciously at this time in the wonderful and inscrutable mystery, both in the word, and in the Sacraments, spiritually through faith. *(t)*

DR. JAKOB ANDREAE'S MARGINAL NOTES: (N) COMMUNICATION OF ATTRIBUTES IS NOTHING TO THESE PEOPLE OTHER THAN A UNION OF NATURES AND PROPERTIES, ALTHOUGH THESE DIFFER AS CAUSE AND EFFECT. <212> (O) MAN BECAME GOD AND WORD [θεὸς καὶ λόγος], WHICH THUS FAR THEY REPROVE IN US, BUT WHAT THEY UNDERSTAND WILL FOLLOW.[27] (P) IS THIS NOT TO DENY OPENLY WITH NESTORIUS THE COMMUNICATION OF ATTRIBUTES? (Q) PERVERSE INTERPRETATION OF THE RIGHT HAND OF GOD AND SESSION AT THE RIGHT HAND OF GOD, CONCERNING WHICH MORE WILL BE SAID IN CONFERENCE. (R) A CONTRADICTION IS MANIFEST IN THE WORDS OF THE THESIS. FOR THEY DENY THAT THE HYPOSTATIC UNION PRODUCES A SACRAMENTAL PRESENCE, BUT HE IS PRESENT TO THE ENTIRE CHURCH BY HIS OWN POWER AND SINCE HE IS ONE PERSON OF CHRIST. (S) WE SAY HE IS IN HEAVEN AND NOT ON EARTH BY THE PROPERTY OF THE NATURE, A FACT THAT DOES NOT AT ALL DIMINISH THE SACRAMENTAL PRESENCE. (T) SINCE THIS MAKING KNOWN DOES NOT HAPPEN WITHOUT A REAL PRESENCE, WHAT IS THE REASON THAT YOU DO NOT GIVE GLORY TO GOD AND SAY IT OPENLY WITH US?

---

27   This annotation in the printed edition is preceded by a "N.B." (*nota bene*).

At Montbéliard, 24 March, 1586.

Signed:

Theodore Beza, Minister of the Church at Geneva.

Abraham Musculus, Minister of the Church at Bern.

Antoine de La Faye, Minister of the Church at Geneva.

Claude Albery, Professor of Philosophy in the Academy
at Lausanne.

Pierre Hübner, Professor of Greek, in the public
Gymnasium at Bern.

<213>

2D. TO THE DOGMAS, WHICH THE COLLOCUTORS JUDGE DISAGREE WITH HOLY SCRIPTURE, ETC.

RESPONSE 1.

We condemn those also (if there are any of this sort) who think that the natures are united through the hypostatic union only as far as the names are concerned, as if through that union it is not Word [λόγος], but is only called man, and in turn think that the man does not exist in reality, but is called God only in name. (a) But we deny that from this union anything is communicated to the humanity other than the union of properties of the Word [λόγος], as if in the Word [λόγος] the humanity is really omnipotent and omnipresent, etc. (b) Because this communication and union is one and the same thing. (c) And as we answered to Thesis 18 and 19, the Word [λόγος] would need to accept something from the humanity in precisely the same way. (d) Therefore those things which they censure here in the first place do not at all pertain to us. But we consider the Communication of Attributes real, as also the union; nevertheless not in respect to the unity of natures, (e) but in respect to a unity of person; and we thus interpret this enunciation, by which God is said to have suffered: God, that is, the flesh united to his Divinity, suffered. (f) We have learned to understand this in fact from the Apostle Peter, who says that CHRIST (that is, the person) suffered in the flesh, that is, in his humanity, not in his Divinity. (g) And in turn we interpret: a man is omnipotent, that is, Divinity united to the humanity, is omnipotent. (h) We do not on this account divide the person with Nestorius, (i) but we distinguish the natures, and their properties, as the definition of hypostatic union demands, against Eutyches. (k) <214> *Finally let Dr. Luther respond to you; these are his words in the sermon for the Nativity on the first chapter of the Epistle to the Hebrews: The humanity of Christ equally and otherwise is holy and natural man; he did not always think all things, say all things, wish or turn his attention to all things, as if some sort of omnipotent man, as those who unwisely confuse the two natures and their workings make of him.*[28] *(l)*

ANNOTATIONS: (A) INDEED, YOU CONDEMN WITH WORDS, BUT YOU ASSERT THE SAME THING IN REALITY, WHICH WILL BECOME PLAIN A LITTLE LATER. (B) WHAT COULD BE SAID MORE PLAINLY? THEY DENY THAT THE HUMANITY IS REALLY OMNIPOTENT IN THE WORD [λόγος]. (C) UNION AND COMMUNICATION ARE FAR DIFFERENT. (D) IT DOES NOT FOLLOW: BECAUSE IT IS SUFFICIENT FOR THE UNION THAT DIVINITY GIVES AND HUMANITY RECEIVES. (E) THERE IS CLEARLY NO COMMUNICATION, IF NEITHER NATURE SHOULD PARTAKE OF THE OTHER, BECAUSE THAT IS ITS PROPERTY. AND THIS WAS PAUL OF SAMOSATA'S ERROR. (F) AN OPENLY NESTORIAN NEGATION OF THE COMMUNICATION OF ATTRIBUTES. (G) A DISTORTION OF PETER'S WORDS, WHICH OVERTURN THE PRIOR ASSERTION. FOR IT IS ONE THING TO SAY CHRIST SUFFERED IN THE FLESH; AND IT IS ANOTHER TO SAY THE FLESH OF CHRIST SUFFERED. (H) WHAT IS HERE ATTRIBUTED TO MAN, EXCEPT A VAIN TITLE? NAY RATHER, IT DETRACTS FROM THE MAN WHAT IS ASCRIBED TO THE DIVINITY ALONE, NAMELY OMNIPOTENCE. *NESTORIANISM.* (I) NESTORIUS SAID THE SAME THING, BUT SINCE HIS STATEMENT WAS MEANINGLESS, THE FATHERS OF THE COUNCIL CONDEMNED HIM OF HERESY. <214> (K) THIS IS NOT TO DISTINGUISH, BUT TO SEPARATE. (L) LUTHER WROTE THESE WORDS ABOUT CHRIST, INSOFAR AS HE WAS IN THE STATE OF HUMILITY, AND IN ORDER THAT HE MIGHT DEMONSTRATE THE DISTINCTION OF THE NATURES IN CHRIST. BY NO MEANS, HOWEVER, DOES HE DENY THAT CHRIST IS AN OMNIPOTENT MAN IN GOD.

RESPONSE 2.

We do not know whether anyone could be so mad as to think in regard to the Word [ὁ λόγος] that it somehow withdrew into itself, (m) when it assumed flesh, and then came back again, after the flesh

---

28   Christmas morning service, third sermon (Hebrews 1.1–12), Christmas postil (1522).

was carried up above every name into its glory once the Ministry of our redemption had been completed. Rather, we teach this, following Paul, that the Word [ὁ λόγος] emptied itself "in a certain manner," not into itself, but insofar as it was almost hiding, sustaining itself though its glory was concealed for a time, just as once again, once the flesh was fully glorified, it received its own former glory back, not into itself, but rather in the "certain manner," which he asked also of his father, John 17:5.

ANNOTATIONS: (M) SCRIPTURES ARE EXTANT WHICH MOTIVATE SOME PEOPLE TO DENY THE DIVINITY OF THE MAN CHRIST.

RESPONSE 3.

We teach that the office of mediator comes together in the whole Christ and the entirety of Christ, but as with the natures, so also with their distinct operations. (n) So the humanity always resided underneath the Word [ὁ λόγος], and still does, however glorified it may be. But the Word [ὁ λόγος] (though insofar as he is the redeemer, he is the mediator between the Church and the Father, whom we have acquired by his blood, and of which Church he is head) is not on this account God equivocally [ὁμωνύμως], or inferior in person to the father.

ANNOTATIONS: (N) BY DISTINCT HE UNDERSTANDS THE AGENTS SEPARATELY, WITHOUT ANY COMMUNICATION, WHICH IS FALSE. HE MAKES NO ANSWER TO THE THESIS.

<215>

RESPONSE 4.

We affirm without blasphemy that Christ's humanity, as ever subjected under the Divinity, cannot be regarded as equal to either the substance [οὐσία] or the power of the Word [ἐξουσία τοῦ λόγου], (o) by which it was assumed, which the reality indicates. Paul also eloquently express this in 1 Corinthians 15, making a distinction about the power of his reign when he says, he is excepted, who subjected all things under the son (1 Corinthians 15[:27]). The Word [λόγος] himself however, even though distinct in person from the father, in office the mediator between the father and the Church, is nevertheless one with the father according to essence, and insofar as he is the son, equal to his father.

ANNOTATIONS: (O) POWER [ἐξουσία] DOES NOT SIGNIFY THE ABSOLUTE POWER OF GOD (WHICH IS THE VERY ESSENCE [οὐσία] OF DIVINITY) BUT RATHER HIS PARTICIPATION.

RESPONSE 5.

Luther answered before you in the passage cited above that Christ the man (that is, according to his humanity) was only capable of as much and could know as much as the Word [λόγος] wanted him to be capable of and to know. (p) And we ought certainly to recognize that Christ the man knew all things and knows them without any change according to his Divinity, but at the time of his humility was ignorant of much according to his humanity, on account of us, none of which is nevertheless unknown to him in his glory. (q)

ANNOTATIONS: (P) LUTHER WISHED TO TEACH NOTHING LESS; THEREFORE LET THIS CITATION BE INSPECTED AND ACCURATELY EXAMINED. (Q) NEVERTHELESS THEY DO NOT WISH OR DARE TO ASSERT THAT HE KNOWS ALL THINGS.

RESPONSE 6.

We affirm the first part of this Article; we denounce the last part. (r)

ANNOTATIONS: (R) MANY PEOPLE REJECT PRESENCE AND OMNIPRESENCE IN OPEN WORDS.

RESPONSE 7.

That has indeed been said falsely against us, as it appears from our response at the earlier Thesis 15. (s)

ANNOTATIONS: (S) DISSIMULATION OF ERROR.

<216>

RESPONSE 8.

We answer also to the undeserved objection against us (if these things are said against us) at Thesis 20. (t)

ANNOTATIONS: (T) THEY ARE SPOKEN ABOUT DANEAU, WHOSE STANDARD WORDS HAVE BEEN RECITED HERE, AND OTHERWISE OFTEN REPEATED.

> *At Montbéliard, 24 March, 1586.*
> *Signed:*
> *Theodore Beza, Minister of the Church at Geneva.*
> *Abraham Musculus, Minister of the Church at Bern.*
> *Antoine de La Faye, Minister of the Church at Geneva.*
> *Claude Albery, Professor of Philosophy in the Academy*
> > *at Lausanne.*
> *Pierre Hübner, Professor of Greek, in the public*
> > *Gymnasium at Bern.*

2E.I. DISCUSSION ON THE PERSON OF CHRIST

Dr. Jakob:

WHO HAS GIVEN A REASON FOR DISPUTING ABOUT THE PERSON OF CHRIST.

Reverend Dr. Beza, your Reverence is not ignorant why it has come to a dispute regarding the person of Christ in our contention over the Lord's Supper.

THE WÜRTTEMBERG THEOLOGIANS URGE ALL PEOPLE TO SIMPLICITY OF FAITH. OCCASION OF THE DISPUTE REGARDING GOD'S OMNIPOTENCE.

Our side showed afterwards in Christ's words that his *will* was in fact to be present in his body and blood in the Eucharist, and to distribute it with the bread, and that it be eaten orally by us. He said, Take and eat, This is my body, etc.; Take, drink, this is my blood, etc. We eagerly urge our hearers, indeed all pious and faithful people, both in our writings and our speech, simply to have faith in the words of Christ's Testament, without any dispute or doubt. We do so now as well. Since Christ is not only truthful, [217] and is not able

to deceive or lie, but is also omnipotent, and with whom no word is impossible, as the Angel says to Mary (Luke 1[:37]). From this point our adversaries have begun to dispute about the power not only of Christ the man, but also about the absolute power of God.

PETER MARTYR'S UNHOLY OPINION ON THE ABSOLUTE POWER OF GOD. LAMBERT DANEAU'S BLASPHEMY IN THE ASSERTION AGAINST DR. JAKOB ANDREAE. BEZA AND HIS PARTY APPROVE THE SAME OPINION IN THE RESPONSES CONCERNING THE LORD'S SUPPER AND THE PERSON OF CHRIST.

For Peter Martyr in his Dialogue expressly wrote: *It cannot happen by any means* that a created thing be everywhere. And not so long ago, Lambert Daneau wrote in a pamphlet published in Geneva: *Christ could not even have wished* that his body be present at one and the same time in multiple locations, since he cannot be so present. And in your own Theses regarding the Lord's Supper, the same is also affirmed. This has been repeated in your Responses concerning the person of Christ, where you contend that on account of this God is not able to be denied omnipotence, even though he cannot be present like this.

The Theologians of our Confession have opposed themselves to this doctrine, and have demonstrated not only the *willingness*, but also the *capability*, by which he not only wishes but also is able to be present bodily in multiple—indeed in all—places in a divine and heavenly way, in which the Lord's Supper is celebrated over all the earth at the same time.

FROM WHOM HAS ARISEN THE CONTROVERSY CONCERNING THE OMNIPOTENCE OF CHRIST AS GOD, BY WHOM IT HAS BEEN KINDLED. WHY CHRIST'S OMNIPOTENCE MUST BE DISPUTED.

From this it is clear that the controversy and dispute regarding the person of Christ *did not arise from us*. Rather, our adversaries have presented not only the occasion for it, but also the reason. For if what Martyr and Daneau and their people say were true, that Christ in his universal power, and even by his own omnipotence, cannot bring it about that his body is truly and really present in multiple, and indeed all, places in which the Lord's Supper is celebrated over all the earth, then it is futile to dispute the matter from the words of the Testament.

THE LUTHERANS DRAGGED INTO THE DISPUTE REGARDING GOD'S OMNIPOTENCE AGAINST THEIR WILL.

But if it should be conceded, and God's power not at all doubted or disputed, that he can be present, as we have always done, and now do also, and indeed will do henceforth, then we would straight-way disregard that disputation, and urge all people to <218> simple faith in the words of Christ, so that when he says, This is my body, they simply believe that it is Christ's body, which he has given to them. And since he bids them eat orally, they should eat, and do so in memory of his death. If our adversaries had remained in this simplicity of faith, we would never have arrived at this Disputation regarding the person of Christ.

Very little mention of this dispute was made, however, in the conference regarding the Lord's Supper, although you mentioned it in the Theses regarding the Lord's Supper, where you introduced certain things about a double divinity and omnipotence. But we have saved it for this place, lest the material and doctrine of different *loci* be commingled and confused, since we decided amongst ourselves from the beginning of the conference not to let anything drop into another article, before the proposed *locus* had been resolved and the conference about it completed.

CHIEF QUESTION IN THE MATTER OF THE PERSON OF CHRIST, NAMELY CONCERNING THE REAL COMMUNICATION OF ATTRIBUTES.

The entire Dispute, though, revolves around one very important question, which concerns the real communication of divine and human properties. If this is explained, I am confident of an answer to all the things that are contained in your Theses and assertion.

IN WHAT MATTERS THERE IS CONSENSUS CONCERNING THE PERSON OF CHRIST.

For we say the following: 1. That in Christ are two natures, divine and human; 2. That in Christ the single natures perpetually retain their own essential properties, even in the union itself, and never lay them aside or lose them;

3. That the properties of one nature can never become the properties of the other nature; 4. That the divine nature cannot be changed into the human, nor the human into the divine; 5. That neither the natures nor their properties are commingled such that they together become a third, which is neither a divine nor a human nature; 6. That the natures are not separated, although the natures and their properties are perpetually distinct and remain so; 7. That in Christ there is one person and not two persons.

<219>

Concerning all these chief points in the doctrine of the person of Christ, as I see it, there is no controversy between us. For we confess the same thing from both sides both in speech and writing.

A TWOFOLD QUESTION REGARDING COMMUNICATION.

But concerning communication there is a question, and it is twofold. The first concerns the Natures themselves. The other concerns the properties of the Natures.

---

1. QUESTION REGARDING THE COMMUNICATION OF NATURES IN THE PERSON OF CHRIST.

For it is asked, whether the union of Natures in Christ's person is like that in which neither nature communicates anything to the other except for its name. For example: Although Christ is Man, he is called God. Is it merely the name of Deity, or is Deity itself communicated to the human nature?

---

2. QUESTION REGARDING THE COMMUNICATION OF PROPERTIES. CHIEF POINT OF THE ENTIRE DISPUTE REGARDING THE PERSON OF CHRIST.

Then it is asked, whether the properties of the natures in the person of Christ are communicated through the union, not merely verbally, but also really, in the abstract, or in the concrete. For example, when we say: God suffered; the Man Christ is omnipotent. In these two questions revolves the chief point of the entire dispute regarding the person of Christ. In these matters we for our part hold the affirmative, namely that there is a real communication of the natures and properties in the person of Christ, that is, in the concrete, and not in the abstract, with the exception of the natures and properties considered in and of themselves outside of the union. Up to this point you have contended for the negative.

We leave now to the judgment of these Gentlemen what has been set forth: whether they themselves wish to take the position of disputant against us? Or whether we ought to take the position of disputant against them? We think it makes little difference whether we take up the part of disputant or respondent, since according to the administration of the disputation, if anything has been objected to by the opposing party, both parties need to dispute and respond and come to resolution.

Dr. Beza:

1. HOW THE WORDS OF THE TESTAMENT MUST BE BELIEVED IN SIMPLE FAITH.

Reverend Doctor, in these matters which it has pleased your worthiness to offer, you have also carefully commended the simplicity of the Christian faith, [220] and affirmed that they sin who depart from this simplicity. This is a nice saying, but it does not pertain to us. For no one of us has ever denied this. And indeed we agree that Christ's words must be believed with very simple faith, since Christ does not lie; rather he is truth itself (John 14[:6]). However in regard to the interpretation of Christ's words in the Eucharist, we are debating what the genuine and real meaning of them is. For we understand and interpret them differently than you.

2. WHY THEY MENTION CREATED OMNIPOTENCE AND DEITY.

Now, we mentioned created and uncreated Divinity and omnipotence. I in fact remember that I read that the real presence of Christ's body and blood in the Lord's Supper could not be established unless the omnipresence of Christ's body were put forward and conceded, the business we are attending to now. I also remember that I read this in your writings. It remains for me therefore to say and explain what our opinion and doctrine is concerning this article, which I will do briefly.

---

3. DR. BEZA'S CONFESSION REGARDING THE PERSON OF CHRIST.

In this we agree, it is true, that in the hypostatic union two natures are united, a divine and a human, without any separation, confusion, or commingling. And indeed they are so united and conjoined that THEY CONSTITUTE one person, not composed of parts, as a man is composed of soul and body, but rather since the Word [λόγος] as an individual assumed a human nature.

---

4. STATUS OF THE CONTROVERSY REGARDING THE PERSON OF CHRIST.

And since the properties are inseparable from the natures, we say that the properties remain sound in their particular natures in this union, and not destroyed or mixed. For just as the substances of the natures, so also the properties of the natures remain sound and distinct. In all these matters I think we agree. But it is asked whether it should be thought that some real communication of properties has happened on account of, and through, this hypostatic union of the natures in the person of Christ, besides those exceptional, singular, and ineffable gifts <221> with which Christ's human nature was adorned above all other saints, and which the Flesh attained from the Word [λόγος] through the personal union, such that the essential properties of divinity are really communicated to the assumed human nature IN SOME MANNER, I see that you think this, and we deny it. So then:

---

5. DR. BEZA'S CONFESSION REGARDING THE COMMUNICATION OF ATTRIBUTES.
6. ONE KIND OF UNION OF NATURES IN CHRIST.

We confess that whatsoever can be communicated to this Man, which the human nature is capable of containing, has been communicated. Since therefore that Man was assumed as God, it is necessary for him to be adapted to the properties of Divinity. But this, such that they are not in the man PER SE, but in the Word [λόγος]. And although we know that in that hypostatic union the divine nature excels in infinite ways and rises above the assumed flesh, nevertheless we say that the Word [Λόγος] is united to the flesh in one way, and that the flesh is united to the Word [Λόγος]. From this it is also said in the same way that Man is God and God is Man. And again, God redeemed the Church by his own blood, God was crucified, or the Lord of glory was crucified. In such a way also is it said rightly in the same way, This Man is God omnipotent, omnipresent, and omniscient.

WHAT ABSTRACT MEANS IN SCHOLARLY DISCUSSIONS.

For just as the properties of humanity are attributed to God, so the properties of divinity are attributed to Man, namely on account of the hypostatic union. And in this way it is also fitting to speak, and so we say that we must speak. Since in fact there is one subsisting thing [ὑφιστάμενον], for this reason also there is one and the same way of communication. But the assertion is false that says, Humanity is Divinity, Divinity is Humanity, although the assertions, God is Man, and Man is God, are true. The foundation of this distinction is the distinction of abstract and concrete. For abstract in scholarly discussions is said to be not whatever is removed from something, but rather what is understood to be the form <222> which accidentally exists in something. In this way justice and the Just differ, the one abstract, the other concrete. Here justice does not mean something abstracted from a just man, but rather the form inhering in a just man. Justice is in fact an accident in a just man, not something abstracted from him.

In this way Man and Humanity differ, the one concrete, the other abstract. So when we speak about humanity, we are not abstracting or removing it from man. In this manner also, when we mention Divinity, we are not abstracting it from God, but we are considering both the divine and human nature, OF WHAT KIND either is in itself, in its very own nature.[29]

---

29   The logic of Beza's argument relies on the cognate Latin words *humanitas < homo; deitas < deus.*

CONCERNING THE PERSON OF CHRIST

PREDICATIONS IN THE ABSTRACT AND THE CONCRETE.

With this foundation established, we therefore say: Just as one cannot speak about the nature, nor can it be predicated of the nature, that Divinity is humanity, Humanity is Divinity, so also can one not say about the essential properties of the natures, that they are either predicated of each other or belong one to the other. For this reason, even if one could say concretely and truly, Man is omnipotent, nevertheless one cannot say truly, humanity is omnipotent.

For in the concrete only those things which are proper to Divinity are attributed to man, and vice versa, those things which are proper to humanity are attributed to God.

Dr. Jakob:
Reverend Dr. Beza, I leave to the judgment of the audience whatever I said about simplicity of faith, and whether you depart from it when you attack the plain, literal meaning [τὸ ῥητόν] in the words of the Testament, and necessarily teach evasion to figure of speech, which you say is Metonymy, by which a noun is put in place of another noun. We think enough has been said about this matter in the preceding conference on the Lord's Supper.

<223>

Concerning whether I or others handed down or wrote about Divinity and a two-fold omnipotence, a created and an uncreated, as you mention here, and also in what way the doctrine of the Lord's Supper depends on the person of Christ, this will be taken up in its own place.

For unless it were the flesh of the Son of God, it could not be the vivific food of life in the Lord's Supper, and even if it were present and being distributed, it would be futile to eat it for this purpose.

So also, as regards what you discussed concerning the personal union of the two natures in the one person of Christ, there is no dis-agreement between us, just as it stands from the brief memorandum I submitted.

I say also that the status of the controversy has been correctly stated by you here, namely, whether the properties of the divine nature have been communicated *in some way* to the human nature *really* in the person of Christ? This the audience should endeavor to remember attentively.

And I would wish moreover that the terms "abstract and concrete" were as well-known to the whole audience as they are to us. Since, though, I fear that they are less familiar to them, we will avoid these and other scholastic terms as much as possible, and speak about the matter at hand in such a way that we may be understood rightly by each and every one in the audience. After all, it is also for their sake that this conference has been established. And so I will respond briefly to those things which you have pointed out concerning the meaning of the term abstract. For the distinction between the terms concrete and abstract is, by God's grace, well-known to me.

You point out that by abstract is not meant something removed or separated from a thing, but the form of the thing itself, and you explain this with the example of justice and the just. Here justice is not separated from the just, since it is abstracted, that is, it is considered just as *it is in itself*, but it remains in a just man, united with him.

ABSTRACTION HAPPENS IN A TWO-FOLD WAY.

To this I respond that something is abstracted from something else in two ways. First, mentally or in thought, when a thing is considered in itself, by reason of its form, either substantial or accidental, with the result that it becomes almost <224> the Idea of the thing from which it is abstracted. And this abstraction happens in individual or singular things.

WHAT ABSTRACT MEANS.

Second is the abstraction which does not happen mentally or in thought only, but also actually, when one thing is so abstracted from another that it is separated and removed. I wish to explain with an example brought up by you. Justice is called abstract, that is, a certain form considered by itself apart from the subject in which it exists. From this subject it can actually be removed and abstracted, with the subject's substance remaining sound. The concrete expression of it is the Just, which signifies the subject having that form. From this it is clear that by the term abstract is meant only one thing, namely, the form, and that either only mentally or actually abstracted.

WHAT CONCRETE MEANS.

Now, concrete can mean two things, namely the form which exists in a certain thing, and the thing in which this form exists. If, therefore, in the Dispute regarding the person of Christ, the term "Humanity" is abstract, that is, signifies the form of a human, but Man is concrete, that is, the thing which possesses this form, just as the just is said to possess justice, and so is said to be the just, then I ask you whether the humanity that the Son *of God* assumed is abstract or concrete, which is called Man? Please answer me honestly.

Dr. Beza:
The Son of God assumed an individual.

Dr. Jakob:
This is not at all an answer to the question I put forward regarding abstract and concrete. For I am asking, since in your opinion humanity is abstract, and Man is concrete (these things should not be at all confused, and we are even rebuked by you under the accusation that we confuse the terms abstract and concrete), whether the Son of God assumed man or humanity?

Dr. Beza:
I say that the Son of God assumed an individual thing.

<225>

Dr. Jakob:
This is not at all an answer to the question I put forward regarding abstract and concrete. For I am asking, since in your opinion humanity is abstract, and Man is concrete (these things should not

be at all confused, and we are even rebuked by you under the accusation that we confuse the terms abstract and concrete), whether the
Son of God assumed man or humanity?

Dr. Beza:
I say that the Son of God assumed an individual thing.[30]

Dr. Jakob:
I ask, then, which predicable among the five is man in?[31]

Dr. Beza:
In species.

Dr. Jakob:
Therefore these two terms "Man and Humanity" are in the same
predicable, which is species, by which is signified form and something like the image of individuals, which the mind abstracts from
individual things, and which conveys all individual things of the
same species.

These forms are not outside the mind, but in the mind only. Thus
man is nothing outside the mind, nor have I ever seen man, that is,
such an abstracted form, but I have seen Peter, I have seen Paul, I
have seen John. But Peter is not a species or an abstraction of man,
but is an individual. So also Paul and John, and so with everyone
else. From this you see that the distinction put forward by you cannot
consist, as you say, of concrete being meant by the term "Man," and
abstract being meant by the term "Humanity," since both terms are
understood under the same predicable.

<226>

---

30   This last exchange is a verbatim copy of the prior one; it is probably a printer's dittograph, mistak-
enly copied from the bottom of p. **<224>**, though the effect is consistent with other passages in which
Andreae repeats questions but fails to get a different response from Beza.

31   A word here about predicates and *praedicabilia*. They are the things that can be said about an object, within a larger discussion of categories (which number something like 10 in classical and medieval
thought). In Aristotle, there are four families of *praedicabilia*: definition, genus, proprium, and accident. In
Scholastic thought there are five: genus, species, differentia, proprium, and accident. E.g., Accident: this
horse is *brown*. Species: Beza *is a man*. Definition: Man *is a rational animal*. Differentia: Man is a *rational
animal*.

Dr. Beza:

I am speaking about the Man, who is an individual thing, and about the kind of humanity, of which the Man is possessed. Therefore humanity is one thing, and the Man is another.

Dr. Jakob:

The Man is not a species, but an individual thing. If in fact you were to add a Demonstrative Pronoun, what is signified is not the species of man, but some certain man, Peter, Paul, John, or someone else. But I asked in what predicable was Man? And here you correctly answered, Species. But species is not an individual thing, but the form or substantial image of an individual thing. For what is Man, other than that which consists of both a body and a rational soul?

MAN AND HUMANITY SYNONYMS.

Now, what is signified by the noun humanity or human nature (since these are synonyms) other than a creature consisting of a body and a rational soul? This is something that no one moderately educated can deny. Hence it has happened that the old orthodox doctors of the Church, especially Augustine, employed the term "Man" for "*humanity*" and understand, by the assumed man, human nature itself. It would be difficult to accuse them of ignorance of the terms abstract and concrete.

USE OF THE TERM ABSTRACT AMONG ANCIENT AND MODERN DOCTORS OF THE CHURCH.

For this reason we disregard the dispute regarding abstract and concrete, which few people understand. For us abstract signifies every thing, whether it be substance or accident, which is abstracted either mentally or actually from the thing with which it is joined, and is considered in itself in the property of its own nature. It is in this way that Luther employed it in this dispute, and likewise we and Brenz always do the same. Thus humanity considered in the abstract means nothing other than the human nature itself, which consists of body and rational soul, which the Son of God assumed, *when it is considered without respect to divinity in and of itself.* [227] This consideration does not differ at all from the consideration of humanity, in any other man, who is not personally united with the Son of God, but is separate from him.

Now, since I say Man is God, I ask you, my dear Beza, whether this proposition is universal or particular?

Dr. Beza:
It is singular, since only this Man is God, who is called and is Jesus Christ.

MAN IS A SPECIES, NOT AN INDIVIDUAL THING. WHEN THE TERM *"MAN"* IS CONCRETE.

Dr. Jakob:
The term "Man" is a universal term, which is attributed to all men. For if it is said that Man is a rational animal, is a creature of God, is mortal, and countless similar things which pertain to human nature, there is no need to add the universal marker *every*, since the term Man does not signify an individual thing but a species, which contains all individual things of the same species under it. It is for this reason that in order for the proposition Man is God to be true, you need to add the Pronoun *"this"* or the proper name of Christ: This Man is God, or the Man Christ Jesus son of Mary is God. Otherwise it is simply not true. From this it is clear to everyone that if the term "Man" were to be put forward without determination, it would not be concrete, but abstract. But if a determination should be added: this Man, the Man Jesus of Nazareth, son of Mary, then this is indeed concrete, and signifies a man of this sort, who is personally united with God, and on this account is and is said to be God.

Dr. Beza:
When I treat man, I am treating the assumed man. But humanity is something far different than Man. For the assertion Humanity is Divinity is false, but the assertion Man is God is true.

<228>

Dr. Jakob:

I have already shown that this proposition, Man is God, *is not true* unless the Pronoun *this* or *that* should be added, and you were to say, This Man (indicating Jesus alone, son of Mary) is God. The reason is that the term "*man*" is not concrete, but abstract, For this reason, concerning the question regarding the person of Christ, it is permissible and correct to employ without distinction in place of Humanity what means exactly the same thing, Man, because it is humanity or human nature.

WHY DISPUTE REGARDING ABSTRACT AND CONCRETE IS NECESSARY. A HIDING PLACE OF ERROR UNDER THE TERM "*MAN*."

Nor would anyone judge that this dispute about the abstract is useless or not in the least necessary in this question. For the thing itself in this conference will teach that under the term Man is put forward a very large hiding place of error, by which our adversaries say that Christ the man is God not literally, but figuratively and by literary device, as will be displayed plainly for all to see in its own place. But I ask something else of Dr. Beza: when we read it written in John 1, The Word became flesh, is the term "*flesh*" in this passage abstract or concrete?

Dr. Beza:
It is concrete.

WHAT DR. BEZA CALLS CONCRETE TERMS. FLESH IS NOT A CONCRETE TERM.

Dr. Jakob:

How can you say that it is a concrete term, since it signifies nothing in Hebrew usage other than an assumed human nature alone? For you call concrete terms in this dispute *those which* signify *a whole person*, not merely another nature. So when it is said, Man is omnipotent, from this you say that Man is a concrete term since it signifies a whole person, which is at the same time God and Man, otherwise it would not be a true assertion. Thus when it is said that God suffered, the term "*God*" is a concrete term according to you, since it denotes

a whole person, which is not only <229> God, but is also truly Man.
If therefore the term "*flesh*" is a concrete term because it signifies a
whole person, which consists of a divine and human nature, it would
follow that the Word had assumed flesh which was assumed before
God had existed. This would be absurd. In the same way therefore
"*word*" is not a concrete term in the assertion, The Word became
flesh, because it denotes a person who is at the same time God and
Man. For otherwise the Word would have been incarnate before it
became flesh. This would likewise be absurd. Thus the term "*flesh*" is
not a concrete term, but means humanity, or human nature, which
are abstract terms, a fact no sane person can deny. For the Word,
that is, the Son of God, who was without assumed flesh from eternity
the second person of the Trinity, became flesh, that is, assumed
flesh into the unity of his person, which it had previously lacked. It
is for this reason that in the assertion, The Word became flesh, Word
means Son of God without flesh, and flesh means Human Nature
without Word, and therefore Human *nature alone*. For the word,
which was nothing except the word, became flesh, that is, true Man.

I pray that all the Audience observe this carefully. Very much in
fact has been built on this point, so that it may understood correctly.
But enough has been said about the term "abstract," what it means
in the question about the person of Christ, something removed and
considered in itself, which nevertheless does not occur actually but
merely in the mind. That is, nature without respect to something
else, whether considered with respect to human or divine, and finally
by whatever name it be called, whether God, or Divinity, or Man, or
Humanity.

Dr. Beza:
*We understand form by abstract terms, not one removed from the
thing in which it inheres, but one considered permanently remaining
in it.*

<230>

Dr. Jakob:

Enough has been said about how this meaning of the term is not germane to this question. A little later I will demonstrate what kind of error is hidden under those terms which you call concrete. For now, let us proceed to the matter at hand, disregarding the technical terms "concrete and abstract."

THE STATE OF THE QUESTION CONCERNING *COMMUNICATION* OF ATTRIBUTES. COMMUNICATION TWOFOLD: 1. OF NATURES, 2. OF PROPERTIES. BEZA'S UNION OF NATURES WITHOUT REAL COMMUNICATION.

The question is whether something has been communicated to the assumed nature by the Divinity or Word [λόγος], not as far as their words are concerned or just in regard to their title, but truly and really communicated properties of Divinity. I pray the whole audience together to incline their attention willingly and carefully. Mention was made above regarding a twofold communication. The one belongs to the natures, which is called the personal union; the other belongs to the properties of the natures, which is an effect of the former. When asked about the first communication, that which belongs to the natures, Dr. Beza always answers in regard to the union of the natures.

DISTINCTION BETWEEN COMMUNICATION AND UNION OF NATURES. COMMUNICATION TWOFOLD. 1. ESSENTIAL COMMUNICATION. 2. PERSONAL COMMUNICATION OF NATURES AND PROPERTIES. WHAT SORT OF COMMUNICATION OF NATURES AND PROPERTIES IN CHRIST ACCORDING TO BEZA. DR. BEZA IN RESPONSE TO THESIS 10. REFUTATION OF THIS OPINION CONCERNING COMMUNICATION. OPINION OF THE FATHERS REGARDING THE PERSONAL UNION. ANALOGY OF RED-HOT IRON. COMMUNICATION OF THE SUBSTANCE OF FIRE AND ITS PROPERTIES IN IRON. COMMUNICATION'S EFFECTS. ANALOGY OF BODY AND RATIONAL SOUL IN MAN.

But there is a vast difference between union and communication. Things can in fact be united which communicate precisely nothing to one another, such that the one receives from the other nothing. Just like these two feather pens (Dr. Jakob was holding two in his hands), if they were joined together and the one was made of pure gold and the other was a goose feather, would communicate nothing to one another. The gold would not give anything to the goose, nor

the goose to the gold, but they would be merely combined and conjoined. This union of these two feather pens, as you see, can happen
without any communication. Now then, communication itself is also
twofold. The one is essential, or natural. And this is purely common
to the three persons of Divinity in the Trinity. For the Father begetting the son from eternity has communicated to him both his essence
and his own essential properties. Thus the holy Spirit proceeding
from both possesses the essence of Divinity with the father and the
son, and his properties are essentially and naturally in common
with them. For the essence and nature of the three persons of the
Divinity is one. Therefore on account of the communication there are
not three omnipotent Gods, but there is one omnipotent <231> God. In
this way the essence of Divinity is communicated to no creature with
its own properties. If in fact it were communicated in this way to a
creature, it would become essentially and naturally God. The other
communication is personal, where there is not merely one nature.
Rather, two different natures meet together in the one person of the
son of God without any confusion, and they are not simply united,
but they are united such that the one communicates to the other
its own essence with its own properties. Thus the Son of God, the
second person of the Trinity, assuming human nature into the unity
of his own person, communicates the essence of his Divinity and
his properties to it. At this point our adversaries say that this communication happens in Christ's person such that each of the natures
communicates itself and its own properties to this *person* which
is called Christ, on account of the running together of the natures
which are united in that person, but not communicated to each other.
Whence this person is called God omnipotent, Creator of heaven and
earth, omnipresent, omniscient, life-maker, the one to be adored.
And on the other hand, mortal Man, who suffered, was crucified,
since he is both, God and Man. For this reason also the properties of
both natures are attributed to this person. But just as the natures are
different and remain distinct even in the union itself, so also do they
do distinctly what is proper to their particular natures. The result is
that the Word [λόγος] does distinctly, without any real communication, what belongs to the Word [λόγος], and the flesh accomplishes
that which belongs to the flesh. But holy Scripture does not teach this

kind of union of the natures in Christ, nor do the Orthodox Fathers, as we will show in its own place. They have in fact not defined the personal union of the two natures in Christ without communication. To explain it they employed the analogies of red-hot iron and of the soul with the body. For two substances run together in red-hot iron, iron and fire. But not in the way that I described when I said two feather pens were united, neither of which communicated anything to the other. For fire communicates itself along with its proper-ties to the iron such that the whole thing is rendered red-hot, as if it were changed into fire. This iron burns; wood is drilled through in a moment by this iron, which the iron would not do without fire, <232> nor fire do without iron. And the iron is not changed into the substance of fire on account of this communication of fire and its properties, nor destroyed, but it is lit up. If fire is removed from the iron, it does not make a hole of this kind in wood, but consumes the wood. Therefore the iron becomes red-hot, and nevertheless its substance is not changed into the substance of fire. Accordingly the rational soul is united with the body, but not without communica-tion. For the soul communicates its own substance with all its own powers to the body. But it is not a union of the sort in which the soul operates distinctly and the body also operates distinctly, but the operations of soul and body are in common, with the result that they accomplish not only one ultimate purpose [ἀποτέλεσμα], that is, one work, but possess in common the action itself, such that the soul works no action at all which is in the body for some time, without the body. This is clear in regard to sense and motion. For the soul does not see without the eye, does not hear without ears, does not taste without the tongue, does not perceive smells without a nose. So also it understands nothing without ideas, as the saying goes: Nothing is understood that was not first in the sense. Experience itself teaches this, when someone is injured in the head such that he loses all his understanding and becomes utterly stupid. From this it is clear that it is not a stark union or combination, but a real communication of the soul, communicated with the body, in which the soul communicates life, sense, and motion to the body, so much that it communicates its entire self to it. Without it, it is no longer called a body, but a cadaver, and so the body is separated from the soul. In the same way that the soul with the body, and the body with the soul, possess in common all actions and passions, so also has the entire fullness of divinity been personally communicated to the assumed nature in Christ, in which he dwells bodily. This otherwise applies to no creature, in whom he dwells either by his essence or by his grace. Nevertheless, the human nature has not been changed into the divine, just as the body does not become the soul, but rather animated. So the assumed body does not become Deity itself, but is Deified, as Gregory of Nazianzus and John of Damascus say.

<233>

NESTORIUS' CONFESSION REGARDING THE UNITY OF THE PERSON OF CHRIST.

Your Reverence says, though, that the Divinity possesses its own actions distinct from the flesh, since they are proper to it. This is precisely the teaching of Nestorius, condemned by the leading Fathers of the Council of Ephesus. For Nestorius never denied the *unity* of the person in Christ, nor ever asserted two persons in Christ, but consistently confessed by mouth *one single* person. For this reason he became incensed with the Council of Ephesus, and complained all the way up to his death that an injury had been done to him, that he had been condemned under this accusation.

WHAT NESTORIUS' HERESY WAS.

But his heresy was this: that he was unwilling to attribute the properties of the humanity, namely being born of a woman, suffering, dying, to the Divinity, as if they were unworthy of God.

NESTORIUS DID NOT WANT TO QUARREL ABOUT WORDS. NESTORIUS JUSTLY CONDEMNED FOR SEPARATION OF NATURES IN CHRIST. NESTORIUS' ERROR NOT SUFFICIENTLY CONDEMNED IN THE COUNCIL OF EPHESUS. HOW GREAT A HERESY THE NESTORIAN ERROR IS. UNION OF NATURES IN THE PERSON OF CHRIST IS TRUE AND REAL COMMUNICATION. COMMUNICATION OF THE WHOLE FULLNESS OF DIVINITY IN CHRIST'S FLESH.

Do not exult, Jews, he said, since you crucified a man, not God. And again, he called Mary Christ-bearer [χριστοτόκος] and the mother of Christ who is the Son of God, but was unwilling to concede that she was θεοτόκος, that is, the mother of God or of God's son. I do not believe, he said, in a two- or three-month old God. And he publicly swore that he did not begrudge the name mother of God for Mary, but taught that it did not suit him, since from it would follow (according to the understanding and opinion of Nestorius) that Mary was prior to Divinity, since indeed every mother is by very nature older than her own son. He contended rather that since Divinity existed from eternity, God could not be born of woman. Because of Nestorius' teaching the Fathers of the Council of Ephesus rightly concluded against Nestorius that he established two persons in Christ, seeing that he asserted that the actions and passions were not common to either nature, but that he attributed them distinctly, in one way to flesh, in another to divinity, without any real communication. Even if it is true, writes Leo, that whatsoever form Christ acts in, is its own thing, nevertheless he attributes this not absolutely and distinctly to only one nature, but to the whole person in Christ. For Leo adds, with the communion of the other form. These are his words: Each form works with the other in communion that which is proper to it, namely the Word works that which belongs to the Word, and the flesh achieves that which belongs to flesh (Leo *Epistle 10 to Flavian*).[32] For this reason Luther <234> says that Nestorius was not sufficiently condemned by the fathers of the Council of Ephesus, since he abandoned no one genuine article of the faith concerning the person of Christ, but corrupted and perverted all of them at the same time, since he stated that merely a man was born of Mary, suffered, was crucified, which completely conflicts with the articles of the Apostles' Creed. For all the articles of the Apostles' Creed on the person of Christ speak expressly concerning the Son of God: I believe in Jesus Christ his only *son, who* was conceived by the holy Spirit, *who was born, who* suffered, *who* was crucified, *who* died, etc., the natural and only-begotten son, I say, of God. Since Nestorius was obstinately attacking these points, he was rightly condemned for heresy. Therefore the union of natures is personal, not a stark combination without communication, but a true and real communication of natures in which one nature gives to the other, and the other receives. Paul embraced

---

32   Leo *Ep* 28 ("Tome").

this communication eloquently in a few words: In him (he says) dwells the whole fullness of Divinity bodily (Colossians 2[:9]). For the Son of God, in whose person this union happened, communicated the whole fullness of Divinity to his assumed nature. For even though God possesses all his own fullness of Divinity everywhere with himself, and even dwells in us through faith (Ephesians 3[:17]), nevertheless he has communicated this to none of the saints. So Christ alone the son of Mary can truly say, All power in heaven and earth has been given to me (Matthew 28[:18]).

Dr. Beza:

The analogy of the two feather pens joined together does not at all pertain to us. We in fact do not teach or believe such a union of natures in the person of Christ. As far as what you have said about Nestorius having believed in the unity of the person of Christ and not to have established two persons, I answer: if he had actually believed in the unity of the person, he would also have confessed the communication of attributes. For this reason what he said about one singular person was pure mockery, or he did not understand what he was saying. And how Pelagius deceived the Churches is known from the Ecclesiastical History.

<235>

WHETHER DR. BEZA SEPARATES NATURES IN CHRIST.

The next point is that Nestorius actually separated the natures and their actions in the person of Christ, which we do not do. For even though we attribute to whichever nature their own properties and distinct actions, we nevertheless do not say on this account that the human nature accomplishes this separated from the divine, or the divine separated from the human, but rather that remaining permanently in the union itself, it accomplishes whatever is proper to itself.

Thus Jesus Christ says that he saw Nathanael under the fig tree. This was accomplished not according to his humanity, but according to his divinity. And while Eutyches did not wish to appear to follow the determination of the Fathers of the Council of Ephesus against Nestorius, he fell into the opposite error and contended that the Divinity suffered. In this way he confused the natures; it would have been better to distinguish divinity and its properties from humanity and its properties.

Dr. Jakob:

The thing itself will inform us that you do assert a stark combination of two natures in Christ without communication, which I explained by means of the analogy of the two feather pens.

NESTORIUS CONFESSED ONE SINGLE PERSON IN CHRIST.

Nestorius' own Letter openly teaches that he did not pretend, but asserted in plain and not at all doubtful words *one single* person of Christ (Nestorius, *2nd Epistle to Cyril, Council of Ephesus*, p. 662. This is the reason that he complained until his death that he had been unfairly condemned by the Council, as the Ecclesiastical History teaches.

For this reason there is a vast difference on this score between Nestorius and Pelagius. Pelagius is said to have recanted on some points, a fact some did not believe. For this reason Augustine wrote to Pope Innocent (Augustine *Ep.* 95 & 96)]. Nestorius on the other hand consistently and at all times confessed his own opinion, but did not understand that he was contradicting himself.

NESTORIUS JUSTLY CONDEMNED OF HERESY BY THE COUNCIL OF EPHESUS.

But since the fathers of the Council of Ephesus understood that the union of the natures and the communication of attributes or properties [236] of the natures were joined together like cause and effect in the person of Christ (for the communication follows from the union), and since they assumed that there was no reason in his confession concerning the one single person, they rightly pronounced that Nestorius had done away with the personal union in Christ and had separated the natures in Christ, that he was attributing the passions in Christ to the human nature alone without any communication, and was separating it from the Divinity. For he wanted to say that God was not born of woman, nor suffered or was crucified.

Although he would not deny that Christ, who was born of Mary, suffered, and was crucified, was true God, the true only-begotten son of God. For under the term "God" he understood the Divinity of the Word [λόγος], which cannot be separated from the person of the Word [λόγος]. For this reason even though he openly and frankly confessed that Jesus Christ is true God, nevertheless he did not want to say that God suffered or was crucified. He said these things were properties of humanity, and so he contended that they should be related to his humanity alone, and never attributed to God. These are his words: When he was about to make mention of his death, lest anyone suspect God the Word of being capable of suffering, he [Paul in Philippians 2:5] uses the word Christ, a way of naming him *in one single person* as of a substance both incapable and capable of suffering, in order that Christ may without risk be called both incapable of suffering and capable of suffering: on the one hand incapable of suffering with respect to his Divinity, on the other hand capable of suffering with respect to the nature of his body (Nestorius, *2nd Epistle to Cyril, Council of Ephesus*, p. 662).

CONFORMITY OF DR. BEZA'S DOCTRINE WITH NESTORIUS' ERROR. THEY CONCEDE NOT EVEN VERBAL COMMUNICATION IN THE NATURES. DR. BEZA IN RESPONSE TO THESES 8 & 9. ASSERTION OF DISTINCT OPERATION IS SEPARATION OF THE NATURES. *RULE*: ACTIONS AND SUFFERINGS OF CHRIST BELONG NOT TO THE NATURES, BUT TO THE PERSON. HOW CHRIST SAW NATHANAEL UNDER THE FIG TREE.

Now your party teaches one single person in Christ, in which two natures come together into one hypostasis, and are united inseparably, but you do not concede that there is any real communication of the properties of the natures between them one to the other, not even a verbal or Grammatical one. This cannot be denied, and your writings openly testify to this. You say that you do not separate the natures even though you say that the operations of the natures are distinct. I respond that Nestorius said the same thing, but the Fathers of the Council of Ephesus proved the contrary. For this is a timeless rule of truth: in Christ <237> actions and passions should be attributed not *to the natures*, but rather *to the whole person*. Whoever does not do this actually professes the heresy of Nestorius, whatever he says and does. Christ does not say, My Divinity saw Nathanael under the fig tree, but he said, before Philip called you, when you were under the fig tree, *I saw you*. This seeing is attributed to the person. But that he saw Nathanael one way as man, since he was united to God, and he saw him in another way as God, for this there was no need that he be united with man. But when you attribute this only to Divinity, by this very act you also separate the natures.

Dr. Beza:
We do not separate the natures, but so long as we attribute distinct operations to the natures we avoid a Eutychian confusion of the natures.

Dr. Jakob:

THE WORD [λόγος] WORKS ALL THINGS *IN, WITH, AND THROUGH* THE HUMAN NATURE.

The thing itself indicates the contrary. For just as the soul in a person, so long as it is in the person, does nothing without the body, but rather does all things through and with the body, though the body can do nothing of itself without the soul, so also in the person of Christ the Word [λόγος] does not do or work anything without the assumed man, but rather as the orthodox Fathers testify, in, with, and through It. Just as Athanasius attests: God the Word [λόγος] united to man performs miracles and works not *independently* or *separately* from the assumed nature, but rather he was pleased in his goodness to work *through* the assumed humanity *in it*, and *with it*, by the working of his own Divine power (Athanasius *dial. 5 de Trinitate*).[33] If therefore only the Divinity saw Nathanael under the fig tree, is this not a seeing independent and separate from the human nature, and in this way dividing the person and separating the natures? Though you say they are united.

---

33   Athanasius, from *De Trinitate Dialogi* (PG 28) (spurious).

Dr. Beza:

Would you have wanted to condemn Nestorius if after speaking in this way <238> *he had sworn that he was not dividing the person in Christ or separating the natures and establishing two persons?*

Dr. Jakob:

HOW NESTORIUS SHOULD BE TREATED.

I would have said to him, if you think the same thing as us, correct your language and examine your thinking. For if you think with the Church you should also speak with the Church. For holy Scripture and the articles of the Apostles' Creed plainly bear witness and say that God, that is the Son of God, was born, suffered, and was crucified.

Dr. Beza:

Nestorius could not distinguish between concrete and abstract. Otherwise he would not have fallen into that error. For it is one thing to say God was born of a woman, suffered, was crucified; but it is something else to say that divinity was born, suffered, was crucified. The former is true; the latter is false, and condemned in the orthodox Church.

Dr. Jakob:

NESTORIUS' CONSISTENT AND PERPETUAL OPINION. HOW THE WORD SUFFERED IMPASSIBLY. GOD AND DIVINITY SIGNIFY THE SAME THING FOR THE ORTHODOX FATHERS. IN WHAT WAY DIVINITY WAS NOT EXCLUDED FROM THE PASSION IN CHRIST.

Nestorius was not too ignorant to understand that God the word was born of woman, not without divinity. Take away divinity from the Word [λόγος], and the Word [λόγος] will no longer be God. For how can God exist apart from his Divinity? This is why the same thing is signified by the term "God" as something eternal and uncreated, indeed Divinity itself. And just as he attacked the going assertions which run, God was born of a woman, suffered, was crucified, so also the one that runs, Divinity was born of a woman, suffered, was crucified. Cyril said to the contrary: The Word suffered impassibly [*verbum passum esse impassibiliter*]. He suffers, he says, when his body suffers, to the extent that it is said to be proper to that which he has communicated his entire self. Yet God himself remains incapable of suffering, to the extent that he possesses the unique property that he cannot suffer. And Vigilius writes that Divinity was pinned with nails, but not transfixed (*Tom 1 Concil. P 636 Vigilius lib 3 cap 3*). Here <239> both Cyril and Vigilius employ the terms God and Divinity as Synonyms without distinction, and attribute in this way the passions of Christ to the Divinity. For whether it is called God or Divinity, it is unique to his nature that he is incapable of suffering and he always remains this way whether apart from the union or exisiting in the union, but because of the personal union made with the passible nature, is never exempt from suffering. Since in fact the assumed body of the Son of God was his own, no manner of suffering without Divinity could befall him that would not also overflow to the Divinity itself. And likewise, certain passions are directly aimed against his divinity, when they said, If you are the Son of God, come down and we will believe in you. It was not only his humanity that heard these things and patiently endured them, but the Divinity itself of the Son of God held up under and endured it, which could have immediately destroyed those very blasphemers.

Dr. Beza:

WHETHER COMMUNICATION OF PROPERTIES IS RECIPROCAL IN THE PERSON OF CHRIST.

I ask you, is the logic [RATIO] of these two assertions the same: The Son of man is omnipotent, and the son of God was crucified?

CAUSE OF COMMUNICATION OF ATTRIBUTES THE SAME, BUT NOT THE SAME LOGIC. CAUSE OF COMMUNICATION OF ATTRIBUTES IS UNION AND COMMUNICATION OF NATURES. LOGIC OF DIVERSITY OF COMMUNICATION OF PROPERTIES IN THE PERSON OF CHRIST. IN WHAT WAY THE DIVINE NATURE RESTED IN THE PASSION OF CHRIST.

Dr. Jakob:

I contend that the cause [*causa*] of these two utterances is one and the same, but the logic [*ratio*] is not also the same for this reason. For the cause of these two assertions is one and the same, namely the union of the natures in the person of the Son of God. In fact unless this hypostatic union had happened, God would never be crucified, nor could Man have become omnipotent. Therefore we hold that from this union the son of man became truly omnipotent and that he is called the Son of God and suffered. But the logic of these assertions is very far different on account of the distinction of the natures, by which they are considered in themselves. For the divine nature is unchangeable, and no perfection or imperfection is able to happen to it. But human nature is changeable, and it can be humiliated and exalted, debilitated and strengthened. It follows from this <240> that Divinity participates in passions in a different manner than Humanity participated in the glory and Majesty proper to Divinity. For human nature can receive omnipotence into itself, but Divinity cannot receive passions in the same manner such that it can be wounded or injured. But the Divinity suffered in its own flesh, just as the Word [λόγος] is said to have rested in the passion with respect to its flesh, that is, not only did it keep its human nature such that it could suffer such things, but the Divinity itself also did not cast off the passions from its own flesh, something it could have done if it had wanted to, but rather allowed them to happen in this way.

Dr. Beza:

I say that not only is the cause [CAUSA] of each predicate and enunciation the same, but that the rationale [RATIO] is the same as well. For just as it is said that God was crucified, so also I say that the man was made Omnipotent. For the natures are and remain perpetually distinct in the union itself, and the unique natures maintain their own distinct properties. These properties do not exceed their subject, but also remain distinct, just as the natures remain distinct. Therefore in the same way, God is said to have suffered, not because he received sufferings in himself, but rather in another way [κατ᾽ ἄλλο], that is, it must be understood according to the human nature, because it suffered. So also the Man is said to have become omnipo-

tent, not because Humanity received omnipotence IN ITSELF, or became a sharer in it, but because it was United with God the word.

Dr. Jakob:

On the contrary, Cyril bears witness with all Orthodox antiquity that Christ's flesh was so richly supplied with divine working that the Divine nature remained, free from suffering.

<241>

Dr. Beza:
Do you then desire to stand on Cyril's opinion?

Dr. Jakob:
I do.

Dr. Beza:
I will therefore recite the opinion of Cyril in which the properties of Divinity are attributed to the Divinity alone in such a way that he denies they are communicated to the flesh.

His words read thus: It were fitting that no other thing be able to vivify, even if it is understood that it is Christ's flesh, as it is flesh, except for the divinity alone (Cyril, DE TRINITATE Book 6). And again, We have therefore not attributed to the flesh, as it is flesh, the power of divine working, but rather to the nature of the word. It can in fact do no things which are proper works OF GOD, UNLESS it is SUBSTANTIALLY God (Book 2, on John 21).

Dr. Jakob:

CYRIL'S PERPETUAL AND CONSISTENT OPINION ABOUT THE COMMUNICATION OF PROPERTIES OF THE DIVINITY. PROPERTIES OF DIVINITY ARE IN NO CREATURE IN AND OF ITSELF. IN WHAT WAY CHRIST'S FLESH IS AND IS NOT VIVIFIC. IN WHAT WAY CHRIST'S FLESH VIVIFIC. METHOD [RATIO] OF COMMUNICATION NOT THE SAME.

Not only in this place, but also as many analogies as you like are found in Cyril, in which he asserts that there no thing can do those things that are proper to divinity *in and of themselves*, unless it is essentially God. But Cyril wanted to teach this, that when the properties of Divinity are attributed to the flesh or Christ's human nature, they are not attributed to Christ's flesh *in as much as the flesh is human*. We attribute the power of divine operation not to the flesh *as flesh* (says Cyril, Book 2, on John 21), but to the nature of the word. But it does not therefore follow that on this account the works proper to divinity are not really communicated to the flesh of Christ. Indeed, Cyril himself asserts the contrary in very plain words, as follows (Cyril, on John, Book 4, chapter 23): You do not foolishly deny altogether that flesh is vivific. For if *only* is understood, it can vivify nothing at all, to be sure, since it lacks the power to vivify. But when <242> you have carefully examined the Mystery of the incarnation, and have learned that *life* dwells in the flesh, even though *within itself the flesh* is capable *of nothing, in and of itself*, you will believe *nevertheless that it has become vivific*. For since it has been joined with the life-giving Word, *it has been made wholly vivific. God's word* joined to its corruptible nature does not diminish it; rather it is itself elevated *to the power of the better one*. Therefore although the nature of flesh *as flesh* cannot vivify, nevertheless he accomplishes this: *it undertakes the entire operation of the word*. And again, John of Damascus: The divine nature *communicates to the flesh* its *proper* excellencies, or glorifications, but *in its very self* remains free from the sufferings of the flesh (On the Orthodox Faith, Book 3, chapter 7). It has been manifestly shown by these words that the logic of the expressions is not the same: God was crucified, and a Man is omnipotent. Because the human nature is made a sharer in the properties of divinity in another way than the divinity in the passions of humanity in the person of Christ.

Dr. Beza:

WHAT SORT OF COMMUNICATION BEZA TEACHES WITH HIS PARTY.

Indeed, a communication of properties of both natures in the person of Christ happened, but it did not happen in the natures IN AND OF THEMSELVES, such that the humanity became omnipotent IN AND OF ITSELF. For this was the heresy of Eutyches, which the orthodox Church always condemned. For this reason we also cannot concede it.

Dr. Jakob:

WHAT THE HERESY OF EUTYCHES WAS. CONFESSION OF EUTYCHES REGARDING THE PERSON OF CHRIST.

The Ecclesiastical History bears witness regarding Eutyches, that he believed and taught only one nature in Christ after the ascension into heaven, namely just a divine nature, into which the humanity was absorbed in glory. And Vigilius, writing against the same error, concluded from the properties of the body and the human nature that in Christ was not just one nature, but rather two natures. These are the words of Eutyches to Evagrius: I confess that the Lord consists in two nature before the union; <243> but after the union, I confess his nature to be one. And again, Christ's body did not remain of the same substance [ὁμοούσιος], or similar, to our bodies, but rather was utterly transformed and absorbed into the divine nature.

AMBIGUITY OF THE PHRASE *"IN ITSELF"* WHICH CAN BE UNDERSTOOD IN A TWOFOLD WAY.

As far as the phrase *"in itself"* is concerned, this can be understood in a twofold way. On the one hand it can mean the same as *in and of itself* and absolutely, and in the property of its own nature, without respect to another. In this way, omnipotence does not reside in any creature, nor is it able to, unless it be Divinity itself.

On the other hand *"in itself"* is means that something is actually found *in* something else, in which it is said to be, even if it has arrived from somewhere. And in this way the *power of vivifying*, and other properties of divinity are, and are said to be, *in the assumed humanity*, to which they have been communicated and granted by the son of God through the personal union.

USE OF THE ANALOGIES OF GLOWING HOT IRON AND OF THE SOUL WITH THE BODY. REAL COMMUNICATION DOES NOT ACCOMPLISH CONFUSION OF NATURES, OR ABOLITION OF THE HUMAN NATURE.

But the analogy of soul and body, by which the Fathers explained this Mystery, although it does not square on every point (for no analogy runs on four feet), nevertheless can easily set us straight regarding this one question, just as the other analogy also, of glowing hot iron, by which it is demonstrated that a true and real communication of the substance of fire and its properties never in any way commingles its substances and properties, nor abolishes the substance of the other nature in which this communication happens. Likewise on account of this communication of the soul and its capabilities, the body indeed acquires a new name and definition, that is, it is and is called animated, and the iron when it is fired up is called ignited, nevertheless neither are the natures confused with their own properties, nor is the other nature abolished, namely the body or the iron. So also the humanity assumed by the son of God in this real communication of the essence and properties of the Word [ὁ λόγος] is not abolished or changed into Divinity, but rather acquires a new name and title, which we call Deified. And so it acquires Majesty from the son of God, which is proper to God himself, which Divinity does not lose in this communication, but rather retains *in itself*. But it holds it in common with the assumed man just as it holds it in common essentially <244> with the Father and holy Spirit. This is why this one man Jesus son of Mary can *truly* say, All authority has been given to me in heaven and earth (Matthew 28[:18]), which Peter, Paul, or any other saint cannot say. God nevertheless dwells by his grace in them, retaining in himself the whole fullness of his divinity.

THE CAUSE OF THE ERROR OF BEZA AND HIS BROTHERS.

But on this point you deceive yourselves, thinking that no true and real communication can happen either of the natures or of the properties of divinity unless it should be essential, on account of the sort of unity of divine essence we have said exists in the divinity of Father, Son, and holy Spirit. This is indeed the only thing you attack in this disputation about the communication of attributes, since you falsely believe another sort of communication is not able to exist. Nevertheless this cannot prevail in the personal communication.

The previously mentioned analogies, which plainly teach the contrary, can easily free you from this opinion.

Dr. Beza:

You explain the effect of the union of the two natures with these analogies in such a way that a third something results from the two. Body is in fact not soul, and soul is not body, but rather body becomes animated by its union with a soul. So we call a man a third something, which is neither body only nor soul only, but rather something composed of both, like parts. But in this Mystery of union is not constituted a third something from God and man which is neither God nor man, but rather Christ, who is nothing other than God and man. So also may they be predicated of each other: God is a man, and a man is God in Christ. This cannot be said about a soul and a body. We do not in fact say a soul is a body, a body is a soul. Thus also can it not be said that iron is fire, fire is iron.

<245>

Dr. Jakob:

I said a little while ago that those analogies do not square on all points. Nevertheless, they are the best for explaining communication, and very suitable for explaining that it happens without confusion of natures or the abolition of one or the other. To this end only they were used by the Fathers and introduced into the Church.

DISSIMILARITY BETWEEN THE TWO PRIOR ANALOGIES AND THE PERSON OF CHRIST.

But it is otherwise true that there is a vast difference. For a man consists of soul and body, as if from its own substantial parts, of which neither is complete without the other. A body without a soul is in fact (as we say) a corpse. And a soul has been created by God not as an Angel, such that it may exercise its faculties apart from a body, but rather in and through a body.

WE ALSO CALL THE PERSON OF CHRIST COMPOSITE.

But the person of Christ is composed of two entire, whole, and complete things, not from parts (we can in fact use the term composition, after the example of the holy Councils). For Word [λόγος] is God complete in itself, and a man is not required for its completion. Again, a man is complete as a man, who consists of body and a rational soul. Since therefore neither is part of the other, for this reason, on account of the wondrous union and communication, and most intimate conjunction, by which Word [λόγος] and the assumed human nature were united and communicated with each other, they are predicated of each other, a fact that cannot be said about a soul and a body. And the same way also regarding glowing hot iron: iron and fire would not be predicated of each other, even though they constitute one thing, which is called glowing hot iron.

Dr. Beza:

WHETHER THE HUMAN NATURE ONLY RECEIVED SUBSISTENCE FROM THE WORD [λόγος].

I do not deny that Word [λόγος] communicates its own hypostasis to the assumed nature, and so is personally sustained by it, which happens by the union. But I do not think that this union should be mixed up with the communication of attributes or properties, which you say follows from this union. But we say that the humanity <246> *only received its sustenance from the Word [λόγος], without any communication of properties of the other nature, from which would follow a confusion of the natures. For the human nature is united with the Word [λόγος] in such a way that it acquire from it its subsistence.*

Dr. Jakob:
I deny simply that the human nature received only subsistence from the Word [λόγος].

Dr. Beza:
I say that this communication of subsistence is the foundation of the communication of properties.

Dr. Jakob:

CONSENSUS IN WORDS, NOT THINGS.

I say the same thing. But when it comes to explaining what this communication is, you interpret this communication in a far different way than we do, as has been said above.

Dr. Beza:
We say that the union is of a kind by which the human nature subsists in the person of the Son of God.

Dr. Jakob:
What more do you attribute on account of this union?

Dr. Beza:
We add that it also subsists in properties.

Dr. Jakob:
But how do you explain this subsistence, or what do you say it yields to the human nature?

Dr. Beza:
Great dignity, by which it is elevated over all creatures.

<247>

Dr. Jakob:
But is this supreme dignity a created or uncreated gift?

Dr. Beza:
It is not uncreated, but rather a created gift.

Dr. Jakob:

WHETHER DR. BEZA BELIEVES IN A COMMUNICATION OF ATTRIBUTES. MAJESTY OF THE MAN CHRIST IS NOT A CREATED GIFT.

It is already manifestly apparent that you totally deny the κοινωνίαν ἰδιωμάτων, that is, the communication of properties of the divinity, after Nestorius' example. For if the supreme dignity *is a created gift*, then it is not a property of God, that is, Majesty proper to God, which we proved above with Paul's words was communicated to Christ according to the human nature, who plainly confirms that in Christ dwells the whole fullness of Deity bodily, by which fullness the human nature was given in Christ. But this fullness is not a *created gift*, but rather the eternal and infinite Majesty of God. In the same way also Christ's human nature is seated at the right hand of this Majesty, infinite and proper to God, and not to a created Majesty, as none other than Paul says and the Apostles' creed confirms.

ON THE RESPONSE TO DOGMA 1.

For this reason it is *nothing* except for words and word tricks when you say that you believe that the Man Christ Jesus, son of Mary, is omnipotent, omniscient, and omnipresent. Your explanation set down in your Response plainly shows it. For you say, A man is omnipotent, that is, the Divinity united to the humanity is omnipotent.

HOW DR. BEZA TALKS ABOUT THE OMNIPOTENT MAN CHRIST. ON THESES 6 & 7.

But I ask the whole audience carefully to weigh this amongst yourselves, in what way the Man Jesus son of Mary is said to be and is omnipotent according to the opinion of the Theologians of the other party. They say in fact that the meaning of these words, "A man is omnipotent," is this: Divinity united to humanity is omnipotent. But in what language? In what grammar, may I ask, does man mean the same thing as Divinity? And again, how can a man truly be called omnipotent, <248> to whose humanity, that is, his soul and body, has not been communicated omnipotence? Can this in no way also be rightly said about the humanity, not even in union? just as your Response suggests.

What is stated by this expression, Divinity united to humanity is omnipotent, other than that it teaches that Divinity is so omnipotent that it is not at all communicated to humanity? And that this is your opinion, all may plainly understand, as these your words have been laid out openly in your Response: And so communication, of which mention is made, by which is said, *humanity* is omnipotent by a certain mode, etc., *we say that this is the case not even verbally*, but rather we judge it to be just as false as that the *humanity* escaped from the Divinity in the Hypostatic union.

Therefore whatever is said by you about the communication of properties, by which the man Christ is called omnipotent, omniscient, and similar things, it is your desire that these things should be understood such that you openly say that not even the name of this Majesty could truly be attributed *to Christ's humanity*.

Just as all these things are horrendous to hear, so also I think everyone understands the way they accord with Paul's words set forth above, In him dwells the whole fullness of Deity bodily (Colossians 2[:9]). They testify that the human nature of Christ possesses the fullness of divinity communicated bodily, and is seated in the seat and throne proper to Divinity itself.

Dr. Beza:
Paul in the passage to the Colossians demonstrates against Nestorius that Christ not only possesses the Son of God joined to himself by παρουσία, *that is, by him being at hand, but rather has the most perfect substance of the Word [*ὁ λόγος*]. And so we distinguish habitual grace from the grace of the personal union.*

<249>

Dr. Jakob:

IN WHAT WAY THE SUBSTANCE OF DIVINITY IS UNITED WITH THE ASSUMED
HUMANITY. TESTIMONY OF THE FATHERS REGARDING THE COMMUNICATION
OF THE SUBSTANCE OF DIVINITY IN THE MAN CHRIST. IN WHAT WAY THE
HUMAN WILL IN CHRIST IS OMNIPOTENT.

We have now said many times that the substance of the Word [ὁ
λόγος], as it is in itself and remains forever most complete, is in all
creatures and dwells in the saints through grace. But it is united
to Christ the son of Mary in another way than with the rest of the
blessed saints, that is, it is not understood, except *a posteriori*, that
is, as a consequence of this union, namely by the communication of
Majesty, about which Paul speaks in this passage, which all ancient
orthodox Fathers thought and taught along with us. God (writes
Augustine) is present everywhere, and is everywhere wholly present, and does not dwell everywhere, but rather in his own temple,
to which he is kind and gracious through his grace. His dwelling
however is grasped more by some and less by others. The Apostle
speaks regarding our very head: In him dwells the whole fullness
of Deity bodily. And again Origen: Christ's whole soul receives the
whole Word [λόγος], and walks in its light and splendor (Origen *De
Principiis* Book 2 cp. 6). And again: Christ's soul joined together with
the word of God, was *plainly* capable of containing the son of God.
John of Damascus: Christ's human will naturally *was not omnipotent*.
But truly, and according to nature, the will became that of the Word
of God, *and it is omnipotent* (John of Damascus, On the Orthodox
Faith, Book 3 cp. 18). His commentator explains these words thus:
The divine will has by its very own nature the power to accomplish
all the things it wants to. But the human will of Christ does *not* have
all-accomplishing power *by its own nature, but rather as it has been
united to the Word of God.*

These words of the holy Spirit and the orthodox Fathers speak far
differently about the communication of omnipotence to the human
nature accomplished in Christ than your Response does.

And the matter is so clear that the sense can also grasp the
reason of the consequence. If the human nature has omnipotence,

therefore it is also omnipotent and is called omnipotent, after its own fashion, *truly and really*. But that Christ's human nature possesses omnipotence has been shown more clearly than the light of noonday. <250> How therefore will it not be omnipotent? How great an error is it to assert therefore that it is not even verbally omnipotent, that is, that the name omnipotence does not belong to it?

Dr. Beza:
The Fathers speak about the Hypostatic union, which is the foundation of this communication, and we do not deny that Christ the man is omnipotent, just as God is.

Dr. Jakob:

IN RESPONSE TO 8 AND 9.

But are you not saying that the humanity of Christ became omnipotent, nor that it can become omnipotent in any way, unless it were to become Divinity itself? How then can a man truly be called omnipotent, whose humanity has nothing in common with omnipotence, and cannot contain it or be a sharer in it? Nay rather, to which cannot be attributed even the name of omnipotence, according to your thought and opinion?

Dr. Beza:
It happens on account of the personal union that the humanity subsists in the person of the Word.

Dr. Jakob:
But since the union is one thing, and communication another, how can those things be truly predicated about a man on account of the union which are nevertheless not communicated?

Dr. Beza:

IN RESPONSE TO THESIS 8 AND 9. CONFUSION OF PERSONAL UNION AND COMMUNICATION OF ATTRIBUTES.

There is ambiguity [ὁμωνυμία] in the term communication, which is read one way for the hypostatic union, and another for its effects. Therefore when we admit a real communication, we understand by communication the union of the natures, in which the single natures remain in themselves, and distinct with respect to their properties in the union, quite apart from any other communication.

<251>

Dr. Jakob:

Thus far we have been accused by you in this controversy of confusing union and communication. Now you are yourselves saying that union and communication are one thing.

THE UNION OF NATURES AND THE COMMUNICATION OF ATTRIBUTES ARE NOT ONE AND THE SAME.

But how can the union of natures and the communication of attributes be one and the same thing, which differ as cause and effect? The union of natures is in fact one thing, and the communication of the properties of the natures is another. Just as human nature is one thing and the properties of human nature are something else.

Dr. Beza:

HOW THE PHRASE IN ANOTHER WAY [κατ' ἄλλο] SHOULD BE UNDERSTOOD, ACCORDING TO BEZA.

The union of natures in Christ is a sort of thing by which not only the natures but also the properties of the natures are united. On account of this union the things proper to God are said about the man, and the things proper to the man are said about God, but in another way [κατ' ἄλλο], that is, with respect to the other nature, in which inhere the things proper to the one in and of itself, and do not inhere in this way in the other nature. And so they cannot be predicated about that nature.

Dr. Jakob:

TRUE AND GENUINE MEANING OF THE PHRASE IN ANOTHER WAY [κατ' ἄλλο].

We are also saying that the things proper to the one nature are said and predicated about the other, but in another way [κατ' ἄλλο], that is, not absolutely and in the abstract, but in the concrete, that is, in the personal union with respect to the other nature.

These words, though, κατ' ἄλλο, that is, according to something else, just as also marked phrases used in the Scripture, "according to the flesh," "according to the spirit," we are interpreting differently, and understand differently than you do.

For you understand and interpret thus, when it is said, God suffered, this must be understood κατ' ἄλλο, that is, with respect to the humanity. In this part we have consensus. If in fact God had not become man, this proposition would never have been true: God suffered. Since God in and of himself in his Divinity is incapable of suffering.

<252>

IN RESPONSE TO DOGMA 1.

Then you understand and interpret "in another way" [κατ' ἄλλο] in this way: God suffered, that is, the humanity suffered, which was united to the Divinity, so that the suffering pertains not at all to the Divinity, to such a pitch indeed that not even a verbal communication can be uttered with respect to the divine nature, but it is referred *only to the humanity*, whose property is to suffer.

CORRUPTION AND PERVERSION OF THE ARTICLE CONCERNING THE SUFFERING OF CHRIST.

This explanation is false and a manifest denial of the Apostolic article regarding Christ's passion. For the suffering by which the human race was redeemed is being attributed only to the humanity in such a way that the Son of God is excluded from it, in short, by his own divinity. This is in conflict with the Apostles' Creed which reads thus: I believe in Jesus Christ *his only son, our Lord, who* suffered. And it does not say, whose human nature suffered.

TRUE UNDERSTANDING AND MEANING OF MARKED PHRASES.

But the Fathers interpreted these marked phrases far differently because they followed holy Scripture and the articles of the Apostles' Creed. For the marked phrases demonstrate not only the nature, the property of which is that it is attributed to the whole person, but they also signify the reason why it is attributed to the other nature, namely that it has been personally united with it.

Thus Paul writes about the Son of God that he was begotten from the seed of David. Posited absolutely, this would not be true, since the Son of God cannot be begotten from the seed of man, since he is not at all corporeal but rather indivisible spirit. Therefore Paul adds the marked phrase κατὰ σάρκα, according to the flesh. With this phrase he shows the reason why it is attributed to the son of God, because it is in conflict with his nature, namely to be begotten of human seed.

Since when Mary was conceiving Christ, she did not conceive only a man, but also with the seed of the virgin was the son of God when he was becoming man, and not without the Son of God did he become the son of Mary from the seed of the virgin.

Therefore if anyone interpreted this phrase in the following way, according to your thought and opinion: The Son of God was begotten from the seed of David according to the flesh, that is, flesh united with the Son of God, <253> was begotten from the seed of David after this fashion, such that not even by verbal predication may this pertain to the son of God, then who could truly say that Mary conceived and gave birth to the son of God? Since all these things are said to have come to pass merely from the flesh, without any real communication with the son of God? This was the opinion and heresy of Nestorius.

WHAT THE HERESY OF NESTORIUS WAS.

For Nestorius also thought that the flesh, begotten of the seed of David (that is, of the virgin, who was from the seed of David), had been united with the son of God and what was born of Mary he said was the son of God, not a mere man; but on the other hand, to be born of woman, this he did not want to be said of the Son of God, since it is proper for humanity to be born of woman, but not fitting for God, that is the only-begotten Son of God.

But you are indeed saying about the son of God that he was born of the virgin Mary, but you do so patently after the same fashion as Nestorius, that is to say verbally, nay rather, not even verbally, that if you should look at the divine nature, since it is fitting for flesh alone, which is plainly and openly Nestorian.

Dr. Beza:
Surely therefore you are not saying that the son of God was really begotten of the seed of David, just like his flesh was begotten from the seed?

Dr. Jakob:
We are not saying that or believing that at all. But here is where your error reveals itself, that you think that the son of God could not really become flesh, unless after that fashion by which flesh exists, which is false. For the Word became flesh, says John, and that truly and really; nevertheless it did not become flesh like flesh is begotten from seed.

THE CAUSE OF THE ERROR OF NESTORIUS. THE NESTORIAN CONTROVERSY WAS NOT A BATTLE OF WORDS [λογομαχία].

Nestorius was plainly in the same error, since he could not think otherwise. If the son of God is said to be born of the seed of David and of Mary, then it could not happen otherwise than if the Divinity had assumed its beginning <254> from the virgin Mary, and this way of speaking is manifestly false and impious. Therefore he said that Mary gave birth to Christ the man, who is God, but she did not give birth to God. Here was no λογομαχία, that is, a mere semantic battle, but rather it concerned the greatest matter of all by far: whether the son of God is truly born of Mary, whether the son of God truly suffered, whether the son of God redeemed the human race by his passion? These things Nestorius denied.

And your teaching is the same, when you interpret this proposition in this way: the Son of God suffered, that is, the flesh of the son of God suffered, which was united with the son of God. But the communication of passion (in your opinion) cannot even verbally be attributed to the son of God, since it is proper to the human nature, which is not fitting for the son of God.

Dr. Beza:
We have nothing in common with the error of Nestorius, since we admit this enunciation: God suffered; a man is omnipotent; which Nestorius did not do, but rather attacked them.

Dr. Jakob:

COMPARISON OF THE DOCTRINE OF NESTORIUS AND DR. BEZA REGARDING THE PERSON OF CHRIST. THE OPINION OF NESTORIUS.

You do indeed admit the phrase in order that you may seem to agree with us and dissent from Nestorius, but when it comes to explaining it is discovered that your explanation and opinion are the same as those of Nestorius. For your words are plainly the same words of Nestorius, who says that in the womb of his mother the son of Mary truly was the son of God, and he confessed *not two*, but one son of God and Mary. But to be born of a woman, which is a property of human nature, does not really correspond to the son of God, which you also say, even while you assert that these two propositions are equivalent: The Son of God was born of the virgin Mary, and the flesh united to the son of God was born of the virgin Mary without real communication of property. Concerning this, I implore, let the audience judge.

NESTORIUS DID NOT DENY THE COMMUNICATION OF THE PROPERTIES OF DIVINITY.

But it is much more intolerable that you assert that it is said after the same fashion, [255] and plainly in the same way, that the assumed man is omnipotent, and the Divinity united to the humanity is omnipotent, which *in no way* communicates its own omnipotence to the assumed humanity. Nestorius had expressed this abominable explanation, who fought only against the communication of properties of humanity, which he judged as unworthy of God and not in the least corresponding to God, namely to be born of a woman, to suffer, to be crucified, but he did not at all deny that the assumed human nature had been glorified into God by the glory characteristic of divinity; and he even attempted to distance himself from the charge of flesh-eating [κρεοφαγία] (which Cyril and the Fathers threw in his face) in that he would not deny the communication of the vivific power of Christ's flesh.

Dr. Beza:
When therefore you say that the Divinity suffered, we assert that this is Eutychian, which was also condemned as just as false and erroneous. Suffering is in fact proper only to the human nature, and corresponds to the human nature alone, BUT IN NO WAY to his Divinity.

Dr. Jakob:

DIVINITY INCAPABLE OF SUFFERING *IN AND OF ITSELF.*

We never said that the Divinity suffered *in and of itself* in the property of its essence, and we have never written this, never thought it, and we still do not believe, think, or teach this. For we know that it is incapable of suffering. But we say that it is openly Nestorian and in conflict with the consensus of the Orthodox Church to remove the passion utterly from the divinity on this account, by which we were redeemed. For even though the Son of God does not suffer in the property of the divine essence, nevertheless he suffers, according to the flesh, the passions he really has in common with the flesh, into which every slander abounded, which his enemies poured out upon his flesh and humanity in both word and deed, as he is one person, as was explained above. Otherwise the redemption of the human race would be attributed really only to the flesh, but not even verbally to the Son of God, which we say is impious and blasphemous.

<256>

Dr. Beza:
And we also say that the Son of God has sufferings in common with the united flesh on account of the accomplished personal union.

Dr. Jakob:

CONSENSUS IN WORDS, NOT IN THINGS.

You are speaking with us but not thinking with us. How can you attribute sufferings to the whole person which consists of a divine and human nature when you say that they cannot be attributed to the Divine nature in any way, not even verbally?

Dr. Beza:

ANALOGY OF A MAN.

The whole man is called rational, though only his soul is rational, and not his body as well, which is devoid of reason.

Dr. Jakob:
Is what is proper to a soul in a human body, then, reason and intellect, such that nothing besides a rational soul is required for a rational man?

Dr. Beza:
A man is said to be rational on account of the soul, which alone is rational, not the body as well.

Dr. Jakob:

A RATIONAL SOUL ALONE IS NOT REQUIRED FOR A RATIONAL MAN.

I of course concede that a man is called rational on account of his rational soul. But a disposition of the body is also required for the enjoyment of reason and intellect, which in no way can be denied. For experience teaches that if anyone should receive a dangerous wound to the head, he would obviously become mentally damaged, and suffer a disorder of Melancholy, as there is no enjoyment of reason in the soul, howsoever rational it may otherwise have been in itself. Nor does the soul reason without <257> a body, so long as it is in a body. Therefore the body is also a participant in reason in its own way, though it understands nothing by itself apart from the soul. So Scripture in various places declares that the heart is wise, and not just the soul. The Lord God did not give you a wise heart, etc. (Deuteronomy 29[:4]). This sentence, repeated so often in Scripture, is not in the least improper for the holy Spirit. And from the heart, says Christ, proceed evil thoughts, which are the work of reason (Matthew 15[:18–19]).

Therefore a man is rational and intelligent, only if his soul and body are well, and the soul does not reason alone, but together with the body, just as you can see in simpletons, who though endowed with a rational soul nevertheless do not know how to count.

ACCOMMODATION OF THE ANALOGY OF THE WISE AND INTELLIGENT MAN. WHY THE SUFFERING OF GOD WAS NECESSARY FOR THE REDEMPTION OF THE HUMAN RACE.

So in the work of redemption of the human race, unless there is a real communication of suffering, the *whole* Christ did not redeem us. For if his Divinity is removed from Christ's passion, and you admit no other communication than that which sustained the human nature lest it succumb to suffering, Christ will have this in common with all the saints: if indeed God sustained all the saints in their suffering, lest they succumb. But here the manner is far different, since the sins which offended the infinite God had to be expiated by passion and death. But flesh was not able to satisfy God's infinite wrath by means of its suffering, however much it was sustained by God, but rather it was necessary for the very son of God to suffer, though not in the property of his own substance, but rather according to the flesh, in order that the Church might be redeemed by God's blood. Upon him, God the son, all injuries and slanders have superabundantly been poured out, which his enemies employed against his soul and body. The son of God not only sustained and strengthened the human nature in the midst of them, such that it was able to endure those sufferings, but he himself also endured and sustained them as God, and did not violently push them away.

PATIENCE OF DIVINITY IN TOLERATING WICKED AND IMPIOUS MEN.

But surely tolerating injury and slander inflicted by words and deed, and not pushing them aside, surely this has to be called suffering? That God grieved greatly, just as man did? Surely God was not pleased? Surely God was angry and could have avenged? We often wonder at <258> and preach about God's patience, that he tolerates disgraceful men for so long and does not punish those who blaspheme against the name proper to Divinity itself; how therefore do we so separate the Divinity from the suffering that we assert with Nestorius that not even a verbal predicate is allowed to have a place in this?

DIVERSITY OF COMMUNICATION AND ITS NATURE.

But we demonstrated above that the nature of the communication of God's omnipotence in the human nature of God is far different, since the human nature is capable of containing the divine Majesty in a different way than the divine nature is said to have become a sharer in the sufferings.

HOW SUFFERING OVERFLOWS TO THE DIVINE NATURE.

For the divine nature can on account of its own supreme perfection receive into itself no sufferings. But since it communicated itself to the flesh through union in the Son, by whom it was assumed into the unity of person, for this reason the suffering also overflows into it. But the human nature is fully capable of containing omnipotence, just as Origen says (Origen *De Princ.* Book 4), such that it is also able to receive the fullness of divinity. For this reason the omnipotence is actually able to be effected in another way than the divinity is said to be capable of containing passions.

Dr. Beza:

COMMUNICATION IN BEZA'S OPINION IS NOTHING EXCEPT FOR UNION.
REGARDING THE POURING OUT OF THE PROPERTIES OF DIVINITY INTO THE
HUMAN NATURE.

*I believe in the communication about which I have spoken,
namely the union of the natures and the properties of the divinity
of the Word [λόγος], with the assumed human nature. But if you
prove from all the Fathers, and find in the writings of one or another
of them, that the properties of divinity were poured out or infused
into the assumed flesh, then you will win.*

Dr. Jakob:

I have the witness of as many Fathers as used the analogy of
glowing-hot or ignited iron, that this pouring out into the assumed
flesh happened.

ANALOGY OF IGNITED IRON.

For just as not only the substance of the fire has been united with
the ignited iron, but also its properties, namely the virtue of glowing
and burning has also been entirely poured into the iron, such that
every bit of it glows and burns, <259> so the Word [λόγος] has not only
been united with the human nature, but also pours out into it the
whole fullness of divinity (Colossians 2[:9]). If in fact the Lord poured
out from the holy Spirit particular gifts into the saints (Joel 2[:28];
1 Corinthians 12[:11]; Acts 2[:4]), how would he have not poured out
into Christ the fullness of the entire Deity, to whom the spirit was
give without measure (John 3[:34])? The Fathers imitated this phrase
of the holy Spirit and his words. Cassian says in the recitation of his
confession, to which all the African and Gallic Bishops subscribed,
God mercifully mingled himself with the Human Nature *through
the infusion* of his own power.[34] Hilary, with Theodoret as witness,
Dialogue 2: God mingled himself *through infusion* of his power, just as
his mercy was mingled *with the human nature*, but the human nature
was not mingled with the divine.

---

34   *Conf* 7.13.

HOW OMNIPOTENCE AND THE PROPERTIES OF GOD WERE POURED OUT INTO THE HUMAN NATURE.

But we never use the term *effusion*, as has been imputed to us falsely, as if we teach that what was poured out into the human nature from the divinity was a created omnipotence and divinity, which is equal to an essential Deity and omnipotence. This impious doctrine and opinion has never come into the mind of me, us, or any of our party. This opinion conflicts with the status of our disputation. For such created omnipotence would not be an attribute or property of God.

The fact though is that we have always argued in this disputation, not about the communication of created gifts, but rather about the real communication of attributes, or properties, of the divine nature, that they have really been communicated to the assumed nature.

SLANDER REGARDING CREATED AND UNCREATED DIVINITY AND OMNIPOTENCE.

From all these things it is clear that we have been insulted by all those who attribute in their writings a created divinity and a created omnipotence to Dr. Brenz, and to me, on account of our assertion of a real communication of attributes. They cannot ever point this out in any of our writings. For this reason if such a pouring out of the properties of divinity is attacked by our opponents, it is not our doctrine that is attacked by them, but merely a figment of the imagination of those who speak against us. They will themselves consider how they will render to God an account on the last day, who have falsely spread about in various regions accusations like this, <260> Though often warned, nevertheless they do not cease doing it. But for this reason they do it, lest readers turning their attention to the true and proper status of the controversy rightly inquire into the truth, and comprehend their error.

Dr. Beza:

I remember reading in your and Brenz's writings about ambiguous divinity and ambiguous omnipotence, and I did not understand your words in a different way, but had no intention at all of slandering. The reason I say this is, I love truth and peace. Would that we understood each other better and more correctly, if by any means concord might be decided between us! And I could wish that all published writings that seem to stand in the way of this peace and concord, or to obscure the truth, be destroyed!

Dr. Jakob:

I too could wish that they were all destroyed. The twisted opinion in fact fastens itself in the minds of men who read such things, and they make twisted judgments about our teaching.

IN CHRIST ONLY ONE DIVINITY AND OMNIPOTENCE.

We in fact teach no created divinity or omnipotence in the human nature, nor have we ever taught it, which habitually or subjectively exists in the human nature. Concerning this the preface of the Book of Concord of our Churches bears witness with many words. On the contrary, we recognize in Christ's person *only one divinity and omnipotence*, the eternal essence, which Christ truly and really possesses in common, essentially with the Father and the holy Spirit, but with the assumed human nature personally.

DIFFERENT NATURE OF THE ONE DIVINITY AND OMNIPOTENCE IN CHRIST.

But even though it is one in number, nevertheless the nature of it is diverse, when it is considered in itself and of itself, as nature in itself, and when it is considered in the personal union. It is for this reason that Augustine calls it sharing in and being shared in. Just as Aristotle hands down two definitions of one <261> and the same soul, by which it is considered in itself, as well as in respect of the body with which it is united and communicated to it.

Dr. Beza:

TWISTED EXPLANATION OF THE ANALOGY OF GLOWING-HOT IRON.

We also recognize one omnipotence proper to the eternal Deity in Christ. So also we say that it was united with the flesh, so that on this account we recognize no mode of communication. And we say that what is proper to it acts distinctly in Christ's person. For this reason the natures are not separated. You will find this also in John of Damascus, when he explains the analogy of the ignited metal in a branding-iron. For fire burns in the iron; the iron does not burn. And again, the branding-iron is what cuts in; the fire does not. The iron does what belongs to it, and the fire also what belongs to it. Cutting in belongs to the iron, burning belongs to the fire. In this way Divinity and humanity are united in Christ, and no pouring out of divinity into the humanity happens. For this reason the operations remain distinct too, and God does not do the things that belong to the man, nor man those things that belong to God.

Besides, the soul has certain actions which are not done with the body, or through the body.

Dr. Jakob:

TRUE EXPLANATION OF IT FROM JOHN OF DAMASCUS.

No one in any way denies the distinction of the natures. So also no one denies the distinction of the power working in the operation of each nature. But that the one nature works that which is proper to it without the communication of another power, nether John of Damascus nor any other of the genuine Fathers concedes. John of Damascus says,

> Not according to its *proper* working, but rather on account of the Word being united to it, did the *flesh* of the Lord work divine things, with the Word manifesting through the flesh the work proper to It. For ignited iron also burns, possessing the burning work not by a

natural faculty, but rather obtaining *this* from <262> its union to the fire. Therefore the Lord's very flesh was mortal on account of itself, *and vivific* on account of the hypostatic union to the Word. (John of Damascus, *On the Orthodox Faith* Book 3, chapter 17)

John of Damascus does not say, The Word was working divine things, but the flesh of the Lord was working divine things. The rest of the Fathers have the same opinion; I could produce very many of their testimonies.

Dr. Beza:

UNIQUE FOUNDATION OF DR. BEZA'S OPINION AGAINST THE COMMUNICATION OF PROPERTIES.

No communication of omnipotence is possible, or communication of its properties IN THE HUMAN NATURE, unless the human nature were to be changed into divinity. For this reason these statements are equivalent: Humanity became omnipotent, and humanity became Deity, since Deity, and the omnipotence of Deity, are one and the same thing. If the one is communicated, so is the other.

Dr. Jakob:

REFUTATION OF THIS FOUNDATION. COMMUNICATION OF PROPERTIES DOES NOT PRESUPPOSE CHANGE OF HUMAN NATURE INTO DEITY.

I have demonstrated by means of two analogies from the writings of the orthodox Fathers I produced, namely the glowing-hot or ignited iron, and the union of the soul with the body, that a true and real communication of properties and substances can happen, without any confusion of them or destruction of one or the other. Iron is in fact not destroyed, nor does it lose its substance, when fire is communicated with the qualities proper to it of glowing and burning.

So also it is not necessary for the humanity to be changed into Deity and to become Deity, if omnipotence should be communicated to it by the person of the Son of God.

But omitting those analogies, let us hear from God's word, on which alone our faith rests, to learn whether omnipotence truly and really has been communicated to the human nature in Christ. So I ask, regarding Paul's words, In him the entire fullness of Deity dwells bodily, whether the fullness of Deity refers to a created gift?

<263>

Dr. Beza:
Paul wanted to show in this place that not only names, but two natures were personally united in Christ, namely the divine and human nature.

Dr. Jakob:
This is no answer to the question. The reason is, I am asking whether the fullness of Deity means a created gift? Paul does not say Deity dwells in him, but rather he says, The entire fullness *of Deity.* Clearly he did not wish by this term to speak of something created. It rather embraces all things without measure, which are in God, and which can be said about God. Just as it is written: we have all received from his fullness (John 1[:16]).

The gifts that God distributes to us are all created and measured gifts, according to the measure of Christ's donation; we have received them all, and still receive them, from his unmeasured fullness (Ephesians 4[:7]; 1 Corinthians 12[:7], 14[:1]).

THE WHOLE FULLNESS OF DEITY DWELLS IN THE FLESH OF CHRIST.

It stands therefore that the saying of Paul must be understood not as speaking about created gifts, but about the fullness which is essential and proper to divinity, which we embrace by means of the one term, omnipotence. Paul affirms that this dwells in Christ bodily. All the orthodox Fathers interpret this with respect to Christ *according to the flesh.* For the fullness of Deity cannot dwell bodily in Deity, since Deity is not a body, or something corporeal, but rather is purely singular and indivisible Spirit. For this reason the Fathers said that this fullness dwelt *in the flesh, in the assumed nature, just as in its very own body.*

CONFIRMATION OF THE REAL COMMUNICATION OF OMNIPOTENCE IN THE FLESH.

Therefore I am arguing from the cited passage of Paul in order to prove the communication of omnipotence in the assumed nature.

Whatever the whole fullness of Deity has been communicated to, to this has omnipotence also been communicated. But the whole fullness of Deity has been communicated to the assumed nature in Christ. Therefore omnipotence has also been communicated to it.

<264>

Dr. Beza:

DR. BEZA'S DODGE. CONFUSION OF UNION AND COMMUNICATION OF ATTRIBUTES.

If by communication we understand union, then I concede that not only omnipotence, but also the rest of the attributes of Deity have been communicated to the human nature. For since the human nature has been united with the divine, and both God and man are one person, therefore omnipotence has also been united, which cannot be separated from Deity.

Dr. Jakob:

DIFFERENCE BETWEEN UNION OF NATURES AND COMMUNICATION OF ATTRIBUTES.

It was said and demonstrated above that the union of natures and communication of properties differ amongst themselves quite a bit. For the communication of properties is like the effect and consequence of the union of natures. So even though they occur at the same time, nevertheless they exist by reason of the order of nature as former and latter.

For this reason, as the union of natures is not a bare and simple union, but rather a true and real communication, by which the divine gives and the human receives, so the communication of attributes is not a kind of union, by which the natures communicate none of their own properties with one another, but also a true and real communication, by which the Word [λόγος] itself has also communicated all that belongs to it to the assumed nature.

Dr. Beza:
Union and communication are one thing, and just as suffering was not communicated to the divine nature, such that it possesses it IN ITSELF, so also omnipotence was not communicated to the humanity in Christ such that it possesses it IN ITSELF. In the same way therefore that Deity was crucified, so humanity was made omnipotent. But that is not the case. Therefore neither is this, which you say, that humanity became omnipotent.

<265>

Dr. Jakob:
I have sufficient shown that the Union of natures and the Communication of attributes or properties is not one and the same thing. So I also said above that the nature of these statements was not the same: Divinity was crucified, and humanity became omnipotent, and this on account of the diversity of natures. And I showed for that reason that human nature becoming omnipotent was something far different than divinity suffering or being crucified.

For divinity receives no perfection or imperfection *in itself* on account of the immutability of its own nature. But the human nature can receive *in itself,* and in the person of the son of God truly received, supreme Majesty, which is proper to Deity, just as I have declared by the words of the Holy Fathers.

Dr. Beza:

Dr. Beza attributes only created *gifts* to Christ.

We also confess that the supreme gifts of Deity, which can befall a creature and which the human nature is capable of containing, were conferred upon the humanity of Christ, but that these gifts are not properties of Deity, which are incommunicable, but are habitual created gifts, which Christ's humanity possesses IN ITSELF, by which he surpasses all creatures.

Dr. Jakob:

DR. BEZA'S DOCTRINE REGARDING THE COMMUNICATION OF GIFTS MADE TO CHRIST, THE SAME AS THE QUR'AN.

You are not answering Paul's testimony or my questions at all, whether the fullness of Deity is a created gift. If therefore you persist in the opinion that Christ possesses no other gifts except for created ones according to his humanity, or that his humanity possesses, communicated by the son of God, then it is clear that your doctrine is in this part clearly the same as the Turkish Qur'an, which also attributes the same gifts to Christ, which namely are created, by which Christ surpasses all creatures.

<266>

Dr. Beza:
We have not come here to hear insults; we have nothing in common with the Turkish Qur'an, and the impiety of those who deny that Christ is God. Much to the contrary, they say it is the highest blasphemy if anyone calls Christ God, and we do not say this.

MUTTERING OF THE FRENCH.

After Dr. Beza's exclamation, a great muttering of the French arose, as they heard their confession regarding Christ compared with the Turkish Qur'an, but they calmed down and were appeased once more by the speech of Dr. Jakob.

Dr. Jakob:

Reverend Dr. Beza, the one who speaks the truth is not at the same time insulting. I will in fact recite the words of the Qur'an, which read thus:

THE TURKISH QUR'AN'S CONFESSION ABOUT CHRIST [QUR'AN 2:253].

Of all the Prophets, we elevate some over others, and God spoke to some of them to various degrees, and we especially gave spirit to Christ the son of Mary and granted him power and excellence.

GOD'S SOUL COMMUNICATED TO CHRIST.

Is this not a magnificent confession about Christ? That God is said to have conferred upon him *specially his very own soul*, and to have granted him power over all the rest? What is God's soul in fact but God himself? This is why Bibliander noted in the margin, why therefore do you deny the Son of God?

On this account I pray you not take as an insult what was said by me in my eagerness for the truth, so that all may see and understand what hides under this doctrine, in which real communication of the properties of divinity is denied the humanity of Christ, by which name also his divinity is denied. For what is Divinity other than all his properties? Are all these <267> in it not accidents, but rather substances, that is, the essence itself of Deity? But how can that man be God who possesses from God only his created gifts? I pray pious minds carefully weigh this amongst themselves, and that they all comprehend very well the things that have been brought up by me from the Qur'an, as no slander against any person.

Dr. Beza:

DR. BEZA ACTUALLY DENIES WHAT HE ATTRIBUTES TO THE MAN CHRIST IN WORDS; THE CONFERENCE WILL SHOW THIS MORE CLEARLY THAN THE LIGHT OF NOON.

No one can attribute to the man Christ what we do not attribute to him. For we say that the assumed man is true God, omnipotent, omniscient; creator and ruler of heaven and earth; but we do not say that his humanity is omnipotent. You, however, are always confusing the abstract and the concrete. These are very different from each other. You heap an assortment of insults on us, comparing our doctrine to Muhammadism and the Turkish Qur'an. We therefore ask that we have a conference about the real issue, without any insults of this sort.

Dr. Jakob:

CONCRETE AND ABSTRACT TERMS NOT TO BE CONFUSED. CONSENSUS IN WORDS, NOT IN THINGS. BEZA CONDEMNED BY VARIED GRAMMATICAL CONSTRUCTION [ἀλλοίωσις].

It was shown sufficiently above that I do not confuse abstract and concrete terms. Nor in fact have I conceded that the term "man," presented absolutely, is concrete, which differs not at all from humanity, since it is the species, that is, the form abstracted from individual members, that is suited to them all. But what is hidden underneath these things falsely called concrete, your Theses declare sufficiently. We will speak about them a little later. For you expressly put it forward when you say, The man is omnipotent must be understood in this way: Deity united to the humanity is omnipotent. Likewise the other sentences: God suffered, that is, humanity, or the flesh united to the Deity suffered. From this it is clear that you attribute nothing to the assumed man concerning God's omnipotence, but rather you contend that all these things must be understood only (*only*, I say) in regard to the Deity. This we perpetually deny, and consistently fight against. For varied grammatical construction [ἀλλοίωσις] or switching terms around cannot hold any ground here.

<268>

Besides, it is known to all the audience that we have often been accused by you of Eutychianism in this conference, as if our doctrine about the person of Christ belongs to the same heresy. Nevertheless we always respond calmly to this, and likewise all those times men-tion was made by us of Nestorianism.

Dr. Beza:
I can handle a charge of Nestorianism against us, but I cannot listen to Muhammadism and the Turkish Qur'an.

Dr. Jakob:
Let it suffice that we have said this. After this, since I see that you are offended, I will restrain myself from mention of the Qur'an, and we will conduct the conference peacefully on the matter at hand, just as we have thus far.

Dr. Beza:
The Church of God is not built up by insults. Though they are found in the writings of both parties, I could wish they were all destroyed at the same time, and holy concord be established. I confess in fact that many things have been written by me that I wished had not been written. And I think you feel the same thing too. Let us strive for peace and both abstain henceforth from those harsh writ-ings, until the Lord has granted us pious peace and concord.

Dr. Jakob:
I take no pleasure in insults either, but love peace and am eager for concord. This I think is not in the least unknown to Your Reverence. But on the other hand, you cannot deny that heresies as horrible as possible have been imputed to us in your writings so far, those of the Manicheanss, Arians, Eutychians, Monothelites, which we bring back from the dead, and they have been scattered through many realms in your writings. Our conscience would not let us remain silent about these, of course.

<269>

But as far as I am concerned, I say that I neither regret nor am ashamed of the things that I have written concerning this matter. For I know the things that are true and in accord with the word *of the Lord* and with the analogy of the Christian faith.

Dr. Beza:

We have both sinned in our writings. And God knows whether I came to this match of my own will or in light of being challenged. But the business now is not about those writings; rather, let us seek concord and strive for peace. This is the reason that I did not want to answer Holderus at all, nor have I been willing thus far to hurl back insults. I will rather suppress them by my silence and put a limit on these things. I rather commit the business itself to Christ.

Dr. Jakob:

I submit all my writings on this matter to the Church and to the judgment of all pious men, just as also the writings on the other articles. But I know that I have confirmed the doctrine of our Churches not by human authority, but rather by the most plain and not in the least doubtful testimonies of holy Scripture, and have refuted the contrary doctrine on the basis of the same foundations.

For this reason by God's grace I persist in this argument of mine firm and unmoved, by which I have proved that omnipotence in the person of the son of God has been communicated to the assumed nature truly and really, since the whole fullness of Deity dwells in him bodily. This indwelling is very real communication. To this argument and testimony of Scripture no answer has yet been made to me.

Dr. Beza:

UNIQUE FOUNDATION OF DR. BEZA'S OPINION.

Omnipotence does not befit Christ's humanity, since it is an attribute or property of Deity. On the other hand, it is correctly said in the concrete, The man is omnipotent, since the man is God. In the same way <270> *it is also correct and true to say, God suffered and died.*

Dr. Jakob:

REFUTATION OF THE SAME.

I showed a little bit ago from John of Damascus that these statements differ very much from each other: God suffered, and the man is omnipotent, on account of the immutability of the divine nature which can be neither exalted, nor humiliated, made infirm, or perfected. But the human nature is capable of all these things, and was made a sharer in Christ. *In it* the whole fullness of Deity dwells bodily. Whence even the flesh of Christ is not only called vivific but also really became vivific, since *it drank in the entire power* of vivifying, as Cyril says.

Dr. Beza:

HOW CHRIST'S FLESH IS VIVIFIC ACCORDING TO DR. BEZA.

Christ's flesh is vivific for the reason of merit, that by it we were restored to life, and by it also the life which is in the Word [λόγος] is distributed to us. For this reason Christ is also joined to us in a human nature. But the power of vivifying has not been communicated to Christ's flesh such that it possesses it IN ITSELF and vivifies like God does.

Dr. Jakob:

THE HUMAN NATURE OF CHRIST POSSESSES IN ITSELF VIVIFYING POWER.

Cyril says: Christ shows that his entire body is full of the vivific power of the Spirit, not that he lost the nature of the flesh and was changed into spirit, but rather that supremely conjoined with it, he drank in *the total power of vivifying* (Cyril, Book 4, chapter 24). Also: Our nature, assumed by the son of God, *exceeded* its own *limits*, and in his assumed state was transformed by grace (Book 12, *Thesauri* chapter 15). The assumed flesh does not indeed possess life in itself like the Word [λόγος] possesses by reason of its own Divinity, but it has it dwelling personally in itself, in a manner that no other flesh has life dwelling in itself. Just as it is written: The first man was made into a living soul, but the second man into a vivifying spirit (1 Corinthians 15[:46]).

<271>

Dr. Beza:

DR. BEZA ALWAYS REPEATS HIS ONE AND ONLY FOUNDATION.

It must be proved that the humanity became Deity before it can be proved that the human nature became omnipotent. If that is proved, so also will be the communication of all properties, since the nature of all the properties in God is the same. But I especially ask the reason why eternity and infinity also have not been communicated to the assumed nature by the Word [λόγος]?

Dr. Jakob:

I proved by Paul's plain words and demonstrated through a syllogism that omnipotence was communicated to the human nature and that it was nevertheless not necessary for the human nature to be changed into Deity. Since in fact the whole fullness of Deity dwells bodily in the human nature, and from this fullness omnipotence is not excluded, but is rather included, therefore it is really communicated. It is just like a soul with all its powers communicated to the animated body, without the body being changed into a soul.

But you are asking the reason why eternity and infinity have not been communicated to the humanity, so that we can say that Christ's humanity is from eternity, is infinite, in just the same manner we say that it is omnipotent, omniscient? I answer that the manner and mode of the divine attributes and of their communication is not the same. The reason I say this is that in the divine essence certain substantial actions are energetic, such as wisdom, power, life, justice, mercy, etc. But there are others which (as Athanasius says) are occupied with and reflect the essence of Deity, and are not energetic, such as being from eternity, being essentially infinite, incorporeal, immaterial, and the like. These are said to be communicated to the humanity, since Deity itself was communicated, and they cannot be separated from it. But the humanity is not specifically designated by these attributes, since they are not actions perfecting the human nature, like the proper ones mentioned in the first order <272> perfect it, and it is specifically designated by them. On this account, even though the human nature possesses communicated eternity and an infinite essence, dwelling in *itself* bodily, just as with omnipotence, nevertheless it is not called infinite and eternal just as it is truly called omnipotent.

Dr. Beza:
I concede the entire argument, if it should be understood in the concrete, namely, that the man is omnipotent. But from there it does not follow that humanity became omnipotent.

Dr. Jakob:

The term "man" is not concrete.

We have now many times said the term "man" is not concrete, since it is a species or form which is not concrete, but is called abstract.

Dr. Beza's word-tricks regarding the man Christ.

Besides, it is also not a concrete term in your usage, which means an *entire* person, but rather just another nature considered in the abstract, just as you openly declare in your response, when you say: Man is omnipotent, that is Deity united to humanity is omnipotent. Most people would in fact understand that Man, which consists of body and rational soul, and is united to the word, is omnipotent, just like the words sound. But you do not in the least either understand or interpret in this way. On the contrary, you teach that here we must necessarily resort to a figure of speech, since you confidently affirm that this usage cannot be true, if the proper meaning of the term "*man*" should be retained. But I ask, pray, in what Grammar or tongue is this found? Hebrew, Greek, Latin, French, or German, in which man means the same thing as Deity united to humanity?

Let the audience carefully remember, therefore, those things that were said above about abstract and concrete terms, and how badly and unsuitably, contrary to the holy Spirit's rules of Grammar <273> in any language, they befit this mystery, and the horrendous error lurking that persuades people to believe that the true assumed man is neither God nor is omnipotent.

BATTLES OF WORDS [λογομαχίαι] MUST BE AVOIDED IN THE CHURCH.

Therefore omitting the terms "abstract and concrete," which neither the Lord nor the Prophets nor the Apostles used, which are nowhere found in holy Scripture either, nor are understood, perhaps, by all the audience, as scholastic terms, we will use those words to explain this mystery which the holy Spirit used in holy Scripture. Just as Paul carefully advised his disciple Timothy not to fight about words, which profits nothing except the ruin of your hearers who do not understand these things, and without care easily can be led into error by them.

Dr. Beza:
We need to put these limits on this disputation, otherwise this controversy is difficult to explain.

Dr. Jakob:
It ought to seem amazing of course to everyone that the holy Spirit, who preached so copiously and perspicuously in the old and new Testament about Christ God and man, would be so at a loss for words that he could not teach and explain from the writings of the Prophets, without the terms "abstract and concrete," who Christ is and what has been communicated to the man Christ, that is, according to his humanity.

And I will of course tolerate the use of these terms in this controversy during this conference, provided the audience understand, and they be correctly suited to the business at hand, which is not the case with you. The analogy of the ignited iron is clear, which can be understood by everyone, even people of middling intelligence.

Dr. Beza:

WHETHER THE ANALOGY OF IGNITED IRON IS SUITED TO THIS DISPUTATION.

The analogy about ignited iron does not square up well for explaining this Mystery. [274] *Since the fire is in the iron as in a subject. But the union of natures in Christ's person is something far different. Again, the iron does not burn, but rather the fire in the iron. Thus did Christ raise Lazarus. Though indeed the humanity supplying the voice did something when Christ said, Lazarus, come out, on the other hand it is the Divinity that restored him to life by its own power.*

Dr. Jakob:

THE FIRE IS NOT IN THE IRON AS IN A SUBJECT.

It is patently absurd to say that the fire is in the iron as in a subject. This is in conflict with Philosophy itself and with reason. For only accidents are said to be in subjects, just as whiteness on a wall, justice in a just man. But here two substances are united, and one is in the other with its own properties, and in this way is really communicated to it. For fire is not an accident, but is a substance, no less than the iron itself. For this reason it cannot be in the iron as in a subject, like heat in water, where heat, as an accident, is in the water, as in a subject.

This is the reason that our ancestors and Fathers of the first and purer Church thought this analogy was very suitable for explaining the personal union of the two natures in Christ, when the two natures run together with their own properties and communicate with each other, although it could not attain to or perfectly express the exaltation of the Mystery of the personal union.

Nor could Peter's voice in the same manner raise the dead like the voice of Christ did when he said, Lazarus, come out. For Peter's voice raised the dead by means of a power outside of himself, namely that of Christ, God and man, when he said, I say to you in the name of Jesus, rise. This power was not united with Peter as with the Christ who said, Lazarus come out. The power of divinity united with this voice made Lazarus rise again immediately. Without Christ, Peter's voice could not have done this, even if he had said a thousand times, rise, rise, rise. <275> But the voice of Christ, who was working together with him, made it happen, as it is written: Setting out, they preached everywhere, with the Lord working together in them and confirming their speech with signs that followed. The Lord gave signs, and confirmed their speech, not Peter, Paul, etc.

For this reason I said above also that you made a mistake when you omitted Leo's words, "with the communication of another form," which he put on the earlier ones, namely, one nature or other does in fact what is proper to it, however not apart from, but rather with, the communication of the other nature.

HOW LAZARUS WAS RAISED FROM THE DEAD BY CHRIST.

So Christ's voice did not raise Lazarus without his divine power, nor did the power of God raise him without this voice of Christ, "Lazarus come out." For this reason the voice of Christ can correctly and truly be called and omnipotent voice, and it is really true that it can perform things by the power of the divine nature that would otherwise be impossible for a human voice and for all men.

Dr. Beza:

JOHN OF DAMASCUS DENIES THAT THERE IS ONE END PURPOSE [ἀποτέλεσμα] OF THE IRON AND FIRE, BOOK 3, CHAPTER 15.

I will demonstrate that there is not a communication of actions and operations of the divine and human nature of the kind that Your Reverence asserts by the analogy of the glowing-hot iron. The iron cuts, and not the fire. And again, fire burns, and does not cut like iron, though the body of each of them is one, and there is one end purpose [ἀποτέλεσμα]. The same principle exists in the analogy of the soul and body, because the soul does one thing and the body another, and the actions of the soul and body are thus distinct. So also the actions of the humanity and divinity in the person of Christ are distinct, such that the human nature does one thing and the divine nature another. The human nature sustains pains, but the divine nature supports the human nature, lest it succumb.

Dr. Jakob:

COMMUNICATION OF THE ACTIONS OF THE NATURES DOES NOT CONFUSE THE NATURES.

The actions of the natures are by no means distinct in this way in the case of ignited iron, nor of the body and soul in a man, nor of the natures <276> in the person of Christ, such as is asserted by you here. For the iron without the fire does not cut in this way, nor does the fire without the iron burn in the same way. But in the cutting, just as also in the burning, the iron and fire run together, and accomplish this work together and not separately or distinctly. Thus a soul without a body, and a body without a soul, accomplishes nothing and executes none of the things which is proper to either one, such that the action of the body is distinct from the action of the soul. Rather they accomplish all things conjointly, not by themselves or separately. Divinity is and remains indeed perpetually distinct from the humanity after this fashion, and is not mixed together with it, just like iron is not mixed with fire, or the soul with the body. But the passions and actions are common to both, and attributed to the whole person, even though in light of the diversity of the natures and properties, which remain distinct, they run together in operation and action.

These things can easily be understood by everyone. There is no treachery here, no trope or figure of speech. On the contrary, these are matters explained and perspicuous, visible and palpable.

IN WHAT WAY DIVINITY IS SAID TO HAVE SUFFERED.

Thus iron burns more strongly and causes more pain than just fire without the iron. And ignited iron penetrates and cuts more swiftly and in a different way than if just cold iron (by its own nature) is employed for cutting something. So by the passion of Christ, God and man, the sins *of the entire world* could not have been expiated unless the divinity had been joined together with the humanity in the passion itself as well, not just to support it, but *in suffering* (I say suffering in the way that was explained above), so that it may truly be said that the least of his passions must not be referred only to his humanity, but also to the Deity itself. These it nevertheless did not sustain in itself in the same way as the human nature did. This notwithstanding, *it truly endured* and patiently suffered to the highest degree the impiety and the deed of the Jews, and did not repel violently those insults that he could have repelled violently had he wished to.

Separation of actions separates natures. Christ's flesh alone did not redeem us.

But when the actions and passions are attributed distinctly in this way to the natures, <277> such that one is said to work something or one to suffer, which the other does not work or does not suffer, here immediately the personal union is destroyed, the natures are separated, and two persons are established. Moreover, from this it would follow that we were redeemed from our sins by the suffering of Christ, since suffering pertains only to the human nature, with which the divinity has no real communication at all, and *not* the son of God, but rather only his human nature had redeemed us. That, or we have not yet been redeemed, since redemption from sins is not a matter of the flesh alone, but of the son of God, but not of the son alone without flesh, but rather a work of the incarnate Son of God.

Dr. Beza:

Resurrection of the dead a work of divinity alone, according to the opinion of Beza.

Resurrection of the dead is the work of divinity alone, and cannot be attributed to Christ's humanity. So Christ's divinity alone raised his body from the dead. But this is the supreme dignity of humanity in Christ, that it subsists in the person of the son of God. No other testimony of Scripture can be produced by which it may be proved that the properties of Deity were given or communicated to the humanity in Christ besides created gifts.

Dr. Jakob:

CHRIST'S DIVINITY DID NOT RESUSCITATE THE DEAD WITHOUT THE COMMUNICATION OF HUMANITY.

It is plainly novel and unheard of in the Church of God that the resurrection of the dead is a property of Deity such that it is not communicated to the humanity assumed by the Son of God. For even though it is true that humanity cannot vivify by itself in a spiritual way, as it were, as also it could not revive a dead body, nevertheless to assert that it cannot do so by the communication of divine power is not only absurd, but also plainly impious, and goes so far as to deny Christ himself.

WHETHER CHRIST'S BODY WAS RESUSCITATED BY DEITY ALONE.

But as far as the dead body of Christ himself is concerned, it cannot be denied that the soul separated from his dead body was neither dead nor separated from the son of God, since it had been sustained by his father, <278> and Christ committed it into his hands while dying. Therefore since it had remained a sharer in this power even while his body was dead, what intelligent person would dare to exclude it from the resuscitation of his body? Since Christ himself says, I have the power to lay down my soul, that is, my life, and to take it up again. Therefore just as Christ laid down his body, when he himself wished, not only according to the divinity, but also his *soul* willed, and not when it pleased his enemies, so the same soul of Christ, united to the Son of God, took up again the same body when he willed, namely on the third day, just as he had said. This power was given to the soul of no man, that when he willed, it could be united again with its body, and so rise again as a man. But that hour should be waited for by all people who are in their graves, in which all will hear the voice of Christ Jesus, God and man, and will rise again from the dead, some to life, some to judgment (John 5[:19–29]; 1 Thessalonians 4[:13–18]).

And Christ the Man, that is, according to his humanity, possesses thereafter the supreme dignity, that his humanity subsists in the Son of God, that is, having become one person with him, he is a sharer in this infinite power, which is true of no other creature, not even angelic ones.

TESTIMONIES OF SCRIPTURE, OMNIPOTENCE HAS BEEN COMMUNICATED TO THE HUMAN NATURE.

But it is entirely false to say that no testimony of Scripture can be produced that says omnipotence and other attributes of God have been communicated to the human nature in Christ, except that which was brought up from Paul a little bit ago, and was totally unrefuted. I will in fact confirm it with another no less prominent testimony, when he says, To me has been given all authority in heaven and on earth (Matthew 28[:18]). Who is the one who says *to me*? The Man Jesus, Mary's son. To this one was given all authority in heaven and on earth. Paul confirms the same thing when he says, We who believe according to the working of the power of his virtue, which he worked in Christ, reviving him from the dead, and seating him and his right hand in the heavens above every principality and power, and virtue, and dominion, and every name which is named not only in this age but also in the age to come, and subjected all things under his feet (Ephesians 1[:22]).

<279>

Again, Peter says, Therefore let the whole house of Israel know that God made him Lord and Christ, *this Jesus*, whom you crucified (Acts 2[:23]). And again, He gave him the name above every name, that at the name *of Jesus* every knee should bow in heaven, earth, and under the earth, etc. (Philippians 2[:10]).

Again, We shall all sit at the *tribunal* of Christ (Romans 14[:10]), for it is written: As I live, says *the Lord*, let every knee bow to me (Isaiah 49[:23]). Together all these testimonies confirm that omnipotence was communicated to Christ the man, seated at the right hand of omnipotent power and Majesty of God and exalted, by which it has been granted him to rule over and govern the entire World, creatures visible and invisible subject to him.

Dr. Beza:

BEZA IN RESPONSE TO THESIS 2.

All the authority, about which Christ speaks at Matthew 28, "To me has been given all authority in heaven and on earth," is not to be understood in regard to the omnipotence of God, but only in regard to Christ's Dominion, which was given to him according to his humanity after the exaltation to the right hand of God. For all this authority is utterly different from that which is essential in God, and considered distinctly. This is nothing other than the power to administer created things according to God, which among the gifts conferred upon Christ's flesh should be attributed to habitual grace.

Dr. Jakob:

Since against the testimonies of Scripture I have brought up, you bring up nothing but an interpretation by which you say that the power is utterly different from that which is essential in God and is considered distinctly, I ask that you produce just one testimony of holy Scripture, the old or new Testament, by which you are willing and able to prove this interpretation of you and your colleagues.

<280>

Dr. Beza:

BEZA CANNOT PROVE HIS INTERPRETATION BY MEANS OF TESTIMONIES OF SCRIPTURE.

There is no need because the matter is clear. If the essential power of God had been really communicated to the humanity, it would follow that it would have been changed into Deity, and have become Deity. This cannot happen.

Dr. Jakob:

I require a plain testimony of holy Scripture, at the very least just *one*, by which you may prove this interpretation of yours. But you are offering a theory, which has no less need of proof. Therefore I very lovingly beseech you, that you prove by *one*, just *one* testimony of

Scripture, that what you are saying is true: If the essential power of God were communicated to the human nature, humanity would have become Deity. It is not in fact sufficient to say this; instead, you need to prove it.

Dr. Beza:

The matter is so clear that it needs no proof. Because God's power is infinite. But the human nature is finite. Therefore it is not capable of containing or sharing in infinite power.

Dr. Jakob:

I still hear no testimony of Scripture, but rather just a philosophical principle, that the finite is not capable of containing the infinite. This has its own place in Philosophy and the natural sciences. But it cannot hold a place in this mystery. For I have proved above, in Paul's words, that the whole fullness of Deity (*which is infinite*) dwells bodily in Christ's flesh (*which is finite* and remains so) (Colossians 2[:9]). This could not happen, nor indeed could it have happened, if this philosophical principle were holding place here.

This is the reason I still ask you to offer *one, one* I say, just *one* testimony of holy Scripture, by which <281> you may prove that you are showing, if omnipotence had been communicated to humanity, that it would have been turned into Deity, and would have become *Deity* itself. If Your Reverence cannot show this, our opinion remains firm and unmovable, that God's essential omnipotence was really communicated to the human nature in Christ, according to the testimonies of Scripture that have been brought up. In this regard Christ speaks in Matthew 28[:18] when he says, *To me* (the man *Jesus* of Nazareth, Mary's son) has been given all authority in heaven and on earth.

Since you deny this, it is clear to everyone that you establish two persons in Christ, with Nestorius, even though you confess with your mouth, with Nestorius himself, one single person.

Dr. Beza:

Nestorius did not earnestly confess one singular person in Christ, but only pretended. But we earnestly confess only one person in Christ, and believe in two natures, distinct in their essence, properties, and operations. And we do not separate the natures, but rather say that they are united, even though we distinguish their actions. For Eutyches, since he wished to avoid this separation of natures, fell into the opposite error, namely into the confusion of natures and properties, and said that the divinity was crucified. We must beware of this, lest this happen to us too.

Dr. Jakob:

HOW NESTORIUS WAS CONVICTED OF THE ERROR OF SEPARATION OF NATURES.

It has been clearly demonstrated above that Nestorius did earnestly assert one singular person in Christ, in the very words of Nestorius himself. But from his denial of the real communication of properties follows the separation of natures, and two persons are established. Two hundred Fathers of the Council of Ephesus, with Cyril as leader, showed this publicly to Nestorius himself. I trust that it has been shown, sufficiently and more than sufficiently, that you are doing the same as him. In what remains, <282> I will show and prove what follows no less clearly. For whoever denies the consequence of a good conclusion also denies its premise. Since therefore the real communication of properties and operations is denied by your party, for this very reason also the true personal union which is the cause of this communication is denied by you, even though you should say in your mouth and your words, with Nestorius, that it is *one and singular.*

But how Cyril said that the Word of God suffered impassibly, and how Vigilius wrote that the Divinity was pinned with nails but not pierced, has been said above.

Dr. Beza:

We in no way deny, but consistently affirm, the personal union of the natures in the person OF CHRIST. But we do deny that the communication of attributes or properties of divinity in the human nature follows from this. This cannot hold a place unless the humanity should be changed into Deity. This is Eutychian, and was condemned by the Church.

Dr. Jakob:

It was said above that the *Ecclesiastical History* testifies about Eutyches that he had believed and taught only one nature in Christ after the assumption of the human nature, and that humanity was absorbed into the Deity (*Concord* vol. 1). Therefore his heresy is nothing to us.

NESTORIUS WAS CONDEMNED VERY JUSTLY OF HERESY.

But there is nothing keeping us from saying that Nestorius was confessing one singular person in Christ, so as to prevent his very Just condemnation of heresy by the Synod of Ephesus, namely that he established two persons on account of his denial of the communication of attributes. For if he had fully thought in his heart in the same way as the Church, but had not been able to express the thought of his mind, <283> nevertheless he was condemned rightly on account of his stubbornness, since he was so often warned, and yet he was unwilling to speak in accord with the church, with which he wanted to appear to agree.

The proof of my syllogism regarding omnipotence therefore still remains unmoved, which I posited above: to that which the whole fullness of divinity has been communicated, to the same has also been communicated omnipotence. To Christ's humanity has been communicated the entire fullness of Deity. Therefore omnipotence has also been communicated to the same. In this communication the supreme consolation for pious minds has been deposited.

HOW GREAT A CONSOLATION OF THE PIOUS HAS BEEN DEPOSITED IN THE COMMUNICATION OF CHRIST'S OMNIPOTENCE.

For even if the absolute, infinite power of God were sufficing for us in cross and calamities, and even in our supreme trials, nevertheless this is formidable for us without a mediator. But when our conscience, afflicted and supremely troubled, and in like manner oppressed by enemies, considers that the power of heaven and earth has been placed in the hand of a man who is our brother, redeemer, savior, and helper in all tribulations, then it takes hold of greater assurance and doubts not at all that it will be freed.

But enough about these things. The Honorable Prince, heeding the supper hour, is advising us to conclude and to reconvene tomorrow at the seventh hour to resume the conference.

<284>

2E.II. 26 MARCH, 1586, 7:00 A.M.

Dr. Jakob:

---

1. THE HUMAN NATURE IN CHRIST IS TRULY OMNIPOTENT.

Reverend Dr. Beza, yesterday we carried out our conference peaceably and on friendly terms about God's first attribute, namely his omnipotence. We proved, by plain testimonies of holy Scripture, that it had been communicated truly and really to the assumed human nature in Christ, with the result that it also truly is, and is said to be, omnipotent.

---

2. POWER COMMUNICATED TO THE MAN CHRIST IS NOT A CREATED GIFT.

I demonstrated also that the power given to the man Christ in time was not a created gift in the man Christ, but was itself God's essential omnipotence, since indeed there is only one omnipotence in Christ, not two, just as there is also only one divinity. And the fullness of divinity, under which omnipresence is also comprehended, means nothing other than the essence of divinity, and whatever is and is said to be God, which dwells bodily in the assumed nature. Whence Christ also said, All authority has been given to me in heaven and on earth (Matthew 28[:18]). This authority is God's eternal and infinite power, concerning which, Daniel 7[:27] speaks. Created power does not suffice for governing heaven and earth.

GOVERNING OF HEAVEN AND EARTH A POSSESSION OF THE WHOLE CHRIST.

Therefore not only does his divinity now govern heaven and earth, things visible and invisible, but also Christ's assumed humanity, for which he requires that eternal and infinite power which was given to him by the personal union and really communicated to him. Against this statement, if Your Reverence has anything more from Scripture, I ask that he bring it forward for all to see. I am prepared to answer each and every thing for the sake of my poverty. For our faith rests not on human reason, but on God's word alone, which has been comprehended in holy writ.

<285>

Dr. Beza.

POINTS 1–4.

We acknowledge the words brought forward from Scripture. But there is a question about the sense and interpretation of those words. Every interpretation of holy Scripture's testimonies ought to be brought back to the analogy of faith. Now that I have stated this, I respond that we do not deny anything less than that the essence of divinity was united to the man, as also those things which are in God were united with him hypostatically. But it is one thing to say, Things were given to a man, and another, things were given to his humanity. For in the hypostatic union his natures remain distinct, just as also their properties. And that which is a characteristic is not in common. On account of this we say that to Christ the man was given created power, not uncreated, which if it were communicated, was not the characteristic of divinity.

POINT 5.

In the Matthew 28 passage, All authority has been given to me, we ascribe this to created power, which was conferred upon the man Christ. Nor does what is objected stand in the way, that a man is not able to govern heaven and earth by means of created power. God can in fact confer upon the assumed human nature as many and as much as he wants. For this reason we say that Christ is Lord of all things according to his humanity, with the exception of the one who established him as Lord (1 Corinthians 15[:28]).

Dr. Jakob:

POINT 1.

We agree without any hesitation whatsoever that every interpretation of holy Scripture and its testimony must be referred to the analogy of faith.

POINT 2. COMMUNICATION OF OMNIPOTENCE DOES NOT CONFLICT WITH THE ANALOGY OF FAITH.

But that which conflicts with the analogy of faith, which we teach about the man Christ and his omnipotence, truly and really communicated to his humanity by the personal union, <286> we have not yet heard this. For this reason the analogy of faith openly confirms our teaching, which bears witness that his humanity is located at the right hand of God the father.

POINT 3.

For that which is brought forward, that in the hypostatic union itself not only natures, but also their properties, remain distinct, has been advanced beyond all controversy. But this does not keep those things which are the proper to divinity from being any less personally communicated.

POINT 4. IN WHAT WAY OMNIPOTENCE REMAINS PROPER TO DIVINITY, EVEN WHEN COMMUNICATED.

And Divinity's omnipotence does not cease to be a proper to it, even if it be communicated personally to the assumed human nature. For if the second person of the Trinity, God's Son, which is incommunicable and is defined to be, has been truly communicated to the human nature, then how is the essential property particular to him also not able to be communicated, with the result that what belongs only to him nevertheless remains? The analogy of glowing-hot iron displays the same thing. For the properties of glowing and burning remain proper to fire, which never are separated from it naturally, wherever there is fire. Nevertheless they are really communicated to iron. In such a way does God's essential omnipotence remain proper to Deity, even if it is really communicated to the human nature in the person of God's Son, which the Son of God assumed into the unity of person.

POINT 5.

It is said indeed that Christ's words must be understood as created power, but there is no proof of this. And although it may be true that God is able to impart power, as much as he wants, nevertheless Scripture openly testifies that this is not created power, but eternal and infinite power, by the participation of which Christ's human nature is able also to see and judge the hidden places of hearts. This is not a property of created power.

JOHN OF DAMASCUS, BOOK 3, CHAPTER 19.

And we showed yesterday, not in our own words, but in those of John of Damascus, that this is not created power but participation in the infinite power of God. By this power with the Word [λόγος], the assumed humanity has dominion over all things in heaven, earth, and hell. Flesh (he says) *communicates* to the Divine operation of the word to the same degree that divine operations were being performed through the organ of the body. Thus his holy *mind* also performs its natural operations. <287> However *what communicates* to the Divine operation of the word and arranging and governing of the universe is *also the mind of God, understanding and knowing, and arranging, not as the mere mind of man, but as* established and united *to God*, according to hypostasis. The glory (says Cyril), which he always had *as God, is what he has sought as man*, and these things are not said about him because he was ever destitute of his own glory, but rather because he wished to raise *his own temple into the glory* which is always present to him *as God*. Please, what could be said more clearly about the real communication *of glory*, which is proper to divinity, and under which omnipotence is also understood?

On this account I still ask that Dr. Beza produce just one clear testimony of Scripture by which he may demonstrate that this power given to the man Christ was created power. This he cannot do.

Dr. Beza:
I produce the analogy of faith, which teaches that the properties of the divinity are and remain incommunicable even in the personal union itself. And when we say that God is omnipotent, we understand that by This that God exists IN HIMSELF and through himself, and remains alone.

Then there are the rays of divine omnipotence, and these rays are created qualities which emanate from the substance of the divinity into the humanity of Christ. Of course they are created gifts, and the most absolute, perfect, and highest ones conferred upon Christ's humanity, which must be distinguished from the absolute powers of God.

<288>

Dr. Jakob:
I ask that it be demonstrated to me from the analogy of faith that the communication of omnipotence in the assumed human nature goes against this analogy.

Dr. Beza:

ARGUMENTATION FROM THE ANALOGY OF FAITH AGAINST THE COMMUNICATION OF OMNIPOTENCE.

The analogy of faith teaches that Christ assumed a true body in the womb of the Blessed virgin Mary, and a true human nature, finite and circumscribed, and retains these essential properties that belong to him even in the union. These do not admit of the real communication, but rather destroy directly the human nature of Christ and change it into Divinity.

Dr. Jakob:

This is not the analogy of faith, but rather a syllogism of human Philosophy, solicited against the analogy of faith.

For even though it is true that the analogy of faith teaches that the assumed human nature of the Son of God is truly a finite and circumscribed human nature, similar in every way to ours with the exception of sin, a fact that also our senses prove and bear witness to, nevertheless the same analogy of faith teaches at the same time that this human nature was personally united with the Son of God in the womb of his mother, and exalted over all creatures. Indeed in the first place, thanks to the union, at the point of conception the whole fullness of divinity dwelt bodily in this assumed nature, which includes omnipotence, or rather is expressed by this term whole [*tota*].

In the second place, the same analogy bears witness that this same human nature has been seated at the right hand of the power and Majesty of God the omnipotent Father, on the throne proper to Divinity, *who is himself Omnipotence.*

Therefore this Philosophical conglomeration of Beza's opposes the analogy of faith itself, though it was made from the analogy of faith itself but through the fallacy of division. For this very analogy testifies to both: <289> that the humanity of Christ retains in itself those things proper to humanity, and at the same time has become a sharer in the omnipotent Majesty of God. These are able to stand simultaneously. For these things are not contrary or contradictory, but different and distinct, which do not overturn each other.

A MIDDLE POWER OF CHRIST IS NOT ABLE TO BE PROVED FROM THE HOLY SCRIPTURE.

For this reason I insist once again, and ask of Your Reverence, that you offer one testimony of Scripture by which you may prove your interpretation and opinion that it was not the very omnipotence of God that given and communicated to Christ the man or his humanity, but rather merely a created power, that is, some middle power between the angels, the blessed saints, and God, which is greater than the power of the angels and the blessed saints, but less than the power proper to God. I will say this: I want it to be proved to me by just one clear testimony of Scripture.

Dr. Beza:
Your reverence should prove your own opinion from holy Scripture.

Dr. Jakob:
I have proved my opinion, not with one, but with several clear testimonies of Scripture, against which Your Reverence has brought up nothing other than interpretation, and you have made your interpretation about a created power. You have been able to prove this interpretation, however, by no testimony of Scripture. This I still implore you to do.

Dr. Beza:
I contend that it is communicated in no other way than through being united. For this reason God is in fact man, and in the same way Man is God and omnipotent, etc.

Dr. Jakob:
It was demonstrated previously that the union of the natures and the communication of properties is not the same thing, but that they differ just as cause and effect do. Likewise we also said that the difference in the communication of divine and human properties is like this, <290> despite there being a single cause of each. But Your Reverence should prove that the power which holy Scripture predicates as having been given to Christ the man is a quality, that is, a created gift.

Dr. Beza:

WHETHER THE POWER OF CHRIST IS A CREATED GIFT.

The gifts of God are the qualities of God's essence (1 Corinthians 12[:4–6]). There are varieties of gifts, but the same Spirit; there are varieties of service, but the same Lord; there are varieties of activities, but the same God, who works all things in all people. Therefore also in Christ power is a quality that is given.

Dr. Jakob:

DISTINCTION BETWEEN GIFTS OF THE SAINTS, AND GIFTS CONFERRED UPON CHRIST'S HUMANITY.

These are particular gifts which God distributes to the members of Christ, according to the measure of Christ's giving; for this reason they are qualities. But holy Scripture bears witness that the spirit was given to Christ *without measure* (John 3[:34]). Therefore it cannot be understood about qualities, which all have been measured. The fullness of the whole divinity dwells in Christ bodily (Colossians 2[:9]), not special or particular gifts conferred upon him, as upon other saints. John of Damascus says, The divine nature communicates *its own excellent properties to the flesh*, which is omnipotent, as it truly is done according to nature by God's will (John of Damascus, Book 3, chapter 7 and chapter 18). And Ambrose. God does not in fact grant participation to the Apostles *of his own throne*, but to Christ is given participation of the divine throne according to his humanity. Prove the contrary from holy Scripture.

Dr. Beza:
I confess the omnipotent Divine nature united to Christ's flesh, and deny any other communication than by union.

Dr. Jakob:
I still hear no testimony of Scripture against communicated <291> omnipotence. The foundation of this communication is union, but it is not itself the communication of properties.

Dr. Beza:
We have heard Cyril, Thesauri Book 2 to the contrary: those things which are proper to the divine nature alone should also be attributed only to the divine nature, lest the natures be confused.

Dr. Jakob:

REGARDING THE COMMUNICATION OF PROPERTIES, THE LASTING AND
CONSISTENT OPINION OF CYRIL.

Cyril's words are plain and perspicuous; moreover to this opinion
other further words of the same author can be brought to bear. He
teaches by them, if anyone were attributing what is proper to the
divine nature absolutely and without respect to any union with the
divine nature of the Word [ὁ λόγος] to the humanity of Christ, that the
humanity by this communication of properties would be destroyed,
and that it would change into the divine nature. But the best of his
words is Cyril himself as interpreter, who explains his own opinion
openly in the words that follow, which were also brought up yesterday. You do not altogether ignorantly deny (he says) that the flesh is
vivific. For if it should be understood alone, it can clearly in no way
vivify; it consequently stands in need of vivification. But when you
have examined the Mystery of the incarnation, and recognized the
life dwelling in the flesh, even though the flesh in itself can do nothing in and of itself, nevertheless, you will believe that it has become
vivific. (Cyril on John, Book 4, chapter 23.)

Dr. Beza:
On account of the union we say also that the man is omnipotent.

Dr. Jakob:

CONSENSUS IN WORDS BUT NOT IN REALITY. IN RESPONSE TO THESES 8 AND 9.

These are words. The reason I say this is that by "Man" you
understand only the divine nature, and that by way of a figure of
speech, which is called Metonymy, in the same way that it was stated
in your response: A man is omnipotent, that is, the Divine nature
united to the human nature is omnipotent, without any real communication having been made to the humanity. This is false, as we have
now said and proven many times.

<292>

Dr. Beza:

PERVERSION OF LUTHER'S WORDS. IN RESPONSE TO DOGMA 1.

Luther himself found fault with those who teach that the man Christ is omnipotent. These are his words from his Christmas sermon on Hebrews 1. The humanity of Christ, just as with any other holy and natural Man, DID NOT ALWAYS think all things, say, wish, turn his attention to all things, just as some make an omnipotent man out of him, by unwisely confusing the two natures and their workings.

Dr. Jakob:

Luther's words are not at all in conflict with our teaching whatsoever, which is the teaching of Luther himself, nay rather, that of the holy Spirit. Luther consistently emphasized it in his assertion about the Lord's Supper, and confirmed it with the plainest testimonies of Scripture.

LUTHER ON THE COMMUNICATION OF CHRIST'S KNOWLEDGE. LUTHER IN THE CHURCH POSTIL ON THE DOMINICAL LETTER ON THE FEAST OF CHRIST'S NATIVITY.

For in the passage cited by you, Luther finds fault with the interpretation of Christ's words at Mark 13[:32]: "About that day and hour no one knows, neither the Angels in heaven, nor the son, only the father," which some people bring up out of context.

> There is no need (says Luther) of the interpretation here: the son does not know, that is, he does not wish to know. What does this interpretation mean? Christ's humanity, like also any other holy and natural man, did not always think all things, etc. And after these words he adds: Just as he did not always see all things, hear, and perceive all things, so also he did *not always* regard all things in his heart, but rather as the spirit led him and assisted him. He was full of grace and wisdom such that *he could* judge and teach all things

which had been set forth before him, and that for this reason, that the divinity, which alone knows all things, was present in him personally. In sum, whatever has been said regarding Christ's humiliation and exaltation must be attributed *to the man,* since the divine nature cannot be humiliated or exalted.

Thus far Luther's words, which plainly confirm our opinion and provide not even the weakest defense of Dr. Beza's opinion.

<293>

Nor in fact does Luther deny that Christ is an omnipotent man; rather he finds fault only with the false interpretation of Christ's words, which Christ spoke about himself while in the state of humiliation. He wished to show by them that he did not know all things according to the human nature in the same way as he did according to the Divine nature. Since in fact the Divine nature is unchangeable and the knowledge of God is his essence, for this reason just as he is not able not always to be God, so he is not able not always to know *all things.* But since human nature is changeable, and possesses from somewhere else the capacity to know all things, namely, just as Luther says here, from the personal presence of the Divine nature, which did not always reveal itself through the human nature in the state of humiliation, for this reason he teaches that that interpretation is false, he does *not* know, that is, *he does not wish* to know, though he plainly says that he was nevertheless able to know all things. He did not in fact pretend not to know the day and hour of the last judgment, but rather *truly* did not know when he was saying these words, since he had emptied himself, as Paul says. Ἐκένωσε, says Paul, he emptied himself on the basis of his humanity. This emptying or evacuation was in no way a pretense in the man Christ, but happened earnestly and really. Just as also he responds to the sons of Zebedee, It is not *mine* to give, to have this one sit at my right hand and the other at my left; he speaks not simply, but rather on the basis of his emptying. For the same Christ will situate some at his right hand and others at his left, and will say, Depart, come (Matthew 25[:41]). For this reason he said all these things in the form of a slave, as if he were saying, Now I am not present on account of this reason.

But this emptying or evacuation presupposes a preceding filling up of infinite gifts, such that he possessed according to his humanity that majesty, but did not wish to seize it. He was full (says Luther) of grace and of wisdom, such that he was able to understand all things, etc. And this is the communication of omnipotence, concerning which we will say more a little later in our treatment of the omniscience of the man Christ.

But I ask, my dear Dr. Beza, whether these two propositions are equivalent: God is omnipotent; Man is omnipotent? Since in fact according to your opinion there is no <294> communication of omnipotence in the human nature, how therefore is a man omnipotent? Or can he truly be called omnipotent? You assert that it is is said truly, only to deny most stubbornly, that omnipotence has been communicated to the humanity.

Dr. Beza:

IN WHAT WAY THE MAN CHRIST BECOMES GOD AND OMNIPOTENT ACCORDING TO BEZA.

I do not say that these propositions are equivalent. For God is said to be omnipotent according to a different principle, namely in the way of what is proper to him, and essentially IN AND OF HIMSELF. But a man is said to be omnipotent not because omnipotence has been communicated to the humanity, but rather since it has been united to the omnipotent divinity, which alone is and remains omnipotent, such that it does not communicate its own power to any creature, not even to the humanity of Christ.

So we say: That man is God. We understand by the term man, though, the Divinity or the Son of God in this manner: The Son of God, who was united to the humanity, and his Divine nature, is God. The Divine nature in fact has not been communicated to the humanity.

Dr. Jakob:

In response to your answer to our Thesis 8 and 9, I reply that it is horrible to hear what you believe and teach: that humanity receives no communication of omnipotence, not even verbally; that not only the thing itself, that is, God's omnipotence, but not even the name of omnipotence, can truly be attributed to Christ's humanity. For how can this man truly be called omnipotent, whose humanity, soul and body, has not only failed to have omnipotence communicated to it, but does not even receive the name of omnipotence? I ask the audience please to be willing to weigh this matter carefully, how the holy Scripture harmonizes and agrees with the testimonies drawn from it that plainly attribute to Christ not only *the name* but also the very fact, that is, Majesty proper to divinity and omnipotence.

<295>

Dr. Beza:
Dr. Brenz has explained that the passage in John 1, "The Word became flesh," is not about the union of the natures, but rather about the communication of the properties of divinity, and the nature of the gifts, by which Christ surpasses Peter, otherwise there would be one union of divinity with Peter and Christ. These are his words: So the distinction between Christ and Peter cannot simply be drawn from the indwelling of the Son of God, but rather from the communication of his properties.

Dr. Jakob:
I simply deny that Brenz asserts that the same union of divinity is in Peter as is in the assumed Man Christ. For when he was arguing against Peter Martyr (who had written that it is sufficient that the Deity, though immense and infinite in its own hypostasis, supports and *sustains* the humanity wherever it will be), he added these words: certainly should you rightly examine Martyr's position regarding the personal union, which I mentioned above, you will find that he makes the union between the Son of God and the son of Mary the same kind of union as that between the Son of God and all creatures, or anyhow between him and Peter and Paul and all the Saints.. It simply is not true that Brenz asserted the same union of Christ and Peter with God, like the one that he demonstrated follows from the description of Peter Martyr, which is the most absurd position of all,

that it is sufficient for the Personal union that it *supports and sustains* in its own hypostasis.

WHY THE HYPOSTATIC UNION OF TWO NATURES IN CHRIST IS DEFINED BY THE COMMUNICATION OF ATTRIBUTES.

But this is the reason he defined the personal union by the communication of attributes: the Mystery of the hypostatic union is established in such a way that it cannot be defined *a priori*. Therefore in those places in which we there are not specific differences, we replace them with things that are more known, whether properties or accidents, or operations. These things are distinguished from one another such that what they are can be understood by other means.

<296>

UNION OF THE RATIONAL SOUL WITH THE BODY. WHY TWO DEFINITIONS OF SOUL HANDED DOWN BY ARISTOTLE. WHENCE THE UNION OF SOUL WITH THE BODY IS UNDERSTOOD.

The union of the soul with the body is this sort of thing that we cannot know *a priori*. Therefore we define it *a posteriori*, that is, from the communication of the soul's powers with the body, by means of which the body lives, feels, moves around. Aristotle hands down two definitions of soul because of this, even though there is otherwise only one definition of each thing. The first definition is that by which he describes the soul as it exists in and of itself, by reason of its own powers. But he hands down the second according to the way in which it is united to the body, and communicates itself with its own powers. The soul, he says, is the act of the physical Organic body that has life in power. And again, The soul is that by which we live, feel, move around, and understand. And since we see the soul exercising none of these powers without the body as long as it is in the body, without which powers even the body is able to do nothing, but rather is like a stone or a block, we understand from this resulting communication of the union, as it were, how much of a union it is, and how close the conjunction of body and soul is.

WHY DR. BRENZ AND DR. JAKOB ANDREAE DEFINED THE PERSONAL UNION BY THE COMMUNICATION OF ATTRIBUTES.

So since we understand the Mystery of the personal union of the divine and human nature in Christ much less, like people who have no knowledge of ourselves, Dr. Brenz and his Colleagues, having followed the lead of the holy Scripture and Holy Fathers, described this miraculous union by the communication of divine Majesty, by which we distinguish between Peter and the man Christ may be observed, who otherwise have many things in common.

THE UNION OF THE WHOLE PERSON OF CHRIST WITH PETER.

The reason I say this is that it cannot be denied that the whole divinity, which is indivisible [ἀμέριστος] and not divided into parts, was not only entirely in Peter but was also dwelling in him, which in number is no other divinity that that which is in Christ. It does not in the least follow, though, that the same mode of union and conjoining of God was with Peter which is in the man Christ.

WHENCE THE DISTINCTION OF THE UNION OF THE DIVINITY IN CHRIST AND PETER MUST BE ASSUMED.

From where, though, must this distinction be assumed, which cannot be perceived either by the eyes of the body or by the mind?

Indisputably from the effect that follows from this hyper-wondrous union, which has been explained in holy Scripture, namely, by the communication of Majesty, which holy Scripture attributes to the man Christ, <297> and which is attributed otherwise to no other person at all, no matter how holy and excellent. For the man Christ says, Young man, I say to you, Get up, and immediately he rose up (Luke 7[:14]). Peter does not speak after the same fashion, but says, I say to you, in the name *of Jesus Christ the Nazarene*, rise and walk (Acts 3[:6]). We conclude from this that Peter raised the dead by one principle, and Christ by another.

But you say, What raised the dead? I answer: The omnipotent power of the divine nature, a property of which is to raise the dead.

Why then does the man Christ simply say, Young man I say to you get up, and immediately, at the voice of Christ, the young man gets up? But Peter did not simply say, I say to you get up, but he says, *In the name of Jesus* get up and walk, when nevertheless the divine power is one and the same, by which they were raised? Here we notice a distinction between the union of the divinity with Peter and with the assumed man, that the man Christ raised the dead by means of a proper power, and Peter by means of an alien power,[35] and performed miracles.

HOW THE ASSUMED MAN'S OMNIPOTENCE IS AT THE SAME TIME PROPER AND COMMUNICATED.

Since the omnipotent power of divinity has been communicated to the humanity of Christ, it belongs to his humanity alone, or to him as man, and was proper to him *in contrast with other saints* so that the man Christ might raise the dead by the power, proper to him with respect to those powers, and nevertheless communicated by the divine nature, which on account of the lack of this communication Peter could not perform, but was always compelled to add, *in the name of Jesus.* Just as we read that the Apostles prayed that the Lord stretch out his hand to perform healing and signs and prodigies by the name of *his holy son Jesus.* From this real communication effected in Christ it is understood that the union of divinity with the assumed man in the person of Christ is something far different from what it is with Peter.

REFUTATION OF FALSE DOCTRINE IMPUTED TO DR. BRENZ.

This was the intention and opinion of Dr. Brenz, in the meeting of Peter with Christ, when defining the personal union through communication of the divine Majesty in Christ, and he wanted to distinguish is from other unions of God with blessed men. <298> But he never at all taught the same union of divinity with the humanity of Christ and Peter, such that he located the distinction merely in degree or

---

35 "Proper" and "alien" power: *virtus propria* and *virtus aliena. Propria virtus* carries the idea of being common to, proper to, or connected to the identity and nature of an individual, and is distinct from an external or alien quality or potency.

number of gifts. Just as it is attributed to the same Brenz, resting in the Lord, and to me also, as if we teach or taught that the divinity was only present to the man Christ by his presence [παρουσία], just as to the rest of the saints, whom he surpassed in terms of the degree of gifts, and being similar to God by means of created power and wisdom, is called God and equal to God. None of these things were ever even dreamt by Brenz or me.

WHY BRENZ DEFINED THE PERSONAL UNION THROUGH THE COMMUNICATION OF ATTRIBUTES.

But by this conferred Majesty, he wanted to guide people in a certain way to the miraculous and ineffable union of the divinity with the assumed man Jesus, son of Mary, a union which differs entirely in type from every other union of divinity with holy people. In this the spirit was given to Christ not to a certain measure, but rather without measure. Nor was the power a certain created power, but rather the *whole* fullness of Divinity was communicated to him, from which fullness we all receive gifts, according to the measure of Christ's giving. (John 3[:34]; Colossians 2[:9]; John 1[:16]; 1 Corinthians 12[:27]; Romans 12[:3–8])

Dr. Beza:
I say that we do not deny that omnipotence was given to this man, since the man is God, but I deny that it was given to the humanity. For just as it cannot be said, Humanity is Divinity, so also it cannot be said, humanity is omnipotent.

Dr. Jakob:
These things have now been heard and repeated by you several times, and how you understand Divinity alone apart from humanity under the term "Man" and trick your reader, has been shown from your responses. But I ask for *one*, only *one* testimony of holy Scripture, by which you may prove your interpretation, by which you assert and emphatically repeat so many times, if omnipotence had been communicated to the assumed humanity by the Son of God, that it had been changed into Divinity. Please prove this.

<299>

Dr. Beza:

This is the same as if anyone were asking me for a testimony of Scripture to prove that we are in Montbéliard. The matter is plain and clear, and so is in need of no testimony of Scripture.

Dr. Jakob:

I have openly and clearly proved the contrary from Scripture, and have demonstrated it by the comparison of molten iron. To this witness you brought up nothing other than an interpretation contrary to the plain text, and you can prove it with no testimony of Scripture, namely that the power given to the man Christ is a created quality and a created gift.

Dr. Beza:

BEZA'S ARGUMENT FROM THE MEMBERS TO THE HEAD.

It is certain that all gifts given to men are created qualities. For this reason Christ is the head of the body, which is called the Church; therefore it is certain also that the gifts of his humanity that were given are created qualities, in the number and excellence of which the humanity of Christ surpasses not only all blessed men but also the Angels.

Dr. Jakob:

REFUTATION OF THIS ARGUMENT.

I deny the conclusion simply. To all the pious and faithful have been conferred created gifts, since they are not united with God hypostatically. And holy Scripture openly bears witness that all the gifts of the members of Christ's body have been measured out, and that the Lord has not given the whole to a single person, but according to the measure of the giving of Christ, as much as is sufficient for each. But to Christ he has given the whole without measure, the Holy Spirit and even Christ himself testifies about himself: And the whole fullness, not of created gifts, but of the whole divinity, says Paul, dwells in Christ. To these words of the holy Spirit the conscience of a pious person can safely cling, and in them find rest, while in regard to your interpretation he is always compelled to doubt whether it is true or false, as it is confirmed by no testimony of Scripture. But since it can be proved with no testimony of Scripture that the power given to Christ's <300> human nature is a created gift, then let us also see about the remaining attributes of God, which are omniscience, omnipresence, vivification, and religious adoration (for these all are proper to Divinity) whether they also have been communicated to the assumed humanity of Christ.

Dr. Beza:

DR. BEZA'S CONFESSION CONCERNING THE COMMUNICATION OF ATTRIBUTES OF THE DEITY.

What need is there to speak about each and every single thing? Since the nature and communication of all of God's attributes is the same. If in fact you were to demonstrate that one of God's proper attributes had been communicated, I think there would be no dispute about the rest.

Dr. Jakob:
I trust that I have demonstrated that the omnipotence of divinity has been communicated to Christ's assumed humanity, by plain testimonies of Scripture clearer than the light of noon. Concerning this, let judgment rest with the audience.

But then you are not ignorant that certain people attribute omnipotence and omniscience to Christ's humanity, but make the argument denying that omnipresence has been communicated. Indeed it is for this reason that this must be said about those matters.

Dr. Beza:

IN WHAT WAY DR. HESYCHIUS' OPINION CONDEMNED BY BEZA.

I know that Doctor Hesychius does this, but he is entirely mistaken and proceeds foolishly. For if one property of divinity has been communicated to the divine nature, all the rest have been communicated. If you have demonstrated it about one, I wish in no way at all to argue or dispute with you about the rest.

Dr. Jakob:

Come then, and let us confer peaceably about the rest also, and most of all for the sake of the audience, that they may see and understand that we for our part attribute nothing to the man Christ or his humanity, <301> which cannot be proven and demonstrated by the plain testimonies of holy Scripture (on which alone our Christian faith rests).

Dr. Beza:
As it is agreeable, so let it be.

Dr. Jakob:

II. CONCERNING OMNISCIENCE. OMNISCIENCE TRULY AND REALLY COMMUNICATED TO THE HUMAN NATURE IN CHRIST.

We assert that omniscience is really communicated to the man Christ, that is, to his humanity. But that this our doctrine is true I confirm by means of this argument. To whomsoever the spirit has been given without measure, to this one omniscience has been given. But to Christ the man, that is, according to his humanity, the spirit was given not according to measure. Therefore omniscience was also given to him. Proof of the lesser proposition: in John 3[:34–35] it is written, "Whom God sent, he utters the words of God. For God gives the Spirit without measure. The father loves the son, and has given all things into his hand."

Dr. Beza:
I concede that all the gifts of the holy Spirit have been given to Christ without measure, which are created qualities. And so I concede as well that now Christ KNOWS ALL THINGS in glory, which

he did not know prior in his state of humility, that is, emptiness, since he now possesses the government of all things.

Dr. Jakob:

I ask then whether the human spirit of Christ, that is, Christ's soul, now in glory, knows all things which God knows?

Dr. Beza:

I am in no doubt that even now he knows ALL THINGS, WHICH he did not know before, since he was in the state of emptiness. And I said above, Luther distinguishes in the sermon for the Nativity between the cognition of Christ's <302> humanity and divinity, that Christ was ignorant of many things according to his human nature, which he knew according to his divinity. And Luther himself confesses that he often erred in this matter and in other passages of Scripture that attribute to the nature things that are proper to the person, and vice versa.

Dr. Jakob:

WHETHER LUTHER REVOKED HIS DOCTRINE REGARDING THE PERSON OF CHRIST.

What year did Luther write these things? The reason I ask is that these same words of Luther are brought out and mentioned by your brothers with this chief goal in mind, to prove that Luther himself revoked his doctrine regarding the person of Christ. But above all the things which he wrote about the person of Christ in the Greater Confession regarding the Lord's Supper, and in the book titled, the words of Christ "This is my body," still persist firm and unmoved. And so I ask, what year did he write these things?

Dr. Beza:
I do not know.

Dr. Jakob:

WHEN LUTHER WAS A YOUNG MAN HE OFTEN MADE ERRORS IN HIS STUDY OF SACRED LETTERS.

In the dedicatory Epistle to the Count of Mansfeld, the time when Luther wrote these things was noted. Namely, it shows that in the year of our Lord 1521 that Postil was published, which had been written in the preceding years. How therefore could Luther retract them from these words, which he wrote in the year 1527 and 1528, that is, six or seven years afterward? Later writings are not in fact corrected by earlier ones, but rather earlier ones by later ones. Therefore the sense of Luther's words in his Church Postil is: he confesses he was still a young man in sacred letters, that he often made mistakes in the meanings of Scripture of this sort, and attributed to the nature what belongs to the person.

COMPARISON OF LUTHER'S WRITINGS, IN THE WAY OF TIME.

But in his later writings he labored no longer under this ignorance, but rather solidly disputed against the enemies of the truth from a true and genuine interpretation of the testimonies of holy Scripture, and defeated these same opponents with the word of the Lord. For he interpreted Scripture <303> with Scripture, which is the best mode of interpretation. Moreover, he demonstrated in his explanation of the right hand of God, not from human interpretations but rather by means of the very plain words of holy Scripture, that the omnipotence proper to the divinity was truly and really communicated to Christ according to his human nature. And the rule of Luther suggested above is especially necessary for all who study the sacred letters, young people in particular: Do not attribute to the natures what belongs to the person, lest we confuse or separate the natures, concerning this elsewhere.

WHETHER CHRIST'S SOUL EVEN KNOWS AND SEES THE THOUGHTS OF MEN.

But I ask once again, whether Christ's soul, now in glory, knows all things, even the thoughts of men?

Dr. Beza:
I do not know. From the revelation of divinity he can know as much as he wants to know and as much as he needs to.

Dr. Jakob:
So also the Heidelberg Theologians once wrote, that Christ knows as much as he wants to know and as much as he needs to for exercising judgment. Indeed to possess the knowledge of God himself and the knowledge of the works of God, it were fitting that he know so much. This statement in the ears of pious men is not only hard, but plainly impious. As if Christ according to his humanity possesses a not yet perfect knowledge of God and of his works?

Dr. Beza:
I am not ignorant of what they wrote; let them answer for themselves. I say that Christ according to his human nature now knows all things WHICH HE WANTS TO KNOW.

Dr. Jakob:
Does the man Christ want to know all things?

Dr. Beza:
I do not know. I have not had a conversation with him about this.

<304>

Dr. Jakob:
Is Christ the man knower of hearts [καρδιογνώστης] according to his human spirit, that is according to his soul, that is, in his soul?

Dr. Beza:
No.

Dr. Jakob:
When he was dwelling on earth, did he not see the thought in the hearts of men with his human spirit? And again, it is fitting for him to know the thoughts of men, since he is going to be the judge of the

living and the dead, and will judge and punish the thoughts of their hearts which are contrary to his divine will and law.

Dr. Beza:

God alone is καρδιογνώστης, *that is, examiner of hearts. But he communicates to the humanity what he wishes. His soul has knowledge, which is a quality, as much knowledge as the Divinity desires. Thus the Divine nature of Christ, when Christ was dwelling on earth locally and visibly, saw the thoughts of hearts and revealed them to the human nature, as much as he wanted and when he wanted. Such now is also the nature of his glory, though most excellent, as much as is able to be delivered from above into a creature, but a quality nevertheless and a created gift.*

Dr. Jakob:

HOW GOD SAW AND KNEW ALL THINGS.

We do not understand how God sees the thoughts in the hearts of people. He does not in fact glance through a window like we do, such that he sees what is happening on earth. He writes in the Psalm, You have understood my thoughts from far off (Psalm 139[:2]). So also it is not being asked about Christ how he saw the thoughts of men, but rather whether he also saw them as a man? You answer that he possesses something from the revelation of divinity. But this was not the question at all. <305> The Evangelists bear witness about the man Christ, though, that he saw the thoughts of the Pharisees and of others with whom he was conversing, especially wicked people. Why, he says, are you thinking evil in your hearts? (Matthew 9[:4]; Mark 2[:8]; Luke 5[:22]) Christ therefore, in so far as he is a man, is knower of hearts [καρδιογνώστης], and knows the thoughts of men, not only as God, but also as a man.

Dr. Beza:

The knowledge of God is absolute. But the knowledge of man is the quality, by which a man knows those things which God reveals.

Dr. Jakob:

DIFFERENCE BETWEEN KNOWLEDGE IN THIS AND IN THE FUTURE AGE.

Our knowledge in the next age will not be like this, the kind of knowledge you are sticking on Christ himself. As the Apostle bears witness: knowledge will be torn down; for we know in part and prophesy in part, but when what is perfect comes that which is *partial* will become void. Now I know in part; then I shall know, *even as I am known* (1 Corinthians 13[:8–10, 12]). If therefore what is partial in us will be destroyed, and just as we have been known by God, we will know, much the less should "*the partial*" be attributed to Christ's humanity in the knowledge of God and his works.

Dr. Beza:
Since Christ's humanity is a creature and finite, his knowledge also is a finite quality, even though it surpasses the knowledge of all creatures.

Dr. Jakob:

KNOWLEDGE WAS GIVEN TO CHRIST WITHOUT MEASURE.

But this finite humanity possesses in itself bodily the indwelling infinite fullness of Deity, and receives the spirit without measure (Colossians 2[:9]; John 3[:34]). Therefore it cannot be a quality or finite knowledge, but rather the infinite knowledge proper to God himself. For whatever lacks measure is immense and infinite. The spirit, <306> which Christ received according to the man, was given without measure. Therefore his knowledge and understanding are infinite and without measure.

Dr. Beza:
Spirit is taken to mean gifts of the holy Spirit. We read in John 7[:39]: "The spirit was not yet, that is, the gifts of the holy Spirit."

Dr. Jakob:

Even though I would most readily concede the point to you, that "Spirit" should be read as gifts of the holy Spirit in this passage, because it is understood more rightly about the revelation of the holy Spirit than about the gifts of the holy Spirit, nevertheless the limitation laid out at John 3 plainly indicates that the saying of Christ cannot be understood as about created gifts as John 7. For the term spirit is not used absolutely, as in the passage you brought up from John, but there is added: *without* measure. By these words it is clearly distinguished from created gifts. For nothing is without need or is without measure except for *God alone*.

Dr. Beza:
Is the Holy Spirit essentially given to the humanity of Christ?

Dr. Jakob:

The term "Essentially" is ambiguous. I say that in this passage the Holy Spirit himself is understood, not the created gifts of the holy Spirit, which are not the Holy Spirit, but rather the effects of the holy Spirit, his workings in the saints. This holy Spirit was given to Christ the man without measure, according to the word in John 1[:33]: "Upon whom you see the Holy Spirit descending and remaining upon him." If therefore the Spirit given without measure were a created gift, then the Holy Spirit, the third person of the Trinity, would be a created something, which is absurd and plainly impious to say.

Dr. Beza:
You are going over to the Spirit from the person of the Son. You said in fact that the humanity possesses infinite and uncreated gifts from the divinity of the son and the communication of it, but now you are attributing and ascribing those things to the Holy Spirit.

<307>

Dr. Jakob:

HOW THE SAME GIFTS WITHOUT MEASURE WERE GIVEN BY THE SON OF GOD
AND THE HOLY SPIRIT TO THE HUMANITY OF CHRIST.

This conferring of gifts which is attributed to the Holy Spirit
effects no confusion of persons. Since the Holy Spirit is in fact the
common Spirit of the Father and the Son, whatever gifts the holy
Spirit confers to the assumed human nature is the work of the entire
divinity, Father, Son, and holy Spirit, from whom the holy Spirit
receives it.

Therefore the assumed humanity possesses from the divinity of
the son infinite power and knowledge through the conferred holy
Spirit, as we read: Upon whom you see the holy Spirit descending
and remaining. It does not say: Upon whom you see the gifts of
the Holy Spirit descending. Since therefore he possesses this Spirit
without measure (John 3[:34]), John says: From his fullness we have
received; what is infinite is not measured or created.

Dr. Beza:
*Do you therefore want Christ to be omniscient also according to
his human spirit?*

Dr. Jakob:

CHRIST OMNISCIENT ACCORDING TO HIS HUMAN SPIRIT.

I think so. For I do not want to possess half a Christ, but *the whole
one*, God and man, and especially the man, about whom the Epistle
to the Hebrews bears witness: We do not have a Priest who cannot
sympathize with our weaknesses, but one tempted in all ways, but
without sin (Hebrews 4[:15]). And again: *Because* he himself suffered when he was tempted he is *powerful* to help those who are
being tempted (Hebrews 2[:18]). The greatest temptations though are
inward, in the hearts of the pious, and these Christ does not see if
he is not, in so far as he is man, καρδιογνώστης, that is, examiner of
hearts. The greatest consolation for us would have been lost in temptations of this kind.

Would that I might in fact worship Christ the man, and pour out my misery into his lap; nevertheless if he does not know the thoughts of my heart, what consolation, I ask, would be laid up for me in the man Christ?

<308>

Dr. Beza:
The Christ who is omnipotent, omniscient, and omnipresent is not half but whole. But the whole of Christ is not omnipotent. For the divinity alone is omnipotent, but the human nature is not omnipotent.

Dr. Jakob:
We have shown above that when our adversaries speak, they offer deceptions and nothing more than words: The whole Christ is omnipotent, omniscient, omnipresent. For without the humanity Christ is not the whole Christ, but rather merely Word [λόγος]. But humanity also is required of the whole Christ. When they openly exclude the humanity from omnipotence, how can the whole Christ God and Man be, or be called, omnipotent?

Dr. Beza:

SOPHISTIC GAME IN THE TERMS WHOLE AND ENTIRE [*TOTUS, TOTUM*].

The term "WHOLE" ["TOTUS"] is the description of a person, which is omnipotent. But the word "ENTIRE" ["TOTUM"] refers to natures, of which one only is omnipotent, namely the divine nature, but not the human nature. So we say that the whole Christ is omnipotent, but not the whole of Christ, that is, his humanity also.

Dr. Jakob:

DECEPTION AND SOPHISTRY LYING HIDDEN UNDER THE TERM WHOLE [*TOTUS*]. CHRIST WITHOUT THE HUMAN NATURE IS NOT THE WHOLE CHRIST. THE WHOLE CHRIST AND THE WHOLE OF CHRIST EQUAL TERMS.

Deception hides under the term *whole*. For if you were frankly to use this term *whole* about Christ, it would mean a person who consists of two natures, and not merely one nature. If someone were therefore to say, The whole Christ is omnipotent, and were to understand this only about the divine nature, to the exclusion of the human nature, it is blatant deception and Sophistry. For the divine nature alone is not the whole Christ, but rather the human nature is required as well for the whole Christ. So *The Whole Christ* and *The Whole of Christ* <309> are equivalent terms, since the whole of Christ is nothing other than the Son of God and the assumed man, and the whole Christ also is nothing other than the Son of God with the assumed human nature. Just as Augustine bears witness in clear words: Take, says Augustine, the whole Christ, the word, the rational mind, and the flesh. (Augustine *Tractate on John* 23)[36] This is the whole Christ.

WHOLE AND ENTIRE [*TOTUS ET TOTUM*] SYNONYMS. THE WHOLE CHRIST ALSO OMNIPOTENT. HOW IT CANNOT BE TRULY SAID THAT THE WHOLE OF CHRIST IS NOT OMNIPOTENT.

Therefore the whole Christ, God and man, is omnipotent, if we should consider the natures in the way of the personal union, yet with respect to the natures, if they should be considered by the property of essence, it is not considered in the same way. For the Word [λόγος] or the divine nature of the Word [ὁ λόγος], whether considered in the union or outside the union, is always omnipotent and omniscient *in and of itself*. But the human nature is not omnipotent and omniscient *in and of itself*, but rather by reason of the union and the participation effected which it possesses from the omniscient son of God, in order that it too may be made omniscient. But when it is said, The Whole of Christ is not omniscient, the Natures are not being considered by reason of the union but rather in and of themselves, and it true to say that the Whole of Christ is not omnipotent, since the human nature in and of itself, that is, by the property of its nature, is not omnipotent, but only by reason of the union and in the union.

This is the true and genuine meaning of this saying: Christ is omnipotent, omniscient, and everywhere *whole*, but not *wholly*. If anyone would interpret this otherwise, as our adversaries do, it would be sophistry and he would deceive simple hearts.

---

36   Tractate 23 on John (John 5.19–40).

Dr. Beza:

BEZA'S FALLACY OF DIVISION.

When it is said that the whole Christ is omnipotent, I understand the Son of God not to be separated from the humanity but rather to be united personally with it. But nevertheless I can without opposition say that he is omnipotent, even though his human nature is not omnipotent.

Dr. Jakob:

THE WHOLE CHRIST IS OMNIPOTENT CAN BE UNDERSTOOD IN TWO WAYS.

This is a new fallacy, called fallacy of division. For the term <310> "Whole" in Dr. Beza's declaration does not refer to the predicate, "he is omnipotent," but rather to the subject "Christ." This results in this meaning: The whole Christ, that is, the Son of God not separated from the humanity, but rather united with it, is omnipotent. In this way the declaration is true, even though it is understood to be about only one nature. But when the term *"whole"* is referred to the predicate "omnipotent," in this way: Christ is omnipotent entire, then it is false, if it is understood to be only about one nature. This is what our adversaries are doing.

Dr. Beza:
The gifts of Christ the man, among which are numbered also knowledge and the gifts of the rest of the saints, differ according to greater and lesser, but all are God's created gifts all the same, no less in Christ than in the saints.

Dr. Jakob:
I will never concede that the gifts of Christ and of the saints differ only according to the degree of more or less. The reason I say this is that Christ the man possesses from the personal union that he was anointed with the oil of the holy Spirit ahead of his brothers, and this is not degrees of gifts. For the knowledge of Christ the man differs entirely from the knowledge of the saints. Our gifts were distributed

one by one according to the measure of the giving of Christ, that
is, just as Christ the man meted out and distributed them, who
ascended on high in order that he might give gifts to men. But the
spirit was given to Christ the man without measure. (Ephesians 4[:7];
1 Corinthians 12[:11]; 14[:25]; Romans 12[:3]; Psalm 69[68:18])

Dr. Beza:

DR. BEZA'S METONYMY.

*The effect takes the name of the cause, with the result that spirit
is understood for the gifts of the Holy Spirit, all of which Christ
possessed at the same time to the highest and fullest degree in his
humanity. Since Deity is in his humanity in a twofold way, namely
as Word [λόγος] and Holy Spirit, which does not get delivered from
above to other saints. In fact none of them possessed all the gifts of
the holy Spirit, and they all were not given to anyone except for the
man Christ.*

<311>

Dr. Jakob:

CHRIST THE MAN IS OMNISCIENT.

The words of the Baptist overturn this interpretation: God gives
the spirit without measure (John 3[:34]). For if you were to collect
all the gifts of all the saints into one mass, just as numerable as are
the saints themselves, so also would the gifts be able to be counted,
if they were all to run together in the one man Christ in the way that
our adversaries are talking about. But the Baptist says, The spirit
has been given to the son without measure. Therefore there is no
way this can be understood about created gifts, but rather about
uncreated gifts of the holy Spirit himself, by which is understood his
sharing in the knowledge that is divine and proper to God, which was
conferred wholly upon the man Christ, so that now he also knows
what God knows, and nothing is hidden or concealed from him which
he does not know.

Dr. Beza:

If this kind of knowledge had been communicated to Christ's humanity, it would follow that the humanity had been made the Divinity, which is impossible.

Dr. Jakob:

Offer one, one I say, testimony of Scripture by which you may prove this opinion, namely that the knowledge that is in the man Christ is a created gift, or that his is not able to become omniscient except the humanity be transformed into Divinity, and I am prepared to answer you. It is in not in fact sufficient to say this, but you need rather to prove it, not by means of human Philosophy, but instead by the word of God drawn from holy Scripture, which bears witness. In Christ all the riches of wisdom and knowledge have been hidden, and that without measure. A person's conscience and faith rest on these testimonies more safely than on arguments and interpretations of human reason, which are obviously and plainly opposed to the word of God.

Dr. Beza:

When you say that the spirit was given to the Son without measure, I say that this applies to Christ alone. But it is also said about us that <312> we are one spirit with Christ. And again, Romans 8[:14], Those who are led by the spirit of God are Sons of God. Therefore you are attributing one divinity of the Spirit to Christ the man, and another to the saints, who are Christ's members, and sharers in the same spirit.

Dr. Jakob:

ONE SPIRIT IN THE MAN CHRIST AND THE SAINTS, BUT NOT ONE AND THE SAME WAY OF COMMUNICATION.

The divinity of the holy Spirit is indeed one in the man Christ and in the other saints, who are Christ's members, but the participation in the same or rather the communication is not one and the same. For in the man Christ all things are without measure, that is, uncreated, immense, and infinite; in all other saints however, Christ's members, all these communicated gifts are created, measured, and finite. This communication, by reason of the particular gifts, differs not only in degrees and number of gifts, but also wholly in kind, just like the union of the humanity accomplished with the Son of God in Christ also differs. Christ himself, also God and man, is the bestower and dispenser of these gifts to the saints, which all his members receive from his infinite fullness.

III. REGARDING OMNIPRESENCE OF CHRIST ACCORDING TO THE HUMANITY. IN RESPONSE TO THESIS 13 AND 14.

But since no testimony of Scripture is being offered by which it may be proved that the Knowledge of the man Christ is a created gift, let us proceed to another Thesis from your response, namely concerning the omnipresence of Christ the man, which you call in your writings Ubiquity, in which we assert that Christ is not only in his own Divinity, but also in his own assumed human nature, present everywhere. This doctrine you reject and condemn as a novel dogma unheard of before in the Church. But I will point out and prove the doctrine with illustrative testimonies of holy Scripture no less than I did the communication of omnipotence and omniscience accomplished really in the humanity of Christ, if only we have faith in the express words of the Holy Spirit. The argument goes like this:

<313>

ARGUMENT FOR THE OMNIPRESENCE OF CHRIST THE MAN.

Whoever fills all things is present everywhere. The man assumed by the Son of God into the unity of his person fills all things. Therefore the assumed man is present everywhere.

DR. OSIANDER RECITED THESE WORDS FROM THE BOOK.

The major premise is proved first by the testimony and authority of Jeremiah 23[:23–24] whose words read thus: Do you think I am a God who is near, says the Lord, and not a God far off? If a man hides himself in secret places, do I not see him? declares the Lord. Do I not fill heaven and earth? And the passage from Isaiah: Heaven is my throne, and the earth a stool for my feet (Isaiah 66[:1]). The proof of the minor premise, Ephesians 4[:6] Christ ascended over all the heavens so that he might fill all things, which is said about Christ the son of man, that is, with respect to his human nature. From this it follows that Christ the man, who ascended above all the heavens, now fills all things and is present to all. Whence indeed his very sweet promises: I will be with you all the days, up to the consummation of the age (Matthew 28[:20]). And again, Where two or three are gathered together in my name, *there I am in the midst* of them (Matthew 18[:20]).

Dr. Beza:

WHETHER GOD ALONE FILLS ALL THINGS.

To the major premise of the syllogism I answer that he who fills all things is true God, but not man. On this account, I do not simply concede about Christ, but instead about the true God only. Whoever therefore is not God, about him I do not concede, just as about the humanity of Christ, which is not God. For God fills all things, but not humanity.

WHETHER THE HUMANITY OF CHRIST ALSO FILLS ALL THINGS. HE BROUGHT UP HERE THE WORDS OF VIGILIUS, ORIGEN HOMILY 13 ON MATTHEW.

In the minor premise it is said that Christ fills all things, and it is proved from Paul's words in Ephesians 4[:10], who testifies that Christ ascended in his humanity above all the heavens to the degree that he filled all things. To this minor premise I answer that the word "fill" does not refer to the substance of either the divinity or the humanity, but instead to the office of Christ. The Apostle wanted to show and teach that the office of Christ had now been consummated, that is, all things had been fulfilled by Christ, which pertained to his office. [314] For the ascension of Christ into heaven put a limit upon Christ's Ministry discharged on earth. For this reason, once all the things mandated him on earth by the father had been discharged, he ascended into the heavens so that he might show that nothing remained which had yet to be fulfilled. Thus Christ also employed this word of fulfilling when he was being baptized by

John. Do not hold back, he said, It is in fact fitting to do thus, to fulfill all righteousness (Matthew 3[:15]).

Dr. Jakob:

TRUE EXPLANATION OF PAUL'S WORDS (EPHESIANS 4).

The very plain words of Paul's text clearly disagree with this explanation and interpretation and do not concede what Beza asserts here. For the words of Paul that precede those just mentioned attest that what is being treated here is the presence of Christ in his ascension; clear mention is being made not about the consummation of his office, but rather about the higher and lower regions. His words read thus: But what does it mean that he ascended except that he first descended to the lower parts of the earth. The one who descended is the same one who ascended above all the heavens so that he might fill up all things. Thus far the words of Paul. Here the terms on high, to the lower parts of the earth, above all the heavens, ascending, descending, express no part of Christ's office, but rather speak only about the various presence of Christ whatever his motive may be.

CONCERNING CHRIST'S ASCENSION NOTHING CARNAL TO BE THOUGHT.

But it should be carefully observed that Paul does not say that he ascended into the heavens or toward the heavens, but above the heavens. Indeed, he further adds, above all the heavens, lest we think carnally about Christ's ascension here.

NEITHER CHRIST'S DIVINITY NOR HIS HUMANITY FILLS ALL THINGS LOCALLY.

We are also taught by this that the term "fill" in Ephesians means the same thing that it does in Jeremiah 23, namely, true presence, by which the God and man Christ is said to be present everywhere, even if it is attributed in another way to Christ's divinity than to his humanity. For the divinity fills up all things itself, by itself, without respect to another. But the humanity does not fill all things by itself or by the property of its own nature, but does so with respect to and in participation with his divinity and majesty which it needs.

Regarding either nature, we say that this must nevertheless not be accepted and understood carnally, physically, or locally.

<315>

HOW GOD FILLS ALL THINGS WITH HIS OWN ESSENCE.

For although the essence of divinity may be infinite, which essentially fills heaven and earth, and is present to all created things, nevertheless since God is not great by mass and quantity, but by virtue, no bodily extension or diffusion that is local should be imagined, by which the divine essence is present in creatures, like straw in a bag or bread in a breadbox. Rather, as Augustine says, he is both present everywhere and fills all things *in himself*, and human reason and understanding does not grasp the mode of presence (Augustine, *Epistle 57, to Dardanus*).

HOW THE OMNIPRESENCE OF CHRIST'S HUMANITY OUGHT TO BE THOUGHT ABOUT. CHRIST'S HUMANITY IS NOT COEXTENSIVE WITH HIS DIVINITY. ABSURD REFUTATION OF THE OMNIPRESENCE OF CHRIST'S HUMANITY.

Therefore since it is attributed to Christ's humanity that it also, itself, fills all things with the divinity, with which it has been personally united, as soon as we begin to think about this filling, a local extension into all places must be far removed from our thinking. We should think instead about its participation with the divine majesty, to which Christ's flesh is said to have ascended, and to have been seated at the right hand of God's power, which is neither a place, nor in a place, but fills heaven and earth and all things. And since the divinity is not extended or diffused, also no coextension or diffusion of Christ's humanity should be imagined, but the majesty should be regarded, which established heaven as his throne, and earth as his footstool. If someone were to understand all these things about God physically and locally, what absurd and impious thoughts would arise in the minds of people regarding God himself, if I were to say them about God himself or about Christ's humanity?

CARNAL, GROSS, AND ABSURD ANALOGIES AGAINST THE OMNIPRESENCE OF CHRIST'S HUMANITY. 1. ANALOGY OF THE ORBITS AND PLANETARY BODIES, AND A SILLY ARGUMENT AGAINST THE MAJESTY OF THE MAN CHRIST.

Once all these things have been necessarily laid out, all your arguments disappear, which have carried the dispute along thus far against that spiritual and heavenly presence of Christ's humanity and his omnipresence, by which Christ is said to fill all things even just as a man. Your writers have employed various analogies to explain and refute this. Comparing the divinity to orbits or heavenly circuits on the one hand, and on the other, Christ's body to planetary bodies, they have reasoned in this way: in what manner an orbit or heavenly circuit of a planet is always where a planetary body is, since it never deviates from its own orbit or circuit. But on the other hand, to the contrary, where a planet's orbit is, there is not also a planetary body; <316> since a planet's orbit is larger than the planetary body. In such a way is the divinity present, wherever the assumed man is, but not the converse, that where divinity is, there also is the assumed man.

---

2. ANALOGY OF A GEM IN A RING. 3. ANALOGY OF ANTWERP AND THE OCEAN.

They explain the same thing by way of the analogy of the gem in a ring as well. And at the Maulbronn Colloquy, the Heidelberg theologians formed their argument against us after this fashion, by analogy and the example of Antwerp and the Ocean: as it does not follow that the Ocean runs round the entire earth, and Antwerp is connected to the Ocean, therefore Antwerp also runs round the entire earth; so also it does not follow, if on account of the connection of the Word with the assumed humanity, we should wish to assert that the humanity itself is also present in Christ everywhere, wherever the divinity is present.

GROSS AND CARNAL CONCEPTIONS CONCERNING THE MYSTERY OF THE INCARNATION, CHRIST'S DIVINITY, AND HIS HUMANITY.

These analogies which are found in your writings and those of your brothers point out how gross, carnal, absurd, and false are the conceptions about the mystery of the incarnation of the Son of God, and not only regarding the presence of his humanity in all places, but also of Christ's divinity.

NOTIONS CONCERNING THE PRESENCE OF DEITY IN THE CREATURE. CARNAL CONCEPTIONS REGARDING THE PRESENCE OF CHRIST'S HUMANITY, IN THE ADMINISTRATION OF ALL THINGS.

For they make God after the fashion of a planetary orbit, and the Ocean, represent him as having been extended and diffused, as if he is great by the measure of mass and quantity. From here they say: the humanity is not *coextended* to the divinity. In fact Peter Martyr and many others employ this word. But *coextended* presupposes *extended*. However, since the divinity has no need of *extension* on account of its presence in heaven and on earth, by which he fills all things, neither has it been extended. So, please, what is the reason that Christ's humanity is said, besides, also to have been coextensive with his divinity, if it is said that Christ's humanity fills all things, with the divinity?

<317>

CARNAL CONCEPTIONS REGARDING THE PERSONAL UNION.

Next, they fashion such a union of natures in Christ that, just as the body of a Planet receives nothing from the revolution of its own orbit, and a gem from the circular shape of a ring, and Antwerp from the breadth of the Ocean, but are united and joined only at extremities and surfaces, so also they say the assumed human nature shares nothing with God's Son and things proper to his majesty, but is only united with it.

REFUTATION OF THE MOST ABSURD ANALOGIES ABOUT THE PERSON AND NATURES IN CHRIST.

The absurdity of this is plainly refuted by at least one clear testimony of Scripture, which was explained abundantly a little bit ago. For Paul bears witness that in the assumed Man, namely in Christ, *all the fullness of Deity dwells bodily* (Colossians 2[:9]). Under the term fullness of Deity, though, it has been laid out that the whole divinity is understood, beyond any controversy, and there is no way this can be denied. If this is true, how can these analogies remain and at the same time somehow disparage the presence of Christ's humanity?

Do your people argue and dispute from them against the universal presence of Christ's humanity? Is the whole Ocean in the city of Antwerp? Is the whole ring in a gem? Is the whole revolution of an orbit in a planetary body? Are all the limbs contained in the head of the body? Are all the branches in the trunk of the tree?

It is therefore a false and utterly carnal fancy, as concerning the universal presence of the Deity itself, so also with that of Christ's humanity. This does not wrestle against our doctrine, which is the teaching of the holy Spirit, but rather against its own carnal and very gross formation of these matters.

WHENCE ADJUDICATION OF THE CONTROVERSY REGARDING THE UNIVERSAL PRESENCE MUST BE SOUGHT.

Therefore to understand and decide this controversy, there is need first and foremost for us to consider rightly omnipresence of divinity. The omnipresence is attributed also to humanity by participation and communication with divinity, which it has from divinity and union with the person of the Son of God.

HOW GOD IS PRESENT EVERYWHERE IS UNKNOWN.

Concerning this presence, however, we are not able to say what and of what sort it is, but only what and of what sort it is not. For this divinity is present to all creatures, and the creatures themselves make this known by their own <318> wondrous effects and properties, and Scripture plainly attests that God is above all things, through all things and in all things, to the degree that he fills all things, heaven and earth (Ephesians 4[:10]; Jeremiah 23[:24]; Isaiah 66[:1]). Where will I flee from your spirit?, asks David (Psalm 139[:7]). But *how* he is present, we do not understand.

For if we should accept locally, and think about or reason these things out naturally or carnally, into what absurdities will we not fall? For a circumspect man, arguing from Physical or local presence, would say if he is in all things, then he is not above all things; if he is above all things, he is not in all things. For *in* and *above* mean different places. Therefore although he is present by neither one of these modes, it is right to say that he is nevertheless truly and really present: above, below, outside of and within all things, nowhere either included or excluded. We know too that it is commonly and truly said, God is within all things, not included, outside of all things, not excluded, above all things, not elevated, below all things, not reduced.

However, the Word [λόγος] did not assume a human nature and join it to itself just as a planetary body does so to its own orbit, or Antwerp to the Ocean, or a gem to a ring, or limbs of the human body have been joined to the head, or branches to the stump of a tree. Therefore we reject all those analogies in consideration of this Mystery. For as long as they are stuck in our minds, we will conceive of nothing right or true and in accordance with holy Scripture. These analogies have occupied the minds of many people, and because they have, they cannot for this reason grasp this mystery, nor listen to its true explanation, nor subject themselves to it.

But since we have rejected these conceptions, only the word of God remains, which makes its declaration about that wondrous presence of Deity in all creatures. The mode of this presence is perceived by neither the senses nor reason, but faith alone understands it, which leads the intellect captive and utterly abstains from investigating this Majesty.

Then, since holy Scripture teaches the same things, that the Son of God assumed a human nature into the unity of his person, and that the all the fullness of Deity dwells *in* him bodily, <319> and has caused that nature to have a share in his own proper Majesty, that he has stationed it at the right hand of power and of the Majesty of God the omnipotent Father, on that throne that fills heaven and earth. And he plainly bears witness that he ascended toward the heavens, into the heavens, and above all the heavens, in order that he might fill all things. What reason is there to doubt even a bit that communicated majesty? And attach a meaning so alien to the plain testimonies of Scripture and those things that it makes known so magnificently regarding the man Christ's Majesty to which Christ has been exalted according to his flesh? I beg the pardon of my hearers, as I have been so wordy in explaining our opinion, so that it may be understood why controversy exists. After this I will be briefer.

Dr. Beza:

Our party employed the analogies mentioned, wanting to signify these things: the humanity, since it is circumscribed, does not extend as far as the divinity does, with the result that it remains in the union itself finite, circumscribed, and organic. Whence it does not follow that the divinity does nothing outside of it. Likewise, it is not so constrained by the humanity that it is unable to act outside of it. I say that the man Christ fills all things, and is present everywhere, but not his humanity.

Dr. Jakob:

Consensus in words, deception in referents.

We have now demonstrated that those analogies are very silly. They cannot be applied to Christ's divinity nor to his humanity, nor to the personal union of the natures. It is also false to say that the divinity does anything outside of the assumed flesh, since *in it, with it,* and through *it* he does all things, as was proved above. When you say besides this that the man fills all things, there is no answer for this point. For your answer (in which you explain the phrase) teaches sufficiently that by the term Man you understand only the Deity, when <320> you say: The man Christ fills all things. In fact this means the same thing to you, that the Divine nature united to his humanity fills all things. This is clearly a fraud and deception, by which simple Christians may think that you think the same thing that we do, when you merely speak with us in the same words, but meanwhile, nonetheless, understand and think something else.

Dr. Beza:

Objection sought from the proprium of the body.

Even if the divinity is not extended or diffused into all places, since it is spirit, it is everywhere whole. It nevertheless does not follow that the humanity is also present everywhere with the divinity, since it is united to the divinity in the person of the Word. For the property and truth of Christ's body does not admit it. It cannot be truly and essentially present, unless by extension in local and physical circumscription, by which it is extended after the fashion of the orbit of planets with the divinity, so that it may be present to it in any place.

REFUTATION.

The sort of union the human nature has with the person of the Word or the Son of God is also the sort of mode of presence. But the union is not local, but personal, by which the Word [λόγος] dwells with all the fullness of divinity, bodily in the assumed human nature, without which or outside of which he does nothing, but does all things *with it, in it, and through it,* just as the orthodox Fathers bear witness. Therefore there is no need of local diffusion or extension for that universal presence. Since Christ's flesh possesses *within itself* that which offers this real presence to his humanity, not outside of itself, as your gross analogies falsely emphasize. If therefore the Word [λόγος] is present everywhere, why not also the humanity, in which the Word [λόγος] dwells bodily with all the fullness of Deity?

<321>

Dr. Beza:
The Word [λόγος] has been assumed in the humanity in such a way that it is also outside it in the rest of the creatures, nor is it distributed into parts, such that here is part of the Word [λόγος], and there is another part; but the entire Word [λόγος], which is whole in the assumed humanity, is also the same whole outside of it. For this reason on account of that union, it is not necessary, nor does it follow, that wherever the Word [λόγος] is, there also is his humanity. For the truth and property of true body, of the kind that the Son of God assumed, does not allow or admit that.

CHRIST'S HUMAN NATURE IS NOT LOCALLY PRESENT ANYWHERE.

Dr. Jakob:

If you were to speak about the truth of Christ's body, and the local circumscription of it, and what sort of mode of presence, I would easily concede to you that it is in a way that Christ's human nature is not present anywhere locally and circumscribed. I say this because there has never been a controversy between us about this local presence, just as our writings openly bear witness.

QUESTION, WHETHER CHRIST'S HUMANITY IS ANYWHERE PERSONALLY PRESENT WITH THE WORD [λόγος].

But since the personal union is not local, but personal, by which the Son of God is united not locally, but personally, with the human nature, I ask whether the Word [λόγος] keeps the assumed humanity present anywhere with him personally, that is, after the fashion by which it has been personally united to him? With the result that he is not God and man in one place, and in another is only God without humanity, just as he was from eternity, but is anywhere entire God and man, wherever the Word [λόγος] is? Please answer me categorically here, and then it will be apparent to everybody what every Christian man of this party believes or does not believe.

Dr. Beza:

IN RESPONSE TO THE 13TH AND 14TH THESIS.

Omnipresence necessarily presupposes an infinite essence. Therefore we are able to recognize that there is precisely one Divinity, and there are four modes of being, as they say, that are proper to it, yet this is in no way applied to Christ's humanity,[37] <322> despite it being hypostatically united and even now glorified. Because Christ's body perpetually retains its circumscription.

Dr. Jakob:

The question has not been answered at all. I am asking about his humanity, in the ever-permanent, circumscribed property of its nature, whether the Word [λόγος] personally possesses anywhere

---

37   Referring to a concept from Aristotle's *Posterior Analytics* I.4.

present this finite and circumscribed human nature, assumed into the unity of his person, such that he is God and man anywhere, and not in one location only in the way a human being is present. Answer this.

Dr. Beza:
Wherever the Word [λόγος] is, it is united with the human nature. And there is no place such that it is separated from its human nature. But it always has it personally united to it, though the human nature is contained in a certain and circumscribed place, and is not present everywhere, where the Word [λόγος] is present.

Dr. Jakob:
Answer has still not been made to my proposed question, namely whether the Word [λόγος] personally keeps humanity with him anywhere?

Dr. Beza:
Assumed humanity is always present to the Word [λόγος] or Son of God, since it is not separated from him. And the Son of God, because he has assumed it, never puts it down. It does not follow from this, though, that he is present in all those places where the Word [λόγος] is, on account of the truth and circumscription of the human nature which is in one place, indisputably in heaven and not on the earth.

<323>

Dr. Jakob:
Is the Word [λόγος] present to us on earth?

Dr. Beza:
It is present.

Dr. Jakob:
And on earth does he not keep the human nature present with him?

Dr. Beza:
Indeed he does keep it present with him, but the nature itself remains circumscribed in heaven.

Dr. Jakob:
Is that mode of presence true and real, by which the Word [λόγος] on earth keeps the assumed man present with him, or is it rather fictitious and imaginary?

Dr. Beza:
Christ's body is in heaven, and not on earth; he cannot be in heaven and on earth at the same time.

Dr. Jakob:
Therefore you see, my dear Beza, that you should necessarily establish that the Word [λόγος] in heaven alone is God, and man is where Christ's humanity is. Nevertheless he is not in all of locations of heaven, but merely in one place, where the assumed man is. However outside of heaven he is mere Word [λόγος] without his own humanity. You do not dare say this plainly, however, since you understand the absurdity into which you are falling.

In response to the 4ᵗʰ Thesis.

The cause of this error is that in the article concerning the Lord's Supper, you asserted regarding Christ's body: It is not possible for the substance of Christ's humanity, regardless of how much it is glorified, to be really on the earth and established as present, *in any way other than local and physical circumscription.* This is false.

But we also have never believed, taught, or written that the presence of Christ's body and blood is physical and local, still less his entire humanity on earth, in countless locations.

<324>

Therefore the question still remains undiscussed, which you were supposed to answer conclusively, though this has not happened yet: since the union is not local, but is nevertheless real, can the true and real presence of Christ's humanity exist, by virtue of the union, without damage to its locality, in such a way that wherever the Word [λόγος] is, on account of the unity of the person the assumed human nature is also there? Not locally though, but rather personally; not just in word or name, but truly and really?

CONCERNING OMNIPRESENCE OF THE HUMANITY OF CHRIST, CATEGORICAL ASSERTION OF THE WÜRTTEMBERG THEOLOGIANS.

With Paul, we consistently and fearlessly hold and assert the affirmative, when he says: Christ ascended above all the heavens (but he ascended according to his humanity, which cannot be denied, who according to his Divinity has always been in heaven) *in order that he might fill up all things* (Ephesians 4[:10]) that is, be present in all things.

Christ also confirms this when he says, I am with you all the days, up to the consummation of the age (Matthew 28[:20]). And again, Where two or three are gathered in my name, I am in their midst (Matthew 18[:20]). Now as we do not investigate the mode of presence, so can we not grasp the mode of the personal union by means of reason and human intellect, as it is ineffable and inscrutable, and God himself alone knows it. But let it suffice for us that we possess on earth, according to these plain and not in the least doubtful testimonies of Christ and Paul, not half but the whole Christ present, and especially Christ the man, our brother, helper in all tribulations, in whatever place we are.

Dr. Beza:
The divine and human nature are so united in the person of Christ that the natures always remain intact, and their properties distinct. Therefore even if we should say, The Divinity is someplace were the humanity is not, nevertheless we are not on this account dividing the person or separating the natures. Because just as it is the property of divinity <325> *to be everywhere, so it is the property of humanity to be circumscribed in a particular place. Since therefore the human nature of Christ soundly retains this property even in glory, I do not*

see how he can be present in another way than by physical and local circumscription.

BEZA'S OPINION AGAINST THE MODE OF PRESENCE IN THE MYSTERY.

Regarding the personal presence, the thing you say, I am indeed familiar with the union of the human nature with the Son of God and I believe it, but I do not see and am not able to believe in any other true and real presence of the substance of the humanity of Christ on earth than a local and physical one, which I say is now in heaven, and is nowhere else. I also say that Paul's words should be taken to refer to the office of Christ, and not to omnipresence, when he says that Christ ascended above all the heavens in order that he might fill up all things.

Dr. Jakob:

No one is doubting or speaking against the fact that the human nature retains its own properties in the personal union and in glory. The question is rather whether the same human nature, with its properties intact, can be adorned with divine glory and the majesty proper to Divinity. What we have just proven about omnipotence and omniscience, that they have been really communicated to the assumed nature, we have demonstrated with plain testimonies of Scripture in a way more clear than the light of midday.

THE SUM OF ALL THINGS IN THE CONTROVERSY ABOUT THE LORD'S SUPPER.
THE GOVERNMENT OF ALL CREATURES NECESSARILY PRESUPPOSES PRESENCE.
DISTINCTION BETWEEN CHRIST'S GOVERNANCE AND AN EARTHLY RULE.

I leave to the judgment of all the audience and pious men, there-fore, whether they themselves also believe that God possesses no other mode of presence than a local and physical one, by which the assumed man may truly and really be present in every place with the Word [λόγος]. I do not think in fact that there is anyone in this entire auditorium who would dare assert this and so undermine this mode of divine omnipotence. Nor in fact does Paul attribute a merely idle presence to Christ according to his humanity, but rather an especially industrious and efficacious one, Ephesians 1[:1–2], when he says, Establishing <326> him at his right hand in the heavenlies, above every rule, authority, power, and dominion, and every name which is named not only in this age but also in the age to come. And again, You have placed all things under his feet. (Psalm 8[:6]) Now in saying this, that he subjected all things under him, he leaves nothing that is not subject to him (Hebrews 2[:8]). *But now* (says the Epistle to the Hebrews) *we do not see that all things are subjected to him.* For this reason governance, dominion, and the administration of all things visible and invisible, in heaven and earth, necessarily presupposes his divine and heavenly presence. For it is not an absent Christ but the present man Christ who governs all these things that have been subjected to him, unless we should wish to convert the reign of Christ to an earthly one, in which not the king himself, but rather his prefects and vicars rule by his authority in all those places to which the king does not go or where he himself is not present.

Dr. Beza:

God can do many things which he does not do, since he does not wish to. He does not wish a thing simultaneously to be and not be, to be at the same time local and illocal, or not local. Since Christ therefore perpetually keeps his human nature, a property of which is local circumscription, he does not wish for it to be present in heaven and earth and everywhere at the same time. Otherwise he would be acting contrary to his truth, which God himself is.

Dr. Jakob:

I have now demonstrated the words of Paul and Christ, that *Christ* wished to fill all things with his own humanity. It is for this reason, says Paul, that he ascended, to fill up all things, not only according to his divinity, of which he was not lacking in the ascension, by which already he filled up all things from the moment of the foundation of the world, but with his own *flesh*, as Oecumenius says, whose words are these: He ascended above all the heavens, in order that he might fill up all things, even though (he says) <327> he already filled up all things by means of his *bare* divinity. And so in order that he might as incarnate fill up all things with his *flesh*, he descended and ascended.

CONTRADICTORY THINGS CAN BE ATTRIBUTED TO THE SAME THING IN A DIFFERENT RESPECT.

And in this presence of Christ's humanity, God does not act against the rule of truth by which it is said that God does not wish something simultaneously to be and not be. For not only different, but also contradictory things can be attributed to one and the same thing in a different respect. It does not follow from this, nevertheless, that something is for this reason simultaneously existent and non-existent.

HOW THE HUMANITY OF CHRIST SIMULTANEOUSLY LOCAL AND ILLOCAL. HUMANITY OF CHRIST EXISTS ILLOCALLY IN GOD.

In such a way are the contrary terms local and illocal attributed to Christ's humanity, but in a different respect. For his humanity is called local, and it is and always remains so by the property of its nature. But it is illocal by reason of the person of the son of God. For the humanity is one and the same in number, and though in heaven locally it is in God illocally, and has been united with the Son of God illocally. No sensible person, much less pious person, can deny this. For God is neither a place nor in a place. It is therefore necessary that the way that something is in God is illocally. Nevertheless, it does not follow that because the humanity exists illocally in God (since there is no place in God), then it cannot exist locally in heaven.

We can therefore truly say with Paul and Christ that the same humanity of Christ is in heaven locally and in a circumscribed way, that is, by the property of the human nature, which always remains, in the nature of which substance we will be likewise formed in the resurrection, and that it is at the same time illocally on earth with the Son of God in the way it is in God, that is, personally united with the Son of God.

Here there is no hint of contradiction. These contrary things are not simply attributed to one and the same thing, but attributed in a different respect.

It is a manifest fallacy of converse accident, to jump as you do from the qualified assertion to the general conclusion, when you argue in this way: The Humanity of Christ is not present on earth by means of physical location and circumscription, therefore *he is not present in any way.* For we have already demonstrated that he is truly present. We in fact believe in no <328> Christ on earth who is only God and not also man. *How* he is present, though, we attribute to divine power, wisdom, and truth, who says *I am with you* (Matthew 28[:20]). He did not say, My divine nature is with you.

Dr. Beza:
From where will Christ come?

Dr. Jakob:
He will come from heaven.

Dr. Beza:
Therefore the term "to fill up" pertains not to the universal presence, but rather to the consummation of the office of Christ. The divine nature fills up all things; the human nature is not omnipresent.

IN PAUL, TO FILL UP MEANS PRESENCE, NOT CONSUMMATION OF OFFICE.

Dr. Jakob:
I deny very simply that the term "to fill up" in this context means consummation of Christ's office according to Paul. For when Scripture speaks about the filling up of those things that pertain to the office of Christ, it adds, in order that what was written might be fulfilled. But here there is mention of no fulfilled Scripture, but rather it speaks plainly about the descent and ascension and filling up of his presence.

HUMANITY OF CHRIST DOES NOT FILL UP ALL THINGS LIKE THE DIVINITY DOES.

As to the next point, it is true that the humanity does not fill up all things like the divinity, since divinity does so of itself and by the property of its own essence, but the Human nature by the personal participation and communication of the divinity itself communicated to it. Nothing is done here concerning the circumscription of the human nature, and it is not eliminated by the communication of this majesty. This majesty is not local, and thus the presence of this majesty is not local.

Dr. Beza:
Circumscription of the human nature in Christ does not admit a presence of this kind, <329> *which is proper to God alone, in the fourth mode.[38] And the human nature according to the property of its own nature, as it remains finite and circumscribed, is thus contained in merely one place, and cannot be present at the same time in heaven and on earth.*

Dr. Jakob:
You should therefore produce *one* testimony of Scripture, at least *one* (I say), that disallows the truth of the body, and I would believe you. For I have proved by plain words of Scripture that the human nature is capable of containing and has been made a participant in *the whole* fullness of divinity. Therefore why not of this presence as well? For God, in order that he may be present to the creature, does not step outside of himself.

Dr. Beza:
The analogy of faith proves and confirms that it cannot happen.

Dr. Jakob:
Enough has been said above regarding the analogy of faith, that it does not fight against us. But I challenge you to prove it with a testimony of Scripture, just *one*. I am hearing none. Since you can

---

38   Referring to a concept from Aristotle's *Posterior Analytics* I.4; cf. footnote 24 (p. 251).

produce none, therefore, I leave judgment to the audience. But I hope that I have demonstrated, since Paul testifies that Christ ascended above all the heavens in order that he might fill up all things, that by this it is understood he is speaking about the present governing of creatures and not about the consummation of office, which was charged to him on earth by the Father.

CONCERNING THE OFFICE OF MEDIATOR IN HEAVEN.

Dr. Beza:

The office of mediator exists not only to reconcile us to God the Father through his passion and death, but also to act as mediator in the heavens, where he still intercedes for us with the Father. <330> *And again, it is his office also to invite us to be with him, as it is written: Father, I it is my wish that where I am, they be also with me whom you have given to me, so that they may see my glory (John 17[:24]). Before the ascension of Christ this was not yet fulfilled. Christ now fulfills this in heaven; he ascended for this reason.*

HOW CHRIST IS OUR MEDIATOR AND ADVOCATE IN HEAVEN.

Dr. Jakob:

As far as the office of mediator and its parts is concerned, it is a silly notion about Christ that imagines him prostrate or a suppliant on this knees, stretching his hands to the Father to intercede for us, and praying to the Father on our behalf. Rather the virtue of his death and resurrection appears before the Father in place of continuous intercession in Christ, and this is before God the Father in place of most efficacious prayer. Because of this we invoke the Father in true faith and trust in Christ, and our prayers follow.

For this reason Paul says that Christ now fills up all things after his ascension. He refers to his presence in heaven and on earth, and to the administration of his rule, which he received from the Father over all creatures visible and invisible, who gazes upon the affliction of the pious as a man, not from a distance, but rather being very present he sees and defends and protects them against evil.

Dr. Beza:
Show that humanity has become Divinity, and we will concede that it also is omnipresent.

COMMUNICATION OF MAJESTY DOES NOT TRANSFORM HUMANITY INTO DIVINITY.

Dr. Jakob:

I just now demonstrated that omnipresence happens by participation of the divine Majesty, but nevertheless it is not transformed into Divinity for this reason, nor does it become Divinity. Let your Reverence offer *one* (*one* I say) testimony of Scripture by which he may prove that Majesty proper to divinity, really communicated to Christ's humanity, which holy Scripture commends, <331> is a created gift. Prove it, please, with at least one testimony, and I will be content. For we ought in sacred matters that concern the salvation of our souls to affirm or deny nothing without the word of God.

Dr. Beza:
I did prove it by the analogy of faith, which I think is sufficient, which teaches that the Son of God assumed a true human nature with all its essential properties, and never set it aside. Besides, this majesty is a gift, and so created, since all gifts are created.

Dr. Jakob:

That this majesty is a gift no one has denied, since it is a property not of the human nature, but rather is added to the human nature by the divinity of the Son of God. But let Dr. Beza demonstrate, where is it written in holy writ that it is a created gift? For Christ does not send us to human reasoning but rather to the Scripture. Where is it written?

Dr. Beza:

The whole Christ is everywhere and omnipotent, but not the whole of Christ. You always confuse the abstract and the concrete, and you attribute to the humanity that which should have been attributed to the man. But demonstrate that the humanity becomes Divinity.

Dr. Jakob:

In regard to that trite and common saying, that the whole Christ is everywhere, but not the whole of Christ: Enough has been said by me above in what way it is true or false, and in what way it can be applied to this business, but it has not been refuted by you. In a similar way it has also been shown that we do not in the least confuse the abstract and concrete. On the other hand we have demonstrated clearly that you consider concrete things that are abstract.

<332>

So also there is no need for us to show that Humanity has become Divinity; enough has been said, seeing as this transformation of natures in no way follows or can truly be deduced from the communication of majesty.

Dr. Beza:

I request that it be proved to me that the substance of Christ's humanity fills up all things.

Dr. Jakob:

THE SUBSTANCE OF CHRIST'S HUMANITY FILLS UP ALL THINGS. UNIQUE CAUSE OF THE ERROR AND CONTROVERSY REGARDING THE PRESENCE OF CHRIST'S HUMANITY IN THE LORD'S SUPPER, AND REGARDING UBIQUITY.

I already proved it. It was not in fact the accident of the humanity of Christ that ascended above all the heavens, but its substance, in order that it might fill up all things. But Dr. Beza is mistaken (begging his pardon) on this point, since he thinks that Christ's humanity cannot fill up all things by means of its own substance unless it should happen physically, locally, and in a circumscribed way. If this opinion could be taken away from you, the road to concord in this entire controversy would be an easy and unobstructed one.

EXPLANATION OF CHRIST'S WORDS, JOHN 3.

The son of man when he was speaking on earth with Nicodemus was (says Christ) in heaven. He does not say Son of God, lest he be understood to speak about the divinity alone, but rather says son of man. But he was not in heaven physically, locally, and in a circumscribed way, but instead by means of *the unity* of person, as Augustine says, that it, on account of the personal union by which Christ is not only in heaven in his own humanity, but has become higher than the very heavens (Hebrews 7[:26]).

Dr. Beza:
Son of man is one thing, humanity is another. For we do not in the least deny that the son of man was in heaven when he was speaking on earth with Nicodemus, but rather we deny that his humanity was in heaven.

Dr. Jakob:
If in Christ's words nothing is attributed to his humanity, when he says: The son of man who is in heaven, then Peter was also in <333> heaven when he was dwelling on earth. For the divinity, which is on earth and dwells in Peter himself, was also in heaven. But we have demonstrated from your Theses above, that by son of man you understand nothing other than Deity. For just as in this formula-tion, Man is omnipotent, you understand by man only Deity united to humanity, so also by son of man do you only accept the same divinity as is this sentence: The son of man is in heaven, that is, the divinity (which is united with the humanity, when the Son of God is called Man) is in heaven. No one of true faith and understanding will approve of this. If this had been the meaning of Christ's words, he could have said them in another way.

But let us continue on to the communication of vivification, which is no less proper to divinity than the properties just now mentioned. I think in fact that our audience has understood sufficiently that you can bring against the omnipresence of Christ's humanity no testimony of Scripture, nor prove the interpretation advanced by you of Paul's words, who so plainly testifies that Christ ascended in his humanity above all the heavens *in order that he might fill up all things*; furthermore that this should in no way be understood to refer to the fulfillment of his office, but rather openly proclaims his presence in the administration of heaven and earth.

Dr. Beza:

We are arguing in so many words about the parts, that is, the several properties of divinity, whether they have really been communicated to the assumed nature, when we could expedite it in a few. For unless you were to show that the Humanity has become Divinity, you will labor in vain about every single attribute of divinity, that you may show that they are communicated ot the assumed humanity.

Dr. Jakob:

WHY THERE IS A DISPUTE REGARDING COMMUNICATION OF EVERY SINGLE ATTRIBUTE OF DIVINITY.

I explained at the beginning the reason why we argue about every single attribute and the communication of them. [334] Namely, in order that the entire audience may understand that we, for our part, in our Churches and Schools, ascribe nothing to Christ's humanity of which we do not possess clear and manifest and not in the least doubtful testimonies of holy Scripture.

POINT 4. REGARDING VIVIFICATION AND ITS COMMUNICATION IN THE FLESH OF CHRIST.

But it is especially necessary that we be certain about the communicated virtue of vivifying, since we desire and receive Christ's flesh in the Lord's Supper for no other reason than for vivification. Christ's body is in fact not food for bellies which like veal is passed through the throat into the belly, but it is taken by mouth in order that it may be for us the food of eternal life, which Christ earned for us by his passion and death.

WHENCE CHRIST'S FLESH HAS BECOME VIVIFIC.

Christ's flesh does not possess this virtue, however, in itself, but rather by means of participation, that is, communication of the divinity of the Word [λόγος], that is, of the Son of God. Since it belongs to Divinity alone to vivify, what in fact does God possess that is more proper to him? Go ask the 200 Fathers of the Council of Ephesus. I argue in this same way.

CONFIRMATION THAT CHRIST'S FLESH IS VIVIFIC.

If Christ's flesh is vivific, it vivifies by means of participation with power proper to Divinity alone. But Christ's flesh is truly vivific. Therefore it vivifies by means of participation with power proper to Divinity. Or:

Whatever really vivifies, the power proper to Divinity has been communicated to it. But Christ's flesh truly and really vivifies. Therefore the power proper to divinity has been communicated to Christ's flesh.

The major premise is proved, since it is proper to God alone to vivify. This is denied by no one.

The minor premise is proved by John 6: My flesh truly is food. But not food for bellies, rather for eternal life.

Dr. Beza:
If you accept communication for union, that Christ's flesh is united with the power of vivifying, which is proper to divinity, I concede the entire argument.

1. HOW CHRIST'S FLESH IS VIVIFIC IN DR. BEZA'S OPINION.

And meanwhile I do not deny that Christ's flesh is also truly [335] *vivific, Since the Son of God has filled up and brought to perfection all things in and through the flesh which were necessary for us for obtaining eternal life.*

2.

And the next point is that since he is ὁμοούσιος *with our flesh, that is, of the same substance, and we are made members of Christ who is the head of the body, whence life flows into us, only by communication of the flesh which he assumed into the unity of his person.*

WHETHER THE POWER OF VIVIFYING INHERES IN CHRIST'S FLESH.

But as for some power or virtue of vivifying inhering in Christ's flesh, on account of which communicated power it has become and is said to be vivific, this we thoroughly deny. Cyril confirms our opinion in this regard, Book 6 on the Trinity: It is meet and proper that no other thing or creature be able to vivify, even if it is known to be Christ's flesh IN SO FAR AT IS FLESH, except for the nature of Divinity alone.

In these words Cyril attributes this power not to Christ's flesh, but to divinity alone, as if the virtue was the incommunicable property of the Son of God.

Dr. Jakob:

IN WHAT WAY CHRIST'S FLESH IS NOT CALLED VIVIFIC.

I ask that the same words of Cyril be recited and shown me again, which are clearly not at all in conflict with our opinion. Cyril in fact proposes the same things not once, but repeats and stresses them several times and abundantly.

If in fact divinity and flesh should be compared together in the nature of their properties, vivifying is a property of divinity alone, such that Christ's flesh lacks this virtue, by which it cannot vivify itself, but receives its life from divinity in order that it may also live. For this reason, if you were to consider the property of the nature of flesh, it never is, was or will be vivific, but rather lacks vivification itself. What more do you want? But if you were to consider the same flesh in the union and by reason of the personal union in Christ, not only does it live in God, just as we live, <336> who grants life to us all, as it is written: in him we live, move, and exist, but it also has *in itself* the power of vivifying, communicated to it by divinity. As it is written in John 5[:26–27]: He granted the son to have life *in himself* and he gave him the power to make judgment, *because he is the son of man*. This power was communicated to no other heavenly or earthly creature. As it is written: The first man Adam was made into a living soul; the last Adam into *a vivifying spirit*.

CYRIL'S PERPETUAL OPINION REGARDING THE VIVIFIC FLESH OF CHRIST.

And I will show by his own very clear words that this is Cyril's perpetual opinion, as he is the best interpreter of his own words, which read thus:

> You do not ignorantly deny that *the flesh* is altogether *vivific*. For if it should be understood *by itself*, *nothing* at all can vivify, since it lacks vivifying power. But since you have examined, with commendable care, the mystery of the incarnation, and know him dwelling *in the flesh*, even though *flesh is not at all able to do this by itself, nevertheless you believe that it has become vivific*. For since *the flesh* has been joined together with the vivifying word, *it has become entirely vivific*. For it has not dragged *the Word of God* joined to it down to its own corruptible nature, but rather *was itself elevated to the virtue of the greater*. Therefore even though *the nature of flesh as it is flesh* is unable to vivify, nevertheless this it does, *since it undertakes the whole operation of the Word*. For it is a body, not of any man you wish, whose flesh cannot produce anything (not even Paul's or Peter's or the rest), but rather *the body of life* itself, of our savior Jesus Christ, *in which* the fullness of Deity dwells bodily, is able to do this.[39] For if honey makes the things with which it is mixed sweet, since

---

39   This sentence in the printed edition is specially marked with a "N.B." (*nota bene*).

it is naturally sweet, will it not be foolish to think that the vivific nature of the word has not given to the Man, in whom it dwells, the power of vivifying? Indeed because of these things the flesh of all the rest can do *nothing, but Christ's flesh*, since the only begotten Son of God dwells in it, *alone* can vivify. (Cyril on John, Book 4, chapter 23)

Thus far Cyril.
<337>

CYRIL'S TESTIMONIES REGARDING THE VIVIFIC FLESH OF CHRIST.

These words of Cyril are so clear, perspicuous, and plain, that they need no interpretation, nor allow your interpretation. By them he bears witness openly that the communicated power and virtue of vivifying is in Christ's flesh, by which it not only lives, like Peter and Paul, but can also vivify others. In addition to this opinion a great many similar sayings of his are found, a few of which we will recite.

DR. JAKOB RECITED THESE SAYINGS OF CYRIL FROM NOTES.

Christ's body vivifies, and restores to incorruptibility by its own participation. For it is not the body of some other person, but *it is the body of life* itself, retaining the power of the incarnate Word, and full of the power of the one by whom all things exist and live. (Cyril on John, Book 3, chapter 37)

I have refilled my body with life; I have assumed mortal flesh, but since naturally *existing life*, I dwell in it, *I have reshaped my whole life*. (Cyril on John, Book 4, chapter 18)

Again: *The nature of flesh* itself cannot *of itself* vivify; for what could it possess greater than the nature of Deity? It is not understood *to be alone* in Christ, but rather has the Son of God joined to itself, *who is life consubstantially*. When therefore Christ calls his flesh vivific, he attributes the power of vivifying *not to it, but to himself*, that is, to his own spirit. For his spirit vivifies on account of itself, *to the power of which the flesh* ascends through the joining together. But *how* this happens, we cannot understand with the mind nor say with the tongue, but in silence accept *it with firm faith.* (Cyril on John, Book 4, chapter 24)

Again: The flesh of life having become the flesh of the only begotten *was translated to the power of life.* (Cyril on John, Book 10, chapter 13)

POWER OF VIVIFYING ONE WAY IN DIVINITY, ANOTHER WAY IN HUMANITY OF CHRIST.

With these words Cyril not only attributes the power of vivifying to Christ's flesh, but at the same time also shows the manner of difference that is attributed in one way *to the Word*, that is, to the Son of God, and in another way to the flesh. It is attributed to the Word as proper to it essentially and naturally, but to the flesh, as it is joined personally to the word.

<338>

EXPEDIENT PATH TO HOLY CONCORD.

But would that we all equally followed Cyril's example, and accept with firm faith that which we cannot understand with our mind or utter with our tongue. In such a way could pious, holy, and God-pleasing concord be easily established in this supreme article of Christian faith; nay rather, it would already have been established.

For if Christ's flesh, *as it is flesh*, were being considered also in Christ, it cannot vivify, just like mine or the flesh of another person, since it is like the essence of our flesh in every way with the exception of sin. But since it has been personally united with the divinity of the Son, *who is life*, for this reason it drinks in this power (as Cyril says), such that it has also been made truly and really vivific by means of the communication of this *life*.

Dr. Beza:

In the quoted passages, Cyril attributes the vivific virtue and power to Christ's flesh since it behooves us to become members of Christ THROUGH it. This Christ won for us by his passion and death in THE FLESH AND THROUGH THE FLESH, and became flesh of our flesh and bone of our bones.

Next, I deny that by the term "drinking," he understands some power poured into Christ's flesh, as you want the flesh apart from Deity to possess THE POWER, poured out from the divinity, OF VIVIFYING IN ITSELF, which does not vivify less than Deity itself, by its very own virtue. This we do not concede, but totally deny. For the power of vivifying is proper to Deity in such a way that it cannot be communicated to Christ's flesh nor to any creature, except it be changed into Deity.

Dr. Jakob:

In the quoted testimonies and passages, Cyril does not call Christ's flesh vivific by reason of merit, but rather [339] attributes the power and virtue of vivifying to the operation proper to divinity, communicated to Christ's flesh through the indwelling. To this point, we refer the audience to the passages of Cyril just quoted, and commend them to their judgment. For the words of Cyril cannot be clearer.

THE POWER OF VIVIFYING BELONGING TO CHRIST'S FLESH NOT SEPARATE FROM DIVINITY.

Next, Dr. Beza speaks about the power or virtue of vivifying having been poured out into Christ's flesh, as if it has been poured out from the separate substance of the divinity of the Word [ὁ λόγος], that is, of the Son of God, and from there, into the assumed humanity, as if someone were to pour out oil from one glass into another. On this point, he should know that this opinion or thought never crossed our mind.

One power of vivifying in Christ.

For there is one life in Christ, one vivifier, that is, one vivific power and virtue in Christ, namely the eternal, infinite one proper and essential to divinity. There are not two, one eternal and essential, proper to divinity, and the other, created, and separate from the essential divinity, poured out into the human nature, by which the humanity has become vivific *in itself in the way* that the Son of God possesses the vivific virtue *in himself.* Far be it from us, I say, that we ever have thought such a thing about the man Christ, not to mention believed, spoken, or written! Likewise we spoke above also about the twofold omnipotence, the eternal uncreated and the created divinity, all of which are falsely attributed to us.

Power of vivifying essential to God, communicated to Christ's flesh.
Power of vivifying is the work of the whole Christ.

On the contrary, we say that the life, the power and virtue of vivifying proper and essential to divinity, has been really communicated to the human nature of Christ by the personal union and joining together with the word, such that now following this accomplished union and glorified human nature, this life, which is the Word [λόγος] itself, the Son of God, does not work distinctly in such a way that the power of this operation is not communicated to the humanity. We say rather that the flesh of Christ works and effects the life and vivification by means of the real and true communication of the virtue of vivifying.

<340>

Thus the Fathers of the Synod of Ephesus teach us to come forward to receive the Eucharist and to eat Christ's flesh not as the body of some common person or even of a sanctified man, but rather the proper body of Life itself, which on account of this communication of the virtue of vivifying, which it has in *itself,* is also truly vivifying food. Without this real communication, the eating of the body of Christ in the Lord's Supper, which happens orally, would be mere Capernaitic flesh-eating [κρεοφαγία] and cyclopic carnage of Christ's flesh. The Fathers accused Nestorius of this, though he himself denied the charge, that he only took issue with the communication of the properties of humanity.

IN WHAT WAY CHRIST'S FLESH IS SAID TO HAVE LIFE *IN ITSELF*.

The words of the Fathers of the Council of Ephesus read thus: And so we come forward for mystical blessings and are sanctified, made participants in the holy flesh and precious blood of the savior of us all, receiving it not as common flesh, which it is not at all, nor even as the flesh of a sanctified man, joined to the Word according to the unity of dignity, or as if possessing a divine indwelling, *but as truly the vivifier*, and flesh become proper to the word itself. For the life existing naturally *as God* confessed that the flesh, since it is one with his own flesh, is the vivifier. So therefore, although it may be said to us, Amen I say to you, unless you eat the flesh of the son of man, nevertheless we ought not to think about this as the flesh of *one* of us. For in what way will the flesh of a man be able to be vivific *according to its own nature? But as truly become proper to it*, which the son of man became for us. Thus far the words of the Fathers of the Council of Ephesus. Besides, the audience of the Colloquy should recall that the phrase "*in itself*," which we explained above, is ambiguous, when it is said that the flesh of Christ possesses the virtue of vivifying *in itself*, or rather it does not possess this. For it is understood in two ways as proper to the place in which the phrase is attributed. Divinity alone possesses the power *in itself* in this way of speaking, but otherwise it means communicated power, as when Paul says of Christ: The whole fullness of Deity dwells in him bodily, that is, *in his flesh*, <341> just as all the Orthodox Fathers interpret. But no one doubts that by fullness of divinity is contained also life, or the power of vivifying. For this reason also it is truly and correctly said that Christ's flesh has life *in itself*, even though divinity possesses it in itself in another way than his humanity or his flesh possesses it in itself. Scripture speaks the same way, nay Christ himself, when he says, he gave the son to have *life in himself*, and gave him power also to make judgment, *since he is the son of man* (John 5[:26–27]).

IN WHAT WAY THE POWER OF VIVIFYING COMMON TO EITHER NATURE.

Since therefore Christ has life in himself in a twofold way, namely as God and as man, for this reason the operation of vivification is attributed *not distinctly* to only one nature, that is, only to the divinity nor only to the humanity, but rather to both at the same time. And indeed it is ascribed to either *in itself*, but to the divinity only *through itself*, and to the humanity only on account of the joining together with the word.

Now that this ambiguity of the phrase has been explained, everyone understands that nothing is deprived the Deity by the communication of vivification in the flesh of Christ which is proper to it, nor is anything attributed to the humanity of which it has not become capable of bearing or sharing. And so the whole Christ, God and Man, works vivification in the mysteries.

But since your Theses plainly say that the power of vivifying proper to divinity has not been communicated to the assumed nature, I am asking and begging for at least *one* testimony of holy Scripture to be offered by you, by which it may be proved that the vivific power in Christ's flesh is not proper to divinity but rather some created thing?

Dr. Beza:

WHETHER THE POWER OF VIVIFYING PROPER TO DIVINITY HAS BEEN COMMUNICATED TO CHRIST'S FLESH.

That which is proper cannot be communicated. The power and virtue of vivifying, about which you are speaking, is proper to divinity. Therefore it cannot be communicated to the assumed human nature. <342> *For if it is something in common, it ceases to be proper. If it remains proper, it cannot be communicated. When the man Christ is called Jehovah, the power of vivifying is attributed to him. Therefore we do not deny that it is attributed to the man, but we do not say that it is attributed to the humanity or else humanity would be Jehovah or divinity, which I want proved to me.*

Dr. Jakob:

I hear reasoning and interpretation, but no testimony of Scripture by which it may be proved that the power of vivifying *in the flesh* of Christ is some created thing, and not a power and virtue proper to divinity itself. I am looking for only *one* testimony of Scripture by which it may be proved or by which it may be possible to be proved.

CYRIL EMPLOYS ABSTRACT TERMS IN REGARD TO THE COMMUNICATION OF VIVIFICATION.

Now, I produced four or five patent testimonies from Cyril, in which he ascribes the power of vivifying to Christ's flesh. In these he employs not the concrete term, as you call it, "man," but rather the abstract one, "flesh." Christ's flesh (he says), Christ's body, the nature of the flesh, vivifies. The body of life was transformed to the life of God; flesh was drawn to the virtue of life, and ascended, etc.

Dr. Beza:

WHETHER THINGS THAT ARE PROPER CAN BE COMMUNICATED SUCH THAT THEY NEVERTHELESS REMAIN THINGS THAT ARE PROPER.

What is proper can be communicated in no way, and can be in common with something else in no way, unless it ceases to be something that is proper. For what is in common and what is proper are opposites, and cannot subsist simultaneously or be predicated about one and the same thing.

Dr. Jakob:

WHAT SORT OF THING IS THE COMMUNICATION OF PROPERTIES. ANALOGY OF IGNITED IRON.

It was demonstrated above, before your eyes, that things that are proper can be communicated without confusion, by the analogy of ignited iron. Even though the fire communicates to the iron the power of glowing and burning, which are and remain properties of fire, and are never in iron as they are in fire, nevertheless they are communicated to the iron truly and really, and are in it through the union, and make the iron, by their communication, what it could not be without this communication. Nor <343> on this account does the power of glowing and burning become proper to iron, or cease to be proper to fire.

Thus the operation of vivification, that is, the power and virtue of vivifying, remains proper to divinity, and is never proper to the humanity of Christ; nevertheless it is, notwithstanding, truly and really communicated to the same. For Christ's flesh does not vivify by means of some nature, inherent, inseparable, created virtue of vivifying, but rather by means of the virtue proper to divinity and communicated to it, it does the things that divinity does. For this power of vivifying cannot be separated from divinity, since it is essential, and essentially proper to God. But if the divinity were separated from the flesh of Christ (which nevertheless will never happen), the power of vivifying would also be separated from Christ's flesh. Just as all virtues and operations of the soul are separated from the body when it is separated from the body. This, I think, all the audience can understand.

Dr. Beza:
You should prove that the humanity of Christ became Deity; then you will have proved also, and I will concede, that it has in itself the power and virtue of vivifying, just as Deity has.

Dr. Jakob:

V. REGARDING THE RELIGIOUS ADORATION OF CHRIST'S FLESH, THAT IS, HUMANITY.

Since you can bring forward exactly no testimony of Scripture against us either regarding the communication of the attribute of vivification proper to Divinity, which attribute we have manifestly demonstrated was communicated to Christ's flesh according to the plain words of Christ and the indubitable testimonies of the Fathers, let us proceed to the last attribute of God, which is *religious adoration*. And we will prove that it also has been truly and really communicated to the flesh of Christ, that is, his humanity. If anyone does not call upon him *with one adoration*, with the son, as the true object of adoration, we consistently and fearlessly assert that he destroys the unity of the person of Christ and with Nestorius separates the natures in Christ. My argument proceeds in this way.

<344>

SYLLOGISM. SEPARATION OF ADORATION SEPARATES THE NATURES IN CHRIST.

Whoever directs his adoration in Christ to Deity alone, this man separates the natures and divides the person. You teach that religious adoration should be directed to Deity alone, as the sole object of adoration. Therefore with Nestorius you separate his natures and divide his person.

Dr. Beza:

DR. BEZA'S ONE PERPETUAL ANSWER TO THE QUESTION ABOUT THE COMMUNICATION OF GOD'S ATTRIBUTES. ANALOGY OF A KING CROWNED, CLOTHED IN PURPLE, AND HOLDING A SCEPTER.

None of us teaches that the man Christ should not be worshiped, but we deny only that the humanity should be worshiped. For the man is one thing and the humanity is another. The man Christ is to be worship since he is GOD. But the humanity, that is, the flesh of Christ, is not God. Therefore it is not also an object of worship, even though it has been personally united to the Word [λόγος]. We worship the whole Christ, but not the Whole of Christ, that is, the humanity with the Deity. We will explain this with an analogy. I worship a King or Prince clothed in purple, crowned, holding a scepter in his right hand. In that worship I do not pay heed to the crown which he wears on his head or to the purple with which he is dressed or to the scepter which he holds in his hand. Nevertheless I do not separate the crown, the purple, or the scepter from the King. So also in the religious adoration of Christ, we direct our invocation to the Son of God, that is, to his divinity, as to the sole, proper object of religious adoration, and not to his humanity. Nevertheless we do not separate the humanity from the Deity of the Son of God. For we distinguish the natures and their properties; we do not separate them.

Dr. Jakob:

Reverend Dr. Beza, I humbly and reverently ask not only your dignity, but also especially the Honorable Prince, Count Frederick, and the rest of the Gentlemen of the audience, that ³⁴⁵ they be willing patiently to offer their ears to me while I recite a few passages from the book which I have in my hands.

THE BLASPHEMOUS DOCTRINE OF LAMBERT DANEAU REGARDING THE RELIGIOUS ADORATION OF CHRIST'S FLESH, PAGE 415.

This is a book by Lambert Daneau, printed in 1581, Titled *Examination of the book of Dr. Chemnitz regarding the two natures in Christ.* The following words appear, which I want briefly to read.

RELIGIOUS ADORATION SHOULD NOT BE DIRECTED TO CHRIST'S FLESH EVEN IN THE UNION ITSELF.

First of all, therefore, our position must be explained briefly, which is emphatically this: That the whole Christ is indeed to be worshiped and called upon by us lest we divide the person of Christ (which is unique, consisting of both natures), or separate it. But worship ought not be directed *to the whole of Christ*, lest we confuse the natures which remain in the person unconfused, or regard the human as equal to the divine. Both our worship and invocation are in fact not rendered or directed properly and of themselves to the flesh *of Christ itself*, that is, to the human nature, *but rather to the Deity of Christ itself*, nor indeed as it subsists by itself and separate, outside of the assumed human nature (as Nestorius understood, and Cyril refuted in his Anathemas), but instead as it is ever joined together with the same assumed nature in one person, and remains united. For in the same way when we praise anyone (for example Apollo, the fellow-worker [συνεργός] of Paul) as blessed [εὐλόγιον] and endowed with the greatest faculty of reasoning and understanding, we indeed praise the whole man

himself, who consists of body and soul, and we celebrate and proclaim him. Nevertheless the praise and
proclamation of that person's reason and intelligence
pertains only to his mind, which nevertheless remains not
separately and in itself, but rather conjoined together
with its own body. In such a way do we offer our adoration and invocation indeed to the whole Christ (who
is God and man) but nevertheless the praise in and
of itself, and the invocation and worship, *we offer not
to the whole of Christ, but rather to his Deity, and this we
regard*, even though it does not subsist piecemeal [ἀνὰ
μέρος], that is, not having a hypostasis of its own, by
itself, outside of the human nature. In summary therefore, while we worship Christ, and call upon him <346>
(though here we are talking about religious worship
and adoration, but not civil adoration and and invocation, a point on which we agree with Chemnitz),
neither our invocation nor adoration is directed at, in and
of itself, *or looks toward,* the flesh of Christ itself, *even
though it remains in the union of the person.*[40] And these
are some of the many reasons for our opinion.

**1. THE ONE WHO PLACES HIS TRUST IN THE MAN CHRIST AND WORSHIPS HIM
IS CURSED, ACCORDING TO DANEAU.**

---

1. First. The man is cursed (says the Prophet, speaking as the very person of God) who puts his trust in
   man, and makes flesh his arm (Jeremiah 17:5). Now
   the flesh of Christ is true flesh, and the man Christ
   is true man. But the one who adores or calls upon
   any man in religious worship puts his trust in him
   whom he thus calls upon and worships. Therefore
   he who directs his worship to the flesh of Christ
   itself has been cursed by the mouth of God himself.

---

40   This sentence in the printed edition has a printer's mark in the margin connected to a "N.B." (*nota bene*).

2. Second. They are true Idolaters who serve, that is adore or call upon those, who by nature are not Gods (Galatians 4[:8]). Now Christ's flesh is not by nature God, even though it is hypostatically united to the true God. Therefore those who direct their invocation particularly to it are true Idolaters. But this *word nature* is of such great significance in this passage of Paul, that even if Chemnitz's construct of the real communication of the essential properties of Deity into the assumed human nature were true, nevertheless the result would not be that on this account Christ's flesh was an object of worship, which it would be God by Grace and not by nature.

3. Those who worship Christ's flesh condemned, according to Daneau.

3. Third. Those who adore or call upon their own fellow-slaves who are from among their brothers in religious worship are chastised by the holy Spirit himself through his angel and condemned (Revelation 19:10; 22:8). And Christ, as man, is fellow-slave and one of our brothers, even if he is the firstborn. Therefore as man, Christ should not be adored or called upon.

4. Fourth. Only God should be adored (Revelation 19:10). But Christ's flesh is not God. Therefore.

Those who worship Christ's flesh are blasphemers according to Daneau. Horrible to hear.

5. Fifth. He who calls upon a creature or adores one with religious worship, [347] is a blasphemer against God (Deuteronomy 4:6; 10:17; Matthew

4:10). Christ's flesh remains a creature, even though it is glorified and in the union of the person of Christ (Augustine on John, sermon 58), *therefore he who directs his worship to it blasphemes God.*

6. Paul, though he says Christ should be adored, explains that it is to be attributed to him by reason of his nature, calling him God (Romans 9:5). Therefore Christ, as God, *and not as man*, should be adored.

GLORY OF ADORATION HAS NOT BEEN COMMUNICATED TO CHRIST'S HUMANITY, ACCORDING TO DANEAU.

---

7. The Lord says (Isaiah 43[42:8]), I will not give my glory to another. Therefore the glory of God should not be given to him. And this is the glory of God: religious worship.

FALSE.

---

8. This was once the error of Nestorius: he taught that Christ, as he is man, should be worshiped together with the Word. Therefore he is a Nestorian who teaches and stresses the same thing today.

FALSE. ALL THE FATHERS TEACH THE OPPOSITE. WHETHER CHRIST'S FLESH AN OBJECT OF WORSHIP. QUOTATION OF DANEAU, P. 419.[41] FALSE AND IMPIOUS HUMAN REASONING. QUOTATION OF DANEAU, P. 420. SOLE FOUNDATION OF DANEAU AGAINST THE RELIGIOUS ADORATION OF THE FLESH OF CHRIST. IF WE BELIEVE DANEAU, CHRIST'S FLESH NOT TO BE WORSHIPED EVEN IN THE UNION ITSELF. NOT EVEN UNITED WITH THE WORD IS THE FLESH AN OBJECT OF RELIGIOUS WORSHIP. HORRIBLE TO HEAR.

---

9. All the Orthodox Fathers teach that our invocation and adoration *should not be directed* to the flesh of Christ itself, *even as it remains in the*

---

41   This annotation in the printed edition is followed by a "N.B." (*nota bene*).

hypostasis of the Son of God, *but rather to the very* Deity of the Son. Therefore he contradicts the Orthodox Fathers and the pious and learned ancient practice of the Church who desires and thinks and says, when Christ is adored or called upon, that *the flesh of Christ itself is also* an object of this sort of adoration and invocation. And a little later, But I ask, how can it happen that, if Christ's human nature, just as the divine also, should be worshiped and adored, that it would itself not also be divine, that is, God? And would it follow logically that the distinction between the natures still remain preserved? And a little later, Chemnitz first of all works partly from the very solid and unvanquished foundation by which it is said that no creature ought to be worshiped, and partly by the making sport of the very true and suitable analogy of the crown by which the King is adorned, and which is greeted along with the King himself. Therefore (says Chemnitz), Christ's flesh should not be adored **<348>** *apart from the union.* But who ever said this or thought this? Much to the contrary, the Fathers themselves, whose testimonies I have offered, deny, and clearly so, that Christ's flesh, even as it remains in the union, ought to have our adoration directed to it. Therefore Chemnitz seeks precedence, and perverts the Fathers, while he wishes to twist their opinions to his own, though they teach so clearly that not even united to the Word [λόγος] is the flesh in Christ an object of our worship. And the reason is, since the flesh of Christ, *even in the union*, is true flesh, and truly creature. And so *it is never to be adored with religious worship.*

Thus far the words of Daneau, read from his book.[42]

---

42   This sentence in the printed edition has a printer's mark in the margin pointing to this section.

CONSIDERATION OF CHRIST'S HUMANITY TO BE FAR REMOVED IN RELIGIOUS ADORATION OF CHRIST, ACCORDING TO DANEAU.

He also wrote in a pamphlet, published not so long ago at Geneva, titled Assertion, etc., that the consideration of Christ's humanity in religious adoration was not only not necessary, but even *ought to be removed far away from that adoration, lest worship,* which is owed to God alone, be attributed also to it. His words are (pp. 38–39): No consideration of flesh or human nature is necessary. Much to the contrary, *it should be utterly removed* from religious adoration of God and the divine nature, even *in Christ himself.* Since this *honor* is owed *to God alone* (Deuteronomy 6[:14–15]; Matthew 4[:10]).[43] Thus far the words of Daneau.

DANEAU'S BLASPHEMOUS OPINION REGARDING THE ADORATION OF CHRIST. WHAT DANEAU MEANS BY THE WORDS *PARTICULARLY* AND *OF ITSELF* [*PROPRIE ET PER SE*]. DANEAU'S HORRENDOUS AND ABOMINABLE DOCTRINE REGARDING THE WORSHIP OF CHRIST.

Honorable Prince and gentlemen of the Audience, I pray humbly and with all my strength that these words be weighed carefully. Their meaning is this: that in religious worship and the invocation of Christ, every thought should be directed to the divinity alone as the sole object of religious worship, such that the divinity alone is *the one* object of religious adoration. But whoever should join the divinity and the humanity of Christ in his religious worship and invocation, and say the two are at the same time the object of worship, such that he trusts not only on the divinity but also on the assumed man, and call upon him with one religious adoration, this man has been cursed by God's decree as an Idolater, a blasphemer, and condemned, since he attributes to the creature <349> what ought to be attributed to God and his divinity alone. And lest anyone think, when he says: The Human nature is *not particularly and of itself* an object of religious adoration, that he means this about the human nature considered without respect to the union, and as if a separate thing, he explains himself in clear words what is meant by these terms "particularly and of itself," or what he wants to be understood, namely that the

---

43   This annotation in the printed edition is followed by a "N.B." (*nota bene*).

human nature of Christ is *in no way* an object of worship, considered *even in the union itself*, because it is a creature and *not by nature* God, since in the union itself it is also remains creature, and for this reason can *never* be called upon without Idolatry. This is why he clearly proposes in express words: *never to be adored with religious worship*. I am in no way slandering but rather have recited his words in good faith, his very public words, just now recited, and am briefly explaining the meaning they teach, without the least bit of corruption or distortion. This teaching regarding the worship of Christ, Honorable Prince and gentlemen of the audience, is quite horrendous to hear. That no confidence should be placed in the man Christ; that whoever should do so has been cursed by God's decree; that he is not to be called upon by us in temptations, trial, and afflictions; though nevertheless the supreme consolation has been deposited for us in the man Christ, that is, in his humanity, since without this Mediator no access to God would lie open to us in our prayers. The Son of God alone, however, without his humanity, is not the Mediator. Rather, as often as we think about the Mediator, it is necessary that his humanity also come to mind with pious thoughts. As it is written, There is one God, and one Mediator of God and men, *the Man Jesus Christ* (1 Timothy 2[:5]).

Therefore in worshiping him we speak not only with his divinity, as Daneau falsely and impiously teaches, with the humanity removed (indeed inseparable from the divinity, but merely separated from it in the mind, lest it become a sharer in this honor and worship), but rather we direct our invocation to the very human Spirit of Christ as to <350> the true object also of this religious worship, with one prayer, not separate prayers, as if to our Priest, who tempted according to the flesh, we believe is able to suffer our temptations and help us, as the Apostle says (Hebrews 2[:18], 4[:15]).

For even if the human nature is and remains creature, even in the union itself, nevertheless the Lord deemed it worthy to be assumed into the unity of his person, and placed it at God's right hand of power and Majesty, such that it may not be removed in our thinking from the religious worship of the Son of God, but rather no less worship should be directed to it than to the Deity itself, *since* it has been united personally with the Son of God and has been seated on the throne proper to God at the right hand of the omnipotent Father.

THE WHOLE CHRIST IS WORSHIPED BY MEANS OF ONE ADORATION, DEITY AND HUMANITY.

Likewise Stephan, when he saw Christ standing at the right hand of God, is said to have prayed: *Lord Jesus, receive my spirit* (Acts 7[:59]). Stephan did not see divinity. So he directed his invocation not to the Deity alone, but also to the man, whom he did see standing at the right hand of God, as to the true object of his worship, whom he trusted was true God, and he did not turn his invocation away from the humanity. So also do we call upon him with one adoration, not separately God and separately man, but the Whole Christ. He is Whole, God and man, the object of religious worship, proper indeed to divinity, but communicated to his human nature.

IN ADMONITION REGARDING THE BOOK OF CONCORD.

When therefore it is said that the humanity of Christ is not an object of religious worship, that he does not hear our prayers in heaven according to his humanity, as the Heidelberg Theologians said plainly, it deprives pious consciences in the midst of trial and calamities the greatest part of consolation, which is intolerable in the Church of God, and openly condemned by Anathema in the eighth Council of Ephesus as impious and blasphemous. These are its words: If anyone dares <351> to say that the assumed man must be worshiped alongside, glorified alongside, and named alongside God the Word, *such that* he worships *one with the other*, and does not rather worship Immanuel with one worship, and apply one glorification to him, in as far as the word became flesh, let him be Anathema.

ANALOGY OF A KING, ROBED IN PURPLE, CROWNED, AND WIELDING A SCEPTER, MOST UNSUITABLE.

As far as the analogy of the King's Diadem, scepter, and purple robe is concerned, which you say is very fitting, we respond that it is by far most unsuitable, and the reason is twofold: since the King's Diadem, purple robe, and scepter have no understanding, nor do

they constitute with the King one person. Therefore a person ador-
ing the King and bending the knee does not speak to the King's
diadem, scepter, and purple robe, nor bend his knee to them, nor is
the honor of his adoration directed to those things, but rather to the
King himself.

But Christ's humanity is not like a diadem, a scepter, or a purple
robe, but rather is necessarily required to constitute the person of
Christ, without which nature the Son of God is not Christ, though he
is king, and remains king, even if he lays aside his diadem, purple
robe, or scepter, which he is also accustomed to do.

For this reason when I worship Christ, not only is the Deity the
object of my religious adoration, as Lambert Daneau impiously
asserts, but the humanity with the Deity is the object, and thus properly the *Whole* Christ, God and man, whom I adore equally as Lord
and brother and my flesh in this way: Behold Lord Jesus Christ, I am
your flesh. But you, lifted up to such high majesty nevertheless do
not despise me, but have deigned to acknowledge me as your brother.
Therefore I place into your lap my misery, that you may be to me a
helper in this my tribulation in which I have found myself.

ANALOGY OF THE SOUL AND HUMAN BODY IS MORE SUITABLE TO THE
ADORATION OF CHRIST.

Therefore an analogy by far more suitable, which the Fathers
employ, is that of the body and soul of a man: "Just as flesh and
rational soul (says the Athanasian Creed) [352] is one person, so God
and man is one Christ." In the invocation of him, that is, the adoration of him, we speak not with the soul alone (if he were a King), nor
with the body alone, but rather with his body and soul, regarding not
only his soul but also his body as an object of adoration, and we also
observe precisely the attitude of his body, whether the King listens
with a calm expression to our petition, which not only the soul hears,
but the body as well.

This analogy is (I say) very suitable and fitting, by which the
communication of the honor of adoration may be explained, which
one and same honor is presented not only to the Deity but also to

the flesh, that is, to the humanity of Christ, in religious invocation. It is expressed in this way, that not divinity alone, but also his
humanity, indeed the Whole Christ, God and Man, pays heed to and
understands our prayers, and not by the property of his own human
nature, or else Peter and Paul would also hear us, but rather by the
communication of the property of divine Majesty, which was communicated to the human nature, truly and really in Christ, in the
Personal union by exaltation to the Throne proper to divinity.

Meanwhile the opposing party denies this communication of
properties of divinity in the assumed humanity of Christ; they fall
into this offensive and horrendous error as they teach that Christ
according to the human nature does not regard our prayers, since
this is proper to the omnipotent nature alone, and so as a result he
should not be called upon either according to his humanity. This is of
course horrendous to hear in the Church of God.

Dr. Beza:
This is preaching, not disputing and debating.

Dr. Jakob:
I was a little too prolix in explaining the teaching of our Churches
regarding the true and religious adoration of Christ, [353] which I
judge necessary, and has been not in the least annoying to the members of the audience. After this I will practice brevity, as much as I
can.

Dr. Beza:

EXCUSE AND APPROVAL OF DANEAU'S BOOK AGAINST RELIGIOUS ADORATION
OF CHRIST'S FLESH. SEE IN BEZA'S RESPONSE AT THESIS 20. CYRIL IN JOHN,
BOOK 2, CP. 92, ON THESE WORDS: WE WORSHIP WHAT WE KNOW. CYRIL TO
THEODOSIUS ON THE RIGHT FAITH.

If Daneau were here, he would have something he could answer.
These duties have not been given to us such that we can answer
on his behalf. But you will find nothing in him other than that the
humanity is not to be worshiped, since flesh is not God. You are
taking abstract things as concrete, and saying that it is the same

*thing if it should be said, The Man Christ is to be worshiped, and
the Humanity of Christ is to be worshiped. The former, Daneau
concedes; the latter on the other hand he denies, and we do too. It
cannot be concluded because of this therefore that Daneau means,
The Man Christ is not to be worshiped, that is, called upon. For The
Whole Christ is adored, but not the Whole of Christ. Abstract and
concrete terms should not be confused, and a distinction between
the natures and properties, against a Eutychian confusion of the
natures and properties, ought to be maintained. We read that Cyril
did this carefully, who left us his writing on John, Book 2, cp. 92,
as follows: The humanity, says Cyril, considered simply IN ITSELF
and not in the relation counts itself among those who worship, and
Christ also worships, AS MAN, after he became Man. But he is
always worshiped with the Father and the Spirit since he is true
God according to his nature. And again, Should we should worship
Immanuel as a man (in himself, namely, considered absolutely in the
union)? No. This in fact would be nonsense, both a deception and
also a mistake. In doing so we would in fact differ in no way from
those who worship the creature alongside the maker and author.*

Dr. Jakob:

DANEAU'S WORDS AND MEANING ARE IMPIOUS AND BLASPHEMOUS AGAINST
CHRIST.

Daneau's words recited from his book are patent, plain, and <354>
perspicuous., when he says: Christ's flesh is true flesh, and the Man
Christ is *true man*. But whoever *adores any person* with religious
worship places his trust in the one whom he calls upon and adores.
And he adapts the Passage of Jeremiah to Christ *the man*, not without very great blasphemy: Cursed is the man who *places his trust in a
man*. What plainer slander and blasphemy could therefore be uttered
against *the man* Christ?

CONSENSUS IN WORDS, DISAGREEMENT IN REALITY AND UNDERSTANDING OF
THE WORDS. A HIDING PLACE OF ERROR UNDER THE PROPOSITION "MAN IS TO
BE WORSHIPED" IS EXPOSED. WORDPLAY IN THE PHRASES BEING USED.
DECEPTION OF SIMPLE MEN.

But the distinction you make between man and humanity, the proposition you concede when it is said, The Man Christ should be worshiped, but you deny, when it is said, The Humanity of Christ is Omnipotent or to be worshiped, is nothing other than word tricks, as was said and shown just a bit ago. What, pray tell, is man without humanity? Remove body and soul from a man, what will remain? A name without the thing. If Christ's humanity even *in the union itself* (which Daneau repeats and emphasizes over and over again) is not to be worshiped, how ever can it be said truly by you that the man Christ is to be worshiped? For just as you interpreted and explained these pronouncements above: Man is omnipotent, omniscient, omnipresent, that is, the Deity joined to the humanity is omnipotent, omniscient, omnipresent, so also you interpret and explain this proposition: Man is to be worshiped. But I do not think there is any one in this gathering who would not understand that this is pure word trickery, contrived for the purpose of deceiving simple people, such that when they hear you also saying that Christ should be worshiped, they may think that there is no difference between us in this matter, though we disagree to as great an extent as the heaven is distant from the earth.

RESPONSE TO THE COMMON SAYING, REGARDING *THE WHOLE* CHRIST, AND *THE WHOLE OF* CHRIST.

We answer the same thing also to the saying that has been brought up by you so often: The Whole Christ should be worshiped, but the Whole of Christ should not be, since his humanity should not be worshiped. Here once again we call upon the judgment of the audience, whether the Christ is whole without his humanity? Or is humanity not also required for the Whole Christ? <355> Since Christ's whole person consists not only of divinity but also of humanity, then without humanity he is not Christ. Therefore the entire audience sees and feels palpably that what you are asserting is quite false: that the Whole Christ is worshiped, if his humanity is removed from our thoughts and not worshiped with religious adoration at the same time.

To the Words of Cyril we answer: they are quite true, just as all the other ones also, which you have brought forward from this author on the topic of vivification. For just as Christ's flesh *as flesh* cannot vivify, so also Christ's humanity *in itself*, without respect to its union with the divinity, should not be worshiped.

REFUTATION OF THE PERVERSION OF CYRIL'S WORDS. HOW THE RESPECT OF THE UNION SHOULD BE UNDERSTOOD IN CYRIL AND THE FATHERS. FALSE INTERPRETATION OF THE RESPECT OF THE UNION WITH THE WORD. BEZA IS DECEIVED BY THE ANALOGY OF THE KING'S PURPLE ROBE.

But Cyril did not interpret or explain the respect as Dr. Beza interprets and explains it. For Cyril understands by respect of union a communication of dignity and honor of worship, a real one made in the human nature. Christ (says Cyril) always receives worship and adoration from the Angels. He was in fact always God. But now they also worship *him as man* (Cyril on the Epistle to the Hebrews 1). Chrysostom explained it in clearer words: It truly is great, amazing, and full of wonder *that our flesh* is seated above and worshiped by Angels and Archangels, Cherubim and Seraphim. Frequently do I turn this about in my mind, and *undergo ecstasy* (Chrysostom on Hebrews 2). But Dr. Beza and his party interpret the respect without the communication of this honor, just as if someone were speaking with the King's hat, scepter, or purple robe, when he addresses the King. And as much as a hat, that is, a crown or diadem, a scepter, or a purple robe actually hears and understands, just so much also does Christ's humanity hear in the heavens when we call upon Christ, since it belongs only to the omnipotent nature to listen to the thoughts and sighs of all hearts (which are very effective prayers, even if the lips do not move), and this is not communicated to any creature, no, not even Christ's human nature, according to your opinion. Indeed, this is why this honor of invocation or of religious adoration is suited to him. We judge that this assertion is not only false, but also plainly impious.

<356>

HOW THE ADVERSARIES FALL INTO ERROR REGARDING WORSHIP.

But they fall into that error because of a twisted application of the analogy of the king's vestment or coronation, as if the purple robe's union with the King is the same as that of Christ's humanity with the Son of God. Even if they do not say it, nevertheless they make their arguments against the Religious worship of Christ's flesh by this analogy contrary to us after this fashion, and defend the horrible error.

GENUINE MEANING OF CYRIL'S WORDS.

But when Cyril says that the humanity counts itself among the worshipers and that Christ worships *as a man*, again, it would be absurd if we should adore Christ *as* the man Immanuel, not simply, but according to what it says and means, namely, if we should understand the man Christ merely by reason of the property of the human nature, without respect to the communicated divine Majesty. In fact, in the same book Cyril says to Theodosius, I am of the opinion that Christ's humanity must not be deprived of divine glory, should it be understood and spoken about in Christ.

For in so far as *he is a man*, and in as much as *he is a man in and of himself*, he worshiped God the Father just as another man, with hands raised to heaven, and for this reason was also numbered among those who worship. And in so far as he is considered *a man in and of himself*, he is not Immanuel, but only in so far as he has been personally united and joined together with the Son of God.

But since as Mediator and intercessor he has prayed for us, but he is not a Mediator as man only, but also as God, to the point that he is at the same time God and Man, in order that he might fulfill this office of Mediator, he emptied himself by reason of the communicated Majesty, in order that he might as God and man worship, and at the same time as not only God and the Son of God, but also as man, not drive away his worshipers. So Peter says, You are the Christ, the Son of the living God. Though his disciples called upon him in the boat as a man (they did not in fact speak only with his divinity), he did not drive them away as blasphemous idolaters, but rather commanded the winds to clear away, and did so to the supreme astonishment of the people who attributed this miracle <357> to a man. Who is this, they said, whom even the sea and winds obey?

But here again Dr. Beza messes around with equivocation, that is, the ambiguity of the terms "*in itself*" which refer to Christ's humanity in such a way that he excludes it altogether from worship, whether it is understood in the union or apart from the union. Cyril does not do this. For this reason it is absurd, a deception and error, just as Cyril says.

HOW CHRIST'S HUMANITY IS OR IS NOT WORSHIPED *IN ITSELF*.

Though his humanity is in fact not worshiped in *itself* as his divinity, which as it is adored does not lack the humanity, nevertheless this *very humanity* is worshiped *in itself* by reason of the union, that is on account of, or through, its union with the Son of God, who placed this humanity on his own Throne, proper to divinity, and communicated to it *equality of glory*, just as the Fathers plainly bear witness in the explanation of the words of the Psalm: Sit at my right hand. In Theodorus, dialogue 2, Athanasius: He has a body, to whom the Lord says: Sit at my right hand.

CHRIST GOD AND MAN, MEDIATOR IN HEAVEN AND EARTH.

So today also in heaven he acts as Mediator with the Father, and intercedes on our behalf. But it does not in any way follow on this account, which they falsely conclude, that Christ's humanity, existing in heaven, cannot be worshiped without blasphemy by us existing on earth. He does not in fact act as intercessor and advocate by means of bending his knees before God in a servile fashion, as was done on earth, but in consideration of his merit. He is Mediator between the Father and sinners by merit not only of his humanity but of the Whole Christ, God and man, even as he is at the same time God and Man, and not as man only.

I have seemed perhaps once again to preach. But not only had our teaching to be explained, but also the ambiguities of phrases had to be pointed out, and the genuine meaning of Cyril's words delivered, which you draw out under ambiguous phrases to an alien and purely contrary meaning. For this reason I beg your pardon for my wordiness, which I have of necessity frequently had to employ in the Colloquy. I trust that it has not been disagreeable to the members of the audience, as they desire to know the truth.

<358>

Dr. Beza:

Christ's flesh, that is, his humanity, should not be worshiped, since it is not Deity, that is, God. Nothing should be worshiped which is not God. This honor is proper to God alone, as it is written: You will worship the Lord your God and serve him only (Matthew 4[:10]). We do not deny that the man Christ is to be worshiped, but we do not concede that the humanity of Christ should be worshiped IN ITSELF.

Dr. Jakob:

CONCERNING THE PHRASE, FLESH IS GOD.

This phrase, Flesh is God, is not ours, which Daneau attempts to thrust upon us, so that he can accuse us as innovators on some pretext. Rather it belongs to John of Damascus, not in the least a condemnable Ecclesiastical Writer, if we also trust the consensus of your Orthodox Author, since he infers this phrase from the words of John the Evangelist. If in fact what John says is true, The Word became flesh, then this proposition is also true: Flesh became the Word of God, where flesh means a man. These are the words of John of Damascus: Διὰ γὰρ τὴν καθ' ὑπόστασιν ἕνωσιν, ἡ σάρξ τεθεῶσθαι λέγεται, καὶ θεὸς γενέσθαι, καὶ ὁμὸς θεὸς τῷ λόγῳ.[44] That is, For on account of the union according to hypostasis, the *flesh* also is said to be deified, *and became God, at the same time God with the word.* You have therefore, my dear Beza, once for all time, not in my words, but in the words of John of Damascus, a response to the objection you and your associates have made so many times against us regarding the phrase *Flesh is God.* You cannot throw this back at us as the authors. For John

---

44   This is actually Cyril of Alexandria, *De sancta trinitate* (PG 77).

of Damascus writes plainly that *flesh becomes God*, and at the same time God is with the Word. What more do you want?

Next, it has been said many times that in this expression, Man is God, Man means a true man, from the substance of the Blessed virgin Mary, assumed by the Word [λόγος] into the unity of his person. For this reason it is false and corrupt if it be said to be equivalent to this proposition: The Son of God is God, who was joined together with this <359> man. Since therefore the assumed man is true God, not by the property of the human nature, but on account of the personal union with the Son of God, and is not two sons, but only one son, for this reason, removing any objection about humanity having been changed into divinity, nevertheless this man is truly God. For this reason the Son of God cannot be worshiped except you worship the humanity at the same time as and with the same prayer also, unless you should want to pull the humanity away from the Son of God and divide the person. That these things are true, even those of middling ability can understand.

But an error of this type also lies hidden under the terms "*in itself*," as has been said sufficiently above, lest anyone be deceived. They are set in opposition to the personal union, on account of which this honor of worship is not verbally, but rather really, attributed to the human nature. This honor is not suited to it by itself, outside of this union.

Dr. Beza:
It is one thing to worship a man, and another to worship the humanity.

Dr. Jakob:
I say that these are the same thing, just as they are really the same thing in Christ. For the Son of God assumed the man, and the Son of God assumed the humanity. And the orthodox Fathers employed either phrase to mean the same thing.

Dr. Beza:

I do not concede that they are the same thing. We worship a King in a purple robe, but we do not worship the purple robe.

Dr. Jakob:

I commend this to the judgment of the audience then. And we have demonstrated that the analogy of the King and the purple robe is not only unsuitable, but also absurd, and that its application to Christ's flesh is impious. Rather, offer *one* testimony of Scripture which proves that the humanity ought not be worshiped even in union with the Word [λόγος]?

<360>

Dr. Beza:

You will worship the Lord your God, and serve him only. Flesh, that is, the humanity of Christ, is not the LORD GOD. Therefore it ought not be worshiped.

Dr. Jakob:

For what reason are you able to reject the holy Spirit's phrase, and say that flesh is not God? When John says, The Word became flesh? When we take and interpret flesh to mean man, which you cannot deny. And for this reason even among all the Ecclesiastical Writers, these expressions are equivalent: The Word became flesh, God became man. And again, a man is God, Flesh is God, since flesh here in this sentence of Scripture means the whole man, just as I demonstrated quite plainly a little bit ago from John of Damascus.

Dr. Beza:

But John does not say, The flesh became Word, but rather he says, The Word became flesh.

Dr. Jakob:

But after the Word became flesh, I ask, whether these propositions are not interchangeable: Word became flesh, and Flesh became Word? God became man, and man became God?

Dr. Beza:
Scripture does not speak this way.

Dr. Jakob:
Right. For when John says, The Word became flesh, he wanted to signify that the Word, that is, the Son of God, existed before he had become flesh. But the flesh, that is, the assumed man, did not exist before it was assumed. But at that very <361> moment when the man began to be, he was God. Therefore the nature of correspondence of these propositions is the same, namely, the union of the person, however much the condition of the Word and the Flesh may not be the same. But after the Son of God became man, holy Scripture not only plainly says that this man is God, but also attributes to him the properties of the Deity, among which manifestly is reckoned also religious worship. In this regard, Psalm 72: And all the Kings of the earth will adore "the King."

Dr. Beza:
Flesh is not God. Therefore it is not to be worshiped.

Dr. Jakob:
If flesh means man, as we take John 1, when John says, the Word became flesh, then this proposition is equivalent to it: God became man. I respond, it is not only a false, but also a blasphemous and condemned expression, should someone say that flesh is not God, since it openly denies that man is God, which is understood by the noun *flesh.*

WHICH PHRASES THE CHURCH HAS CONDEMNED.

Indeed, the Church has condemned these propositions: Deity is humanity, humanity is Deity, and rightly, since in these the natures are predicated about themselves reciprocally in an absolute way, that is, without respect to the personal union, which is false. For even though a communication of natures has happened, nevertheless it did not happen in an absolute way, but rather it happened in the person of the Son of God, in which they were united.

But this proposition is never condemned by the Church: The flesh of Christ became God (where this term *flesh* means man). Rather, it is used and fought for by John of Damascus (Book 4 on the Orthodox Faith, cp. 19).

WORD-BATTLES [Λογομαχίαι] SHOULD BE AVOIDED IN THE CHURCH.

But we do not want to quarrel over the phrase, in light of the precept of Paul, when he sternly warns: You should adjure them before the Lord not to strive over words; it profits nothing except the destruction of your hearers (2 Timothy 2[:14]). Regarding this phrase, therefore, they should not strive with John of Damascus, <362> who used it piously. Let us talk about the thing itself. The question is in fact, when "Flesh" means true assumed man, whether the assumed flesh, that is, the human nature, ought to be worshiped?

Dr. Beza:
I reject this proposition: Flesh should be worshiped, for the same reason I reject this proposition: Flesh is God.

Dr. Jakob:

TESTIMONIES OF THE FATHERS REGARDING WORSHIP OF CHRIST'S FLESH.

You are fighting therefore not only against the express Word of God, but also with all of antiquity, which attests in plain words that Christ's flesh is to be worshiped.

Augustine (Regarding the words of the Lord, sermon 58): If Christ is not by nature God, but a creature, then he should be neither worshiped nor adored as God. Why is it therefore that you do not reject *his flesh*, which is creature, while at the same time *you adore it with the divinity, and* are devoted *to it not less* than to the Deity? I worship *the Lord's flesh*, rather, the humanity perfected in Christ, since it was assumed by the divinity and united to the Deity.

The same author, in the words of the Psalm (On Psalm 98): Worship his footstool; his footstool is the earth; and Christ assumed earth from earth, since *his flesh is from the earth and from the flesh of Mary* he received his flesh. And since he walked here in the very flesh, and gave his very flesh to us to eat for our salvation, though no one eats the *flesh* unless he has previously worshiped it, we discover how *the Lord's* footstool of this kind is worshiped, *and not only do we not* sin in worshiping it, but we would be sinning by not *worshiping it*. John of Damascus (Book 4, cp. 3): Christ's flesh is not adorable according to its own nature. But *it is adored* in God incarnate in the Word, not on account of itself, but rather on account of God the Word being joined with it according to hypostasis.

And again, Chrysostom (on Hebrews 2): He says that *our flesh is adored by the angels*, which as often as he thinks about it, causes him to experience Ecstasy. [363] Here Your Reverence, my dear Beza, hears that flesh is adored, that humanity is adored. What more do you want?

Dr. Beza:
The Fathers also speak inappropriately from time to time. The man is adored, not the humanity.

Dr. Jakob:
But what certainty will there be at the end about those things which should be believed and done, if we are to retain the proper sense of words neither in the words of Scripture nor in the sayings of the Fathers, and they all speak inappropriately in your opinion, when we place their very plain words in opposition to you?

Dr. Beza:
Scriptural diction was not unknown to the Fathers, and they also imitated it.

Dr. Jakob:
Scriptural diction is clear, and so is that of the Fathers. If it pleases you therefore to depart from them, and to attach an alien meaning to each utterance, we will have nothing sure in our religion. But I do ask, my dear Beza, whether the man Christ, that is, Christ

according to the flesh, or by reason of his humanity, also hears our prayers on earth.

Dr. Beza:
I think so, if he wants to.

Dr. Jakob:
This is not certainty of faith. Rather, it is fitting that we know for sure that he hears our prayers even before we begin to pray, and direct our prayer to him, otherwise we will pray in vain.

<364>

Dr. Beza:
The flesh, that is, the humanity of Christ, is worshiped relatively, but worship is not directed to the flesh itself, but rather to the Deity of the son, who hears the prayers and witnesses the groaning of our hearts.

Dr. Jakob:
Here relation does not hold a place, the way you understand it, as was said a little while ago. For it is not the sort of relation that a purple robe has to the King, as you fashion it when you say that the humanity of Christ is worshiped relatively. Rather the humanity is the object of adoration with the divinity, when we call upon Christ, such that religious worship is directed not less to the humanity itself than to the divinity. But since we hear the same thing from you all the time, not without annoyance to the audience, I do not see what more can be said about this matter. So let it suffice for us that your point is not proven nor has been proved by any testimony of Scripture, your point being that if the flesh, that is, the humanity of Christ, should be worshiped religiously, then by necessity it has to have been changed into divinity and Deity itself. In fact it is able to become a sharer in this honor and glory, just as it truly became a sharer in it, even if the true humanity remains in the person of Christ. We say that whoever withdraws this honor from the humanity of Christ divides the person of Christ with Nestorius, and separates the natures.

VI. Regarding the proposition: This man is God; whether it is true without a Figure of Speech. Blasphemy of the Heidelberg theologians in their admonition.

But we can append one thing as an Epilogue. For the Heidelberg Theologians write that this proposition can never be true: This man is God, but that it is impossible if the proper meaning of the endings of the subject and predicate, with their connecting verb, and again the proper meaning of the individual words, is retained. *Namely, Man* means man, *God* means God, *is* means it truly is, such that true man is true God. And so they contend that it is absurd, as if somebody should say, A cow is an ass, unless it is understood and explained by way of Figure of Speech. Since the species are different, <365> they cannot be talked about or predicated interchangeably. This, without doubt, is your meaning (so far as I have been able to gather in this disputation regarding the person of Christ), which I desire to hear from your Reverence.

Dr. Beza:
The Heidelbergers do not need our explanation or defense; they will answer for themselves. What is it to us what they have written?

Dr. Jakob:
In your Orthodox Consensus are read the following words:

> If ever they will dare truly to defend, with Luther, this
> expression: *That man is the Son of God*, what is to be
> understood by the subject *That man* is not the very Son
> of God, but rather the nature of the assumed human-
> ity, just as those sayings of Luther rashly seem man-
> ifestly to signify.

And in the preface of the same orthodox Consensus:

First, we cannot grant them that every Figure of Speech is excluded by the substantive verb *is*. Even John the Evangelist writes, The Word became flesh. This expression says something more than if he had said that the word was flesh. Nevertheless if anyone should wish to cling rather obstinately to the letter, he would fall into heresy; he will deny the Deity of Christ; the result will be that the Deity suffers mutation and is changed into the human nature. *It is therefore necessary to resort to a figure of speech.*

Thus far the words of the Orthodox Consensus (Fol 18, fasc. 2, first edition). I want to know whether your Reverence also approves of this sentence or condemns it. For this is what they want: that these expressions, Man is God, Word was made flesh, should be interpreted not literally as the words read, but rather figuratively and metaphorically, and not to be able to exist and be real in any other way. In like manner also in the words of Christ, This is my body, you contend that there is a figure of speech in it, and that it cannot be true without a figure of speech.
<366>

Dr. Beza:

DEFENSE OF THE AUTHOR OF THE ORTHODOX CONSENSUS.

Do you think that the author of the Orthodox consensus was so unlearned a person that he would deny that God is man and man is God? He was a religious man and now dwells with God. But as far as this point is concerned, our people do not deny this proposition: Man is God, but they teach how it must be explained.

EXPLANATION OF THE PROPOSITION, MAN IS GOD, ACCORDING TO BEZA.

We say that it is a figurative expression, which you call an unusual one, when it says, This man is God, since it is not a usual or regular predication in which disparate things are predicated together about themselves, as for example God about a man, since one species is not the other.

For this reason the word IS is interpreted by the word "assumed." Whence then also those expressions, God is mortal, suffered, was crucified, and expressions similar to these. Since God, that is, the Son of God, supports in his hypostasis the man, that is the flesh, which is mortal, suffered, and was crucified.

Dr. Jakob:

An expression is not figurative or metaphorical just because it is unusual and is said to be. For a figure of speech holds a place only in those expressions in which the proper meaning of the single terms cannot be retained intact by the analogy of faith.

IN JOHN'S WORDS *THE WORD BECAME FLESH* THERE IS NOT FIGURE OF SPEECH.
1. WORD. 2. FLESH. 3. *BECAME*.

What necessity obliges us, pray, as in the words of the Evangelist? The Word became flesh: must we retreat from the proper meaning of the terms and necessarily flee to a figure of speech? Or in what term is there a figure of speech? For "Word" properly denotes in this passage the eternal Son of God, and nothing else. And then, "Flesh" means man, a Scriptural usage, used by the Hebrews. Finally the word *"became"* [367] means substantially [ὑπαρκτικῶς], namely, that this Word truly and really became what it was not before, namely flesh, that is, man. The result is that the Word, that is the Son of God, truly and really became *man*, which before was just Word, and was not man.

If then in this expression, This man is God, the term *man* means a true man, properly and not figuratively or metaphorically, which consists of a body and a rational soul, namely Jesus the son of Mary of the seed of David, and the second term *God* means the true and eternal, essential Son of God, and that also properly, not figuratively or metaphorically, and the Third, the Word *is*, retains its own proper meaning, by which something that is expressed is said actually to be and exist, then Where, or in what term, will there be a figure of speech? If the utterance (according to your definition) is metaphorical, or if there must necessarily be recourse to a figure of speech? There is no need (no need, I say) that compels us to resort to a figure of speech, unless we should wish absolutely to deny the true incarnation of the Son of God and the unity of the person of Christ. For the Word truly and really became flesh, and God truly and really became man, truly I say and really, without any figure and without any metaphor.

Dr. Beza:

Surely you are not therefore saying that the Word was changed and converted into flesh? It would certainly follow if you were to accept the words of John, the Word became flesh, without a figure of speech.

Dr. Jakob:

But surely the Word cannot truly and really become flesh in any way except for being changed into flesh? How, pray, will you prove this? Surely there is not just one mode by which something is said truly to become, and no other one than it, by which a substance is changed into another substance? Or does it seem to you that <368> the Word did not really become flesh, unless the Word was transmuted into flesh, and God into a person, that is was transubstantiated and changed into one?

Dr. Beza:

Nevertheless you also say that this predication is unusual. Why therefore could it not be called figurative or metaphorical?

Dr. Jakob:

It is an unusual instance, and for this reason is called an unusual predication. But it does not follow from the fact that it is not regular that it is figurative or metaphorical. For between a regular and figurative, that is, metaphorical, predication is a third predication, which is called unusual. Since the thing, namely, the Mystery of the incarnation, is an unusual thing, and was unknown to Aristotle, it is not subjected to the rules of his Organon just as of other Dialectica.

EVERY FIGURE OF SPEECH TO BE REMOVED FROM PREDICATIONS IN EXPRESSIONS ABOUT THE PERSON OF CHRIST.

The truth therefore remains unshaken that these expressions, The Word became flesh, and God became man, should be understood literally without any figure of speech, and the proper, customary and Grammatical, true and genuine meaning of every single term should be retained.

MISUSE OF THE DOCTRINE OF ARISTOTLE IN THE DOCTRINE CONCERNING THE PERSON OF CHRIST.

If Aristotle had heard and believed in this Mystery, he would have led his intellect captive in submission to Christ, and would have strictly advised that the rules of his Organon and Dialectica should not in the least be adapted to it.

VERY TRUE RULE IN PHILOSOPHY REGARDING PREDICATIONS.

For in things that are subjected to the senses and reason and human intellect, this rule is very true: Whatever is predicated about another thing is predicated and said either properly and regularly or figuratively and metaphorically. But in this Mystery this rule is not valid.

REASON FOR THE BLINDNESS OF THE JEWS AND TURKS, THAT THEY DO NOT ARRIVE AT A TRUE KNOWLEDGE OF CHRIST.

And indeed this matter and this Mystery troubles and impedes the Jews and Turks still, wretched and blind, keeping them all the more from coming to a knowledge of Christ. Since they cannot comprehend how true God is true man, and true man is true God, by means of human reason and intellect, <369> for this reason also the can neither believe this Mystery nor do they wish to. And they take them for blasphemers who allow themselves to be persuaded of such things so manifestly absurd to human reason, such that they believe and confess that Jesus son of Mary is true and natural God, the Omnipotent Creator of heaven and earth.

MISUSE OF THE DIALECTIC RULE REGARDING DISPARATE THINGS.

This doctrine the Turkish Qur'an affirms to be blasphemy and by far the most horrible lie, confirmed by the misuse of this rule: that disparate things cannot be predicated really and truly about one another, unless figuratively and metaphorically.

But if it has been conceded that these expressions, The Word became flesh, and This Man is God, are not true if we should follow the literal sense, but to the contrary, we must necessary resort to a figure of speech, what absurdity, pray, would not follow? Or into what labyrinths of error would we not finally blunder?

ABSURDITIES THAT ACCOMPANY FIGURATIVE PREDICATION IN THE ARTICLE REGARDING THE PERSON OF CHRIST.

If in fact the Word did not become flesh except by a figure of speech, and a man is not God, except by a figure of speech, then we will have a metaphorical and figurative Christ, not a true Christ, who is truly and really neither man nor God. And will the Son of God not truly and really, but metaphorically and figuratively instead, have been born of the virgin Mary, suffered, crucified, died, and buried? By this reasoning the Son of God did not truly and really redeem us from our sins by suffering, but instead did so metaphorically. Would he not therefore be not a true, but rather merely a figurative, Redeemer and Savior? And would the man Christ not be truly and really, but figuratively omnipotent, figuratively omniscient, figuratively present everywhere on earth, figuratively ruling all things in heaven and on earth, figuratively vivifying, and finally figuratively fit to be worshiped?

In like manner we would have a metaphorical and figurative Lord's Supper, too, in which would be distributed not things that were present, but rather things that foreshadowed and signified such things as remained in heaven, such that we would have to fly up to them into heaven in our thoughts if we wanted to have them present and enjoy them.

<370>

FIGURATIVE THEOLOGY RENDERS EVERYTHING IN SCRIPTURE UNCERTAIN.

What, finally, is there that is certain in all of Scripture, or where will the literal sense remain? If we must necessarily have recourse to a figure of speech in all the sayings regarding Christ, the Lord's Supper, and the other Sacraments?

FIGURATIVE LORD'S SUPPER. HYPERBOLE IN THE TESTIMONIES OF THE FATHERS.

When in fact we produce the word of Christ, This is my body, etc., the immediate answer is that these words should not be understood according to the plain, literal meaning [κατὰ δ' ῥητόν], that is, as they read, but rather should be explained by a figure of speech: This means my body, it is a figure, it is a sign of the body of Christ. If we offer the words of Christ's Testament: This is my blood, the answer is that these words should not be understood as they sound, but rather we must retreat to a figure of speech, which is called Metonymy: This is a sign of my blood. But if we produce plain testimonies from the Writings of the Fathers (to which we are sent back in order that we may destroy the genuine sense of Christ's words) which retain the plain, literal sense [δ' ῥητόν] of the words of Christ's Testament: This is my body, etc., and their literal sense, and acknowledge no figure of speech in them, then they throw not only metaphor at us, but also hyperbole. These are your words:

> Chrysostom says, You see *him* (Christ), you touch him, But really it is fitting for you to call this rather a hyperbole, by which the supreme truth of perception is overly stressed; you should show us whether to be seen and to be touched are identical or with a sign, which you contend are invisible and valid [ἀπερίγραπτον]. (Beza, *Contra Westphal.*, Volume 1, folio 250)

Again, when Cyril brings up that we are not only joined together spiritually through faith with Christ, but also communicate bodily with Christ's flesh, and that Christ dwells in us by natural participation, which is a blessing of Mystical virtue, Your Reverence answers (Volume 1, folio 273), I concede all these things, even though it stands that Cyril in order that he might safeguard the union of natures against Nestorius, spoke hyperbolically [ὑπερβολικῶς] from time to time, if anyone should push hard on his particular words.

And in the same place (Volume 1, folio 293). Hence those holy hyperboles of the ancients, and of Chrysostom especially, were for this reason stressed very frequently by them, [371] that they might teach the souls of the faithful to distinguish the Sacraments from matters destined for common usage, and to apprehend in true faith the eternal things proposed spiritually in the Sacraments. Thus far your words.

If therefore all the sayings are figurative and hyperbolic which Christ himself, or the Apostle Paul, or the Fathers and Doctors of the purer, primitive Church handed down so plainly, regarding this real presence of Christ's body and blood in the Lord's Supper, and regarding the real communication of natures and divine Majesty in the person of Christ, then what, pray, will remain certain and firm in either of these articles of faith, and how can a Christian person's faith rest securely in them?

Dr. Beza:
Sacramental expressions and ways of speaking, both in the old and in the new Testament are customary and usual, and were not unknown either to the Apostles themselves or even to the Fathers and Doctors of the primitive Church. And the analogy of faith teaches to understand and explain them in such a way, unless we should wish to deny the truth of the body and the human nature in Christ, and fall into the Eutychian heresy.

Dr. Jakob:
Concerning those sacramental expressions and ways of speaking, it was explained sufficiently in the instituted conference and it was openly demonstrated that the thing itself is completely different and that there cannot be a place for figures of speech in expressions of this kind. Let it be enough for us to have demonstrated by the plain words of Christ and clear testimonies of holy Scripture, absent any human interpretation, the truth of the doctrine of our Churches. We leave the judgment and choice to the audience, whether they want to stand on simple faith in the words of Christ's Testament, with Paul's explanation of the Lord's Supper, and embracing the plainest

testimonies of holy Scripture regarding the person of Christ, the real communication of divine Majesty <372> *in the* human *nature*, whose literal meaning the Fathers of the purer old Church retained, and carefully stressed to their hearers, or whether instead to follow figures of speech and hyperboles in place of the very plain text, human interpretations that do not stand amid weightier proofs.

Dr. Beza:
We do not lead our hearers by a figure of speech that is not in God's word. Rather we will instruct them how it must be understood, lest we sin against the analogy of faith.

Dr. Jakob:
Reverend Dr. Beza, the Honorable Prince Frederick desires to know whether you have more that you would like to propose on this article regarding the person of Christ. If not, he thinks that our business on this article ought also to be concluded, and that we ought to proceed to discussion about Predestination.

Dr. Beza:
Reverend Sir, I do not see anything left in this article, but I would desire that an end be put on the disputation. We in fact did not think that there would be a disputation about other articles (but rather only about the Lord's Supper and the person of Christ). We will be entering a very deep abyss if we have to discuss Predestination. Nor is it wise to discuss this article in the presence of everybody, lest by chance more are offended than educated, since they cannot understand those things. But I nevertheless am not avoiding it. Besides, we would happily return home to our Churches for Easter. Let there be consensus in these two articles. The doctrine of Predestination sows no discords in our Churches. But if the Prince should wish nevertheless to hear our opinion on Predestination, we will explain it privately; <373> there will be no need to institute a new disputation for the sake of it in the presence of everybody.

Dr. Jakob:
We will easily be able to expedite it in this conference in one hour.

Dr. Beza:
The sheer volume of what has transpired has ruined my memory. But we will read the Theses you provided on Predestination, and we will respond.

3

26 March, 1586, 3:00 p.m.

Dr. Beza:

THE REASONS WHY DR. BEZA CAME TO MONTBÉLIARD WITH HIS BROTHERS.

Honorable Prince, most merciful Lord, and the rest of you most courteous audience. Two reasons brought us here: First, that we might testify that we earnestly seek a resolution of the controversies which to date have troubled the wretchedly afflicted, and more than enough distressed Churches; Second, that we might satisfy the holy plan of the Honorable Prince, Count Frederick.

Now a new disputation is proposed, regarding Predestination, which cannot be expedited in the space of one hour, day, or month, as easily as it seems to some. Because of this, we have in a brief note brought together our thought and petition, and humbly ask that the Honorable Prince, Count Frederick, deign to read it.

<374>

Supplication of Dr. Beza and His Colleagues, to the Honorable Prince, Count Frederick, by means of which Beza broke off the Colloquy the first time.

TO THE HONORABLE PRINCE AND LORD, FREDERICK, COUNT OF WÜRTTEMBERG AND MONTBÉLIARD, ETC., OUR MOST MERCIFUL LORD.

THEY WORRY THEMSELVES OVER THE PUBLICATION OF THE COLLOQUY. THEY DECLINE A DISPUTATION REGARDING PREDESTINATION. THE STING OF THEIR CONSCIENCE IN THIS ARTICLE. THIS DOCTRINE APPLIES TO ALL CHRISTIANS.

Honorable Prince, in order that we might submit to your holy desire, with the consensus of our highest Magistrates from the Republics of Bern and Geneva, we arrived here in order to engage with Dr. Jakob Andreae in a conference from God's word in a peaceful and friendly way regarding the controversy about the Lord's Supper. No mention of a conference instituted on other topics was made in the letter of your Highness. But we think that we have done our part to discharge our duty in this regard, which we think is clear from both writings of the Gentlemen's colloquies, the one on the Lord's Supper, the other on the person of our Lord Jesus Christ, with our responses to each, gathered with those same writings. Nor have we resorted to any human calculations, but rather turning to the testimonies from the word of God, and interpreting them according to the analogy of faith, we used these to confirm the matters which the Reverend Dr. Collocutors used in support of their position. But the rest of the things that were said here and there by them and us were not written down by chosen notaries and secretaries, and we requested from the beginning that this entire conference be conducted with writings sent back and forth, and signed with the signature of the collocutors. <375> Nevertheless, the Reverend Dr. collocutors did not concede to this; we judge that they must keep no faith at all. We point this out for this reason: so that the same thing may not happen that has happened on too many other occasions, namely, if by chance they get published, a deed we do not in the least want to have happen, that some will misuse them for the purpose of giving fuel to those wretched discords which are not able to be totally quelled to this day, which nevertheless we hope can, little by little, be laid to rest and extinguished. For the rest, as far as the proposed Theses on Predestination are concerned, we cannot enter upon this disputation (we say this begging the pardon of Your Honorable Highness), not only because it is strange and different from that reason for the sake of which we came here, but also for two other reasons above all, which we would wish to explain carefully to Your Highness. One is that it would not be possible for this disputation on Predestination to be carried out in half an hour (as the Dr. Collocutors and Your Highness have promised), but rather not even in a whole week.[45] This we know for certain, being fully aware of what great importance this very serious disputation is. We however cannot be away from our Churches for so long a time. The other reason is that this disputation could not be held in a public meeting without serious offense to those who are not capable of bearing such a great mystery, whether they agree with our opinion or the contrary one, whence a new seedbed of dissension can arise. As a result, this disputation ought to be debated in the schoolrooms, among well-trained Theologians, rather than in a public meeting of just anyone.

Nevertheless, in the meantime, if Your Highness desires more fully to understand our opinion on the Theses of the Dr. collocutors, we promise that upon our return to our Churches, we will, together with our Colleagues, take a look at them and carefully write out our opinion.

<376>

As for what remains, Honorable Prince, lest so many labors have been undertaken in vain by Your Highness, paying the cost without any fruit, we pray Your Highness as humbly as possible in God's

---

45 The marginal note directed at this statement in particular: "The impiety of their doctrine has in a few words been thereby demonstrated."

name, and ask the Dr. collocutors on behalf of Christian charity, that
it be noted down afterward on both sides, on a common document,
which matters from the two previous conferences we agree on. I pray
we enter discussion observing some Christian conduct by which it
may happen, though this controversy cannot now be expedited, as we
were especially hoping; nevertheless my prayer is that all this anguish
and bitterness, both in discourse and in writing (by which the spirits
of both sides were being exacerbated more and more, and an opportunity for derision presented to our common adversaries) be entirely
removed, so that in the meantime the Lord may bestow better things,
and each party propose its own doctrine for its own flocks, eager to
abstain from those hostile and hardly Christian people belonging to
the Zwinglians, Calvinists, Sacramentalists, Ubiquitarians, and the
rest of those notorious groups,[46] so that we may pray for each other
to the Lord from the heart and from the mouth, in order that he may
finally grant to us full consensus also in those matters.

**THERE IS NO LESS CONTROVERSY ABOUT THE EATING OF THE WORTHY THAN OF
THE UNWORTHY. A SHAMELESS PROPOSITION.**

Next, we ask this too, that since we manifestly agree on the
subject of the sacrament, on those points which are truly essential,
just as in the true reception of the things signified, the true body and
blood of the Lord, though as yet there is not agreement between us
regarding the mode of Sacramental presence, nor the eating of the
unfaithful, for the sake of whom it were unworthy for the pious to
be separated from each other, that the brothers of our Confession,
retaining their own confessions without any prior examination from
another, be allowed to receive the holy Supper from the hands of
others, and thus cultivate and bear witness to mutual fraternity.

<377>

But if we can procure this from Your Highness, we will judge it
has rendered us the great fruit of this conference. And we will await
the great deed about to be done for the Churches by Your Highness

---

46   The marginal note directed at this statement in particular: "We cannot bestow this on them."

in order to restore a fresh peace sometime to them, to the great and remarkable glory among all Christian Churches with Your Highness.

> *At Montbéliard, 26 March, 1586.*
> *Signed:*
> *Theodore Beza, Minister of the Church at Geneva.*
> *Abraham Musculus, Minister of the Church at Bern.*
> *Antoine de La Faye, Minister of the Church at Geneva.*
> *Claude Albery, Bachelor and Professor of Philosophy*
> *   in the Academy at Lausanne.*
> *Pierre Hübner, Professor of Greek, in the public*
> *   Gymnasium at Bern.*

After the petition had been offered, Beza was ordered to withdraw for a little while with his brothers and the rest of the audience, until the Prince, Count Frederick, should read what was written and be able to deliberate what had to be done next.

Therefore after his Highness read his petition and spoke with the Württemberg Theologians, he ordered him to be answered in a few words by Dr. Jakob, as follows.

<378>

Dr. Jakob:

THE RESPONSE OF THE HONORABLE PRINCE, COUNT FREDERICK, TO THE PETITION OF DR. BEZA AND HIS BROTHERS.

The Honorable Prince, Count Frederick, our Most Merciful Lord, has read your petition and carefully weighed it. And of course his Highness prays for and desires nothing more, if it could happen in any way, than that we proceed publicly in the established conference regarding the remaining controverted articles. The entire audience would be able to understand from this in what points we agree and disagree.

But the reason that his Highness did not make mention of the remaining articles in his letters is only that the remaining controversies were frankly thus far unknown to his Highness. Nor indeed is his Highness passing judgment on a decision of the Church or some great fruit from this Colloquy that needs to be hoped for, if some consensus should be established in one and another article, but in the rest which are no less important, such as especially the article on Predestination, there should remain pernicious disagreement.

THE DOCTRINE OF PREDESTINATION IS USEFUL, NECESSARY, AND FULL OF CONSOLATION.

His Highness would therefore desire, if it be possible, that by the grace of the holy Spirit, a full agreement and holy concord be established regarding all controversies, or that it be shown clearly at least by either party in what matters some discord remains, what is the consistent and perpetual doctrine of each party in the individual articles, and on what foundations they rest from either side. But especially, the doctrine of Predestination in the Church of God is not only useful, but also very necessary. Testimonies about it meet us everywhere in the explanation of holy Scripture, and indeed, it is quite full of consolation when in the midst of extreme temptations. We are taught by it that our eternal salvation has not been placed in our hands (by which we could fall the more swiftly, on account of the corruption of our nature, than our first parents in the state of innocence), but rather it is located in the hand of God, according to Christ's word: No one will snatch my sheep from my hand (John 10[:28]).

<379>

TRUE INSTRUCTION ON PREDESTINATION VERY NECESSARY.

It is especially necessary therefore for those who listen to our preaching to be rightly instructed. If in fact we should be in error, and explain it incorrectly according to the analogy of faith, not only will the path be laid open for the Epicurean life, but also an occasion will be given for desperation for those consciences afflicted and tempted by Satan.

For this reason it ought to be known not only to erudite and learned men, but also to people who are less well-educated, for Christ's voice rings in the ears of all, set forth each and every year in the expositions of the Evangelists, Many are called, but few are chosen (Matthew 20[22:14]), in order that they may learn for certain that they stand and have never been excluded from the number of the elect.

TEACHING ABOUT PREDESTINATION TO BE SET FORTH NOT ONLY IN THE SCHOOLS BUT ALSO IN THE CHURCH. SCOPE OF THE WHOLE OF SCRIPTURE. RULE.

For this reason this doctrine of Predestination should not be relegated to the schools in such a way that there is no need to set it forth for uneducated and unsophisticated people. Rather it is very necessary that it be explained to them thoroughly after the manner of common people, lest thwarted by Satan they succumb and perish. For whatsoever has been written (says the Apostle) has been written for our instruction, in order that through patience and *consolation* we may have the hope of the Scriptures (Romans 14[15:4]). Therefore whatever part of Christian doctrine is treated in such a way that it destroys Christian hope, it is certain that it is not being taught correctly.

But since our Lords once and for all decided to return to their Churches for the feast of Easter, and do not want to converse any longer either about the rest of the controverted articles, his Honorable Highness leaves this for your judgment and discretion.

THE HONORABLE COUNT FREDERICK ASKS THAT THE THESES OF THE WÜRTTEMBERGERS BE PUBLICLY READ ALOUD, REGARDING PREDESTINATION, BAPTISM, AND THE REFORMATION OF TEMPLES.

But, before there is any departure by anyone, since besides the article on Predestination, there are still two others left, namely

Baptism and the destruction of Temples and Icons, in which, especially in regard to Baptism, there is disagreement between us no less than that in regard to the Lord's Supper, it has seemed good to his Highness to decree that our Theses be read out publicly to all those in the audience, which we have written briefly already on the three mentioned articles, and what opinion we embrace and what is the opinion of our Churches regarding each single one. <380> After these Theses have been read out publicly and presented to you, then our Lords will be able to report back to your brothers in Geneva and Bern and to answer them also whenever it seems good to you, about how things stand now for all those who hear, regarding the doctrine of the Churches of the Augsburg Confession, and regarding the true state also of the controversies in each single article in which there is contention between us.

SUMMARY OF THE DOCTRINE OF PREDESTINATION OF DR. BEZA AND HIS BROTHERS.

For regarding Predestination, the opposing party teaches that an eternal, hidden, and unchangeable decree has been made by God, to the effect that he does not want a very large part of the human race to be saved or to come to a knowledge of the truth, but rather that he has created, ordained, and destined them for the purpose of eternal damnation, and does not want them to repent, to believe the promises of the Gospel, and to be saved. He would want the merit of Christ's death and blood to profit them nothing, seeing as it does not pertain to them; indeed he neither suffered nor died for them. We publicly condemn this teaching as erroneous and false, that it removes every consolation from afflicted and troubled consciences, and clearly destroys the use of the entire Ministry of word and Sacraments.

SUMMARY OF DR. BEZA'S DOCTRINE OF BAPTISM.

They also teach about Baptism that Baptism is not a washing of regeneration, but rather merely his sign and seal, and that not all infants who are baptized are regenerated, but that innumerable children of the baptized are eternally damned who have not been included in the hidden decree of God and the number of those to be saved, whom God also never wanted to be saved and regenerated.

STATUS OF THE CONTROVERSY REGARDING THE REFORMATION OF TEMPLES AND ICONS.

There is also controversy between us regarding the destruction of temples and icons, whether images which seem to furnish an opportunity for Idolatry ought to be removed from the eyes before they are removed from the heart. And whether true preaching of the Gospel and practice of the Sacraments can be celebrated in those temples in which the Pontiffs worked their Idolatry. Should they be totally overthrown, <381> demolished, and new ones built? For there is no controversy between us nor any question that those images which stand out publicly for the purpose Idolatry ought to be removed from view and destroyed.

THE WÜRTTEMBERG THEOLOGIANS ASK THAT THE COLLOQUY BE CONTINUED.

But if our Lords therefore wish to have no conversation at all on the topic of Predestination on account of the bottomless pit of this disputation, as it seems to them, though not in the least to us, we leave it to the judgment and discretion of our Lords whether they would wish to proceed with a peaceful conference regarding the remaining two articles, namely on Baptism and on Temples and icons. And this is especially important for your sake and the sake of your Churches, since you are not unaware how great is the odium you incur, at least nominally, since you are compelled to heart that in prior years so many temples were utterly overthrown by your people in France and Belgium, which many people think could have been more appropriately passed over.

Dr. Beza:

DR. BEZA BEGS OFF PUBLIC RECITATION OF THE THESES OF THE WÜRTTEMBERG THEOLOGIANS REGARDING PREDESTINATION, BAPTISM, AND ICONS.

Honorable Prince, as far as I can understand, it seems good to Your Highness that the written Theses of the collocutors be set forth

*publicly and recited before all the audience on the topics of Predesti-
nation, Baptism, and the destruction of temples and icons. But we
ask that this public recitation not occur, but rather that it be permitted us to bring the Theses of the collocutors home with us, where we
will respond just as soon as we have collected our thoughts with our
brothers.*

*For if, as Your Highness wills, it should happen that the Theses
of the Dr. collocutors just mentioned should be recited publicly, but
we do not respond immediately to them all, an opinion could stick in
the minds of the audience which would be grave for us.*

*For as far as I hear in the sermon of the Reverend Lord Doctor,
we do not teach the thing at which their Theses are directed.* <382>
*When they are recited, therefore, the audience members will think
the matter stands as such and that this is our doctrine which they
embrace and condemn in their Theses. Regarding the destruction of
Temples that happened in riots and war, no one of us approved all
those things that we could not anticipate and avert. For this reason
it will belong to us to explain our opinion in our own words, and
from our own books, and then the audience and speakers will be able
to make their judgment from that.*

*You have books which you have brought with you. We lack these.
You came prepared and ready for disputation on these articles; we
have not thought about them. A disputation about Predestination
is the most serious of all save that regarding Christ. A conference
on the topic should therefore be done carefully and attentively. It is
one thing, that is [ὅτι ἔστι], to set the topic before peoples' eyes; it
is another to treat the reasoning and arguments. Since not all people
are capable of handling this doctrine, and very many people use this
disputation inappropriately, we must carefully avoid these risks.*

Dr. Jakob:

Reverend Dr. Beza, the Honorable Prince, Count Frederick, has heard what you mentioned just now. But just as I said from the start, so now also His Highness bids me repeat. His Highness would altogether desire that the conference here established would be continued on the remaining three proposed articles and brought to completion.

Indeed, his Highness is of the opinion that when Your Reverence was advised about these matters by the Lord Baron, Lord Vesines, he told you there was no need for recourse to many books. All these things are in fact doubtless understood and very well-known by Your Lordship as a veteran Theologian. And we can truly swear for our part that we have not brought with us *even one book or tract* or any writing regarding these articles either.

<383>

But since we have brought with us a spirit that loves the truth, and one that is eager for peace and holy concord, if a strong peace and concord is at all to be established between us, we think it would have to be necessary for us to confer also regarding these three articles. This is the reason we put our opinion down in very brief, distinct, and clear Theses during the time we had to wait here before your arrival, so that we might then the more readily explain the controversies once the conference had begun.

His Highness entreats us the more to make this happen. But if you wish to persist in your opinion and are unwilling to converse and confer any further, his Highness permits you to carry our Theses home with you.

Dr. Beza:

We can truly swear that when we came here we had no idea that we were going to treat Baptism, nor the overthrow of Temples. We would also like to have a conference on these articles scheduled and to be able to proceed. But since it cannot happen on account of the reasons we have mentioned, we ask that those Theses not be read, lest something stick in the minds of the audience, as if we teach the things that are put forward in your Theses. Or that it explains our position, our opinion, in our words. Rather, we will bring them back home, so that we may respond in a measured way and perhaps more suitably than if we should also have a disputation on them now.

Dr. Jakob:

WHY COUNT FREDERICK DID NOT WANT ALL THINGS TO BE SET FORTH IN WRITING.

The Honorable Prince, Count Frederick, resolves the following: if all things had had to be prepared in writing, then there would have been no need in the least for our meeting together. For to this important end was this peaceful and friendly conference established: that the entire audience may hear from the mouth of both parties what is their consistent and perpetual opinion, which cannot be as easily perceived in writing or published books, <384> or known or judged, particularly in matters where either party complains that things have been attributed to them unjustly by their opponent, which they never thought or taught.

And the readers of the writings of both parties have been so disposed, whenever something meets them in Beza's writing about which they have doubt, the thought immediately occurs that they desire concerning this thing now to listen to Dr. Jakob, to hear what he would answer these things. And on the other hand, those who read my writings would want meanwhile, when in difficulty, to listen to Dr. Beza. The Honorable Prince, Count Frederick, trusts that the audience's desire has been satisfied in this Colloquy in regard to two articles. I think all have understood, enough and more than enough, what is the consistent and perpetual opinion of each party, and what the foundations of either doctrine, especially with the result that consensus has not been reached. His Highness would have wanted the same thing to happen in the remaining articles, which no doubt the remainder of the audience requests as well. For the living voice has some kind of latent energy that penetrates the minds of men and sticks more resolutely than if it should be committed to letters.

THE HONORABLE PRINCE, COUNT FREDERICK, EAGER FOR CONCORD AND PEACE.

But since his Highness sees that you persist in your intention, he also cannot do otherwise, and commends the entire business to God Almighty. Nor would he have spared any expense had it been possible to establish concord in all the controverted articles, if only the pious, holy, God-pleasing truth of heavenly doctrine be kept unharmed and inviolate in every way. Nor does his Highness doubt that our Lords will think carefully at home regarding the entire business, especially about the two articles about the Lord's Supper and the person of Christ, which will be seen hereafter to advance the propagation of truth and holy concord. And we very lovingly pray also that our Lords do this.

IN WHAT WAY THE DOCTRINE AND FOUNDATIONS OF THE WÜRTTEMBERG THEOLOGIANS WERE PREPARED.

All people will be able easily to perceive from these matters on which either side has conferred that in the assertion of our doctrine we have proposed not arguments of human reason or human inter-pretations but rather the perspicuous, clear, and manifest word of God, and have urged and do urge each and every single person to lead his understanding <385> captive, into obedience to Christ, and humbly to subject it to the word of the Lord, and simply believe it. They would then never be deceived or tricked, but rather would walk securely and most safely, and not succumb to temptations; rather, they would boast and triumph over the Devil.

STRIFE OVER THE LORD'S SUPPER AND THE PERSON OF CHRIST DID NOT ARISE FROM THE WÜRTTEMBERG THEOLOGIANS.

And it is known to all that the unfortunate and pernicious strife over the Lord's Supper and the person of Christ did not in the least arise from us, nor did we give any reason or opportunity for it to rise. We have always maintained, and still maintain, without disputation, the simple and literal sense of the words of Christ's Testament. And we unremittingly advise all pious and faithful people to do the same, urging them emphatically to reject all figures of speech and literary devices.

WHO GAVE REASON AND OPPORTUNITY TO THE CONTROVERSY ON THE LORD'S SUPPER AND THE PERSON OF CHRIST.

Some from your party began to attack our doctrine and still have not stopped. They have tried to draw us away from the express words of Christ's Testament to literary devices and figures of speech. These people had of necessity to be resisted, and granted no concession, for fear the Testament of Christ be corrupted and his very plain words get twisted into an alien sense. And we continue to do so for the sake of the faith and our Ministerium, and to stand guard, unless we should be willing to render the most unfavorable account to God and our savior Jesus Christ.

THE WÜRTTEMBERG THEOLOGIANS EAGER FOR PEACE AND CONCORD. HOW A PIOUS, HOLY, AND GOD-PLEASING CONCORD SALUTARY FOR THE CHURCH CAN BE RESTORED.

We will be eager, though, for peace and public tranquility, as much as can happen without harm to conscience and with truth kept inviolate. Nor will we give any cause for larger distractions, but rather as much as is in us, we will give attention to putting the controversies to rest more than letting them break out afresh. This can happen in no other way than by a genuine and public declaration of the truth of heavenly doctrine.

FALSE TEACHERS IN THE CHURCH NEED TO BE RESISTED.

We ourselves also see, and reality and experience testify, that it has not been advanced much by writing. Rather, when errors get scattered which creep in like a cancer, as Paul bears witness, and occupy the hearts and minds of simple and innocent people, then they must always be resisted, just as the Apostle teaches (2 Timothy 2[:14–19]).

<386>

AFFECTION AND LOVE OF THE WÜRTTEMBERG THEOLOGIANS FOR THE FRENCH CHURCHES.

We are gravely and fiercely affected by the misery of the French Churches, and not only grieve for them inwardly, but we also pray for them without ceasing, and exhort our Churches to public prayers, and we have God himself and our Churches and our audience as witness that we beg and pray that God would finally bring to an end those evils and endow holy peace and concord. And now we do the same thing also, and will do so as long as we live. Nor ever do we ever promise for our part that we will be absent from them in all those matters which will seem to advance pious peace, tranquility, and eternal salvation.

ADDRESS TO THE AUDIENCE, THAT IN ALL CONTROVERSIES OF RELIGION THEY REGARD ONLY GOD'S WORD, AND NOT ALLOW THEMSELVES TO BE DRAWN AWAY FROM ITS SIMPLICITY BY ANY INTERPRETATION.

To conclude, we urge the audience, each and every single one, especially as they reflect on their eternal salvation, not only in light of the present controversies that have been stirred up, but also in all the remaining contentions of religion, *to rely* on the Interpretation of no man, this or that one, but rather *to rely on only the word of God alone*, to cling consistently to it, and not to allow themselves to be led astray from it.

CONSISTENCY AND FIRMNESS OF FAITH IN *ONLY THE WORD OF GOD*. WHEN CONCORD IS STRONG.

For in such a way their faith will remain firm and unmoved against all temptations and rages of the Devil, and their minds will grow more firm and be joined together when *one teacher* is recognized by all as the only teacher and leader, and all will hang on his word, and not on what our experience and reason is able to grasp.

For the pious do not indulge in their scrutiny in the holy mysteries, but rather they allow their understanding to be subject to obedience to Christ, and they take their thoughts captive, and they allow themselves to be taught by the word of the Lord alone.

CONCORD TO BE ASKED OF GOD BY PIOUS PRAYERS.

And we hope finally in accordance with pious prayers that a holy, God-pleasing concord salutary for the Churches may be established. May the eternal God, the Father of our Lord Jesus Christ, accomplish and grant this, through the holy Spirit. Amen.

Dr. Beza:

BEZA'S THANKSGIVING.

Honorable Prince, we give great thanks to Your Highness for this most holy decision of yours, and for your eagerness to promote holy concord. And we pray you not think we are refusing this conference for any other reason <387> than that we think it most righteous and safe to conduct the business in writing. We will pray God to be willing to promote this your holy desire and to bless more and more the whole of the Württemberg family.

PRAISE OF THE MERITS OF THE HONORABLE WÜRTTEMBERG PRINCES IN THE FRENCH CHURCHES.

For I know the French Churches by name and often by experience, and the remarkable piety and goodwill with which Duke Christopher of blessed memory, and that of the father of Your Highness, were endowed. We obtained envoys and very useful letters from them; I can honestly say as a result that, after God, very many people owe their salvation to them. Since Your Highness follows in their footsteps, it falls to us to acknowledge you with thanks, and offer prayers in proportion to our gratitude, praying for the salvation of Your Highness and for every blessing and increase. And we hope that these our prayers will not be in vain.

WHY DR. BEZA AND HIS BROTHERS ASKED FOR THE BUSINESS TO BE DONE IN WRITING.

As far as the conference is concerned, we asked to do the business in writing, not so that the gathering would understand nothing;

rather we judged our arguments could be understood the more comprehensively and circumspectly in writing.

THEY PREDICT AND PROMISE MUTUAL GOODWILL.

But the speech of the Reverend Dr. Jakob Andreae reinvigorates us, which promises us goodwill. Nor will the French Churches make themselves appear unworthy on this account. For we will strive to show equal goodwill as well, and what we are doing, we will be eager to do better.

I can swear by the grace of God that the Ubiquists, the Lutherans, and similar voices have been heard in our gatherings and lectures. For we are accustomed to set forth our opinion and recite our arguments simply, and to explain your opinion, when we differ from it, without any bitterness.

<388>

But would that the things which have been written by both sides in prior years with a spirit of such great acrimony be abolished from the collective memory, by common agreement. This is our prayer and cry, and lest our prayer should appear to be in vain, I would dare to promise that we will go forward demonstrating everything both by our interpretive work and also the work we present, and take care that neither a saying nor a writing will arise in our Church which might disturb the Church.

Afterwards, therefore, the Theses on the three remaining articles were shown Dr. Beza and his brothers by the Württemberg Theologians, and the will and desire of the Honorable Prince, Count Frederick, was not unknown to them, that he was looking for a continuation of the colloquy, and many of the French were also urging and requesting the same thing. After they had deliberated on the matter privately amongst themselves, they took care to indicate to the Württemberg Theologians, that on the following day, which was 27 March, they would converse peacefully about the fifth Article, which is on the reformation of Temples and Papist Icons, and on the following days the other two remaining articles, namely Predestination and Baptism, with the same discretion as was observed in the prior articles. This was most pleasing to the Württemberg Theologians, but especially to the Honorable Prince, Count Frederick.

<389>

4

27 March, 1586

Dr. Jakob:

Reverend Dr. Beza, seeing as we ought to meet in a calm and friendly conference for the rest of the day about the fifth article, namely regarding reformation of Temples and Images, it pleases the Honorable Prince, Count Frederick, that the same method be observed which we followed in the preceding articles, namely that we first publicly recount the Theses we drew up before the conference begins, so that the Audience may have some taste of the scope towards which the whole conference is aimed.

4A. THESES OF THE WÜRTTEMBERG THEOLOGIANS REGARDING PAPISTIC TEMPLES, IMAGES, ORGANS IN THE CHURCH, AND THEIR REFORMATION, WHICH DR. LUCAS OSIANDER RECITED.

These are placed outside of controversy.

THESIS 1.

Temples intended for divine worship, in order that in them the word of the Lord may be taught and heard, the Sacraments distributed and received, must be purged when they have been contaminated with Idolatry, according to the word of the Lord.

<390>

THESIS 2.

Images, whether paintings or sculptures, by which histories and sacred things are represented, are adiaphora.

THESIS 3.

Images that stand for Idolatry should be taken away and abolished.

THESIS 4.

STATUS OF THE CONTROVERSY.

But it is asked whether what is done throughout Papistic Temples should be destroyed on account of Idolatry: the Temple itself, and the altar decorated with Images, sacred histories not in the least Idolatrous, and intended for the distribution of the body and blood of Christ in the Eucharist. And also, whether the Music Organs should be eliminated from Temples as though they had been forbidden by God. In this question we embrace and defend the negative position.

THESIS 5. THESE ARE THE FOUNDATIONS OF OUR TEACHING AND ASSERTION.

Christ taught in the Jerusalem Temple, which place he otherwise called a den of thieves. And we read that the Feast of Dedication was happening (John 10[:22]), not the destruction of the Temple.

Paul preaches Christ to the gentiles at the altar consecrated to the unknown God at Athens (Acts 17[:22–34]). And we do not read elsewhere in the Acts of the Apostles that such a thing was attempted either by the Apostles or by their hearers.

THESIS 6.

Images, whether sculptures or paintings, were not absolutely forbidden in the law, but for the reason of divine worship, lest they stand for Idolatry.

For if God had wanted to forbid in his law (since he says, You will not make for yourself a graven image, neither anything resembling what is in heaven above, nor what is on the earth below, nor those things which are in the waters under the earth, Exodus 20[:4]) all Images (even outside of the danger of adoration and Idolatry), <391> he certainly would not have given instructions for the two gold Cherubim to be made on the ark of the covenant, Exodus 25[:19–20], and on the curtain, Exodus 26[:1], but instead in the Jerusalem Temple constructed at the Lord's command, Solomon made two Cherubim in the Holy of holies, 1 Kings 6[:23–28]. And on the holy lavers Cherubim and Lions were on the side, 1 Kings 7[:29], and in the same place, twelve bulls under the cast sea. All these things were continually seen in the temple. Nevertheless, these Images did not constitute sin against God's law, so long as no one worshiped the Images. Moses even offered a bronze snake for the Israelites in the desert to look at, Numbers 21[:4–9], which Hezekiah would not have destroyed had not the people of Israel worshiped the serpent with incense, and used it for Idolatry (2 Kings 18[:4]).

Moreover, how great a distance is there from the depiction of the Image of God which Isaiah relates: I saw the Lord sitting on a throne, high and lifted up, Isaiah 6[:1]? And how about Daniel depicting God the Father for us as the ancient of days? Whose vestment was white as snow, and the hairs of his head like fine wool. And then he depicts the son of man, approaching the ancient of days, Daniel 7[:13]. Are these not depictions? Therefore should we remove the Images which are worshiped, this will be sufficient for this part of the divine law; there will be no danger from the rest of the Images and depictions.

THESIS 7.

St. Paul's prescription regarding not offending the weak should be carefully observed, and Idols should be removed from the minds of men by the word of the Lord before they are removed from their eyes, etc.

THESIS 8.

As far as Organs and Musical instruments are concerned, the clear word of God stands: Praise the Lord with strings and Organ. Praise him with fine sounding Cymbals. Praise him with Cymbals of jubilation (Psalm 150[:5]). The example <392> of the most pious Kings, David, Solomon, Hezekiah, Josiah, etc., testify to the same thing: their instrumental Music in the Temple was not reproved by the holy Spirit, but was rather commended (3 Kings [1 Kings] 10[:12]; 2 Chronicles 20[:21]; 2 Chronicles 29:35).

4B. WE JUDGE THAT THE FOLLOWING DOGMAS ARE NOT IN AGREEMENT WITH HOLY SCRIPTURE, ETC.

DOGMA 1.

The Gospel cannot be taught in a Temple in which forbidden and Idolatrous rites have been celebrated.

DOGMA 2.

The Lord's Supper cannot be celebrated on an altar which previously served for the abomination of the Papal Mass.

DOGMA 3.

In place of a stone altar, a wooden table must necessarily be established in temples, on which the Lord's Supper may be celebrated, although Christ together with his disciples nevertheless used not a table, but reclined on the ground after the manner and fashion of the gentiles.

Dogma 4.

Removal of Images must be permitted to the masses, and has been entrusted to the piety and wisdom of Kings, Princes, and the regular Magistrate of each place.

Signed:

Dr. Jakob Andreae

Dr. Lucas Osiander

Even though the Response of Dr. Beza and his brothers was not recited at this session, as it had not been written down, but was finally delivered afterward, we nevertheless judged that it would not be unappreciated by the Reader if it were inserted here. So may the pious reader the more easily be able to understand more fully what was in fact <393> the consistent and certain opinion of either party, and judge which party advanced the friendly conference instituted around this article with strong and immovable testimonies of the truth.

4c. Response to the Theses
regarding Images.

To Thesis 1.

We agree. (a)

MARGINAL ANNOTATIONS OF DR. JAKOB ANDREAE BY WHICH BRIEF ANSWER IS MADE TO DR. BEZA'S THESES, DELIVERED FOLLOWING THE TERMINATION OF THE CONFERENCE. (A) THAT THEY DESTROYED VERY MANY OF THE RICHEST TEMPLES AND OVERTURNED THEIR FOUNDATIONS, THIS MADNESS THEREFORE WAS NOT ZEAL, OR AT LEAST NOT ZEAL ACCORDING TO KNOWLEDGE.

To Thesis 2.

We acknowledge that painting and sculpture has a great use in civil affairs; this is not our business. But experience itself shows that its use in representing sacred histories, even if it is in and of itself a matter of indifference [ἀδιάφορος], is more harmful than profitable,

(b) on account of the propensity of the human mind for Idolatrous worship. It is not by accident this custom did not exist either under the old covenant (c) or for more than three hundred years after Christ, (d) such that things other than those that were written in the holy word of God were written or sculpted or painted. To be sure, although Bishop Paulinus of Nola (e) had brought in the custom of painting walls with sincere zeal, we see that it came to pass that this was rightly forbidden, expressly by the Council of Elvira. (f) And the Letter of Epiphanius is extant, translated by Jerome from Greek to Latin, from which it is clear that it was intolerable in that era for an image of Christ or any saint to stand in the holy sanctuary.

ANDREAE'S ANNOTATIONS: (B) THIS IS A FALLACY OF ACCIDENT. IT DOES NOT HAPPEN BECAUSE OF THE FAULT OF PAINTINGS OR SCULPTURES, BUT BECAUSE OF THE NEGLECT OF BISHOPS AND MINISTERS OF THE CHURCH, BY WHOSE FAITHFUL ATTENTION ALL THESE THINGS CAN BE EASILY GUARDED AGAINST. (C) WHERE THERE IS NO LAW THERE IS NO TRANSGRESSION. PAINTINGS AND SCULPTURES ARE FORBIDDEN ONLY AS THEY STAND FOR WORSHIP, EXODUS 20[:4–6]. (D) THEY WERE FORBIDDEN TO DO THIS BY NO DIVINE PRECEPT, BUT RATHER EVERYTHING IN THESE TIMES OF PERSECUTION WAS THROWN INTO CONFUSION, WITH THE RESULT THAT THEY WERE NOT THINKING ABOUT THESE THINGS. THEREFORE THIS WAS CUSTOM, NOT PRECEPT. (E) PAULINUS OF NOLA SHOULD NOT BE CHARGED WITH IMPIETY, BUT RATHER ACCUSED OF NEGLECT IN TEACHING PASTORS AND BISHOPS. THEY COULD EASILY HAVE GUARDED AGAINST ALL THESE THINGS THAT TURNED OUT BADLY. (F) REGARDING THE ELVIRA COUNCIL AND THE LETTER OF EPIPHANIUS, SEE BELOW IN THE ACTS OF THE COLLOQUY.

<394>

TO THESIS 3.

We think that not only images of this kind which people clearly use, but also those by reason of which they can be attracted to Idolatry, (g) which are looked at in holy places, should be taken away. We are generally agreeing with God's express word, where speaking of his worship he forbids not only that they be adored, but even that they be made. (h) Augustine in fact says it very well, commenting on Psalm 113[115:4–7]. Statues, which have a mouth, eyes, feet, ears, but do not speak, nor see, nor hear, nor walk, have more power for bending down the unfortunate soul than for correcting it.

ANDREAE'S ANNOTATIONS: (G) REGARDING THESE IMAGES THERE IS NO CONTROVERSY BETWEEN US. WE ALSO THINK EXACTLY THE SAME THING. (H) THERE IS ALSO CONSENSUS IN THIS, THAT FOR WORSHIP, GOD NOT ONLY FORBIDS THAT THEY BE ADORED, BUT ALSO THAT THEY BE MADE.

TO THESIS 4.

The destruction of temples, of which we do not in the least approve, is different (i) than the removal of manifest Idols, (k) which people either used at that time or that it is probable they will be unable to avoid using. As far as the Organ is concerned, we do not in the least condemn Music, but when there is harmonious singing, which is not understood in the mind, (l) the matter itself shows what the consequence of this is, that assuredly, a great part of the worship of God is changed, little by little, into alluring strains, and minds are not fed with the word of God, (m) but rather their ears are caressed with empty noises.

ANDREAE'S ANNOTATIONS: (I) SO MANY PEOPLE WEAK IN FAITH HAVE BEEN OFFENDED BY THIS DESTRUCTION THAT THE TEACHING OF TRUTH HAS BEEN REJECTED, WHICH THEY BEGAN TO TASTE BUT RETURNED TO THEIR VOMIT. MOREOVER, THE ENEMIES OF THE TRUTH HAVE BECOME MORE PERSISTENT IN FIGHTING AGAINST IDOLATRY. (K) WE AGREE THAT IDOLS SHOULD BE REMOVED. BUT THE EDIFICATION OF THE CHURCH NEEDS TO BE OUR CAREFUL ATTENTION AND BUSINESS IN REGARD TO THOSE THINGS THAT HAVE BEEN PAINTED OR SCULPTED FOR THE PURPOSE OF REPRESENTING SACRED HISTORIES. WE MUST CONTINUE TO ACT IN THIS FASHION CONTINUALLY, ESPECIALLY FOR THE SAKE OF THE WEAK. (L) HARMONIOUS MUSIC IS A SINGULAR GIFT OF GOD, THE PRINCIPAL USE OF WHICH OUGHT TO BE DIRECTED TOWARDS THE WORSHIP OF GOD, AS THE EXAMPLES OF THE PIOUS KINDS SHOW. (M) MUCH TO THE CONTRARY, THE MINDS OF THE PIOUS ARE ROUSED TO PIETY, AND TO OFFERING DEVOTEDLY THE WORSHIP THEY OWE TO GOD.

TO THESES 5 AND 6.

It is rightly taught that the destruction of temples is not at all necessary, and ought not heedlessly be approved of. (n) But what is said here about the Jerusalem temple in no way pertains to this. (o) It is just not true that when Christ was teaching in it, it was contaminated with any idols or sculptures or paintings, since the Jews of that time would have preferred to suffer extreme penalties, whatever *they might be, rather than that the image of an eagle be set up in it. It could even be debated whether Christ would have allowed them to be seen in the temple, who so zealously threw out of the temple those who were selling and buying, and <395> overturned the tables of the money changers; even though they could not be adorned with any images, they could nevertheless have some decorative ornament.*

ANDREAE'S ANNOTATIONS: (N) WE CAN IN NO WAY APPROVE OF THOSE FOLLIES OF PEOPLE, WHEN THE REMOVAL IS THE BUSINESS OF THE MAGISTRATE OF EACH PLACE. NEVERTHELESS, WISDOM WITH PIETY IS DEMANDED IN THIS MATTER, LEST ANYTHING HAPPEN UNSEASONABLY OR WITH OFFENSE TO THE PIOUS. (O) MUCH TO THE CONTRARY, IT VERY MUCH PERTAINS TO THIS. FOR DESTRUCTIONS OF TEMPLES HAVE COME ABOUT IN FRANCE AND BELGIUM MORE ON ACCOUNT OF IMPIOUS TEACHING AND PAPAL MASSES THAN ON ACCOUNT OF IDOLATROUS IMAGES. THEY CORRESPOND ESPECIALLY FOR THIS REASON TO THE JERUSALEM TEMPLE AT THE TIME OF CHRIST.

But we deny what you have said about images not having been forbidden in the law absolutely but rather for the purpose of worship, if it is understood as a ceremonial precept, like the observation of the Sabbath. (p) And we prove it by means of the everlasting and precise observation of this favorable precept in the ancient, purely Christian Church, which nevertheless dispensed with ceremonial laws. They observed the rule with the Cherubim, too; it was exactly as if they had not been put in the temple, even outside the gaze of all the Priests, and they were put forth as types of the Majesty of the Messiah who rules over the angels themselves, the truth of which we now maintain.

ANDREAE'S ANNOTATIONS: (P) WE ARE NOT REFERRING GOD'S PRECEPT REGARDING FORBIDDEN IMAGES TO CEREMONIAL LAWS, BUT RATHER TO THE FORBIDDEN WORSHIP OF GOD, AND WE TEACH THAT GOD'S PRECEPT READS THAT IMAGES SHOULD BE NEITHER FABRICATED NOR WORSHIPED. (Q) IT IS OF NO CONSEQUENCE THAT PEOPLE DID NOT LOOK AT THE IMAGES. WE ASK RATHER WHETHER BY THE EXAMPLE OF THOSE THINGS IT IS PERMISSIBLE TO PAINT IMAGES OR CARVE A SCULPTURE. IS IT IN AND OF ITSELF AN IMPIOUS THING? THESE EXAMPLES ARE SUITED TO THIS QUESTION, AGAINST THE ERROR OF THOSE WHO THINK THAT PAINTING OR SCULPTING IMAGES IS FORBIDDEN BY GOD WITHOUT EXCEPTION.

But the other images, like the lions and the bulls, pertain in no way to this matter, (r) since they were like decorations of holy Vases, lacking any danger of Idolatry, and besides this, constructed in this way by the express word of God. Finally, the outcome explains the brass serpent, which was not supposed to be shown to the eyes of everyone, (s) and would that Christian Magistrates imitate the example of the Church in destroying those things (t) in which the Christian Church has been most despicably profaned, by far less excusable ornamentation, and especially in images of the cross and the crucifix. (u) Paul declares how they ought to be depicted and seen by Christians, Galatians 3[:1]. (x) We say the same thing about Prophetic visions, (y) which the Lord showed his servants not at all for this reason: that he wished to be described b them or seen by them in another way than verbally. In words, things are never changed like they are in artists' paintings.

ANDREAE'S ANNOTATIONS: (R) THE NATURE OF THESE IMAGES IS THE SAME, WHICH WERE BROUGHT UP FOR THIS PROPOSED SCOPE AND QUESTION, JUST AS WAS SAID ABOUT THE CHERUBIM. (S) THERE WAS NO SIN IN EXPOSING THE BRONZE SERPENT TO THE EYES OF ALL; INSTEAD THE SIN WAS PRIESTS WHO DID NOT TEACH THE PEOPLE RIGHTLY BY THE DOCTRINE OF MOSES. THUS THERE WAS NO DANGER IN THE PUBLIC SPECTACLE, THROUGH WHICH PIOUS PEOPLE COULD DAILY STRENGTHEN THEIR FAITH. (T) PIOUS PRINCES IN OUR TIME HAVE IMITATED THE EXAMPLE OF HEZEKIAH IN REMOVING IMAGES THAT WERE STANDING OUT IN PUBLIC FOR WORSHIP. AS FOR THE REMAINDER WHO ACTED MODERATELY, THEY VERY MUCH SERVED THE EDIFICATION OF THE CHURCH. (U) THERE IS NO DANGER IN THE IMAGES OF A CROSS AND THE CRUCIFIX, SO LONG AS THE PEOPLE ARE RIGHTLY TAUGHT. BUT WHEN TEACHING IS CORRUPT, NOTHING SOUND OR SINCERE IS LEFT, WHETHER IMAGES ARE PRESENT OR ABSENT IN TEMPLES. (X) EVEN AN EXTERNAL PICTURE DOES NOT CONFLICT WITH THE DEPICTION OF CHRIST CRUCIFIED IN THE EPISTLE TO THE GALATIANS 3[:1], WHICH SINCE IT IS NEITHER COMMANDED NOR FORBIDDEN, MUST BE CONSIDERED AS AN ADIAPHORON. AND THEY SHOULD NOT BE CONSIDERED AS PAPISTIC TEMPLES IN WHICH THE IMAGES OF THE CRUCIFIX ARE STILL FOUND, IF THE PEOPLE ARE PIOUSLY AND RIGHTLY TAUGHT. (Y) WE ALSO SAY THE SAME THING. BUT MEANWHILE, FOR NO REASON CAN IT BE TAUGHT THAT IT IS IMPIOUS IF THEY SHOULD BE DEPICTED IN THIS FASHION, JUST AS THEY WERE RECOUNTED IN THE WORD BY THE HOLY SPIRIT.

<396>

TO THESIS 7.

Attention indeed needs to be given to removing idols from the minds of Idolaters themselves little by little. But we deny on the other hand that the disease of such rank superstition needs to be fostered. (z) We do not understand, for how, pray, would objects that stand before their eyes not be fostered in their minds, such that they be motivated to retain that superstition?

ANDREAE'S ANNOTATIONS: (Z) IF A SOUND TEACHING OF THE GOSPEL IS TO BE GIVEN TO PEOPLE, THERE IS MORE DANGER IN HASTE THAN IN DEFERRAL AND LENGTHIER DELAY IN REMOVING IMAGES. FOR IDOLS HAVE TO TAKEN AWAY FROM PEOPLES' MINDS BY THE WORD OF GOD BEFORE THEY ARE REMOVED FROM THEIR EYES. A PRECISE TIME FOR THIS CANNOT NOR SHOULD BE DEFINED.

TO THESIS 8.

This certainly was quite a large part of Levitical worship, (a) established by God's authorship, not the maxims of men. As for the rest, if this mandate of God should pertain to them, it would have to be established in all Christian Churches.

ANDREAE'S ANNOTATIONS: (A) INSTRUMENTAL MUSIC WAS INDEED EMPLOYED IN LEVITICAL WORSHIP, BUT THE PIOUS KINGS HAD NO EXPRESS AND SPECIAL MANDATE OF GOD ABOUT IT, WHO ESTABLISHED IT SINCE IT HAD BEEN ESTABLISHED BY MOSES AND HAD NOT BEEN OBSERVED. FOR THIS REASON, ALL THE TESTIMONIES WHICH HAVE BEEN BROUGHT FORTH FROM HOLY SCRIPTURE BY THE WÜRTTEMBERG THEOLOGIANS, ON BEHALF OF INSTRUMENTAL MUSIC NEEDING TO BE RETAINED IN TEMPLES, PERTAIN TO EVERYONE. AND THEY DO BADLY WHO ELIMINATE IT FROM CHURCHES AND TEMPLES AS IF IT WERE FORBIDDEN BY GOD.

4D. ON THE DOGMAS.

Those things condemned by the Reverend Doctors in Conference, and rejected by the above Theses, concern neither us nor other Christian churches, in our opinion. (b) Nevertheless we say, even though it is in and of itself a matter of indifference [ἀδιάφορος] to have a structure of stone which they call an altar, or a common wooden

table in the use of the holy Lord's Supper, nevertheless it is not prob-
able that Satan could have ever transformed the Sacrament of the
Lord's Supper into that horrible sacrifice of offering Christ anew, (c)
had Christian Churches lacked altars. <397> *And would that the name*
Sacrament of the altar had never been used.

ANDREAE'S ANNOTATIONS: (B) IT IS ABUNDANTLY SHOWN BELOW IN THE COLLOQUY THAT THESE DOGMAS ARE SPREAD ABROAD BY ZWINGLIANS AND CALVINISTS AND SUPPLIED IN THEIR WORK. (C) SACRIFICE GAVE BIRTH TO THE ALTAR, NOT THE ALTAR TO SACRIFICES. CONCERNING THIS POINT EVEN MORE WILL FOLLOW IN THE CONFERENCE ITSELF.

Signed:
Theodore Beza, Minister of the Church at Geneva.
Abraham Musculus, Minister of the Church at Bern.
Pierre Hübner, Professor of Greek, in the public
*   Gymnasium at Bern.*
Antoine de La Faye, Minister of the Church at Geneva.
Claude Albery, Bachelor and Professor of Philosophy
*   in the Academy at Lausanne.*
At Montbéliard, 29 March, 1586.

4E. DISCUSSION ON TEMPLES AND IMAGES

Dr. Jakob:

WÜRTTEMBERG THEOLOGIANS ARE NOT PROTECTORS OF IDOLS.

Reverend Dr. Beza, we did not write and propose our Theses with the thought that we wanted to undertake a defense of Idols, for the very recitation of the Theses openly demonstrates that we detest and openly condemn all idols and their worship no less than you.

PROFIT OF ARGUMENT AND CONFERENCE REGARDING THE FIFTH ARTICLE.

But since by not only the unseasonable demolition of images, but also the laying to waste and destruction of Churches, so many among the French and in Belgium have been offended and frightened away from the teaching of the Gospel by actions of this kind, who have not yet truly been established in the doctrine of Christ, and, what is most alarming, confirmed in their impiety have even perished in both body and soul in eternity, we thought our admonition to you would not be unappreciated, that we meet in a peaceful and friendly conference about what we think ought to be done. But we do not think that you for your part differ much or at all from our opinion. So we hope also that the accommodation of our differences in this controversy, if there is any, will be easy. At the same time, the audience should be advised to understand what Magistrates and their subjects must do in this matter, lest while we seem to draw conclusions about the repeal of images for the salvation of souls, <398> many fall headlong into very present and eternal destruction.

Dr. Beza:

DR. BEZA DOES NOT APPROVE THE DESTRUCTION OF TEMPLES AND IMAGES THAT HAPPENED IN THE FRENCH CIVIL WARS.

I confess that I was confused by the proposed disputation, that you decided to propose these things about temples and images. I do not in fact think that anything can be produced by which it can be established that those dogmas which are condemned in your Theses stack up against us or can be attributed to us.

We do not deny that in France things of this sort have happened in riots and civil wars that have arisen because of a certain zeal, but not beyond measure, to our knowledge. But I do not think that it can be shown or determined against us that those things were approved by our confession and teaching. I myself can testify to this, since this war concerned me from its beginning all the way to its conclusion. I can testify that my colleagues and I often admonished and urged Princes and Dukes in word and deed to hinder these attempts and what was turning into disorder, but we warned in vain and could accomplish nothing.

Therefore since our business is now just about those things which are taught in our churches, and not the civil strife in France or Belgium or anywhere else, we are surprised that this question has been mingled together in this treatment.

But since it has seemed good to you to do this in your Theses, we do not want to oppose it, and we will leave those things which lie outside of controversy and turn our attention to those about which there could be some doubt. For there are certain things that have been written by you in those Theses about which we could inquire. If it is alright, then, I will follow the order of your Theses, and respond to them one by one, so that where we agree or disagree may come to light, as well as what our opinion is <399> *about each and every one. I will do so briefly, too, since our departure time, which is at hand, compels us.*

Dr. Jakob:

Reverend Dr. Beza, the speech of Your Honor was pleasing to us, by which you testify that you and your colleagues do not in the least approve of the outrageous conduct and disorder in the overturning of Temples, and that you never have approved of it as it was happening in years past in the civil conflict among the French and Belgians.

WHY MENTION WAS MADE OF THE OVERTURNING OF TEMPLES IN THE THESES OF THE WÜRTTEMBERG THEOLOGIANS.

But on the other hand, we can affirm solemnly that some mention was made of them in our Theses, and that we did it for this reason, since we were not in the least doubtful that inconsiderate actions of this kind would be not at all approved of by you, in order that a public testimony of your consensus, for your part, might stand before others by which your Churches may be the less oppressed by this reputation, to which actions of this sort are attributed and imputed as if they were approved by them. They will on this account be able easily to be exculpated and excused in the view of all truly pious people.

But since your Honor thinks that certain things were proposed in our Theses, concerning which a conference seems not unprofitable, we ask that these be put forward by you peacefully, and we will answer them with moderation.

Dr. Beza:
I will first recite the individual Theses, and indicate in what points we are perplexed.

These have been placed outside of controversy.

Thesis 1 of the Württemberg theologians.

Temples intended for divine worship, in order that in them the word of the Lord may be taught and heard, the Sacraments distributed and received, must be purged when they have been contaminated with Idolatry, according to the word of the Lord.

<400>

Dr. Beza:

THERE IS NEED OF PUBLIC TEMPLES AND APPOINTED TIMES.

We agree. Since the Lord is in fact a God of order and not of confusion, we think there is need of public places and appointed times, where and when the Church may gather together for hearing the word of God, for receiving the Sacraments, and for public prayers, so that they may happen both in order and decently according to the admonition of the Apostle. For this reason we say that there is need of temples.

Thesis 2.

Images, whether paintings or sculptures, by which histories and sacred things are represented, are a matter of indifference [ἀδιάφορον].

Dr. Beza:

DR. BEZA DOES NOT DISAPPROVE OF SCULPTURES AND PICTURES AND THEIR ARTISTS.

We have never disapproved of pictures or sculptures; they are of great use in representing sacred histories as well as in civil affairs, especially in describing and depicting plants. So we do not disapprove those arts, but recommend them and affirm that they should be exercised as useful to the Republic.

REGARDING PICTURES AND IMAGES IN SACRED PLACES.

But as far as images are concerned, whether painted or sculpted, though we do not reject their use when sacred material or histories are represented, nevertheless we do not admit them in holy places without hesitation. Nor do we judge it prudent especially that sculpted Images be set up in Temples, not because it is impious in and of itself, or because we think it is not allowed, but rather because of the sad appearance of the Churches we see in Temples of the Papists, which took its origin from the use of Images and pictures.

BISHOP PAULINUS' DEED TURNED OUT BADLY. IMAGES ABROGATED IN THE COUNCIL OF ELVIRA.

Bishop Paulinus of Nola instituted Images with a good enough intention, but it turned out badly. For even though no one could disapprove of his zeal [401] or criticize it, nevertheless the outcome shows that he should have abstained from pictures. The pictures resulted in them being used for worship, and at length made their way to the altar and occupied the place of Christ, and Christ was finally pushed away from it. This is why the Council of Elvira in Spain abrogated images, as Canon 36 shows: Pictures ought not to be in the Church lest what is painted on walls become an object of worship or adoration. Let them be more prudently located outside the temples and the holy sanctuaries, rather than in the temples themselves. St. Augustine also confirms this in Psalm 114: The resemblance of a form (he says) draws hearts away, and the imitated image of members kidnaps the hearts of mortals with a certain weak disposition.

In addition, there is the custom of the ancient Church, which lacked pictures, a custom from which we ought not rashly depart.

IN THE EPISTLE OF EPIPHANIUS TO JOHN, BISHOP OF JERUSALEM.

Your Eminence is familiar with the Epistle of Epiphanius translated by Jerome, who was contemporary [σύγχρονος] with Chrysostom. In it he writes that he arrived at a certain villa and there found in the Church a canvas hanging on the outer doors of the Church, with an image painted in color of a hanging man, probably an image of the crucifixion. He cut down the canvas and advised that the dead of the poor be rolled up and carried away in it. Those who murmured against the deed said, if you wanted to cut it down, fair enough, you should give another canvas and change it, which he promised he would do. From this it stands that at the time images were an unknown thing in temples. Therefore it is fitting that we also be wise about the examples and dangers of the times past and, as much as we can, stand guard against any opportunities for Idolatry.

USE OF IMAGES IN TEMPLES A MATTER OF INDIFFERENCE [ἀδιάφορον].

For this reason, though I completely concede that the use of images in which sacred things and histories are represented in temples is a matter of indifference [ἀδιάφορον], nevertheless since people easily abuse them when they are seen in sacred <402> places, I think they do wisely who eliminate all these things from temples. And the primitive Church was able for three hundred years to do without the use of images. So can we. And the thing itself shows what happens after eight hundred years, after they were introduced into temples and sacred places. They ought rightly to move us not to accept their use in such great light of the Gospel. For we see how difficult it is to recall people from them now who cleave to them, and do not allow themselves to be pulled away from them.

We therefore accept your Thesis; nevertheless we think that they act prudently who take away this stumbling stone, lest people fall. For there is a danger that someone will cleave to pictures, as we see has happened.

For this reason then, I do not disapprove of your Thesis, but nevertheless, let us not on this account think that they acted less than prudently who removed painted and sculpted images for the reasons just mentioned.

*King Hezekiah in the same way acted piously in that he demol-
ished the bronze serpent to which the people offered sacrifices (2
Kings 18[:4]). We should act in this way in fact, lest people strike
their feet upon those stones. But I am speaking about those places in
which all these things have been done in order.*[47]

Dr. Jakob:

IMAGES EITHER PAINTED OR SCULPTED ARE A MATTER OF INDIFFERENCE
[ἀδιάφορον].

Reverend Dr. Beza, it is very nice for us to hear that Your Honor
approves also of the second Thesis. In this part there is consensus
between us. Images are in fact by their nature, either painted or
sculpted, matters of adiaphora. We can be absent from them without
sin, and we can also have them, provided abuse is not admitted,
expressly forbidden by the word of the Lord, which is worship or
adoration, which should in no way be given to images.

WHAT WAS THE CHIEF CAUSE OF IDOLATROUS WORSHIP OF IMAGES. NATURE
PRONE TO IDOLATRY.

But Your Honor added something about the danger, and advised
that we should act cautiously and carefully lest an opportunity for
Idolatry be given, especially in temples and sacred places, and confirmed it with a historical recitation <403> of Bishop Paulinus of Nola,
Epiphanius, Augustine, the Council of Elvira, and the custom of the
ancient Church, showing how much damage painted or sculpted
images caused the Churches in as many places as possible. For this
reason you judge that it is most prudent that they be eliminated and
removed from temples and sacred places. I answer: it is true that our
nature is corrupt, and to a high degree prone to Idolatry and inclined
to it. For this reason I agree in this, that we should act cautiously and
carefully in this matter, lest any opportunity for Idolatry be given to
painted or sculpted images.

---

47   This sentence in the printed edition is specially indicated with "N.B." (*nota bene*).

But we think that the fact that they were introduced into temples and sacred places with a good intention, and turned out unfortunately, and posterity perverted them into Idolatrous worship, is not the fault of using painted or sculpted images, but rather of neglect of the teachers of the Church, who did not perform their office of teaching.

USE OF IMAGES IN TEMPLES AND SACRED PLACES.

For even if images can be retained without impiety and apart from offense to God, in which are represented sacred matters and histories, and which are extant throughout holy Scripture, and call to mind for the illiterate the stories of the deeds (which is a unique use of images in temples and other places, whether sacred or profane), nevertheless if ministers of the Churches do not perform their office by teaching, I confess that the slip to forbidden worship is easy.

But at the same time, I do not see that on this account they must all be abolished from temples and sacred places, and eliminated without any discretion, provided pastors of the Churches perform their duty vigilantly and carefully. If in fact the word of God is heard rightly and purely in temples and all sacred places, there is no danger in images, which merely represent sacred things, and call them to mind for people ignorant of them.

WHETHER IMAGES AND PICTURES DISTRACT PEOPLE FROM HOLY SCRIPTURE. IMAGES AND PICTURES IN SAXON CHURCHES, WITHOUT ANY SUPERSTITION.

But Your Honor states that those who cleave to images are distracted from holy Scripture more than they are put in mind of it, and called to it. I say that the case is this: When I was traveling through almost the entirety of Saxony, where as you know I lived for many years, I saw the principal Churches, indeed most among them, and in them, just a few or none at all of the painted or sculpted images <404> were removed or eliminated from temples and public sacred places. And what is more, they still retain the whole panoply [πανοπλία] of vestments, which they used in years past in the celebration of the Papal Mass. Nevertheless there was not one person there found, so

I heard, who was given to the superstition and Idolatry of the Papist Roman religion.

LUTHER'S MODERATION AND PRUDENCE IN REFORMING THE CHURCH.

Luther in fact, of pious memory, cleansed Churches in those locations by means of the word of the Lord alone from the beginning, and through this one Instrument of the holy Spirit dragged away all idols from the hearts of his hearers, with which the minds of men had been preoccupied, before he ever removed even the smallest ones from their eyes. For an idol in the world is nothing, as the Apostle testifies, 1 Corinthians 8[:4], but instead they reside in the hearts of people, created by Satan. Once these have been eliminated from hearts, there is no more danger from images.

WHEN IMAGES SHOULD BE REMOVED FROM PEOPLES' EYES.

But since all people are not affected equally, and all hearts of people cannot immediately or in a moment be changed at the same time, for this reason a precise time cannot be set or prescribed for when all these things should be removed from peoples' eyes.

WHY LUTHER WORE A HOOD FOR SO LONG. OPINION ABOUT THE MONASTIC CULT.

Thus Luther for many years wore the monastic hood or habit. He was not in the least unaware of what peoples' opinion was regarding the monastic vestment, by which they imagined that sins could be hidden from the sight of God, just as chief men were convinced that their dead bodies should be buried dressed in such a habit so that they might share in all the merits of the monastic order.

LUTHER CAUSED MORE DAMAGE TO THE ROMAN PONTIFF BY HIS MODERATION THAN OTHERS BY THEIR CARELESS ZEAL.

By this moderation Luther edified the Churches and disparaged Popery more than those who, after scarcely one or two meetings, took away with a two-edged sword (as the Germans say) everything that people made use of for the forbidden worship of God.

We experienced the same thing in the Dukedom of Württemberg, where in the first year after the light of the Gospel was introduced and lit, and Papal Idolatry abrogated, images were removed throughout all the temples before <405> the imagination of their worship was pulled away from the minds of men. This is why it has come about that very many people were so offended by this unseasonable reformation undertaken with a two-edged sword (as they say) that neither listened to Evangelical assemblies nor approached their Sacraments any longer, but rather clung to their Papist Idolatry till their final breath, despising the teaching of the Gospel and the true use of the Sacraments. This was the fruit of the unseasonable reformation in which everything was destroyed with no regard given to the weak in faith.

THERE IS NEED OF PRUDENCE IN GETTING RID OF IMAGES.

Since therefore painted and sculpted images by which sacred matters or histories are represented are by their nature matters of adiaphora, there is need of prudence both in retaining and in abrogating them, lest the weak be offended and they be frightened away from the teaching of the Gospel, or superstitious people be entrenched and become stubborn in their own impiety.

TWO CLIFFS IN RETAINING AND GETTING RID OF IMAGES. MANY SALUTARY THINGS DESTROYED WITH THE ABROGATION OF IMAGES.

But there is less danger when pure and genuine doctrine is heard, by which all people are called away from Idolatry to the true worship of God in daily meetings, should they be retained, than if they should be abolished rashly and unthoughtfully. Because of this, we think that the Magistrate of each place sins less, and takes counsel to the advantage of the salvation of souls far better, if they have endured them longer than if they have unseasonably abrogated them. Indeed, he sins against Christian liberty no less if people should be taught that these must necessarily be abolished than if they should be persuaded that they must necessarily be retained. If in fact they are matters of indifference [ἀδιάφορα], as is the consensus between us, why could one be urged necessarily over the other? It happens all the time with the majority of things of this kind that are abrogated with careless zeal, even other things, together with images, which were introduced by our Ancestors not rashly or with impiety, that it is better for them to be retained, at least for the sake of order and decorum, than that they can be erected again not without offense to many people, which were once abrogated and eliminated as impious and superstitious or Idolatrous, though they were not in the least impious in their own nature, or contrary to the word of God. Neither of these things happens when the matter is entrusted to the madness of the people so uncritically, even if they happen by the Magistrate's authority.

<406>

THE WORD OF PIERRE VIRET ABOUT THE CRUCIFIXION OF CHRIST.

Pierre Viret wrote in another place that the crucified Christ is better represented by a cow than by a painted or sculpted image. This speech unnecessarily offends pious people, even those not too much given to favor images at all. We think therefore that we should stay away from sayings and deeds of this sort, and endeavor instead to retain purity of doctrine. Then there will be no danger in images of this kind which are retained in temples, that they may see that this house or temple has been constructed for this purpose alone, namely for knowing Christ crucified. In this matter, all thoughts about Political and Economic affairs ought to be silent, and minds should be dedicated to divine worship.

Dr. Beza:
This whole business can best be described as resting on two points, namely, the prudence of pastors and the consideration of circumstances. For it is certain that an object inspires meaning. Therefore so long as they are retained in the eyes of people, Idolatry is retained, such that people cleave to them. The custom was observed in certain places that images of this kind were retained for four years after reformation. But I do not want to fight with anyone about these things or reprove the deeds of other people; let us just be on guard against all opportunities for Idolatry, as much as possible.

Dr. Jakob:

I am of the opinion that a precise time for abolishing images cannot be set, but I think instead that we must always have regard for the edification of the Church, where there is more danger in unseasonable destruction than if they should be retained for the present, as has been said.

Dr. Beza:
I will therefore proceed to the third Thesis, which reads thus.

THESIS 3.

Images that stand for Idolatry should be taken away and abolished.

<407>

Dr. Beza's Response.

WHICH IMAGES SHOULD BE REMOVED FROM TEMPLES.

If I understand Your Honors correctly, you do not mean in this Thesis images which people abuse but rather those that have been put out for the purpose of Idolatry and have been carried into the Churches for this purpose, and there is no other use for them. If this is your meaning, many images will stand which ought to be abrogated. For I think that they also should be removed which can tempt people to Idolatry.

King Hezekiah did not permit the bronze serpent to stand (a memorial of the blessing offered to the Israelite people in the desert), because it was tempting people to Idolatry (2 Kings 18[:4]). Why could we not therefore also, for the same reason, take away images from sacred places, so that similar Idolatry may be guarded against, and the people not tempted to it.

YOUNG WOMEN IN PROSTITUTES' GARB PAINTED IN TEMPLES.

I think therefore that the abuse of images is greater than the true use of them in temples, whatever their nature may be, whether painted or sculpted. I do not know the reason they are painted in so many places. In fact, in Papist temples throughout France and Italy and in other places, young women are painted in the garb of prostitutes, such that men are undoubtedly invited to prayers by them.

Because of this I would prefer, without any prejudice, that the custom of the first and purer Church would be observed, in which there were NO images at all.

TRUE DEPICTIONS OF CHRIST'S IMAGE.

But I would be willing to have the passion of Our Lord Jesus Christ, and Christ crucified, depicted for Christians by the preaching of the word, just as we read him depicted by Paul to the Galatians (3[:1]). Christ Jesus was depicted before your eyes (he says), and among you as crucified. This is the true depiction and image of Christ crucified, if he should be depicted after this fashion, and the merit of his death preached to the people. But the rest of the images, either painted or sculpted, call people back to earthly things, to which by nature they are inclined, and which destroy the Churches. For Idolatry has crept into the Churches with images, and with them <408> even the very Sacraments have devolved into idols, to such a degree that the Papists worship not in the way of the Sacrament, but rather in the way of an idol. This is the way it turns out for the consecrated host in the Corpus Christi Feast and in the daily Papistic Masses.

And so if we should compare the use and abuse of images, use will not compare to abuse. This is why they should, in our opinion, be done away with. Nevertheless I do not want to prescribe anything for so many very learned and religious men, but instead think that they act better in the meantime who remove them all together and call people away from them. If in former times a Christian person happened to catch sight of an image in private houses, he would not have endured it, but perhaps would have removed it zealously, not according to knowledge.

Dr. Jakob:

THAT IMAGES REPRESENTING SACRED THINGS CAN BE RETAINED IN THE CHURCH OF GOD.

I will respond briefly for the purpose of declaring consensus. We think that images, by which sacred matters and histories are represented, can be retained in temples with a healthy and unharmed conscience so long as people do not use them the wrong way, for Idolatry. Therefore they should *not necessarily* be destroyed on account of abuse, as if unless they were abolished the Churches would not seem in the least to be cleansed and reformed according to the prescription of God's word. For if they are matters of adiaphora, then they should not be removed of necessity, nor should they be retained of necessity.

WHICH IMAGES HAVE TO BE ABOLISHED.

And King Hezekiah would never have destroyed the serpent had he not seen the people making sacrifice to it. For this reason we think that things that stand out publicly for worship of this kind also ought to be abolished.

FILTHY PICTURES AND IMAGES TO BE ABOLISHED.

As far as painted or sculpted images are concerned, painted or placed on altars, that depict young women in the dress of prostitutes, with a great part of their body naked, so that those performing the sacrifice and the Monks may celebrate their private Masses so *devotedly* in the sight of them, we can truly testify that in the Dukedom of Württemberg, <409> in the most famous Monasteries where these were seen, they were taken away and destroyed together with the others.

STATUS OF THE DISPUTATION REGARDING PAINTED AND SCULPTED IMAGES.

For this reason there is between us no disagreement or controversy. Instead, I ask only this, whether such an image, one or more, namely of Christ crucified, can be retained in the Church, without superstition and impiety, or not? For if such circumstances happen, about which Dr. Beza has spoken, then we think that they all ought to be demolished and abrogated at the same time. In this matter also I judge that there is consensus between us.

Dr. Beza:
Let us proceed then to the fourth Thesis which reads thus.

THESIS 4.

But it is asked whether what is done throughout Papistic temples should be destroyed on account of Idolatry: the Temple itself, and the altar decorated with images, sacred histories not in the least Idolatrous, and intended for the distribution of the body and blood of Christ in the Eucharist. And also, whether the Music organs should be eliminated from temples as though they had been forbidden by God. In this question we embrace and defend the negative position.

Dr. Beza:

THAT TEMPLES AND ALTARS PROFANED BY THE PAPISTS CAN BE RETAINED.

Reverend Doctor, I do not think that this matter needs to be treated with a lot of words between us, since we agree that temples and the altar intended for the use of the Lord's Supper can be retained. For even if they were used for their Idolatry, nevertheless we can use them for holding holy meetings and for the true use of the Sacraments. Thus we also retain the same temples at Geneva and in other places for the use for which <410> they were constructed and established in the first place. In the same way altars can also be retained for the use of the Lord's Supper.

THE GREAT AND HIDDEN POWER OF MUSICAL HARMONY. THE MOST EXCELLENT USE OF MUSIC.

As far as Organs are concerned, we know that the great force of its arts of Music and Harmony exists to move the souls of men. And we do not see a more excellent use for the Organ than that these arts be directed to and serve for the celebration and praise of the divine name, and for moving and rousing the souls of men to the true worship of God.

But we see what has happened in Papacy. For organs do not speak, and only the harmony is heard, without understanding. This affects only the ears and not the mind, for which cantors are employed. The common people do not understand what is being sung by the organ or the different voices of the Musicians, but the mind is held only by the harmony which strikes the ears.

WHAT MUSIC THERE IS USE OF IN TEMPLES. CHANTING OF THE PSALMS IN TEMPLES IS APPROVED OF.

But the use of this Music in temples is what is understood by all people, when the mind perceives what sounds in the ears, and what things are sung are understood in this way, and the chant has been adapted to that which is sung. Such is the practice of chanting the Psalms in the Church which we do not in the least disapprove.[48]

WHY IT SEEMS THAT FIGURATIVE[49] MUSIC OUGHT TO BE REMOVED FROM THE CHURCH.

But when there is playing of the Organ or other Musical instruments in the Church, or there is singing in different voices, such that it is not understood by the people, then only a sound is held in the ears, and they think more about the sound than about the things that are being sung. For this reason we remove that Music of which we see there is no good use in the Church. We do not in the least deny that in private homes there is good use for it, but in the Churches the

---

48   The French Protestants chanted the metrical psalter of Clément Marot (1496–1544), which Beza completed after Marot's death.

49   I.e., mensurally notated, often polyphonic (as opposed to monotonic chant); coined by 16th century German critics of music.

whole mind ought to be fixed on those things which lead forward to God and his true worship.

THE USE OF THE ORGAN AND OTHER INSTRUMENTS IS A MATTER OF INDIFFERENCE [ἀδιάφορον].

It is also well-known that Organists often play lewd, Trite pieces on the organs. This likewise should not happen in the Church. We do not deny that these Musical instruments are likewise matters of indifference [ἀδιάφορα], <411> which we can use or do without, without offense to God.

I proceed therefore to the following Thesis.

Dr. Jakob:

I will interject a few things for the sake of bearing witness to our consensus. For I understand this much, that Your Reverence judges that organs in temples are a matter of adiaphora, which have been neither commanded nor prohibited by God, and we also agree in this.

THE USE OF FIGURATIVE MUSIC AND THE ORGAN IN TEMPLES.

But you add that hearers have regard only to the sounds and the harmony, and not the things which are being sung about, whether it happens with an organ and instrumental Music or with a human voice, and for this reason there seems to be no good use for figurative Music in temples, since only the ears are affected and not the mind. I answer that the things themselves which are sung in figurative Music are not unknown to all, but rather are well-known to the educated, and those who have learned Latin or even Music, and the things themselves are brought to mind in the harmony. I can solemnly affirm this about myself, that I very much delight in figurative Music and the organ, and that not only do my ears perceive the sound but also that my mind is wondrously affected by the harmony, and is roused to prayers or giving or listening to sermons with a more ardent spirit, when an Ecclesiastical canticle is being played with a very sweet harmony either on the organ or by cantors, even before the preacher mounts the pulpit, according to the traditional way it is accustomed to be sung. For this reason I affirm that I feel effectively the divinely appointed power of harmony that inheres in figurative Music, which you spoke about at the beginning. I have heard the same thing also from many other pious men, Laymen too, ignorant of the art of Music, that they experience the same thing for themselves.

DAVID REPELLED THE EVIL SPIRIT OF THE LORD IN SAUL BY THE USE OF THE CITHARA, 1 SAMUEL 18[:10].

Besides, the history of David is well-known, when he was in Saul's presence, while he was being troubled by an evil spirit of the Lord, and David played the cithara, and repelled the wicked spirit with the harmony. This harmony was not only striking the ears of King Saul, but affecting his soul also, such that he was freed from the evil spirit for a time and was calmed. It is not written that David sang, but only that he played on the Musical instrument, and what sort it was.

<412>

HOW GREAT THE POWER OF FIGURATIVE MUSIC IS.

Therefore the power of figurative Music's harmony should not be condemned, which repressed the evil spirit of the Lord, and penetrates to the soul, even if that which is played or sung is not understood by everyone. They who understand also the sacred things which are sung together with the harmony, experience and feel this power much more in themselves.

MISUSE OF MUSICAL ORGANS DOES NOT DESTROY THEIR TRUE USE.

But as far as the misuse of organs in temples is concerned, when profane and impure things are played on them from time to time, this is a fallacy of accident,[50] and I judge that the true and legitimate use of organs in temples should not be at all abrogated on account of misuse. Otherwise we would have to forbid the use of wine to all since many abuse it to the point of inebriation.

---

50   I.e., arguing from what is true by accident to what is true by the nature of a thing; cf. p. 460, annotation (b).

For this reason when Organists play shameful things which are not at all decent for a Church meeting, they should be severely checked lest they do so henceforth, and we should pay careful heed lest the temple be profaned more than God be celebrated, but let all things in the Church take place decently and in good order.

WHAT HAS GIVEN THE REASON AND OCCASION FOR THE DISPUTE ABOUT ORGANS.

But this has given an occasion and reason for this question such that we proposed it, that in many places not only has merely the use of song and Musical organs in temples been abrogated as a matter profane and not in the least God pleasing, but in the temple itself horses have been called for, so that the universal body of organ Music might be driven out in ropes and chains in a single action as something profane, and eliminated from the temple. As if organ Music had been forbidden by God in temples, and could not be retained with a good conscience without offense to God. But since it is true that they are adiaphora, and not only licit but also honorable ornaments of temples, let them be used only for the celebration of the divine power, which is not only not forbidden, but is also expressly commanded, Psalm 150[:3–4]. Praise the Lord with trumpet sound; Praise him with lute and harp; Praise him with tambourine and dance; Praise him with strings and pipe; Praise him with sounding cymbals; Praise him with loud clashing cymbals.

<413>

So also, when the *ark of the Lord* was being led back from , David was playing with the entirety of Israel in the presence of *God*, with all virtue, in chants, and citharae, and lutes, and tambourines, and cymbals, and trumpets (1 Chronicles 13[:5–8]).

Dr. Beza:
Since we have consensus in this matter, I am not willing to add anything further. Let us proceed therefore to the fifth Thesis, in which the foundations of your opinion about the use of temples and images is put forth.

Thesis 5.

Foundations of the teaching of the Württemberg theologians
concerning images and musical instruments in temples.

Christ taught in the Jerusalem Temple, which place he nevertheless otherwise called a den of thieves. And we read that the feast of
dedication was happening, not the destruction of the temple.

Paul preaches Christ to the gentiles at the altar consecrated to
the unknown God at Athens (Acts 17[:16–34]). And we do not read
elsewhere in the Acts of the Apostles that such a thing was attempted
either by the Apostles or by their hearers.

Dr. Beza's Response.

Difference between the Jerusalem temple and other temples. The
Jerusalem temple a type of Christ (John 2).

---

*We judge that the nature of the Jerusalem temple was different
than that of our temples. For not only was it built to this end, that
it would be the certain place in which they would gather together
for hearing the word of God and rightly performing their sacred rites
according to God's mandate, but also it was something ceremonial.
Indeed that temple foreshadowed Christ, as is known from the John
2 passage: Destroy this temple, etc. (John 2[:19]).*

*Nevertheless, it is well that these things are brought up, that it is
understood that temples profaned by false Papistic worship can be
retained by Christian people without abuse. Just as the temple here
at Montbéliard, profaned by false Papistic worship, is now devoted
to the pure and genuine word of God, <414> that it may here be taught
and heard and the Sacraments rightly administered.*

Dr. Jakob:
There is consensus, and I think of nothing in which we disagree
in this part.

Dr. Beza:
I will therefore read the sixth Thesis.

THESIS 6.

Images, whether sculptures or paintings, were not absolutely forbidden in the law, but for the reason of divine worship, lest they stand for Idolatry.

For if God had wanted to forbid in his law (since he says, You will not make for yourself a graven image, neither anything resembling what is in heaven above, nor what is on the earth below, nor those things which are in the waters under the earth, Exodus 20[:4]) all images (even outside of the danger of adoration and idolatry), he certainly would not have given instructions for the two gold Cherubim to be made on the ark of the covenant, Exodus 25[:18], and on the curtain, Exodus 26[:1].

But in the Jerusalem Temple, constructed at the *Lord's* command, Solomon made two Cherubim in the Holy of holies, 1 Kings 6[:23]. And on the holy lavers Cherubim and Lions were on the side, 1 Kings 7[:29]. And in the same place, twelve bulls under the cast sea.

All these things were continually seen in the temple. Nevertheless, these images did not constitute sin against God's law, so long as no one worshiped the images.

Moses even offered a bronze snake for the Israelites in the desert to look at, Numbers 21[:8–9]. Hezekiah would not have destroyed it had not the people of Israel worshiped the serpent with incense, and used it for Idolatry.

Moreover, how great a distance is there from the depiction of the image of God which Isaiah relates: he saw the *Lord* sitting on a throne, high and lifted up, Isaiah 6[:1]?

<415>

And how about Daniel depicting God the Father for us as the ancient of days? Whose vestment was white as *snow*, and the hairs of his head like fine wool.

And then he depicts the son of man, approaching the ancient of days, Daniel 7. Are these not depictions? Therefore should we remove the images which are worshiped, this will be sufficient for this part of the divine law. There will be no danger from the rest of the images and depictions.

Dr. Beza's response.

WHY IMAGES WERE NOT ALLOWED TO BE BROUGHT INTO THE JERUSALEM TEMPLE.

Bringing in an image into the Jerusalem temple, no matter how small, was abominable in the time of the old testament, so long as the true and pure worship of God endured among the Israelite people, and it was not allowed for any reason. This is clear from Ezekiel's vision.

IN WHAT WAY THE LAW ABOUT NOT MAKING IMAGES SHOULD BE UNDERSTOOD, EXODUS 20.

But as far as the law itself is concerned, You will not make for yourself a graven image, nor any likeness of anything under heaven above, etc., the LORD forbids two things: the one, that they be made; the other, that they be worshiped. Nevertheless this was not imposed on consciences except by reason of divine worship, namely lest they be made with this goal in mind, and lest those things that have been fashioned be adored.

But what you bring up about the two Cherubim which were placed in the Holy of holies, there was no danger in these, since they were apart from any human observation, and were not seen by the Priests even, except for the high priest, and him only once a year, when he entered into the Holy of holies.

WHY THE TWO CHERUBIM WERE PUT TO USE ON THE MERCY SEAT.

But the LORD established these two Cherubim around the ark and the mercy seat, since they were a type of Christ, whom they were representing, by which he wanted to signify the man Christ whom the Angels would honor, on whom they desire to gaze (1 Peter 1[:12]), so that all would understand how great must be the Messiah who was to come.

<416>

As far as the oxen and lions are concerned, those were decorations of the building. There was no danger that these would be used for worship or adoration either. Besides these things Moses and Solomon made nothing for which they had not received a command from God. Therefore these things which are mentioned in your Theses also came to pass by way of divine precept and mandate.

Nevertheless I think it is fine to conclude from this that sculptures in and of themselves are not condemned by God. But I do not think that images ought to be located in holy places unless we pay very cautious heed lest they give occasion for idolatry.

To what is said about King Hezekiah's deed, I answer that if he had demolished and done away with the serpent long before, the people would not have been able to offer it incense and abuse it in Idolatry. But God wanted to signify by King Hezekiah's pious deed that they had not done wisely who had preserved this bronze serpent. Indeed it could have been preserved, but it not have been set out in public for the gaze of the whole people whom it invited to idolatry. But whatever the case may be, I nevertheless see also that in this Thesis there is consensus between us; therefore let us advance to the next Thesis.

Dr. Jakob:

THAT IMAGES WERE FORBIDDEN ONLY BY REASON OF WORSHIP.

As far as this Thesis is concerned, I also see that there is agreement between us. For the opinion of your Honor is that Images were forbidden only by reason of worship, and not simply by divine law. Their nature is in fact and remains adiaphora, provided we do not abuse them for worship.

WHY BRINGING IMAGES INTO THE JERUSALEM TEMPLE WAS NOT ALLOWED.

We are also agreed that bringing the smallest image into the temple of the *Lord* was not permitted to the Israelites on account of this most prevailing reason, that the temple itself with the place of atonement and those things that had been built around it, where a type and a prefiguring of Christ the Messiah to come, which they were representing. The *Lord* taught the people so sternly that this representation not be obscured, <417> lest they get mixed up with other statues and images. And so the Jews did right to cleanse the temple after it had been profaned with idols by Antiochus.

REGARDING THE BRONZE SERPENT, ETC.

And I do not think that the pious Kings who came before King Hezekiah sinned in preserving the bronze serpent as a memorial for the sake of the blessing shown. And I do not think it was always set out in public. Though it also should be numbered among the figures and shadows that represented Christ, as is plainly said in John 3[:14–15]. Thus it should not be doubted that Solomon and David made pious and correct use of this bronze serpent. They did not in the least wish to destroy it, since it was giving no cause or occasion for idolatry.

But afterward the Kings became idolaters, when the law of Moses was abandoned and the true worship of God neglected. They also misused the bronze serpent, just as all other things which their mad-ness, their spirit of fornication, supplied them.

But passing over all these things, there is consensus between us, that the bronze serpent was in its nature an adiaphoron after it performed its office in the desert. The people could have retained it with a good conscience so long as they were not infected with idola-trous worship. But after idolatry arrived, King Hezekiah did right to destroy it. The same also should be done with images if by them idolatry is put into effect; they should be removed from the sight of men and done away with.

Dr. Beza:

WHETHER THE IMAGE OF THE CRUCIFIX SHOULD BE REMOVED FROM TEMPLES ON ACCOUNT OF THE ABUSE OF PAST YEARS.

I hardly think that the Pontifical party misused any image more than the crucifix, for which reason I ask whether it is right if images of the crucifix be removed from sacred places? For the Papists are so mad that they not only offer it Incense, but even adore it with intolerable idolatry. O cross, they say, etc.

(Dr. Beza here recited an especially impious and Idolatrous prayer, which has not been recorded.)

<418>

I myself have seen and heard these things, and I confess that my whole body begins to shudder in horror as often as I think about those deeds. For our hope is placed in the true cross OF our LORD JESUS CHRIST, not in an image. For this reason I confess that I WHOLE-HEARTEDLY DETEST THE IMAGE OF THE CRUCIFIX. It is the image of the cruelty of the Jews against Christ, AND SO I CANNOT BEAR IT. Hezekiah is praised for destroying the bronze serpent to which divine worship was being offered (2 Kings 10 [18:4]), and so I think they should be praised also who do away with the image of the crucifix as well, for the purpose of guarding against the same idolatry, and eliminate them from all temples and sacred places. But let us advance to the next Thesis.

Dr. Jakob:

WHETHER THE IMAGE OF THE CRUCIFIX SHOULD BE REMOVED FROM TEMPLES.

Our business is about the danger and safety of souls, lest they receive any detriment from the use of images. Therefore your Reverence has asked about the image of the crucified Christ, whether it should be removed forthwith since the Pontifical churches misuse it for idolatry?

I answer in the same way I also answered above, that idolatry is not taken away when the things are removed from the gaze of men and their eyes, which they abuse for that purpose, since an idol is in the heart, as the Apostle bears witness (1 Corinthians 8). When it is removed from the heart, an image which is set out as a representation of sacred things does no harm at all. And the world is of such a mind that at the instigation of the Devil, to the degree that things are better and more excellent, they abuse them the more.

ABUSE REIGNS OVER ALL THINGS, EVEN THOSE MOST EXCELLENT. *RULE:* USE OF A THING SHOULD NOT BE DONE AWAY WITH ON ACCOUNT OF ABUSE.

For what is more excellent than the word of God, which is contained in the writings of the Prophets and the Apostles? But how grossly have Idolatrous men abused it for the purpose of their own contentious impiety? Therefore this rule must be observed: Use of a thing should not be done away with on account of abuse, otherwise the best things too must be rejected. Just think of the abomination of the Papist private Mass; <419> what did the Papists not abuse? The Lord's Prayer, the Apostles' Creed, the Apostlic Epistles, the Gospel, etc. All these were compelled to serve this idol. Surely all these should not on this account be rejected and eliminated from temples?

NO DANGER FROM IMAGES IN THE SAXON CHURCHES.

I have spoken also about the Saxon Churches, in which not only an image of the crucifix, but also very many other images, possibly even of those whose souls are in hell, still survive in the Churches. Nevertheless no one uses them for Idolatry. For if the word of God should ring out purely, there is no longer any danger from images. But when they are removed from the eyes, before idolatry is rooted out from the hearts of men by the word *of the Lord*, the danger to souls is greater in their obstinacy, because then they are unwilling to hear the word any longer. Examples of this have been witnessed in the Duchy of Württemberg.

CONDUCT MUST BE PRUDENT IN ABROGATING IMAGES.

Nor can a precise time for conversion be prescribed for people. For one man comes at the third hour, another at the sixth, the ninth, and some even come at the eleventh hour into the vineyard *of the*

Lord, towards all of whom must be exercised patience and charity in matters of adiaphora, as much as religion and conscience can bear. The salvation of one soul is to be preferred to the entire world, and we must take pains towards this goal, lest someone be offended by a rash action in matters of adiaphora. The public voice of the Gospel can easily remedy all these evils, provided the nature of the weak is considered. In its own time, the outer cleansing of temples follows this voice with the edification of the Church, provided not only that no one abuses images of this kind any longer, but also that they themselves, who had once been addicted to them, desire that they be done away with. They regard them in that place as if they were not present.

Dr. Beza:

There is a vast difference between the word of God and the abuse of images. For the word of God is necessary for us, and we cannot do without it. Images on the other hand are not necessary, <420> and we can do without them. What Augustine said to the pious Magistrate about the Donatists can be said correctly about images also.

And though it is true that it is not for us to prescribe a precise time of conversion for people, and in the reformed Saxon Churches, since the Papist church is no longer there, to what end therefore are the images, or what good use is there in them? Perhaps there are more who pretend consensus in doctrine, since the Magistrate is Christian, but once he were removed, what do you think would happen? And the picture of the Ancient of days in Daniel was not put forward as if it were a picture. Though I would not deny that depiction of this sort is not sin, but rather an adiaphoron.

Dr. Jakob:

DOCTRINE OF CHRISTIAN LIBERTY SHOULD BE PRESERVED IN THE CHURCH.

The doctrine of Christian liberty must also be carefully preserved in matters of adiaphora, even though there can be sin in excess just as much as in defect, but especially when freedom is closely joined with a stumbling-block, whence the Apostle: If eating scandalizes my brother, I will never eat flesh again, lest I scandalize my brother (1 Corinthians 8[:10–13]). Since therefore Your Reverence also is of this opinion, always considering the nature of the weak, and he concedes that all these things are in their nature adiaphora, then there is also consensus between us in this. All things must be directed towards edification and not towards destruction.

Dr. Beza:
We do approve of written, as opposed to painted, images, such as are the visions from Daniel and Isaiah the prophet, which the Lord wanted to be perpetual. For pictures do not speak, but the word of God always speaks, and for this reason it should remain in the word, and not <421> be stuck in a picture. This notwithstanding, we nevertheless really do consent that pictures of this sort are an adiaphoron.

Dr. Jakob:
If the description of God put forward in Daniel and Isaiah the prophet were to be painted, does Dr. Beza think that ought to be numbered also among the adiaphora?

Dr. Beza:
I concede that it is an adiaphoron, provided no occasion is given for idolatry. But I am going on to Thesis 7.

THESIS 7.

St. Paul's prescription regarding not offending the weak should be carefully observed. And idols should be removed from the minds of men by the word of God before they are removed from the eyes of men.

Dr. Beza's response.

WHEN WE MUST HAVE REGARD FOR THE NATURE OF THE WEAK IN FAITH.

The Apostle's rule about the weak in eating those things that had been sacrificed to idols is most sure and we do not at all doubt it. But since his observation is twofold, we think that the nature of the weak in faith must be regarded lest they be confirmed in their infirmity and depart into obstinacy. For this reason we ought to take heed lest the things objected to cause them harm. This is why I think it is better if the instruments of idolatry were to be removed and taken away from their eyes.

Dr. Jakob:

I agree. If only it should happen with regard to reason and in its own time, lest there be any danger in regard to the weak.

Dr. Beza:
I proceed to the eighth Thesis.

<422>

THESIS 8.

As far as Organs and Musical instruments are concerned, the clear word of God stands: Praise the Lord with strings and pipe. Praise him with fine sounding cymbals. Praise him with cymbals of jubilation. The example of the most pious Kings, David, Solomon, Hezekiah, Josiah, etc., testify to the same thing. Their instrumental Music in the temple was not reproved by the holy Spirit, but was rather commended.

Dr. Beza's response.

HOW THE PRECEPT ABOUT PRAISING GOD WITH THE ORGAN SHOULD BE UNDERSTOOD.

I refer those precepts about strings, organ, and cymbals to ceremonial worship, which was instituted in the old Testament. And I think that Music used to be something other than what it is now, and perhaps those who could reduce it would not be missing the mark. Now, I do not think they should be forbidden from being instructed, like the rest who do not use these, who think they do not profit for edification. In summary, I do not think we are obliged to restore organs in the temple. Let them be used where they can and for whom they are pleasing. But I do not think that they necessarily ought to be played because of a precept and command OF GOD. We have the especially resounding word of God and the Sacraments. If external things can also be used for edification, so be it. But I do not think these are prescribed for us as in a mandated law of God, nor, I think, is this your opinion either.

Dr. Jakob:

WHETHER INSTRUMENTAL MUSIC WAS INSTITUTED BY KINGS BY GOD'S MANDATE. *THE HUMAN VOICE.* FIGURATIVE MUSIC IS ALSO APPROVED BY GOD.

We agree: the Kings of the old Testament, David, Solomon, Hezekiah, Josiah, did not possess a special mandate to institute instrumental Music in the temple, but did this in view of their own piety because of the general mandate which was brought forward in our Thesis: In what the Lord instructs, as in all things, which can set out from man, let them be directed to <423> the celebration of the name of God. Since therefore the human voice is distinct and numbered among the most excellent of God's gifts, therefore it ought also to be directed towards praising God, lest we be thought less in this regard than the birds, who celebrate *God* perpetually with their very sweet singing. But even when they employ instrumental Music, it is also approved by God, as the holy Spirit plainly bears witness in the words of the Psalm we mentioned.

USE OF MUSICAL HARMONY AMONG THE UNSKILLED.

Besides this the masses, roused by the harmony, run to hear sermons, which they would otherwise neglect in great number. For this reason also they serve the edification of the Church.

WHY MENTION WAS MADE OF THE ORGAN AND OTHER MUSICAL INSTRUMENTS IN THIS DISPUTATION.

For this reason we make mention of all these things, as was said above, since in certain places they have sent for horses and eliminated organs from the Churches as if they were forbidden by God and had been not at all legitimate in temples of Christians. But there is consensus between us: by their nature, having Musical organs or not having them is an adiaphoron. This has been left to the judgment of each Church.

Dr. Beza:
We actually do agree, though I would add this: The positions of the Levites, the Cantors, in the old Testament, had been distributed by instruction of the holy Spirit. For this reason the Music was introduced by the precept and mandate of God in a way that had a certain end. But we also can use them well for exciting enthusiasm for listening to the word OF THE LORD. Let us proceed to the examination of the dogmas which have been placed under your Theses.

\<424\>

The Württemberg Theologians think the following dogmas are not in accordance with holy Scripture.

DOGMA 1.

The Gospel cannot be taught in a temple in which forbidden and Idolatrous rites have been celebrated.

DOGMA 2.

The Lord's Supper cannot be celebrated on an altar which previously served for the abomination of a private Mass.

DOGMA 3.

A table made of wood, in place of a stone altar, must necessarily be established in temples, on which the Lord's Supper may be celebrated. Although Christ together with his disciples nevertheless used not a table, but reclined on the ground after the manner and fashion of the gentiles.

DOGMA 4.

Removal of Images must not be permitted to the masses, but it has instead been entrusted to the piety and wisdom of Kings, Princes, and the regular Magistrate of each place.

Dr. Beza's response.

As far as temples are concerned, I laid out our opinion above, namely, that the Gospel can be taught in temples in which Idolatrous rites have previously been celebrated. For this reason, that Thesis does not concern us.

THAT THE LORD'S SUPPER CAN ALSO BE CELEBRATED ON AN ALTAR.

Next, as far as altars are concerned, there is no assumption about whether the Lord's Supper is celebrated on a stone altar or on a wooden table. For this is a matter adiaphora. But on the other hand the thing itself shows how astute our enemy is. For had altars never been constructed, the LORD'S Supper would never have been perverted into a sacrifice. For altars gave birth to sacrifices from our perspective.

<425>

For this reason, even if I do not condemn the thing itself, that the Lord's Supper is celebrated and distributed on a stone altar, I nevertheless say that Satan has used this opportunity to pervert the Sacrament of the Eucharist as we see it into a sacrifice. For where there is no altar, there is no sacrifice. And Paul mentions the table of the Lord, not the altar.

A MARBLE ALTAR HAS BEEN TRANSFERRED FROM LAUSANNE TO BERN.

But I am not opposed to the Lord's Supper being able to be celebrated on an altar. For a marble altar has been transferred from Lausanne to Bern, and the Lord's Supper is celebrated on it.

Dr. Jakob:
The altar did not do this, but rather the pernicious teaching of Pastors and Bishops perverted the Lord's Supper into a sacrifice.

They should have been on guard not to depart from the words of Christ's Testament, and his holy institution. Moreover, Paul also calls the altar of Idolatrous gentiles tables of which he would not have the Corinthians be sharers (1 Corinthians 10[:18]).

But that there are many who share the opinion that celebrating the Lord's Supper on an altar on which a Papistic sacrifice was formerly offered is not in the least an adiaphoron, I am happy to recount briefly a true history.

HISTORY OF THE CONTROVERSY BETWEEN A CERTAIN PRINCE AND A COUNT, CONCERNING A TABLE AND AN ALTAR IN A TEMPLE.

There was a certain Count of your confession who possessed common jurisdiction in a certain Church with a certain Prince of our Religion. Therefore since the Associate was judging that he had more of a right in that Church, he made sure that the altar was destroyed and that a table be built in the temple. The Prince found out later about this, and ordered that the table be removed and an altar be constructed again. The Count in return took care a second time in return that the altar be destroyed, and the table restored. The Prince likewise a second time ordered that the table be taken away and the altar restored. I do not know whether this happened a third time. But the count later heeded the Prince's strictness, and left off from his course, such that the altar remained in the temple in place of the table. <426> This shows that it is very necessary for people to be taught rightly about the matter. For if the Count had thought it was an adiaphoron to celebrate the *Lord's* Supper on an altar or on a table, this contest and strife would never have arisen between himself and the Prince, with so great an offense and stumbling block to the subjects of his land.

Dr. Beza:
The ancients did not recline on the ground, but rather they also had tables. But I do not wish to fight about this.

Dr. Jakob:

The custom and daily habit of the Oriental people even up to today confirm that custom. They do not use tables but take their food reclining on the ground.

Dr. Beza:

It is outside of controversy that all things in the Church ought to be done in good order, according to the saying of the Apostle: let everything be done in order and decently (1 Corinthians 14[:40]).

Therefore as it concerns the demolition of statues that has already taken place, I would not want rashly to condemn their zeal in these actions. For though they seem to have done these things less rightly, nevertheless it appears later that they acted piously, whom we have just now seriously reproved. We read likewise the extraordinary deed of Phineas, son of Eleazar son of Aaron the Priest, who aroused by zeal, took up a dagger and stabbed an Israelite man with his Moabite harlot (Numbers 25[:6–8]). For this reason I would not wish rashly to condemn those particular cases.

Dr. Jakob:

INTEMPERATE BEHAVIOR IN OVERTURNING TEMPLES NOT TO BE APPROVED OF. EPILOGUE OF THE COLLOQUY CONCERNING THE CHURCHES' IMAGES AND ORGANS.

Each and every person will render to God an account of their own deeds. But <427> we testify that that intemperate behavior is not approved by us in the least. I thank *God* moreover for our consensus in this article. For we did not propose these dogmas thinking that you were of a contrary opinion; rather, your Churches have a general reputation that is badly understood, that churches have been over-turned in those disturbances, and images reduced to rubble, and this was done by the mob. For this reason it is helpful that all know that that confusion is approved not at all by you, but that all things are to be recalled to order, especially so that the people may be educated and rightly instructed, that Images in and of themselves are in their nature adiaphora, and if they do not stand in public for Idolatry, such things can be retained without offense to God, by which holy things are represented. As for the rest, the pious Magistrate ought vigilantly and prudently to act, lest the weak in faith be harmed, or occasion be granted for Idolatry. However they should especially not permit this license to the indiscriminate mob, that they vent their rage against images and in abolition of them, do such things as can create a stumbling block for the weak.

May the *Lord* grant that in the remaining controversial Articles we may likewise find complete consent. Amen.

<428>

5

Concerning Baptism

Dr. Beza:
We come now to the Theses you wrote concerning Baptism, in which certain ones pertain to the general question about the substance and fruit of Baptism, what its virtue is, and in what things it consists. But certain ones particularly concern the Baptism of infants, whether they should be baptized who have been born in the Church.

Dr. Jakob:
The Honorable Prince, Count Frederick, wishes our Theses to be delivered publicly before we undertake the conference.

Dr. Beza:
I am fine with this.

Dr. Lucas Osiander therefore recited the following Theses.

5A. CONCERNING BAPTISM

Placed outside of the controversy.

1. Baptism consists of water and God's word.

2. Baptism has replaced circumcision.

<429>

3. Baptism is to be conferred even upon the infants of Christians.

4. But it has come into controversy: Whether Baptism is a washing of regeneration and renewal in the holy Spirit, or whether it is merely a sign by which adoption is signified and sealed?

5. In this question our assertion is this: Baptism is not merely a sign, but is truly a washing of regeneration.

6. The foundations of this faith and our confession are these:

Christ loved the Church and gave himself for her in order that he might sanctify her, cleansing her with washing of water in the word (Ephesians 5[:26]).

Unless someone has been born again of *water* and the Spirit, he is not able to enter into the kingdom of God (John 3[:5]).

He saved us not because of works of righteousness which we have done, but according to his mercy, through the washing of regeneration and renewal of the holy Spirit (Titus 3[:5]).

As many of you as have been baptized have put on Christ (Galatians 3[:27]).

We who have been baptized in Christ Jesus have been baptized into his death; we have been buried with him through Baptism into death, so that just as Christ rose from the dead through the glory of the father, so also we may walk in newness of life (Romans 6[:4]).

<430>

5B. WE JUDGE THAT THE FOLLOWING DOGMAS CONFLICT WITH HOLY SCRIPTURE.

1. When it is taught that a latent virtue is not bound or attached to the Sacraments, by which the Holy Spirit confers grace to the baptized, but has divinely joined to these things merely this gift, to confirm as sacred and bear witness to us of God's goodness.

2. That they are foolish who bind together the Holy Spirit what he accomplishes in us with the Sacraments. They are employed rather for this reason, that they may seal adoption in the infants of believers, and also faith in adults.

3. That regeneration or salvation does not depend on baptism.

4. That these are improper or figurative forms of speaking: 1. Baptism is a washing away of sins. 2. Baptism washes away sins. On the other hand, that this is a proper form of speaking: Baptism is a sign of the washing away of sins.

5. That although Baptism by the Apostles was a washing of sins and renewal, and the same is called a washing away, it must not be understood literally.

6. That Baptism is a very sure pledge of the washing away of sins, of regeneration, renewal, and finally adoption, in the elect, in whom alone its virtue is evident.

<431>

7. That not all infants who are baptized have a share in the grace of Christ and are regenerated.

8. That infants lack faith and nevertheless ought to be baptized.

9. That the working of the covenant depends neither on baptism nor any acquisitions.

10. That children of the faithful are not baptized so that they may become sons first, who prior to this were estranged from the Church. They are rather received into the Church by it as a solemn sign, since they were already beneficiaries of the promise before they belonged to Christ's body.

11. In an extreme case of emergency, it is not permissible for women to baptize infants.

Signed:
Dr. Jakob Andreae
Dr. Lucas Osiander

Even though the responses of Dr. Beza and his brothers were not recited here, nevertheless it seemed good to insert them in this place so that the pious reader may more easily compare them with the Theses of the Württemberg Theologians and understand the conference that follows.

<432>

5C. ON THE THESES CONCERNING BAPTISM.

ON THESIS 1.

What we perceive to be wanting in this Thesis is the particularly neglected part of this Sacrament, namely the blood of Christ, (a) of which the water is a sacramental sign. (b) But we say that it should not in the least have been neglected, since it is essential to the rites of this holy work described by the Apostle, Romans 6:4–5; Colossians 2:12. (c)

DR. JAKOB ANDREAE'S MARGINAL NOTES, IN WHICH A BRIEF RESPONSE WAS MADE TO DR. BEZA'S THESES AFTER THE COLLOQUY WAS CONCLUDED. (A) SINCE FROM THE START IT HAD SEEMED GOOD TO LAY OUT THOSE THINGS THAT WERE ENTIRELY OUTSIDE OF THE CONTROVERSY, THE FIRST THESIS WAS ALSO GENERALLY LAID OUT THAT BAPTISM CONSISTS OF WATER AND GOD'S WORD. BY THE TERM "WORD OF GOD," HOWEVER, WHAT OUR OPPONENTS DESIRE IS INCLUDED HERE, NAMELY, THAT A WASHING FROM SINS DOES NOT HAPPEN WITHOUT THE BLOOD OF CHRIST. (B) WATER DOES NOT SIGNIFY THE BLOOD OF CHRIST, BUT IS THE INSTRUMENT THROUGH WHICH WE ARE WASHED FROM SINS, REGENERATED, RENEWED IN CHRIST'S BLOOD BY THE VIRTUE OF THE HOLY SPIRIT. (C) THE ESSENTIAL RITE IS INDEED COMPREHENDED IN THE WORD OF GOD: BAPTIZE. WE ARE THEREFORE CHASTISED WITHOUT CAUSE, AS IF IT HAD BEEN OMITTED BY US.

ON THESIS 2 AND 3.

We agree.

ON THESIS 4.

We assert that both of those things, namely a seal of adoption and regeneration, are offered by God, and indeed also the remission of sins, in Baptism rightly administered. (d) Though they are not always received by everyone, (e) nor at that very time when baptism is administered. (f)

(D) The doctrine of Dr. Beza and his brother concerning Baptism is exactly the same as his doctrine concerning the Lord's Supper, namely that regeneration, sealing, and remission of sins are offered, but not conferred, to all the baptized. (E) Here are excluded those whom they say have been created and ordained by God to eternal damnation already from the point of their conception and birth, whom God does not wish to be regenerated and saved. (F) They say this becausee they teach that there are elect who are baptized, who do not immediately become regenerated, but rather sometimes not until extreme old age. This is because for them Baptism is merely a sign of regeneration, but not a washing of regeneration, such that all infants who might be baptized, are also necessarily regenerated and renewed. More concerning this in the article on predestination.

On Thesis 5.

We do not teach that Sacraments are mere signs, (g) but we nevertheless deny that what belongs to the holy Spirit alone is attributable to external action. (h) (i) <433> Just as they are not separated, but distinguished, by John, Matthew 3:11, and by Peter, 1 Peter 3:2 [3:21], so also the Apostle speaks about the whole Ministerium: the one who plants and the one who waters are nothing.

(G) Indeed you do not assert this in words, but you do so actually in your explanation of the words. This is because you locate the substance of the Sacraments merely in signifying. (H) Even though there is a distinction between the external action of Baptism and the interior power of the Holy Spirit, nevertheless on account of God's ordaining, the power of the Holy Spirit, whose proper work is regeneration, is rightly attributed to external action. But this separation smells like the error of the Schwenckfeldians. (I) They make two Baptisms, while they exclude water from the proper work of Baptism, which belongs to the Holy Spirit.

ON THESIS 6.

We approve all these testimonies of holy Scripture, by which both the institution of Baptism and its effects are declared in those who do not reject the benefits offered them by their own unworthiness. (k)

(k) HERE THEY EXCLUDE ALL PEOPLE, BOTH THOSE BAPTIZED AND THOSE YET TO BE BAPTIZED, WHO HAVE BEEN ORDAINED TO ETERNAL DAMNATION BY GOD'S ETERNAL AND HIDDEN DECREE, BEFORE THEY DID ANYTHING GOOD OR BAD. FOR THEY AFFIRM THAT THESE PEOPLE WOULD NEVER BE REGENERATED, THOUGH THOUSANDS BE BAPTIZED, WHICH IS HORRENDOUS TO HEAR.

5D. ON THE DOGMAS WRITTEN UNDER THE ABOVE THESES

ON DOGMA 1 AND 2.

We think that attributing some latent virtue to water (even if sacramental), (l) other than that of sacramental signification which is never void or empty (because it has to do with God promising), (m) is manifest Idolatry. (n) To be sure, even the power of forgiving sins (which belongs not even to Angels), and of renewing the human heart, is thus transferred to water, even if it is sacramental. (o)

(L) IF EVERY LATENT POWER IS REMOVED FROM THE WATER OF BAPTISM, WHAT IS LEFT, MAY I ASK, OTHER THAN EMPTY SIGNS? THIS CONFLICTS WITH THE SUBSTANCE OF BAPTISM. FOR WHAT REGENERATES IN BAPTISM BY DIVINE INSTITUTION IS NOT THE HOLY SPIRIT WITHOUT WATER, NOR WATER WITHOUT THE HOLY SPIRIT, BUT THE HOLY SPIRIT THROUGH THE WATER, AND WATER BY VIRTUE OF THE HOLY SPIRIT. (M) THE WATER OF BAPTISM IS NOT MERELY FOR THE PURPOSE OF SIGNIFICATION, BUT FOR A REAL DELIVERY OF REGENERATION, AS AN INSTRUMENT THAT HAS BEEN INSTITUTED BY GOD. FOR THIS REASON THIS ASSERTION IS OPENLY FALSE AND IMPIOUS. (N) WE DOUBT NOT IN THE LEAST THAT THIS IS BLASPHEMY AGAINST CHRIST, THE AUTHOR OF BAPTISM. FOR THIS DOCTRINE OF BAPTISM IS NOT IDOLATRY, BUT WORSHIP OF GOD, AS WAS LAID OUT A LITTLE EARLIER. (O) THIS LATENT POWER OF REGENERATING IS NOT ATTRIBUTED TO WATER SIMPLY, OR RATHER IN AND OF ITSELF, BUT RATHER BECAUSE DIVINITY HAS BEEN AFFIXED TO THIS IN BAPTISM.

<434>

ON DOGMA 3.

We are surprised that one thing has been neglected here from the particular ends of Baptism, namely the remission of sins. (p) But we keep our salvation from Baptism this far, (q) that we neither commence the foundation of salvation itself from it, nor the lack of it, but judge that people are excluded from salvation by contempt.

(P) REMISSION OF SINS IS COMPREHENDED IN THE TERM "SALVATION." FOR THERE IS NO SAVING WHERE THERE IS NO REMISSION OF SINS. (Q) THIS RESPONSE IS CLEARLY IMPIOUS. IT DEPRIVES BELIEVERS OF EVERY CONSOLATION WHICH THEY HAVE LAID UP IN BAPTISM AS A FOUNDATION OF SALVATION, ACCORDING TO THE WORD OF CHRIST: HE WHO BELIEVES AND HAS BEEN BAPTIZED WILL BE SAVED.

ON DOGMA 4 AND 5.

As often as what belongs to a signified thing is attributed to external action (of the sort that in baptism is CHRIST'S blood and the holy Spirit's work, which is an interior cleansing, through Christ's blood), we affirm that it is a sacramental Metonymy. (r)

(R) WE OPENLY CONDEMN THIS METONOYMY, JUST AS IN THE LORD'S SUPPER, WHICH SUBVERTS THE SUBSTANCE OF THE SACRAMENT OF BAPTISM. FOR THE WATER OF BAPTISM WAS INSTITUTED BY CHRIST NOT FOR THE PURPOSE OF SIGNIFYING REGENERATION, BUT RATHER FOR THE PURPOSE OF CONFERRING IT. HERE NO METONYMY, NOR EXCHANGE OF ONE TERM FOR ANOTHER, HAS ANY PLACE.

ON DOGMA 6.

We assert that a whole baptism is always offered to whichever adults are baptized. But the interior one is received only by those who confess true faith, (s) either at the very time when they are baptized, or when this happens to them through God's grace. Nor in fact do we refer the efficacy of Baptism to that moment when it is performed, (t) but rather, the very benefits of Christ offered in it are sometimes derived from it later, as in the case of Cornelius (Acts 10[:25–47]). Just as Abraham was justified before he was circumcised, meanwhile we affirm that it follows in those, namely, who do not have faith, but will have that which they confess when they are baptized in their own time.

(S) THEY CONTRIVE A DOUBLE BAPTISM, AN INTERIOR AND EXTERIOR, ALTHOUGH BAPTISM IS ONLY ONE, WHICH CONSISTS OF AN EXTERNAL THING, NAMELY WATER, AND AN INTERNAL THING BY VIRTUE OF THE REGENERATING SPIRIT. (T) THIS IS A CLEAR AND PLAIN PROFANATION OF THE DIVINE NAME IN THE ACTION OF BAPTISM, BY WHICH THE VIRTUE OF BAPTISM IS CONTINUALLY REJECTED UNTIL OLD AGE.

<435>

ON DOGMA 7.

We think that it is absurd to say that infants are renewed such that they become new people, with the old man killed; it is absurd to say this at that very time when they are baptized, or before the age of adulthood, or even before the time they have acknowledged and accepted Christ through faith. (u) Nevertheless we assert that adoption of the covenant in which they are born is sealed in them, and the grace of remission of original sin; only let them not deprive themselves of these benefits when they have become adults.

(U) THIS IS ALSO A PATENTLY FALSE AND IMPIOUS ASSERTION, WHICH DENIES THAT INFANTS BORN AND BAPTIZED IN THE CHURCH ARE REGENERATED.

ON DOGMA 8 AND 10.

Even though infants lack their own faith, especially actual faith (seeing as it comes from the hearing of the preached word, Romans 10[:17]), (x) nevertheless from the formula of the covenant, I will be your God, and the God of your seed, Genesis 17:7, those who have been included by their parents through faith, for themselves and their children (for which reason also they are called holy, 1 Corinthians 7:14), are worthily baptized, and are thought probably to be presented with the fruit of adoption, (y) though the final, hidden verdict is left to God. (z)

(x) This assertion is no less clearly false and impious, in which it is affirmed that infants lack their own faith, contrary to the express word of Christ, Whoever offends *one of these smallest ones who* believe in me. And infants believe more easily than adults, since the use of reason impedes more than promotes faith, 1 Corinthians 2[:1–5]. (y) They are thought to be children of God not probably, but certainly, and baptized infants are presented with the fruit of adoption, since God cannot deceive with His promise. Therefore they who teach such doctrines about Baptism put in its place a dubious consolation and totally subvert the virtue of Baptism, and profane the very Sacrament instituted by Christ. (z) They are heeding their own impious dogma concerning God's hidden decree against the greatest part of the human race, which God is unwilling to be regenerated through Baptism.

On Dogma 9.

The answer to this is above, at Theses 1 and 2.

On Dogma 11.

Baptism is part of the public Ministerium, which is forbidden to women by the express word of God, (a) and also to private persons. Nor can they seem to have spurned Baptism, either, <436> who die unbaptized through no fault of their own. Nor can any necessity happen to transgress the laws of the insistent public ministerium. (b)

(A) It is not permitted for women to speak *in the Church*, that is, to give sermons in the company of men (1 Corinthians 14[:33–35]). But when there is no man present, both preaching and baptizing in a case of emergency is permitted, since in Christ there is no male nor female, but all are *one* in Christ Jesus (Galatians 3[:27]). <436> (B) There is no law extant in the Word of the Lord which prevents women in a case of emergency either from teaching or from baptizing.

Signed:
Theodore Beza, Minister of the Church at Geneva.
Abraham Musculus, Minister of the Church at Bern.
Pierre Hübner, Professor of Greek, in the public
Gymnasium at Bern.
Antoine de La Faye, Minister of the Church at Geneva.

Claude Albery, Bachelor and Professor of Philosophy
in the Academy at Lausanne.
At Montbéliard, 29 March 1586.

5E.I. CONFERENCE CONCERNING BAPTISM.

Dr. Beza:
If it is alright, we will follow the order which we observed in the preceding article, that we respond to your Theses one by one, and if we want to, briefly add something.

Dr. Jakob:
This is fine by me.

CONCERNING THE SUBSTANCE OF BAPTISM, IN WHAT THINGS IT CONSISTS.

Dr. Beza:
In the first Thesis, Sir, I ask: what do you understand there by the word Baptism? The external action with water, or an internal action of the Holy Spirit, or an interior and exterior Baptism together at the same time?

Dr. Jakob:
By Baptism we understand all those things that pertain to the substance of Baptism and are of necessity required, namely the external Element and the word of God's command and promise.

<437>

Dr. Beza:
We also say that external Baptism consists of an external Element and word. For this reason we affirm that this Thesis of yours is true about external Baptism. But with reference to interior Baptism, we say that it is an insufficient description of Baptism. Since Baptism consists not only of word and Element or sign, but also of the thing signified, namely Christ's blood, which is especially needed in Baptism.

For the action of Baptism, as far as the Element of water is concerned, meets the eyes, though the word of promise meets the ears. But just as we have said about the Lord's Supper, that not only do the external signs of bread and wine meet the eyes and other external senses, but the thing signified is presented and offered to the mind, namely, the body and blood of Christ, so also Baptism (since the property of Sacraments is the same, which consist of signs and things signified) consists not only of an external Element and word, but also of the thing signified, namely, Christ's blood, which cleanses us from all sins. This blood is represented by the water of Baptism (1 John 5[:6–8]). The rite of the external action of Baptism reminds us of this, concerning which Paul preaches in Romans 6[:3–4], when he says, *Or are you unaware that whoever of us have been baptized into Christ Jesus have been baptized into his death? We were therefore buried with him through Baptism into death, so that just as Christ was raised from the dead through the glory of the Father, so we also may walk in newness of life.*

SIGNIFICATION OF THE EXTERNAL RITE IN BAPTISM.

For through immersion into the water of Baptism, mortification of the old Adam and joining in the death of Christ is represented. But by emerging, a spiritual resurrection is represented, by which we rise again from the death of sin to righteousness and newness of life. The blood of Jesus Christ presents all these things to us. They are represented through the action of Baptism <438> and offered to the baptized. And this inner action is performed by the Holy Spirit by virtue of Christ's blood. For this reason the blood of Christ should necessarily have been added, in which Baptism consists, not less than it does of word and water. You say in your Thesis, however, that Baptism consists only of word and water, though on account of the signification of Christ's blood it also should have been added. I am speaking, though, not about a bare signification, but rather a representation of the kind by which the thing signified is offered also, and presented with its external sign.

Dr. Jakob:

Only one Baptism.

Reverend Dr. Beza, I wish to respond not in my own words, but those of the Apostle Paul, who writes this way to the Ephesians: One Lord, one faith, one Baptism, one God and Father of all, who is over all, and through all, and in all (Ephesians 4[:5–6]). It is clear from these words of the Apostle that there is only one baptism, and not two, an inner and an outer, as you have distinguished. This one Baptism consists of water and Spirit, just as Christ says: Unless someone is born again of water and spirit, he cannot enter the kingdom of heaven (John 3[:5]). For water without the Spirit is not a Baptism, nor is spirit a Baptism without water, but water with the spirit and spirit with the water joined together with Christ's word, under which word in our first Thesis we understand the holy Spirit, which it embraces. Christ also instituted Baptism by this word. Baptize them, he said, in the name of the Father, Son, and holy Spirit (Matthew 28[:19]). These things make a Baptism, which is a washing of regeneration and renewal in the holy Spirit (Titus 3[:5]).

In what way Sacraments are different from each other. Baptism.

This is why it is asked in vain whether we understand by the term Baptism merely an external, and not at the same time an internal Baptism, since there is only one Baptism, not <439> two Baptisms, one inner, the other outer. Next, as far as a common property of the Sacraments of Baptism and the Lord's Supper is concerned, even though Christ's blood coincides in all things, nevertheless the property of all Sacraments is not for this reason the same throughout. They in fact differ, not only with respect to their Elements, but also with respect to their formal cause, which is taken from the word and its ends or effects. For in Baptism we are regenerated, not reinvigorated; in the Lord's Supper we who have been born again are reinvigorated, not regenerated. Again, in Baptism the holy Spirit regenerates us through water in Christ's blood; in the Lord's Supper, however, Christ reinvigorates us with his own body and blood.

Even though on this account the application of Christ's blood in both the Sacrament of Baptism and the Lord's Supper is for the imputation of grace if they are received in faith, nevertheless as single Sacraments they have their own certain properties and definitions, distinct from each other, expressed in the word.

Therefore since Christ has joined water with spirit and spirit with water, when he says, Unless anyone has been born again of water and Spirit, and does not say, unless anyone has been born again of water only, nor of spirit only, and repeats the same thing in the institution of Baptism, when he says, Baptize them in the name of the Father, Son, and holy Spirit, for this reason we cannot acknowledge two Baptisms, the one inner, which is signified by the outer, the other outer, which signifies and represents the inner. Rather we acknowledge one Baptism only, not two.

THE EFFECT OF BAPTISM NOT TO BE CONFUSED WITH ITS SUBSTANCE. SPIRIT AND WATER NOT TO BE TORN APART IN BAPTISM.

Furthermore, we ought not confuse Baptism's effect, which is regeneration, with Baptism's substance, which consists of water and Spirit. For regeneration is one thing, and Baptism is another, which consists of water and Spirit, by which regeneration happens, according to Christ's word in Baptism. For the holy Spirit regenerates through the sprinkling of water done in the name of the entire Trinity. And for this reason the Spirit and the water in Baptism <440> must in no way be torn apart, which have been joined together in this action by the word of Christ, and remain joined together such that in this action Baptism cannot be called, or be, one without the other. These are the substantial things in Baptism, without which Baptism cannot exist.

Dr. Beza:
Paul's words from the Epistle to the Ephesians do not seem to me to be cited in a way suitable to this point. He warns us in these words not to follow different religions, but that we all remain under the one Christ. And we also acknowledge that there is only one Bap-

tism, and we are not saying that there are two types of Baptism. For there is one Baptism.

Dr. Jakob:

The very matter at hand shows that Paul's words have been cited suitably by me. For it is not being asked where Paul was looking back to or to what end he wrote these words, but it is enough that he says that Baptism is *one*. You, however, make two Baptisms, an outer of water, and an inner of spirit, which loudly contradicts Paul's words.

Dr. Beza:

But what is the reason, when you make the holy Spirit a part of Baptism, that you do not also put it in this Thesis in which you say, Baptism consists of two things, the Element and the word; why do you pass over the holy Spirit?

Dr. Jakob:

The reason we did not expressly put the holy Spirit in this Thesis is that from the start we wanted to put in only those things in which there was consensus between us, as was also done in the prior articles. For we thought that you would never <441> deny that Baptism consists of a word and an Element, according to the widely known saying of Augustine, Let the word approach the Element, and it is a Sacrament. Now, we are not unaware how these are understood by you and us, and how differently they are understood. On the contrary, when we were writing those Theses, the conversation we had about it amongst ourselves was that it would have to be explained whenever we came to the controversial Theses. Only this axiom, solid and outside of controversy, was put there, Baptism consists of word and Element, because no understanding person can deny it. But what the word embraces, and what is understood by it, that is another question, explained in the other Theses that follow. Besides this, the holy Spirit is comprehended and included as the principal and substantial part of baptism (if I may say so) in the word. For just as in the Lord's Supper, the body and blood of Christ are included in the word of the Testament: Take, eat, this is my body; Take, drink, this is my blood; so also in the word of Baptism the holy Spirit is included, and joined together with the external Element of water, by which Christ bids us baptize. For if anyone were sprinkled thousands and thousands of times over with water, they would never be washed from their sins. But when the word of God approaches the water, and the holy Spirit through the word of God, and this water is sprinkled in the name of the Father, Son, and holy Spirit, then finally the one baptized is washed from sins, regenerated, and renewed, and becomes wholly a new person.

Dr. Beza:
Why do you attribute the holy Spirit to Baptism rather than to the Lord's Supper?

Dr. Jakob:
Because the word of God expressly teaches this, and it pleased God so to do it, who ordained that the holy Spirit regenerates in Baptism. <442> The body and blood of Christ, on the other hand, spiritually reinvigorate us in the Lord's Supper.

Dr. Beza:
The way you establish signs in the Lord's Supper and the thing expressed by the word of Christ, namely that the body of Christ given for us and the blood of Christ poured out for our sins, is the same way you also confess that it is necessary that you establish in Baptism the signs and the thing comprehended by the word. Why therefore do you not put Christ's blood here rather than the holy Spirit? For we are cleansed of our sins by Christ's blood, without which no purging from sins can happen. For Christ's blood is the thing of the Sacrament in Baptism, just as was declared above, that is necessarily required for Baptism, and there is no cleansing and purging from sins in Baptism in another way, which is required for the inner Baptism.

Dr. Jakob:

REGENERATION IS THE WORK OF THE THREE PERSONS OF THE DIVINITY IN BAPTISM. THE HOLY SPIRIT THE THING OF THE SACRAMENT IN BAPTISM.

What should be thought and said about each of the Sacraments is just as God's word says. We are not speaking an empty word, but rather it truly contains what it says. This is Christ's word in Baptism: Baptize them in the name of the Father, the Son, and the holy Spirit. This word embraces the presence of the three persons of the holy Trinity, Father, Son, and holy Spirit. For this reason also the work of regeneration in Baptism is the work of the whole Trinity. Since Father, Son, and holy Spirit are working regeneration and renewal, for this reason Christ attributes this work of regeneration particularly to the holy Spirit, when he says, Unless one has been born again of water and the Spirit. Therefore in Baptism we say that the thing of the Sacrament is the holy Spirit, who regenerates people to eternal life by the virtue of Christ's blood.

BAPTISM IS NOT DUPLEX.

This is therefore our opinion: it can never correctly or truly be said <443> that one Baptism is outer, and the other is inner. For he was never truly baptized who was merely washed with external water. Since Baptism, just as it is not water only, so neither is it Spirit only, but water and Spirit at the same time. For this reason Baptism also is correctly called a spiritual water. Just as also the bread of the Lord's Supper is not a common bread, but the bread *of the Lord*, and it is Christ's body which the word of Christ's Testament joins together sacramentally with the bread, when he says, this is my body.

THE LORD'S SUPPER ONE, NOT TWO.

Therefore just as there are not two Lord's Suppers or a duplex Lord's Supper, the one outer, the other inner, so also there are not two Baptisms, the one outer, the other inner, but rather there is only baptism, consisting of an internal and external thing, namely water and Spirit, joined together by the word of the Lord, which joined together at the same time make one Baptism, instituted by God.

Dr. Beza:
We are not yet disputing the whole business, but talking here only about the parts of Baptism. And I am not establishing two

Baptisms. For just as in the use of the Lord's Supper, which is one, there is an inner eating and an outer (since besides the bread the faithful receive and eat the Lord's body by faith, and thus have something more inward that others do not have, who lack true faith), so also in Baptism, those who are truly faithful and elect are not only sprinkled and washed with water, but are sprinkled inwardly with Christ's blood, which does not happen for the unfaithful.

WHAT IS EXPRESSED BY GOD'S WORD IN BAPTISM.

But I ask you to explain to me clearly what you understand Baptism to consist of, in this Thesis, through God's word. Does it consist of Christ's blood? Since indeed Father, Son, and holy Spirit are not a part of Baptism, for this reason it is necessary to understand Christ's blood, which is represented sacramentally and efficaciously by the water of Baptism.

<444>

Dr. Jakob:

Christ is the best interpreter of his own words. He expressed his intention in very few words in John 3, saying, Unless someone has been born again of water and Spirit, he cannot inter the kingdom of heaven (John 3[:5]). In these words Christ makes no express mention of Father, or Son, nor even of the son's blood, but of the holy Spirit only, as there was no need. For Father and Son and holy Spirit are one very simple spirit. However he has joined together water with the Spirit, and attributes regeneration to both, namely in this way, that the Spirit regenerates through water unto eternal life. For this reason, having followed the manifest words of Christ, we say that Baptism consists of water and the Spirit, which are joined together by Christ's word, by which he instituted baptism.

Dr. Beza:

But what will happen concerning Christ's blood in Baptism? Or where will you locate it?

Dr. Jakob:

The blood of Jesus Christ the Son of God (says John) washes us from every sin. By the sprinkling of it the holy Spirit regenerates us through the water of Baptism. This water is an organ and instrument of the holy Spirit, by which he works regeneration. The holy Spirit therefore regenerates and renews us through the sprinkling of water in the name of the holy Trinity poured over an infant, those immersed into it, by the virtue of Christ's blood. This sprinkling was foreshadowed in the old Testament under various means, in which the people were sprinkled by the blood of sacrifices and washed in water (Exodus 25[24:8]).

Dr. Beza:

You mention sprinkling with Christ's blood. Therefore just as the body is sprinkled with water, so also we say that the soul is sprinkled. [445] *For this reason the water of Baptism represents the blood of Christ, which should not be excluded from Baptism.*

Dr. Jakob:

THE WATER OF BAPTISM WAS NOT INSTITUTED FOR A REPRESENTATION OF CHRIST'S BLOOD.

Christ did not say about the water of Baptism, This is my blood. Nor did he say, the water represents my blood. But he did say, Unless someone has been born again of water and Spirit. We should concur in these words. And it is for this reason that we cannot assert that the water of Baptism has been instituted and ordained by Christ in order that he might signify and represent his blood. But God's word speaks merely about the sprinkling of water, in the name of the Trinity. Here there is no representation described, but a washing of true and real regeneration. For just as in the Lord's Supper bread and wine were ordained not for a representation, but for the delivery of Christ's body and blood, so also the water of Baptism has been ordained not for a representation, but for the delivery of a spiritual washing of regeneration in the name of the Trinity. The baptized are truly regenerated there; the instrument of this regeneration is water, through which the holy Spirit works, by the virtue of Christ's blood, that which Christ has merited by his own blood.

THE RITE OF IMMERSION OR SPRINKLING OF WATER IN BAPTISM IS NOT REPRESENTATIVE ONLY.

And even though the rite of immersion or sprinkling in Baptism is a certain representation of spiritual mortification and regeneration, it nevertheless was not instituted for the sake of representing, but rather of accomplishing regeneration, lest we seek out and trust in shadows and figures rather than body and truth. Paul's line applies to this: Christ loved his Church and gave himself up for her, in order that he might sanctify her, washing her *with a washing of water in the word* (Ephesians 5[:26]). Here the Apostle Paul described the substance of Baptism, as our first Thesis has it, in these two parts, namely water and the word.

Dr. Beza:

WHETHER BAPTISM IS A WASHING OF REGENERATION.

A washing of water is only a signification and representation <446> of a spiritual washing, in which the soul is washed, that is, is cleansed from sins, which happens through the blood of Christ. The external and Elemental water of Baptism signifies and represents this washing. But it is not itself a washing or bath, nor can it deliver or accomplish this.

Dr. Jakob:

The words of the Apostle Paul I recited just now plainly fight against this, and cannot concede your false interpretation, when he says, *He cleansed his Church in a washing of water in the word* (Ephesians 5[:26]). In which word? In that which the holy Spirit joined with the water. For he did not wash her symbolically, but really. And he plainly said, λουτρῷ, that is, by a washing of water, by which he wants to teach that the merit of Christ's blood that was poured out is applied to the baptized person through the sprinkling of the water of Baptism. Without this application, the pouring out of Christ's blood accomplishes no benefit for an infant who has neither been baptized nor regenerated for a purging from sins, according to Christ's word, Unless someone has been born again of water and Spirit, he cannot enter the kingdom of heaven (John 3[:5]).

Dr. Beza:
The noun "washing" in Baptism, when referring to the soul, is understood figuratively and metaphorically, since a soul is not washed with water, but only a body. Therefore since baptism is called a washing, it is necessary only that it signify the spiritual washing that is inward through the sprinkling of Christ's blood. This is why Baptism is not correctly defined by you when you exclude Christ's blood, which is the substantial part of Baptism. So in Baptism the visible and the invisible coincide. The visible thing is water, signifying or representing Christ's blood, and the invisible thing is the blood of Christ, represented by the water. Just as also the external rite of the visible sprinkling of water, signifying <447> *and representing the invisible sprinkling of Christ's blood, which happens through faith.*

Dr. Jakob:
I have said several times now that two things are necessary for Baptism, water and Spirit. You want tear apart and separate these things in Baptism, and establish a duplex Baptism, though it is only one. This is in fact because water alone, or the sprinkling of water, is not Baptism, but rather water with the Spirit. And for this reason there is no figurative language here, no metaphor, no signification of the kind you say holds a place, but rather it *is, is, is* a washing of regeneration.

IN WHAT WAY THE SOUL IS CLEANSED THROUGH THE SPRINKLING OF THE WATER OF BAPTISM.

For even though water does not extend to the soul, nevertheless since the Spirit extends its virtue through the water, and that whole action is spiritual, and the water is not a washing of dirt from the body, it does not do the work in this action, but body and soul are washed equally from sins, and they are not imputed, and the Spirit is regenerated, who also draws the flesh with it into obedience to God; it pleased the holy Spirit that invisible things be administered and accomplished through external and visible things, not merely represented or signified, as was also mentioned above concerning the Lord's Supper.

IN BAPTISM BODILY AND SPIRITUAL THINGS MUST BE DISTINGUISHED, NOT TORN APART.

And in order that I may embrace everything in a few words, the visible and invisible things in Baptism should be distinguished rather than torn apart, or the visible changed into bare signification of spiritual regeneration, which regeneration you claim merely to be signified. You deny, however, that Baptism is *actually* a washing of water of regeneration. This is false.

Dr. Beza:
Why, though, do you pass over in that Thesis this spiritual regeneration?

Dr. Jakob:
I did not at all do this, but rather embraced it under *the word of God* in which it is included.

<448>

Dr. Beza:
But why do you pass over Christ's blood, which is the substantial part of the Sacrament of Baptism, without which no washing from sins happens, which the sprinkling of the water of Baptism represents and offers?

Dr. Jakob:

CHRIST'S BLOOD COMPREHENDED IN THE WORD.

I say that it is similarly comprehended in God's word. For we are baptized into Christ's death, which God's word teaches. And the holy Spirit cleanses hearts from sins by the virtue of Christ's blood, and regenerates the person and renews his mind. For this reason Augustine says, Word draws near to Element and becomes Sacrament. Whatever therefore is present besides the external element in Baptism has been included and comprehended in *the word*.

Dr. Beza:

DESCRIPTION OF BAPTISM.

The Fathers did not employ the term Sacrament according to a single meaning. Rather, its common usage is as external signs, by which sacred things are represented and offered. And St. Peter describes true Baptism, which makes us saved, not by removing the dirt from the flesh, but rather that a good conscience may respond well to God, through the resurrection of Jesus Christ (1 Peter 3[:21]). However you define only the exterior Baptism, which consists of water and the Word. And you omit the interior Baptism and the blood of Christ, which is the true Baptism, which the exterior Baptism of water represents.

This is affirmed by the third chapter of John's gospel: Unless one has been born again of water and Spirit. He describes not the substance but the effect only of the true interior Baptism, which is regeneration, something water cannot accomplish.

Dr. Jakob:

WHEN THE TERM SACRAMENT IS USED ONLY AS SIGN. BAPTISM OF WATER AN ANTITYPE [ἀντίτυπον] OF THE WATER OF THE FLOOD. EXPLICATION OF THE 1 PETER 3 PASSAGE.

I am not unaware of the various meanings of the term Sacrament in the writings of the Fathers and Doctors of the Church. But when <449> the Fathers from time to time employ it only as sign, they mean just a part of the Sacrament, not its entire substance. Augustine does this very frequently, but discussing the Lord's Supper he nonetheless testifies that it consists of two things, the visible bread and wine, and the invisible body and blood of our Lord Jesus Christ. And Peter's reference diametrically opposes your opinion, where he compares the Baptism of water with the water of the flood, and calls Baptism of water the antitype [ἀντίτυπον] of the water of the flood, not that it is itself a type of spiritual washing which it merely represents. For such a type was the water of the flood, but he calls it antitype [ἀντίτυπον]. For a type [τύπος] indicates the foreshadowing of a thing, but antitype [ἀντίτυπος] indicates the thing signified by the type. And in this reference Peter makes the flood and preservation of Noah a type of Baptism in the same kind of way, such that Baptism is the antitype [ἀντίτυπον] and corresponds to the type [τύπος], that the water of Baptism may be destined for a nobler use, namely that a conscience may be made saved through it, that is, having acquired the remission of sins and obtained the grace of God, it may respond well before God. By this way of reasoning there is not one Baptism that is interior and the other exterior, but one and the same Baptism consisting of water and Spirit, in which body and soul are washed spiritually, but nevertheless truly, from sins, regenerated, and renewed. And at John 3 Christ not only preaches about the fruit and effect of Baptism, but describes the substance of Baptism at the same time, in what parts it consists, namely water and Spirit, joined together by God's word, neither of which is a Baptism without the other.

But the reason that we did not explicitly state in this Thesis what things coincide in Baptism is this (as was our answer a little earlier), that we merely stated in the first place those things that are entirely outside the controversy. As you also cannot deny, Baptism consists of God's word and water. Should one or the other in fact not be there, it is not a Baptism. It belongs to another place to state what should be comprehended under the word of God.

<450>

Dr. Beza:
Why did you not also say the same thing about the Lord's Supper, that it consists of the word of God as well as bread and wine? Rather, you put the body and blood of Christ in place of the word of God, when it comes to understanding what the Lord's Supper involves.

Dr. Jakob:

Because in the words of institution of the Lord's Supper, the body and blood of Christ are expressly put forward: Take, eat, this is my body; Drink, this is my blood. This did not happen in the words of institution of Baptism, where no mention at all is made of Christ's blood, but of the Trinity alone, in whose name baptism must happen.

Besides this, in the Sacraments of the new Testament there are not significations or types [τύποι], that is, figures and shadows which signify things that are absent, but rather antitypes [ἀντίτυπα], that is, the things themselves signified and represented by shadows and figures, and the word of Christ has been spoken: *This is my body; This is my blood.* It is for this reason that we also laid out the substantial parts of the Lord's Supper, joined together by the word of Christ's Testament, just as we also expressly joined together water and the Spirit in the following Theses.

Dr. Beza:

But in fact I am proceeding to the next Thesis, the second. I concede that Baptism has succeeded in place of circumcision, though there should have been a distinction between the circumcision of the heart and the external circumcision of the flesh.

Dr. Jakob:

ONE CIRCUMCISION, NOT TWO.

It was enough simply to say circumcision in this place, since there are not two circumcisions, but one only, which God entrusted to Abraham.

<451>

Dr. Beza:

CONCERNING THE PHRASES: IN THE HOLY SPIRIT, AND THROUGH THE HOLY SPIRIT.

We also endorse the third Thesis. For infants born in the church have to be baptized; no one on our side doubts that. For this reason

*we proceed to the fourth Thesis, in which we would prefer to say
through [PER] the holy Spirit rather than IN the holy Spirit. Since in
fact Baptism consists of a sign and a thing signified, we say that we
are regenerated by the holy Spirit through Baptism.*

Dr. Jakob:

WHY *IN* THE HOLY SPIRIT SHOULD BE STATED RATHER THAN *THROUGH* THE
HOLY SPIRIT.

This applies to the phrase which we used in the fourth Thesis,
whether Baptism is a washing of regeneration and renewal *in the Holy
Spirit*, in place of which you would prefer that it be said through the
holy Spirit. I answer that it is the holy Spirit's phrase, used by the
Hebrews. And among those who speak the Latin language, "through"
["*per*"] means for the most part the instrumental cause. But since
the holy Spirit is the principal efficient cause of regeneration, which
he works through water as through an instrument, in Christ's blood,
for this reason we put forward the particle *in* rather than *through*.
We nevertheless have no wish to quarrel with anyone, so long as it
consists of this, that we do not attribute this work *to mere water*, but
to the holy Spirit through the water.

WHETHER BAPTISM IS A WASHING OF REGENERATION. IN THE APOLOGETIC
PREFACE, A.5. IN BAPTISM THE WORD *IS* TO BE UNDERSTOOD WITHOUT A
LITERARY DEVICE. *IS*. WASHING. REGENERATION. BAPTISM IS NOT A BARE SIGN
OF ADOPTION.

The reason we put forward this Thesis, which embraces the
status of the controversy, is especially this: that in your Orthodox
consensus, as you call it, it was expressly stated that when it is said
that Baptism is a washing of regeneration and renewing, it is not
at all to be understood literally, but rather (as in the words of the
Lord's Supper and manners of speaking about the person of Christ)
recourse should be made to a literary device, namely because it is not
regeneration, but only signifies and represents regeneration, of which
it is also a seal, but merely in the elect. We condemn this as openly
false, and we consistently assert that the word "is" must be received
and understood really, substantially [ὑπαρκτικῶς], that is, in the

same way as the rest of the words are, not through a literary device but literally, just as <452> they literally sound in their own natural and proper meaning. For the term "Baptism" means not water only but water with the Spirit, and the whole action instituted by Christ. The word "*is*" means the same as truly and really is, not signifies, prefigures, foreshadows, represents. Washing is understood rightly when a person is really washed with water. Renewal and regeneration articulate a real regeneration and renewal. Where therefore, or in what term, is a figure of speech? What refuge must so necessarily be sought according to that consensus that is not at all orthodox, which is also your opinion? No, I say no necessity compels us to do this. On the contrary, the property of Baptism does not admit such a figure of speech at all. For as many infants as are baptized truly and really are adopted as the sons of God, regenerated, and renewed. Just like the one who was not in God's grace before, that is before Baptism was received, is received after Baptism into God's grace and truly adopted as a Son of God. Adoption is not only signified there, but *really* conferred. For the holy Spirit is present in that sprinkling of water. Baptism offers what bare water without the holy Spirit could not offer. For this reason there is no figurative signification of adoption here, but true communication of adoption. For a baptized person receives in Baptism, and possesses after Baptism has been done, that which he did not possess before Baptism was received. It is in fact just like an infant who had not been circumcised on the eighth day would have his soul erased from God's people, in spite of having been born of pious parents, since he made God's pledge void, as the words of Moses expressly read: The male, the flesh of whose foreskin has not been circumcised, his *soul will be erased* from his people, *because he has made my pledge void*. The same should be judged also about Baptism. The Lord for this reason nevertheless did not prescribe a certain time for it. Baptism is not for this reason a bare sign of adoption, but adoption itself is conferred through it. For at that very moment in which an infant was circumcised, he was also adopted as a Son of God. He indeed received the external sign of this adoption <453> in the removal of the flesh of his foreskin, but the removal alone could not bestow God's great blessing, unless the word had drawn near through which the holy Spirit was the one making the adoption happen and the seal of the same. Just as now he is also efficacious in the new Testament through Baptism, and applies to us and seals the adoption acquired by Christ's blood and merit through this Sacrament of Baptism.

Dr. Beza:

Concerning the power and efficacy of the Sacrament of Baptism.

We do not teach that Sacraments are bare signs, but we deny that as much power should be attributed only to the external action as you attribute to it. This belongs to the holy Spirit alone. Besides this, we say that in a Baptism administered rightly, remission of sins and regeneration is not just signified but offered and presented to all the baptized, though they are not received by all who are baptized.

For Baptism of water represents regeneration and adoption such that latent power has not been affixed to it. Otherwise all people who are baptized would also be regenerated and renewed. And Baptism of water is not a washing of regeneration and renewal, but rather merely signifies and represents it. The proof of this is the life of those who, though they have been baptized, nevertheless have not been born again, nor renewed, but rather allow the old man with its desires to reign in them, entirely slaves to sin.

Nor in fact must the efficacy of Baptism be attached to that moment when a person is baptized, but the very benefits of Christ himself offered in it, the blessings of regeneration and renewal, sometimes precede it, as in the case of Cornelius, but other times we say they follow later, namely in those who do not have faith, but will receive in due time what they profess by mouth when they are baptized.

<454>

Dr. Jakob:

WHETHER BARE SIGNS ARE PUT FORWARD IN THE SACRAMENTS. IN RESPONSE TO DOGMAS 1 AND 2. WHETHER THE HOLY SPIRIT EXERTS HIS POWER IMMEDIATELY IN THE ACT OF BAPTISM. METONYMY HAS NO PLACE IN BAPTISM.

I am not unaware that you consistently deny that bare signs or empty significations and representations are but forward in the Sacraments of the new Testament, since you say that the things signified are offered and presented at the same time with the signs. But it was shown above in the space devoted to the Lord's Supper that bare signs were actually established by you on earth. Since you believe in no real presence of these things on earth, which you say are signified in the Lord's Supper through bread and wine. Likewise you affirm in this space devoted to Baptism, since indeed you state in your Theses that it is manifest Idolatry *if* we attribute *any virtue to the water other* than sacramental *signification*, however much we call it sacramental. But whether this is not establishing bare signs without the thing signified, we commend to the judgment of the audience. Then you say that things signified are offered and presented in no other way than by signifying and representing. This similarly establishes no real presence, but merely a relation of the sign to the thing signified, one of which, namely the sign, is on the earth, and the thing signified in heaven, or otherwise not present, but rather to follow only after a long time. This also we commend to the judgment of our audience, whether this does not assert bare signs. If in fact this relation adheres to all signs, the things you dispute here simply only signify and represent. But that in a legitimately administered Baptism the holy Spirit does not exert the power latent in Baptism at that time when a person is baptized, this is exceedingly novel to me and remarkable to hear. And of course this very assertion plainly confirms that you are putting forward bare signs in the use of the Sacraments. Take away from the Sacraments the substance of the things signified, in fact, and also their effect and use—what, I ask, are left, except for bare signs? You say this happens not only in the Baptism of the damned (who indeed have been baptized, but in your opinion have never been regenerated or endowed with the holy Spirit), but also of the elect. Then you say that the effect of Baptism follows, not at the time when a person is baptized, but after a long time has gone by. <455> However the reason for this error is that you divide one Baptism into two Baptisms, an interior and an exterior, though Scripture is ignorant of these two Baptisms and proclaims only one Baptism. There can be no place for metonymy in this, unless we should wish to assert bare signs, something not even you want to appear to do.

Dr. Beza:

God however wanted in no way to institute, but rather to abrogate the representation of washings which were used in various ways in the old Testament. All these have now been abrogated through Baptism, when by Christ's very blood we were sprinkled through the water of Baptism, body and soul, in the name of the Trinity, purged of every impurity, and considered clean before God. Dr. Beza:

IN WHAT WAY BEZA DOES NOT ESTABLISH BARE SIGNS.

The do not seem to us in the least to be bare signs, which have joined to them such efficacious significations and representations. The things signified are not only represented by them, but at the same time offered and presented with the signs. For as the body is washed with water, so also is the soul cleansed from sins by Christ's blood, through the interior Baptism of the Spirit. This Baptism of the Spirit is the true Baptism, which the outer Baptism of water signifies and represents, and seals adoption, even if it does not happen at once, at the time when a person is baptized.

Dr. Jakob:

Signification or representation of a thing is one thing, and delivery of the thing is another. In baptism adoption is not only signified and represented, but also delivered, and offered for the present. Representation or signification differ therefore from the delivery of a thing as much as our opinion differs <456> from yours. For Baptism, since it is a washing of regeneration, is not merely signified and represented by the sprinkling of water, but is delivered in the sprinkling

of water, as we have said; for this reason also it offers regeneration in
that action.

IN WHAT WAY SIGNIFICATION CAN HAVE A PLACE IN BAPTISM. IN RESPONSE TO THESIS 3 AND 4.

But as far as signification or representation is concerned, if the
parts of Baptism should be compared with each other, after its own
fashion we can tolerate saying that water is a sign of blood, and its
sprinkling, or immersion could be called a signification or representation of spiritual mortification and regeneration. But this water
and its bare sprinkling is not Baptism, but merely part of Baptism.
For since Baptism is only one in number, and consists of water *and
Spirit*, not water only, nor Spirit only, but water and Spirit at the same
time, your sacramental Metonymy which you fashion can have no
place here, by which one thing is assumed for another, or attributed
to something which belongs to something else. Rather, one and the
same effect is attributed at the same time to both, namely the Spirit
and the water. Since what truly regenerates and renews a person is
not water without Spirit, nor Spirit without water, but Spirit through
water, and water by virtue of the holy Spirit. Here must every figure
of speech be totally excluded, and accepted in no way, concerning
which your Orthodox consensus argues falsely.

Dr. Beza:

CONCERNING THE TERM SACRAMENT. THE WORD OF THE GOSPEL. BAPTISM. DEFINITION OF BAPTISM.

---

*The definition of Baptism is assumed sometimes more narrowly,
and other times more widely. Sometimes the external signs alone
are understood, which signify and represent the things. Sometimes
it embraces the thing signified and its effect at the same time with
the signs. Just as the Gospel is sometimes the proclaimed external
word, and other times means God's internal and eternal Word.
So in Baptism that external washing, which happens through
the sprinkling or immersion of water, is called a Baptism, but the
spiritual immersion represented by it is the true Baptism. For this
reason this sort of definition* <457> *is causal, when a thing is defined*

by its effects, as when Baptism is called a washing of regeneration and renewal of the holy Spirit.

DEFINITION OF BAPTISM ACCORDING TO BEZA.

We therefore join together the thing signified, that is, the effect with the sign, when we say that Baptism is a sign signifying and sealing the adoption of the sons of God. We follow Paul in this, who said about Abraham, And he received the sign of circumcision, a seal of the righteousness of faith (Romans 4[:11]), lest we attribute more to a sign than is fair, namely, that it belongs to a thing, that is, the efficacy of the inner Baptism, which belongs to the holy Spirit, and ought to be attributed to him alone. Thus, speaking about Sacraments, we state the Genus first, namely the sign, then we add the efficacy, which the sign signifies and represents, which meets the eyes.

Dr. Jakob:

DIFFERENCES BETWEEN SEALING AND DELIVERY OF A THING. HOW ADOPTION IS SEALED THROUGH BAPTISM. BAPTISM IS NOT A WASHING OF REGENERATION METAPHORICALLY.

It has been said many times by us now that bodily and external things must indeed be distinguished in Sacraments from spiritual and internal ones, but not torn apart and separated. And again, sealing something is one thing; delivery of a thing is another. For sealing is confirmation of a thing delivered. Therefore in Baptism, adoption is not sealed in the future, following a long time after, but in the present, or in adults before adoption was conferred. The holy Spirit confers adoption through the water of Baptism, or confirms it if already present. From this it is said to be a washing of regeneration not metaphorically, figuratively, by way of Metonymy, but truly and really. For at the moment that an infant is baptized, he is truly a son of God regenerated, and attains to the adoption of the sons of God.

It is like a Prince granting a servant to a certain fief. Not only does he hand over letters, but he also seals them with his own signature. The signature of the Prince is not the thing itself, but presupposes the thing comprehended in the letters, which he confirms by sealing them. Thus Baptism is a washing of regeneration for infants, <458> not an uncertain or future regeneration, after a certain number of years should follow, but a present one, and done in this very act of adoption, with the result that we can say with certainty, This infant is truly a child of God, since he was baptized in the name and into the death of Jesus Christ.

This applies to the reference from Paul about the circumcision of Abraham. He says that it was not only a sign, but a seal [σφραγίς] of the righteousness of faith. Here when Paul does not separate the external sign, namely, the removal of the skin, from the word of the pledge, by which adoption had been bound, he does not also say that adoption and righteousness of faith follow long after, but rather the seal of the present thing was its signature and confirmation. Thus Baptism is also a seal, a signature, and a real confirmation of present cleansing and adoption. It does not only signify and represent what will follow at some unspecified time of its own.

Dr. Beza:
Then I ask, sir, whether Cornelius was adopted before he was baptized?

Dr. Jakob:
He was, but it is one way with infants, and another with adults, who have believed by means of the heard external word.

Dr. Beza:
If therefore infants believe, are they already adopted before they undergo baptism?

Dr. Jakob:

REFUTATION OF THE ARGUMENT OF THE ANABAPTISTS ABOUT THE FAITH OF INFANTS.

No. For before infants are baptized, we cannot affirm that they believe, since faith is given to them in baptism. Therefore in the reception of baptism, infants are at the same time adopted as children of God, and the adoption is sealed on them. For this reason we speak against the Anabaptists, who dwell in the error that, since infants actually lack intellect, it is impossible for them to believe. We say the contrary: not only is it possible, but very easy, for God to work faith in infants, even without the benefit of human reason. Indeed also <459> it really happened and was demonstrated in John the Baptist, who recognized Christ when he was still in the womb of his mother, and leapt at the voice of Mary the mother of God, in the womb of his mother Elizabeth. But that he also wonderfully conferred and does confer this grace on infants either circumcised or baptized, Christ himself testifies when says, Let the little children come to me (Mark 10[:13–16]). They are brought to Christ through Baptism (Matthew 28[:19]), and unless they be born again of water and Spirit (John 3[:5]), we cannot promise the kingdom of God to them. Therefore they become sharers in Baptism of both things, namely regeneration or adoption, and the seal of the same, with the result that they are truly called sons of the Most High. Here there is nothing metaphorical or figurative, but the thing itself is conferred. The baptized infant is changed in soul and body, and regenerated; from the old man has come the new, from the unrighteous the righteous, from the defiled the holy, from the child of hell the child of the heavenly kingdom. But even though we cannot comprehend it from the external sense of the eyes, nevertheless heeding the word of God we do not doubt surely what is attested about this work of God, namely that baptized infants are gifted with the grace of adoption, faith, and the holy Spirit.

Dr. Beza:

WHY LITTLE CHILDREN ALSO WITHOUT FAITH MUST BE BAPTIZED, ACCORDING TO BEZA'S OPINION.

Even though infants lack their own faith, namely actual faith, nevertheless we think they must be baptized on account of the formula of the covenant which was spoken to Abraham and his posterity: I will be your God and the God of your seed after you. And the faith of the parents suffices since they take hold of this promise in both their own name and that of their children, so they are justly baptized.

THE EXAMPLE OF JOHN THE BAPTIST UNIQUE.

The example which is brought up, of John the Baptist leaping in the womb of his mother, is unique. Nowhere else in Scripture is there a place where God works in the same way among all infants of Christians in an identical manner.

<460>

And they were children in the covenant, concerning whom Christ was saying: Let the little children come to me, since the kingdom of heaven belongs to such as these, but not to all of them. For God left in his hidden judgment which infants he wanted to gift with his grace. And so we can affirm that baptized infants are only PROBABLY gifted with the fruit of adoption.

Dr. Jakob:

INFANTS AND CHILDREN EQUAL WITH RESPECT TO SPIRITUAL INTELLIGENCE.

No one is saved by means of someone else's faith, so it is necessary for infants to possess their own faith. Just as it is written: It is impossible to please God without faith (Hebrews 11[:6]). Also, the righteous will live *by his own faith* (Habakkuk 2[:4]), not somebody else's but rather his own. And Christ plainly says that the children that he talked to the disciples about believed. Anyone who causes one of these little ones to stumble, *who believe in me*, it would be better for him to have a millstone tied on his neck and be drowned in the depth of the sea (Matthew 18[:6]). More confidence should be attributed to these words of Christ about the distinct faith of infants and children than if some adult were to affirm a thousand times that he believed. And there is no reason for anyone to object that those children were not infants. For even if the little one, that child, the one that Christ placed in the midst of his disciples, was not lying in a cradle, still there is no difference between that one and the infant who is lying in a cradle, with respect to the spiritual capacity in the intellect, if they should be compared with adults. Neverthless, without any consideration for this, Christ plainly says, *the ones who believe in me.* This word of Christ needs to be heeded, and we need to put more confidence in it than the judgment of our blind reason that thinks otherwise regarding the faith of infants.

Dr. Beza:
If therefore infants believe, then they must have been adopted as children of God before they were baptized.

Dr. Jakob:
Not at all. For they are in fact baptized in order that they may be adopted. Just as <461> in the old Testament they were getting circumcised in order that they might be received into the covenant, which did not happen if circumcision was neglected (Genesis 17[:10]). Since a fleshly birth does not save them, just because they were born to believing parents. For whatever is born of flesh is flesh, that is, is damned. For this reason it is necessary to be born again of Spirit and water in order that they may be deemed in the covenant (John 3[:5]); faith is necessary for its salutary reception.

Dr. Beza:

Regarding whether Simon Magus believed.

I ask you, Doctor, whether Simon Magus also believed when he was baptized?

Dr. Jakob:
He certainly did. Scripture in fact openly testifies to this
(Acts 8[:13]).

Dr. Beza:
*But he had no part in Christ's kingdom; how therefore did he
have faith, or truly believe?*

Dr. Jakob:

SIMON MAGUS WAS ABLE TO LOSE HIS FAITH.

The grace which he received in Baptism he could again lose
through his own impiety. It can in fact happen that someone who
truly believes again loses faith and the holy Spirit, which had been
given by God in Baptism.

Dr. Beza:

WHETHER SIMON MAGUS BELIEVED.

---

*Simon Magus pretended to believe, but he did not believe. This is
why he is called accursed.*

Dr. Jakob:
Let us see and hear Luke the Evangelist himself regarding Simon
Magus, speaking about his faith, who says thus: But when they
had believed Philip preaching about the kingdom of God, men and
women were baptized in the name of Jesus Christ, *then Simon himself
also believed* (Acts 8[:]13). This is the plain testimony, by which Luke
testifies that Simon himself believed.

\<462\>

Dr. Beza:
*The holy Spirit says that even hypocrites believe; in this way
Simon Magus also pretended to believe, but really lacked faith.*

Dr. Jakob:

The text contradicts you. For Luke testifies that after Simon believed and was baptized, he clung to Philip, and seeing the signs and great powers come to pass, he was wondrously amazed. And even though afterwards he was tempted by Satan and wanted to purchase with money the power of laying on hands so that people could receive the holy Spirit, upon which Peter called down a curse: May your money perish with you, nevertheless the same Luke testifies that the same Simon begged the Apostles to intercede before the Lord for him. Please pray for me, he said, to the Lord, that none of the things you have said may come upon me. Simon would never have done this if he had not truly believed.

Dr. Beza:

The faith by which it is written that Simon believed was not true faith, but rather pretend faith; he pretended to believe, but really he did not.

Dr. Osiander:

Reverend Beza, I beg the pardon of the Honorable Prince, Count Frederick, and the audience, for interrupting with a word. If you always make sport of all the plain testimonies of holy Scripture after this fashion through interpretations, what will we have for certain in the whole of holy Scripture left at the end? For example: Simon believed, that is, he pretended to believe.

Abraham Musculus:
His heart was not upright.

<463>

Dr. Jakob:

WHETHER THOSE WHO HAVE TRUE FAITH CAN LOSE IT.

Can it happen or not that the truly regenerate fall into fornication or some other disgraceful act? What must one do certainly to lose faith and the holy Spirit?

Dr. Beza:

It is certain from Peter's curse that Simon's heart was not upright before the Lord. And so Peter also told him: There is not part for you or lot in this speech.

Dr. Jakob:

Could it happen or not that he again lost the faith that he earlier possessed true in his heart? Since Luke openly testifies that he believed?

Dr. Beza:

No, if in fact he had possessed true faith, he never would have lost it. For those who once have been gifted by God with true faith are never able to lose it any longer.

Dr. Jakob:

WHETHER THE HOLY SPIRIT IS LOST THROUGH MORTAL SINS.

Then I ask whether David lost faith and the holy Spirit when he committed adultery with Bathsheba, Uriah's wife?

Dr. Beza:

He did not lose it at all; rather, he kept it.

Dr. Jakob:

I have not read this in holy Scripture or any Church Writer. It even conflicts manifestly with Paul's words when he says: If you live according to the flesh, you will die (Romans 8[:6]). If they are able to die, then they are able also to lose their faith. When he has it and keeps it, so long as he possesses it, he cannot die. In the same way no one is saved without it, and so long as a person retains it, he cannot die.

<464>

Dr. Beza:

ANALOGY ABOUT THE DRUNK MAN.

I am saying that David retained faith and the holy Spirit, and did not lose it, amid the perpetration of adultery. I will make this clear with an analogy. A drunk man does not lose his intellect or reason, even though for as long as drunkenness occupies his head, reason does not make itself known, but he is rather similar to a brute beast. And in the same way that fire is covered with ashes, but is not in the least extinguished, but hides, so also grace, faith, and the holy Spirit, in the falls of the Elect, are hidden for a time such that they are not perceived, until they return to themselves and acknowledge their sin, and work repentance. This also happened in David's adultery, in which God's grace was hidden for a time, but was not lost.

Dr. Jakob:

REFUTATION OF THE ARGUMENT FROM THE ANALOGY ABOUT THE DRUNK MAN.

This example you offer about the drunk man represents not a similarity, but a difference. Reason and human intellect is in fact the essential power of the soul, the use of which is reason itself, even if a person loses it for a time. That is, the power of the soul is not lost so long as he is and remains a man. But the way of God's grace, faith, and the holy Spirit is something else entirely, which are not essential parts of a person, but rather are gifts of God. Therefore just as they have been given by God, so also can they be lost, and that they truly have been lost as a matter of fact, holy Scripture openly testifies. Do not cast me away from your face, and take not your holy Spirit from me. *Restore to me* the joy of your salvation, etc., prays the Psalmist (51[:12]). Nor either is the appearance of flames hidden under ashes, but straightway they are extinguished, and in this way also are lost.

Dr. Beza:

Just as drunkenness can take away the use of reason for a certain time, but not reason itself, so also can sins perpetrated among the Elect take away the enjoyment of the holy Spirit, faith, and God's *grace for a certain time, <465> but not the grace of God itself, or faith and the holy Spirit, which remains in them and does not withdraw from them, as also it did not depart from David.*

Dr. Jakob:
I could not wish to for a thousand florins, no, not even for the whole world, to put such things before my hearers, things so manifestly impious. Namely, that those who perpetrate sins against conscience, fornicators and adulterers, if they should be elect, would retain faith and the holy Spirit in the very act of their sin.

Dr. Beza:
I would wish to die if I were teaching otherwise. And will you present me a person who is without some failing? In whom exists no flesh? Can it happen that someone is such a fornicator that he is scarcely aware that he fornicates? Surely he would not lose the holy Spirit on account of this?

Dr. Jakob:

DISTINCTION BETWEEN VENIAL AND MORTAL SINS.

Distinguish between failings of human weakness and manifest wickedness against the law of God. The former are in fact venial sins, that is, sins not imputed to those who believe and are elect, according to the passage: Seven times a day the righteous man falls, and rises again (Proverbs 24[:16]). For these ones the holy Spirit is not lost. But the latter are mortal sins, according to the passage from Paul: If you live according to the flesh, *you will die.*

Dr. Beza:
No sin is venial; rather all are mortal, that is, worthy of death. This distinction of sins therefore cannot have a place here, as it is Papistic.

Dr. Jakob:

It is indeed true that all sins are worthy of eternal death, but not-withstanding, the holy Spirit distinguishes weaknesses <466> that do not drive out the holy Spirit from those that are manifest disgraceful actions. By these faith and the grace of the holy Spirit is lost after Baptism has been received. For there are certain sins which drive out the holy Spirit, concerning which Paul speaks in the passage just cited: If you live according to the flesh, you will die (Romans 8[:6]). And again, the works of the flesh are manifest, which are fornication, filth, lewdness, lust, etc. *Those who do such things* do not attain the kingdom of God (Galatians 5[:21]). There is another type of sins that even the elect cannot lay aside until they die, but they fight against them continually to the last breath of their life, so long as they sin not by intention but against their will. Paul offers his own example of this to the whole Church: But if I do, he says, that which I do not want to do, it is no longer I who do it, but rather the sin that dwells in me (Romans 7[:17]). So someone is especially prone to wrath by the cor-ruption of his nature, while another can scarcely, or with difficulty, be provoked to anger. When therefore he becomes angry against his will, he does not on this account nevertheless lose faith and the holy Spirit, even though wrath is a mortal sin, that is, worthy of death (Matthew 5[:21–22]). Paul's passage applies to this: There is therefore now no condemnation for those who are in Christ Jesus (Romans 8[:1]). And: Blessed are those whose sins are covered (Psalm 32[:1]). But David's adultery and fornication was something else: when someone destroys a member of Christ, and makes a whore out of a member, he certainly does not retain the spirit of Christ, nor does he remain a member of Christ. For this reason Paul does not simply say there is no condemnation for those who are in Christ Jesus, but he adds, who do not walk according to the flesh. With these words he plainly shows that those who are in Christ, if they walk accord-ing to the flesh, pass away from God's grace and are condemned. When I become angry, then I do not know what I am doing. But when someone fornicates, he does what he wants to do, and drives out the holy Spirit. For this reason, when David not unwillingly, but rather willingly committed adultery, he certainly would have remained con-demned if in his sin he would have died before his act of repentance.

<467>

Dr. Beza:

Far be it from us that we should say that all sins are equal, like the Stoics think. Indeed they are all mortal by their own nature, but they become venial in the elect (with the exception of one, concerning which John says that one should not be prayed for, which is the sin against the holy Spirit, 1 John 5[:10]). But they in whom true faith exists (which you say the elect can lose) are not able to lose it; rather it hides, like fire hidden under ashes.

Dr. Jakob:

Therefore I ask this one thing only: If David had died after committing adultery in his own self-assurance, before he heard the preaching of repentance from the Prophet Nathan, would he have been saved or condemned?

Dr. Beza:

Since David was in the number of the elect, he could not fall away from God's grace. And in this way they return to the path in their own time, however many are elect, even if at the time, like David, they should be sinning. For the gifts of God are not to be regretted [ἀμεταμέλητα], that is, God does not change his mind about the gifts which he has conferred to his elect. And so they cannot fall away from God's grace.

Dr. Jakob:

IN WHAT WAY GOD'S GIFTS ARE NOT TO BE REGRETTED [ἀμεταμέλητα], THAT IS, WITHOUT CHANGE OF MIND. THE TRUTH OF GOD IN HIS OFFERED GIFTS.

I think this way: if Nathan had not reproved David, David would not have repented; he would never have been saved. The reason I say this is that after Nathan's sermon, he finally said, I have sinned. And after he received absolution, The Lord has taken away your sin, <468> then he finally prayed, And take not your holy Spirit from me. It had certainly been taken away from him so long as he lived in self-assurance. Therefore Paul's words regarding God's gifts are being cited not rightly and not consistently with the analogy of faith. For Paul does not want this: that God not be able to take away his own gifts from those who truly believe, of which he bears witness by his own example when he says, I beat my body and subject it to slavery, lest so long as I preach to others I become reprobate. But there is no doubt that Paul was truly regenerate, and had true faith. He nevertheless bears witness that he could so preach unto the salvation of others that he himself would become reprobate if he did not chastise himself. For this reason the opinion of these words of Paul is in no way at all what is affixed falsely and perversely to those in this place, namely that God's gifts are such that without repentance he does not take away gifts once given from those to whom he has given them. But that he cannot lie and is unable to deny himself, this proclaims the truth of God. This applies simultaneously to the pious and impious, to whom God offers his grace equally. If therefore people should not accept it, or reject it once accepted, God himself is nevertheless in himself without repentance, and stretches out his hand all day long, as the Prophet says (Isaiah 65[:2]), to all sinners, and through his emissaries bids us and those who have lapsed shamefully to return to grace with God (2 Corinthians 5[:19]). Therefore God conferred this grace to us one time in Baptism, and he never repents of it. Just as also spouses who have once been married, who are separated for a time, do not get married again in church, but rather a reconciliation happens by virtue of the earlier marriage bond, by which they were originally married, so also those who are once baptized, even if a spiritual divorce has been committed, nevertheless are not baptized all over again, but rather by virtue of the Baptism once received a reconciliation happens through true repentance, by whicih sinners again return to grace with God, which they lost by sin. If a man divorce his wife (says Jeremiah), and she departing from him marry another man, would she return to him again? Will the wife not be polluted and contaminated? But you have fornicated with many lovers; nevertheless return to me, says the Lord (Jeremiah 2[:26]).

<469>

Just as there was therefore no need of a new circumcision for those returning to God through repentance, so also there is no need of a new Baptism for those working repentance, who lost God's grace, faith, and the holy Spirit after they received Baptism. For God does not change, but remains firm in his promises. In fact, even if someone should reject God's grace, and lose faith and the holy Spirit, if he should rise in repentance and turn back to God, he is received by him again into grace who is in the way of his gifts without regret [ἀμεταμέλητος], that is, without change of mind.

Dr. Beza:

HORRIBLE TO HEAR.

God ordained to grace and eternal life, in his eternal and hidden counsel, those to whom he also gives faith and the holy Spirit. They also retain it and do not at all lose it, even though they should sin from time to time, as happened to David. For such people to be sure ultimately return to themselves, and finally are not cut off from the grace of God. But the Lord did not choose others in this way, despite thousands being baptized by the external Baptism of water. Though this be the case, nevertheless neither faith nor the holy Spirit are given them, but rather they perish by their own fault, abandoned by the just judgment of God.

But as far as the substance of Baptism is concerned, and its effect, when it is called a washing of regeneration, it is not always necessary that the effect follow at the same time as when they are baptized. Since it declares this very end of Baptism to such a degree, it nevertheless remains a true Baptism, even though regeneration is not in the least the consequence in the reprobate and those not elected to eternal life.

It is in fact just like the Gospel is the power of God for salvation (Romans 1[:16]), in its own nature, that is, the power of saving is offered, which is not only signified but is also truly offered, nevertheless the power does not bring itself to bear simply and immediately to all [470] who hear the Gospel, but to a few, namely those who are contained in the number of the elect. Just as also in the Lord's Supper the body and blood of Christ are offered to all, and neverthe-

less are not received by all, but rather only by those who believe, so also the grace of adoption is offered to all in the Baptism of water, which the good and evil, the elect and the reprobate, receive without distinction. But the effect brings itself to bear only in the Elect, but not immediately at the time when they are baptized; rather the holy Spirit sometimes does not work his operation until old age.

Dr. Jakob:

Reverend Dr. Beza, we decided at the beginning of the Colloquy not to mingle controverted articles about which we had to meet in conference, but rather to treat them one by one in their own place. We will for this reason put off what you have said here about the elect, that at least the virtue of Baptism and regeneration brings itself to bear in them, to its place and conference on predestination.

HOW THE CONSOLATION OF ADOPTION ACCOMPLISHED BY BAPTISM SHOULD BE SOUGHT.

But I ask only one thing at this point: how can somebody who is troubled in his conscience and beset by the greatest temptations seek consolation from the Baptism once received? If it is not certain that he has been adopted in Baptism?

The reason I say this is that according to your opinion, not all who are baptized are regenerated, but merely those who have been elected and ordained by God's eternal decree to eternal life.

Dr. Beza:

That not all who are baptized are regenerated to eternal life is not the fault of God, but rather of impious men to whom God owes nothing, if they should be left in their impiety.

<471>

THE SOURCE FROM WHICH BEZA TEACHES TO SEEK CERTAINTY OF ACCOMPLISHED ADOPTION.

But the consolation that we have been adopted should be sought from the effects of the holy Spirit, namely when we feel such movements of the holy Spirit in us that bear witness that we have been truly regenerated and adopted and are sons of God.

Dr. Jakob:

But what will happen in in the midst of supreme temptations, when such movements of the holy Spirit are not only not felt, but contrary thoughts also are inspired by Satan, which threaten nothing but despair? Since we in fact sin horribly, we therefore can hold out no hope of grace from God. Whence therefore must firm consolation be sought? Since he finds in Baptism (according to your teaching) no consolation, which you teach is not a certain testimony of adoption in all who have been baptized, but rather in the elect alone, and in those ordained by God's hidden will to eternal life. How therefore is such a conscience able to be cheered? If he should in fact be left to the internal movings of the holy Spirit, which he does not feel, but rather the contrary, desperation will increase, not diminish. It is necessary therefore to run to the word and Sacraments, and they should be made us of more than those ruminations that cause despair. If our hearts condemn us (says John), God is greater than our heart (1 John 3[:20]), and speaks to us and acts through the word, confers in Baptism the grace of adoption to all who are baptized, and seals it in them. In these things a firm consolation must be sought, where it is found for certain. Just as can be seen in David's Single combat with Goliath, when David placed every consolation and very certain hope of victory against Goliath in his circumcision, which he had received in his infancy. Who is this uncircumcised Philistine, he said, who works shame upon the front line <472> of the living God (1 Samuel 17[:26]). And again, This uncircumcised Philistine will also be like one of them, who dared to curse the army of the living God (1 Samuel 17[:36]). It is as if he were saying, This Philistine, since he is not circumcised, is not with God in grace. But I am circumcised, and therefore am in God's grace. His assistance to me is most certain. Armed with this consolation, David stepped forward to engage Goliath, and overthrew him, and slew him. This consolation would have been not at all certain and firm, had David been of the opinon that adoption had not been entirely accomplished through circumcision. We would say the same thing also, to be sure, about Baptism:

if your teaching about Baptism is true, that not all who are baptized are adopted as sons of God, then no consolation has been or is left for us in this.

Dr. Beza:
I am not saying that we ought not seek any consolation in word and Sacrament, but rather I am saying only this: the holy Spirit does not bring to bear through the external Baptism of water the power of the inner Baptism in all people, but rather only in the elect. Therefore when the elect possess this inner testimony of the holy Spirit and feel it, then part of the consolation rests in the external Baptism of water, to which troubled consciences can and ought to run.

Dr. Jakob:

BEZA DEPRIVES THE TEMPTED OF CONSOLATION WHICH THEY HAVE LAID UP IN BAPTISM.

But this is no response at all to the matter. For doubt still remains there, when the feeling and movement of the holy Spirit is not felt in troubled consciences, and it rather turns out for them as David says about himself: I said in my alarm (he said), I have been cut off from your sight (Psalm 31[:22]). Nor can I know for certain whether God made a hidden decree about saving me; what consolation therefore can the Baptism I received bring to me? Which does not have the effect of regeneration joined to it, but rather <473> brings itself to bear in the elect sometimes not until old age? But holy Scripture plainly testifies against this: Baptism is a *washing* of regeneration and renewal in the holy Spirit, and an infallible seal of adoption. And in the midst of those supreme temptations no heed should be given to those internal movements, but rather should Satan be scoffed through Baptism, and repelled with words of this sort: Get away from me Satan, you have no part in me, since I am baptized in the name of the holy Trinity, and am truly adopted as a son of God. I must trust this with the firmest faith, unless I should wish to accuse the whole Trinity of lying, and say that the Baptism I received is an idle ceremony and a jest. The one who believes (says Christ) and is baptized will be saved (Mark 16[:16]); and again, As many of you as have been baptized have put on Christ (Galatians 3[:27]).

Dr. Beza:

IN WHAT WAY BAPTISM IS A WASHING OF REGENERATION, ACCORDING TO BEZA.

We say: Baptism of water is a washing of regeneration, that is, it signifies and represents an inner regeneration. But it does not so signify such that this happens in all people, but rather it points to the end for which Baptism has been instituted, namely, that it may seal grace in the elect, into which they have been elected and ordained by God by his eternal and hidden decree. Just as we said above regarding the Gospel's power unto salvation, and about the signs of the Lord's Supper, by which the power of salvation is offered to all, both the body and blood of Christ, but they are not received except by the elect. Whoever has been counted in their number, though he sin seriously, just as was said about David, he is not cut off nevertheless from the grace into which he was once received by God.

But the difference is observed manifestly in the two examples of David and King Saul. For each of them sinned seriously before the Lord, but David is saved, and Saul is condemned. David was elected by God's eternal decree; Saul on the other hand was created and ordained to eternal damnation.

<474>

Dr. Jakob:
Was Saul also circumcised?

Dr. Beza:
According to the letter, but not according to the Spirit.

Dr. Jakob:

ONE CIRCUMCISION OF DAVID AND SAUL.

The circumcision of David and Saul was one; God's word is the same; the rite and ceremony is one and the same. This cannot be denied. For just as David was circumcised, so also Saul, when he was an infant eight days old, was circumcised according to God's command.

Dr. Beza:

WHETHER CIRCUMCISION IS TWOFOLD OR ONLY ONE.

It is clear from Paul's words that circumcision is twofold, when he says, No one is a Jew who is one outwardly, nor is circumcision outward and of the flesh. Rather he who is a Jew who is one inwardly, and circumcision of the heart is circumcision, which consists of the Spirit, not the letter (Romans 2[:28–29]).

Paul plainly teaches in these words that circumcision is twofold, namely, of flesh and spirit, letter and spirit, one outward, with an external rite, the other internal in the heart and spirit.

I say therefore that Saul was indeed circumcised with a circumcision of the flesh, according to the letter, but not with a circumcision of the spirit, which was far different in Saul than in David.

Dr. Jakob:

Saul's history teaches manifestly to the contrary. It bears witness that Saul was furnished from childhood with special gifts of the holy Spirit, namely holy fear, honor, and obedience to his father, special humility of spirit before all, patience and singular moderation, and wisdom worthy of a King. In addition to this, it is plainly written about Saul that <475> the spirit of the Lord withdrew from him and an evil spirit tormented him (1 Samuel 16[:14]). If the holy Spirit withdrew, then he had it before, and lost it again.

TRUE EXPLANATION OF PAUL'S WORDS ABOUT CIRCUMCISION (ROMANS 2[:28–29]).

Next, St. Paul in no way makes circumcision twofold, but rather reproves in the Jews the abuse and false understanding of circumcision given by God. They were boasting that they were in grace and the true people of God on account of having undergone circumcision, though they rejected Christ and spurned the teaching of the Gospel. This was in open conflict with Abraham's circumcision, in which circumcision was the sign of the righteousness of faith, which consisted not only in the removal of the foreskin, but also in the promise, without which the external ceremony was totally useless, and merely one part of circumcision, and the least part at that.

Paul teaches here that since the Jews neglected the promise, scorned Christ, and condemned his teaching, they boasted in vain about the circumcision they had undergone, since they reject once again the grace received in circumcision, and render their circumcision useless for themselves. And so he calls just the letter a circumcision that is undergone without faith in the promise, which looked back to Christ, by which it was said of Abraham and his seed, all nations of earth will be blessed in your seed. When this word is left out, circumcision is a letter, no, it is nothing, and it profits nothing. And that man is not a true Jew, even if he should be circumcised a thousand times, who rejects this promise, in which he himself was received into grace through circumcision.

Dr. Beza:

It is clear from the words of Paul we have recounted that there are two types of circumcision, the one of the letter and the other of the spirit. And the external circumcision of the flesh was signifying and representing the inner circumcision of the spirit, which was a sign and seal of adoption.

Dr. Jakob:

<476>

WHETHER SAUL WAS ADOPTED AS A SON OF GOD THROUGH CIRCUMCISION.

If the external circumcision of the flesh was a seal of adoption, but Saul (according to your opinion) was not adopted by God as a son, how therefore was the circumcision he underwent a seal on him, or how could it be? For there is no seal for that which does not exist.

Dr. Beza:

External circumcision, as far as God is concerned, offers to all what it signifies and represents. But it does not bring its power to bear in all people, and this is not God's fault, but the fault of the people who despise this grace.

Dr. Jakob:

But it was shown above that Saul did not despise this grace at the time of his circumcision, which he received as an infant in circumcision. The Spirit of God was in fact in him, and he was manifestly showing forth signs of grace until it withdrew from him, and an evil spirit of the Lord tormented him. How great would the sacrilege against God's name be, if it should be said that God sealed the grace of adoption on the infant Saul, but had nevertheless never adopted him?

ANALOGY OF A PRINCE.

If a Prince sealed a parchment with his own seal, on which nothing had been written, and not only promised grace and mercy with the counterfeit, but also inspired hope regarding a very generous fief, how would this deed be in accordance with the honor of a Prince?

SACRILEGE OF GOD'S NAME IN THE BAPTISM OF THE REPROBATE, IN BEZA'S OPINION.

How great therefore the sacrilege of the name of the most holy Trinity, God the Father, Son, and holy Spirit would be, if he sealed grace with the seal of his Sacraments, and swore to a person a very generous hope regarding the eternal life to come, whom he nevertheless deemed unworthy of his grace, and never wished in the past, present, or into eternity to be saved, but rather had predestined to eternal punishment by his hidden decree? <477> Far it be from us, far be it, I say, that we think thoughts so impious and blasphemous about God and his Sacraments in our hearts, which a just Prince would consider as the highest insult if such things were spread around about him.

IN RESPONSE TO THESIS 4.

But if your opinion were true, we would be compelled to confess such things about God, that he was toying with us in Baptism, and not acting seriously, if indeed you are saying that external circum-cision was a seal of grace and Baptism is now a seal of grace in those whom God never loved, nor wished to be saved, just as your responses to our Theses openly testify.

But the Lord speaks far differently about Saul being rejected by Samuel. He does not in fact say, You have been rejected by God, since God never loved you, and you were disapproved of from eternity, created by God and predestined for eternal ruin. Samuel does not saying any of this at all, but says rather, Because of this, that you have rejected the Lord's word, the Lord has rejected you, so that you are not King (1 Samuel 15[:26]).

SAUL HAD THE HOLY SPIRIT, AND LOST IT AGAIN.

Therefore King Saul was truly adopted as a son of God in circum-cision, and adoption was not only signified and offered to him, but was also truly conferred upon him, and he possessed obvious and manifest signs of the holy Spirit dwelling in him, which he afterward lost again by his own impiety, and despite being warned multiple times and called back to repentance, nevertheless he did not come back to his senses or truly work repentance, but rather stubbornly persevered in his contempt of the Lord. This is the reason for his rejection, that he perished not because of God's hidden decree, that God did not wish that he be saved, but rather that his own spite stood in the way of his savior.

ALL THE BAPTIZED ARE ADOPTED AS SONS OF GOD. CAUSE OF THE REJECTION OF THE DAMNED NOT THE HIDDEN DECREE OF GOD.

It is the same way with all infants born in the Church. For how-ever many are baptized, put on Christ, and are truly adopted as sons of God, are gifted with the holy Spirit, and the promise of grace is sealed on them. But when they begin to grow to maturity, it can happen that by the neglect of the parents or their own wantonness, they lose the holy Spirit again, and are robbed of the grace of God they once received. For this reason they cannot transfer the responsibility and blame for their <478> destruction on the hidden decree of God who received them into grace, truly regenerated them, and adopted them as children. Rather, they themselves while they were growing up were not walking according to the spirit, but according to the flesh, and fell away again from God's grace. Regarding this stands the plain testimony of St. Paul, when he says, If you are circumcised, Christ will be of no advantage to you; you are severed from Christ, you who would be justified by the law; *you have fallen away from grace* (Galatians 5[:2–3]). But how can someone fall away from grace who never was in grace before God?

Dr. Beza:

A HORRIBLE STATEMENT: MANY THOUSANDS OF BAPTIZED INFANTS PERISH FOR ETERNITY.

These are interpretations contrary to the clear text of Paul's words, who plainly speaks of a twofold circumcision, namely of the letter and the spirit. For this reason that which is of the spirit should not be attributed to the letter, that is, to the external rite. Since therefore adoption of the sons of God is the work of the holy Spirit alone, and water Baptism cannot bring it about, which does not penetrate all the way to the soul, but rather washes the body only, therefore water Baptism is merely external, a signification and a representation of the spiritual washing, which the holy Spirit alone works through the blood of Christ, and only in the elect. But not so in the reprobate, since they lack faith, and do not receive this grace offered by the representing and signifying. For this reason also Paul removes the power of the spiritual circumcision of the heart from the circumcision of the letter, in which alone the Jews were boasting, shouting: The Lord's temple, the Lord's temple, circumcision, circumcision, just as also they were putting their trust in their sacrifices. And Paul shows that the circumcision of the flesh in not the true circumcision by which the heart is circumcised, but rather is only a representation of it, and an offering, which happens for all the circumcised without distinction, but the holy Spirit brings its power *to bear on the elect alone, whose hearts <479> he circumcises and regenerates. Not so the rest who are damned and are not elect. Just as the sun shines on all, but the blind do not receive the light, the fault does not lie in the light or the splendor of the sun, but rather in the defect of the eyes of the blind, so also adoption is not only signified and represented, but is also offered in circumcision to all who have been circumcised, but the only ones who receive it are the elect, for whom God has opened the eyes that they may see and be saved. The rest are abandoned to the just judgment of God, whom he has not deemed worthy of this grace, and God remains true nonetheless. The same thing also happens in Baptism, which many thousands of infants receive, who are nevertheless never regenerated, but rather perish eternally.*

Dr. Jakob:

Let the whole audience judge whether what I have brought up to confirm our opinion are interpretations or patent testimonies of Scripture without any human interpretation. The opinion of Paul's words is manifest also: he knows only one circumcision, and likewise knows one Baptism in the Church, and does not recognize in place of circumcision what is apart from the spirit. So a sprinkling of water without the spirit is no Baptism at all, which consists not only of water, but also of spirit. This spirit accomplishes regeneration and renewal in the baptized through the washing of water. But it is especially horrendous to hear that you say that many thousands of infants are baptized who were never regenerated but rather perish eternally. And I do not think that there is anyone in this gathered audience who would agree with you in this matter.

In fact everyone doubtless is of this opinion, that before the reception of Baptism, infants are born from their parents carnally with respect to their flesh, that is, their nature, as children of wrath, who would be damned by the righteous judgment of God, <480> unless they should be received into grace through Baptism by God and regenerated. But after they have been baptized in the name of the Father, Son, and holy Spirit, no one at all doubts that all such infants have now truly been adopted as sons of God, whom their fathers commend joyfully to their new mothers to be nursed and brought up as children of God. Here, says the pious father, returned home from the church, to his wife recently delivered of her child, He who was formerly a child of wrath has now been adopted by God and has truly become a child of God through Baptism.

Therefore that teaching and opinion should by no means and in no way be admitted in God's Church, by which you separate the Spirit from the water in external Baptism and teach that you should reserve judgment regarding the grace of adoption and regeneration of infants until you see operations of the holy Spirit, operations of the kind which they may sense, namely, once they have matured, signs that regeneration has happened, and only then can it be declared certainly that he is elect and truly regenerated. This is false. For we ought not to make a conjecture that we have been regenerated in Baptism, but rather we ought to know without doubt and trust and firmly in the confidence of the Baptism we have received. We said above what David did after receiving external circumcision, that strengthened by his circumcision he rose up against Goliath himself with full confidence of divine assistance. You therefore do badly to leave pious parents in perpetual doubt whether their children have been adopted as children of God through the Baptism they received.

IN RESPONSE TO THESIS 8 AND 10 REGARDING BAPTISM.

For according to the responses you put forward in the Theses, this is what you intend: a baptized infant cannot certainly, nor ought to, be declared adopted truly as a child of God or regenerated, *but rather is only probably* thought that these are given them as fruit of adoption, and the final verdict hidden and left to God. Against this are the patent words of Paul: As many of you as have been baptized have put on Christ, Galatians 3[:27].

Dr. Beza:
If I feel the holy Spirit and his operation in me, I can certainly <481> *declare that I have been truly regenerated, according to that saying of Paul: Those who are led by the spirit of God are sons of God. Each of*

us can judge ourselves and declare whether they are regenerated or not, but judgment about others can be doubtful and false.

Dr. Jakob:

Baptism should be the place to run back to in the worst trials regarding God's grace.

It was said above, if the consolation about adoption into the children of God happens, it can only be assumed by the operations of the holy Spirit, such that from a Baptism received in infancy, I should conceive not a certain, but a probable hope only, that I have been adopted as a child of God, that by this doctrine a window is manifestly and without doubt opened for desperation in troubled consciences under trial.

For in the worst trials, even truly pious and elect people feel not only no operations, but those that are plainly contrary, from which they cannot conclude other than that they have been rejected by God. In trials of this kind, it is necessary that they flee to not only the word but also the Sacraments, especially Baptism; Satan too should be resisted since we were baptized and so we have truly also been adopted as children of God. And just as John says, that especially when our heart condemns us, and is full of no other thoughts than that we have been eternally damned, nevertheless we ought to resist thoughts of this kind inspired by the devil, since God is greater than our heart, who in Baptism has offered us not only adoption, but has also actually conferred it on us. Just as he said, He who believes and has been baptized shall be saved. This is a firm and true consolation, which your opinion is not only shaking, but removing whole and entirely, since you concede that no one unless destined, created, and ordained for eternal life in God's hidden decree, has received Baptism, in whom alone the promise of grace has been sealed.

<482>

Dr. Beza:

Beza's consolation in the worst trials regarding God's grace.

As it relates to consolation, we do not deprive consciences of it when afflicted in the worst trials, but rather explain that which is set forth in holy Scripture. So in fact I would say to a person afflicted and troubled: You should not be in doubt regarding God's grace. For since God called you through the preaching of the Gospel to the knowledge of his son, do you not feel sometimes in yourself such operations as would cause you to repent of your sins, place your trust in Christ, make you desire to live devoutly, bear adversities patiently, and aspire to the eternal kingdom of God's son? These operations belong to the children of God, and if you have ever felt them, you should not doubt that you also are in the number of the elect, and that you possess a God well-disposed.

Dr. Jakob:

But if someone does not feel such operations in himself, how will he console himself?

Dr. Beza:

A man under trial should be told that the sun has risen, even if the sun has not yet risen. For just as the light of the sun is not seen at night, but nevertheless the surest hope of it happening can belong to a person that it will rise, so also should a man under trial be told that especially the sun of righteousness has not yet risen, and he himself does not feel such operations, nevertheless this sun also will rise, and he himself will feel at some time such operations which he does not now feel.

Dr. Jakob:

This consolation can offer no benefit at all in temptations, since a tempted man does not know, but rather doubts, whether he is in the number of the elect, in whom alone such a sun will rise, in whom alone God is willing to kindle such impulses. Since he is in perpetual doubt, then, whether the sun will rise for him, he comes to very certain desperation and perishes wretchedly. Just as the example teaches of those <483> to whom true consolation has not been set forth, and who have succumbed in temptations of the same kind. There is not anyone who can draw any consolation from such a

doctrine, in which the fruit and efficacy of Baptism is deemed doubtful for him, if Baptism is only a sign of grace for those who have been
ordained to eternal life by the hidden decree of God, but for others
no, even if they also received it, at least those about whom God made
the opposite decree.

Dr. Beza:

SOLID CONSOLATION OF CHRISTIANS, PLACED IN THE WORD AND SACRAMENTS.

HOW ELECTION OUGHT TO BE JUDGED FROM WHAT HAPPENS LATER, ACCORDING
TO BEZA.

*Regarding our election to eternal life, we can make no judgment
except from what happens later, that is, by those motions of the holy
Spirit, whether we are indeed comprehended in the number of the
elect.*

Dr. Jakob:
Many things have been said by you for the consolation of those
who are ruined by incomparable trials, and you have made no
mention at all of Baptism. Whence nevertheless the beginning of
consolation had to be made in order that a person may think that
he was baptized and adopted, and for this reason has not at all been
rejected by God. On account of this I say that this is a false doctrine,
and intolerable in the Church, which removes the true use of the
word of God and the Sacraments, and prohibits every consolation
to consciences that have faced trials. For our *entire* consolation has
been placed in the word of promise, and the received use of the
Sacraments.

SOLID CONSOLATION OF CHRISTIANS, PLACED IN THE WORD AND SACRAMENTS.

For even though the operations of the holy Spirit are those of
regeneration and the fruit of adoption and its signs, nevertheless
Satan can, in the worst temptations, obscure them, such that a man
so tempted may feel no consolation at all, but experience all the
opposite things. Then must Satan be repelled by the Minister of the
Church from the tempted man in this way.

TRUE CONSOLATION IN THE WORST TRIALS.

You have been baptized as an infant (says the sincere Minister of the Church) in the name of the holy Trinity, and truly adopted as a son of God. This God is truthful, observing his promises; though we should deny ourselves, he is not able to deny himself. For this reason you should not doubt at all that the Baptism received is a true seal of adoption, which is not signified through water, <484> but truly conferred upon you in infancy. This is why you should not doubt at all that you are already an elect child of God and joined with Christ through Baptism, who will not abandon you in trials, but will certainly rescue you from all those things about which you have not the least doubt. For the holy Trinity will not lie to you, which promised its grace to you, offered it, delivered and sealed it. This is why you may say to the Devil, Get behind me Satan, you have no part in me. I know Christ the Savior will be present with me, by whose blood I have been washed from all my sins in Baptism.

Dr. Beza:

ADOPTION OF BAPTIZED INFANTS MUST BE DOUBTED, ACCORDING TO BEZA'S TEACHING, ALL THE WAY UP TO THE AGE OF ADULTHOOD.

The strength and fruit of Baptism ought not to be referred to the definite time when a person is baptized in water. For it is not believable that all are baptized by the spirit inwardly who are sprinkled with water outwardly. But time teaches when someone is regenerated or not, namely when a person has matured, and demonstrates that he has been regenerated or not regenerated by his life and conversation.

Dr. Jakob:

I do not believe that anyone is found among pious fathers, to whom God granted children, who would say to his wife after their infant's baptism, Dearest wife, the son given us just now by God has indeed been baptized, but we do not know, nor are we certain, that he has been adopted as a child of God and received into grace. I do not believe, I say, that there is anyone of our audience who would be at home in this opinion.

Dr. Beza:

BEZA TEACHES ABOUT THE ADOPTION OF INFANTS, BUT THAT THEY DO NOT BELIEVE.

Indeed, I bid everyone be of good hope, but I am not a Prophet, such that I can predict that this boy will be a good man.

\<485\>

Dr. Jakob:

No need. Since God's grace is received in the Sacrament, it cannot lose those who receive Baptism. But here is a question: is an infant adopted as a son of God after it is baptized?

Dr. Beza:

IN RESPONSE TO THESIS 7. ON THESIS 8.

I answer: Infants sprinkled by water Baptism are PROBABLY, probably I say, considered sons of God. But we think that it is absurd to assert that they are renewed at that moment when they are baptized, such that they become new people with the old man destroyed. The reason for this is that children do not have faith, especially actual faith. But they are baptized in the faith of their parents.

Dr. Jakob:

But what certainty of salvation can there be, or what consolation in Baptism, when people are taught that no infants are renewed in Baptism and not only are the reprobate destined to eternal damnation by God's hidden, eternal, unchangeable, and absolute decree, before, after, or even in Baptism, that is, that they are never renewed, even if thousands were being baptized, but also that those who are to be saved are not renewed in Baptism, but that adoption is only sealed, and renewal, or generation, which meanwhile also follows in extreme agony?

Dr. Beza:

IN RESPONSE TO THESIS 6. DR. BEZA'S OPINION ABOUT BAPTIZED ADULTS.

We assert that Baptism entire is given to as many adults as are baptized, but we affirm that the inner Baptism is received only by those who have true faith prior to it, or following some time after. For we refer the efficacy of Baptism not to that time when a person is baptized. Nevertheless it is a benefit for them who have been baptized through faith which they <486> have before the time they were baptized or indeed do not have, but will in their own time.

Dr. Jakob:

I am asking about infants, you are answering me about adults. It has now been said and demonstrated several times that there is one Baptism, not two. So what is fashioned as outer is never given without the inner, nor the inner without the outer.

Therefore since Baptism is one, and it consists of water and Spirit, then the effect of water and Spirit is also one. These two are always joined in Baptism, although the causes do not have the same reason, since the Spirit renews through water, and the water regenerates, renews, and seals adoption by virtue of the holy Spirit joined with it.

WATER BAPTISM IS A WASHING OF REGENERATION BY WAY OF METONYMY, ACCORDING TO BEZA.

But there is no answer to my question when you assert that Baptism is called a washing of regeneration only if by way of the literary device of Metonymy. But what is the reason that not all baptized infants are regenerated? Are not even the elect, at the time when they are baptized as infants?

Dr. Beza:
Since not all people are elect, a fact that adolescence demonstrates. For only the elect are regenerated, and the rest are left in

their sins and misery, in which they were conceived and born, to God's just judgment. God has reproved them in order that he may demonstrate in them his righteousness, and has not chosen them to be saved for life. Since this cannot be judged before adulthood, we say that we have to keep children in good hope until it is demonstrated that they are actually elect.

Dr. Jakob:

Let the whole audience judge whether or not this takes away from the Sacrament of Baptism all its own virtue, and keeps Christian parents in perpetual doubt concerning the adoption of their children as sons of God, depriving them and their children of every consolation [487] which they have stored up in Baptism, and in the same way have left everything in doubt, such that no one may be able to, or should, believe certainly that they have been adopted through Baptism as a child of God. Rather they should hope only *probably* in a regeneration to follow sometime, which cannot happen in baptized infants, seeing as they lack actual faith.

Dr. Beza:

The virtue of Baptism can reveal itself ultimately in the final agony. As the example of the thief teaches, he is not like the one who has been baptized. Nevertheless in that moment when Christ addressed him, he was converted and saved.

Dr. Jakob:

We are not saying that the virtue of regenerating with respect to God is so bound to water Baptism that the holy Spirit is not able to regenerate without water, but we teach that people are bound so to water Baptism that without it we cannot promise hold out for ourselves the promise of salvation and life, if Baptism is something we are able to be connected with. This is in accordance with the saying of St. Augustine: Those who spurn the Sacraments are deprived of the grace of the Sacraments. But it can never be proved that something is sealed by God in Baptism which does not exist.

Dr. Beza:

What is sealed through Baptism will happen in its own time. For just as seed cast to the earth does not immediately germinate, but lies hidden in the earth for a certain time, so also the seed of the Spirit of the inner Baptism remains hidden for some time until it is revealed in its own time who are truly regenerated, and the fruit that will follow in them, and the most certain indications of the regeneration having happened, and in whom they do not follow.

<488>

Dr. Jakob:

Since you have said so many times what even now you have confessed several times, that as many people as you can imagine are baptized, who are never regenerated, since they have been created and destined by the eternal and hidden but righteous decree of God to eternal condemnation, whom God does not want to be regenerated, how is it possible that adoption was sealed on them through Baptism of water, which will not continue eternally? Is this not manifest blasphemy not only of Baptism but also God's name?

Dr. Beza:

The blessing of adoption is offered, but God is not at fault for the fact that it is not received by everyone.

Dr. Jakob:

The gift of adoption is one thing, which is not received, and the seal of its reception is another. For unless it should be received, the seal cannot have a place. Again, how or why is it offered to the reprobate, when God would not wish it, so that it may be received by them?

Dr. Beza:

That fact that it is not received properly belongs not to God but to themselves.

Dr. Jakob:

You have established two things which can never be demonstrated by testimonies of holy Scripture. The first thing you say is,

Since God did not elect all people to eternal life, and on that account did not choose that many thousands of infants be baptized, who are not regenerated or renewed nor adopted into the sons of God, then God decided to abandon them to their own misery in order to declare his own righteousness. More concerning this in the following article regarding Predestination. But the other thing you say is, that infants, at the time they are baptized, are not reborn and renewed, even those who have been elected to eternal life <489> through Baptism, since they lack their own faith. Nor can anyone be certain, even their baptized children, that they have been adopted into the sons of God, but it is at best for them merely something to be hoped, and probably an idea to be entertained, that they are given the benefit of adoption. We openly condemn this and have demonstrated that it is in conflict manifestly with holy Scripture.

Let the audience have the power of judgment, since they have heard the arguments of either party, ways of reasoning, and testimonies produced from sacred writ. They can easily understand from these things and make their judgment. Let them be under obligation to join either party.

Dr. Beza:
We have set out the foundations of our doctrine, its grounds, and the arguments about each point in our Theses, and we entrust them to the judgment of both the audience and all holy men.

5E.II. 28 March, Morning.

Dr. Jakob:
After our business about Baptism yesterday, from what was understood and shown to you from our Theses in writing, I do not see what more we can say. The remaining Theses consist of the same thing which was treated in the earlier ones.

Whether Baptism is able to profit infants without proper faith.

But it does seem good to add one thing in place of a colophon. For it has pleased you to ask, since the Heidelberg Theologians openly write: Water Baptism without faith is an idle and useless ceremony. But you openly assert in your response that infants lack faith, and still think that they ought nonetheless to be baptized. What is the profit of this Baptism, or what can it be, which infants receive without proper (according to your opinion) <490> faith? For if infants do not believe, what can Baptism profit them? It will therefore be an idle ceremony.

Dr. Beza:

WHY BAPTIZED INFANTS LACK FAITH, ACCORDING TO BEZA.

Were our esteemed Heidelberg brothers present here, they would be able to answer quite appropriately to those things which they themselves have earlier written. For the best interpreter of his own words is whoever wrote them. We say nevertheless that if we should speak about faith which is in action, we do not see how infants are able to have faith, since they neither hear God's word nor understand it. Paul however openly bears witness that faith is from hearing God's word (Romans 10[:17]). For actual faith presupposes knowledge of the thing which is believed. But this is infused either in a way that is extraordinary, of which we have no testimony in holy scripture, or in a way that is ordinary, which happens through the external hearing of God's word (Romans 10[:17]). Therefore these two causes are always joined, the efficient principle and the instrumental, when faith is granted or infused in a person, namely, the holy Spirit, and the hearing of God's word. We cannot attribute faith of this sort to infants if we mean actual faith. But if on the contrary we mean they have only the seed or root of faith, this is nevertheless not actual faith, about which Paul is speaking, faith from hearing.

IN WHAT WAY BAPTISM PROFITS INFANTS BAPTIZED WITHOUT PROPER FAITH.

Therefore, even if infants of Christians lack faith, nevertheless Baptism is not on that account useless to them, or an idle ceremony.

It can in fact happen that when a Baptism is administered someone does not believe, but afterwards Baptism begins to profit him when he begins to believe. This faith renders Baptism efficacious, by which the elect are merely sealed. Indeed, it is just as possible that someone may hear God's word, which he nevertheless believes far later. There is no need of a new proclamation, but the earlier proclamation that was made is revived in his heart through the holy Spirit, and from the former hearing of the word, <491> gives birth to faith in what was heard. Besides, infants of Christians are born in the Church, and thus are included in the covenant, according to that word: I will be your God and the God of your seed. This is why we baptize them. But we do not baptize the children of the Turks, unless they should be able to respond to questions and confess openly that they believe. In what way do we read about Philip, who would baptize the Eunuch, before he asked whether he believed? For when the Eunuch was saying, Look, here is water, and what prohibits me from being baptized? Philip said to him, If you believe with your whole heart. He answered him, saying, I believe that Jesus Christ is the son of God. And he baptized him (Acts 8[:26–40]). In baptizing infants in the church of God, however, we presuppose the faith of the Church, in which they are baptized. This is not proper faith, however, which they cannot have on account of deficiency of actual intellect, faith which is only given through the hearing of God's word.

In response to Thesis 8 and 10 concerning Baptism.

Thus in the Baptism of an infant in the Church, therefore, the faith of the Church runs together with the faith of the parents. From this we think, and count all who are born in that covenant, probably to be in the Church and to be numbered among the sons of God. Even infants have been included in this number, though deferring always to the hidden decree of God concerning the elect, whom God has decided to make saved from eternity.

Dr. Jakob:

If I have rightly understood your statement, your worthiness has argued a duplex nature of faith, one part of which is conjoined with understanding, and the other expressed by you after the fashion of a seed. And again, that faith is infused by the holy Spirit in an ordinary, and an extraordinary, manner. We cannot concede this distinction.

FAITH IS GIVEN TO INFANTS IN BAPTISM NOT IN AN EXTRAORDINARY WAY.

For in Baptism faith is given and infused. This happens not in an extraordinary way, but an ordinary one. That this can happen, with the result that <492> it is given also to infants, and the holy Spirit works it in them, we have consistently asserted till now against the Anabaptists by the example of John the Baptist, and proven by the patent word of God. It is written about him that at the sound of the virgin Mary's greeting made to Elizabeth, the infant in her womb leapt with joy.

LEAPING OF JOHN THE BAPTIST IN ELIZABETH'S WOMB OUT OF THE ORDINARY.

What is important about this example, therefore, is that, even though it is extraordinary that he leapt with joy in his mother's womb at the voice of Mary, nevertheless, it is not extraordinary, that God should work faith in baptized infants.

For even if not all baptized infants leap to the same extent in an unusual way in the womb of their mothers, nevertheless God works faith in them, on account of which they are pleasing to Christ and are not probably counted as adopted sons of God, but certainly announced as such. Otherwise Baptism would be an idle ceremony, by which something would be sealed, which would not be.

IN WHAT WAY THE CHILDREN OF CHRISTIANS ARE IN THE COVENANT.

Granted therefore that children of Christians are born in the Church. They are not on account of this, nevertheless, counted as in the covenant, unless they also do, or have done in them, those things which the covenant requires and which are included in it.

FLESHLY BIRTH FROM PIOUS PARENTS ACHIEVES NOTHING WITH REGARD TO ADOPTION OF THE SONS OF GOD.

Since fleshly birth from pious parents achieves nothing with regard to obtaining the kingdom of heaven. Just as it is written: Do not say among yourselves, we have Abraham as our father. For I say to you, God is able to raise up from those stones sons of Abraham (Matthew 3[:9]). And again: Whatever is born of flesh is flesh (John 8:3 [3:6]).

Therefore unless the children be regenerated and born again of water and Spirit (which is in Baptism), those born of pious and Christian parents cannot see the kingdom of God.

CHILDREN OF THE ISRAELITES WERE NOT COUNTED AS IN THE COVENANT APART FROM CIRCUMCISION.

For just as in the old Testament, children were born of pious parents, but were not counted in the covenant unless there were performed in them also those things which were contained in the covenant, namely, that on the eighth day the flesh of their foreskin was circumcised. For every male, says Moses, the flesh of whose foreskin has not been circumcised, that soul will be erased from his people, because he has made my pledge null and void (Genesis 17[:14]).

<493>

INFANTS WHO DO NOT BELIEVE ARE NOT SAVED.

It follows then, not in some probable fashion, but holding fast as a most certain and indubitable consequence, that in the new Testament infants, even those born of pious and Christian parents, are not counted as in the covenant unless they have also been baptized, according to that word of Christ, John 3: Unless someone has been born again of water and Spirit, he is not able to see the kingdom of God. Baptism would profit them nothing, if they did not believe, according to Christ's word: But he who has not believed will be condemned (Mark 16[:16]). And he does not say, He who was baptized, even if he did not believe, will be saved.

BAPTIZED CHILDREN OF CHRISTIANS DO BELIEVE. WHAT SORT OF A CHILD CHRIST SET BEFORE HIS DISCIPLES.

But that which Dr. Theodore from your statement calls seed of faith, this is nevertheless not faith. Christ speaks much to the contrary; he plainly calls it faith, when he says, He who offends one of the least of those *who believe in me*, who believe in me, Christ says. It is right to think that more of faith applies to this testimony of Christ concerning children than to adults themselves, who confess with their mouth that they believe, although they are able to lie and deceive. But Christ does not lie or deceive. Therefore even if we do not see how they believe who lack the benefit of actual understanding, nevertheless Christ and the holy Spirit on this account are not to be denounced as liars. They openly bear witness that those children believe. There were indeed boys who had been circumcised, from whose number Christ set one before his disciples as an example of humility. These boys had not only been born in the Church, but also had received the sign of the covenant. In this sign were they received into grace by God, and gifted with the holy Spirit's faith and grace.

HUMAN REASON AND INTELLECT DO NOT HELP, BUT IMPEDE FAITH.

Nor is it the case that you may predict the benefit of reason or intellect in them, in comparison with other infants. Those children of four or five years, or even older, possess as little understanding in spiritual matters as an infant lying in its cradle. Nor does reason or human intellect help us in obtaining faith. Nay rather, adults are ordered to take it captive human intellect captive (2 Corinthians 10[:5]), in order that they may either acquire faith or retain it (2 Thessalonians 3[:3–5]), which is the most free gift of the holy Spirit (Philippians 1[:19]).

For this reason I would conclude: If infants of Christians lack faith, and are nevertheless to be baptized, I do not see how <494> it can be reconciled that their Baptism is not an idle and useless ceremony, since without faith Baptism profits nothing.

Dr. Beza:
I do not see how it follows: John the Baptist had faith in his mother's womb. Therefore all baptized infants also have faith. This is an argument from the particular to the universal; it does not entail

this conclusion. Going from possible to being is not a valid argument.
Besides, I do not think that the boys about whom Christ says "they
believe" were four or five years old.

Dr. Jakob:
Even if the example of John is on this account unique, seeing
that he leapt in his mother's womb in actual understanding of faith,
nevertheless it is not unique in this, that he was granted faith in his
infancy.

FOUNDATION OF THE DOCTRINE ABOUT THE FAITH OF BAPTIZED INFANTS.

And of course it would not be possible to argue from the example
of John the Baptist to the infants of all Christians, as if from the particular, or rather the unique, to the universal, unless it were extant in
the word of Christ, who confirms that they believe (Matthew 18[:18]).
And Luke expressly bears witness that they were brought forward
to Christ, not merely children [παιδία] age four or five or older, but τὰ
βρέφη, that is, children hanging from their mothers' breasts. Christ
blessed them and announced that kingdom of heaven belonged to
such (Luke 18[:16]).

---

2 THESSALONIANS 3[:2–3]; HEBREWS 11[:3]; PHILIPPIANS 1[:19].

Since faith is therefore a work of God the holy Spirit, without
which no one is able to please God, how easy it is for God to work
faith, indeed, rather more easily in those in whom the flesh does
not so resist as in adults, than in those very adults, where the flesh
always fights back (that is, understanding and reason, which are the
most excellent faculties of the soul in man).

For reason impedes faith in us more than it promotes or confirms
it. For this reason indeed, it ought to be fought against continually,
up to our last breath, as if the most savage enemy of our eternal
salvation.

<495>

Dr. Beza:

Christ's words concerning faith, which is given through the hearing of the word, must be understood to be about adults. The use of reason and actual understanding is required for hearing. For if God's word were to be heard and not understood, it would profit nothing, nor would faith be conceived. Since infants are deprived of this, we cannot assert that they believe.

We baptize them in any case, seeing as they may sometime believe, even if now, when they receive Baptism, they may not, but are deprived of, and are baptized in the faith of their parents and of the Church, that they may be counted as in the covenant, because they were born in this Church (Joshua 5[:2–9]). Otherwise all infants who died uncircumcised at the time of Moses in the desert would have been damned.

Dr. Jakob:

Mark and Luke plainly bear witness that Christ is speaking not about adults, but about children. He says in plain words that they *believe*, and for this reason ought not in the least be made to stumble. Nor should we concern ourselves how they hear God's word, and how faith is infused in them, when they are baptized. It suffices that Christ bears witness to this.

THAT JUDGMENT REGARDING INFANTS OUGHT TO BE BASED ON THE WORD OF THE LORD. THE SIN OF THE ISRAELITES IN NEGLECTING TO CIRCUMCISE THEIR SONS IN THE DESERT.

From now on, we should not base our judgment regarding whether it applies to unbaptized infants on human reason, but on the Lord's word. This is how the word of the Lord reads: The male, the flesh of whose foreskin has not been circumcised, that soul will be erased from his people, *because he has rendered the Lord's pledge null and void* (Genesis 17[:14]). On this account the parents seriously sinned in the desert, just as they did so many other times, because against God's express mandate they did not take care to have their infants circumcised on the eighth day, and for this reason led them on into risk and very grave danger of losing their life and eternal salvation.

But since their camp had to be moved again and again, hurriedly and unexpectedly, and it seemed proper for their children not to be led into risk of their lives, <496> the Lord himself corrected this error in them by miraculously preserving even the uncircumcised, lest they die in the desert without circumcision, but were circumcised before the entrance into the promised land, as we read was done under Joshua at the Lord's command (Joshua 5[:2–9]).

WHETHER MALES, DEAD AND UNCIRCUMCISED BEFORE THE EIGHTH DAY, WERE SAVED.

Likewise, it is not in the least a source of doubt that very many male infants died uncircumcised before the eighth day. Nevertheless damnation is not imputed to them, since they had not attained the day defined by God, on which account parents with uncircumcised children were excused before God and men. Since they did not transgress the Lord's covenant, neither did they render it null and void. We ought also to make the same judgment regarding infants of Christians, when no fault of the parents and no contempt of the Sacrament has happened.

Dr. Beza:
Do you judge, though, from the word of God, that all those who died uncircumcised in the desert perished? Because it is written: His soul will be erased from his people?

Dr. Jakob:

JUSTIFICATION OF CIRCUMCISION'S OMISSION IN THE DESERT.

If it must be judged from the word of God, certainly it cannot be judged otherwise, especially if negligence and contempt for God's mandate had occurred. But they are able in some way to be excused from negligence and contempt of the Sacrament because of their frequent and unexpected journeys. For this reason indeed were they preserved miraculously, lest they die without circumcision, and perish eternally. And it is likely that very few died in the desert, since, except for Joshua and Caleb, all who had left Egypt at the age of manhood died in the desert, though their children grew to such a great and wonderful number.

Dr. Beza:

If you judge that all uncircumcised infants in the desert <497> perished eternally, you accuse Moses and Aaron of negligence, because they did not advise the people about that sin, with the result that they did not take care to have recently born male infants circumcised at the appointed time. We do not read that this was done by them. But I judge this way, that God did not cast aside uncircumcised infants on account of the negligence of their parents. So also the negligence of parents is no way detrimental to the salvation of the infants of Christians, when they depart this life unbaptized.

Dr. Jakob:

MOSES ENDURED MANY THINGS AMONG THE ISRAELITES, WHICH HE WAS NOT ABLE TO CHANGE.

Moses endured many things against his will among the Jewish people, a stiff-necked people, which he was not able to change. For this reason it is not only likely, but is doubtless a fact as well, that Moses and Aaron also put the Israelites in mind of this part of their duty. But the people did not submit to them in place of their own inclination. These the Lord often punished severely.

Dr. Beza:

WHETHER CIRCUMCISION WAS UTTERLY NECESSARY FOR SALVATION.

Therefore you will make circumcision utterly necessary, since it is written, that one, the flesh of whose foreskin has not been circumcised, his soul will be erased from his people. But I do not believe this, nor do I think in this way. For circumcision was put off all the way up to the eighth day, and in the meantime the poor little boy began to die. Surely he had not been erased from his own people on account of this? However if it is possible to be circumcised, and they did not make use of it, but despised it, I also affirm that such ones perished. I think the same thing about Baptism, and that that is how we ought to judge unbaptized infants.

Dr. Jakob:

When an infant dies before the eighth day appointed for circum-cision, both parents and children are excused before <498> God and men, and whatever he may wish to decide about those infants is left to his will. About this we are making judgment outside the word. Since the infant did not render the covenant of the Lord ineffectual, we think also that this is not imputed to him.

BAPTISM OF INFANTS NOT TO BE DELAYED.

Concerning Baptism, however, although no certain time has been prescribed by God when infants of Christians ought to be baptized, Christ very seriously rebuked his disciples who hindered *infants* and children from being led up to him. He so tenderly invited them, saying: Let the little children come to me since of such is the king-dom of heaven. In such a way is it incumbent upon all parents to be most devoted in this concern, that they allow no delay too lengthy to interpose, but that their recently born infants be baptized and received by Baptism into the covenant, with which Christ has made us a promise of eternal life. According that that word of Christ: Unless one has been born of water and the Spirit, he will not be able to enter the kingdom of God (John 3[:5]). This blessing is necessary not less for children than for adults, seeing as they were conceived and born in sins (Psalm 51[:5]), and are by nature sons of wrath (Ephesians 2[:3]). And unless they should be received into grace on account of Christ, there is no hope left to them of obtaining eter-nal life in their carnal birth, though they were born in the Church. For whatever is born of flesh is flesh, that is, worthy of eternal damnation.

IN WHAT WAY BAPTISM NECESSARY FOR INFANTS.

Because of this, we judge that Baptism is so necessary for infants that we think that only unavoidable necessity excuses it. We propose, however, that negligence and contempt merits forgiveness not in the least. We tie salvation in this way to Baptism, just as the words read: He who believes and is baptized will be saved (Mark 16[:16]). And again: Unless one has been born of water and the Spirit, he is not able to enter into the kingdom of heaven (John 3[:5]).

Dr. Beza:

WHETHER UNBAPTIZED INFANTS ARE IN THE COVENANT OF GOD.

If therefore Baptism is necessary for infants, we piously believe it is not with unconditional necessity, otherwise a great many unbaptized would have been damned, who were saved. Therefore it is clear from this that infants <499> *are in the covenant before they are baptized, or even if they were not baptized, but departed without Baptism.*

Dr. Jakob:

IN WHAT WAY INFANTS, DYING IN THE LAST MOMENT OF NECESSITY WITHOUT BAPTISM, TO BE COMMENDED TO GOD.

Pious parents and honest matrons, when they find their infants in such a state of necessity, commend them to God with their pious prayers. And without doubt they are heard, according to His true word: Seek and you will find, knock and it will be opened to you.

And God is not so bound to the water that he cannot work grace without it when called upon, nor does he wish to be.

REGARDING BAPTISM ADMINISTERED BY WOMEN [Περὶ τοῦ Γυναικοβαπτίσματος].

However, in order that newborn infants who are born extremely ill may not fall into this danger, it is permitted even to women to baptize in such a case of necessity.

Dr. Beza:

WHETHER IT HAS BEEN GRANTED TO WOMEN TO BAPTIZE INFANTS IN THE CASE
OF NECESSITY.

Baptizing is part of the Ministry of the Church, which has been entrusted to the charge of men, and not women, nor should it be. For just as it is not permitted to a woman to speak in the Church, so also is she not allowed to baptize. Paul says, Let a woman learn in silence with all submission. I do not permit a woman to teach (1 Timothy 2[:12]). And again, Let women be silent in the Churches (1 Corinthians 14[:34]).

Dr. Jakob:

BAPTISM ADMINISTERED BY WOMEN NOT TO BE CONDEMNED.

It is true that baptizing is part of the Ministry of the Church, and that ordinarily it is entrusted to the charge of men, and ought to be. But it does not therefore follow that, in a case of necessity, women are not allowed to baptize.

A WOMAN IS ALLOWED TO PREACH AND ABSOLVE IN THE ABSENCE OF MINISTERS
OF THE CHURCH. PROCLAMATION OF THE GOSPEL IS ABSOLUTION FROM SINS.

Just as in fact in the case of necessity, when a person happens to be in the final death throes, and is now about to breathe his last, if the Ministers of the Church are absent, or other men appointed out-side this Ministerium, a pious woman is allowed to speak, that is, to console the person about to die with the proclamation of God's word his divine promises, and to absolve from sins (for what is the procla-mation of <500> the Gospel and the preaching of the promises of God's grace delivered in Christ, other than absolution from sins?). She is to do so like this: Trust (brother or sister in agony) that your sins are forgiven on account of Christ, who promised you this in the word of the Gospel, which he sealed by Baptism, who gave you his own body and blood, and the holy Spirit in Baptism, acting as his pledge. In this way women are allowed also to baptize in the case of necessity, when Ministers of the Church are absent, as are all men as well. For which is greater? The word and its proclamation, or the Sacrament of Baptism and its administration?

Dr. Beza:

PROCLAMATION OF THE WORD GREATER THAN THE ADMINISTRATION OF THE SACRAMENT.

God's word.

Dr. Jakob:

IN WHAT WAY AND WHERE IT IS FORBIDDEN FOR WOMEN TO PREACH THE GOSPEL. LET NOT A WOMAN TEACH IN THE CHURCH.

If therefore a woman is allowed to do what is greater in the case of emergency, then she will also be allowed to do what is less. This agrees with the sayings of Paul that have been brought up and contradict us in no way. For Paul does not utterly forbid women to teach. Otherwise they would also be prohibited from instructing their children and family at home, which is done by means of the salutary doctrine of the Gospel, which from time to time women know and understand better than men, even their husbands, or masters, or *patresfamilias*. For this reason he does not say simply: Let not a woman teach, but he adds, *in the Church*, that is, in the public meeting comprised of men and women, where it would be indecent for men to be taught and instructed by women. Rather, it is their obligation to learn in silence from the men. However the situation is different in a case of emergency, when no man or ordinary Minister of the Church is present, and Paul writes about this in another place: In Christ there is neither male nor female (Galatians 3[:28]).

Dr. Beza:

WHETHER WOMEN ARE ALLOWED TO ADMINISTRATE THE LORD'S SUPPER.

I ask, therefore, if women are allowed to baptize in case of emergency, whether they are also allowed to administrate the Lord's Supper? <501> *Since the nature of the Sacraments and the administra-*

tion of them is the same. If therefore women are allowed the one, they will also be allowed the other.

Dr. Jakob:

DISTINCTION OF NECESSITY IN ADMINISTRATION OF BAPTISM AND THE LORD'S SUPPER.

I answer that there is a vast difference between the administration of the Lord's Supper and Baptism in a case of emergency. For the newborn infant whom the mother baptizes in an extreme case of emergency has never been baptized. But the established Christian in agony who is an adult often received the Lord's Supper in the public Church meeting. If he should be reminded by a woman, consoling him with the message of the Gospel, this poses no risk, because it pertains to eternal salvation, especially if he should die and not receive the Lord's Supper. Baptism is however by far of another nature, concerning which Christ's words are extant: Unless someone has been born of water and spirit, he cannot enter and see the kingdom of God (John 3[:5]).

Dr.Beza:
In the absence of Ministers of the Church, it is fitting for men to do such things, not women. They have been, frankly, excluded from the Ministerium of the Church.

Dr. Jakob:

THE CHURCH ORDINANCE OF WÜRTTEMBERG REGARDING THE ADMINISTRATION OF BAPTISM BY WOMEN.

The Church Ordinance of Württemberg expressly regulates the administration of Baptism by women, lest a midwife or other woman baptize an infant except in the most extreme case of emergency. But if a Minister of the Church were not able to be found an honorable man would be called upon so that he could discharge this office of baptizing. However if these are also found to be in short supply, women cannot be prohibited from this Church Ministry by any law or express word of God. Nor should they be, unless we should wish, in the absence of men, to prohibit them and push them away from the duty of teaching the Gospel and of comforting the sick and those struggling with death. Let us leave the judgment about this in the hands of our audience.

<502>

6

Concerning Predestination

Since Theodore Beza had not yet written down his and his brothers' refutations to the Theses of the Württemberg Theologians concerning Predestination, as also those concerning Baptism and the Reformation of Temples, and the Honorable Prince Count Frederick had also bidden that it should be discussed, Dr. Lucas Osiander was ordered to recite publicly the Theses of the Württembergers, which follow. Dr. Beza earnestly asked the Honorable Prince, Count Frederick, however, through principal French audience-members of the colloquy, since the business was taking place with Dr. Jakob Andreae, that he strive after brevity and abstain from the long-windedness which he had employed in his collation of the preceding articles. Dr. Jakob promised that he would do this.

6A. WÜRTTEMBERG THEOLOGIANS' THESES CONCERNING PREDESTINATION

The theses that follow have been placed outside the controversy.

1. That God foresaw from eternity not only the fall of our first parents, but also of all men.

<503>

2. That he foreknew not only those who would be saved, but also chose them from eternity, and predestined them to eternal life.

3. That election happened in Christ, before the world's foundations were laid, that is, that they were being saved through Christ.

4. That the number of those who will be saved is certain in the sight of God.

5. It is asked however whether God predestined his elect to eternal life in such a way that he has destined certain people to eternal condemnation, in fact the greatest portion of mankind, before they were born. The question is whether their eternal destruction was effected by means of his absolute and hidden will, with the result that he does not wish them to work repentance, to be converted, and to be saved.

6. We believe and confess that it is impossible to demonstrate from Scripture what God's hidden will is, that without any regard for unworthiness, he destined a particular individual by the genuine determination of his will, much less that he destined to eternal damnation the greatest portion of the human race to the extent that he does not wish them to repent, be converted, or be saved.

7. The *foundations* of our assertion are these:

Whatsoever things are written, are written for our learning, in order that we may have patience, *consolation*, and the *hope* of the Scriptures (Romans 15[:4]).

God desires all men to be saved and to come to a knowledge of the truth (1 Timothy 2[:4]).

As I live, I do not desire the death of the sinner, but that he be converted and live (Ezekiel 18[:23]).

<504>

Thus has it been written, that it had to be that the Christ suffered and rose again from the dead on the third day, and that repentance and the remission of sins be preached in his name *to all nations* (Luke 24[:47]).

God so loved *the world* that he gave his only-begotten Son, that *everyone* who believes in him should not perish, but have eternal life (John 3[:16]).

He himself is the propitiation for sins, not only for ours, but for the sins of the whole *world* (1 John 2[:2]).

Come to me *all* who labor and are heavy-laden, and I will refresh you (Matthew 11[:28]).

God subjected all things under unbelief, in order that he might have mercy *on all* (Romans 11[:32]).

The Lord does not wish that *any* perish, but that *all* be turned to repentance (2 Peter 3[:9]).

The issue of Predestination of the elect has to be determined neither by law nor by human reason, but from the Gospel alone.

6B. WE REJECT, AS NOT IN THE LEAST FITTING WITH GOD'S WORD, TEACHINGS WHICH TAKE AWAY EVERY CONSOLATION FROM PIOUS MINDS, AS WHEN IT IS TAUGHT:

1. That rejection is the most judicious design of God, in which before all eternity (as they themselves say) he decided, consistently without any injustice, *not to have mercy on those* whom he did not love, but passed them over, by which act, by their just condemnation, he demonstrates his wrath against sins and his glory.

<505>

2. That the efficient cause of rejection is God's design, in which God has been pleased to create certain people and *to raise them up for this purpose*, in order that he might show his power, in order that he be glorified also in them.

3. That God has destined for destruction, with no regard to unworthiness, the reprobate who are not yet born, and that certain people have been set aside by God for righteous judgment.

4. That Adam fell into those calamities of his own will indeed, but nevertheless not only did God foreknow that he would, but also *righteously ordained* and decided that it would happen.

5. That the reason for his decision of rejection and election is on the one hand the eternal mercy on *those whom he has been pleased* to predestine to salvation, and on the other hand his eternal hatred for wickedness, upon *whom he has been pleased to ordain a just damnation.* Why *he destined these*, however, rather than *those*, for salvation or damnation, is for *no other* immediate and primary [προκαταρκτικὴ] reason, *than his own will.*

6. That, even though Holy Scripture declares that the rest of mankind has been delivered over to eternal death in the person of one man, nevertheless *this* can be ascribed *not to their nature*, but has been *designed by God's admirable plan.*

7. That the fact that Adam's fall entangled so many nations together with their children and as many infants in eternal death without remedy, was for no other reason than that it *seemed good to God to do so.*

<506>

8. That God foreknew the destruction that man would endure to the extent that, before he could actually do anything himself, *he so ordained it by his own will.*

9. That Adam would not have been able to fall had it not been for the decree and ordaining *of God.*

10. That *it was fitting* for man to fall from his purity and integrity.

11. That God does not desire those destined for Rejection *to be saved, or the death of his son to be a source of profit for them.*

> *Signed*:
> Dr. *Jakob Andreae*
> Dr. *Lucas Osiander*

To these it seemed good to attach the Responses of Dr. Beza and his brothers, although now at length delivered at the conclusion of the conference, following the same method here as in the preceding articles for the sake of order.

<507>

6C. ON THE THESES CONCERNING PREDESTINATION.

TO THE FIRST.

We generally affirm that the circumstance under which our first parents fell was one of God being neither unwilling nor ignorant, nor even idly prescient of the fact. This is true of everything in the world that has been, or is, or will ever come to pass, by whose will (a) not even the little sparrows are an exception (Matthew 10:39[29]).

ANNOTATIONS OF DR. JAKOB ANDREAE: (A) THAT GOD WAS WILLING THAT OUR FIRST PARENTS SINNED, THAT IS, THAT GOD WILLED THAT THEY TRANSGRESS THE GOD-GIVEN PRECEPT IN PARADISE IN REGARD TO THE FRUIT OF THE TREE OF KNOWLEDGE OF GOOD AND EVIL, THIS IDEA THE HOLY SPIRIT NEVER TEACHES IN THE WHOLE OF HOLY SCRIPTURE.

TO THE SECOND.

We assent, so long as the term choosing (b) or election stands for Predestination. Let it be assumed that according to the decree things follow in due time. And since he who chooses may not receive all things, we say that it necessarily follows that the remainder are passed over by the same decree.

ANNOTATIONS OF DR. JAKOB ANDREAE: (B) THE TERM CHOOSING IS PLACED BY US IN OUR THESIS IN THE MEANING USED BY HOLY SCRIPTURE, BY WHICH IS UNDERSTOOD NOT GOD'S ABSOLUTE DECREE, BUT WHAT IS LIMITED AND CIRCUMSCRIBED IN CHRIST, EPHESIANS 1: HE CHOSE US IN CHRIST JESUS BEFORE THE FOUNDATIONS OF THE WORLD WERE LAID. AND FURTHERMORE IN THIS PASSAGE: HE LOVED US, JUST AS OUR THIRD THESIS TEACHES.

TO THE THIRD.

We assent.

TO THE FOURTH.

We assent, and affirm by the same reasoning that the number of those who have been destined for just damnation (c) is certain in the sight of God.

ANNOTATIONS OF DR. JAKOB ANDREAE: (C) NOT HOWEVER BY THE ABSOLUTE DECREE OF GOD, NAMELY THAT GOD DOES NOT WANT THEM TO BE SAVED, BUT ON ACCOUNT OF THEIR OWN IMPIETY, IN WHICH THEY SPURN GOD'S GRACE, OFFERED IN CHRIST, WHOM GOD THE FATHER WISHES TO BE HEARD BY ALL PEOPLE (MATTHEW 17[:5]).

<508>

TO THE FIFTH AND SIXTH.

We affirm what is denied here, that vessels of wrath (d) have been as destined from eternity as vessels of mercy have been. This is not only because the argument follows the same reasoning as its counterargument (e) (as we have said, the term election (f) itself carries this point), but also because it is declared in the express word of God, both in a few various places, as well as from the profession of the Apostle (Romans 9:11) (g). This decree of God is so far from anyone being able to accuse him of injustice, (h) that God would not even have been unjust if he had predestined no one to salvation, since we are all born sons of wrath and he himself is debtor to no one. <509> *We next say that the condemnation, of those who are abandoned in their corruption by God's eternal decree, (i) is not rightly attributed to this decree. For even though it cannot turn out to be the case that God decreed and the result was that those who perish do so apart from this decree of God, (k) nevertheless the reason (l) for the execution of the decree, that is, the damnation of those who perish, is not the decree of God, but rather their native corruption in which they were born, and the fruits of the corruption, from which it pleases God to exempt only his own who are predestined for salvation. But the greatest number has always been and is the number of those who are perishing, (m) The fact itself carries this point. And the Lord himself shows this, saying, many are called but few are chosen, (n) and few are those who enter the narrow gate. Finally, this must be understood,* <510> *that God (o) does not want them to be converted and saved, not as if they themselves want to be and God resists their desire, but because they themselves also do not wish to be converted, and are not even able to wish it, (p) having been abandoned righteously in their impenitence.*

ANNOTATIONS OF DR. JAKOB ANDREAE: <508> (D) VESSELS OF WRATH HAVE BEEN MADE AND PREPARED NOT BY GOD, OR HIS ABSOLUTE WILL, BUT BY THE DEVIL AND THEIR OWN WILL. ON ACCOUNT OF THIS THEY HAVE BEEN DESTINED FOR THE RIGHTEOUS JUDGMENT OF GOD HIMSELF UNTO ETERNAL DAMNATION. HE NEVER WILLED THEIR DAMNATION. THEREFORE THEY PERISH AGAINST GOD'S WILL BY MEANS OF THEIR OWN WILL. (E) THE REASONING IS NOT THE SAME HERE. FOR THE SOLE AND ONLY REASON FOR THE DESTRUCTION OF THE IMPIOUS IS THE EVIL WILL OF THE DEVIL AND THEIR OWN EVIL WILL. THE REASON FOR THE ETERNAL SALVATION OF THE PIOUS, ON THE OTHER HAND, IS GOD'S WILL REVEALED IN CHRIST, JUST AS THE VOICE FROM HEAVEN SOUNDS: THIS IS MY CHOSEN SON, IN WHOM I HAVE BEEN WELL PLEASED; *LISTEN TO THIS ONE* (MATTHEW 17[:5]). THE FAITHFUL AND ELECT SUBMIT THEMSELVES TO HIM. (F) THE TERM ELECTION DOES NOT IN THE LEAST CARRY THIS POINT, SINCE NOWHERE IN HOLY SCRIPTURE IS TAUGHT AN ABSOLUTE DECREE OF GOD BY WHICH HE HAS CREATED CERTAIN PEOPLE FOR DAMNATION. (G) AT ROMANS 9 PAUL INDEED TEACHES THAT THE BELIEVING ARE SAVED BY THE GRACE AND MERCY OF GOD, NOT *BY HIS ABSOLUTE MERCY*, HOWEVER, BUT BY THE MERCY DECLARED AND DELIVERED IN CHRIST. HE SAYS NOTHING, ON THE OTHER HAND, ABOUT GOD'S ABSOLUTE JUSTICE, BY WHICH HE HAS CREATED AND ORDAINED THE GREATEST PART OF THE HUMAN RACE UNTO ETERNAL DAMNATION, AND THAT HE *DOES NOT WISH* THEM TO BE SAVED. (H) GOD COULD INDEED NOT BE ACCUSED OF INJUSTICE IF WERE TO ACT IN THIS MANNER, BUT HOLY SCRIPTURE DOES NOT TEACH THIS. RATHER, ALL THE PAGES OF HOLY WRIT EMPHASIZE THE CONTRARY, NAMELY THAT GOD *DOES NOT WISH THE DEATH OF ANY PERSON.* <509> (I) THOSE WHO ARE DAMNED ARE NOT ABANDONED BECAUSE OF GOD'S ETERNAL DECREE, BUT ON ACCOUNT OF IMPIETY AND CONTEMPT FOR THE WORD AND GRACE OFFERED IN CHRIST: HOW OFTEN I HAVE WISHED TO GATHER YOUR CHILDREN, *AND YOU WERE UNWILLING* (MATTHEW 23[:37]). (K) NOWHERE IS THIS DECREE EXTANT IN SCRIPTURE. AND TO SAY THIS IS TO PUT WORDS IN HEAVEN'S MOUTH IN A WAY NOT REVEALED FROM GOD, IN ORDER TO OVERTURN EVERY CONSOLATION OF THE PIOUS. (L) SINCE THEY HAVE SAID ABOVE THAT THE FIRST PEOPLE SINNED WITH GOD WILLING, AND LATER FROM THE MOUTH OF THE VERY SAME WE HEAR THAT MAN WAS OBLIGED TO FALL, THEN HOW WAS THE CAUSE OF THE EXECUTION OF THEIR DAMNATION NOT THIS HIDDEN WILL OF GOD? IF IN FACT (ACCORDING TO THEIR OPINION) GOD HAD NOT WANTED THEM TO SIN, THEN THEY WOULD HAVE BEEN FREE FROM THIS JUDGMENT AND HIS DECREE. FOR ANYTHING THAT IS THE CAUSE OF A CAUSE IS ALSO THE CAUSE OF THE EFFECT. (M) THE GREATEST NUMBER IS INDEED THAT OF THE DAMNED, BUT NOT FROM GOD'S ABSOLUTE DECREE. FOR GOD WISHES NO ONE TO PERISH, BUT TO SAVE ALL. BUT SCORN

FOR GRACE OFFERED IN CHRIST AND FOR HIS WORD IS THE CAUSE OF DESTRUCTION, WHICH GOD DOES NOT WISH. (N) SINCE GOD DOES NOT CALL SINNERS TO REPENTANCE INSINCERELY BUT RATHER IN EARNEST, FOR THIS REASON HE CONDEMNS NO ONE BY A HIDDEN DECREE, BUT ONLY THOSE WHO OPPOSE THEMSELVES TO THE ELECTION WHICH HAS BEEN REVEALED IN CHRIST: COME TO ME *ALL*. <510> (O) THIS IS A HORRIBLE TERM, WHICH IS FOUND NOWHERE IN HOLY SCRIPTURE, THAT *GOD IN HIS ABSOLUTE WILL DOES NOT WISH PEOPLE TO BE CONVERTED AND SAVED*. (P) THIS IS A HORRIBLE AND ABOMINABLE TERM, THAT THEY WOULD NEITHER WISH NOR BE ABLE TO BE CONVERTED, BECAUSE THEY HAVE BEEN ABANDONED BY GOD'S HIDDEN DECREE IN THEIR IMPENITENCE. THIS OVERTURNS THE UNIVERSAL DOCTRINE OF THE GOSPEL AND THE USE OF THE SACRAMENTS, AND TAKES AWAY EVERY CONSOLATION FROM TROUBLED CONSCIENCES.

TO THE SEVENTH.

The passage from Romans 15 applies to the universality of the elect (q), and the Apostle does not reckon himself among the others, that is, those destined for destruction, and placed outside the Church.

To the 1 Timothy 2 passage we respond what the Apostle's very point entails, (r) as well as all orthodox Fathers, especially Augustine in as many places as possible. It is shown from their declaration that by the term all people, what is to be understood is not each and every type of person, but rather types of each and every person. For the Apostle is in this passage treating the various states of people, (s) whom the Lord calls to his own Church. And not only would it be thoroughly absurd, but it would also be profane to think, if <511> God wants each and every person to be saved, that he himself is not able to accomplish what he wishes, or to suspend the effect of his divine will from the judgment of mankind.

To the Ezekiel 18[:32] passage we respond that it is an ambiguous statement (u) that differs from the universal in very many respects, and the limitation about conversion shows that this must be understood about those alone to whom is given the grace of conversion, which is characteristic of the elect. (x) They who spurn God's warnings and exhortations he makes through his preached word are nevertheless, however, rendered inexcusable, (y) because they are accustomed to act stubbornly whom God does not convert inwardly. And next to that, convert me and I will be converted. (z)

<512> *To the Luke 24[:47] passage,*

By all nations, it is astonishing that you take this to mean each and every person of all peoples. (a) Even if this were true, nevertheless it could not be truly said of every era, since God did not reveal his salvific will to all nations until after the mission of the Apostles, (b) and now wills that the greatest part of the world live in darkness and perish by his righteous judgment, though ultimately not with a new plan formed. (c) John 3: the human race is not understood universally by the term World, but rather indefinitely. (d) It is applied to those who trust in him, as Christ says: <513> he does not pray for the world, but rather only for those whom his father gave him, and who will believe in his name. (e) 1 John 2, where John says propitiation has been made not only for our sins, but for the sins of the entire world, (f) is interpreted in regard only to the universality of the elect and believing, which now is gathered not only from the race of the Apostle himself, that is, the Jews, but rather with the dividing wall torn down, as the Apostle abundantly explains in the Epistle to the Ephesians, he pours himself out to the rest of the nations.. Just as was promised to Abraham, that all nations would be blessed through his seed. And John seems to have followed these very words of Christ purposely, since that prayer of his is ardent in the extreme, John 17:20: I do not ask on their behalf only, he says, but also on behalf of those who will come to believe in me through their speech. Indeed, just as John said, This is the lamb of God, who takes away the sins of the world. (g) But surely Christ did not take away the sins of the whole <514> world, (h) as you interpret, in the way of each and every single person? And certainly your sentence has appeared to us unsupportable, (i) that Christ died on behalf of the damned, and that men are not damned on account of their sins. (k) Matthew 11, let all be gathered, who labor and are heavy laden, that is, grow tired under the weight of their sins, (l) which certainly is appropriate only for those who recognize that they are sinners and flee to him from whom they hope to be able to be relieved, Romans 11. (m) Context itself shows clearly that the Apostle does not act there concerning single people per se, but wished to distribute the human race into two parts, Jews <515> and Gentiles of course, out of whom God gathers his own Church through mercy, since both the latter group and the former would perish worthily, in order that no one who is saved may be saved in any way other than through mercy. Nay rather is it said that God has included all people under unbelief. He proves what we assert, that to be sure people have fallen into this misery neither with God being unwilling (n) nor accidentally. Nevertheless, every fault must be referred to man's voluntary fall (o) and his descendants thus subjected to sin.

2 Peter 3:9. With these words, God does not wish that anyone (p) perish, it is evident from the preceding, from his whole treatment up to this point, that Peter is addressing only the faithful, to whom he also adds himself. Finally, we approve that this is added, that Predestination of the Elect should be judged not by law and not by human reason, but by the Gospel alone. <516> Only let it be understood from these words, 1 John 3:24, By this we know that we dwell in him and he in us, that he has given us of his spirit. (q)

And 1 John 3:10, by this the sons of God are made known, and the sons of the devil, whoever does not work righteousness and the one who does not love his brother is not from God. (r)

ANNOTATIONS OF DR. JAKOB ANDREAE: <510> (Q) PAUL'S TEACHING ABOUT THE USE OF HOLY SCRIPTURE IS UNIVERSAL. HE DIRECTS ALL THINGS TO THE CONSOLATION OF SINFUL PEOPLE WHO WORK TRUE REPENTANCE, FROM WHICH CONSOLATION NO ONE IS EXCLUDED, BUT *ALL PEOPLE* ARE INVITED TO IT. (R) PAUL'S WORDS ARE OBVIOUS AND CLEAR, BY WHICH HE BIDS PRAYER *ON BEHALF OF ALL* PEOPLE, *BECAUSE* GOD WISHES *ALL PEOPLE* TO BECOME SAVED. FOR THIS REASON IT IS IMPIETY TO EXCLUDE ANYONE FROM THIS UNIVERSAL PROMISE. (S) PAUL DOES NOT ACT THERE FROM THE VARIOUS STATES OF PEOPLE, BUT SPEAKS IDIOMATICALLY ABOUT ALL PEOPLE, ON BEHALF OF WHOM THERE MUST BE PRAYER, BUT ESPECIALLY FOR THE MAGISTRATE, BECAUSE HE CAN BE EITHER A VERY GREAT BENEFIT OR HINDRANCE TO THE SALVATION OR DESTRUCTION OF OTHERS. <511> (T) GOD HAS NOT WILLED BY HIS ABSOLUTE WILL THAT ALL MEN BECOME SAVED. FOR ALL MEN WOULD CERTAINLY BE SAVED IF THIS WERE THE CASE. WHO IN FACT IS ABLE TO RESIST HIS WILL? BUT HE HAS WILLED IT BY HIS RESTRICTED WILL *IN CHRIST*. OUTSIDE OF HIM HE WILLS NO ONE TO BE SAVED. HIM HE OFFERS TO ALL PEOPLE THROUGH THE PREACHING OF THE GOSPEL AND THE USE OF THE SACRAMENTS. WHOEVER OPPOSES HIMSELF

AGAINST HIM PERISHES, NOT BY GOD'S WILL, BUT BY HIS OWN IMPIETY, AGAINST GOD'S WILL. (U) THE THING ITSELF TEACHES THAT IT IS A UNIVERSAL STATEMENT WHEN *THE LORD* SAYS, I DO NOT WISH THE DEATH OF THE DYING, WHOEVER IT MAY BE. THEREFORE IT IS BLATANT IMPIETY AND AN ABOMINABLE DOCTRINE TO MAKE A PARTICULAR OUT OF A UNIVERSAL PROMISE, CONTRARY TO THE EXPRESS LETTER OF THE TEXT. (X) BUT ELECTION IS DEFINED NOT BY GOD'S ABSOLUTE DECREE, BUT IN CHRIST, WHO CALLS ALL PEOPLE TO REPENTANCE. FOR THIS REASON, NO ONE MAY EXCLUDE HIMSELF FROM THE NUMBER OF THE ELECT; RATHER LET US SAY WITH AUGUSTINE: IF YOU ARE NOT PREDESTINED, MAKE SURE YOU ARE. (Y) IN WHAT WAY WOULD THEY NOT BE RENDERED EXCUSABLE? THAT IS, IF WHAT YOU AFFIRM WERE TRUE, THAT BY GOD'S HIDDEN AND ABSOLUTE DECREE THEY HAD BEEN CREATED AND DESTINED FOR ETERNAL DESTRUCTION, WITH THE RESULT THAT GOD *DOES NOT WISH* THEM TO BE CONVERTED, AND SO IT IS NOT POSSIBLE FOR THEM TO BE CONVERTED? THESE THINGS ARE HORRIBLE AND ABOMINABLE TO HEAR IN THE CHURCH OF CHRIST. (Z) THIS PRAYER DOES NOT CONFIRM THE ERROR ABOUT GOD'S HIDDEN AND ABSOLUTE WILL IN DAMNING PEOPLE, BUT TEACHES RATHER THAT CONVERSION TO GOD CANNOT HAPPEN BY HUMAN STRENGTH. <512> FOR THIS REASON HE IMPLORES GOD'S GRACE, OFFERED *TO ALL* PEOPLE, INDEED TO THE WHOLE WORLD. (A) MORE SHOCKING THAT THIS IS DENIED BY YOU, SINCE THE MATTER IS VERY CLEAR, NAMELY THAT UNDER THE UNIVERSAL ADJECTIVE *"ALL"* ARE ALSO UNDERSTOOD EACH AND EVERY PERSON AMONG ALL NATIONS. (B) GOD HAS ALREADY FROM THE FOUNDATION OF THE WORLD REVEALED HIS WILL FOR THE SALVATION OF MANKIND, AND RENDERED THE ISRAELITE PEOPLE DISTINGUISHED AMONG ALL KINGS. THESE PROMISES WERE PRESERVED AMONG THIS PEOPLE. SINCE PEOPLE RUN ACROSS THE SEA IN PURSUIT OF TRADE, THE WORSHIP OF GOD BECAME CARELESS. THEY WILL HAVE TO ACCUSE NOT GOD'S WILL, NOR A HIDDEN DECREE OF HIS REGARDING THE DAMNATION OF PEOPLE, BUT RATHER THEIR OWN IMPIETY. THEY COULD HAVE BECOME PROSELYTES AND BEEN SAVED. (C) THAT THE GREATEST PART OF THE WORLD IS *NOW* TURNED TO THE DARKNESS CANNOT BE BLAMED ON GOD'S HIDDEN AND ABSOLUTE DECREE, BUT HAS ITS SOURCE IN THE WICKEDNESS OF MANKIND. PAUL PLAINLY TEACHES THIS, 2 THESSALONIANS 2[:10–11], WHEN HE SAYS, SINCE THEY DID NOT ACCEPT LOVE OF THE TRUTH *IN ORDER THAT THEY MIGHT BECOME SAVED*, FOR THIS REASON GOD SENT THEM THE WORKING OF DELUSION, IN ORDER THAT THEY BELIEVE A LIE. WHAT COULD BE SAID MORE PLAINLY AGAINST THE OPINION OF GOD'S ABSOLUTE DECREE IN DAMNING PEOPLE? (D) A MANIFEST PERVERSION OF CHRIST'S WORDS AND FALSE INTERPRETATION OF THE TERM "WORLD," WHICH THEY WILL NEVER BE ABLE TO PROVE FROM HOLY SCRIPTURE. <513> BUT JOHN HIMSELF, THE BEST INTERPRETER OF HIS OWN WORDS, TEACHES THE CONTRARY WHEN HE SAYS: CHRIST IS THE PROPITIATION FOR THE SINS *OF THE ENTIRE WORLD*. THERE IS PLACED HERE NOT AN INDEFINITE ADJECTIVE, BUT A UNIVERSAL ONE. (E) EVEN IF THE TERM *"WORLD"* IS RESTRICTED HERE, NEVERTHELESS IT DOES NOT CONFIRM THE ERROR CONCERNING AN ABSOLUTE DECREE OF DAMNATION. FOR HE UNDERSTANDS BY *WORLD* THOSE WHO DESPISE THE TEACHING OF THE

GOSPEL, WHO PUT THEMSELVES AGAINST CHRIST. CHRIST DENIES THAT HE PRAYS FOR THESE. BUT IT DOES NOT FOLLOW THAT CHRIST IN HIS ABSOLUTE WILL DOES NOT WANT THEM TO BE SAVED. (F) JOHN'S WORDS ARE TOO CLEAR TO ADMIT SUCH A MANIFESTLY FALSE INTERPRETATION. HE DID NOT DECIDE ON A COLLECTION AMONG JEWS AND THE NATIONS, BUT SPEAKS UNIVERSALLY ABOUT *THE ENTIRE WORLD*. (G) NOTHING IS MORE CERTAIN THAN THAT JOHN HAS UNDERSTOOD ALL MANKIND BY THE TERM "WORLD," NOT INDEFINITELY, BUT UNIVERSALLY, JUST AS OTHER, NEARLY ENDLESS, PASSAGES OF HOLY SCRIPTURE BEAR WITNESS AND CONFIRM. <514> (H) HE HAS SUFFICIENTLY MADE SATISFACTION FOR THE SINS OF EACH AND EVERY SINGLE PERSON, WITH THE RESULT THAT THERE IS NO NEED FOR A NEW OR ANOTHER SACRIFICIAL VICTIM. IF A THOUSAND WORLDS WERE WAITING TO BE RECONCILED TO GOD, IF I MAY PUT IT THIS WAY, ONE DROP OF BLOOD OF THE SON OF GOD WOULD SUFFICE FOR THEM. BUT SINCE THE GREATEST PART OF MANKIND SPURNS IT, IT IS FOR THIS REASON THAT IT PROFITS THEM NOTHING, AND THEY ARE THE MORE SERIOUSLY CONDEMNED. (I) WE SAY THAT IT IS THE HEIGHT OF IMPIETY IF ANYONE SHOULD SAY THIS. MUCH TO THE CONTRARY, THEY ARE INDEED DAMNED BECAUSE THEY WERE UNWILLING TO BELIEVE THAT CHRIST DIED FOR THEIR SINS, WHICH IS THE SUPREME AND GREATEST SIN. (K) THESE ARE NOT OUR WORDS OR DOCTRINE, BUT RATHER CHRIST'S, WHEN HE SAYS, THIS IS THE VERDICT (THAT IS, THE REASON FOR JUDGMENT AND DAMNATION), THAT LIGHT HAS COME INTO THE WORLD, AND THE WORLD LOVED DARKNESS MORE THAN THE LIGHT. THEREFORE EVEN THOUGH SINS DAMN BY THEIR OWN NATURE, NEVERTHELESS, THEY CANNOT DAMN FURTHER IF YOU SHOULD TRULY TRUST IN CHRIST. THEREFORE PEOPLE ARE NOT DAMNED BECAUSE THEY SIN, SUCH THAT IT IS NOT POSSIBLE FOR THEM TO BE HELPED FURTHER IN ANY WAY; OTHERWISE ALL THE SAINTS WOULD ALSO BE DAMNED, SINCE ALL HAVE SINNED. RATHER, THEY ARE DAMNED BECAUSE THEY DESPISE THEIR REDEEMER AND ARE UNWILLING TO BELIEVE IN HIM. (L) IT IS HORRIBLE TO HEAR SO PLAIN A UNIVERSAL CALLING FASHIONED AS A PARTICULAR ONE, AS IF HE DOES NOT SERIOUSLY CALL ALL WHO LABOR. EVEN TO THINK ABOUT GOD THIS WAY IS IMPIOUS. (M) PAUL'S WORDS ARE CLEAR ENOUGH THAT THEY NEED NO INTERPRETATION, WHEN HE SAYS: GOD HAS SHUT IN ALL THINGS UNDER SIN IN ORDER THAT HE MAY HAVE MERCY ON ALL. FOR JUST AS HE DOES NOT SAY, HE HAS SHUT IN CERTAIN PEOPLE UNDER SIN, BUT RATHER SAYS ALL THINGS, SO ALSO HE DOES NOT SAY, IN ORDER THAT HE MAY HAVE MERCY ON SOME PEOPLE, BUT RATHER, THAT HE MAY HAVE MERCY ON ALL, IN ORDER THAT <515> HE MAY SHOW THAT HIS MERCY IS SERIOUSLY OFFERED TO ALL PEOPLE, AND THAT GOD WANTS ALL MEN TO BELIEVE AND BE SAVED, JUST AS ALL HAVE SINNED. (N) THIS IS ASSERTION IS SIMPLY IMPIOUS, AND HORRIBLE TO HEAR, AND TOTALLY CONTRARY TO GOD'S EXPRESS AND REVEALED WORD. FOR WHATEVER GOD PROHIBITS, HE DOES NOT WILL ANYONE TO DO. THEREFORE OUR FIRST PARENTS TRANSGRESSED THE PRECEPT GIVEN IN PARADISE AND FELL INTO THIS MISERY, AGAINST GOD'S WILL, NOT WITH GOD WILLING IT, BUT RATHER CONTRARY TO HIS WILL. THIS HOLY SPIRIT TEACHES THIS WAY IN HOLY SCRIPTURE, AND THOSE WHO TEACH OTHERWISE, EVEN IF IT WERE AN ANGEL FROM HEAVEN, LET

HIM BE ANATHEMA. (O) IF YOUR DOCTRINE IS TRUE, EVERY FAULT CAN BE REFERRED NOT TO THE PERSON BUT TO THE CREATOR GOD, WHO (ACCORDING TO YOUR OPINION) CREATED AND ORDAINED THEM FOR SINNING AND DAMNATION BY HIS OWN ABSOLUTE DECREE, SO THAT THEY WOULD BE UNWILLING TO DO OTHERWISE, TO BE CONVERTED OR SAVED. THIS IS HORRIBLE AND ABOMINABLE TO HEAR. (P) THIS SENTENCE OF PETER IS ALSO SO PLAIN THAT IT CAN IN NO WAY ADMIT YOUR INTERPRETATION. FOR NOT ONLY IS THE UNIVERSAL ADJECTIVE "ALL" PLACED IN THE SENTENCE, BUT HE ADDS AN EXPLANATION TOO: *WANTING NO ONE* TO PERISH, BUT *THAT ALL* BE TURNED AROUND TO REPENTANCE. THEREFORE BEZA'S DOCTRINE IS HORRIBLE AND BLASPHEMOUS, BY WHICH HE IMPIOUSLY ASSERTS THE CONTRARY. <516> (Q) OFTEN THOSE WHO FEEL THAT THEY ARE BEING LED BY THE SPIRIT HAVE A SENSE THAT IT SO DEBILITATED IN THE MIDST OF TEMPTATIONS THAT THEIR HEART EXPERIENCES THE EXACT OPPOSITE. IF THEREFORE THEY HAVE TO MAKE A JUDGMENT ABOUT THEIR ELECTION ONLY FROM THIS SENSE, THERE WILL BE NO USE FOR THE DIVINE PROMISES OF BAPTISM, THE LORD'S SUPPER, ABSOLUTION, AND EVEN THE ENTIRE MINISTRY OF THE CHURCH. IF INDEED (ACCORDING TO BEZA'S OPINION) *NOTHING* CAN BE DECIDED FOR CERTAIN ABOUT OUR ELECTION TO ETERNAL LIFE FROM ALL THESE THINGS. (R) EVEN THE ELECT CHILDREN OF GOD RUSH FROM TIME TO TIME INTO MANIFEST SINS, JUST AS DO THE CHILDREN OF THE DEVIL, AS DID DAVID INTO ADULTERY, HOMICIDE, ETC. WHERE THEREFORE IS THE CONSOLATION AND CERTAINTY OF THEIR ELECTION? WHENCE OUGHT IT TO BE SOUGHT OR TAKEN HOLD OF? ANY CERTAINTY IN THE UNIVERSAL PROMISES OF THE GOSPEL, IN BAPTISM, IN THE *LORD'S* SUPPER, IN ABSOLUTION, IS NOT CERTAIN ACCORDING TO THE OPINION OF BEZA AND HIS FRIENDS. WHO DOES NOT SEE, THEREFORE, WHAT THE DEVIL INTENDS BY THIS TEACHING? NAMELY, DESPAIR AMONG THE PIOUS, AND EPICUREANISM AMONG DEBAUCHED PEOPLE, WHICH CERTAIN FOLLOWS.

6D. ON THE DOGMAS SUBMITTED.

1.

The first dogma, which you reject, we safeguard as truly a Christian (s) and orthodox one.

ANNOTATIONS OF DR. JAKOB ANDREAE: (S) THIS IS HORRIBLE AND ABOMINABLE TO HEAR, THAT GOD IN HIS ETERNAL DECREE *HAS NOT LOVED* CERTAIN PEOPLE, BUT RATHER HAS ABANDONED THEM TO THEIR JUST CONDEMNATION, AND *HAS NOT DESIRED TO HAVE MERCY* UPON THEM.

<517>

2.

If (t) by the word rejection his decree is understood, then it is said awkwardly that it is God's design, that is, his decree is his efficient cause. But even if you accept by that term the execution (u) of his decree, we confess that what you repudiate is false, as we have shown at the fifth and sixth Thesis.

ANNOTATIONS OF DR. JAKOB ANDREAE: (T) THIS ALSO IS HORRIBLE AND ABOMINABLE, TO ASSERT THAT GOD *CREATED* CERTAIN PEOPLE AND RAISED THEM UP FOR THIS PURPOSE, TO DEMONSTRATE HIS WRATH AND HIS POWER, AND *IN ORDER THAT* HE MIGHT BE GLORIFIED ALSO IN THEM. FOR EVEN IF THE APOSTLE BEARS WITNESS THAT HE RAISED PHARAOH UP IN THIS LIFE IN ORDER THAT HE MIGHT DECLARE HIS POWER IN THIS VERY AGE, NEVERTHELESS WE NEVER READ IT WRITTEN THAT HE CREATED HIM FOR ETERNAL DAMNATION, TO THE SAME DEGREE THAT HE, IN HIS ABSOLUTE WILL, DID NOT WISH HIM TO WORK REPENTANCE AND BE CONVERTED. FOR WHAT IS SAID CONCERNING HIS HARDENING OF HEART WAS NOT AN EFFECT OF HIS ABSOLUTE WILL, BUT RATHER WAS A JUST PUNISHMENT OF HIS PRECEDING CRUELTY, WHICH PHARAOH EXERCISED UPON THE CHILDREN OF ISRAEL IN THE MOST INHUMAN WAY. (U) BY THE TERM REJECTION, WHETHER WE UNDERSTAND IT AS HIS DECREE OR AS EXECUTION OF HIS DECREE, IT IS NEVERTHELESS IMPIOUS TO ASSERT THAT GOD DECREED BY HIS ABSOLUTE WILL THAT HE *DOES NOT HAVE MERCY* ON CERTAIN PEOPLE. THIS OBVIOUSLY CLASHES WITH HIS REVEALED WILL.

3. AND 5.

You attack Paul himself in this dogma, Romans 9:11. For the idea that unbelief (x) is the cause of this divine decree concerning the destruction of some, is just as <518> *false as the idea that foreseen faith (y) or good works are the cause of Predestination or of people being elect, which is the dogma of the Pelagians, as has been said at the same Theses 5 and 6.*

ANNOTATIONS OF DR. JAKOB ANDREAE: (X) AND THIS IS NO LESS HORRIBLE TO HEAR AS WELL, AND ABOMINABLE, THAT DR. BEZA DARES TO DENY THAT *UNBELIEF* IS THE CAUSE OF GOD'S DECREE CONCERNING THE DESTRUCTION OF MANKIND. INDEED, CHRIST OPENLY SAYS, *THE ONE WHO DOES NOT BELIEVE IS ALREADY JUDGED* (JOHN 3[:18]). AND AGAIN, THE HOLY SPIRIT WILL CONVICT THE WORLD IN REGARD TO SIN, *BECAUSE THEY DO NOT BELIEVE* IN ME (JOHN 16[:9]). AND AGAIN, HE WHO HAS NOT BELIEVED WILL BE CONDEMNED (MARK 16[:16]). ON THIS ACCOUNT WE IN NO WAY ATTACK PAUL, WHO NEVER SAYS THAT HE *HAS RESERVED* CERTAIN PEOPLE FOR ETERNAL DAMNATION, AS BEZA

TEACHES. <518> (Y) FAITH IN CHRIST DOES NOT BELONG TO NATURE OR TO OUR HUMAN STRENGTH, BUT IS THE WORK OF THE HOLY SPIRIT. SINCE THEREFORE FAITH IS THE CAUSE OF ELECTION, BY NO MEANS DOES THIS DOGMA SMACK OF THE PELAGIANS, WHO ATTRIBUTED TO NATURE'S STRENGTH WHAT THE HOLY SPIRIT ALONE IS ABLE TO SHOW FORTH.

4.

You yourselves cited what the Apostle said, that God consigned all things under unbelief, Romans 11[:32], although this should necessarily be applied to Adam's fall (z), as to the first ancestor. And it were profane to think (a) that God's most excellent work had fallen into such great misery, with God being either unwilling or indifferent, or that it happened accidentally. We very justly confirm that this fall belongs to the damned, nor besides this do we transfer the blame of Adam's fall to God, (b)<519> which remains entirely a product of his own will. He was not in the least compelled, nor even subject to concupiscence, inasmuch as this had not yet entered the world.

ANNOTATIONS OF DR. JAKOB ANDREAE: (Z) THE APOSTLE NEVER SAYS THAT ADAM FELL INTO THOSE CALAMITIES BECAUSE GOD *JUSTLY ORDAINED AND DECREED IT SO*. IN FACT THE SENSE OF PAUL'S WORDS IS THAT ALL PEOPLE ARE SINNERS, AND GOD WISHES TO HAVE MERCY ON ALL OF THEM, IF THEY RECEIVE CHRIST THROUGH TRUE FAITH. BUT HE DOES NOT SAY THAT GOD HAS ORDAINED THAT ALL MEN SHOULD SIN AND PERISH. (A) THE NOTION THAT MAN SINNED DUE TO GOD BEING UNWILLING OR INDIFFERENT, OR BECAUSE OF HIS LAZINESS, IS A HUMAN ONE. BUT WE SHOULD *NOT* JUDGE OR SPEAK OR THINK ABOUT GOD AND HIS WILL *EXCEPT BY GOD'S WORD*, AND MUST REFRAIN FROM INVESTIGATING HIS MAJESTY. (B) A LITTLE BIT AGO IT WAS SAID, IF THE OPINION OF DR. BEZA AND HIS BROTHERS CONCERNING GOD'S ABSOLUTE DECREE WERE TRUE, BY WHICH GOD HAS ORDAINED AND DECREED THAT MAN SHOULD SIN, WHO WOULD TRANSFER THE BLAME TO GOD UNJUSTLY? THIS IS LEFT TO THE JUDGMENT OF THE READER. INDEED, WE HAVE MORE PLAINLY SET IT FORTH IN OUR FIFTH THESIS USING THEIR OWN WORDS, WHERE THEY SAY: THE PRINCIPAL [προκαταρκτική] REASON *WHY HE DESTINES THESE*, RATHER THAN THOSE TO SALVATION OR DAMNATION, IS *NOTHING OTHER THAN HIS OWN WILL*. THEREFORE HOW IS BLAME TRANSFERRED TO THEM, AGAINST WHOM AN ETERNAL AND UNCHANGEABLE DECREE WAS MADE CONCERNING THEIR DAMNATION <519> BY GOD'S *STARK AND PRIVATE* WILL, WITH NO OTHER PRINCIPAL [προκαταρκτική], PRECEDING CAUSE?

6. AND 7.

The response above refutes this Thesis, also written incorrectly. For either Adam's fall proceeded from some source other than his own spontaneous will, or the stubbornness of his posterity, which flows forth from their own corruption, although neither one came to pass apart from the decree. (c) Hence that very cleverly spoken proverb of Prudentius[51]: No one is guilty, if the fates are in charge of life and what happens; rather the guilty one is the one who willingly dares what he is not permitted to do.

ANNOTATIONS OF DR. JAKOB ANDREAE: (C) SINCE BY GOD'S DECREE THUS ORDAINING IT, THE FIRST PEOPLE HAD TO FALL, AS THEIR WORDS WERE REITERATED BY US IN THE EIGHTH AND TENTH THESIS, HOW CAN IT TRULY BE SAID TO HAVE FLOWED FROM NO OTHER PLACE, THAN FROM THE WILL OF THE PERSON HIMSELF? DR. BEZA AND HIS ALLIES BLATANTLY AND OPENLY CONTRADICT THEMSELVES IN THIS PART.

8.

Since by the order of causes, God knows nothing will be before what he decreed will be, except (which would be most absurd) <520> *we should imagine something existing or happening apart from God's decree, it follows that the decree precedes knowledge, (d) and knowledge is not the proper cause of things.*

ANNOTATIONS OF DR. JAKOB ANDREAE: (D) IT IS ONE THING TO KNOW BEFOREHAND THAT SOMETHING WILL HAVE A CERTAIN KIND OF OUTCOME; IT IS ANOTHER TO ORDAIN BY DECREE. FOR THE FORMER BELONGS TO UNDERSTANDING, AND THE LATER TO THE WILL. IF THE WILL OF GOD IS COEXTENSIVE IN THE SIN OF ADAM, IT CANNOT BE EXCLUDED FROM THE CAUSE. FOR THE ONE WHO WISHES SOMETHING THAT HAPPENS WHILE HE IS ORDAINING IT AND DECIDING IT IS ALSO RIGHTLY CALLED ITS CAUSE.

9.

We have spoken about this at dogma 6 and 7. (e)

---

51   Contra Symmachum 2.471–72.

ANNOTATIONS OF DR. JAKOB ANDREAE: (E) THIS CONFIRMS EVEN MORE NOW THE REPEATED IMPIETY. FOR IF ADAM WERE NOT ABLE TO FALL, UNLESS GOD HAD SO DECREED AND ORDAINED IT, SUCH THAT HE WAS UNDER THE OBLIGATION TO FALL, THEN HOW IS IT THAT THE WILL OF GOD HAS NOT BEEN OPENLY ESTABLISHED BY YOU AS THE CAUSE OF HIS FALL?

10.

That necessity is from the hypothesis, (f) not the nature of Adam himself, just as today the human race has been given up to sin. And so it is said in GOD's word: it was necessary (g) for Christ, the second Adam, to be crucified.

ANNOTATIONS OF DR. JAKOB ANDREAE: (F) THIS HYPOTHESIS, WHICH BEZA CONSTRUCTS WITH HIS COLLEAGUES, IS NOT ONLY FALSE BUT ALSO IMPIOUS, AND IS A BLASPHEMY AGAINST GOD. NAMELY, LIKE GOD HAD MADE AN ABSOLUTE DECREE, OF THE KIND THAT IS CONSTRUCTED BY THE ADVERSARIES, JUST AS IF THEY HAD SAT PRIVY TO THE HIDDEN MIND OF GOD. (G) THIS HYPOTHESIS IS TRUE, THAT *THE LORD* MADE HIS DECREE ABOUT REDEEMING THE HUMAN RACE THROUGH THE BLOOD OF HIS SON. BECAUSE WITHOUT HIS DEATH THIS COULD NOT HAPPEN. BUT IT IS NOT ABSOLUTE NECESSITY, AS IF GOD COULD NOT ORDAIN ALL THINGS IN ANOTHER WAY.

11.

In what sense (h) the thing you condemn here is rightly said in an orthodox way, <521> we have explained at Theses 5 and 6.

ANNOTATIONS OF DR. JAKOB ANDREAE: (H) NO PIOUS SENSE EXISTS IN THESE WORDS, SINCE THE ADVERSARIES SAY AND ASSERT THAT GOD *DOES NOT WISH* THOSE DESTINED FOR REJECTION *TO BE SAVED, OR THAT THE DEATH* OF HIS SON *BENEFITS THEM.* ALL TRULY PIOUS PEOPLE, AND THOSE BARELY EDUCATED IN THE MERE RUDIMENTS OF FAITH AND CHRISTIAN RELIGION CAN EASILY UNDERSTAND AND JUDGE THIS. <521> THIS ENTIRE DOCTRINE OF OUR OPPONENTS NEEDS ACCORDINGLY TO BE AVOIDED, SINCE IT OVERTHROWS THE WHOLE MINISTRY OF THE GOSPEL, CERTAINTY ABOUT THE DIVINE PROMISES CONCERNING CHRIST, BAPTISM, THE LORD'S SUPPER, ABSOLUTION, AND REMOVES ALL CONSOLATION FROM PIOUS AND TROUBLED CONSCIENCES, JUST AS THE CONFERENCE WHICH FOLLOWS TEACHES CLEARLY.

Signed:

Signed:
Theodore Beza, Minister of the Church at Geneva.
Abraham Musculus, Minister of the Church at Bern.
Pierre Hübner, Professor of Greek in the public
    Gymnasium of Bern.
Antoine de La Faye, Minister of the Church of Geneva.
Dr. Claude Albery, Professor of Philosophy at the
    Academy of Lausanne.
At Montbéliard, 29 March, 1586.

Therefore when the Theses of the Württemberg Theologians had been recited, Dr. Jakob proceeded at the bidding of the Honorable Count Frederick.

6E.1 DISCUSSION ON PREDESTINATION

Dr. Jakob:
Reverend Dr. Beza, if your Honor has anything that he wishes to oppose to our Theses regarding Predestination which we have read out and signed, we will also happily hear it, and respond peacefully, just as has happened thus far for our part.

\<522\>

STATUS OF THE CHIEF CONTROVERSY ABOUT PREDESTINATION.

For even if the Theses are many in number, they can nevertheless be collected into a few chief points. I think even to this extent, that the greatest and most important part of the whole business and disputation turns on this one cardinal point: Whether God, in his eternal, secret, and hidden will, made an eternal, absolute, and unchangeable decree that he does not wish the greatest part of mankind to be saved, nor to believe in Christ, and to arrive at a knowledge of him, nor yet that the value of his blood is of any profit to them, but that he has destined them, ordained, and created them, for eternal damnation?

When this question has become untangled, an easy answer will follow for all the remaining points proposed in our Theses concerning this article.

Dr. Beza:
Reverend Doctor, we are here stepping into a deep abyss, and so we ought especially to pray to the LORD that he guide us with his holy Spirit, and direct us in this mystery to the path of truth.

DOCTRINE ABOUT PREDESTINATION UNKNOWN TO HUMAN REASON.

For there is no part of Christian doctrine from which human sense and reason does not recoil in large part. Because of this, I ask again that the LORD'S Spirit be present with us.

I. GOD CREATED MANKIND TOWARD A CERTAIN END.

But let us put forward these principal points: God, like a very wise artisan, whose wisdom in infinite had a certain end designed when he created the world, but especially in the creation of mankind.

If in fact an architect or paterfamilias is not so foolish as to build some house he has in mind before he considers the end to the house he would be build, so much the more should we consider that God, since his wisdom is infinite, had a certain end designed in the creation of mankind. Of this there is no doubt.
<523>

MAN ESTABLISHED FOR GOD'S GLORY.

But even if the ways of the LORD are inscrutable, nevertheless we deduce from these things that have come to pass what was end of the creation of people. God's eternal and unchangeable design, in fact, was also (as regards order) what preceded all causes, that he decreed in himself from eternity to establish all people for his own glory.

God's glory, though, is neither acknowledged nor celebrated unless his mercy and justice are declared. For this reason he made an eternal and unchangeable decree, by which he destined certain people, by pure grace unto eternal life, but certain others he destined by his just justice to eternal damnation, so that he might declare in the former his mercy, but in the latter his justice. Since God had this end designed in the creation of mankind, it was necessary that he also consider the course and way by which he could attain that end, that his mercy and justice might equally be manifest.

II. WHAT SORT OF PERSON HAD TO BE CREATED BY GOD.

Since mercy presupposes affliction, and there could not be a place for mercy or its declaration where there is no affliction, for this reason it was fitting for man to be created such that a place could be in him for God's mercy. Without the preceding affliction this could not happen.

Likewise, since judgment presupposes fault, without which it cannot be executed (for where there is no fault, there is also no place for judgment), for this reason also it was fitting for man to be created in such a way that God could reveal his justice in him, his nature preserved as appropriate to him. For he could not have declared his justice in man unless he had destined him to eternal damnation.

III. GOD'S DESIGN IN ELECTION AND REPROOF.

Therefore God designed and made his unchangeable decree from eternity, preceding all secondary causes, that in the interest of his infinite mercy he wishes to choose some people to be saved in Christ, but to reject some according to his justice, condemned by their own fault.

<524>

IV. WHY MAN WAS CREATED GOOD FROM THE BEGINNING.

In order that he might attain to this end, since he is good by nature, nay rather, is goodness itself, God neither was able nor willing to create man evil. If man had remained in this state, no place would have existed for declaring either mercy or justice in him. Therefore a way had to be found, by which man would be prepared and disposed to either one.

V. WHY MAN WAS CREATED BY GOD CHANGEABLE.

For this reason he created man in an upright state, good, just, holy, but nevertheless changeable, so that left in the hand of his own counsel, he could fall and slip into misery, in which there might be room continuously for both mercy and justice.

VI. WHY MAN WAS NOT CREATED UNCHANGEABLE.

For if he had created people unchangeable, so that they could not slip and sin, God would not have opened up for himself a path for mercy or justice. Since misery had not entered the world, without which God's mercy could not be declared. So also, if sin had not entered the world, God's justice would not have become manifest. For this reason it was fitting for man to be created good, lest God be considered the author of evil, but not unchangeable; rather changeable, such that he could sin (though through no fault of God), so that God could attain to the execution of his hidden and revealed will.

VII. WHY IT WAS FITTING TO BE CREATED MALE AND FEMALE.

It was also fitting to create male and female, from which the human race might continually be propagated, in which the LORD decreed and decided to declare his justice and mercy.

What I have said so far are not human thoughts originating with me, but are the testimonies of holy Scripture, not only about the elect, whom God chose before the foundation of the world, but also about the rejected and reprobate, whom God created for a bad day, that he might declare in them his power and justice (Ephesians 1[:21]; Proverbs 16[:4]; Exodus 9[:16]; Romans 10[:18]).

<525>

601

VIII. The first people sinned without the fault of God.

Therefore after the first people, Adam and Eve, had been created in this way, in an upright state, good, righteous, and both holy and changeable, they sinned in such a way that God was not involved in their fault.

IX. It was fitting that Eve be deceived by the serpent.

It was fitting therefore that Eve be deceived by the old serpent, Satan, such that she transgress the law given by God regarding the fruit of the tree of the knowledge of good and evil, together with her husband.

X. Eve was compelled to sin neither by God nor by Satan.

She was driven to this transgression neither by God nor by Satan, but by her own free will which was good, righteous, holy, complete, and not in the least corrupted, she acquiesced to the serpent's temptation.

Nor did this occur with God being unwilling or ignorant, or INDIFFERENTLY PRESCIENT, apart from whose will not even the sparrows are excepted, nor was it some simple, indifferent permission, which is separated from his will and decree. For since he ordained an end, it is also necessary that he established causes that carry towards that end, unless we contend that the end came about rashly or from causes decided by some other God, as is the opinion of the Manicheans.

XI. Man necessarily sinned by God's providence. Man sinned by free will.

For this reason Man, standing in a state of wholeness, did not fall thoughtlessly. And if not thoughtlessly, then certainly according to God's providence. Since IT WAS FITTING that what God decreed would happen, who planned the way and cause in man's fall such that his glory might be manifested in the declaration of his mercy and his justice, but nevertheless in such a way that God is not involved in the fault. Since man was not compelled to sin, but sinned of his own free will, though he could have and should have resisted the temptation of the serpent that tempted the mind of Eve, against the precept of God. But in order that God might pursue the end of man's creation, IT WAS FITTING that Eve and Adam <526> be deceived by Satan, so that a place could exist for mercy in pardoning transgression.

XII. No room for mercy, unless it should first give satisfaction to God's justice.

But since God could not declare his mercy to sinners unless his justice were first satisfied, which is so great that no creature, created by God however righteous and holy, could endure it, he also discovered a way in his eternal and secret counsel which both would satisfy this justice for the sins of the elect in the sight of God as well as allow a place for mercy for men.

XIII. God's eternal decree concerning the incarnation of God's Son.

As a result the holy Trinity decreed, in the same secret and eternal counsel, that the only-begotten Son of God the Father in the unity of his person, should assume a human nature, in which he might carry out the penalty of sin owed according to God's justice, and make satisfaction by his passion and death for the sins of the elect.

XIV. Christ was able not to die. Augustine City of God.

Now since he was conceived by the holy Spirit and born of Mary without sin, righteous and holy, he was man in such a way that he was able not to die, and just as Augustine says, Christ's bones were very breakable, nevertheless they could not be broken, since God so ordained it that they would not be broken. So also, he died, not at the hour his enemies wanted, but rather at the hour he himself wanted. Just as it is written, They were seeking to arrest him, and no one raised his hand against him, since his hour had not yet come.

XV. Christ's voluntary death.

Nor in fact was Christ's death forced, but rather voluntary, and undertaken not with respect to Christ's debts, but rather on behalf *of the elect, for whose debts the Son of God wished by this death to make satisfaction.*

XVI. COMPARISON OF CHRIST WITH ADAM.

The condition of Adam and Eve was not like this. For Christ could not sin, since he was not only man but also true God, one person. Therefore he was able not to die, though nevertheless by God's decree he died. Just as Peter shows in Acts 2[:24]. But Adam was able not to sin, just as Bernard says: nevertheless he did sin by God's providence. I therefore conclude that God opened a way for himself to have mercy; indeed I say contingently <527> that mankind first fell not out of pressing necessity or compelling need, but freely by reason of his own will, though NECESSARILY WITH RESPECT TO GOD. For God enclosed all thing under sin by his eternal decree, in order that he might have mercy on all, as the Apostle says. Therefore it was fitting that man also sin, not with God's bare and indifferent permission, separate from his will and decree, though nevertheless without the fault of GOD, but rather by his own will, because of which he submitted to the serpent more than God.

XVII. NOTHING SHOULD PROCEED FROM ONE EXTREME TO THE OTHER WITHOUT MIDDLE CAUSES.

But we should take special caution not to rise up from below or descend down from on high, not to run from one extreme to the other while passing over the middles of things, like from God's design to salvation, or much more from salvation to God's design, and again from design to damnation or the converse, passing over the related causes of God's judgment. These causes GOD ORDAINED STEP BY STEP SO THAT BY THEM IT COULD HAPPEN that the entire fault of peoples' destruction would be in them. He curses them justly as reprobate, in so far as they are corrupt. Against the majority of them HE EXERCISES HIS RIGHTEOUS ANGER AS SOON AS THEY HAVE BEEN BORN.

XVIII. GOD ORDAINED THE CAUSES OF DAMNATION OF MAN BY DEGREES. GOD'S WRATH AGAINST INFANTS DESTINED FOR DAMNATION. A HORRIBLE STATEMENT.

For if we were to pass over the secondary and mediating causes, we would easily fall into absurdities. If we were to explain, for example, when Paul says that God shut all things under sin in order that he might have mercy on all, in the following way: Adam fell in order that all men could be redeemed from this misery, how absurd a position would this be, and not in the least consistent with the truth? It would in fact follow that God had changed his decree, will, and design, by which he decided to declare his justice from eternity on certain people, abandoned in their misery. Rather, Scripture openly attests that God has created and prepared vessels of wrath for eternal destruction. Man did not fall therefore so that all men could be restored. Reality shows that not <528> people are saved, but rather the grand majority of people are damned. Therefore it is necessary that the first people who fell did so by God so ordaining it that some may be damned.

XIX. MEDIATING CAUSES OF THE EXECUTION OF GOD'S DECREE RIGHTLY CONSIDERED.

Therefore lest we encroach on this mystery, secondary and mediating causes must rightly be considered as well, which intercede between God's hidden decree and its ultimate outcome, the salvation and condemnation of men.

XX. HOW GOD DECIDED THAT PEOPLE ARE SAVED AND DAMNED. XXI. REVEALING ELECTION. XXII. UNMERITED ELECTION OF GOD.

For since God neither saves all people nor damns all people, the holy Spirit shows the causes, for what reasons and in what ways, he saves and damns. Now we arrive at the topic that needs to be considered: the order of causes in Adam's fall, whom God made saved. For it is not probable that he was damned. For as soon as Adam and Eve sinned, the free and unmerited love of God reveals itself to them as corrupt in themselves, but in Christ, as people destined for election and salvation. For immediately a remedy was laid out for them against sins, death, and damnation, in the promise of Christ the savior to come (Genesis 3[:15]). The seed of the woman will strike the head of the serpent. THE LORD reveals election in this word.

For in Christ election was made according to the Apostle's word: In him we have been chosen, before the foundations of the world were set. And this election is by his free unmerited favor, of which God deemed some men worthy, whom he destined for eternal salvation from eternity.

XXIII. ELECTION PARTICULAR NOT UNIVERSAL.

Now one who chooses does not take all things, but leaves certain things behind. For choose is taking one then and leaving the other. Therefore THE LORD chooses, by his own most free will, those with whom he pleased and whom he wishes to make saved.

XXIV. GOD NOT UNJUST IN DAMNING PEOPLE.

But the fact that he does not choose all people, but rather abandons many in their misery, ordained and destined by the eternal decree of God to eternal damnation, does not allow on this account for God to be accused of any injustice or cruelty. Since he owes no one anything, <529> since in Adam all have sinned, and have been equally worthy of being left in their misery (Romans 9:5 [5:12]). For he could have abandoned all people and received no one.

XXV. CALL OF THE ELECT EFFICACIOUS.

Let us now proceed to the execution of the accomplished election. For just as he chose in Christ those whom he has deemed worthy of his fatherly love according to his eternal design, so also he devised a reason by which he might execute this decree by a certain order of secondary and mediating causes. For those whom he chose (says Paul), these he also called (Romans 8[:30]), and this calling is efficacious, by which he not only calls for true repentance and knowledge of Christ through the Church's ministry by the external preaching of the Gospel, but at the same time also draws their hearts through the Holy Spirit, according to Christ's word: No one comes to me except the Father draw him (John 6[:44]).

XXVI. EFFECTS OF EFFICACIOUS CALLING IN THE ELECT.

The effect of this efficacious calling is the softening of the heart, that is, conversion to God from pure grace. Faith follows this, that is, true trust in Christ, by which the elect take hold of Christ, and apply him to themselves with all his blessings for the remission of sins and eternal life.

XXVII. JUSTIFICATION BY FAITH OF GOD'S ELECT. XXVIII. SANCTIFICATION BEGUN. XXIX. GOOD WORKS OF THE ELECT.

But by faith justification before God is accomplished, which consists of imputation of alien righteousness, that is, in the merit of Christ, and the commencement of sanctification is accomplished as well, by which the elect, endowed with the Holy Spirit, are renewed in the spirit of their mind, and made new men. He also accomplishes good works through them, which are pleasing to God and accepted on account of Christ.

XXX. EXECUTION OF GOD'S DECREE IN PEOPLE CREATED FOR ETERNAL DAMNATION. XXXI. OBSTINACY OF THE DAMNED NECESSARY.

But just as he acts through secondary and mediating causes with the elect for salvation, so also he acts through ordained causes with the reprobate.

For since God's hatred against those corrupted in themselves is righteous, induced by causes that he alone knows, he decided to create them for this end, that he might demonstrate in them his wrath and justice, <530> whom he never loved and therefore does not call in any way or even if he should, nevertheless the call is utterly ineffectual, since the preached word strikes their ears, but does not touch the heart, nor does it inspire conversion. Though their obstinacy is NECESSARY, nevertheless it is also voluntary in those who have not been granted to embrace and believe the spirit of truth.

XXXII. WHAT SORT OF INTELLIGENCE AND FAITH IS AROUSED BY GOD IN THE DAMNED.

And even though there are others besides whose understanding is aroused to those things that ought to be received and believed, which they hear through the preached word, nevertheless this happens because of the generic faith, with which the demons are endowed, and tremble. For the fact that the calling is not universal that all people be saved is obvious from this: there are many people who have never hear the word of God, and to whom it has never been preached.

XXXIII. THE REASON WHY GOD EITHER DOES NOT SIMPLY CALL THOSE TO BE DAMNED, OR DOES NOT DO SO EFFICACIOUSLY. XXXIV. WHENCE OBSTINACY AND PERSEVERANCE OF UNBELIEF.

But the reason that he does not call outright, or the calling is ineffectual, is that God owes no one anything, such that he owes a call to any people or person, but rather it is grace if he should call anyone. But if he should not call, or if he should call them in a way that is not efficacious, that is, he should not draw them through the holy Spirit, this should be attributed to men's wickedness. And human nature, that is, the flesh, is composed in such a way that it is not only not in submission to God, but rather also perpetually fights against him. This is the source of their stubbornness and the obstinacy of their unbelief, though they flatter themselves in such a way that they claim they can see: they neither wish to be called, nor are able to respond.

XXXV. IGNORANCE AND SCORN OF THE GOSPEL.

This stubbornness and obstinacy of unbelief, though, is not from God, but rather from the innate corruption of mankind received from our parents. From it ignorance and contempt for the Gospel also follows. For they are not just unaware of the Gospel, but also horribly despise it, hate it, and persecute it. And they finally rush into unrighteousness, defilement, and crimes of every kind.

<531>

XXXVI. CAUSE AND REASON FOR DIVERSITY OF GOD'S JUDGMENT ON THE ELECT AND THE REPROBATE. ANALOGY OF THE SUN.

But when discussing God's decision regarding both the elect and the reprobate, Holy Scripture bears witness to differences. For glorification belongs to the justified in Christ, and righteous damnation to sinners. Nevertheless the cause of these is not the same, were you to consider the execution of election and the design of God. For the cause of salvation of the elect is in God, but the cause of the destruction of the damned is in the wickedness of man, which is from the devil, not from God, as it is written: *Your destruction is from you, Israel, but your salvation is in me* (Hosea 13[:9]). I would like to clarify this with an analogy. The Sun makes the day, and also the night: the day in itself and by its own light, when it rises and shines, and it also causes the night, but by way of the earth's opacity, since there would be no shade if there were no sun, nor would the night be caused by this shadow. Thus God in his grace and favor on account of Christ, apart from any respect of our works or merits, saves the elect who believe in Christ, but damns the reprobate on account of their wickedness and corruption which they work, and he leaves them in their misery by his righteous judgment.

XXXVII. Cause of the destruction of the damned.

When therefore the glorification of the elect and the damnation of the rejected are placed side by side, this difference must be carefully considered in the execution of God's decree, lest the cause of this damnation be attributed to God, which should be ascribed to the wickedness of man alone. For it is not the decree of God, but rather the wickedness of man and his corruption that is the cause eternal destruction of people who are damned.

XXXVIII. Righteousness of God in saving and damning people.

Therefore the righteousness of God is perceived both in the saved as well as the damned. For whoever have been elected in Christ, are also saved. For Christ's obedience is rewarded with the crown of eternal life, won by Christ's passion and death, and imputed to his members freely. But sinners are punished with the righteous penalty of eternal death, left by God's righteous judgment in their misery.

<532>

XXXIX. GLORY OF GOD SUPREMELY MERCIFUL AND SEVERE IN THE SAVED AND THE DAMNED.

Here the glory of the God who is supremely merciful and supremely severe by his eternal decree becomes obvious and is declared to the whole world. He declares worthy of his grace and mercy those whom he elected to eternal life by his secret decree, and by the same secret but not in the least unjust decision he passed over, and subjected to eternal punishments on account of their malice, those whom he never deemed worthy of his love in his eternal decree, for hidden reasons KNOWN ONLY TO HIM. I wanted to relate this a little more at length so that everyone may understand that we establish the cause of damnation not in God, as certain people think falsely about us, but rather only in the wickedness of people. For the cause of execution of Divine justice as far as the reprobate are concerned is not in God, but rather, as we just said, in people, whom he justly passes over in their impiety, and does not save, which should seem astonishing to no one. And it is not injustice in God, who did not wish the impious to enter the path of salvation, whom he created for damnation. And the things that are done unjustly by them are not sins reckoned to God's account as the one who ordained them to happen, but rather are reckoned to the account of the people who do them. For there is a difference between the two willings, between the willing of God and the willing of man. There was no greater sin then the crucifying of the Son of God. Nevertheless this happened by God's decree, ordaining, and his will. For what if he had passed over all people and had saved no one? Who could find fault with him on this account? Surely the creation does not say to the creator, why do you make me thus? Who are you, says Paul, to respond to God? Does the potter not have the power to make from the same Lump one vessel for honor, and another for shame (Romans 9[:21])?

On this account we should not be amazed that God has abandoned some to their own misery in his hidden and secret will whom he created by his eternal but just decree for eternal damnation, and never loved them. We ought rather to be amazed and give thanks to God <533> *that he is willing to save anyone, rather than censure him for so many people being condemned.*

XL. In what way the gentiles sinned with God willing it.

No reason can be given for the fact that he left the Gentiles to walk in their perverted ways during the era of the Mosaic State than the hidden, secret, and just decree that wants to declare his anger, power, and justice upon them.

XLI. In what way it should be investigated, whether someone is also included in the number of the elect.

But someone says, how will I be able to know that I have been included in the number of those elected to eternal life and the worship of God? I answer: If you wish, whoever you are, to be more certain of your Predestination and accordingly your eternal salvation as well, which you are hoping for against all the insults of Satan, then do not do so from doubts at all or from conjectures sought from human cleverness. Indeed, these are no less certain and confirmed than if you had ascended all the way into heaven itself, and had heard the hidden decree from the very mouth of God: Take special care not to begin from the highest step; otherwise you will not be able to bear the immense light of God. Therefore make a beginning from the lowest steps, search in the word, which calls you to Christ. And when you hear the voice of God resounding in your ears and your mind, which calls you to Christ the only Mediator, CONSIDER AWHILE and carefully EXAMINE, whether you are in Christ, justified and sanctified by faith. These in fact are the marks by which faith is discerned, which is the cause of them. But you will recognize this partly by the spirit of adoption exclaiming within, ABBA, Father, and partly by the force and efficacy of the same spirit within you, if of course YOU SHOULD FEEL IT, and actually show also that the sin that still especially lives in you nevertheless does not rule over you, with the result that you have not willingly given up the reins to shameful and wicked lusts. If from time to time we knowingly and consciously sin, and afterwards hate the sin, not in fear of punishment but rather because we have offended so merciful a father, then we should boldly approach <534> and call upon him. If from these marks we can conclude faith, what is left is that we have been called and drawn to him efficaciously. And from this calling it is again understood that we are of course predestined, since in the eternal counsel of God which he proposed in himself, we were adopted as sons of God. It follows from this, finally, with the very consistent will of God, which relies on itself alone, that we are predestined, such that no one can snatch us from the hand of Christ (John 10[:28]), and therefore it would be unspeakable to doubt that we will persevere all the way to the end.

This doctrine of Predestination does not make God the author of sin or the cause of sin or of the damnation of the reprobate, nor is it full of stumbling blocks, as certain people think, nor does it give birth to perverse thoughts or provide an opportunity either for the contempt of God or for despair.

XLII. IN WHAT WAY AND FOR WHOM THE DOCTRINE OF PREDESTINATION OUGHT TO BE SET FORTH. PAUL'S METHOD OBSERVED IN THE EPISTLE TO THE ROMANS.

Nor is this Milk for children and infants in the Christian religion, but rather solid food. And this doctrine should never be laid out in such a way that it is applied to just any single person. In visiting the sick, they should encourage the consciences of the afflicted by the witness of election, but they should strike the obstinately wicked and insolent with the horrendous judgment in such a way that they nevertheless abstain from the extreme position, since this judgment belongs to God alone. On this account this doctrine is not to be indiscriminately laid out for anyone at all, or carelessly, but it should be prudently considered and seen whether those with whom you are involved in the business are capable of bearing this doctrine and fit for it and rightly disposed, that is, educated beforehand rightly regarding sin, the law, and justification of faith. Paul observed this method in the Epistle to the Romans, and showed the way it should be taught. He teaches in the earlier eight chapters that all men are sinners before God, and were condemned by the just righteousness of God, but God sent his Son, in order that by his suffering and dying he might make satisfaction before God the Father and his righteousness. He ordered it to be proclaimed in <535> all the world and promised that whoever believed would righteous before God and be *saved. After he taught these things, he rose up in the ninth chapter to the explanation of the hidden decree of God made in Christ, and revealed through the preaching of the Word and the Gospel regarding people to be saved and damned, a subject he pursues all the way to the twelfth chapter. In those that follow he treats Ethics.*

BEZA WAS PATIENTLY AND SUFFICIENTLY HEARD BY DR. JAKOB.

But when Dr. Beza had gone on continuously on this topic for nearly an hour and a half, the Honorable Prince, Count Frederick, advised Dr. Jakob not once, but frequently, and more than seven times, to interrupt Dr. Beza's speech, since Beza was being so verbose. But Dr. Jakob refused, and asked his Highness several times to listen to Beza patiently, lest he be able to complain that he had not been listened to enough or sufficiently on so serious a matter and so elevated a topic as Predestination, concerning which he had previously very much refused a conversation and had very much entreated Dr. Jakob's brevity of speech in the conference. For if Beza were dragging out his speech all the way till evening (said Dr. Jakob to the Honorable Count Frederick), he would not mind in the least, since he was prepared to hear him out patiently, and need not fear a waste of time. He would in fact bring the whole business to a conclusion with one or another brief answer, in order that his Highness and all the rest of the audience may understand that this doctrine of Beza and his brothers is in no way in harmony with Holy Scripture, and cannot in the least stand.

<536>

But even though his Highness allowed himself, with difficulty, to be persuaded to listen longer to Beza, nevertheless he swallowed down his annoyance only until, sick of the prolixity of his speech, he interrupted with this exclamation: Dr. Beza, conclusion, conclusion!

Dr. Beza:
Honorable Prince, I have now concluded.

Dr. Jakob:
Reverend Dr. Beza, You yourself will swear with the whole audience that I patiently listened to you speaking, lecturing on this

topic verbosely throughout about an hour and a half. But if you have anything else that you think needs to be added to the things that you have mentioned verbosely now regarding the business of Predestination, I ask that you lay it out, for I am prepared to hear you out sufficiently.

Dr. Beza:
I have nothing further that I would add to those things which have been said by me.

Dr. Jakob:

WHY DR. JAKOB WAS RATHER PROLIX FROM TIME TO TIME IN THIS CONFERENCE.

Since therefore before the conference scheduled about the article of predestination you made a request to Count Frederick through your people that I practice brevity in answering, I will also now happily do this. The reason I seemed to you to have been a little too prolix in the earlier articles was in fact solely that the doctrine of our Churches necessarily had to be a bit more copiously explained, particularly to the French exiles, as our teaching had been dreadfully disfigured in your sermons and writings, and was thus far unknown to them. Our writings on these controversies did not arrive to them. And though I trust that what I accomplished and my verbosity was not in the least disagreeable to the audience, now I will answer your prolix oration briefly, and the explication of the doctrine of Predestination.

<537>

First of all, in regard to the secret, hidden, and unchangeable decree of God, what the Lord has thought, and to what end especially he turned his attention in the creation of man, and how he arranged the mediating steps to achieve his ends, you spoke in such a way that you seemed to me to have been sitting in the secret counsel of God and not only to have heard everything in his presence, which the holy Trinity, the Father with the Son and the holy Spirit, deliberated about regarding the creation of man, but also as if you too had been their adviser.

Dr. Beza:

I am not God's adviser, nor did I explain this matter by follow-ing human ways of thinking, but rather I have explained what the holy Spirit has taught in Holy Scripture. It is not true therefore that you can object to me on the ground of words of this kind.

Dr. Jakob:

Reverend Dr. Beza, I listened very patiently to you for an hour and a half, but you can listen to me offering scarcely three words and answering your speech. I therefore ask you to hear me with patience equal to that with which I heard you. For as much as I can, I will strive for extreme brevity, lest my speech be annoying for any reason to either the Honorable Prince, Count Frederick, or the rest of the audience.

Dr. Beza:
I will listen.

Dr. Jakob:

BRIEF REITERATION OF DR. BEZA'S DOCTRINE AND CONFESSION REGARDING PREDESTINATION.

If I rightly discerned your mind and your position, you undertook to defend and contend on behalf of all the things that we rejected and condemned in our Theses. The summary of your speech was: God is like a very wise architect, who aimed especially at two ends in the creation of man and had set it forth that in the human race, he would declare his mercy <538> and righteousness equally, and reveal his glory as that of a God supremely merciful and supremely severe. On this account he has an eternal, secret, and unchangeable intention that had preceded all secondary and intermediate causes, by which he decreed from eternity to elect certain people, to his glory as that of a God supremely merciful and severe, to be saved in Christ, but to reject others, to be damned by their own fault.

In order that it may proceed to this end, he also prepared a way for himself, and arranged and ordained necessary mediating causes.

Therefore he created man in an upright state, good, just, holy, but changeable, such that he could sin and fall.

IN RESPONSE TO THESIS 1.

Then he fell and transgressed against God's command, while God did was not unwilling, nor ignorant, nor idly prescient, but on the contrary with God willing, since nothing at all has happened, happens, or will happen in the World without the will of God, from which not even the little sparrows are excepted (Matthew 10[:29–31]).

But it was necessary for man to sin and fall in order that in this an opportunity could exist for mercy and justice. For where there is not misery, there also is no mercy, by which man might be freed from the misery. And where there is no fault, there is no sin, and there justice can have no opportunity for inflicting a punishment. Therefore it was *unavoidable* that man fall with respect to the decree and will of God, but with respect to himself it was contingent and of his own will, without any compulsion from God.

Because of the fall, God's unmerited love worked and revealed itself toward them as corrupt in themselves, but in Christ freely as destined for election and salvation, love conceived in the eternal and unchangeable decree of God. Likewise also the righteous hatred of God was revealed towards the corrupted in themselves, fromthe propagation of sin through Adam.

For this reason in the execution of this eternal counsel, God has called them through the proclamation of the word, which is common to the elect and the reprobate. This call with respect to them whom God destined to eternal life by his hidden decree is efficacious, and by the pure grace of God are their hearts softened and converted to God. <539> And the Holy Spirit works faith in Christ in them through the preached word, by which they are justified and sanctified, and finally also glorified, when they are crowned with eternal life on account of obedience to Christ, through imputed faith. But the reprobate are, without respect to these causes, destined to damnation and eternal death by God's absolute design and decree, and either are not called at all, or are not called efficaciously, since God is not willing that they be converted or believe, nor that the merit of Christ's blood profit them at all, nor that they be saved.

Therefore those forsaken by the righteous judgment of God (who owes no one anything) by their own willful hardening not only ignore the Gospel, but indeed scorn it, and thereafter rush into every unrighteousness and defilement, until they are damned by God's righteous judgment and are punished with the penalty of eternal death.

I trust I have reiterated your position in good faith. But I will take up just one point for refutation, and once it has been refuted, your entire teaching on Predestination will crumble. It is this sentence of yours: that God has established an eternal, hidden, unchangeable, and absolute decree, that also precedes all causes in order, that he wished to create the greater part of the human race on earth for the purpose of eternal damnation, and he ordained them to damnation too, and destined them for it. Nor does he wish to call them efficaciously nor that they be converted or believe, nor does he wish the merit of Christ's blood to be of any profit to them or that they be saved, all because he established an immutable decree regarding them, because he wanted to declare his righteousness in them.

We openly and consistently reject this opinion and doctrine as false and as clearly in conflict with the word of God. And we say explicitly that God has never thought up such a decree. For regarding the will *of God*, we teach that this should be determined not by human reason or ways of thinking, but rather by the plain and not in the least obscure word of God. In it, the will of God towards the fallen human race has been expressed and revealed. When this is removed we have no basis at all to think about God's will in either saving or damning the human race. Your word is a lamp to my feet, says the Psalms.

<540>

That we may bring out into the light this will of God from his word and learn it for certain, I ask you just one thing, entreat you to answer me categorically and clearly, namely, whether God ever loved those who now are damned or will be damned in the future.

Dr. Beza:
No.

Dr. Jakob:

This is news to me, and something never heard before. So I coun-
ter with the express testimony of the holy Spirit, that is, the plain
words of Christ himself, John 3[:16]: God so loved *the world* that he
gave his only-begotten Son, in order that everyone who believes in
him may not perish but rather have eternal life. I ask again, what
does the term *the world* mean in these words of Christ?

Dr. Beza:
The elect.

Dr. Jakob:

THE WORLD MEANS THE ENTIRE HUMAN RACE. GOD DOES NOT WILL THE DEATH
AND THE ETERNAL DAMNATION OF THE IMPIOUS.

In these words of Christ, what is undoubtedly and certainly
understood by the term "*the world*," in the judgment and unanimous
consensus of all writers and interpreters of the holy Scripture, the
old ones and the new ones, is the universal human race. But Christ
himself is the best interpreter of his own words, and he confirms this
in the same passage in very plain words when he says, This is the
judgment: that light has come into the world, and the world loved
darkness more than the light (John 3[:]19). Here the term *the world*
cannot be interpreted about the elect only, but rather it is especially
about those who are rejected and damned. For they love the darkness more than the light. And they are damned who, even though
God so loved them that he gave his Son for them, nevertheless
themselves despise and scorn this gift and are judged and damned
on this account. John the Baptist confirms the same thing, who when
he pointed out Christ, <541> said, Behold the lamb of God, who takes
away the sins of the world (John 1[:29]). *Of the world*, he says, not of
the elect. Thus it is written in Romans 5[:10]: For if when we were
enemies we were reconciled to God through the death of his Son, how
much more will we, having been reconciled, be saved in his life. And

2 Corinthians 5: God was in Christ, reconciling the World to himself, not counting their transgressions against them. And he placed in us the word of reconciliation. We function therefore as embassy for Christ, as God exhorting through us. We beg on Christ's behalf: be reconciled to God.

In connection to this is also the passage of Ezekiel: Do I have any pleasure in *the death of the impious*, says the Lord God, and not that he be turned from his ways and live? (Ezekiel 18[:23]). Where the impious are mentioned explicitly, it is explicitly stated that the Lord does not desire their eternal death. It is simply not true that God wills the damnation of the impious, such that he bears witness through the same prophet that he will require the blood of the one who is damned from the hands of the one sent to give him warning. If I say to the impious man, O impious man, you shall surely die, but *you did not tell* the impious man to be on guard (he does not say the elect) from his way, *the impious man himself* will die in his sin, but his blood I will require from your hand. God loved the impious and damned so much that he would require the blood of the damned from the hand of the prophet. And again in the same passage, Why will you die O house of Israel? Since I do not want the *death of the dying*, says the Lord *God*, turn around and live. Here the noun death cannot be interpreted as natural or temporal death, but rather means eternal death, as the preceding words of the Prophet clearly teach, where he does not say, I do not want the death of the elect, but rather the death of the dying, that is, of the one running headlong in the direction of eternal damnation, and who is already dead, that is, is damned, whence he will never be freed any further forever (Luke 16[:19–31]).

In such a way Christ calls all sinners equally to himself, not in a pretend way, but in earnest: Come to me all who labor and are heavy laden and I will give you rest (Matthew 11[:28]). He does not say: Come to me, <542> only if you are someone whom God in his secret counsel decided to save; even though I am also calling the rest, nevertheless it is not the will of me or my Father that they come, listen to me, and believe in me. Far be it from us to think about our savior Christ so impiously!

Paul speaks in the same way: God wills all men to be saved and to come to a knowledge of the truth (2 Timothy 2[:4]). St. Peter not only confirms but also illuminates his words when he says, The Lord is not slow in keeping his promise as some think, but he works patiently on your behalf, not wanting *anyone to perish* but rather that *all* be turned around to repentance. Here he explains perspicuously what he means by the term *all*, when he adds, he does not want anyone to perish. Peter would never have put this in had God wanted *anyone* to perish, and had created and ordained them for eternal damnation by his hidden decree, and had he not wanted them to be turned around to repentance.

He enclosed all things, says Paul, under sin, in order that he might have mercy on all (Romans 11[:32]). He says *on all*; he does not say only *on some*. With this very clear testimonies of Scripture I trust that it has been shown clearer than the light at noon that in Christ's words at John 3, by the term *the world*, what is meant is the entire human race, which God loved, and even the damned, so much that he would demand their blood from the hand of the Prophet, who had not announced to them the judgment of the Lord, but was silent for fear of punishment or hope of some favorable moment lest he lose favor.

FALSE OPINION REGARDING CALLING THAT IS NOT EFFICACIOUS.

On this account what you say about calling that is not efficacious, when God calls the impious, whom he nevertheless does not wish to come and be converted, is your human interpretation, contrary to the word and glory of God. What mockery would it be, if the Honorable Prince, Count Frederick, at the height of the grain shortage, should call all his subjects to himself and promise them a supply of grain, but silently think to himself that he was not willing to give grain to all, and would dismiss most emptyhanded? Would they not all say, truly and rightly, that the Prince had deceived them? This would be unworthy of his <543> person. And it would be much more unworthy to attribute this very thing to Christ in his promises so sweet, by which he draws and calls *all* sinners to himself, such that we would imagine that he does not serious call all sinners to himself, but only those about whom he made a hidden decree that he wanted to save them. These are the things that you say and write, these are the things that are read in your books. With this interpretation all consolation is removed from troubled consciences. For even if Christ says, Come to me *all* you who labor, nevertheless if this interpretation of yours is right, that he only wants certain people to come, who will show you and me, or make you or me more certain, that he wants us to come too? Since you are therefore compelled to be in doubt whether he is calling you too, you will never come to him.

DR. BEZA'S DOCTRINE OF PREDESTINATION LEAVES TROUBLED CONSCIENCES IN PERPETUAL DOUBT.

You make particulars out of all the universal promises of the Gospel (which console us against temptations regarding the particularity of the elect and against the decree of our eternal damnation, with which Satan presses us), so that you always make the term *all* mean only *some*: Come to me all, that is, some of you; God wants all men to be saved, that is, some of them; He has enclosed all people under sin so that he may have mercy *on all*, that is, on some; and those things which are similar to these, partly recited in our Theses. Since this is the case, it is clear to all that this doctrine cannot be tolerated in the Church of God. Where in fact will the consolation which we possess in the universal promises remain firm, if all of them are turned into particulars, and the testimonies of holy Scripture so clear on the matter are perverted by this interpretation? For whatever has been written, says Paul, has been written for our learning, that through patience and consolation of the Scriptures we may have hope (Romans 15[:13]). But this doctrine does not supply consolation, nor does it give hope of eternal life to come, but rather it leaves the conscience and the heart of a person in perpetual doubt whether he be perhaps also in the number of those about whom God has made an eternal and unchangeable decree that the wishes them not to be saved but rather that they have been created, ordained, and destined for damnation <544> by this hidden decree *preceding all causes*. This is a greater and more present danger if according to your opinion many people were not born again all the way up to old age, nor felt any impulses of regeneration, to which they are directed to become more certain of their election. Therefore be it very far from me that I would ever propose this doctrine to my Hearers, whether they be children in need of milk or adult who can stand solid food. Be it far from me, I say, that I would think and teach thus.

Dr. Beza:

Your Reverend Excellency interprets WORLD in Christ's words, God so loved the world, to mean all people. I do not. And I prove this by Christ's words in John 17, when he says, I do not ask on behalf of the world. Therefore Christ does not ask on behalf of everyone, but only on behalf of the elect, whom the Father gave to him. Therefore what is meant by the noun world in John 3 is not all people, but rather only the elect whom God loved, but not the reprobate and damned, whom he never loved.

But when Scripture employs the universal adjectives "EVERY, ALL" ["OMNIS, OMNES"] from time to time, as in the verses of Scripture mention by you now several times in which these adjectives are contained, it is in respect to the gentiles, lest anyone think they pertain only to the Jews, since God prepared vessels of mercy not only out of the Jews, but also out of the gentiles. Augustine testifies in this way as he writes to Simplicianus, and it is manifest in the writings of the Prophets and Apostles. Therefore in passages of this sort when the term "WORLD" is employed, it means the Church, which consists only of the elect as its members, whom God loved in Christ; he has regarded all the rest <545> from eternity under his righteous hatred, and will forever.

Dr. Jakob:

WHEN THE WORLD MEANS ONLY THE REPROBATE.

As far as the John 17 passage is concerned, when Christ says, I do not ask on behalf of the world, I agree that the passage is not to be understood as speaking on behalf of all people but rather in regard to those who scorn Christ and his blessings. I agree because in this passage the elect and the world are opposed by means of clear words, when Christ say, I ask on behalf of them, *"the elect"*; I do not on behalf of the world (that is, those who scorn my word). But in John 3 the position is absolute: God so loved the world. Here the words that follow plainly teach that Christ means not the elect, but rather all people: that everyone who believes, etc. Here he shows the reason that though God loves all people such that he would give his Son for them, why Christ does not benefit them, and why all are not equally saved, since only those are saved who believe, that is, who embrace Christ in true faith. But those who do not believe are at the same time damned, according to Christ's word: he who has not believed will be damned (Matthew 16[:16]). And again, he who does not believe stands condemned already, since he has not believed in the name of the Son of God (John 3[:18]).

But John the Evangelist cannot in the least be censured as an interpreter of Christ's words, who wrote down the words of Christ: God so love the world, and since he knew their meaning best, he explained them in perspicuous and very clear words. His words read thus: If anyone sins, we have an advocate with the Father, Jesus Christ the righteous one. And he is the propitiation for our sins, and *not* only for our sins, but also for the sins of the whole world (1 John 2[:2]). Here the Apostle plainly desired to teach, not only by adding the universal adjective *whole* to the term *world*, but also by combining the elect, which he understands under the term *our*, with the damned, that Christ means all people by the word world (John 3[:16]).

<546>

Dr. Beza:

MANIFEST DISTORTION OF JOHN'S WORDS.

I say that John in this passage (1 John 2) is not combining the elect with the damned, but rather that he is distinguishing Jews and gentiles, such that by the word World, he means gentiles with Jews, but only the elect of either people. The result is that the meaning of John's words is: Christ is the propitiation, not only for the sins of the Jews, that is, the elect who are from the Jews, but also for the elect who are from all the nations, whom John comprehends under the word the whole World. Augustine attests the same to Simplicianus in the second question (Book 1, question 2): We are those whom he has called (he says), not only from the Jews but also from the gentiles. For he has called not all the Jews, he says, but rather from the Jews, and not utterly all people of the gentiles, but rather from the gentiles.

Dr. Jakob:

This is not a refutation of my argument or a confirmation of your interpretation. For John the Evangelist wrote this Epistle not only to Jews, but also to the gentiles, that is, all disciples of Christ who embrace the doctrine of the Gospel, all of whom he means at the same time with the word *our*, but he includes all people and excludes no one with the word *the whole world*. This is quite certain, and undeniable among all truly pious and genuine teachers. Hence the popular saying, Christ died sufficiently for the sins of all people, but not efficiently, because many people scorn this blessing and therefore it does not benefit them at all. Not that Christ does not wish it to benefit all people, but rather that the very great part of the human race, both from the Jews and from the gentiles, care nothing for it, loving the darkness and pleasures of the world more than the light and the truth of the Gospel.

Dr. Beza:

If the Lord wanted his passion and death to benefit all people, <547> one drop of blood would be enough for the sins of the whole world, even of the damned. But Christ did not die for the sins of the damned, otherwise the damned would be saved, whom God created, ordained, and destined for eternal damnation by his eternal but righteous decree for reasons known to him alone. But the Catholic Church is the world about which John speaks here, on behalf of which Christ suffered, was crucified, and died. Christ is her propitiation in his blood, which he poured out on her behalf, not for the impious and damned, for the remission of the sins of the members of the Church, not of the impious.

Dr. Jakob:

BEZA'S DOCTRINE HORRENDOUS, THAT CHRIST DID NOT DIE FOR THE SINS OF
THE WHOLE WORLD.

This is horrendous for the ears of the pious to hear. I could wish
that even one Ecclesiastical Writer, ancient or modern, could be
named who would interpret John the Evangelist's words in this way.
Even then it could be readily shown that all pious minds understand this to be manifestly false, and a patent perversion of John's
words. Indeed, all pious people shudder in revulsion when they hear
this utterance: *Christ* died and made satisfaction, *not* for the sins *of
the whole* World, that is for all people in the World. Who, pray, can
endure this utterance? I am simply reeling in shock, and all the hair
of my body stands up on end when I hear this now.[52] On this account
I say once again, when Dr. Beza teaches that Christ did not suffer for
the damned, nor made satisfaction for their sins, if he can show this
from any accepted Writers ancient or modern, and prove this interpretation of his, I am prepared not only to Recant and revoke my
position, but also suffer the harshest penalty.

<548>

ONLY UNBELIEF DAMNS PEOPLE.

For those who are to be assigned to eternal destruction are not
damned because they have sinned; otherwise all the elect would also
be damned, since all have sinned and fall short of the glory of God
(Romans 3[:23]). Rather they are damned because they are unwilling to embrace Jesus Christ in true faith, who suffered, was crucified,
and died for their sins *no less* than for the sins of Peter, Paul, and all
the saints. This is an eternal and unchangeable truth, against which
the gates of hell will not prevail. Just as Christ openly attests when
he says, This is the verdict: light has come into the world and the
world loved darkness more than the light (John 3[:19]). And again,
The holy Spirit will convict the World of *sin, since they do not believe
in me.* This sin, I say, if it takes possession of a person's mind, and is

---

52   The marginal note directed at this statement in particular: "Here Beza laughed with his brothers
sitting at another table."

not removed, damns, even if the righteousness of the entire World were his. But on the contrary, should anyone believe in Christ truly, the sins of the entire World are not able to press him down into hell. Therefore people die and are damned not because God has established an eternal and unchangeable decree about them, that he does not want to save them, as if he created and ordained them for damnation in order to declare his righteousness, but rather they are damned because they do not apply the benefit of Christ's death to themselves through faith, who died for them and made satisfaction for their sins.

Dr. Beza:

WHETHER UNBELIEF ALONE DAMNS, AND NOT ALSO OTHER SINS.

Well this is plainly novel in my opinion, and unheard of before. You say: People are not damned due to the fact that they have sinned, though sin is the only cause of eternal damnation, the reason why the wicked are left to their malice and damned. I agree at that point, that the death of Christ could suffice for the sins even of the damned, if God had wished that it be of benefit to them. But I still hear in no way that Christ died also for all the damned.

<549>

While Beza was saying these things that were so absurd, horrendous, and plainly impious regarding Christ's death, namely that Christ did not die for the sins of all people and for sinners, the Honorable Prince, Count Frederick, advised Dr. Jakob to bring the conversation to an end. For his Highness had become wearied at hearing such things further.

Dr. Jakob:

CONSOLATION OF THE PIOUS DEPOSITED IN THE SACRAMENTS.

The Honorable Prince, Count Frederick, declares that the conference established on this topic needs to come to an end, since the same things are being constantly repeated, and you keep on proposing such absurdities plainly contrary to the Christian faith and holy Scripture, namely that Christ did not die for all people, and for the sins of the whole World. He thinks therefore that we will argue further only in vain. This is in fact to deny the beginnings and to contradict the very clear testimonies of Scripture on which our faith relies in all temptations, to overthrow it totally, and to snatch away any consolation from pious minds in extreme temptations, which has been deposited in the universal promises of the Gospel and in the Sacraments. For you change all those universal promises into particulars, and in this entire disputation have made no mention of any word of the Sacraments, by which especially our election is sealed and confirmed, and a person ought to be encouraged and strengthened in faith by the same when beset by extreme temptations.

CONSOLATION FROM BAPTISM. CONSOLATION FROM THE LORD'S SUPPER.

For we are baptized, so that we do not doubt our election or salvation. For in Baptism the holy Trinity promises his grace to all individuals who are baptized, that he wishes to be gracious in their sinful circumstance and forgive all their sins freely for on account of Christ, who died not only for their sins, but also for those of the whole world, and made satisfaction for all of them. They take the Eucharist, too, and receive this very body of Christ <550> in the sacrament, which is given for their sins, and they drink this very blood, which was poured out not only for their sins, but also for the sins of the whole World, as a seal of the universal promise. And it is important also for this reason, that they may become more certain that God wants to be gracious to them also through Christ.

Dr. Beza:
We have in no way removed consolation from troubled consciences. We teach that the holy Spirit gives to the elect the spirit of adoption, who bestows his testimony to their spirit, that they are sons of God (Romans 8[:14]). These act by the spirit of Christ, whose impulses the pious feel in themselves. Because of these impulses they can conclude that they are children of God, and comprehended in the number of the elect.

Dr. Jakob:

But why do you not direct troubled consciences back to the universal promises? Again, to the Baptism they received, the reception of the Lord's Supper, so that they make up their mind about the certainty of their eternal salvation in light of these things?

Dr. Beza:

Because not all receive this word, and most people are only baptized outwardly by the Baptism of water, but not washed by the inner water of the Spirit. Again, many receive the bread and wine of the Supper without true faith, but they do not arrive at a participation of the spirit.

Dr. Jakob:

DR. BEZA'S DOCTRINE ABOLISHES THE USE OF THE WORD OF THE GOSPEL AND OF THE SACRAMENTS.

They therefore stay in perpetual doubt, and the promise of universal grace promised in Christ offers no benefit to them, neither Baptism nor the Supper. You apply all these things to the elect in such a way that they make up their mind about them, whether in Baptism the adoption has also been sealed on them. finally based on the impulses of the holy Spirit. For in as much as a person has been persuaded about the hidden decree made in the secret and eternal counsel of God, that God has created and ordained the greater part <551> of mankind to eternal damnation, on whose behalf Christ did not die nor made satisfaction for their sins, nor ever wished the merit of his blood to be of any benefit, he can receive no consolation in extreme temptations from all the promises of the Gospel and from the Sacraments. In fact this opinion always sticks in the minds of people who are tempted: The promises of the Gospel pertain only to those whom God has destined to eternal life in his secret plan and absolute decree, who alone are also sealed in the Sacraments, but those who are left, though they also are called, nevertheless their calling is not efficacious, and in the Sacraments receive only the shell, that is, in Baptism the external water, in the Lord's Supper the bread and wine, but are excluded from the nut inside, since they have been rejected in the secret counsel of God. You write that no other reason is known to us for this secret counsel than his will, since the Lord so willed and it pleased him to declare his righteousness in these things. As you write also: "In an amazing and incomprehensible manner, it pleased God, and he willed, that our first parents sin" (in Vol. 1, *Tract. Theolog.* p. 179). Who therefore will say to you, or whence will you know, whether you are included in the number of the elect or of the reprobate? For you talk about the testimony of the holy Spirit and his impulses, which if the tempted feel in themselves they ought not doubt their election; but everyone understands that consolations of this kind do not remove doubt about God's grace in the midst of extreme those temptations, but rather augment it. For you yourself also agree and write (In Vol. *Theolog. Tract.* p. 192) that understanding is granted to the reprobate and they are aroused by those things to accept and believe what they hear. But this faith is generic, which the Demons possess, and tremble. When therefore the pious are trembling in fear in the midst of extreme temptations, and with David feel in themselves impulses plainly contrary, such that they say, being out of their mind, I have been cast away from your eyes, where then must consolation be found? In a word, it cannot. Because the promises (in your opinion) are all Particular, which you say pertain only to the elect, <552> regarding whom God established a hidden, eternal decree, that he wished to save only them. You do not bid them seek consolation in Baptism either, since God's grace is not in all people who have been baptized, but rather is sealed only on those whom God wished to be saved according to his hidden decree. On this account it is impossible for the tempted to seek certain consolation from Baptism, and for a minister of the word to say to the person beset by those extreme temptations: Trust, brother, baptized in the name of Jesus Christ, you have also been received into God's covenant, in which God promised you eternal salvation, so you have nothing to doubt about his grace. It is impossible, I say, for a minister of the Church to console a troubled person in this way who doubts God's grace, according to your doctrine. Because you teach that Baptism is not a sure sign of adoption in all the baptized, and that not all are regenerated and renewed and adopted in Baptism, but rather that it is only a sign and representation and seal, and just

in those whom God elected, ordained, and destined to eternal life by
his absolute and hidden decree, preceding all second and mediating
causes. Conclusions about this need to be made not from the Baptism
received but rather from the impulses of the holy Spirit; if anyone
feels them in himself then he can conclude that he is also sealed for
adoption in Baptism. Since therefore this doctrine of yours about
Predestination snatches away any consolation from troubled consciences, and you offer nothing except for interpretations contrary
to the patent testimonies of holy Scripture, we publicly attest that we
are not in the least in agreement with you in these matters, just as
also in the rest of the controverted articles treated in this conference,
but rather openly reject and condemn it.

Dr. Beza:
*We have not brought forward interpretations, but rather plain
and manifest testimonies of holy Scripture, by which we have confirmed our doctrine. Our writings demonstrate this too.*

<553>

Dr. Jakob:
We leave it to the judgment of the Honorable Prince, Count
Frederick, and the entire audience, whether you have brought
forward an interpretation or testimonies of holy Scripture in this
conference on the controverted articles, in which you attempted to
attack the plain and manifest testimonies of holy Scripture brought
forward by us for the assertion and confirmation of our doctrine.

BRIEF RESTATEMENT OF DR. BEZA'S DOCTRINES AND INTERPRETATIONS ON
THE CONTROVERTED ARTICLES. I. DR. BEZA'S INTERPRETATIONS REGARDING
THE LORD'S SUPPER.

Since in the article on the Lord's Supper, when we were keeping
to the perspicuous and manifest words of Christ's Testament from
which no one should depart, This is my body, this is my blood, you
immediately proposed an interpretation: This means my body; It is a
sign and figure of my body, absent from the earth, and only subsisting in heaven; This means my blood.

When we were proposing Paul's words regarding the eating of the unfaithful, He who eats and drinks unworthily is guilty of the body and blood of Christ (1 Corinthians 11[:27]), your interpretation is: the impious become guilty of the body and blood of Christ not by eating, but rather by neglecting it, spitting it out, and rejecting it.

Again, when we were producing Paul's text: He who eats and drinks unworthily eats and drinks judgment on himself since he does not discern the body of the Lord (1 Corinthians 11[:27]), your interpretation was heard immediately then: he does not discern the body, that is, he does not distinguish this bread of the Lord's Supper from common bread, which has the name and label of the body of the Lord, whence it is called the body of Christ.

II. Dr. Beza's interpretations in the article on the Person of Christ.

In the article on the Person of Christ, when we were producing the text of John, The Word became flesh (John 1[:14]), and again, You are the Christ the Son of the living God (Matthew 16[:16]), immediately your interpretation was heard: God is man, that is the man united with God, is man, who is carried along and supported by the Son of God.

When it is said, This man (the son of Mary) is God, your interpretation is heard: this man, that is, the Son of God united with the humanity <554> is God. Man is omnipotent, that is the Deity united to the humanity. God suffered, that is the flesh united to the Deity suffered.

III. Dr. Beza's interpretations in the article on Baptism.

In the article on Baptism, when we were producing the text of Titus 3[:5], He saved us through the washing of regeneration of the holy Spirit, your interpretation was immediately heard: that is, a sign of the washing of regeneration, which signifies and represents a washing of regeneration. And again, when we were offering, Unless someone is born again of water and the spirit, the interpretation is heard: Born again, that is, sealed by Baptism of water for a future regeneration that follows later in its own time, and only for the elect, who oftentimes are not reborn until old age.

And again, in the Acts of the Apostles the words of the text regarding Simon Magus are clear: Simon also believed; here your interpretation immediately is added: he believed, that is, he pretended to believe.

And again, the text about Paul in Acts 23 is clear: Christ *was standing near* Paul. Your interpretation: he was standing near, that is, he was appearing to him in a nocturnal vision.

IV. DR. BEZA'S INTERPRETATIONS IN THE ARTICLE ON PREDESTINATION.

In the article on Predestination, when we were arguing against the hidden decree by which you assert that the majority of mankind has been created and ordained for eternal damnation by the hidden and unchangeable decree of God that precedes all second causes (no reason for which can be reported except for the will of the Lord), people whom he never loved nor ever wished nor does wish to be converted, to believe, or to be saved, and when we had produced clear testimonies from holy Scripture, you attempted to evade them all by your interpretation, namely after the following fashion.

God wants all people to be saved (1 Timothy 2[:4]); your interpretation: *all*, that is, *some*, regarding whom he made a decree that he wants some to be saved.

As I live, I do not desire the death of the dying (Ezekiel 18[:23]); your interpretation: I do not desire, that is, <555> I do desire the death of the dying, that is, of the sinner created for damnation.

Repentance and the forgiveness of sins must be preached to *all the nations* (Luke 24[:47]); your interpretation: *not* to all the nations, but rather only *to some*, out of which the Lord elected some by his hidden decree, whom he wished to save.

He himself is the propitiation not for our sins only, but for the sins *of the whole world* (1 John 2[:2]); your interpretation: Of the whole world, that is, of only the elect in the World.

So often have I wished to gather your children, and you were unwilling (Matthew 23); your interpretation: I have wished, that is I have not wished to gather you, since I created, ordained, and destined you for eternal damnation.

God so loved the World (John 3[:16]); your interpretation: World, that is, only the elect in the world.

Come to me all who labor and are heavy-laden (Matthew 11[:28]); your interpretation: *all*, that is, *some*, namely, only the elect, whom I decided to save; I do not want the rest to come.

God enclosed all things under unbelief, in order that he might have mercy *on all* (Romans 11[:32]); your interpretation: *all*, that is, *some*, namely the elect.

The Lord does not want *any* to perish, but *all* to be turned around to repentance (2 Peter 3[:9]); your interpretation: all, that is, some, namely only all the faithful and elect; he wants the rest to perish, whom he created and ordained for destruction and eternal damnation, whom he never loved, nor wanted, nor does want still to be saved.

Christ died for all people; your interpretation: for all people, that is, *for some people*, since he died only for the elect. And six hundred other similar statements.

But are these not interpretations? They make a shambles of the plainest testimonies of holy Scripture in the most important articles of our religion (in which our salvation consists), and return things that are utterly useless to us.

<556>

Though I kept asking for these interpretations to be proved, not once, but frequently, especially in the article on the Person of Christ, none was brought forward, but rather either the interpretation was repeated, or a false reasoning was reiterated by you.

Since all these things have been refuted by us, not by means of a human interpretation, but rather by means of plain and very firm testimonies of holy Scripture, it is clear to everyone, for our part, that the word of God and the text of holy Scripture stands, but you have only interpretation. We advise all pious people to guard themselves against this Theology, and all the audience to fly from it. For not only is the substance of the Sacraments snatched away from us, that is, Christ from the Sacraments, but together with the Sacraments, the word of divine promises about the unmerited remission of sins is removed. Where there is no use of holy Scripture and Sacraments, there will be no further encouraging troubled consciences, to the point that the certainty of our entire eternal salvation to come is utterly overthrown.

Dr. Beza:

You put yourself in the place of a judge, and pronounce just as if you were seated on a Throne before a tribunal, and judgment about religion were placed in your power and commended to you alone by God. But it is not fair that your role is judge. Since therefore you play this part in the presence of Christ as judge, for this reason this does not in the least correspond to you. We do not assert explanations, much less do we deny the truth and substance of the Sacraments. But we have proved our teaching about the Lord's Supper as many times with the testimonies of the holy Spirit as there are extant testimonies in the Scriptures about the truth of Christ's real and natural body, about his ascension into heaven, and about his return for judgment. For our part, we also possess the testimonies of as many Churches and Martyrs as possible, who sign our teaching and confession with their own blood, and perhaps <557> more for our part than you do for yours. Consider this also: you for your part are not at peace. What Chemnitz, Hesychius, and others teach, and where they disagree with you, you are not unaware. They do not work together with you on all points.

But I pray to the Lord that he not charge this much to us. It is granted us to trust and to suffer, and we are grieved that we do not have consensus. We nevertheless desire to cultivate fraternity with you, since the feebleness of human judgment is great. May the Lord open our mind and yours, that we may see more clearly; he will reveal in his own time, for they rightly trust.

Dr. Jakob:

I have established that I am not the judge, and I have said these things not sitting before a tribunal or on a Throne of judgment. All the audience of this Colloquy will be witnesses, especially the Honorable Prince, Count Frederick, that do the judgments of those guys, in this conference not once, but as often as I have made my appeal, and laid out in the judgment of each and every person, as when it was not possible to come between us, let them judge themselves, either part has confirmed its own doctrine by gloss or the express word of God. That I still seek from each and every single person that they consider carefully about the entire business, and examine and judge the teaching of either party not by human explanations but by the word of God. And do not let them focus on which party seems to have more or fewer standing, but rather which comes closer to God's words, and let him rest on that alone.

CONSENSUS OF THE WÜRTEMBERG CHURCHES WITH THE CHURCHES OF THE AUGSBURG CONFESSION.

As far as our consensus is concerned, this is expressed in the book of Concord which we doubt not at all, as it rests on no human explanation but on the express and completely unanimous word of God. Dr. Chemnitz, Dr. Hesychius, and other erudite Theologians in great number, and Ministers of the Churches, Academies, and schools have subscribed to it.

But even if we should see that you disagree with us and still do not change your opinion, we nevertheless will not on account of this leave off <558> praying to the Lord on your behalf, that he open your mind and illuminate you with his holy Spirit so that you may understand, repent of error, and allow yourselves to be taught by God's Son and his open, simple, perspicuous and plain word. This will in fact be the unique and only way to establish a pious, holy, and God-pleasing concord. If I appear perhaps to have said anything too harshly of which I am nevertheless not aware, may your Lordships consider not

that this arose from base passion but rather that my mind and heart
shrink from teaching that is opposed to the truth. And I hope that
our audience will bear us witness that for our part, we proposed all of
our matters peaceably, and have wished not to vitiate, but rather only
to warn, that all may be on guard against that doctrine which is so
ripe in producing new errors, and that the audience may understand
where Satan leads, if he seduces us from the word to explanations
so that he snatches from us not only the substance and true use
of the Sacraments, but also the entire Gospel together with Christ,
and despoils us of every consolation which we have laid up in Christ
alone and no one else.

Dr. Beza:
We will pray to the Lord on your behalf that you grow in charity.

7

Conclusion of the Colloquy

After the colloquy was brought to a close in this way, the Württemberg Theologians asked Dr. Beza and his brothers to deliver them the responses to their Theses on the three last articles: 1. On Temples, Icons, and Organs, etc.; 2. On Baptism; 3. On Predestination. This happened on the next day. But the Württemberg Theologians had wished that the same order would be preserved with them, and their responses also to the Theses delivered before the conference and publicly recited as well, just as had been in observed in the two preceding articles, so that the plenary conference could be drawn up in order from each individual piece.

<559>

But since the many things discussed in the colloquy were collected and written down in their Response, The Christian Reader will be able easily to comprehend that the language used was the same both in writing and in the conference. That which the Christian Reader could understand also from their writings, which were delivered to the Württemberg Theologians by Dr. Beza and his brothers, have also been inserted above in their own place.

On the next day, which was 29 March, the Honorable Prince, Count Frederick, with his counselor and noble court and the rest of his ministers returned to the place in why the conference had taken place between Dr. Beza and Dr. Jakob.

As soon as the Württemberg Theologians had given his Honorable Highness as much thanks as they could for the fact that his Highness had spared no expense to have removed this very large stumbling block of dissension and to have holy concord restored by any way possible, for his longsuffering patience, and for listening to the collocutors of both parties compare their positions on the controverted articles for the entire time.

But even if his Highness did not achieve the end which he most wanted, nevertheless they had no doubt that this colloquy would not be bereft of fruit. His Highness could know for certain because of it what was the consistent and perpetual position of each party, and on what foundations either party relied. From this he could easily understand, too, which party offered human interpretations and opinions, and which the word of the Lord, and by its simple, <560> perspicuous, and plain interpretation confirmed their doctrine. And they promise that his Highness will be repaid superabundantly by God for discharging this office of piety shown to the Church of God. And they would comment his Highness to God's protection, with his very pious wife and very sweet children, and promise their eternal heartfelt gratitude.

Dr. Beza does the same with those he had brought with him from Geneva and Lausanne, and not only they, but also Abraham Musculus, with the Senator of Bern and the Professor of Greek in the Gymnasium at Bern, and they raised their prayers and promised to make public among their people the Honorable Prince's piety, clemency, philanthropy, and eagerness for peace and truth. The Honorable Prince, Count Frederick, answered them through his Highness' Secretary, N. Binningerus, in French, in order that he could be understood by the French who were involved in the colloquy with this address:

<561>

7A. RESPONSE OF THE HONORABLE PRINCE FREDERICK, COUNT OF WÜRTTEMBERG, ETC.

Dr. Beza, the Honorable Prince Frederick, Count of Württemberg and Montbéliard, etc., my most merciful Lord, has commanded me to respond briefly to your speech and explain to you that his Highness had hoped, to be sure, for a different outcome from the scheduled Colloquy, namely, that the minds of the dissenting parties might more closely be joined together in the doctrine of the genuine and uncorrupted truth in the conference that took place. This indeed was the content of the great and ardent prayers raised not only by his Highness but also as many other pious men as possible. Just as the prayers of his Highness are still occupied with nothing more than to be able to see both pious peace at last, and concord in this controversy. Though he does not in the least <562> *doubt that this Colloquy that was held will fail to bear fruit, but rather it will produce something in its own time.*

But since it could not happen in a different way in this convention, he commends the entire business to the Divine will, and cannot think otherwise than that the hour and time destined by God for the resolution of this controversy had not yet come, and that perhaps God had not wished for concord to be fixed in this first meeting.

But his Highness hopes that God Almighty for his infinite goodness and wisdom will show a path and a way in the meantime by which some convention can be scheduled again from which perhaps more usefulness could return to the Church of God than just happened. For this reason his Highness will not cease to ask God the Father of our Lord Jesus Christ and present his pious prayers to him.
<563>

But his Highness graciously thanks you, Dr. Beza, and your Colleagues, for the fact that you approached this conference with so ready a spirit, and asks that you be contented with virtuous treatment.

But since in four important articles no concord was established, for this reason at their departure they put together a brief note, which follows.

When a Colloquy had been established by the Honorable Prince and Lord, Lord Frederick, Count of Württemberg and Montbéliard, etc., our most merciful Lord, at the request of French exiles, between Dr. Jakob Andreae and Dr. Theodore Beza, as in his holy zeal he was eager for

Christian concord, these men conducted a friendly and peaceful conversation in the presence of his Highness and the chief French exiles on the topics of 1. the Lord's Supper; 2. the person of Christ; 3. the reformation of Temples and Icons; 4. Baptism; 5. Predestination. But the Theologians on both sides swore from the beginning that they would conduct the business they were conducting as private individuals, with no prejudice of any Church.

But even though in the fifth Article (which treats Temples and Icons) the Theologian of either party agreed to the point that they resolved business about these matters was adiaphora, provided all things be directed to the edification of the Church and the prevention of Idolatry, nevertheless in regard to the four <564> remaining articles consensus could not be reached at this time except in a few points; in hindsight we now see that since beginning of those controversies no resolution has been achieved between the parties.

But the theologians of either party in the aforementioned articles rely on those foundations which are comprehended in their respective writings, and they do not back down from them. Nevertheless they promise to be careful that nothing be justly missing in them that could be able to effect holy peace and God-pleasing concord (with the glory of God, heavenly truth, and the salvation of the Church preserved.) And since the things that were said in the Colloquy on both sides were not recorded by secretaries, if there are any annotations from either party, we do not want them to have any force and authentic authority of Protocol.

Done at Montbéliard, 29 March, 1586.

Württemberg Theologians.

Dr. Jakob Andreae
Dr. Lucas Osiander
Württemberg Political Counsellors.

Johann Wolfgang von Anweil
Dr. Frederick Schütz

Genevan Theologians.

> *Theodore Beza*
> *Abraham Musculus*
> *Antoine de La Faye*
> *Pierre Hubner*
> *Dr. Claude Albery.*

Politicians of Beza's party.

> *Antoine Maris*
> *Samuel Mayer, Senator of the Republic of Bern*

<565>

But as far as Protocol is concerned, of which mention was made in the Colloquy's recess, as they call it, this is what happened. In order that the conference might foster a freer discussion, and that neither party was obligated to watch their words, no demands were made as is accustomed to happen from time to time in disputations, especially when the passions rule, but it was decided from the beginning of the Colloquy that the business take place on both sides without what was said by either party being taken down by Notaries used for the purpose, but rather each and every person was free to take notes on whatever they wanted, even the audience. From the party of Dr. Jakob, Dr. Lucas Osiander, and M. Caspar Lucius, preacher of Montbéliard, took notes on what they could follow by pen. Those who were of the party of Dr. Beza had the same freedom. But the Genevan Theologians and the one from Bern very eagerly and anxiously asked that the notes taken by either side at the Colloquy not have any force and authentic authority of Protocol. But even though the Württemberg Theologians were wondering why they acted so eagerly in asking this (for it made no difference to them what was written down by either party, since they were ready to give their reasoning on each and every topic from their side in the Colloquy that was talked about both in individual conversations and on all the articles), nevertheless they did not have difficulty consenting to this, since it had been agreed from the start. But the position of either party, noted frankly in this description, was attributed without any bad faith or slanderously on the side of this or the other party. Not only did all the audience who were present the whole time at the Colloquy and the collocutors pay attention well and hear it, but especially the Honorable Prince, Count Frederick. But the writings also <566> of either party were confirmed by their own hands on the individual articles. In like manner also books that exist on these controverted articles, which have been publicly issued by the Theologians of each party, will attest to this.

7B. FAREWELL ADDRESS OF THE THEOLOGIANS

DR. BEZA'S FAREWELL TO DR. JAKOB AND DR. OSIANDER.

When all these things had been completed and while the Honorable Prince, Count Frederick with his Counsellors and Ministers of court were still present, Dr. Beza addressed Dr. Jakob and Dr. Osiander to say farewell to them with their colleagues. He testified again to his will and intention, saying he came to this conference eager for peace and truth. And for this reason it grieved him a great deal that peace and concord in the controverted articles could not be established, but he did not utterly despair that concord could not ever happen in the future on the controverted articles for this reason. For after they had just now listened to each other both sides would think carefully about this whole business in the fear of the Lord. They would also pray to the Lord to open the eyes of both sides and enlighten their minds so that whichever party should be in error may return to the way and allow themselves to be taught by the Spirit of the Lord. In the meantime, until this should happen, he asked that both sides abstain from bitter writings, until the Lord should grant peace. He saluted Dr. Holderus and the rest of the Theologians; they acknowledged Beza with his theological colleagues as brothers, willing to extend the right hand of brotherhood to them, and in turn said that they would strive to show them that concord and peace was dear to them as well.

Dr. Jakob:

RESPONSE OF DR. JAKOB AND DR. OSIANDER TO DR. BEZA'S FAREWELL.

We swear in turn that our intention and will was the same as yours and that of your Colleagues, and that a passion for a pious, holy, and God-pleasing concord has never left us nor ever will by the grace of God. <567> Therefore we have heartfelt grief no less than Beza and his brothers that in this peaceful and friendly conference consensus was not reached on the controverted articles. Nor was this our fault, since we testified at length that we clung to the simple word of the Lord, omitting all human interpretation. And again, if they could do this, now, even now, pious, holy, and God-pleasing concord would have been established.

And there is no other path for establishing it than rejecting their own human opinions. In these Mysteries they should lead their intellect captive, into obedience to Christ, and subject themselves to the word of the Lord in the simplicity of faith. And when they have rightly understood what our position is on each controverted article in the conference that was held, and that we do not in the least teach or defend the errors that Dr. Beza objects to in those published writings of his, but rather openly condemn and despise them in each and every controverted article, under which charge they have nevertheless been publicly paraded, though falsely, throughout foreign Churches, now that our innocence has been learned and demonstrated, we also do not yet despair of reaching a holy concord. We ask Dr. Beza and his brothers and colleagues carefully to consider all these things.

We and our people also wish to pray to God earnestly for you, that he open your eyes and enlighten your minds by his holy Spirit so that you can see the truth and subject yourselves to it.

But how can we offer you the right hand of brotherhood, since you are not unaware that you are guilty of the most horrible of errors and the most loathsome heresy in your writings from the perspective of the Church? I am confused about how we could acknowledge you as brothers or want to? If we acknowledged brotherhood like

this it would be aspiring to fraternity with those who call back condemned heresies <568> from Hell and thrust them upon the Church
of God. No, it has been shown in this conference that you dwell in
these and in errors as loathsome as possible. Since you still persevere in them, our interpretation is that we cannot acknowledge you
as brothers, and so even less would we suffer offering you the right
hand of brotherhood. We attest that bitter writings have not in the
least been approved by us. But you are also not unaware that errors
need to be rejected. But we will take care, should it come up again
in writing, to let a gentle and tender tone bring those errors to the
light, as much as we can while preserving the truth and the glory
of God. But we will discharge all the obligations of polite manners,
which you have experienced and commended more than once among
the Württemberg Theologians, just as also among the Württemberg
Princes of their Church, and for this reason we will not unwillingly
extend you the right hand of polite manners.

Dr. Beza:
*Since you refuse to extend us the right hand of brotherhood, and
you do not wish to acknowledge us as brothers, I also do not want
the right hand of friendship.*

Dr. Jakob:
Then let us part ways.

<569>

8

Appendix:

IN WHICH IT IS TAUGHT WHAT WAS DONE IN THE MATTER OF THE COMMUNICATION AND PROTESTATION OF THE FRENCH EXILES, AFTER THE COLLOQUY HAD BEEN HELD AT MONTBÉLIARD.

Dr. Beza and his Colleagues had asked in a humble Petition (which has been attached to these acts), among other things, this also, that the brothers of their Confession, maintaining their Confession without any prejudice of another, might be allowed to receive the holy Supper from the hands of others and so cultivate and witness mutual brotherhood. But to this part of the humble petition, the Honorable Prince and Lord, Lord Frederick, Count of Württemberg and Montbéliard, etc., had not yet answered before the Colloquy came to an end. But when the discussion had come to an end, Dr. Beza and his Colleagues, now preparing to depart and getting dressed at their inn for their journey, were from time to time pressing the Honorable Prince for an answer, his Highness sent his decision about this matter to them at the inn. His decision was not dissimilar to the one which he had given to the French around the feast of Christmas in the presence of his Highness and his Counsellors and courtiers. The Superintendent of Montbéliard announced it out loud and it was afterward also shown them in writing. We will first recount his opinion, then we will append another which was given by Dr. Beza and his Colleagues. However, the following is the first Decree of the Honorable Prince.

The First response of the Prince Frederick, given to the French before the Colloquy.

After the Ministers of the Churches (a) of Montbéliard made the Honorable Prince, their Lord, Lord Frederick, Count <570> of Württemberg and Montbéliard, more certain about this Writing, (b) his Highness gave this answer: that he needed to indicate by those things that his pious and pure Confession publicly stands out more than sufficiently; if they should wish to communicate under that, they would be more than welcome, but if not, they themselves could abstain and take care of their conscience in this way. No one should be excluded moreover, if they approach for the sake of a preparatory meeting. (c) Enacted in the Citadel, 17 December, 1585.

> *Signed:*
>
> *Frederick Count of Württemberg, etc.*

(A) There are two Churches there, German and French. The primary pastor is German, and he performs the duty of superintendent; <570> he examined, together with his German colleague, and three ministers of the French Church, the writing of the French. (B) In this writing the French had sought to be admitted to the Lord's Supper under their Confession. (C) This was held at night, and treated the substance and use of the Lord's Supper.

Another response which was given to the French exiles, after the Colloquy, is as follows.

That is, to permit the French what had not been permitted earlier, as the Epistle says in its nonsense.

To the petition of Dr. Beza and his Colleagues, where they ask that the brothers of their Confession, retaining their Confession without prejudice of the other, be allowed to receive the holy Supper from the hands of others, the Honorable Prince and Lord,

*Lord Frederick, Count of Württemberg and <571> Montbéliard,
etc., answers that the confession and church order of his Highness is publicly extant; if they should wish to approach the holy
Lord's Supper according to that Confession and church order,
then they would on this account be willing to open their opinion
to the Minister of the Church of Montbéliard, and would not
allow it to be repelled. Enacted at Montbéliard, 29 March, 1586.
(Frederick Count of Württemberg and Montbéliard, etc.)*

After this Decree was promulgated, on the first day of April, which
was Friday, before the Feast of Easter, after the Envoys of either party
had already departed, certain Ministers of the French Churches (to
whom hospitality had been granted at Montbéliard together with the
other French Exiles) approached and asked that at least this clause be
added to the Prince's decree, that the French be unwilling to condemn
their own Confession by communing. And, if it were not possible for this
to be obtained from the Honorable Prince that these things be inserted
in the written decree, they begged that the Minister of the Church of
Montbéliard recite these words publicly before the people from the
pulpit, or standing at the altar. In this matter those French Ministers
certainly did not follow Dr. Beza's counsel, who had just written the
French exiles not to offend the Church at Montbéliard in any way, but
rather commune there without a lot of argument. But the petition of the
French Ministers in exile was too much; they could achieve nothing at
all, in spite of soliciting the Superintendent of Montbéliard, even in the
wee hours of the night. They in fact got this answer from him: that the
Honorable Prince wished them strictly to observe the mandate once given
and signed, and not to depart from it even a hair's breadth. When they
received this answer, one of the French Ministers <572> left the city with
several of the French early on the following Sabbath, looking elsewhere
for people of his own Confession with whom he might commune.

NOTE WITH RESPECT TO THE SIMPLE AND PIOUS PETITION OF THE LORD VESENES.

The rest of the French exiles, though, who had remained at
Montbéliard, called the French Ministers of this Church to them, and then
Lord Vesenes (who had sat at Dr. Beza's table in the Colloquy and had

listened very carefully), addressed the French Ministers of the Church
at Montbéliard in favor of this position: that he and his French brothers
desired most longingly and with goodwill to commune together with the
Church at Montbéliard. He asked they not be excluded from the communion of the holy Supper, and because of externals not be kept away from
Christ's Church, in the name of which so many thus far had endured
persecutions.

These words, which seem to contain in themselves a protestation, were indeed heard by the French ministers but not accepted or approved.

The French Minister Dr. Richard Dinot (whom since then the Lord
has called from this life) wished to respond to this speech, but a certain
Minister of the exiles interrupted him and said that the Lord Vesenes had
not correctly and entirely declared the intention of the French Lords, and
that they in fact were asking that they be admitted to communion of the
Lord's Supper *under their own confession.*

The French exiles were summoned back to the Confession of the Germanic churches, which differs significantly from the French.

Dr. Richard Dinot answered him that no one up to that point had
been excluded from the French Church at Montbéliard, whether he had
come to Montbéliard from Geneva or anywhere else, provided he had
offered himself to the reception of the holy Supper after having heard
and approved their sermons beforehand. Why therefore was he now
excluding the French exiles, many of whom had already communed
with them before? Nor in fact was he in doubt that the French exiles had
sufficiently understood the simple Confession of our Churches from their
many sermons and those of their Colleague. They of course knew it quite
abundantly from the Augsburg Confession and its Apology, and from the
Confession of Duke Christopher of Württemberg which had been offered
to the Council of Trent, and from the concord of Dr. Luther and Dr.
Bucer which was made at Wittenberg in the Year 1536, from which pious
Confession neither he himself nor his Colleague could depart on account
of the fact that it was in conformity with the word of God and was well-
established upon it. He said further that the things that were sown here

and there against the Confession, were mere slanders, lies, and obvious falsehoods.

DINOT RIGHTLY DISTINGUISHED BETWEEN THE CHURCHES THEMSELVES AND THE ERRONEOUS OPINIONS WHICH THE MINISTERS OF THOSE CHURCHES DEFEND. FOR OFTEN THE PEOPLE HAVE PURER EARS THAN THE PRIESTS HAVE LIPS AND HEARTS.

A certain French Legal Adviser (who had often before taken the Lord's Supper in the Church at Montbéliard), together with other **<573>** exiles, interrupted and answered: If they disapproved of the Confession and sermons of the Ministers of the Church of Montbéliard, they would never have tried to ask that they be allowed to commune together. In the meantime however they could not repudiate their own French Confession and condemn the other Churches (either in the realm of France or elsewhere). Dr. Richard Dinot answered him that neither they nor their Colleagues had ever condemned any of the Churches of Christ; nay rather, they put their best home in them always. Nevertheless he could not keep it a secret (if he wished to speak the truth) that the Confession of the French people, especially in article 38, was still ambiguous and insufficient, since it could not be understood who were the Sacramentarians of whom the Confession makes mention.

IRENAEUS REGARDING HERETICS: SAYING THE SAME THINGS, NEVERTHELESS NOT THINKING THE SAME THINGS.

To these points Floretus, a Minister of the French exiles, answered and explained the ambiguity of the French Confession in this way: that by Sacramentarians is meant those who were so rejecting signs that they were saying that they were bare, *not joined with the things themselves which they signify*, though Jesus Christ said nevertheless, This is my body, This is my blood. Here the good Richard Dinot (judging from his candor regarding Floretus), reckoning that he was listening to a Lutheran, answered, What therefore was keeping them back any further and impeding the French exiles (seeing as they felt this way) since what they want is to approach the Lord's Supper with the rest of the faithful?

Afterwards Floretus addressed Richard's Colleague, Samuel Cucuel, the Minister of the French Church of Montbéliard, and asked whether he had anything that could contradict his Colleague's words? Samuel responded that he had nothing indeed; nevertheless he was really wondering why they kept on being willing to reiterate so often the words *under our French confession*. Did the Confession of the Church of Montbéliard not meet their approval? Or did they condemn it?

NOTE: YOU ARE HEARING AGAIN THE LUTHERAN CONFESSION, WHICH ANOTHER FRENCH MINISTER HAD NOT BEEN GOING TO APPROVE, WHO HAD LEFT MONTBÉLIARD WITH HIS PEOPLE.

But immediately Floretus excused himself and his people lest they seem to condemn the Confession of Montbéliard and, repeating the sentence of the Legal Adviser (about whom we spoke above), said: We would not desire to commune with you if we did not approve of your Confession. Nevertheless it is an insult to us (said Floretus) that we are being accused of rendering the Sacraments null and void; we in fact firmly maintain that the bread and wine are not only signs but rather *instruments, through which the true body and blood of Christ are distributed*. But meanwhile (said Floretus) it remains that you, Samuel <574> Cucuel, have rather often publicly rejected Transubstantiation, Consubstantiation, Ubiquity, and the local extension of the body of Christ. Do you still, Cucuel, persist in this opinion? Samuel Cucuel assented to these things.

Finally it was asked of the two French Ministers of Montbéliard, whether they wished to present the Lord's Supper to certain French according to their mode and form, namely, that they offer them the bread into their hands and not into their mouth. To these things Samuel Cucuel answered that nothing could be changed for their sake in the rite of administration of the Lord's Supper, for it could easily happen that the simple people would be offended by this change. The French were indeed insisting on the point even more, but since they were not achieving anything, they acquiesced and declared their opinion, that the ceremony would not impede them from approaching the Lord's Supper.

But once the Ministers of Montbéliard had departed, and were simply ignorant of the all the things which were done by the French afterwards (a fact that the witnessing Minister, Samuel Cucuel, righteously affirms), the French, inviting Notaries and certain citizens of Montbéliard, composed a certain Instrument in secret with such frankness (naturally) and sincerity, that the Honorable Prince and Lord, Lord Frederick, Count of Württemberg and Montbéliard, etc., had very serious and just reasons to disparage and criticize any of that Instrument's trustworthiness, authority, or value (in the preface of this work). It was in fact composed not only in the absence of those whose presence, whose knowledge of what really happened, and whose consensus was required; certain things were also inserted that had absolutely not been mentioned in the presence of the Ministers of Montbéliard, and were not approved by their consensus. The charge was that the Instrument differed a lot from the truth of the thing done.

Since however Christ very truly said: Nothing has been hidden which will not be sometime revealed, it was not possible for that Instrument to lie hidden for long, created illegally and to damage the truth. And indeed, at the revelation of the same, that counterfeit Eusebius Schönberg furnished an opportunity with the publication of his Letter, though quite in vain. He first made mention of the Instrument, citing it as a source of proof. Once the Epistle was read in fact, those to whom the Republic's governance had been committed in Prince Frederick's absence finally found, after a careful and diligent search, **<575>** supplies of that secretly composed Instrument. When they had been shown to the Honorable Prince upon his return, his Highness thought the matter so injurious, clandestine, rash, and not done in good faith, that he was seriously annoyed and violently moved because of it. Nor would the author of that Instrument have endured without punishment his rashness and malice, had death not removed him from human affairs before the return of the Prince.

The Honorable Prince Frederick judged that all these things should be brought to light so that the public testimony of the truth concerning the Acts of the Colloquy of Montbéliard might survive for all posterity, so that the meaninglessness of that Schönbergian Letter (in which there were almost as many lies as there were lines) might become known, and finally so that the Person of his Highness might be vindicated from every false and sinister suspicion, as if deflected by the pious, pure, and first unaltered Augsburg Confession. And indeed his Highness, by the publication of these Acts, was eager to promote true and firm peace of the Churches (which cannot be established or exist except in demonstration of the truth itself), but not to impede it. His Highness offers fervent prayers that an auspicious outcome answer his holy zeal, that for the opposing party, the eyes of their mind may be opened by the virtue of the holy Spirit, that they may acknowledge, love, and embrace heavenly truth. And in order that his Authority may stand together with this Appendix also, his Highness, in public testimony of the truth, has signed it with his own hand. Done at the Castle at Montbéliard, on the 11 day of February, in the Year of Christ, 1587.

Frederick, By God's Grace Count
of Württemberg and Montbéliard, etc.

Works Cited throughout the
Acts of the Colloquy of Montbéliard

Andreae, Jakob

Solida Refutatio compiliationis Cingli-
anae, Quam Illi Consensum
Orthodoxum Sacrae Scripturae
et Veteris Ecclesiae, de controver-
sia sacramentaria, appellarunt,
in lucem ediderunt, & aliquoties
recoxerunt. Tübingen: George
Gruppenbach, 1584.

Aristotle

Collected works — *Operum . . .*
Graecè & Latinè. [Geneva:]
Guillaume Laimarie, 1597.

Anal. — *Organi . . . pars prima eaq.*
analytica (Basel: Eusebius
Episcopius, 1577). — *Prior*
Analytics (LCL 325).

Metaph. — *Duodecim libri metha-*
phisice. Leipzig: Martin Lands-
berg, 1499 — *Metaphysics*
(LCL 271, 287).

Organum, siue Logica, À Doctiss.
hominibus, Ioach. Perionio,
Nicolao Grouchio, Firmino
Durio, Latinè conuersa. Quorum
haec est series: Porphyrii insti-
tutiones ad Chrysaorium. Lib. I.
Aristotelis Categoriae, seu Prae-
dicamenta. I. Περὶ ἑρμενείας,
id est, De Interpretatione. I.
Priorum Analyticorum, II.
Posteriorum Analyticorum, II.
Topicorum, VIII. De reprehen-

sionibus Sophistarum, I. Basel:
per Ioannem Oporinum,
[1559] — *Posterior Analytics*
(LCL 391)".

Physics – *Libri physicorum octo: cum*
singulorum epitomatis . . . Aver-
roeque eius exatiss. interprete: ac
M. Anto. Zimare . . . interprete.
Et hec et alia eius opera. Lyon:
Scipion de Gabiano, 1520 –
Physics (LCL 228, 255).

Athanasius

De Trinitate Dialogi (PG 28)
(spurious).

Augustine of Hippo

Collected works — *Omnivm*
Opervm Primvs Tomvs [–Deci-
mvs]. Paris: Claude Cheval-
lon, 1531; *Primvs [–Decimvs]*
Tomvs . . . D. Avrelii Avgvstini
. . . Cvivs Praestantissima In
Omni Genere monimenta.
Basel: Froben, 1569.

De civit. Dei — *De civitate Dei*
(CCSL 47–48) — *The City of*
God (FC 8, 14, 24).

John — *In Johannis evangelium tracta-*
tus (CCSL 36) — *Tractates on*
the Gospel of John (NPNF[1] 4).

Letters — *Epistulae* (CCSL 34, 44, 57, 58, 88) — *Epistles* (NPNF[1] 1).

Psalms — *Enarrationes in Psalmos* (CCSL 38–40) — *Explanations of the Psalms* (ACW 29–30).

Serm. 2 De verb. Domini — *Sermo 137* (PL 38).

Bernard of Clairvaux

Collected works—*Opera . . . omnia.* Basel: Johann Herwagen, 1552 (PL 182–85; Sancti Bernardi Opera, ed. J. Leclercq. Romae: Ed. Cistercienses, 1957–98)— *Sermo in Coena Dominica* (PL 183).

Beza, Theodore

De Coena Domini, plana et perspicua tractatio. In qua Joachimi Wesphali calumniae postremum editae refelluntur. Geneva: Robert I. Estienne, 1553.

Κρεωφαγία *sive Cyclops: onos sullogizomenos sive sophista; dialogi duo de vera communicatione corporis et sanguinis Domini, adversus Tilemanni Heshusii somnia.* Geneva: Conradus Badius, 1561.

Quaestionum et responsionum Christianarum libellus, vol. 1 [Anchora]: Vignon, 1571

Volvmen Tractationum Theologicarum, In Qvibvs Pleraqve Christiana Religionis dogmata aduersus hæreses nostris temporibus renouatas solidè ex Verbo Dei defenduntur. Anchora: Vignon, 1576

Brenz, Johannes

De maiestate Domini Nostri Iesu Christi ad Dextram Dei Patris, et de Vera Praesentia Corporis & Sanguinis eius in Coena. In hoc scripto respondetur Petro Martyri, & Henrico Bullingero, Cinglianis dogmatis de Coena Dominica propugnatoribus. Frankfurt-am-Main: Peter Braubach, 1562.

Recognitio Propheticae et Apostolicae Doctrinae, de Vera Maiestate Domini Nostri Jesu Christi, ad dexteram Dei Patris sui omnipotentis. Tübingen: Ulrich Morhard, 1564.

Calvin, John

In Evangelium secundum Johannem, commentarius. Geneva: Robert I. Estienne, 1553.

Cassian, John

Conlationes XXIV (CSEL 13) – *The Conferences* (NPNF[2] 11)

Chrysostom, John

Collected works – *Opera . . . tomus primus [– quintus].* Basel: Hieronymus Froben & Nikolaus Episcopius, 1558.

Hebrews – *In Epistulam ad Hebraeos argumentum et homiliae* (PG 63) – *Homilies on the Epistle to the Hebrews* (NPNF[1] 14).

Matthew – *In Matthaeum homiliae* (PG 57–58) – *Homilies on the Gospel of St. Matthew* (NPNF[1] 10).

Councils

Tomvs . . . Conciliorvm omnivm, tvm
generalivm, tvm provincialivm
atqve particvlarivm, qvae iam
inde ab apostolis vsque in prae-
sens habita, obtineri potuerunt,
magna insignium Synodorum . .
. accesione adeo nunc auctorum,
ut in Tomos 4. distributa sint.
Coloniae Agripinae: Calenius
& Quentel, 1567 (Joannes
Dominicus Mansi, ed. Sa-
crorum conciliorum nova et
amplissima collectio. Paris: H.
Welter, 1901–27).

Cyril of Alexandria

Opera . . . In Tomos Quinque digesta.
Basel, 1566.

Commentarii in Iohannem (Pusey,
S. P. N. Cyrilli . . . in d. Joannis
evangelium. Oxford, 1872) –
Commentary on John, 2 vols.,
trans. David R. Maxwell.
Downers Grove, Illinois: Inter-
Varsity Press, 2013–2015.

De recta in dominum nostrum Jesum
Christum fide ad imperatorem
Theodosium (PG 76).

De sancta trinitate dialogi vii
(PG 75).

Explanatio in Epistolam ad Hebraeos.
(PG 74).

Thesaurus – Thesaurus de sancta
et consubstantiali Trinitate, in
Opus . . . Thesaurus nuncupatus,
quatuordecim libros complec-
tens: et de consubstantialitate
filii & spiritus sancti cum patre,
contra hereticos luculentur
disserens. [Paris: Wolfgang
Hopyl], 1514 (PG 75).

Damascenus (John of Damascus)

Ιωαννου Του Δαμασκηνου Εργα . . .
Ioannis Damasceni Opera Omnia . . . Item, Ioannis Cassiani
eremitae non prorsus Dissimilis
Argumenti Libri Aliquot. Basel:
[Sixtus & Sebastian Henricpe-
tri, 1575].

Orthod. fid. – Expositio fidei ortho-
doxae (PG 94) – An Exact
Exposition of the Orthodox
Faith (NPNF[2] 9).

Lambert Daneau (Danaeus, Lambertus)

Examen libri Chemnitiani de duabus
naturis in Christo. Geneva,
1581.

Epiphanius of Salamis

Epistula ad Iohannem Hierosolymita-
num (PG 43).

Gregory of Nazianzus

Sancti Gregorii Nazianzeni . . . Opera
. . . Graecè & Latinè coniunctim
edita . . . Jac. Billivs . . . contulit,
emendauit, interpretatus est,
una cum doctißimis Graecorum
Nicetae Serronij, Pselli, Nonij,
& Eliae Cretensis commen-
tariis. Aucta est haec editio
aliquammultis . . . Gregorij
Epistolis . . . ex interpretatione
Fed. Morelli. Paris: Claude
Morel, 1609.

Gregory of Nyssa

Adversus Eunomium (PG 45) –
Against Eunomius (NPNF[2] 5).

Herdesianus, Christoph

*Consensvs orthodoxvs sacrae script-
vrae et veteris ecclesiae, de sen-
tentia et veritate verborvm coena
Dominicae.* Tiguri: Froschover,
1578.

Irenaeus

*Libri quinque Aduersus portentosas
haereses Valentini & aliorum,
accuratius quàm antehac emen-
dati, additis Graecis quae re-
periri potuerunt.* Geneva: Jean
LePreux and Jean Petit, 1570
– *Adversus haereses* (PG 7) –
Against Heresies (ANF 1).

Leo the Great

Epistolae (PL 54) – *Letters*
(NPNF[2] 12; FC 34).

Luther, Martin

*Festival Sermons of Martin Luther:
The Church Postils: Sermons for
the Main Festivals and Saints
Days of the Church Year; Winter
and Summer Selections,* trans.
by Joel R. Baseley, 2 vols. in 1.
Dearborn, MI: Mark V Publications, 2005.

Origen

Περὶ ἀρχῶν or *De principiis*
(GCS 22) – *On First Principles*
(ANF 4).

Prosper of Aquitaine

*Pro Augustini Doctrina Responsio-
nes Ad Capitula Objectionum
Vincentianarum* (PL 45:1679,
1843–50).

Prudentius, Aurelius

Contra Symmachum. (PL 60) – Prudentius vol. 2 (Loeb Classical
Library 398), Cambridge,
MA: Harvard University Press,
1953.

Tertullian

Adversus Praxean (CCSL 2) –
Against Praxeas (ANF 3).

Vermigli, Peter Martyr

*Dialogvs De Vtraqve In Christo Nat-
vra: Qvomodo coeant in unam
Christi personam inseparabilem,
ut interim non amittant suas
proprietates.* [1561].

Viret, Pierre

*De la source et de la difference et conu-
enance de la vieille et nonuelle
idolatrie et des vrayes et fausses
images et reliques et du seul et
vray mediateur.* [Geneva:]
Antoine Reboul, 1559.